NATURAL AND TECHNOLOGICAL DISASTERS: CAUSES, EFFECTS AND PREVENTIVE MEASURES

The Pennsylvania Academy of Science Publications
Books and Journal
Editor: Shyamal K. Majumdar
Professor of Biology, Lafayette College
Easton, Pennsylvania 18042

1. *Energy, Environment, and the Economy,* 1981. ISBN: 0-9606670-0-8. Editor: Shyamal K. Majumdar.

2. *Pennsylvania Coal: Resources, Technology and Utilization,* 1983. ISBN: 0-9606670-1-6. Editors: Shyamal K. Majumdar and E. Willard Miller.

3. *Hazardous and Toxic Wastes: Technology, Management and Health Effects,* 1984. ISBN: 0-9606670-2-4. Editors: Shyamal K. Majumdar and E. Willard Miller.

4. *Solid and Liquid Wastes: Management, Methods and Socioeconomic Considerations,* 1984. ISBN: 0-9606670-3-2. Editors: Shyamal K. Majumdar and E. Willard Miller.

5. *Management of Radioactive Materials and Wastes: Issues and Progress,* 1985. ISBN: 0-9606670-4-0. Editors: Shyamal K. Majumdar and E. Willard Miller.

6. *Endangered and Threatened Species Programs in Pennsylvania and Other States: Causes, Issues and Management,* 1986. ISBN: 0-9606670-5-9. Editors: Shyamal K. Majumdar, Fred J. Brenner, and Ann F. Rhoads.

7. *Environmental Consequences of Energy Production: Problems and Prospects,* 1987. ISBN:0-9606670-6-7. Editors: Shyamal K. Majumdar, Fred J. Brenner and E. Willard Miller.

8. *Contaminant Problems and Management of Living Chesapeake Bay Resources,* 1987. ISBN: 0-9606670-7-5. Editors: Shyamal K. Majumdar, Lenwood W. Hall, Jr. and Herbert M. Austin.

9. *Ecology and Restoration of The Delaware River Basin,* 1988. ISBN: 0-9606670-8-3. Editors: Shyamal K. Majumdar, E. Willard Miller and Louis E. Sage.

10. *Management of Hazardous Materials and Wastes: Treatment, Minimization and Environmental Impacts,* 1989. ISBN 0-9606670-9-1. Editors: Shyamal K. Majumdar, E. Willard Miller and Robert F. Schmalz.

11. *Wetlands Ecology and Conservation: Emphasis in Pennsylvania,* 1989. ISBN 0-945809-01-8. Editors: Shyamal K. Majumdar, Robert P. Brooks, Fred J. Brenner and Ralph W. Tiner, Jr.

12. *Water Resources in Pennsylvania: Availability, Quality and Management,* 1990. ISBN 0-945809-02-6. Editors: Shyamal K. Majumdar, E. Willard Miller and Richard R. Parizek.

13. *Environmental Radon: Occurrence, Control and Health Hazards*, 1990. ISBN 0-945809-03-4. Editors: Shyamal K. Majumdar, Robert F. Schmalz and E. Willard Miller.

14. *Science Education in the United States: Issues, Crises, and Priorities,* 1991. ISBN: 0945809-04-2. Editors: Shyamal K. Majumdar, Leonard M. Rosenfeld, Peter A. Rubba, E. Willard Miller and Robert F. Schmalz.

15. *Air Pollution: Environmental Issues and Health Effects,* 1991; ISBN: 0-945809-05-0. Editors: Shyamal K. Majumdar, E. Willard Miller, and John J. Cahir.

16. *Natural and Technological Disasters: Causes, Effects and Preventive Measures*, 1992; ISBN: O-945809-06-9. Editors: Shyamal K. Majumdar, Gregory S. Forbes, E. Willard Miller, and Robert F. Schmalz.

NATURAL AND TECHNOLOGICAL DISASTERS: CAUSES, EFFECTS AND PREVENTIVE MEASURES

EDITED BY

S.K. MAJUMDAR, Professor of Biology
Lafayette College
Easton, PA 18042

G.S. FORBES, Associate Professor of Meteorology
The Pennsylvania State University
University Park, PA 16802

E.W. MILLER, Professor and Associate Dean (Emeritus),
The Pennsylvania State University
University Park, PA 16802

R.F. SCHMALZ, Professor of Geoscience
The Pennsylvania State University
University Park, PA 16802

Founded on April 18, 1924

**A Publication of
The Pennsylvania Academy of Science**

Library of Congress Cataloging in Publication Data

Bibliography
Index
Majumdar, Shyamal K. 1938-, ed.

Library of Congress Catalog Card No.: 92-080386

ISBN-0-945809-06-9
Copyright © 1992 By The Pennsylvania Academy of Science, Easton, PA 18042

Printed in the United States of America by

Typehouse of Easton
Phillipsburg, New Jersey 08865

PREFACE

Natural and technological disasters are a normal part of life. In every disaster, the physical and social infrastructure fails to protect people from conditions that threaten their well-being. The basic reason for concern with disasters is thus to reduce human suffering and social disruptions. In order to lessen the vulnerability of human communities to disasters, a world-wide concern is being implemented in the 1990s which has been designated the International Decade for Natural Disaster Reduction. In order to reduce the adverse effects of disasters it is necessary to utilize all branches of knowledge. In addition to scientific and engineering applications to solve problems, there must be the contributions of the social and human sciences. Some people believe that the physical sciences and engineering technologies can provide adequate solutions to problems of disasters. Certainly much progress has been made in constructing earthquake resistant structures as well as structures that will withstand wind, water, and other disaster events. The implementation of all solutions, however, takes planning within specific political, economic and sociocultural contexts. Natural hazard reduction programs that ignore these social dimensions are destined to fail.

This volume is divided into five parts beginning with chapters that consider the problems of disasters and the challenges of reducing their devastation. The second part deals with natural disasters such as earthquakes, volcanic eruptions, hurricanes, thunderstorms, tornadoes, floods, droughts, and wildfires. This is followed by chapters on technological disasters such as industrial disasters, oil spills, radioactive waste deposits, mine fires, toxic and hazardous waste sites, and airplane disasters. Part four is devoted to risk assessments and preparedness such as insurance, emergency management services, preparedness and planning, and risk communication. The volume concludes with chapters on human value consequences such as consequences of floods, ethical dilemmas, and high risk technology and post-traumatic stress disorders.

This book will be of interest to scientists and engineers as well as social and human scientists. It provides a perspective on both the human and the physical aspects of disasters. Because of the universal character of disasters, this volume has special value to the general public.

We express our deep appreciation for the cooperation and dedication of contributors, who recognized the need for disaster reduction and the ways to cope with disasters after they occur. Gratitude is extended to Lafayette College and The Pennsylvania State University for providing facilities to the editors for their work. The editors extend heartfelt thanks to their wives for their encouragement and help in the preparation of this book.

Shyamal K. Majumdar
Gregory S. Forbes
E. Willard Miller
Robert F. Schmalz
Editors
May, 1992

Natural and Technological Disasters: Causes, Effects and Preventive Measures

Table of Contents

VII

Part Three: Technological Disasters

ACKNOWLEDGMENTS

The publication of this book was aided by contributions from The Pennsylvania Power and Light Company, Allentown, Pennsylvania.

Natural and Technological Disasters: Causes, Effects and Preventive Measures. Edited by S.K. Majumdar, G.S. Forbes, E.W. Miller, and R.F. Schmalz. © 1992, The Pennsylvania Academy of Science.

Chapter One

1990's: INTERNATIONAL DECADE FOR NATURAL DISASTER REDUCTION

WALTER W. HAYS

U.S. Geological Survey
Reston, VA 22092

INTRODUCTION

This paper describes the atmospheric, hydrologic, and geologic natural hazards (Figure 1) the United States will face during the 1990's and the program it will undertake to cope with them. The U.S. program will be a part of the International Decade for Natural Disaster Reduction (IDNDR), a program endorsed by the United Nations in 1989.

The United States is 1 of the 155 nations that are expected to have programs in the 1990's to reduce loss of life, human suffering, and economic losses from earthquakes, volcanic eruptions, severe storms (hurricanes and tornadoes), floods, landslides, wildfires, tsunamis, and drought.

The United States is planning a balanced and comprehensive research and applications program as part of the IDNDR. This program is timely because every State and Territory has communities that are at risk from one or more of the natural hazards, and economic losses and casualties are increasing rapidly due to population growth, urbanization, and the concentration of industry and infrastructure in areas prone to recurrent natural hazards. Moreover, the nation's inventory of building wealth is growing at a rate of $400 billion per year from new public and private construction. At this rate, approximately $4 trillion of new inventory requiring hazard resistance will be added during the 1990's.

The IDNDR is both an unprecedented opportunity and a challenge. The opportunity is to use planet Earth as a laboratory and the interactions of natural hazards with society as the experiments to deepen our understanding of the physical and

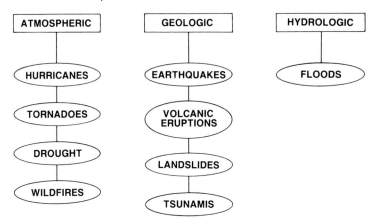

NATURAL HAZARDS
(DURATION OF SECONDS TO YEARS)

FIGURE 1. Natural hazards that will be addressed in the U.S. Decade program. All hazards are rapid onset except drought.

social aspects of natural disaster reduction. The challenge comes from the fact that such a multidisciplinary effort has never been undertaken on a global scale for individual natural hazards, let alone for multiple natural hazards.

In 1989, the United Nations' International Ad Hoc Group of Experts suggested that by the year 2000, planet Earth should expect approximately: a) 1,000,000 thunderstorms; b) 100,000 floods; c) tens of thousands of landslides, damaging earthquakes, wildfires, and tornadoes; and d) several hundred to several thousand tropical cyclones, hurricanes, tsunamis, drought episodes, and volcanic eruptions. Coping with the share of these events that strike the U.S. is the challenge.

The consequences of natural hazards are grave as evidenced recently by two disasters in 1989: Hurricane Hugo (U.S. Weather Service, 1990) and the Loma Prieta earthquake (State of California, 1990). Other recent regional impacts came from floods in Arkansas, Texas, Ohio, and Washington; tornadoes in Kansas, Nebraska, New York, Alabama, Indiana, and Illinois; wildfires in California and Wyoming; earthquakes in California; hurricanes along the Gulf and Atlantic coasts; volcanic eruptions in Hawaii and Alaska; and drought in the Midwest and California. At present, average annual losses from natural hazards reach $20 billion.

CHARACTERISTICS OF NATURAL HAZARDS IN THE UNITED STATES

Floods

Floods happen more frequently than any other natural hazard. They occur annually in every season of the year from heavy rainfall, often in association with thunderstorms, hurricanes, and tornadoes, and cause direct losses of about $4 billion per year. All States have communities that are at risk from flooding. Flash floods are the most dangerous because they are hard to forecast. Riverine flooding in the more than 6 million miles of the Nation's river systems is easier to forecast and is caused by heavy rainfall and/or rapid snowmelt. Storm surges generated seasonally in hurricanes inundate thousands of miles of vulnerable Gulf of Mexico and Atlantic coast. Urbanization, deforestation, wildfires, and other human and natural actions which change drainage patterns often increase flood severity.

Landslides

Landslides also occur annually and impact every State and Territory. California, Alaska, Washington, Utah, Kentucky, Tennessee, Ohio, West Virginia, Puerto Rico, and American Samoa have the most extensive and frequent problems. Landslides, manifest as falls, topples, slides, spreads, and flows of rock and soil, are triggered by meteorological or seismological events. Landslides cause direct losses of about $2 billion per year throughout the Nation.

Severe Storms

Severe storms (hurricanes, tornadoes) occur annually, but they are seasonal and more restricted geographically within the nation than floods or landslides. Almost every year, about a dozen hurricanes strike the Gulf and Altantic coasts in late summer and autumn. They can have wind velocities that reach 210 miles per hour, generate as much as 30 inches of rain in a few days and produce a storm surge of up to 25 feet in coastal areas. Several hundred tornadoes strike the interior of the Nation annually. Although all States are at risk from tornadoes, they strike most frequently along "tornado alley" in Oklahoma, Texas, and Kansas with wind speeds that reach 300 miles per hour.

Wildfires

Several hundred wildfires, or uncontrolled conflagrations, occur annually throughout the nation. In the Western States, they occur maninly during or after hot, dry summers. Lightning causes many wildfires, but others occur as a result of sparks from campfires, arson, and sometimes from fires triggered by earthquakes or lava flows.

Drought

The frequency of drought episodes depends on atmospheric conditions and can vary from once every several years to once every several decades. All regions of the nation are vulnerable to drought. Past episodes of severe drought, like the current episode in California, have highlighted the importance of continuous monitoring   ·

to provide early warning of changes in soil moisture and impending water shortages.

Tsunamis

Tsunamis are large destructive ocean waves generated by some submarine earthquakes, and sometimes by an underwater volcanic eruption or landslide. They can be very destructive at great distances from the source as well as near the source as they cause inundation, wave impacts on structures, and coastal erosion. They strike Hawaii more frequently than any other part of the Nation. However, Alaska, California, Washington, Oregon, Puerto Rico, and the Virgin Islands have also experienced destructive tsunamis in the past 150 years.

Earthquakes

Earthquakes, one of the most destructive natural hazards as a single event, happen relatively infrequently in comparison with floods, landslides, and hurricanes. Earthquakes, which can strike in more than 100 seismogenic zones throughout the nation, are most destructive near the source where they generate strong ground shaking and can trigger extensive permanent ground failure (e.g., liquefaction, surface fault rupture, and landslides). In the western United States, these effects are limited to a portion of a State, but in the East they can extend over several States. Secondary effects such as flooding from dam failure, fire, and aftershock sequences can be even more damaging then the primary effects. Moderate-magnitude earthquakes (i.e., magnitude 5.5 to 7.0) occur every few years in California and Alaska; whereas larger earthquakes recur about once every century. Recurrence intervals are longer in the eastern United States for the same size earthquakes.

Volcanic Eruptions

Volcanic eruptions are restricted to Hawaii and parts of Alaska, Washington, Oregon, California, Nevada, Utah, Wyoming, Arizona, and New Mexico in the western United States. The most destruction occurs near the source, but they generate lahars (i.e., mud flows generated by melting of snow and ice), ash fall, lava and pyroclastic flows, and lateral blasts which can affect broad geographic areas. The frequency of small volume eruptions is about once every century, and large volume eruptions about once every 1,000 to 5,000 years. Very large-volume eruptions, which are rare, recur over much longer time intervals.

U.S. PROGRAM

Recommendations for the research and applications elements of the U.S. Decade program have been prepared through the separate but complimentary efforts of a 17-member multidisciplinary, national committee convened in 1989 by the National Academy of Sciences' National Research Council (NRC) and a committee of the

Federal Government's science and disaster-reduction agencies. These dual efforts (Hays, 1990; National Research Council, 1987; 1991) call for coordinated action at the local, State, and Federal Government levels which could involve as many as 30,000 local jurisdictions and several million people. Because the state of knowledge and state of preparation for natural hazards varies widely in each local jurisdiction, all local jurisdictions will be encouraged to adopt and enforce policies during the 1990's that will reduce their potential losses from natural hazards (Figure 2).

LOSS REDUCTION MEASURES

FIGURE 2. Community goals in the U.S. Decade program.

Communities face a potential disaster when their populaces live and work in buildings exposed to natural hazards. The most hazardous locations are:

- in or adjacent to seismogenic zones capable of generating damaging earthquakes,
- along coasts where hurricanes, storm surges, or tsunami flood waves strike,
- near active volcanoes,
- on unstable slopes susceptible to landslides triggered by meteorological or seismological sources,
- in floodplains subject to inundation.
- in regions prone to tornadoes, and
- along wilderness/urban interfaces vulnerable to wildfires.

Communities have five broad options for coping with recurrent natural hazards. They are:

1. *Preparation* — use of basic knowlege about the natural hazard to plan for it and to mitigate its physical effects through building and land-use regulations.
2. *Prediction and Warning* — use of basic knowledge about the natural hazard to predict the occurrence and/or consequences of future events and to warn the populace at risk.

3. *Intervention* — use of basic knowledge to evacuate and/or intervene while a natural hazard is in progress in order to suppress its physical effects and to lessen societal impacts.
4. *Recovery* — use of basic knowledge gained from past experience to restore the essential community services to normal rapidly and economically and to correct deficiencies in building and land-use regulations and siting, design, and construction practices.
5. *Emergency Assistance*— use of basic knowledge to provide effective search and rescue assistance immediately after a natural hazard strikes a community.

The U.S. program will involve specialists from many different disciplines and will consist of a wide variety of research and applications projects (Figure 3). Some projects will be cooperative national and/or international endeavors designed to collect and analyze scientific data, and to share experiences on risk reduction techniques. Others will be technology transfer, knowledge utilization, or demonstration studies. Post-disaster investigations (e.g., post-earthquake investigations, Figure 4) will be an important element of the U.S. Decade program.

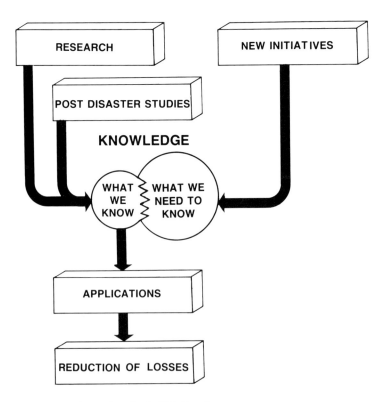

FIGURE 3. Strategy for projects in the U.S. Decade program.

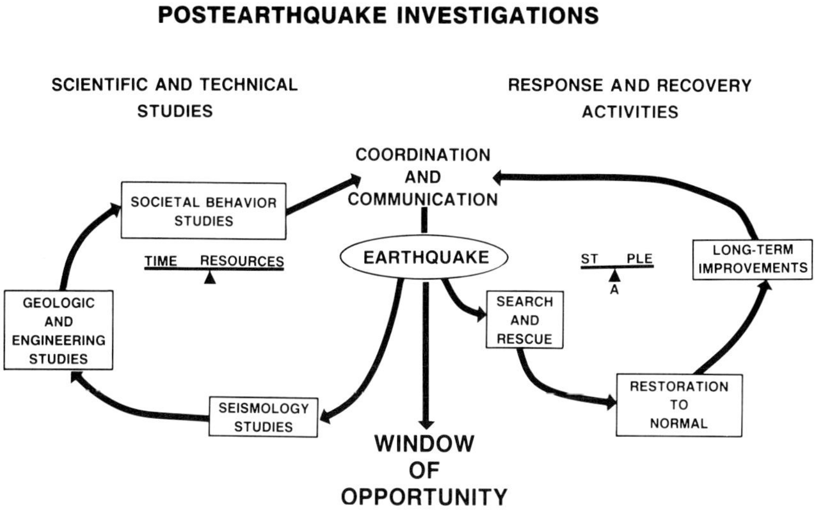

POSTEARTHQUAKE INVESTIGATIONS

FIGURE 4. Illustration of the activities that are initiated after a damaging earthquake to learn from and to cope with it. (ST = Social/Technical, PLE = Political/Legal/Economic, and A = Administrative. Origin must balance factors during the response and recovery process).

Technology transfer will be an important component of the U.S. program because the knowledge base and the capability of practitioners varies widely across the Nation. Each community needs to increase its capacity for enacting new or improved:

- hazard and risk assessments,
- preparedness plans and building and land-use regulations,
- prediction and warning systems,
- planning, siting, design, and construction practices,
- awareness, training, and education programs for all sectors of society, and
- implementation of loss reduction measures based on lessons learned from post-disaster investigations throughout the world.

Hazard and risk assessments are the starting points for communities to define realistic actions to reduce economic loss, human impacts, and loss of life and injuries from natural hazards. Such assessments can be used to improve their capabilities in preparedness, mitigation, prediction and warning, emergency response, and disaster recovery. The goal for each community is to answer the following questions:

- Where have natural hazards happened in the past?
- How severe were the physical effects (e.g., inundation, wind velocity, storm surge, slope failure, ground shaking, etc.) triggered in past events?
- How severe are physical effects expected to be in future events of various sizes?

- How frequently on the average do events capable of generating various levels of a particular physical effect occur?

The corresponding questions are needed for risk assessments:

- What damage will the physical effects of the various natural hazards cause to buildings and lifeline systems in the community?
- What has the community done in the past to control damage, deaths, injuries, economic loss, and loss of function from these effects?
- What societal, scientific, and technical actions can be initiated now to reduce the vulnerability of existing buildings and lifeline systems in the community?

Preparedness plans and mitigation measures need to be a part of society long before a natural hazard strikes the community. The goal is to construct hazard-resistant structures and to preplan for the requirements of emergency managers and the populace during the emergency assistance and the recovery periods. Mitigation measures (e.g., building and land-use regulations) have a goal of controlling damage to the physical development, loss of life, and societal disruption.

Prediction and warning systems are designed to provide all sectors of the population with information on the location, birth and development, severity, onset time, and duration of an impending natural hazard so that the people can evacuate or take other actions to lessen or suppress the anticipated physical effects. Reliable predictions and warnings give the community more options for reducing loss of life and damage to property. A prediction is based on science and depends on continuous monitoring in space and time of the causative mechanisms. It is a neutral statement which indicates that accumulated observations of the physical phenomena signal the imminent occurrence of a hazardous event (National Academy of Sciences, 1975). A warning is an interpretation of a prediction that takes public policy into account (National Academy of Sciences, 1975). It is a public declaration that the normal routines of life should be altered for a period of time to deal with the danger posed by the imminent event. Warnings depend heavily on timeliness, public information systems, and credible sources for their success. Two basic questions are at the heart of the science for predicting the time, place, and severity of a natural hazard. They are:

1. Why does a specific natural hazard occur and what are the precursory signals?

and

2. When it does occur, what will happen?

The answers to both questions involve the detection, measurement, and evaluation of changes in the physical environment. The answer to the first question "why," can be formulated from the answers to a series of interrelated questions which address the three critical elements of a prediction and warning; i.e., "where," "when," and "how severe." The answer to the second question, "what will happen," forms the warning that is communicated to the populace. This message should be designed to provide the threatened population with information about the threat and what can be done to prevent, avoid, or minimize it.

Hurricane Hugo and the Loma Prieta earthquake illustrate the value to society of good prediction and warning systems. Hurricane Hugo was identified, predicted, and tracked continuously by the National Weather Service from its birth in the Atlantic Ocean, to its sweep through the U.S. Virgin Islands and Puerto Rico, to its landfall at 12:20 a.m. on Friday, September 22, 1989, 10 miles north of Charleston, South Carolina, and its eventual decay to a storm category (Figure 5). Warnings were based on weather observation networks which included satellites, Doppler radars, and manned and automated surface and upper-air networks of meteorological and hydrological stations and on computer simulations of storm movement. Only 28 people from the Caribbean to the United States were killed because of effective evacuation procedures implemented on the basis of the warnings (U.S. Weather Service, 1990).

FIGURE 5. Predicted path for Hurricane Hugo.

In contrast, the Loma Prieta earthquake struck Northern California without any warning at 5:04 p.m. on Tuesday, October 17, 1989. Only its location in the Santa Cruz mountains and its size had been predicted in a 30-year forecast made by the U.S. Geological Survey in 1988 on the basis of the seismic cycle (Figure 6). The Loma Prieta earthquake caused property damage of $5.6 billion, 62 deaths, 3,757 injuries, and left 8,000 people homeless (State of California, 1990).

GAPS IN SEISMICITY 1/69—8/89

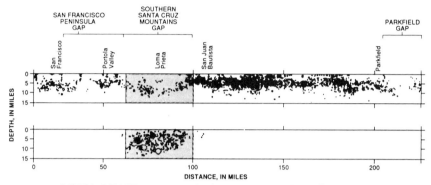

LOMA PRIETA EARTHQUAKE AND AFTERSHOCKS

FIGURE 6. Predicted and actual location of the Loma Prieta earthquake.

TECHNOLOGY TRANSFER

Technology transfer, the transfer of knowlege and know-how for societal use, will be an important component of the U.S. program and the IDNDR. Experience from the U.S. National Earthquake Hazards Reduction Program (NEHRP) has revealed the primary factors that constrain technology transfer (Hays, 1988) (Figure 7). They are:

- apathy (Der Heide, 1989),
- differences in perspectives of scientists/engineers and practitioners/decision-makers (Szanton, 1981), and
- continued use of ineffective technology transfer techniques (Hays, 1988).

Apathy, which causes knowledge to be unknown, unused, or ignored, has the following symptoms: 1) lack of awareness of the potential threat by sectors of the

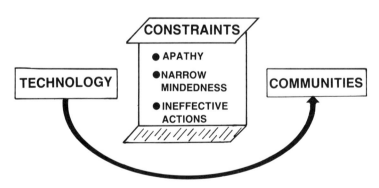

FIGURE 7. Factors that constrain technology transfer.

public; 2) underestimation of the risk to the community by public officials, businesses, or individuals; and 3) overreliance on the Federal and State government technology, luck, or personal ability to cope with a "hypothetical" problem.

The "law of apathy" can be stated as follows:

The status quo on risk reduction will be maintained until external forces compel change.

Technology transfer also lags because scientists/engineers and practitioners/decisionmakers have different perspectives, namely:

1. The ultimate objective of scientists/engineers is the respect of their peers; whereas, it is the approval of the contracting officer or the appointing official, voters or stockholders that matters to practitioners/decisionmakers.
2. The time requirement of scientists/engineers is long; whereas, it is short for practitioners/decisionmakers.
3. The most valued outcome of scientists/engineers is original insight; whereas, it is a reliable solution for practioners/decisionmakers.
4. The way results are expressed is obtuse and highly qualified for scientists/engineers; whereas, it is simple and absolute for practitioners/decisionmakers.
5. The preferred form of conclusion of scientists/engineers is multiple possibilities with emphasis on the uncertainties; whereas, it is the "best" solution with the uncertainties submerged for practions/decisionmakers.

The "law of narrowmindedness" can be stated as follows:

Scientists/engineers and practitioners/decisionmakers view risk reduction differently until external forces compel them to work together as partners to solve the problems faced by their community.

Technology (i.e., knowledge and know how) is transfered when correct assumptions are made about human behavior. For example, technology transfer will fail when the assumption is made that:

1. There is a "general public," instead of sectors of the public.
2. Mailing a technical report is sufficient for communication with all sectors of the public.
3. Scientists/engineers and practitioners/decisionmakers should not interact until the end of a research project.
4. Practioners/decisionmakers cannot understand or use complex scientific and technical information produced by scientists/engineers.
5. Practioners/decisionmakers will not invest in or use technology unless a scientific consensus has been reached.
6. Practioners/decisionmakers only want the "worst case" scenario for which scientists/engineers often have little consensus.
7. There is no "window of opportunity."

The "law of ineffective actions" can be stated as follows:

Transfer techniques based on false assumptions about human behavior will be ineffective and fail until external forces compel modifications that accommodate reality.

To overcome the factors that constrain technology transfer, the nation will continue its efforts to improve understanding of human and societal behavior, and seek to use external forces to cause relevant change in scientists/engineers and practitioners/decisionmakers. Experience in national and international programs has shown that the most effective external forces are:

- Recent damaging natural hazards such as flooding, earthquakes, hurricanes, or volcanic eruptions which cause a "window of opportunity."
- Creation of an institutional process where individuals or organizations have responsibility and accountability for risk reduction.
- Training to imporve professional skills, to "train the trainer," and to develop self capability.
- Legislation that establishes legal liability and a schedule for compliance.

EVALUATION OF U.S. PROGRAM

The progress of each local jurisdiction, which has the constitutional right to choose some, all, or none of the proposed elements of the U.S. Decade program, will be evaluated. A number of important qualitative changes can be measured as indices of accomplishment. Some of the easiest to measure are:

- The number of publications, maps, and products that deepen understanding of the physical and social aspects of natural disaster reduction and transfer technology.
- The number of local jurisdictions that: a) adopt and enforce risk reduction policies based on new or improved hazard and risk assessments, b) exercise their emergency response and recover plans, c) pass legislation to strengthen the enforcement of building and land-use regulations, or d) strengthen unsafe schools and hospitals and other essential facilities.
- The number of organizations in each local jurisdiction that establish training programs.
- The changes in professional practices that are based on the lessons learned from post-disaster investigations.

Some activities involving long-term changes in professional practices of planning, siting, design, and construction should also be measured, but they will require a longer monitoring period than the 1990's. The ultimate measure is to determine if societal impacts, loss of life, and economic losses from natural hazards in the United States decreases in the 21st century as a consequence of actions implemented during the 1990's.

CONCLUSION

The United States will benefit from the IDNDR because every State and Territory has communities that are at risk from one or more of the natural hazards which recur at intervals, ranging from every year for floods, landslides, tornadoes, hurricanes, and wildfires to once every few years for damaging earthquakes in California and drought episodes in some regions for the nation and once every century or longer for major earthquakes in Alaska, California, and the Mississippi Valley area or large volcanic eruptions in the Pacific Northwest and Alaska. By increasing the fundamental knowledge base and accelerating applications that reduce their risk, every community in the nation will be safer in the 21st century.

REFERENCES

Der Heide, Erik A. 1989. *Disaster Response: Principles of Preparation and Coordination.* C.V. Mosby Co., St. Louis, 363 pp.

Hays, Walter W. 1990. Perspectives on the International Decade for Natural Disaster Reduction: 1990-2000. *Earthquake Spectra,* v.6, pp. 1-20.

Hays, Walter, W. (Editor). 1988. Applications of Knowlege Produced in the Natural Earthquake Hazards Reduction Program: 1977-1987. *U.S. Geological Survey Open-File Report 88-13-B,* 50 pp.

Hays, Walter W. (Editor). 1981. Facing Geologic and Hydrologic Hazards: Earth-Science Considerations. *U.S. Geological Survey Professional Paper 1240-B,* 88 pp.

International Ad Hoc Group of Experts. 1989. *Implementing the International Decade for Natural Disaster Reduction, Report Prepared for the Secretary-General of the United Nations,* 58 pp.

National Academy of Sciences. 1975. *Earthquake Prediction and Public Policy, Report of the Panel on the Public Policy Implications of Earthquake Prediction.* Washington, D.C., 142 pp.

National Research Council. 1991. *A Safer Future: Reducing the Impacts of Natural Disaster,* National Academy of Sciences. Washington, D.C.

National Research Council. 1987. *Confronting Natural Disaster. An International Decade for Natural Hazard Reduction.* Natural Academy of Sciences. Washington, D.C., 60 pp.

State of California. 1990. *Competing Against Time, Report to Governor George Deukmejian from the Governor's Board of Inquiry on the 1989 Loma Prieta Earthquake.* North Highlands, CA, 264 pp.

Szanton, Peter. 1981. *Not Well Advised.* Russell Sage Foundation and Ford Foundation, 81 pp.

United Nations. 1989. *International Decade for Natural Disaster Reduction, 44th Session of the General Assembly, Resolution 44/236,* 6 pp.

U.S. National Weather Services. 1990. *Natural Disaster Survey Report, Hurricane Hugo, September 10-22, 1989.* National Oceanic Atmospheric Administration. Washington, D.C., 68 pp.

U.S. Geological Survey. 1988. Working Group on California Earthquake Probabilities, 1988, Probabilities of large earthquakes occurring in California on the San Andreas fault. *U.S. Geological Survey Open-File Report 88-398,* 62 pp.

Natural and Technological Disasters: Causes, Effects and Preventive Measures. Edited by S.K. Majumdar, G.S. Forbes, E.W. Miller, and R.F. Schmalz. © 1992, The Pennsylvania Academy of Science.

Chapter Two

HUMAN RESPONSE TO NATURAL AND TECHNOLOGICAL DISASTERS

E. WILLARD MILLER

Professor of Geography and Associate Dean for Resident Instruction (Emeritus)
College of Earth and Mineral Sciences
The Pennsylvania State University
University Park, PA 16802

INTRODUCTION

The human race has suffered catastrophes from the earliest times. Records show that humans have always tried to understand these cataclysmic events. In time, man has attempted to develop themes and explanations in order to justify his fears and powerlessness. These beliefs have been incorporated into the culture of the people. While modern man has gained scientific insights into many natural and technological disasters, catastrophes are still frequently looked upon as "acts of God." As civilization has advanced the complexity of man-made disasters has increased. It is the purpose of this chapter to discuss some of the human responses to natural and technological calamities.

DEFINITION AND DIMENSION OF DISASTERS

According to Thorndike and Barnhart's Comprehensive Desk Dictionary, disaster is an "event that causes much suffering." Webster's New Universal Dictionary uses such words as, "calamity, a sudden serious misfortune, or an unfortunate event." Disasters may be sudden and dramatic events such as an earthquake, or they may develop gradually, such as a prolonged drought, with the ultimate destruction of the agricultural capacity of a region. Thus, their duration may vary tremendously from a few moments to years in time (Raphael, 1986).

PSYCHOLOGICAL ASPECTS OF DISASTERS

Most disasters are reported in statistical terms such as the value of property destroyed, the number of persons made homeless, or number of dead and injured. While these figures are important they do not reveal such vital human emotions as terror, anguish, fear, and despair. The emotions of a disaster are usually not temporary but are remembered and relived over time. Although people survive the trauma of a disaster and continue to function in an apparently normal fashion, there may be painful emotional scars. At the same time, the individual may gain new strengths and understandings that result from the mastery of the challenge. In the testing of individual behavior at times of disaster, they may find that they were a great deal more courageous than they had thought they would be, but in contrast, the opposite can occur. Encounters with death frequently make people reevaluate their own lives and what is important to them and the people with whom they are associated.

STAGES OF A DISASTER

Most researchers recognize that there are several stages to a disaster (Tyhurst, 1950; Wolfenstein, 1957). The first stage of *risk assessment and preparedness* recognizes that a disaster is possible. This is a time of attempting to make a risk assessment and, if possible, prepare to reduce the effects of the disaster. The actual disaster may begin with a period of *warning,* such as changes in weather indicating an approaching hurricane, followed by the direct *impact* when the disaster strikes. In many disasters a warning does not occur, such as an explosion at a factory or an earthquake. The impact stage may last only a few seconds, such as in an earthquake, or it may persist over years, as in a prolonged drought. The impact stage is the time of destruction and death. The next stage is the *survival and inventory of damage.* In this stage there is an evaluation of what has occurred and the initial assessment of how to proceed. It is critical that it occurs as soon as the impact stage ends in order to rescue human casualties. Finally, there is the *recovery* period that may take a prolonged period of time.

Disasters normally have not only a time dimension, but also a spatial dimension. Disasters can occur in a vast area such as a hurricane in the Gulf of Mexico, or be confined to a tiny area such as lava from an erupting volcano. The time of rescue and rehabilitation may vary greatly depending upon the size and destruction within an area. There is usually a rapid movement of essentials such as medicine and food. An important aspect of the time dimension is the development of an information network so that messages can be sent about victims and their well-being (Raphael, 1986).

Risk Assessment and Preparedness

It is usually impossible to prepare a risk assessment of most technological disasters such as an unexpected explosion in a factory or a nuclear accident such as Chernobyl (Tyler, McGraw, 1983). For natural disasters, geographers, meteorologists, volcanologists, and ecologists are increasingly able to provide highly scientific risk estimates of the possibility or probability of disaster. For example, earthquake and volcanic zones are well defined, and while it is not possible to give precise timing of an earthquake or volcano eruption, warnings can be provided of an impending disaster.

In the evaluation of risk assessment a series of steps are necessary if the information is to be effective. These include the amount of predictive knowledge accumulated, how it is assessed, who has access to it, and the control over its dispersal. If a disaster is not likely to occur the information may be only important to relevant scientists. However, in this system of information distribution lies one of the key problems. For example, the government and other authorities may have access to relevant information, but for many reasons may not distribute it to the general public. To illustrate, due to specific guidelines to ensure safety of buildings and bridges in a zone of potential disaster they may, to a large extent, be "disaster proofed." Thus the threat of functional failure may be so unlikely and unpredictable that any disaster preparedness becomes extremely difficult, if not impossible.

If preparedness for disaster is to be effective, a system of communications must be adequate (Petek, Atkinson, 1982). Preparedness information is normally directed at either vulnerability reduction and thus possible disaster prevention or for the initial planning of post-impact response. Over the years a large number of groups from the local to the national level, have developed plans that are concerned with disaster preparedness. Operationally, many of these groups function with legislative backing and at a variety of resource levels. They usually are empowered to determine the extent of a possible disaster and special powers may be given to provide assistance on preventing, or lessening the effects of the disaster. Because disaster preparedness legislation controls the actions of people before a disaster occurs, compliance may be limited for the concept of control is alien to the value of individual freedom. For example, people continue to build homes on floodplains and on the slopes of active volcanic mountains.

In recent times insurance and special financial inducements have aided in promoting preparedness (Berren, Beigel and Barker, 1982). These efforts are frequently directed toward the safety of the individual. For example, a particular design and material used in a home may lessen its destruction in a hurricane, or if a house is built above the floodplain the insurance rate will be lower than if it were subject to flooding. These economic factors in preparedness are, however, only moderately well developed and certainly not uniformly used.

There are also psychological and social factors that are frequently intangible that influence preparedness for disaster. If the danger occurs rarely many people will ignore the destructiveness of its consequences. Others may accept the danger, but because they believe they can do nothing, they disregard its existence. In contrast, some individuals will undertake personal missions dealing with preparedness. For example, some people have dedicated their existence to the antinuclear movement (Tyler, McGraw, 1983).

The cost of preparedness is not a minor factor in preparing for a disaster. When disasters are rare there may be the perception, which can be correct, that the cost of insurance and material items is too great, when balanced against the risk (Petek, Atkinson, 1982).

There are also cultural variables in that societies view disaster in different perspectives. Mileti (1980) contrasts American and Japanese preparedness for earthquake disaster. The Japanese view preparedness as an opportunity to respond to disaster before a disaster occurs. In contrast, the Americans tend to view preparedness as an intrusion on their freedom of choice and do not respond until convinced that there is a high risk danger.

Warning and Impact

The warning that a disaster is impending is one of the most critical aspects for protection of human suffering and material destruction in a region. When the warning does not occur, there is the potential for catastrophes (Raphael, 1986). Because disasters are rare most people do not recognize that one could occur. When a person has experienced a disaster, they are much more likely to respond to early warnings. In contrast, if a warning is given and the disaster does not occur, there is a tendency to take the next warning less seriously (Wolfenstein, 1957). Each individual has a personal perception of disaster that has developed over time relating to specific memories or fantasies that are acquired by personal experience. Special fears may enlarge the importance of traumatic events such as an injury or even a death (Janis, 1962).

After the initial warning signal of a potential disaster, there is usually a period of dramatic waiting (Quarantelli, Dynes, 1973). At the moment of impact there is the terror of helplessness. If it is a major disaster, survival is the primary goal. It is entirely possible that death will appear imminent with the ultimate feeling that "this is it." Regardless of the outcome, this is an emotional experience that will be remembered for a lifetime. For each type of disaster the fear will be different. If it is a flood the fear of drowning may be overwhelming; if an earthquake, the fear of crushing and asphyxiation may be realistic.

In a disaster, there may be a feeling that the individual has been forsaken by God and man (Wolfenstein, 1957). In the desire for relief, prayer may be spoken the first time in years or people may pray to a God that they previously did not acknowledge. In a disaster there is almost always the desire to escape. Escape, however, is controlled and usually is not expressed in panic behavior. Sometimes a person will exhibit super-human power and strength in preserving not only his own safety, but the safety of others. Many individuals will rise to heights of valor in using their own bodies to protect loved ones who are weaker or older. This behavior is universal in all types of natural and technological calamities. During a disaster there is a desire to be with other persons. There may be fear and concern about the welfare of family members and people will undergo great hardship to protect those that are loved most.

Panic behavior in which there is disorganized activity and loss of control of emotion varies less frequently in disasters than might be expected. Panic occurs when communications are lost with others and what to expect in the future. Panic reflects nonsocial behavior and in a disaster the human desire to protect others appears to overcome the irrational panic urge (Quarantelli, Dynes, 1973).

If the disaster is prolonged a person may develop what has come to be known as the *disaster syndrome*. Under these conditions the individual is unable to respond rationally. The person will appear dazed, apathetic, and stunned and may wander around aimlessly. In this condition the person may not be able to recognize existing dangers. During this period of disfunction, which may last from several hours to days, the person may need psychiatric aid for recovery of normal activities (Tyhurst, 1950).

A major consideration during the impact stage is how long will it last and can I survive a prolonged period of stress. The will to survive may take a number of directions. During this period people may take refuge with others and this human attachment provides incentives to survive as a group (Henderson, Bostock, 1977). Individuals are normally overly concerned about the welfare of close relationships such as a wife, mother, sister, or friend.

During a disaster an individual develops an innate desire to survive. It is simply a will to live. Under these conditions the individual responds in ways that may not be characteristic under normal conditions. A physical and moral strength appears as an intense desire to defeat the forces that are trying to destroy him.

At times of stress the human mind will devise strategies of survival (Weisalth, 1982). Experiences of the past may be recalled that provide a means of focusing on a present problem. An intellectual endeavor may be a defensive attempt to avoid the recognition of the real danger, but at the same time provide a mechanism for survival. Through willpower a person may shut out the feelings of danger. This involves a sense of unreality as if this could not happen to me. At this time there may be a concentration of thoughts that have no relation to the present danger but recall such aspects as memories of the pleasant past or thoughts of the hereafter. There may be a feeling that the present situation is paying for past sins, or prayer may be offered calling for the protection from a deity as an omnipresenet force.

Finally, there is sometimes a feeling of hope during the impact stage. A good leader can mobilize hope to provide a motivating force necessary to take the necessary actions for survival. In the feeling of hope there is always the anticipation that the disaster will end. In essence, hope functions to assist survival by controlling mood (Raphael, 1986).

Survival and Inventory of Damages

As soon as the impact lessens the spontaneous inventory begins. The initial task is to take care of the injured and dying. Individuals who were in the midst of the disaster may still be experiencing shock and are disoriented. Nevertheless, the full emotional impact is not likely to be experienced in this initial stage of rescue. When the devastation becomes apparent the emotional release may begin. The victim's physical state is also important for persons may have sustained injuries and need help. The confrontation with disaster makes all persons equal in their basic humanity to help others (Raphael, 1986).

In the period following the disaster the psychological responses are usually termed post-traumatic reactions. These are normally manifested as involving the reliving and reexperiencing of the event. These reflections of the immediate past are frequently accompanied with tremors, palpitations, and even extreme anxiety and panic. During sleep they take the form of nightmares involving death and injury. Many people will not experience post-traumatic reactions, but when it does occur the time of stress may be indefinite. During the stress period, however, the individual may have difficulty with interpersonal relations, concentration at work, capacity for pleasure, guilt about survival and/or an intensification of symptoms by symbolic events.

Of all survival problems, the coping with the death of a loved one may be most difficult. In a disaster themes of death are particularly intense. The impact of the shock is so overwhelming that the individual may direct his activities to aid those who have survived. There is frequently a feeling of guilt by those who have survived. Regrettably the trauma period may last for an extended period of time.

The emotions of an individual who is experiencing a tragedy may change very rapidly. After the initial shock has been felt, rescue activities may provide a release of pent up emotions. This becomes particularly important when there is a massive need to aid individuals and possibly save lives. An individual may assume a leadership role that was unknown in the past. This is particularly important where the discharge of physical activity may contribute to the return of emotional control.

There are a number of other activities that are important in the period immediately following the impact stage. There is frequently a need to describe what occurred. This is sometimes expressed by "talking through" the incident. In the concrete expression of words the individual can escape personal feelings. The meaning of the experience can be articulated and the recognition of mastery can be achieved. The descriptions of others may make it possible for an individual to gain a better personal perspective of the disaster. The talking through, however, can operate in two directions. In one role, an emotional release may be experienced. In contrast, the person may repeat endlessly the experience of the disaster and lock in the traumatic event with little or no emotional release (Quarantelli, 1978).

A form of release from emotional pressure may be expressed through tears. Emotionally this is most difficult for men, particularly in cultures where men do not cry. The first time an individual can cry, not in relief, but in sorrow, may be the turning point in achieving a normal future. Expression of grief may thus be a part of the recovery process. Tears may express not only what an individual went through but for the death and suffering of others.

Besides emotional suffering there may also be problems created by loss of personal possessions. Vital and symbolic treasured possessions may be destroyed. These may include papers, documents, photos, and other items that cannot be replaced.

Survivors always say that "material possessions are of no importance compared to losing a life." While there is fundamental truth in this statement, the loss of personal possessions has a significant impact and may delay recovery for many months (Raphael, 1986).

The reaction to the loss of a home may also have a devastating effect. To many a home symbolizes identity and the continuity of life, not just for the individual, but for the family. It is, thus, far more than the monetary loss that the destruction of a home symbolizes. In order to salvage some mementos there is normally a searching through the ashes or ruins for prized possessions. Even small things may have important emotional links with the past. There is often a sense of anger, of "why me?" connected with the loss of a home, especially if nearby homes are left undamaged. At times anger is repressed with the loss of a home because there is a feeling that others have suffered more (Krim, 1978).

If the disaster covers a fairly large area with the destruction of whole neighborhoods, people may lose their sense of place (Barton, 1969). They have thus lost their community and with it, their communality with relatives and friends. The sense of a neighborhood and friendliness is gone resulting in purposelessness and disorientation. This type of dislocation leads to a loss of community spirit. There is a feeling that the past may never be recovered as a post-disaster environment is created (Erickson, 1976).

Recovery

After the initial assessment of the disaster is made the long process of recovery begins. Of immediate concern is the provision of adequate shelter until homes can be rebuilt. This is the time when outside organizations, both private and governmental, must play a critical role. It is also a time of many complications when adjustment to the losses brings frustrations.

There are many types of stress during the recovery period. A devastated area may have to be evacuated. It may, however, be difficult to persuade people to leave their homes, even though the house may be nearly destroyed. The home becomes a symbol of protection, safety, and sanctuary. Evacuation may only occur when outside authorities make this drastic decision. At this time, family support may be crucial in moving loved ones to a new location (Cobb, 1976). The initial evacuation may be to a temporary shelter such as a tent or a large auditorium. This form of public emergency shelter may be satisfactory for a few days, but in terms of physical facilities is rarely satisfactory. As soon as possible the disaster victims must go to homes of family members or close friends. Kinship networks respond readily in times of disasters (Bolin, 1982).

After the initial response for shelters, the problems are not necessarily solved if there is an extended period before a new residence is found. People may complain that there is too great crowding and that there is no privacy. Thus an extended period of recovery may have many personal problems. If the new home is far from the original community there may be the feeling of loneliness of living in an alien world. Most people do not realize the importance of a home environment until it no longer exists. Further, the dislocation usually means that the new place provides a lower quality environment. Smaller quarters and at times many of the necessities, such as a toilet, may not function well.

After the initial relocation there still exists many problems. Such questions arise as, what will happen to me? How long will it take to be normal again? What aid can I get from private and public agencies? If these, and many other questions, are not answered a feeling of insecurity develops. A sound information system is essential to the welfare of people who have experienced a disaster (Bolin, 1982).

Besides the problems of coping with the physical aspects of the disaster there may be emotional problems. These may include ongoing anxiety, psychosomatic effects, general distress and post traumatic reactions. These may appear as feelings of exhaustion, lack of sleep, family tensions, social withdrawal, inability to concentrate and excessive preoccupation with the disaster. When these symptoms occur psychiatric help is required. This type of help may be needed for an extended period of time.

MANAGEMENT OF DISASTERS

In recent years there has been a growing desire to develop systems of hazard management. Three concepts have evolved as a function of the public policy-making process. As a consequence a number of private organizations and public agencies have developed for policy formulation and assistance.

The private organizations are of two general types. The first type are those that exist privately to fulfill roles in some phase of community emergency management. Examples are Red Cross, Disaster Relief Programs, Mennonite Disaster Service, and local search and rescue groups. The second type of organization has special equipment and/or expertise potentially useful in emergency management (American Red Cross, 1975).

Traditionally the private sector's role in emergency management has focused on the response-and-recovery phase and has involved providing either material or skills. Special skills are normally contributed by organizations with disaster management structured into their functions. They include sheltering and feeding evacuated populations.

In recent years private organizations have also become active in the mitigation and preparedness phases of emergency management. For example, the Red Cross has initiated an active program in preparedness for a nuclear attack. The effectiveness of these endeavors can be of great importance in preparing a community to respond to a disaster. During a disaster a private organization may implement its established plan of providing aid and have its own plan of determining priorities.

In essence, the private sector engaged in hazard management performs these functions: it identifies and articulates citizen concerns related to emergency-management issues, it supports volunteers in all phases of emergency-management, and it contributes special skills and materials to emergency-management problems (Perry, Mushkatel, 1984). The private organization is increasingly taking an active role in identifying emergency management needs. By this means the private agencies influence the total components of the emergency management system.

Government at all levels—local, city, county, state and federal—have responsibilities for emergency relief. The public policy that has gradually evolved is a product of the interaction of all govenmental bodies. When there is an agreement on procedural policies there can be a considerable degree of cooperation among the governmental units. On the other hand, when there are disagreements, intergovernmental relations may be strained and emergency policies poorly developed and implemented (Raphael, 1986).

The state governments play a major role in emergency management for they are responsible for the safety of their citizens. States have two definite roles to play in hazard management. First, they must be active in hazard management programs. This preparedness is regulated through laws, statutes and regulations. Secondly, the state government has the responsibility of coordination between all governmental agencies from the local to the federal. In this way the state can place all its resources into a total system. Most states, such as the Pennsylvania Emergency Management Agency (PEMA), now have an office of emergency management and a network of operations across the state.

The role of the federal government has increased in recent years. In 1979 the Federal Emergency Management Agency (FEMA) was established to serve as a focal point for federal efforts. FEMA participates in some hazards and emergency activities directly. It also encourages hazardous management activities in other agencies. FEMA's matching of local and state needs with appropriate federal resources is one of its major goals. FEMA's authority is derived from legalization, regulations, and executive orders. It can influence these components through establishing rules, using its influence in the establishment of executive orders, and through financial assistance. (Perry, Mushkatel, 1984). FEMA's efforts are particularly important as a source of long-range recovery resources. It also sponsors research and distributes information for all types of disasters. In conclusion, the federal government promotes hazards and emergency management among other public and private sectors, coordinates activities among these sectors, and provides resources for hazardous and emergency management.

RETROSPECT

Disasters are a fundamental part of the fabric of life. Although each individual must cope with a disaster within his own framework of references, there are common threads that help an individual and a community through an event that is beyond the natural order of day to day occurrence. At all social levels, from the individual to the community, the sharing of a calamity provides both emotional release and the healing of deep wounds.

The formal procedures of reports, documentation, and analysis provides a systematic framework that gives order to a chaotic event. In this way the disaster is evaluated and provides a basis for understanding how a disaster may be survived.

This reformulation of the past may be represented concretely by ceremonies and memorials commemorating how humans reacted, sometimes in super-human ways, to a calamity. Out of these endeavors it is hoped that people will learn how to be better prepared to cope with the problems of a calamity. In the final analysis the forces of either a natural or technological disaster may be so overwhelming it is impossible to prepare and even more impossible to predict human response to forces that are beyond human control.

REFERENCES

American National Red Cross. 1975. *Disaster Relief Program.* Washington, DC: American Red Cross National Headquarters.

Barton, A.H. 1969. *Communities in Disaster: A Sociological Analysis of Collective Stress Situation.* Garden City, NY: Doubleday.

Berren, M.R., A. Beigel and G. Barker. 1982. A Topology for the Classification of Disasters: Implications for Intervention. *Community Mental Health Journal.* 18(2):120-134.

Bolin, R.C. 1982. *Long-term Family Recovery from Disaster.* Monograph No. 36. Boulder, CO: University of Colorado, Institute of Behavioral Science.

Cobb, S. 1976. "Social Support as a Moderator of Life Stress," *Psychosomatic Medicine.* 38-300-14.

Cornell, J. 1976. *The Great International Disaster Book.* New York: Scribner.

Erickson, Pat, Thomas Drabek, William Key, and Juanita Crowe. 1976. "Families in Disaster," *Mass Emergencies.* 1:206-213.

Fritz, Charles E. and Harvey Williams. 1957. "The Human Being in Disasters: A Recent Perspective." *Annals.* 309:42-51.

Henderson, S. and T. Bostock. 1977. "Coping Behavior after Shipwrecks." *British Journal of Psychiatry.* 131:15-20.

Janis, Irving. 1962. "Psychological Effects of Warnings," in G. Baker and D. Chapman, eds., *Man and Society in Disaster.* New York: Basic Books.

Krim, A. 1978. "Urban Disaster: Victims of Fire," in Parad, H.P. and others, eds, *Emergency and Disaster Management: A Mental Health Sourcebook.* Baltimore: Charles Press.

Mileti, Dennis S. 1980. "Human Adjustment to the Risk of Environmental Extremes." *Sociology and Social Research.* 65:327-347.

Miller, E. Willard and Ruby M. Miller. 1990. *Environmental Hazards: Radioactive Materials and Wastes.* Santa Barbara, CA: ABC/CLIO.

Perry, Ronald W. and Alvin H. Mushkatel. 1984. *Disaster Management: Warning Response and Community Relocation.* Westport, CT: Quorum Books.

Petak, W.J. and A.A. Atkisson. 1982. *Natural Hazard Risk Assessment and Public Policy: Anticipating the Unexpected.* New York: Springer-Verlag.

Quarantelli, E., ed. 1978. *Disasters, Theory and Research.* Beverly Hills, CA: Sage.

————— and R. Dynes. 1973. "When Disaster Strikes." *New Society*. 23:5-9.

Raphael, Beverley. 1986. *When Disaster Strikes*. New York: Basic Books.

Tyhurst, J.S. 1950. "Individual Reactions to Community Disaster: The Natural History of Psychiatric Phenomena," *American Journal of Psychiatry*. 107:764-769.

Tyler, T.R. and K.M. McGraw. 1983. "The Threat of Nuclear War: Risk Interpretation and Behavioral Response." *Journal of Social Issues*. 39:25-40.

Weisalth, L. and A. Sund. 1982. "Psychiatric Problems in Unifil and the U.N. Soldiers Stress Syndrome." *International Review of the Army, Navy and Air Force Medical Services,* 55:109-116.

Wolfenstein, M. 1957. *Disaster: A Psychological Essay*. Glencoe, IL: Free Press.

Natural and Technological Disasters: Causes, Effects and Preventive Measures. Edited by
S.K. Majumdar, G.S. Forbes, E.W. Miller, and R.F. Schmalz. © 1992, The Pennsylvania Academy
of Science.

Chapter Three

RADIOACTIVE WASTE: MYTH AND REALITY

ROBERT F. SCHMALZ

Professor of Geology
The Pennsylvania State University
University Park, PA 16802

INTRODUCTION

Radioactive waste includes all waste materials, whether liquid, solid or gas, which
are either inherently radioactive or which are contaminated by radiactive nuclides.
(Some materials with very low levels of radioactivity such as home smoke detec-
tors and certain LCD watches are regarded as "Below Regulatory Concern," and
are treated as ordinary domestic or industrial trash.) Large volumes of radioactive
waste are generated by the military as by-products of nuclear weapons manufacture and research. For reasons of national security (in part) such waste is managed
exclusively by the federal government, and the information available concerning
the quantity produced, its nature or its disposition is incomplete. Accordingly, this
article will address primarily the management of non-military waste, but the reader
should bear in mind that this represents only a fraction of the total radioactive waste
generated annually in the United States.

THE RADIOACTIVE WASTE STREAM

Non-military radioactive wastes include such diverse materials as intensely
radioactive spent fuel assemblies from nuclear reactors, liquid scintillation
"cocktails," uranium and thorium mine waste and mill tailings, depleted industrial

neutron and gamma-ray sources, certain types of medical and research waste, filter materials and ion-exchange resins, and mildly contaiminated protective clothing and cleaning materials from industry, research laboratories, hospitals and power plants. In terms of volume, the waste stream is dominated by protective clothing and clean-up materials. Despite their very small volume, however, and because of their very intense radioactivity, spent reactor fuel assemblies contribute the largest portion of the radioactivity in the civilian waste stream (Singh, 1989).

REGULATION AND MANAGEMENT

Federal regulations divide the waste stream into four categories: (i) high-level waste including spent nuclear fuel, (ii) transuranic waste (TRU), (iii) uranium and thorium mining waste and mill tailings, and (iv) low-level radioactive waste (LLRW).

The management of high-level waste, composed predominantly of spent fuel and the radioactive liquid and solid wastes produced in reprocessing such fuel, is the responsibility of the federal government. Although nuclear fuel is no longer reprocessed in the United States, moderate quantities of reprocessing wastes, both liquid and solid, were generated by experimental plants until 1977. Substantial progress has been made in stabilizing these waste materials in the form of synthetic rock-like materials ("Synroc"), glass or ceramic pellets (Hoffman, 1989; Ringwood, 1978). Spent reactor fuel assemblies are held in "temporary" storage at reactor sites, awaiting siting, design and construction of a permanent federal repository.

Transuranic waste, that is, waste materials containing radioactive elements with atomic number greater than 92, is produced almost exclusively by the nuclear weapons industry, and is managed by the government, for reasons of both security and convenience.

Although less strictly regulated in the past (Collé et al, 1980), uranium mine and mill wastes now are managed directly by the government or by the mine operator under strict government supervision ("Uranium Mill Tailings Radiation Control Act of 1978" (PL 95-604)).

Low-level radioactive wastes (LLRW) are defined as all waste materials which are inherently radioactive or which are contaminated by radionuclides and *which are not high-level waste, spent nuclear fuel, uranium mine and mill tailings or TRU* (PL 96-573; PL 97-425). (Many persons are critical of this definition, on the grounds that it does not say what constitutes LLRW but specifies instead what *is not* LLRW. In fact, of course, in this form the definition is far more comprehensive than any attempt to specify *all* forms of low-level waste could possibly be.) Since enactment of the Low-Level Waste Policy Act in December, 1980, responsibility for managing LLRW in the civilian waste stream resides with the individual states. Historically, however, most forms of radiactive waste were treated little differently from ordinary waste. As a result, the activities of many mining, industrial and research facilities prior to and during World War II led to environmental contamination by radio-nuclides escaping from landfills, storm- and sanitary sewers, industrial holding ponds, etc. (eg.: US DOE, 1981). The ecological significance of such contamination has been fully appreciated only recently (Collé et al, 1980; Gangopadhyay et al, 1987). In conjunction with the development of nuclear weapons during World War II, the federal government assumed authority over and responsibility for virtually all aspects of the nuclear industry, including waste management. But by mid-century, however, increasing use of radionuclides in industry, medicine and research made it clear that continued management of civilian-generated radioactive waste by the government would become intolerably burdensome, and would afford no meaningful benefit in terms of national security. The federal government therefore authorized the development of commercial facilities for the disposal of certain non-military radioactive wastes. The facilities were to be licensed by the US. Atomic Energy Commission (now the Nuclear Regulatory Commission) and operated under its supervision. Between 1962 and 1971, six such facilities were opened, three of which continue to receive wastes at the present time (Table 1). These commercial disposal facilities were permitted to accepted only low-level radioactive waste (LLRW). Spent fuel, TRU's, high-level wastes, mine and mill tailings and all military wastes were to remain the responsibility of the federal government.

COMMERCIAL LLRW MANAGEMENT EXPERIENCE

The commercial LLRW disposal facilities were (and continue to be) highly controversial. Enthusiastically supported by some host communities as economic boons, they were vigorously opposed by others, particularly environmental groups (eg.: CNSI, undated (a); Smith, 1984; Sierra Club, undated). All of the commercial facilities disposed of wastes by shallow land burial. Liquids and mixed wastes (mixed hazardous chemical and radioactive waste) were accepted for disposal, almost any form of packaging was permitted, and operational procedures (stacking, back-filling and capping in particular) were lax by modern standards. Despite these implied faults, however, the design and operation of the commercial LLRW disposal facilities were held to far more exacting standards than were ordinary "sanitary landfills" of the period. In general, operational precautions focused on minimizing exposure of personnel, while siting and engineering standards emphasized long-term environmental effects.

TABLE 1
Commercial LLRW Disposal Facilities in the United States

Location	Opened	Closed	Volume (thru 1980)	Remarks
Beatty, NV	1962	open	3,182,000 cubic feet	
Maxey Flats, KY	1963	1978	4,770,000 cubic feet	
West Valley, NY	1963	1975	2,360,000 cubic feet	
Richland, WA	1965	open	2,180,000 cubic feet	
Sheffield, IL	1967	1978	3,196,000 cubic feet	Filled.
Barnwell, SC	1971	open	11,425,000 cubic feet	

(Clancy et al, 1981)

Unfortunately, it soon became apparent that the design and operational requirements, rigorous as they were by prevailing standards, were insufficient to ensure total containment of the wastes. In several cases, radioactive contaminants were detected in monitoring wells located around the disposal site boundaries. The observed concentrations were closed to the threshold of detectability, well below the level considered hazardous, and contamination was in most cases confined to the site itself and its surrounding buffer zone (Anon., 1986; Cartwright, 1982; Grant, 1982; Kelleher et al, 1983). Nonetheless, the fact that any radioactive material had escaped from the disposal facility justified public concern. Without intending to minimize that concern, it is important to acknowledge two relevant factors which may have caused the public to over-react: first, the widespread public apprehension about any form of radioactivity, and second, the peculiarity of radioactive materials which makes them detectable in concentrations which are orders of magnitude lower than the detectability thresholds of most other environmental contaminants. The first factor stems from the mysterious and frightening qualities of radioactivity - radiation cannot be detected by any of the senses, its effects are rarely evident at once, and the consequences of exposure (among them radiation sickness, cancer and possible genetic damage) are viewed with particular dread. Even experts disagree about the radiation dose at which these effects may be initiated (BEIR, 1972; RERF, 1987). As a result, in the eyes of the public any exposure to radiation is generally regarded as an unacceptable hazard. Environmental activists, particularly those opposed to nuclear power, have exploited this public concern, sometimes irresponsibly.

The second factor, the environmental detectability of radionuclides, results from the extremely sensitive instrumentation which is available to detect and identify radioactive isotopes (Jester et al, 1985). We can easily identify and accurately measure the concentration of such contaminants in the environment at levels far below (often several orders of magnitude below) the level at which we can detect or identify may common organic toxins and carcinogens, for example. Consequently, an apprehensive public, already sensitized by the fear of cancer, may react vigorously to reports of radionuclide contamination even at levels which barely exceed normal background, while ignoring very real health threats posed by non-radiogenic contaminants in food, water or air. Both factors continue to aggravate the socio-political problems of radioactive waste management (Bord, 1985, 1989; Friedman, 1985).

Experience gained in the operation of commercial low-level radioactive waste disposal facilities during the 1960's gave rise to stricter performance standards and led to improved siting, design and operating procedures for shallow land burial facilities (Schmalz, 1987). The largest LLRW disposal facility in the United States, that operated by Chem-Nuclear Systems, Inc. at Barnwell, S.C., has experienced no serious problems through twenty years of continuous operation (Smith, 1984). The development of waste overpacks such as the "SUREPAK" © design proposed by Westinghouse, and a similar design proposed for use in North Carolina and Pennsylvania by Chem-Nuclear Systems (and already pilot-tested at Barnwell) should provide even more effective waste confinement and facilitate retrievability should recovery of a particular waste package ever become necessary (Westinghouse Corporation, 1987; CNSI, undated (a), (b), 1990).

Alternative LLRW disposal methods have been extensively tested elsewhere: above-ground storage, earth-mounded bunkers, and deep-mine repositories have all proven satisfactory (see Salander et al, 1980; Lavie & Barthoux, 1982; Carter & Rao, 1984; Bennett & McAneny, 1985; Schmalz, 1989). Most current LLRW disposal plans focus on above-grade engineered facilities utilizing cement overpacks in an earth-mounted bunker (CNSI, undated (a), (b)). Successful facilities of this general type have been used in Europe for several decades (Bennett & McAneny, 1985). Although none has yet been built or licensed in the United States, such facilities are being designed for several of the LLRW regional compacts organized under the provisions of the Low-Level Waste Policy Act. Although costly to build and to operate (disposal costs are estimated to be on the order of $150/cubic foot in 1990 dollars), there is every reason to believe that these proposed waste facilities will provide an extra margin of safety, and will ensure effective containment of low-level radioactive wastes for 300 to 500 years.

CURRENT STATUS OF LLRW MANAGEMENT

Under the terms of the Low-Level Waste Policy Act, the states were required to provide for safe disposal of all LLRW generated within their borders, either individually or through regional "compacts," by January 1, 1986. The Act was subsequently amended to provide more time for the organization of compacts and the licensing of disposal facilities ("Low-Level Radioactive Waste Policy Amendments Act of 1985"). The 1985 Amendments Act established "milestones" which states (or compacts) were required to meet to avoid penalties and waste disposal surcharges. Despite these inducements, progress has been slow. As yet, no state or compact has a licensed LLRW facility in operation (except those states which were host to one of the commercial facilities operating prior to 1980); most have not progressed beyond the preliminary site selection phase; several have not yet approved enabling legislation. In Pennsylvania, eleven years after the enactment of the Low-Level Radioactive Waste Policy Act (PL 96-573), only the first two milestones have been met on schedule. A compact has been formed (with West Virginia, Delaware and Maryland), and Pennsylvania has been identified as the initial host state for the Appalachian States LLRW Compact. Pennsylvania has enacted the necessary enabling legislation (Title 25, PA Code Chapter 236), and Chem-Nuclear Systems, Incorporated, has been named to build and operate the facility. As of this writing (June, 1991), however, preliminary regional screening, the first step in identification of potential sites, has not yet been *authorized,* and probably will not be started before mid-fall, 1991. When regional screening is completed, three areas will be selected for detailed evaluation requiring twelve months (or longer), and if found to be suitable, they will be submitted for approval by the Department of Environmental Resources. Following final site selection, design of the proposed facility, operating procedures and environmental impact analyses must be prepared to support the license application. Clearly, although Pennsylvania has probably made greater progress than the host state for any other compact, there is no possibility whatever of accepting wastes for disposal by the federally mandated deadline of January 1, 1993. Failure to meet the milestones of the Low-Level Radioactive Waste Policy Amendments Act has already cost the citizens of Pennsylvania millions of dollars in penalties and surcharges, and there seems to be little prospect of having a licensed facility in operation before access to out-of-state disposal facilities *at any cost* may be denied in 1996.

MANAGEMENT OF HIGH-LEVEL WASTES

The federal government has not been significantly more effective in resolving the problems of high-level radioactive waste disposal than the states have been in managing low-level waste. Groundwater contamination by leakage from waste storage tanks and lagoons has been reported at both Richland, Washington, and the Savanna River Plant in South Carolina (Cook 1981; Mellinger, 1990). Experimental reprocessing of spent (nuclear) fuel was stopped in the United States by the Carter Administration in 1977. Although reprocessing is again permitted (even encouraged) today, the volume of high-level reprocessing waste in storage is relatively small (approximately one billion Curies). Under the authority of the Nuclear Waste Policy Act of 1982 and the 1987 Amendments to the Act, the federal government has assumed blanket responsibility for the disposal of all high-level waste, including spent fuel and reprocessing wastes, as well as mine and mill tailings and TRU. Many means of disposing of these high-level wastes have been proposed and investigated. The wastes have been stabilized in the form of fused glass, synthetic cements, ceramic materials and SYNROC (Ringwood, 1978). Cannister designs and materials have been evaluated for convenience of handling, strength, thermal properties (high-level wastes generate substantial amounts of heat) and long-term corrosion resistance. Possible disposal sites have been investigated in the deep sea bed, in mined repositories, in salt diapirs, in layered volcanic sequences, etc. - and under climatic conditions ranging from the humid northeast to the southwestern desert (Roxburgh, 1987). Experimental studies carried out in the Climax Mine at the Nevada Test Site were augmented by environmental evaluations at Yucca Mountain, Nevada, (welded tuff), Deaf Smith County, Texas, (salt), and Richland, Washington (layered basalt) (cf: US DOE, 1988). The selection of Yucca Mountain for a high-level waste repository in 1987 was immediately opposed by environmental groups, scientists, the Nevada government and even by some agencies of the federal government, on environmental and legal grounds. A drilling program for site evaulation and preliminary engineering studies has been delayed by legal challenges, and most observers anticipate that each subsequent step in the design and construction of the HLW repository will experience similar delays. Thus, almost forty years after the first commercial power reactor began operation at Shippingport, Pennsylvania, in 1956, the federal government has not even identified a site for the high-level radioactive waste disposal facility it is committed to provide.

THE RADIOACTIVE WASTE DISASTER

Despite the problems in managing both low- and high-level radioactive wastes summarized above, there have been no cases of serious environmental contamination, few known illnesses (industrial radiation sources have been mixed with metal scrap on several occasions), and no serious property losses attributable to radiation and resulting from mismanagement of radioactive wastes. Why, then, is the management of radioactive waste included in a volume on "Natural and Technological Disasters"? There are two reasons. First, because of the magnitude of the potential damage which improperly managed radioactive wastes might cause, and second, because our failure to deal with the waste we create is, in a very real sense, a disaster in itself.

In the United States we generate approximately 75,000 cubic meters (2.8 million cubic feet) of low-level radioactive waste annually. Of this, nearly two-thirds is generated by nuclear power reactors, the remainder being principally derived from industrial sources. Medical and research wastes contribute a very small fraction. Although small compared to the volume of ordinary domestic trash or hazardous waste, the LLRW represents nearly one-half million Curies. The quantity of high-level radioactive waste is also small. Annual production in the United States (exclusive of mine waste and mill tailings) is on the order of 5740 cubic meters (215,000 cubic feet), of which 5500 cubic meters is defense-related high-level waste and TRU. Spent fuel from power reactors makes up only 240 cubic meters or 4% of the total. To put these quantities in perspective, it may be helpful to observe that we produce 60 million tons of hazardous waste annually in the United States of which less than 0.01% is radioactive waste derived from nuclear power plants (Yasinsky & Bolmgren, 1985; Dornsife, 1985).

Despite its small volume, the potential environmental and human health hazard represented by radioactive waste is very great. High-level reprocessing and defense wastes include extremely toxic nuclides (principally plutonium) and organic solvents which may be carcinogenic. Liquid reprocessing wastes are held in double- or triple-walled underground tanks, some of which have leaked in the past, and may confidently be expected to leak in the future. Stabilization and final disposal of these extremely hazardous materials awaits the completion of the federal high-level nuclear waste repository, optimistically scheduled for 1998. Highly radioactive fuel rod assemblies from commercial power reactors are presently stored at the reactor sites, but most power plants anticipate exhausting their storage space long before the turn of the century. Moreover, power reactors are often located close to the urban areas they serve, and where cooling water is abundant. In such locations, temporary storage facilities for spent fuel may be exposed to flood or storm damage, and any escaping contaminants are likely to be rapidly dispersed. Clearly, the ideal location for a nuclear reactor is unlikely to be the optimum location for relatively long-term storage of hazardous radioactive wastes.

The volume of hazardous radioactive waste will continue to grow. Even if we were to cease all nuclear activities immediately, decommissioning existing nuclear facilities alone would generate millions of cubic feet of waste. So long as we fail to provide a secure and environmentally sound repository for the waste, the probability of accidental release will grow and the magnitude of the potential disaster will increase. Almost fifty years have elapsed since large-scale generation of radioactive waste began. Our failure to provide for its safe disposal is morally reprehensible and a social, environmental and political disaster. Its potential environmental damage, health and genetic effects are on the same scale as many of the greatest recorded natural disasters.

REFERENCES

Anon. (1986). *Geotechnical and Geohydrological Aspects of Waste Management.* Boston. A.A. Balkema, c1986, 558 pp.

BEIR (1978). *The Effects of Populations of Exposure to Low Levels of Ionizing Radiation: Report.* Washington, D.C. NAS/NRC Committee on the Biological Effects of Ionizing Radiation (BEIR). 1972. 200 pp. + bibliography.

Bennett, R.D. & C.C. McAneny. *Inspection of Low- and Intermediate- Level Radioactive Waste Disposal Facilities and Research and Development Projects in France, Sweden and West Germany, 30 April-16 May, 1984.* Vicksburg, MS. Geotechnical Laboratory, USAE Waterways Experiment Station. July, 1985. 143 pp. + 4 appendices.

Bord, R.J. (1985). Problems in Siting Low Level Wastes: A Focus on Public Participation. Chapter 14 *in* Majumdar, S.K. & E.W. Miller, Eds., 1985. pp. 189-202.

Bord, R.J. (1989). Siting hazardous facilities: Problems and prospects. Chapter 26 *in* Majumdar, S.K., E.W. Miller & R.F. Schmalz, Eds., 1989, pp. 300-312.

Carter, T.J. & P.K.M. Rao. *Fifteen Years of Radioactive Waste Management at Ontario Hydro.* Toronto, Ont. Ontario Hydro. (Preprint).

Cartwright, K. (1982). A geological case history: Lessons learned at Sheffield, Illinois, *in* Yalcintas, M.G. (ed.), volume 2, 1982. pp. 67-82.

Clancy, J.J., D.F. Gray & O.I. Oztunali. *Data Base for Radioactive Waste Management: Volume 1. Review of Low-Level Radioactive Waste Disposal History.* Washington, D.C. U.S. Nuclear Regulatory Commission, 1981. (NUREG/CR-1759, vol 1).

CNSI (1990). *Pennsylvania Low-Level Radioactive Waste Disposal Facility Proposed Siting Plan Executive Summary.* Harrisburg, November, 1990. Chem-Nuclear Systems, Inc. 11 pp. (CNSI-PA-90-002).

CNSI (undated) (a), *Southeast Compact Low-Level Radioactive Waste Disposal Facility. Proposal to the North Carolina Low-Level Radioactive Waste Authority. Volume 1: Summary.* Raleigh, N.C. (undated). 27 pp.

CNSI (undated) (b). *Proposal to the Commonweath of Pennsylvania, Department of Environmental Resources for the Appalachian States Low-Level Radioactive Waste Compact Regional Disposal Facility. Volume II, Executive Summary.* Harrisburg, PA (undated). 15 pp.

Collé, R. & P.E. McNall, Jr., Eds. *Radon in Buildings: A Proceedings of a Round-table Discussion of Radon in Buildings Held at NBS, Gaithersburg, MD, June 15, 1979.* (SP-581). Washington, D.C., US Department of Commerce, 1980. 77 pp.

Cook, J.R. (1981). *A survey of radioactive effluent releases from byproduct material facilities.* Washington, D.C. Office of Nuclear Materials Safety and safeguards, U.S. Nuclear Regulatory Commission. 1981. 1 volume (NUREG 0819).

Dornsife, W.P. Classification of Radioactive Materials and Wastes. Chapter 1 *in* Majumdar, S.K. & E.W. Miller, Eds., 1985. pp. 1-9.

Friedman, R.S. Political considerations of nuclear waste disposal policy. Chapter 15 *in* Majumdar, S.K. & E.W. Miller, Eds., 1985. pp. 203-215.

Gangopadhyay, A. & S. Chatterjee (1987). Effects of industrial chemicals and radioactive materials in biological systems. Chapter 31 *in* Majumdar, S.K., F.J. Brenner & E.W. Miller, Eds., 1987. pp. 431-444.

Grant, J.L. (1982). Geotechnical measurements at the Maxey Flats, Kentucky, low-level radioactive waste disposal site - lessons learned. *in* Yalcintas, M.G. (Ed.), volume 2, 1982. pp. 51-166.

Hoffman, W.D. West Valley, New York: Nuclear Fuel, Nuclear Waste, Nuclear Technology. Chapter 7 *in* Majumdar, S.K., E.W. Miller & R.F. Schmalz, Eds., 1989. pp. 71-77.

Jester, W.A. and C. Yu. Environmental monitoring of low-level radioactive materials. Chapter 23 *in* Majumdar, S.K. and E.W. Miller, Eds. 1985, pp. 294-311.

Kelleher, W.J., J. Lyons, K. Tong, W. Greenman & T. Waldman. *Report: Investigations of a Low Level Waste Burial Site at the Western New York Nuclear Services Center.* Albany. Power Authority of the State of New York. 1983.

Lavie, J.M. & A. Barthoux (1982). The management of low and medium level radioactive waste in France. *in Waste Management, '82.* Proceedings of the Symposium on Waste Management, Tucson, AZ, March, 1982.

Majumdar, S.K. & E.W. Miller, Eds., *Management of Radioactive Materials and Wastes: Issues and Progress.* Easton, PA. Pennsylvania Academy of Science. c1985. (355 pp. + 2 appendices, index).

Majumdar, S.K., F.J. Brenner & E.W. Miller, Eds. *Environmental Consequences of Energy Production: Problems and Prospects.* Easton, PA. Pennsylvania Academy of Science, c1987. 522 pp. + index.

Majumdar, S.K., E.W. Miller & R.F. Schmalz, Eds. *Management of Hazardous Materials and Wastes: Treatment, Minimization and Environmental Impacts.* Easton, PA. Pennsylvania Academy of Science, c1989. 463 pp. + index.

Mellinger, G.B., Ed. *Nuclear Waste Management, III.* Westerville, OH. American Ceramic Society, Ceramic Transactions, volume 9 (series), c1990. 590 pp. + index.

RERF (1987). *US-Japan Joint Reassessment of Atomic Bomb Radiation Dosimetry in Hiroshima and Nagasaki, Final Report.* Hiroshima. Radiation Effects

Research Foundation (RERF), 1987. Volume 1, 430 pp.

Ringwood, A.E. *Safe Disposal of High-Level Nuclear Reactor Wastes: A New Strategy*, Canberra, Aust. Australian National University Press, c1978. 62 pp. + bibliography.

Roxburgh, I.S. *Geology of High-Level Nuclear Waste Disposal, An Introduction.* London, Chapman & Hall, c1987. 206 pp. + bibliography, glossary, index.

Salander, C., R. Proske and E. Albrecht. (1980). The Asse salt mine: the world's only test facility for the disposal of radioactive waste. Interdisciplinary Science Reviews, vol. 5, pp. 292-303.

Schmalz, R.F. A "Bathtub" Primer - Lessons from West Valley, New York. Chapter 24 *in* Majumdar, S.K., F.J. Brenner & E.W. Miller, Eds., 1987. pp. 349-368.

Schmalz, R.F. Low-Level Radioactive Waste Management Options. Chpater 16 *in* Majumdar, S.K., E.W. Miller & R.F. Schmalz, Ed., 1989. pp. 177-191.

Sierra Club (undated). *Insecure Landfills: The West Valley Experience.* Radioactive Waste Campaign Fact Sheet, Buffalo, N.Y., Sierra Club Radioactive Waste Campaign.

Singh, K.N. *Appalachian States Compact Low-Level Radioactive Waste Management Survey - 1987.* Harrisburg, PA. Commonwealth of Pennsylvania, Department of Environmental Resources. March, 1989. 23 pp + 5 appendices.

Smith, R.L. (1984). Low Level Radioactive Waste Disposal at the Barnwell Waste Management Facility, *in Low Level Waste Disposal Handbook,* Electric Power Research Institute, c1984. (NP-2488-LD).

US DOE. (1981). *Canonsburg Information Book.* Washington, D.C., U.S. Department of Energy, UMTRA-DOE/ALO. April, 1981. 56 pp.

US DOE (1988). *Site Characterization Plan, Overview (Yucca Mountain Site, NRDA, Nevada).* Washington, D.C. U.S. Department of Energy. 1988. 130 pp. + glossary, appendix.

Westinghouse Corporation (1987). *State of Illinois, Low-Level Radioactive Waste Disposal Site, License Application.* Westinghouse Waste Technology Services Division, Waltz Mill, Madison, PA.

Yasinsky, J.B. & C.R. Bolmgren. Radioactive Waste Management - A Manageable Task. Chapter 7 *in* Majumdar, S.K. & E.W. Miller, Eds., 1985. pp. 73-96.

Natural and Technological Disasters: Causes, Effects and Preventive Measures. Edited by S.K. Majumdar, G.S. Forbes, E.W. Miller, and R.F. Schmalz. © 1992, The Pennsylvania Academy of Science.

Chapter Four

MODELLING, REMOTE SENSING, AND PREDICTION OF NATURAL DISASTERS: AN OVERVIEW

GREGORY S. FORBES[1]
and
ROY GREENFIELD[2]

[1]Associate Professor of Meteorology
and
[2]Professor of Geosciences
The Pennsylvania State University
University Park, PA 16802

PART I. DISASTERS OF METEOROLOGICAL ORIGIN

Hazardous Atmospheric Phenomena

The atmosphere is capable of producing a variety of hazardous phenomena and conditions. Some occur during short periods of highly disturbed weather, and are hazardous because of violent winds or excessive precipitation. At the other extreme, the atmosphere can generate hazardous conditions by an abnormal persistence of "fair" weather: prolonged periods of clear skies can cause drought, crop failures, water emergencies, and health-threatening heat waves. Prolonged stagnant periods can lead to dangerous buildups of pollutants.

Hazardous atmospheric phenomena have a variety of sizes and durations, depicted in Figure 1. Worthy of note is that there is a direct relationship between size and longevity: the smallest phenomena are also the most fleeting. Disaster-producing "maxi" tornadoes are typically 100-500 m wide and persist for 10-50 minutes as they travel across the countryside. Individual intense thunderstorm downdrafts called "microbursts" that have caused numerous airplane accidents are typically 1-3 km in diameter and have a life cycle of about 10 minutes. The typical thunderstorm that produces damaging wind and hail is about 40 km wide and lasts an hour or more.

People often confuse the definitions of tornadoes and hurricanes, but Figure 1 shows that hurricanes (called typhoons in the western Pacific) and their weaker precursor tropical storms are vastly larger in size—typically greater than 500 km in diameter—and exist for several days to several weeks. Someone in the vicinity of a tornado can usually see both its leading and trailing edges simultaneously, whereas it may take several days for the full width of a hurricane to drift over a site. Hurricanes form in the subtropical latitudes, whereas tornadoes typically occur in the mid-latitudes.

Winter storms over land or ocean and river-flood-producing rainstorms are affiliated with low-pressure systems, called "cyclones", typically about 1000 km in

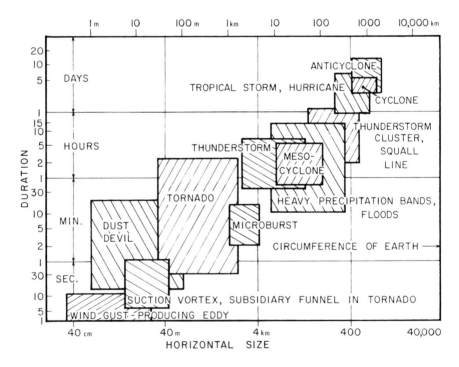

FIGURE 1. Diagram showing typical sizes and durations of various atmospheric phenomena.

diameter (though the heaviest precipitation is usually confined to a corridor about 100 km wide). Air pollution episodes and drought are usually associated with high pressure systems (also called "anticyclones") about 1000 km in diameter that persist over an area for several days to several weeks.

This chapter, obviously, cannot deal thoroughly with the prediction of each phenomenon. Instead, it seeks to enable the reader to better understand (1) some of the atmospheric conditions that are critical for the development of the various hazardous atmospheric phenomena, (2) the knowledge and technology that enables these conditions to be detected or predicted by weather forecasters, and (3) technology upgrades in progress that are expected to lead to unprecedented accuracy of predictions and warnings of hazardous phenomena and conditions by the middle to late 1990s.

Weather Forecasts, Advisories, Watches and Warnings

It is probable that man has always had an interest in the weather, and it is known that certain types of local weather observations were recorded as early as the fifth century B.C. Judging from recorded folklore, sailors and farmers developed crude weather forecasting techniques based upon current conditions and their recollections of the weather that ensued during analogous situations in the past. Fundamental to the progress of weather forecasting, however, were advances on several fronts: measurement capabilities, scientific understanding, and data handling technologies. The thermometer and barometer were invented in the 1600s, and humidity and wind instruments developed in the 1800s completed the set of tools needed to obtain measurements of near-surface variables crucial to weather prediction.

Once measurements were available, rapid advances were made in the understanding of the atmosphere. By 1845, the set of 7 mathematical equations (called "the primitive equations") were known which represent the laws governing the atmosphere and its changes. Use of these equations to predict the future state of the atmosphere would have to wait a century for two technological breakthroughs: development and implementation of a network of balloon-borne radiosondes (1940) to measure conditions from the surface to 10-15 km, and development of computers powerful enough to be able to even crudely handle the immense number of computations required by the involved equations (late 1950s).

In the interim, a key to the progress of weather forecasting was the recognition in the 1700s that not all weather variations are caused locally; instead they are caused by the movement of large organized weather systems over thousands of kilometers. Once this discovery (often credited to Daniel Defoe in England and Benjamin Franklin) became widely recognized, scientists began efforts to create networks of weather observations. Such networks became potentially applicable to weather forecasting in 1849, when reports began to be distributed by telegraph (another technological breakthrough crucial to the progress of weather forecasting).

Weather forecasting for the public in the United States began as a routine in 1869 when observations and forecasts (termed "probabilities") were issued in the *Cincinnati Weather Bulletin*. Congress created a National meteorological service in 1870 within the Army Signal Service, whose primary function was telegraphy. It was replaced by the United States Weather Bureau, formed within the Department of Agriculture in 1891, transferred to the Department of Commerce in 1940, and renamed the National Weather Service (NWS) in 1970.

General forecasts describing the weather for approximately the next 36h are issued to the public several times per day from 52 NWS Forecast Offices across the United States (Philadelphia and Pittsburgh in PA). Separate forecasts are usually issued for each of several subdivisions or "zones" within each Office's area of responsibility, reflecting different topography, geography, and position with respect to the travelling weather systems. The zones are still much larger than the area affected by individual rain showers—so that not all portions of the zone receive precipitation—giving rise to the need for precipitation forecasts in the form of probabilities.

The NWS also bears the responsibility for issuing a hierarchy of special messages—advisories, watches, and warnings—when hazardous weather situations are present or are expected to develop. Hazardous situations include floods and flash floods, severe thunderstorms, tornadoes, hurricanes and tropical storms, gales and high winds (of concern to recreational boaters), and severe winter storms. Government weather services of other countries also issue such special weather statements, although the number and types of messages differ.

The *"advisory"* is the least urgent hazardous weather message, and is usually issued 6-24h before an event is forecasted to occur. This type of message is meant as an information item, most often issued in regard to recreational boating and air pollution. It is occasionally used to heighten public awareness when a particularly severe thunderstorm outbreak is expected.

A *"watch"* is issued when the hazardous phenomenon has not yet developed over the region, but when conditions are favorable for the development within the next 0-6 hours. It signifies that people should go about their normal activities, except for periodically checking to see if threatening conditions have developed. In severe thunderstorm situations, watches are issued for an area about 200 x 400 km. In order to avoid needless "cries of wolf", a watch is usually issued only about an hour before severe weather develops (except for winter storms, when the lead time is longer). The National Severe Storms Forecast Center (in Kansas City, MO) issues all severe thunderstorm and tornado watches for the Nation and the National Hurricane Center (in Miami, FL) has responsibility for all tropical storm and hurricane watches and advisories.

The most urgent messages are called *"warnings"*, and are issued when the phenomenon is present over the region or is moving into the region. People are urged to immediately take safety precautions, summarized in the warning statement. These are usually issued for a county (30 x 50 km) and for up to an hour. Warnings are issued by NWS Forecast Offices and by additional NWS Offices (in PA: Allentown, Erie, Harrisburg, Scranton, and Williamsport), which further subdivide the areas of responsibility.

NWS forecasts and messages are distributed directly to the public via NOAA Weather Radio, transmitted at frequency of about 162.5 MHz. A tone-alert system is part of these broadcasts, by which alarms in the receivers are activated when a warning is issued. Unfortunately, most households are not equipped to receive these broadcasts. The NWS can also activate the Emergency Broadcast System of radio stations when conditions are especially severe. NWS forecasts and messages are also sent electronically on various data and information circuits (e.g., NOAA Weather Wire), from which they are picked up and conveyed to the public by most radio stations, television stations, and newspapers. In addition, private meteorologists and meteorological consulting firms can also receive the data and guidance products from the NWS and use them to prepare their own forecasts. The consequence is that several different "opinions" can sometimes be obtained by switching television channels. This type of meteorological free enterprise system is not nearly as common outside the United States. Fortunately, within the United States only the NWS issues severe weather watches and warnings.

Forecasts and Advisories: Conditions Favorable for the Development of Hazardous Atmospheric Phenonena — Conceptual Models

Weather forecasts are based partly upon observations from around the world—collected at the National Meteorological Center (NMC) in the Washington, DC area, and redistributed electronically in map and data form back to the Forecast Offices.

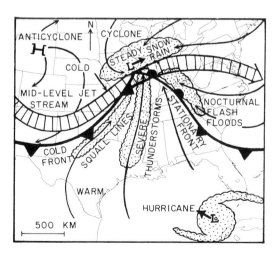

FIGURE 2. Schematic diagram showing typical locations of various atmospheric phenomena with respect to mid-latitude cyclone (L), anticyclone (H), and fronts. Hatched, meandering arrow represents the belt of strongest winds at 5-6 km; single curving arrows represent near-surface winds. Bold short arrows represent movement of mid-latitude cyclone and hurricane entering the mid-latitudes. Geography is shown merely to help visualize sizes. Fronts are shown by thick line, with movement toward classification symbol: semicircle, warm front; triangle, cold front.

The NMC also prepares and transmits two forms of guidance products that are used in making forecasts: (1) numerical model predictions and (2) statistical forecasts based upon a blend of observations, numerical model predicted values, and empirical relationships derived from several years of recent weather records and numerical model predictions. Most other countries of the world have weather services which function similarly.

Many nations use numerical models to solve the primitive equations and generate predictions once or twice daily of the future states of the atmosphere for periods of 1-10 days. Despite using some of the largest computers in the world, the models can only make calculations for points about 100 km apart and at 15 levels in the vertical. This means that most of the thunderstorm phenomena of Figure 1 cannot be predicted by the models. Further, except at the surface, the input data are spaced at least 400 km apart over land and are virtually non-existent over the oceanic 72% of the globe. This generally means that only cyclones and anticyclones (and "noise") exist during the first few hours of the prediction, though smaller phenomena can develop in time. The models are typically more accurate in the "free atmosphere" aloft than near the surface—the lower boundary of the models. For these and other reasons, the numerical model predictions must be viewed as fallible guidance, rather than inevitable outcomes. Forecasters adjust the model predictions based upon known weaknesses and systematic errors, and make use of knowledge of the evolution of the surface weather in relation to conditions aloft. They also make use of conceptual models, including rules that relate the most probable location of hazardous phenomena to the positions of cylcones, anticyclones, and fronts.

Figure 2 is a schematic diagram illustrating typical locations of development of various hazardous weather phenomena, with respect to cyclones and anticyclones that alternate throughout the middle latitudes. Also shown are fronts, which mark the warm side of a narrow zone of transition between a warm air mass and a cold air mass. Since cold air is denser than warm air, the movement of a front is determined by the direction of movement of the air on its cold side. A front is classified as a cold front when the cold air is advancing; as a warm front when the cold air is retreating; as a stationary front when the cold air flows parallel to the front. Also shown schematically is a meandering current of strong winds 5-6 km above the surface which induce the movement of the cyclones and anticyclones around the hemisphere in mid-latitudes. The wind speeds in this current are usually greatest at 9-12 km, where the current is referred to as the jet stream.

To understand the formation of precipitation, it is necessary to recognize that atmospheric pressure is greatest near the surface and decreases with height, because pressure represents the weight of the air above the measurement level. Clouds and precipitation form when air rises and expands (in the lowered pressure at the higher altitude). The expansion causes a cooling, and water vapor condenses. Conversely, sinking air warms, clouds evaporate, and relative humidity decreases.

Widespread precipitation is associated with cyclones, because the air above a cyclone rises at a rate of a few cm/s as low-level air converges toward the center of the cyclone. The ascent is not spatially uniform, and one zone of maximum ascent typically occurs above the warm front, where air from the warm sector glides up over the front (which slopes northward with height). Another zone of maximum ascent typically occurs near and to the north and west of the surface cyclone center, where the low-level convergence is strongest. When temperatures are below 0°C at all levels, heaviest snow occurs beneath the zones of maximum air ascent. Blizzard conditions sometimes occur on the west side of an intense surface cyclone, where strong winds drive a blinding snow, and usher in bitterly cold conditions as the cyclone exits the region.

Rainfall amounts generated from cyclone-scale ascent are not typically enough to cause flooding, unless additional complicating factors are present: (1) a considerable snowpack and rising temperatures as the cold air retreats can contribute additional runoff to streams and rivers from melting snow and ice, especially (2) if the cyclone becomes stationary over the area; (3) embedded bands of showers or thunderstorms can develop in the warm air mass as it glides upward over the warm frontal surface, causing heavy rainfall rates that may even cause flash flooding. During the summer a significant percentage of flash floods develop in the region north of a stationary or warm front, where a southerly flow of air from the warm air mass glides up the frontal surface, triggering a prolonged period of thunderstorms. These events often occur at night, when the northward flow tends to be fastest at levels several hundred meters above ground, and when wind speeds decrease with height.

Other thunderstorm-related phenomena—flash floods, hailstorms, tornadoes, and windstorms—tend to occur from lines or clusters of thunderstorms which develop in the southerly airflow ahead of the cold front. These storms occur when the vertical distribution of temperature and humidity is "unstable", i.e. where it is warm and humid near the surface and cool aloft, and where temperatures decrease with height at a rate in excess of 6°C per km. Usually these conditions occur in the regions east of surface cyclones, where flows of moist air originating over subtropical and tropical oceans migrate poleward to latitudes where it is colder and drier aloft. If there is some initial upward impetus which displaces a bubble or plume of near-surface air upward, in these conditions the bubble/plume becomes buoyant and will accelerate upward until it encounters a layer that is stable. In severe thunderstorms, this may not occur until the updraft hits the lower portion of the stratosphere, at altitudes of 12-16 km. Strong thunderstorm gusts and tornadoes tend to occur when pre-storm winds are strong at all levels, while thunderstorms are more apt to cause flash flooding on days when winds above the 3 km level are weak.

Large high-pressure systems, as shown in Figure 2, are typically accompanied by "fair" weather: few clouds and little precipitation. At altitudes above the surface anticyclone, air descends gently (a few cm/s). Because the subsiding air warms, the atmosphere becomes more stable and thunderstorms may be inhibited. If these conditions persist, drought may develop. The stabilization also inhibits vertical mixing and dilution of pollutants emitted into the atmosphere and, combined with the weak winds near the center of an anticyclone, can allow buildups of pollutant concentrations to hazardous levels. Air pollution events are typically associated with a single stagnant anticyclone, whereas a series of high pressure systems that dominate a region for weeks or months (alternating with comparatively weak low-pressure systems) can yield a drought.

Severe Thunderstorm, Tornado, and Flash Flood Watches and Warnings

The task of preparing severe weather watches and warnings is fundamentally different from that of making forecasts and advisories. The NWS objective is to zoom in on the threatened area as the danger becomes imminent. In many cases, the severe weather that ultimately develops will only affect 1% of the advisory area. In preparing watches, then, the forecaster tries to anticipate specific locations where strong thunderstorms will develop. This often occurs where (1) air flows up hillsides, (2) suface or cloud cover inhomogeneities cause local hot and cool spots to develop or (3) zones of horizontal air convergence force near-surface air to ascend. Evaporation and reduced insolation from clouds over ground wetted by the previous day's rain showers can inhibit showers and focus development on the adjacent sunny regions. Satellite imagery is especially useful in detecting the edges of cloudy areas of this type, and in detecting the initial cloud lines that form in the convergence zones—also called mesoscale boundaries.

In the warning stage, in the case of thunderstorm phenomena, the problem becomes one of detecting and determining which handful of storms are the dangerous ones out of perhaps as many as 100 candidates at any particular time in the area of responsibility. The tools available for the more pinpointed warnings are three types of remotely sensed data: (1) weather radar images and animated video "loops", (2) satellite images and loops, and (3) lightning detection network data. These devices first became available to the forecaster about 1950, 1960, and 1980, respectively. To help get "ground-truth" information to compare to the remotely sensed data, the forecaster turns to data from automatic rain and stream gauges, observations from manned and automated weather stations and reports from spotter networks and the public. Some of the Nation's worst tragedies, such as the Galveston hurricane-flood of 1900, could have been minimized with today's technology, because satellite and radar would have detected the storm before it struck, and the hurricane watch would have allowed time for evacuation of the public to safety.

A New Era

The NWS has just begun a reconfiguration that will place greater emphasis on watches and warnings for hazardous phenomena, made possible by continuing technological advances. Deployment of a network of Doppler weather radars is underway and will continue through the mid-1990s. The Doppler capability of these radars enables the forecaster to not only see where it is precipitating and how heavily, but to also see where strong winds accompany the storms. Wind and tornado hazards will be detected with unprecedented efficiency.

Forecasts will benefit from another measurement system: the wind profiler. Wind profilers remotely sense the winds from near the surface to in excess of 10 km at least once per hour. A network being tested over the Midwest will greatly augment the amount of upper-air data available for input to numerical weather prediction models and that should, in turn, lead to greater accuracy in the details of the resulting predictions. Further, as computer systems are developed with greater speed and more memory, numerical weather prediction models will be able to make predictions having progressively more small-scale detail. Researchers today use 1 km resolution numerical models of thunderstorms, but their domain is limited to about 100 x 100 km. In time these will be nested within the larger-scale models to give optimum forecasts.

The technological advances will, in principle, allow deaths and injuries from severe weather to be significantly reduced. For the potential to become a reality, however, non-meteorological factors must also improve. In developing nations, state-of-the-science technology and forecasting may not be economically feasible, and the public may not have the options of moving to safety even if warned of imminent danger. Within the United States, individuals must realize that their fate ultimately rests in their own hands. The public must become more involved in preparedness planning, conscientiously keep alert for NWS messages and threatening weather, and be prepared to take immediate safety measures when warned of imminent danger.

REFERENCES

Ray, P.S., ed. 1986. *Mesoscale Meteorology and Forecasting.* American Meteorological Society, Boston. 793 pp.

Ruffner, J.A. and F.E. Bair, eds. 1979. *The Weather Almanac.* Avon Books, NY. 728 pp.

Whitnah, D.R. 1961. *A History of the United States Weather Bureau.* Univ. of Illinois Press, Urbana. 267 pp.

PART II DISASTERS OF SOLID EARTH ORIGIN

Description of the Solid Earth

The surface of the earth is undergoing continual changes. These continual changes in the solid earth cause many types of hazards. These include earthquakes, volcanoes, tsunamis, landslides, and sinkholes.

Before discussing the underlying causes of the changes in the earth's surface, we need to describe the major geographic features of the earth's surface. Figure 3 shows a map of the surface with major geologic features marked. About ¾ of the earth's surface is covered by the oceans. Most of the oceans are about 5 km deep. In the oceans there is a series of long ridges that rise about 2 km above the normal ocean depth. The total length of these mid-ocean ridges is 50,000 km. As an example of these ridges, the Mid-Atlantic ridge runs parallel to the North American eastern coastline, half way between North America and Africa. The ridges are offset at intervals. These offsets are known as transform faults.

There is also a series of areas termed trenches, where the oceans are as deep as 11 km. Trenches are found near the Aleutian Islands, the western coast of South America, the Philippine Islands, and the Japanese islands. There are also islands such as Hawaii that are believed to have a special means of formation which will be discussed below.

A simplified description of the layering of the solid earth is the following. The top 100 km of the earth is rigid and is termed the lithosphere. The lithosphere is underlain by a 3000 km thick layer called the mantle. The mantle is composed of hot rocks. These rocks behave viscously and can flow like a fluid such as very thick oil. Below the mantle is the earth's core, the outer part of which is a dense fluid.

Convection in the mantle is continually changing the arrangement of the earth's surface. Through such processes as radioactive generation of heat, the material near the bottom of the mantle becomes hot and expands. This begins the process of convection by which the hot, light material rises and a pattern of convection cells forms. A diagram of a convection cell is given in Figure 4. On one side of the cell, the material is light and rises towards the surface. Near the surface the material cools and becomes more dense. This dense material sinks downward into the mantle on the opposite side of the convection cell.

Modern ideas of the earth envision the top layer, the lithosphere, as broken into a series of plates. A typical plate is the South American Plate. This plate consists

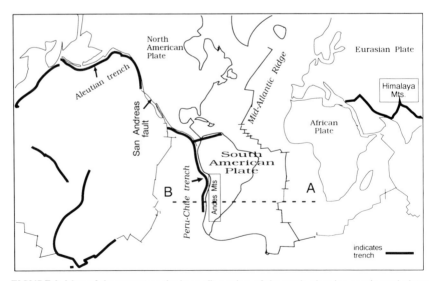

FIGURE 3. Map of the current geologic configuration of the earth, showing continental plates (labeled by name), mid-oceanic ridges (thin jagged lines), and major trenches (thick lines). Selected mountain chains and transform faults are also shown. The location of a cross-section from points A to B (Figure 4) is shown by a dashed line.

of the South American continent together with the portion of the Atlantic Ocean that is west of the Mid-Atlantic Ridge. The western edge of the plate is formed by the Peru-Chile trench. Each plate moves as an almost rigid body on top of the mantle. The earth's continents are affixed to and move with the lithosphere plates.

The boundaries of the plates are of three types. The first type is the mid-ocean ridge. Here the convection cells are bringing up hot material from the mantle, which cools and forms new ocean crust. The continents are drifting apart in connection with the formation of this new oceanic crust. The second type of boundary is the trench. Here the crustal layer on one side of the trench is being forced down into the mantle under the crust on the other side of the trench. The downgoing crust is termed a downgoing slab. At the trench, crust is being destroyed. For example, at the Peru-Chile trench, the Pacific Ocean crust is being thrust under the west coast of South America. This thrusting is forcing up the Andes mountains. In Japan and other places the downgoing crust pushes up an island chain. The Himalya mountains are a variation of the trench type of boundary; here the continental crust of India is pushing below the main continental crust of Asia. The third type of boundary is termed a transform fault. Examples of transform faults are seen as offsets in the Mid-Atlantic ridge. At transform faults one side of the fault is moving horizontally with respect to the opposite side. The San Andreas fault system in California is an example of an unusually long transform fault.

Solid Earth Hazards

Earthquakes are the most destructive disasters due to earth motions and are caused by the sudden breaking of crustal rocks. Most earthquakes can be related to the motions of the plates discussed in the previous section and occur at the boundaries between the lithospheric plates. The most destructive earthquakes are associated with transform faults or with trench plate boundaries. At transform faults one plate slides horizontally past the adjacent plate. Some of the largest earthquakes

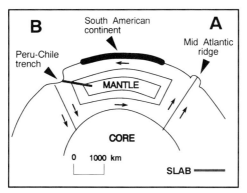

FIGURE 4. Vertical cross-section through the earth from points A to B of Figure 3, depicting layered structure and motions in mantle convection cell.

have occurred near ocean trenches where one plate is being thrust under another plate. These include the great earthquakes in Chile (1960) and the 1964 Alaska Good Friday earthquake. Earthquakes occurring along the mid-ocean ridge systems are not normally extremely large. Moderate sized earthquakes also occur in conjunction with volcanic activity.

The California earthquakes are cased by motions along the San Andreas transform fault system. The ground to the west of the fault is moving north realative to the east side at a rate of about 5 cm per year. Between earthquakes much of the fault is locked, and the motion occurs by deforming (straining) the rocks around the fault. When the strain becomes too great, the rock fails at the fault, and an earthquake occurs. This can be likened to stretching a rubber band until it snaps.

Geological studies have been used to find the recurrence time between large earthquakes on particular faults. The horizontal motion on a fault like the San Andreas causes an offset of a stream bed each time an earthquake occurs. The rate at which this offset occurs and the offset that occurs between earthquakes can give the average recurrence time between earthquakes. Typical average recurrence times for large earthquakes at individual places are 200 years. However, the individual recurrence time for successive earthquakes may vary between 150 and 300 years. Based on this type of observation, a methodology has been developed to allow identification of places where an earthquake is likely to occur over the next few decades. This type of statement is termed an earthquake forecast. The United States Geological Survey recently developed a map giving earthquake forecasts for the Northern California fault system. Similar studies have been done for trench boundary earthquakes in such places as Alaska and Japan.

There are some earthquakes called intra plate earthquakes that occur in the middle of lithospheric plates. Some of these, such as the 1812 New Madrid earthquake sequence in Missouri, have the potential to be extremely destructive. For earthquakes which occur on lithospheric plate boundaries, the rate of motion which strains the rock to the point of failure is well understood. But it is not known how strain changes with time in the interior of plates. Thus, the time between intra plate earthquakes is hard to estimate. However, this time is known to be much greater than the 200-year average time between plate boundary earthquakes.

Short term predictions of earthquakes are very important for saving lives. When it is possible to predict that an earthquake will occur within a period of days, the population can evacuate unsafe structures, get off highways that could collapse, and take other precautions to keep safe. A number of countries including China, Japan, Russia, and the United States have for many years sponsored programs to achieve short-term prediction.

The basis of short-term predictions is that when rocks became strained close to the failure point, they will undergo rapid changes in properties because cracks form. Phenomena reflecting these rapid changes can then indicate the rock is approaching failure, and an earthquake is imminent. Many types of phenomena have been observed before some earthquakes. In some cases there is an unusual series of foreshock earthquakes before a very large one. Changes in the velocity at which seismic waves travel have also been observed. Other precursory phenomena are the uplift of the surface, changes in the earth's electrical properties, increases in the concentrations of the radioactive gas radon, strange types of animal behavior, and changes in water well levels.

Such precursory phenomena have been observed before some large earthquakes, but unfortunately they have not been observed consistently. An extreme example of the inconsistency of the short-term predictive phenomena is the contrast between two earthquakes that occurred in China in the middle 1970's. In 1975 the Chinese successfully made a short-term prediction of the February 1975 Haicheng earthquake, which saved many thousands of lives. In contrast, no short-term prediction was made before the great 1976 T'ang-shan earthquake, which took hundreds of thousands of lives. With the present state of knowledge, these short-term predictive phenomena can only be used to predict a fairly small fraction of destructive earthquakes worldwide and have been of very limited use in California.

The motions of faults are monitored in several ways. The most important is with seismographs. These instruments measure the wave motions of the ground caused by earthquakes. Many countries maintain systems of seismograph stations. From these records seismologists can tell how big an earthquake is and how the fault broke. They also monitor foreshock events. There is a global network of approximately 80 seismometer stations that continually monitor moderate to large earthquake activity world wide. In the United States there are a number of regional networks that look more closely at local earthquakes. There are about 1500 seismographs in these networks; approximately half are in California. Also important is the use of geodetic strain meters. These measure how the distance between points on the earth is changing. With them scientists can tell how the earth is straining.

Volcanoes occur where hot material is being forced out of the earth under pressure. The first type of area where volcanoes occur is near trenches where the lithosphere is being forced back into the mantle. The forcing of the material into the mantle generates heat by friction and causes high pressure. Examples of areas where this is happening are the Andes Mountains, Central America, the Washington state area, Japan, the Philippine islands, and Italy. Volcanoes that have violent explosive eruptions are found near trenches.

A second type of area is along the mid-ocean ridges, where new ocean floor forms by volcanic activity. The eruptions near ridges are not violent and are in the ocean and so are not of danger to man.

The third type of area is above mantle hot spots. Hot spots are thought to be places where thin plumes of light, hot material are coming up from deep in the mantle. This material fractures the lithosphere and through volcanic action forms the islands. Hot spot areas include Hawaii, the Canary Islands, Yellowstone Park, and Iceland. Iceland is unusual because it is on the Mid-Atlantic ridge and is also believed to be above a mantle hot spot. The volcanoes caused by hot spots are not explosive but generate large slow-moving volumes of lava, which can destroy property.

There are often warnings of volcanic activity. Modest-sized earthquakes often occur before and during volcanic activity. These earthquakes are thought to reflect fracturing as hot molten rock forces its way towards the surface. The earth can also bulge upward, which indicates possible volcanic activity.

Tsunami are destructive sea waves that are most often triggered by large earthquakes and, occasionally, by volcanic eruptions or landslides. A great earthquake such as the 1964 Alaska earthquake can raise the level of the sea floor by several meters. This displaces the water which then sets up a wave. The wave can hit the shore near the earthquake, and in Alaska the water reached as high as 40 m above the normal sea level. The waves can also travel large distances, often going across the Pacific ocean. The speed of the waves in the deep ocean is about 600 km/hour. In the deep ocean, the waves are less than a meter high. However, as the wave approaches shallow water, the wave piles up and can reach heights of 20 m. This high water can go far inland and has caused many deaths and great destruction thousands of miles from the earthquake source.

A Tsunami warning system has been set up to warn of approaching tsunamis. Since the generation and travel of tsunamis are reasonably well understood, seismic stations monitor for earthquakes that occur under the ocean and that are likely to generate tsunamis. When such an earthquake is observed, water level gauges are use to tell if a tsunami sea wave has been generated and to chart its progress. When appropriate, warnings are given for people to evacuate low areas that might be flooded.

Landslides, rockslides, and mudslides can occur when a rock mass is close to being unstable. This occurs when the slope is too steep for the cohesive strength of the material. If the slope is close to being too steep, a slide can still be triggered by strong vibrations such as occur from an earthquake. The buildup of subsurface water pressure can also initiate a landslide by lubricating the plane on which the land slides.

Sinkholes are a geologic hazard that causes property damage and occasionally loss of life. Sinkholes occur in areas where the rock near the surface, usually limestone or dolomite, can be easily dissolved by water. A large cavern may form below a surface soil layer, and the soil layer can fail suddenly. Sometimes there is a slight subsidence of the surface before the sinkhole forms, but in some cases the sinkhole can form suddenly with little warning. Sinkholes most often form when an area undergoes a change in the level of the water table, such as can occur when underground water is removed. Geophysical methods such as ground electrical conductivity measurements or ground probing radar can be used to look for sink holes.

REFERENCES

Smith, D.G., ed. 1989. *The Cambridge Encyclopedia of Earth Sciences.* Cambridge Univ. Press, Cambridge. 496 pp.

Press, F. and R. Siever. 1985. *Earth*, 4th Ed. Freeman, New York. 656 pp.

Bolt, B.A. 1988. *Earthquakes.* Freeman, New York. 282 pp.

Natural and Technological Disasters: Causes, Effects and Preventive Measures. Edited by S.K. Majumdar, G.S. Forbes, E.W. Miller, and R.F. Schmalz. 1992, The Pennsylvania Academy of Science.

Chapter Five

TOO CLOSE TO THE TREMORS OF THE EARTH

CHARLES A. LANGSTON

Department of Geosciences
Penn State University
University Park, PA 16802

The earth never lies flat, but is always thinking, it finds a new feeling and curls over it, rising to bury a toad or a great man, it accounts for a fallen meteor, or stones rising from two hundred feet down...

Robert Bly

THE MOVING EARTH

Earth is in motion. Not just the motion of her trip around the sun or the daily rotation which gives us day and night, but a slow, ponderous seething which has been going on for four and half billion years. In the very early beginnings of Earth, the left-over material of stars congregated, melted and differentiated into the major layers of the iron rich and molten core and the stoney crystalline mantle. A very thin crust of lighter elements formed on top of it all and began floating like rafts on the deep ocean of the mantle. At first, it is very likely that the mantle was very similar to an ocean, being molten and fluid-like, but as the early earth cooled, the mantle, like the crust, crystallized and slowed. The events which formed the core and the mantle also concentrated the hot, radioactive elements in the core so that, even today, the core of the earth remains the primary source of heat within Earth.

Although the mantle cooled and crystallized, it only slowed its fluid-like motions. In the conditions of extreme high pressure and temperature within the earth and with a hot core at the base heating it from below, the mantle still behaves like a fluid displaying eddies and currents which move over times of 100 million years and distances of thousands of kilometers. The motions themselves are quite slow, amounting to only a few centimeters per year but their consequence for the floating outer crust of the earth and those who live on it, are profound.

Today, the slow fluid motions of the mantle manifest themselves by forming and moving large, 100 km thick plates. Born by upwelling magma at the mid-ocean ridges, the plates start off paper-thin but thicken as they cool and move away from their birth place. In the Pacific Ocean basin, the plates are composed of a thin dense crust about 7 km thick, on the average, attached to a layer of the mantle which slides as a unit over deeper and partially molten mantle. The region of the earth defined by the deepest extent of the plates is called the *lithosphere* with the partially molten zone underneath called the *astenosphere*. Under continents, the lithospheric plate is composed of crust about 35 km thick with some indications of the ultimate depth of the lithosphere being as great as 150 to 200 km in places.

The plates behave as if rigid and experience relatively little deformation as they move away from mid-ocean ridges, until they interact with other plates at their edges. The major plates of Earth (there are about 10 of them) have the continents imbedded within them, dragging North America and South American away from Europe and Africa and firmly planting India into Asia. Figure 1 shows the configuration of plates as seen today.

The theory of Plate Tectonics is only about 25 years old yet has become the major paradigm for the earth sciences. It very effectively describes the relative motions of the continents over geologic time as well as integrating many previously disparate geophysical observations. In particular, earthquakes are a natural consequence of the interaction of two plates when they encounter each other.

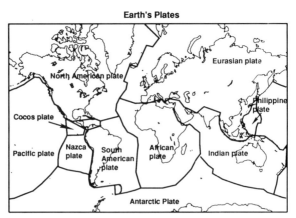

FIGURE 1. A schematic figure showing the continents and boundaries of the major plates of Earth. Plate boundaries are the centers of earthquake, volcanic and other geologic activity.

THE SOURCE OF EARTHQUAKES

The theory of Plate Tectonics allows three basic kinds of interactions (see Figure 2). When plates form at mid-ocean ridges or spreading centers, the brittle cracking near the surface can result in a geologic structure called a *graben* which is bounded by *normal* faults. Catastrophic movement on these normal faults give rise to small or moderate earthquakes. As a plate slides away from the ridge it may be adjacent to another plate sliding in the opposite direction. The fault between the two sliding plates is called a *transform* fault which is also an example of a *strike-slip* fault. Catastrophic slip on transform faults can give rise to moderate to large earthquakes, depending on the length of the fault. However, the largest earthquakes are associated with the most violent interaction of plate tectonics which takes place where two plates collide. A direct collision between two plates forces one to sink under the other. This process produces a *subduction zone* with major *thrust* faults. Most subduction zones are located along the rim of the Pacific Ocean. Remarkably, the sliding of the lithosphere over the asthenosphere causes no discernable earthquakes. This is fortunate since nearly every point on Earth's surface is underlain by these largest of faults forming the base of the plates.

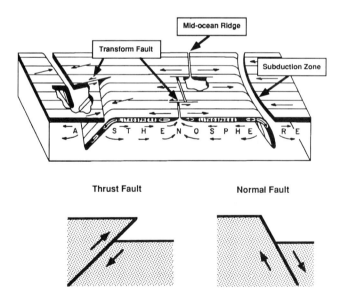

FIGURE 2: The upper figure shows a cartoon of the basic geometric relations of plate interactions and the location of the lithosphere and asthenosphere. Plates are born by cooling of upwelling magma at mid-ocean ridges and are destroyed at subduction zones where they are reincorporated into the mantle (asthenosphere and below). Offsets in ridges and subduction zones produce transform faults which are examples of strike-slip faults. Normal faulting occurs at mid-ocean ridges and thrust faulting occurs in subduction zones. The two lower figures show how these faults slip in cross section. (upper figure modified from Issacks et al, 1968. Reprinted by permission from the American Geophysical Union.).

Plate Tectonics has been very effective in explaining the location where most earthquakes occur. Earthquakes associated with the interactions of plates are usually termed *Interplate earthquakes,* and comprise most of the earthquakes which occur in the world. However, not all is perfect with the theory of Plate Tectonics, and earthquakes, some very large, can also occur within the interior of the major plates. These events are termed *Intraplate earthquakes* and are problematical for both earthquake scientists and for society. Intraplate earthquakes are the result of internal deformation in the plate and represent a frontier area in the science of earthquakes. Compare Figure 1 which shows the location of plate boundaries with Figure 3 which shows the *epicenters* (locations) of destructive earthquakes of this century. Most earthquakes congregate near the plate boundaries.

As Plate Tectonics has become a major unifying principle in the earth sciences so too has the *fault* model become the standard for explaining motions due to earthquakes in the science of Seismology. The fault model, coupled with the known steady motions of the plates, can be used to predict the type (e.g., strike-slip vs. thrust motions), relative size and intensity of shaking of earthquakes in Interplate seismic zones. And even where little is known of the history of major faults within Interplate or Intraplate zones, the fault model allows Seismologists to interpret observed strong ground motions close to the source of the earthquake or very weak ground motions far from the earthquake to infer information on the kind and intensity of faulting.

A *fault* is a discontinuity between two masses of rock. There is often a zone of crushed rock which defines the fault which is termed *fault gouge.* However, the gouge zone is generally thin compared to the length of the fault and is usually ignored in most Seismological studies although physical properties of the gouge zone are probably very important in controlling the ultimate strength (or resistance to slip) of the fault. As two plates move against each other, stresses build up near the

Destructive Earthquakes 1900-1988

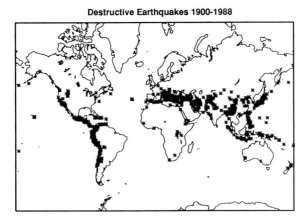

FIGURE 3. Destructive earthquakes for the time period 1900-1988. These events caused deaths or major damage. Events were taken from Nelson and Ganse, 1980, and data reports from the U.S.G.S. and International Seismological Centre.

fault. Eventually the stress exceeds the frictional resistance to slip of the two sides of the fault. An *earthquake* is the result of near-instantaneous slip of a section of a fault when the frictional resistance has been overcome and stresses in the surrounding rock volume relax. The two sides of the fault slip until enough stress has been relieved so that frictional resistance again dominates. The extent of fault breakage or *rupture* over the length and depth of the fault is controlled by irregularities in the shape and/or strength of the fault.

THE QUAKING IN EARTHQUAKES

Slip on a fault is very localized in earthquakes, but the effects from seismic waves that radiate away are not. Like ripples on a pond after a stone is tossed in, the movement of each side of the fault causes waves to travel outward using the immense elasticity of rock in the earth as a sounding board. These seismic waves faithfully reproduce the motions of the fault when very close but progressively become weaker and disperse in time as they travel away.

Figure 4 shows a collection of seismic observations from the 1989 Loma Prieta earthquake in northern California. This event was assigned a local magnitude of 7.1 by the U.S. Geological Survey and ruptured a section of the San Andreas fault system south of San Francisco. It was a very destructive earthquake in terms of property damage (approximately $60 billion) and caused 60 deaths, most from a collapsed freeway section. The figure shows seismogram observations of the velocity of the ground at several different distances from the event.

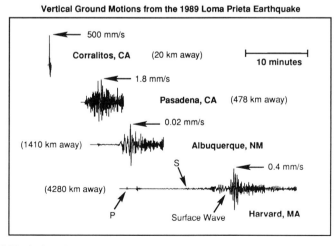

FIGURE 4: Vertical motions of the ground at four different distances from the 1989 Loma Prieta earthquake. The figure shows seismograms which display the velocity of the ground with time. Time runs to the right. Note that ground motions at Corralitos were very short in duration compared to the other seismic stations. The ground motions also decrease dramatically the further the station is from the earthquake.

Immediately after a portion of the San Andreas fault ruptured, seismic waves propagated to the surface at Corralitos, California, directly above the *hypocenter* or focus of the earthquake. The seismic waves moved the ground at Corralitos with accelerations of nearly one half that of gravity, but with velocities comparbale to a person walking slowly, and ground displacements of only about 7 inches or 20 cm. Duration of intense shaking was about 15 seconds. Corralitos was only about 20 km from the initial point of rupture yet, all things considered, experienced only a few percent of the actual motions which occurred on the fault surface. The Loma Prieta earthquake was widely felt and caused much damage but it is amazing to consider how short and how small ground motions need be to produce such destruction. As the waves propagated to further and further distances, they became much smaller and much more drawn out in time. Indeed, by the time the Loma Prieta earthquake could be observed in Harvard, Massachusetts, the seismic waves were at most 1/100th the size of those at Corralitos and lasted well over one half hour.

The reasons for such dramatic changes in the size and duration of seismic waves from an earthquake are easy to understand. When a seismic wave travels through the earth the wave front generally becomes larger and larger like the example of ripples on a pond. Since energy in the wave is conserved and was provided by the fault at the inception of the earthquake, the increasing size of the wavefront demands that the constant amount of energy be smeared out over the growing front of the wave. This results in smaller wave motions with distance from the earthquake. This principle is the same as that describing the dimming of light from a light bulb with increasing distance.

Another effect which contributes to the general decrease of ground motions with distance from an earthquake is the dispersal of seismic waves in time. There are three general types of seismic waves which can be observed in the seismic recordings of Figure 4. The first arriving, or Primary wave, is called the P wave, for short, and is simply the acoustic sound wave that travels through the earth. The S wave (from Secondary or Shear wave) is a wave that exists in solid materials and represents the propagation of a rotational disturbance in the solid. In general, the S wave travels about 60% of the speed of the P wave. Thus, after traveling many thousands of kilometers, the S wave arrives at a seismic station many minutes after the P wave. The third class of seismic waves to propagate away from an earthquake are the Surface waves. They are often the largest waves to be observed and are closely analogous to the ripples on the pond, although they represent ripples on the surface of Earth. These waves are even slower than the S waves. Taken together, the various speeds of these waves initially generated by the earthquake serve to stretch the weak ground motions over a much longer time span than the movements which occurred on the fault.

These simple observations point out a fundamental principle in mitigating hazards from earthquake shaking - that simple avoidance of a dangerous fault is half the battle in avoiding damage. Distance does wonders in reducing the shaking of an earthquake. Unfortunately, with increased population and increased land development in Interplate areas, like the Pacific Rim countries of the world or California in the U.S., hazards mitigation becomes a complex engineering problem in structure design with careful consideration of the location of faults and their likelihood of movement.

MEASURING THE SHAKING

The size of an earthquake can be gauged in many ways. The technology for recording ground motions has advanced much farther than scientific knowledge for understanding the physical dynamics of the earthquake source. Both very large and very small ground motions can be recorded with high fidelity as shown by the example of Loma Prieta data in Figure 4. Even with such complete data, earthquake size is described by an empirical measure of one or two of the largest oscillations on a seismogram. These measurements have been performed for thousands of earthquakes since inception of accurate ground motion recordings.

The *local magnitude* or *Richter scale* is probably the most well known number quoted for an earthquake by the media. It was developed in the 1930's by Charles Richter at the Caltech Seismological Laboratory for earthquakes in Southern California. Since then, the scale has been extended to other areas of the world where seismic stations can record motions from nearby earthquakes. Local magnitude is based on a simple reading of the maximum amplitude of the earthquake recording adjusted for distance using an empirical correction factor. Since the logarithm of the amplitude is used in the mathematical formula for local magnitude, a change in ground displacement by a factor of 10 results in a change in local magnitude by 1. A magnitude 6 earthquake, for example, produces waves ten times larger than a magnitude 5 earthquake at the same distance.

Other magnitude scales have also been developed when seismic data can only be obtained from stations very far (thousands of kilometers) from an earthquake. Two such scales are the body wave magnitude scale, mb, and the surface wave magnitude scale, Ms. These scales have been developed by similar empirical means through measurement of the maximum amplitudes of first arriving sound waves and later arriving surface waves from many earthquake events. The magnitude for a particular earthquake is determined by taking measurements from as many stations as possible and averaging the individual determinations of magnitude. This is done to ensure that vagaries of the properties of wave propagation through the earth and biases in the amplitude of seismic waves due to the type of faulting are empirically averaged out to yield the most reliable measure possible.

Amongst seismologists, there is an informal size designation of earthquakes in terms of magnitude. A microearthquake usually cannot be felt and is generally less than magnitude 3. A small or minor earthquake can be between magnitude 3 to 4.5. Moderate events, between 4.5 and about 6, could cause some local damage. Large events are within the range of 6.5 to 7.9 and can be very damaging. Events greater than magnitude 8 are known as great earthquakes and are major geological events as well as being quite destructive in populated areas. The local magnitude 7.1 Loma Prieta earthquake was a large earthquake, but the 1906 San Francisco

TABLE 1
Selected Levels of the Modified Mercalli Intensity Scale
(abridged from Richter, 1958)

III. Felt indoors. Hanging objects swing. Vibration like passing of light trucks. Duration estimated. May not be recognized as an earthquake.
V. Felt outdoors; direction estimated. Sleepers wakened. Liquids disturbed, some spilled. Small unstable objects displaced or upset. Doors swing, close, open. Shutters, pictures move. Pendulum clocks stop, start, change rate.
VII. Difficult to stand. Noticed by drivers of motor cars. Hanging objects quiver. Furniture broken. Damage to masonry D, including cracks. Weak chimneys broken at roof line. Fall of plaster, loose bricks, stones, tiles, cornices. Some cracks in masonry C. Waves on ponds; water turbid with mud. Small slides and caving in along sand or gravel banks. Large bells ring. Concrete irrigation ditches damaged.
VIII. Steering of motor cars affected. Damage to masonry C; partial collapse. Some damage to masonry B; none to masonry A. Fall of stucco and some masonry walls. Twisting, fall of chimneys, factory stacks, monuments, towers, elevated tanks. Frame houses moved on foundations if not bolted down; loose panel walls thrown out. Decayed piling broken off. Branches broken from trees. Changes in flow or temperature of springs and wells. Cracks in wet ground and on steep slopes.
IX. General panic. Masonry D destroyed; masonry C heavily damaged, sometimes with complete collapse; masonry B seriously damaged. Frame structures, if not bolted, shifted off foundations. Frame racked. Serious damage to reservoirs. Underground pipes broken. Conspicuous cracks in ground. In alluviated areas sand and mud ejected, earthquake fountains, sand craters.
X. Most masonry and frame structures destroyed with their foundations. Some well-built wooden structures and bridges destroyed. Serious damage to dams, dikes, embankments. Large landslides. Water thrown on banks of canals, rivers, lakes, etc. Sand and mud shifted horizontally on beaches and flat land. Rails bent slightly.
XI. Rails bent greatly. Underground pipelines completely out of service.
XII. Damage nearly total. Large rock masses displaced. Lines of sight and level distorted. Objects thrown into the air.

earthquake was one of this century's great earthquakes rupturing 300 km of the San Andreas fault.

A second and older way to measure the size of an earthquake is to tabulate the severity of damage after the event. This is done by assigning a Roman numeral to the kind of damage seen or reported in an area based on the Modified Mercalli Intensity scale. Table 1 displays the Modified Mercalli scale. Obviously, an earthquake can only be rated if there are people living in the epicentral area and the severity of damage can depend on many factors independent of the actual size of the earthquake. For example, if an area has well engineered buildings and other major structures which can withstand severe earthquake shaking compared to an area in a less developed nation, then the same amount of shaking can produce completely different intensity levels. In the United States, the U.S. Geological Survey canvases an earthquake damaged area through field visits and mailed questionnaires to map the spatial variation of intensity. The resulting map for an earthquake is called an *Isoseismal map* and is related to many cultural and geological conditions.

There have been many studies linking earthquake magnitude with the Modified Mercalli intensity and the size of Isoseismal map areas. Generally, as the maximum observed intensity increases so does magnitude. As magnitude increase, so does the area of damage. However, the overall size of felt areas from earthquakes also depends on the region. For example, large earthquakes in the central U.S., like the 1811-1812 New Madrid events (3 magnitude 8 earthquakes) were felt at distances 100 times greater than the 1906 San Francisco earthquake. These differences are due to the great differences in efficiency of propagation of seismic waves in the two regions.

EARTHQUAKES AS DISASTERS

Earthquakes are a natural consequence of the large-scale motions of the plates and have undoubtably occurred over all of the history of Earth. In fact, most large earthquakes that do occur are hardly even noticed except through long-range detection by sensitive seismic instruments. It is a surprising statistic that, on the average, 2 earthquakes per week occur somewhere in the globe that are magnitude 6 or larger. However, like many aspects of the workings of Nature, earthquakes can be devastating if they happen near population centers and may cause long-range effects which eventually impact on population centers.

Earthquakes can induce damage in a number of ways. If structures are situated directly on a fault which moves in an earthquake, differential motion of the two sides of the fault can simply cause those structures to fail. Actually, very little damage occurs in most large earthquakes from direct fault movement. Images of the fault opening up to swallow a building or poor, unsuspecting pedestrians make for exciting grade-B movies but do not actually occur in reality. Indeed, there are many examples of structures situated on or within a few feet of a fault which withstand fault movements very effectively. Hazards from actual fault motions can be effectively mitigated by avoiding building on the fault, as required for example in California. However, roads, pipelines, power lines and some major structures like dams can be severely damaged by direct fault motions since faults are often unavoidable in their construction.

Strong ground shaking caused by the seismic waves propagating away from the fault can be large enough and of enough duration to induce building failure. Even when a structure can withstand the shaking, the contents of a building can be dangerous to the occupants if not properly secured. Millions of dollars worth of damage can result in an earthquake simply through equipment and materials falling on the floor off of shelves and desks, not to mention the hazards to perons trying to avoid these objects.

Perhaps the greatest danger from earthquake shaking is due to failure of the ground under structures. In areas where the ground is composed of loosely consolidated muds, artificial fill or deep soils, strong shaking can cause dramatic settling, slope failure, landslides and can even turn seemingly solid ground into something the consistency of molasses. These secondary effects caused by the earthquake can cause much of the damage. In the 1964 Good Friday Alaskan earthquake

(Ms 8.1), 75 homes in Turnagain Heights, a residential section of Anchorage, were destroyed when the ground they were built on failed in an extensive landslide. In another example, the May 18, 1980 eruption of Mount St. Helens in Washington State was triggered by a small earthquake which caused the entire north slope of the volcano to fail in a massive landslide exhuming the magma within.

Earthquakes which occur offshore can make extremely devastating seismic sea waves called *tsunamis.* These waves are produced when the sea floor is uplifted or fails in an undersea landslide. Although the size of a tsunami is not significantly different from typical sea waves in the open ocean, once they encounter the shore, their run-up can be many meters causing widespread destruction in coastal zones many thousands of miles from the causative earthquake. A 50 foot high tsunami, associated with two large earthquakes, helped destroy Lisbon, Portugal, in 1750. The tsunami associated with the 1964 Alaskan earthquake caused much destruction locally and also destroyed waterfront areas in Cresent City, northern California, over 2500 miles away.

These direct hazards from earthquakes are compounded by secondary, often worse disasters which are set up by the initial earthquake destruction. These include the age-old scourges of humanity - fire, famine and disease. The most famous example in the United States is the fire which destroyed San Francisco, California, in the 1906 San Francisco earthquake. Although the city was severely damaged by the earthquake shaking, the resulting fire caused by spreading of small fires started in the earthquake and compounded by broken water mains caused much more complete destruction.

Figure 3 shows a compilation of significant earthquakes from 1900 to 1988. These are important earthquakes which caused deaths or were costly in damage. Note that most occur where expected - near the boundaries of the great plates of Earth. There were over 1,270,000 deaths from these earthquakes but most losses occurred in just a few major events (Table 2). On the average, there are about 14,000 deaths per year due to earthquake disasters. The costs in human suffering are staggering but the

TABLE 2
The Most Destructive Earthquakes 1900-1988
(Nelson and Ganse, 1979; Bolt, 1988; USGS Preliminary Determination of Epicenters, International Seismological Centre)

Date	Magnitude	Region	Deaths
July 27, 1976	7.6	Tangshan, China	240,000
December 16, 1920	8.5	Kansu, China	200,000
September 1, 1923	8.3	Kwanto, Japan	99,331
May 31, 1970	7.8	Peru	66,794
December 28, 1908	7.5	Messina, Italy	58,000
May 22, 1927	8.0	China	40,912
December 26, 1939	8.0	Erzincan, Turkey	32,700
January 13, 1915	7.5	Avezzano, Italy	32,610
January 25, 1939	8.3	Chillan, Chile	28,000
May 30, 1935	7.5	Quetta, India	25,000
December 7, 1988	6.7	Spitak, Armenia	25,000

death rate is less, on the average, than from traffic fatalities in the United States. So far, history has shown that is it much more hazardous to drive on the freeways of a major city than to experience even a large earthquake in this country.

The difference in scale of an earthquake disaster can be illustrated by the October 17, 1989 Loma Prieta earthquake in California and the December 7, 1988 Spitak, USSR, (Armenia) earthquake. Both earthquakes were about the same size in terms of magnitude, Ms 6.9. The Loma Prieta event was a large earthquake associated with slip on the San Andreas fault near Santa Cruz, California. It caused approximately $6 billion of damage throughout the greater San Francisco area, 62 deaths, 3757 injuries and 8000 homeless. The Spitak earthquake was associated with slip on faults of the Caucuses Mountains in Armenia. Destruction was extensive with 25,000 people killed, 19,000 injured and 500,000 homeless. Damage was estimated to be $16 billion. Although every earthquake is different, in terms of the kind of faulting involved and details of movement on the fault, the great difference in casualties between these two earthquakes can be simply ascribed to quality of building construction in the two areas. Engineering studies of building collapse in Leninakan, Armenia, showed that the combination of poor building design and dangerous ground conditions caused by thick layers of poorly consolidated soils were important factors in explaining the magnitude of the disaster. Indeed, much of the damage that occurred in San Francisco proper from the Loma Prieta earthquake was also due to poor ground conditions in the Marina district. This area was built upon artificial fill and sand which metaphorically acts like a bowl of jello when shaken by seismic waves.

The differences in damage and deaths between these two large earthquakes illustrates that much can be done to alleviate earthquake hazards simply by building appropriately. A well-known engineer commented on the destruction in Armenia at the time by saying that "earthquakes don't kill people, buildings kill people". In the United States, earthquake areas in California, Utah and New England have building codes which require certain standards to be maintained to ensure that new buildings can withstand expected levels of earthquake shaking. Old buildings and structures built before 1930 are generally not under such codes so are potential hazards in future earthquakes.

EARTHQUAKE PREDICTION

Major earthquakes are ephemeral phenomena occurring once in many years, even in very active tectonic areas, and usually lasting less than a minute. Because these geologic processes build up over such long times, earthquake scientists only have a short historical earthquake record to study. Historical accounts of earthquakes can go back several thousand years as seen by descriptions of earthquake effects in the Old Testament. Some countries, like China, have fairly complete records of large earthquakes for over 1000 years. These reports are important and can be supplemented by geological studies which can date the occurrence of large earthquakes using carbon radioisotopes in material taken out of fault zones. Yet most areas only have less than 100 years of data. What these records show is that the occurrence of earthquakes is quite complex and not currently predictable in a deterministic sense.

The location of earthquakes can be usefully predicted in terms of Plate Tectonics theory and the fault model. Large faults with geologically recent movements are recognized as important sites for future earthquakes. However, earthquakes appear to occur randomly in time. The historical record of earthquakes in an area can be used to infer the probability of occurrence of another earthquake in some future time by using the science of statistics and assuming that the processes that caused the past earthquakes are still operating. Finding the probability of occurrence is called *forecasting*. *Prediction* is reserved for definite estimates of the time, place, and magnitude of an earthquake which can be used in short-time preparation for the event in order to mitigate hazards.

How does this work? As an example, take the occurrence of earthquakes east of the Rocky Mountains in North America. This area has experienced the largest Intraplate earthquakes anywhere in the world with the 1811-1812 New Madrid events in the Missouri-Tennessee area. A magnitude 7 earthquake destroyed Charleston, South Carolina, in 1886. Approximately 10 destructive earthquakes have occurred along the St. Lawrence River in Canada since the early 1600's. These events, taken with the instrumental record which shows many smaller earthquakes in the last 40 years, can be used to find the average recurrence interval for an event of a certain magnitude.

To take a simple example of how this is done, imagine that the in-laws are coming for a visit some four-day holiday weekend. You also know they will visit your family for only one of those four days. Making the imperfect analogy between a visit from the in-laws and the occurrence of an earthquake, an estimate of your chances of a visit on the first day is a probability of one in four or 25 percent. After the first day without in-laws appearing, with three days left, the chances of your in-laws coming the next day go up to one in three or a 33 percent probability. At the end of the second day the chances are higher. With only two days left, the chances go up to one in two or a 50 percent probability they will appear on the morrow. At the end of the third day, if they haven't already shown up, you are certain they will appear the next day — earthquake.

The earthquake problem is an open ended one and there is no guarantee that one will happen in any particular area. But, as time passes the probability of an earthquake occurring in any one place does increase. Seismologists estimate that a destructive earthquake of magnitude 6 or larger has about a 64 percent chance of occurring east of the Rocky Mountains in the next 30 years. These odds are almost as high as those for an earthquake of magnitude 7 or larger in the San Francisco Bay region over the same time period.

There are many stories which come out of the drama surrounding a destructive earthquake involving strange animal behavior or strange physical phenomena like unexpected lights in the sky. There are also tantalizing hints from scientifically-documented observations that there are physical processes which occur near the fault before some earthquakes. However, these kinds of experiences often prove to be unique or simply cannot be understood because scientific observations have not been collected for the next earthquake which may occur in the next hundred years. A true science of earthquake prediction in still years away, barring any unexpected breakthroughs, and will only proceed as more data is collected for each earthquake. Until such predictions are realized, the hazards of large earthquakes can be significantly reduced by using sound engineering principles, common sense and planning. Earth will continue its motions, both slow and catastrophic. It is our job to learn to live on our moving planet.

BIBLIOGRAPHY

Bolt, Bruce A., *Earthquakes,* W.H. Freeman and Company, New York, 282 pages, 1988.

Bly, Robert, quotation from "Finding an old ant mansion", in *The Man in the Black Coat Turns,* Harper and Row, New York, 65 pages, 1981.

International Seismological Centre, *Regional Catalogue of Earthquakes,* Thatcham, Newbury RG13 4NS, Berkshire, United Kingdom.

Issacks, Brian, Jack Oliver and Lynn Sykes, Seismology and the new global tectonics, *Journal of Geophysical Research,* vol. 73, pages 5855-5899, 1968.

Nelson, John B., and Robert A. Ganse, *Significant Earthquakes 1900-1979* (map), National Geophysical and Solar-Terrestrial Data Center and World Data Center A for Solid Earth Geophysics, Boulder, CO, 1980.

Richter, Charles F., *Elementary Seismology,* W.H. Freeman and Co., San Francisco, 768 pages, 1958.

Thiel, Charles C. (ed.), Competing Against Time, Report to Governor George Deukmejian from The Governor's Board of Inquiry on the 1989 Loma Prieta Earthquake, State of California, Office of Planning and Research Information Center, 1990.

U.S. Geological Survey, *Preliminary Determination of Epicenters - Monthly Reports,* Golden, CO.

Walker, Bryce, *Earthquake,* Time-Life Books, Alexandria, Virginia, 176 pages, 1982.

Ward, Peter L., and Robert A. Page, The Loma Prieta Earthquake of October 17, 1989, in *Earthquakes and Volcanoes*, pages 215-237, vol. 21, 1989.

Natural and Technological Disasters: Causes, Effects and Preventive Measures. Edited by S.K. Majumdar, G.S. Forbes, E.W. Miller, and R.F. Schmalz. © 1992, The Pennsylvania Academy of Science.

Chapter Six

CONFLAGRATIONS: DISASTROUS URBAN FIRES

ROBERT F. SCHMALZ

Department of Geosciences
The Pennsylvania State University
University Park, PA 16802

Late last night, when we were all in bed,
Mrs. O'Leary took a lantern to the shed.
When the cow kicked it over,
She winked her eye and said,
"There'll be a hot time in the old town tonight!"

(Folk ballad, anonymous)

INTRODUCTION

Near the close of the last glacial epoch, about 5,000 years ago, humankind made a great technological advance on which virtually all subsequent development was based: we began cultivating plants and domesticating animals to provide a reliable and continuing supply of food. The practice of producing food rather than simply gathering what was naturally available, led to vastly increased efficiency. In most areas, an individual dependent upon hunting and gathering could sustain himself (or herself) and perhaps one or two dependent children; agriculture and animal husbandry made it possible for a single producer to supply food for ten or more persons. Those not actively engaged in producing food, relieved of the burden of hunting and gathering, were free to dedicate part of their time to specialized activites — to become tool-makers, basket-makers or ceramists, to supply minor specialized dietary supplements by catching fish or gathering salt, herbs or spices, to investigate the environment, to consider questions of philosophical or intellectual importance, to establish religion, or to develop the arts. The benefits of this increased efficiency could be realized, however, only if people joined together in communities for mutual support and devised a system of commerce by which goods and services could be exchanged equitably. So the first commercial centers — incipient cities as we know them — were begun (see, for example, Bibby, 1961).

Because of the rich soil, relatively level terrain, and easy transportation, many of the earliest "cities" were established on river floodplains and piedmont plains along the coast. It soon became evident that the benefits of urban living were not without cost. Whether on the banks of the Yangtze, the Indus, the Nile or the Eurphrates, many of these early cities and the fields upon which they depended must have been devastated by floods almost as soon as they were built. There are records of extremely destructive floods along the Yellow River in China and in the Nile valley dating back more than 4000 years; the frequency of flood myths in literature of virtually every culture suggest the importance of these natural disasters (Ceram, 1952).

Early city dwellers doubtless soon found that floods were not the only hazard associated with urban living. The closely-packed houses of the primitive cities, dependent upon open fires for heating, light and cooking, were much more vulnerable to fire than the isolated and often very simple shelters of hunting and gathering peoples. Many of the early "proto-cities" must have experienced frequent destructive fires. This would be particularly true of communities in high latitudes where wood was the building material of choice, and where heating was essential throughout the long cold winters.

URBAN CONFLAGRATIONS

We have no records of the earliest urban fires, but there is abundant evidence of destructive fires in the archaeological record. The frequent references to fire in mythology and early religious writings offer further evidence of its importance. Modern cities (those built since the beginning of the Christian Era) appear to be only slightly less vulnerable to urban conflagration than we imagine the earliest cities of the Fertile Crescent to have been. No major city in the west has escaped repeated fires, and most have suffered repeated destruction. Venice, despite its dominantly stone construction and generous supply of water was almost completely destroyed by fire in 1106; Dresden burned to the ground in 1491; Moscow burned in 1752 and again in 1812. (The fire in 1812 was set as part of what may have proved to be an excessively zealous effort to drive Napoleon's troops from the city.) Constantinople was perhaps the incendiary champion of Europe and the Near East; it was destroyed by major fires in 1750, 1756, 1782, 1784, 1870 and again in 1954, when the losses exceeded $200 million. On several occasions in the mid-18th century, there were two or more fires in a single year. Perhaps changing the name to Istanbul may improve its luck!

Before discussing urban conflagrations in detail, it is perhaps important to define the term, "conflagration" and to justify the inclusion of such fires in a volume on Natural and Technological Disasters. Webster defines a conflagration as "a raging, destructive fire". The Oxford English Dictionary is only a little more explicit: "(1) the burning up of anything (1825), (2) a great and destructive fire; the burning of a town, a forest or the like (1625)." Some authors restrict the term to exceptionally large and destructive fires which involve unrelated buildings and which are not confined by ordinary bariers such as streets or open ground. A forest fire or prairie fire would be considered a conflagration if of sufficient extent, but in the more common usage (and in the sense that we shall use the term here), a *conflagration* is *a raging and destructive fire which causes substantial loss of life and property*. By this definition, a conflagration is clearly a form of disaster, but will necessarily be restricted to areas where property and people are concentrated. Is a conflagration, then, a natural or a technological disaster? The question is further complicated by the fact that large destructive fires may be initiated by natural processes (volcanic eruption, earthquake or lightning, for example), but in many cases are the direct result of human activity, both accidental and deliberate. Rather than attempting to resolve these questions, we may examine a number of relatively recent conflagrations to learn something of their causes and their consequences. For the purposes of this discussion, we will recognize three types of urban conflagration.

TYPE I CONFLAGRATIONS

The Great Fire of London, September 2-5, 1666

In the middle of the 17th century, the population of London was probably close to 490,000, making it the largest city in Europe. It had survived repeated fires and floods, and such other disasters as the Black Death of 1348. Plague struck the city again in 1625, killing an estimated 40,000 persons, roughly ten percent of the population. After the trials of the Regicide (1649), and the terrors of the Commonwealth (1649-1660), an even more severe epidemic, the Great Plague, swept the city in the fall of 1664. The first report of plague appears in the Bill of Mortality on November 2, and the number of deaths reported grew rapidly thereafter. At the peak of the epidemic in mid-1665, 7,000 deaths were reported in a single week. By the end of December, 1665, when the epidemic appeared to be subsiding, approximately 75,000 persons had died, and even larger numbers had fled the city to avoid infection. By 1666, as a result of the combined effects of the plague and twenty years' of political instability, large areas of the city were deserted. Most buildings were of "half-timber" construction or built entirely of wood, and roofs were usually made of wood or straw-thatch. The city was ripe for burning (Besant, 1903; Leason, 1961).

In the early morning hours of September 2, 1666, fire broke out in the house of the king's baker on Pudding Lane near London Bridge. The cause is uncertain; an overheated bake-oven, or a soot-choked flue, perhaps. It may have been the result of an accident or simple carelessness. The fire spread rapidly, and continued to burn for four days and nights. Approximately 80% of the city is thought to have been destroyed, including most civic and public buildings, the Royal Exchange, the Customs House and the Guildhall. The original St. Paul's church burned as did 87 parish churches and 13,200 houses. No estimate is available of the number of deaths which resulted from the fire directly, but the fact that large parts of the city were deserted probably helped to keep the number relatively small (Bedford, 1966; Bell, 1920; Reddaway, 1940).

The Great Fire of London is a typical example of an accidental urban conflagration which spread outward from a single ignition point, driven by the wind. Such conflagrations feed on combustible material in their paths, and if uncontrolled, generally die out when they reach a natural barrier like a large river, when they advance into a region of insufficient fuel such as the edge of a built-up area, or when rain douses the flames or changing winds drive the fire back into an area already burnt. The relatively slow rate of advance typical of wind-driven conflagrations generally allows timely evacuation of areas on the path of the fire. Consequently, fires which cause enormous property damage may be responsible for disproportionately few deaths. These general characteristics occur repeatedly; a more recent, but typical example being the fire which destroyed much of Chicago in 1871.

The Chicago Fire, October 8-9, 1871.

Little more than a glorified army depot in 1833, by 1871 Chicago had grown into a major metropolis. Lying at the junction of the Michigan and Illinois Canal and of four important railroads (the Galena, Michigan Central, Illinois Central and Michigan Southern), it was a port city, a major meat-packing and agricultural market, and the principal railroad junction of the nation. Bounded on the east by Lake Michigan, the city extended south into the industrial center of South Chicago, west past the stockyards to rich farmlands, and north through elegant residential neighborhoods along the lake shore to open prairie land. Two-thirds of the buildings were built of wood, and in the central district, houses, office buildings, warehouses and industrial structures were packed closely together (Colbert and Chamberlin, 1871).

The summer and fall of 1871 had been extremely hot and dry. There had been less than 2″ of rain since the fourth of July. On the evening of October 8, a hot, dry southwest wind was blowing across the city. The fire began on the southwest side of the city, somewhere near the intersection of DeKoven and South Jefferson streets, where a memorial stands today. Just how the fire started is not known; the story of Mrs. O'Leary and her cow (sometimes embellished with details about cream to make a late-night oyster stew), may be apocryphal, but in an age of kerosene lamps, an overturned lantern seems as likely a cause as any. Fanned by the moderate (less than 30 mph) wind, the fire spread east- and northward, covering an airline distance of more than two miles in six and one-half hours, burning everything in its path. Its rate of advance was slow enough to allow ample time for evacuation of the area ahead of the fie, and even to allow some sight-seers to observe its progress. The spread of the fire was constrained by Lake Michigan on the east. In the south, explosives were used to create a fire-break to stop the fire's advance, and in the north and northwest, the fire was slowed by open prairie and finally extinguished by rain late on the 9th of October.

The fire had burned more than 2,000 acres in 27 hours, destroying at least 18,000 buildings and causing more than $196,000,000 damage. Although 90,000 persons were driven from their homes, the City Coroner estimated that only about 300 persons had died as a result of the fire (Miller, 1990).

SUMMARY: TYPE I CONFLAGRATIONS

The Chicago fire and the Great Fire of London are typical examples of what might be termed a "Type I" urban conflagration. The characteristics of fires of this type include, (i) accidental ignition by human agency, (ii) single point of initiation, and (iii) wind-driven dispersal. They are often self-terminating (usually because of natural or artificial barriers or by the exhaustion of suitably concentrated combustible materials). They commonly result in very large property losses, but ordinarily do not cause large numbers of fatalities. Today, as a result of increasing industrial use of volatile and unstable chemical agents, explosions are sometimes the initiating event in Type I urban fires. Fatalities attributable to the initiating explosion or to the incidental release of toxic materials may cause greater loss of life than would ordinarily result from a Type I fire. The pier explosion at Texas City, Texas, in April, 1947, is an example. Five hundred sixty-one persons were killed, most of them died in the explosion itself.

TYPE II CONFLAGRATIONS

Type II urban conflagrations differ from the first type in that they originate as the direct result of some precipitating natural disaster. The initiating event may be a volcanic eruption, a landslide, a wind storm or, in unusual circumstances, a flood, but large urban fires are most commonly associated with earthquakes. Two familiar examples illustrate the characteristics of Type II conflagrations.

San Francisco Earthquake and Fire, April 18-19, 1906

San Francisco was an established seaport serving central California by the beginning of the 19th century, but it did not grow rapidly until the discovery of gold in 1848. The city is located adjacent to extensive timber lands, and most of the city's buildings were constructed of wood. Several major fires destroyed parts of the city between 1830 and the end of the century; fires were particularly common during the decade 1849-1860, when the rush to the gold fields left scores of ships abandoned in the bay, and hundreds of houses empty in the city. Earthquakes contributed to the city's misfortunes, those of 1864, 1898 and 1900 being especially destructive. By 1905, San Francisco was a major commercial center which served not only much of the western United States, but was the gateway to the Pacific as well. Closely-packed wooden buildings remained, particularly along the waterfront and in the adjacent business and industrial districts, but in the city center and the Nob Hill residential area, many had been replaced by modern masonry structures. The city was a terminus of the transcontinental railroad as well as a major seaport. A system of electric interurban and trolley cars, with cable cars in hillier parts of the city, provided modern public transportation at low cost. Underground mains and overhead wires distributed illuminating gas and electric power throughout the city, and most of the city streets were illuminated by lamps on elegant iron standards. Abundant pure water was brought into the city from Crystal Springs, Lake Honda and the San Andreas Reservoir through iron pipes up to 44 inches in diameter, and distributed throughout the city by a system of underground mains and pumps. A modern sanitary sewage system collected the city's wastes and carried them to a disposal point off shore. Despite its many modern features, however, the city was a fire-trap. The National Board of Fire Underwriters summarized the situation in 1905:

"In view of the exceptionally large areas, great heights, numerous unprotected openings, general absence of firebreaks and stops and highly combustible nature of the buildings, the potential hazard is very severe. The above features, combined with the almost total lack of sprinklers and modern protective devices generally, make the probability alarmingly severe. In fact, San Francisco has violated all underwriting traditions by not burning up." (quoted in Bolt, *et al*, 1975).

The evening of April 17th, 1906, the Tuesday after Easter, was marked by a gala performance of *Carmen* by the Metropolitan Opera Company. The performance was attended by delighted fans of Enrico Caruso and most of the socially-conscious residents of Nob Hill. Many apparently made a night of it, and were still in their evening clothes when disaster struck on Wednesday morning.

Many residents of the city were wakened at 5:12 AM on April 18 by a rumbling sound, ". . . like an approaching train . . .". A moment later, a second, much more severe shock struck the city, and according to a newspaper account by James Hopper, one heard, ". . . the crash of falling buildings, the rumble of avalanches of bricks and the groans of tortured timbers." The shaking continued for more than a minute, and was sufficiently violent to cause Hopper's bureau to move about the room, ". . . with sudden bold advances and as sudden shy retreats — with little bows and nods, with little mincing steps." (Andrews, 1963). Subsequent studies showed that in that 60-70 seconds of violent shaking, along a 270 mile segment of the San Andreas fault, the land lying to the west of the fault had moved northwestward (relative to land farther east) as much as 40 feet (Bolt *et al*, 1975). The energy released was enormous and today would be compared to that of several hydrogen bombs. The initial rumbling was followed by vigorous shaking, then the surface of the ground seemed to rise and fall like waves on a pond; trees and buildings began to sway from side to side. Masonry buildings were literally shaken apart, casting heaps of bricks and rubble into the streets of the city (Himmelwright, 1906). Wooden buildings collapsed, cracks opened in the ground, hillside soil began to slide downslope carrying crumbling buildings, and breaking water, gas and sewer mains. Overhead wires fell into the streets, disrupting communications, interrupting power and starting minor electrical fires. Along the waterfront, docks and warehouses slipped beneath the sea. When the shaking stopped, there were several moments of quiet as clouds of dust rose above the city, then came the first signs of fire. Most people had no realization that the most severe disaster was just beginning (Wilson, 1906). The fires were small and scattered at first, starting where debris was ignited by overturned cook- or heating stoves or where gas escaping from broken mains was ignited by electrical sparks. The San Francisco fire department was well organized, disciplined, and quick to respond to many of these small fires, despite the fact that most streets were obstructed by rubble or fleeing residents (most in nightclothes, but some still wearing the formal attire of Tuesday evening's opera performance). When they reached the fires, however, the firefighters found that hydrants would deliver no more than a trickle of water which soon gave out entirely. The pipelines from Crystal Springs, Lake Honda and the San Andreas Reservoir had all ruptured, and thousands of service lines connecting individual structures to the mains had broken — the city was essentially without water (Berlin, 1980). The closely-packed wooden buildings without sprinklers and the absence of open space to serve as firebreaks made it possible for the fires to grow quickly, joining one another, until most of the city was ablaze. By four o'clock Wednesday afternoon it was evident that the only hope of controlling the fires was by using explosives to create firebreaks. The firefighters were untrained in the use of explosives, and the military personnel available were inexperienced in fighting fires. Using dynamite until the supply was exhausted, and then gunpowder which was more difficult to control, the soldiers and firemen attempted to limit the spread of the fires. Buildings were emptied (although it was reported that some occupants were so stupified by drink or opium that they could not be evacuated) then blown apart (Andrews, 1963). Unfortunately, in many cases the explosions simply scattered burning debris, spreading the fires; in others, especially when using gunpowder, the debris was ignited by the explosion itself. The spread of the fire was finally checked by destroying virtually every structure east of Van Ness Avenue. When fully extinguished, after raging unchecked for three days, the conflagration had destroyed an area of more than 500 city blocks, nearly double the area burned in Chicago in 1871. The fire was responsible for approximately 80% of the total damage and for the destruction of more than 28,000 buildings. Property damage exceeded $500,000,000, but remarkably, only approximately 700 lives were lost to the combined agencies of earthquake and fire (Berlin, 1980; Erickson, 1988).

Similar, though less extensive fires followed the Lisbon earthquake of 1751 and the New Madrid (Missouri) earthquakes of 1811-1812. The Type II conflagration which destroyed Tokyo and Yokomama in September, 1923, was also initiated by an earthquake, but that fire exhibited a characteristic which made it vastly more costly of human life.

The Great Kanto Earthquake and Fire, September 1-2, 1923

At two minutes to noon, September 1, 1923, a massive earthquake occurred off the southeast coast of Honshu. The epicenter is believed to have located near Oshima Island at the entrance to Sagami Bay. Cities bordering the Bay were severely shaken by three exceedingly violent shocks just a few minutes apart, then subjected to more than 170 aftershocks during the ensuing six hours (Bolt *et al*, 1975). Although more than a dozen resort towns and fishing villages located along the shore of Sagami Bay and its northeastward extension, Tokyo Bay, were devastated by the earthquake and the seismic seawave which it generated, the greatest losses of life and property were concentrated in the cities of Yokohama and Tokyo. In Yokohama, virtually every building of consequence was demolished in the initial shock; in Tokyo it is estimated that 80% of the central city was destroyed (Leet, 1948; Berlin, 1980).

Both cities were undergoing modernization with the construction of new western-style buildings, but the residential areas of both were still dominated by houses built in the classical Japanese style, crowded together with virtually no intervening space. These structures, with heavy tile roofs supported by weak, flexible wood and paper walls responded to earth motion like unstable inverted pendulums. Open fires or small charcoal-burning stoves (*hibachi*) were used for both heating and cooking. Fire protection and fire-prevention devices were virtually unknown.

The timing of the earthquake was particularly unfortunate. Throughout both cities cooking fires had been lit to prepare the noon meal. Although we have no way of determining accurate numbers, scores and scores of houses must have collapsed in the first tremor. Thousands of people may have been killed or injured and trapped in the debris, and hundreds of fires broke out as the building materials were ignited by overturned *hibachi*. Near Yokohama, the railroad embankment and an entire trainload of school children slid down a slope and vanished into the sea. The storage tanks at the Imperial Navy fuel depot above the city burst and fuel oil pouring down the slope and floating on the water of the Bay soon caught fire. It was in Tokyo, however, where the destruction was most appalling. Fires which broke out immediately in every part of the ruined city were fanned by strong winds. They quickly spread and joined together, sweeping across the city. Terrified residents fled before the flames, seeking safety along the shore of Tokyo Bay, along the banks of the Sumida River and in the open ground of Uena Park, the Imperial Palace Plaza and surrounding the Army Clothing Depot. By four o'clock the heat of the fires became so great that the rising air column formed a cyclonic vortex — a fire-driven tornado with winds whirling at speeds in excess of 100 miles per hour. This raging firestorm moved back and forth across the city at 10 to 20 miles per hour. The heat beneath it was so great that unburned debris over which it passed burst into flame. Beneath the vortex, reduced atmospheric pressure and depleted oxygen made death by suffocation as great a hazard as the danger of burning. Driven by winds generated by its own heat, its movement was erratic and unpredictable; the flames repeatedly returned to areas which had already been burnt. Shortly after four o'clock the firestorm swept down the course of the Sumida River, killing many of those who had sought safety along the River bank, and more than 38,000 of the people who had found shelter on the 250 acre plot surrounding the Clothing Depot (Andrews, 1963; Berlin, 1980; Bolt *et al*, 1975).

The firestorm grew less and less violent in the early evening, and twenty-four hours later the fires in Tokyo had died out for lack of combustible materials. In Tokyo, Yokohama and nearby coastal villages, 140,000 persons had been killed by the earthquake, the fires and the seismic seawave which inundated the coast. An estimated 350,000 houses, mostly built of wood, had been destroyed, and more than half the brick buildings in both cities were destroyed as well. One of the few buildings to survive essentially undamaged was the new Imperial Hotel, designed by an inexperienced and relatively unknown American architect, Frank Lloyd Wright. The hotel was scheduled to celebrate a grand opening at a luncheon the day of the earthquake. The spacious public rooms, fresh bedding and abundant food supplies served hundreds of survivors, and most importantly, the decorative pools in the Hotel garden assured an abundant supply of water for drinking and fire protection, just as Wright had planned that they should (Jacobs, 1965). The area of near-total destruction measured almost 90 by 50 miles — an area substantially larger than the areas destroyed in the Great Fire of London, the Chicago Fire and the San Francisco earthquake and fire combined. Certainly the most costly fire in recorded human history, the great Kanto earthquake and fire must be regarded as one of the greatest disasters of human experience (Busch, 1962; Erickson, 1988; Leet, 1948).

SUMMARY: TYPE II CONFLAGRATIONS

The fire which destroyed Tokyo and Yokohama in September, 1923, differs from other Type II urban conflagrations in its enormous extent, but more significantly in the overwhelming cost in human life. At least two hundred times as many persons perished in the Great Kanto fire as died fifteen years earlier in San Francisco; almost five hundred times the number killed in Chicago in 1871. Certainly, the larger area consumed and the greater population density typical of the Japanese cities were important contributing factors. The most important single cause, however, was the development of the firestorm which swept repeatedly across the city of Tokyo on the afternoon of September 1st. Firestorms did not occur in London, Chicago or San Francisco, nor was there a firestorm associated with the six-day conflagration which followed the 1972 earthquake in Managua, Nicaragua. (Five thousand persons died in Managua, but most were killed by collapsing structures. (Bolt *et al*, 1975; Berlin, 1980). Firestorms, when they occur, typically increase the cost of a conflagration in both property and (especially) in human life many fold. Fortunately, such firestorms require a peculiar combination of conditions only some of which are characteristically associated with Type II conflagrations. When abundant highly combustible fuel with relatively low flash point is combined with multiple ignition points, high ambient temperature and inherently unstable meteorological conditions, firestorms may result. High concentration of flame, relatively long duration and extremely high temperatures are required, and these are rarely achieved in urban envirnments with modern fire control and prevention methods. Indeed, firestorms today are more commonly associated with forest or prairie fires than with urban conflagrations (Chandler, 1983; Collins *et al*, 1990).

TYPE III CONFLAGRATIONS

Type III conflagrations differ from either Type I or Type II in that they are deliberately set. Like conflagrations of the second Type, they usually start at many points simultaneously, and may lead to the development of firestorms with consequently high cost in human life. Obviously, to deliberately start an urban conflagration, with the potential of destroying hundreds of millions of dollars worth of property and causing the deaths of hundreds or thousands of persons could be considered only under extreme duress — as a act of war or as a punitive measure of exceptional nature. Biblical references to "scorched earth" and total destruction of cities suggest that the military use of conflagrations is not a new concept. We have, however, far too many examples of the deliberate destruction of cities by fire in this century.

The attempts to destroy Warsaw, London or Coventry by Germany and the firebombing of Hamburg, Kassel, Stuttgart, Darmstadt and Dresden in Germany and Tokyo in Japan by U.S. and Allied forces in World War II are examples which are, if anything, too fresh in many memories. Other, more recent wars afford equally unhappy examples — those in Korea, Viet Nam, Afganistan, and most recently, Iraq, all involved some Type III conflagrations.

Type III urban conflagrations, being deliberate, hostile acts, deserve little discussion here, but it is clear from the U.S. experience in World War II, fires of extremely destructive scale can be initiated by incendiary bombing. It is also clear that on a massive scale such fires can generate firestorms. The strategic effectiveness of such fire-bombing of urban targets and its psychological effect on civilian and military personnel is very much less clear. Brief summaries of two examples should suffice to illustrate these points.

The German Luftwaffe attempted to break the spirit of the British civilian population by massive bombing and firebombing of London and Coventry. The bombing caused enormous property damage and substantial loss of life, but its effect was, if anything, to strengthen the resolve of the British people, and to unify many other nations in Britain's defense (Churchill, 1953). The firebombing of Dresden by Allied forces in 1945 is said to have killed 135,000 civilians, but its effect in shortening the War is debatable. The same could be said for the even more massive bombing attacks on Hamburg on the nights of July 24, 27 and 29, 1943 (Shirer, 1960). The attacks concentrated on areas of 18, 17 and 10 square miles, respectively, and are believed to have killed between 60,000 and 100,000 persons. The bombing on July 27-28 was sufficiently intense that it resulted in a firestorm like that which devastated Tokyo in 1923. In the three raids, 300,000 dwellings were destroyed, and at least 750,000 persons were left homeless. Despite their cost to both sides, however, the benefit of the raids on the Allied war effort, if any, is unclear.

SUMMARY: TYPE III CONGLAGRATIONS

Type III conflagrations differ from conflagrations of the first and second Types only in that they are initiated deliberately. Single-site fires (like Type I) are rare, simply because Type III fires are extraordinary acts of war, and the perpetrator ordinarily has the means to confuse his enemy and increase the effectiveness of the tactic by initiating fires at multiple points simultaneously. Conflagrations of Type III may trigger exceedingly destructive firestorms, but even in the absence of firestorms, Type III conflagrations are usually very costly of lives and property for both victim and aggressor. In view of the uncertain effectiveness of urban conflagrations in warfare, it may be that specific efforts to intitiate such fires in the future will become less common. Unfortunately, large-scale conflagrations as incidental consequences of massive conventional or nuclear bombing attacks remain highly probable.

CONCLUSION

Urban conflagrations may be divided into three major types. The characteristics of each type are as follows:

Type I — accidental ignition by human or natural agency;
single point of initiation;
slow spreading (relatively), wind driven;
often self-extinguished;
extensive property damage;
limited loss of life.

Type II — accidental ignition by natural event
(rarely by human agency)
multiple points of initiation;
rapidly spreading;
commonly precipitate firestorm(s);
self-extinguished (often);
very extensive property damage;
loss of life very great.

Type III — deliberately set;
single or multiple point inititation
(latter more common);
usually an act of war;
self-extinguished;
massive loss of property and life;
uncertain military value.

Excluding fires of the third Type, we may anticipate that urban conflagrations will continue to occur in the future. Incendiary accidents are inevitable, and regardless of any effort to reduce the use of inflammable building materials, fuel will continue to be abundant in the urban environment. It seems unlikely, therefore, that conflagrations can be completely eliminated, but by applying principles learned from major fires of the past, we may be able to prevent the recurrence of holocausts like those that destroyed London, Chicago, San Francisco and Tokyo.

Within structures, the restricted use of combustible materials, fire blocks, fire-doors, sprinkler systems and automatic alarms should be mandated by building codes. Structural "chimneys" (elevator shafts, stairwells, etc.) should be enclosed, and wherever possible, structures should be equipped with standpipes and reservoirs to provide emergency fire-fighting water in the event that municipal supplies are interrupted (Legget, 1975).

The buildings themselves should be separated by wide streets, open land, rivers and other natural blocks to intercept the spread of fires. Rivers, lakes and artificial ponds may be used both to enhance the urban scene and to provide emergency water supplies. It may be necessary to provide high-pressure water lines, completely isolated from domestic supplies, for fire-fighting purposes. Isolation valves must be incorporated into water supply mains and natural gas lines so that damaged and leaking sections can be promptly isolated to minimize water pressure losses, to limit areas of interrupted service, and to control the escape of combustible and potentially explosive fuel. Electric power lines must also be divided into redundant networks so that damaged portions can be isolated while maintaining service elsewhere. Above all, buildings and the cities themselves must be planned with emergency management in mind — structures designed to resist fire and to withstand those natural phenomena which may precipitate disaster (Anon. 1967; Hall, 1979).

Finally, emergency personnel must be trained to deal with all sorts of emergency, and the general public must be sufficiently educated in emergency procedures to be able to assist, rather than interfere with the task of preventing and if necessary controlling an urban conflagration.

REFERENCES

Andrews, A. 1963. *Earthquake.* London. Angus & Robertson. 204 pp. + index.
Anon. 1967. *Municipal Fire Administration.* Chicago. Institute for Training in Municipal Administration. 343 pp. + 8 appendices, index.
Bedford, J. 1966. *London's Burning.* London. Abelard-Schuman.
Bell, W.G. 1920. *The Great Fire of London in 1666.* London. John Lane. 387 pp.
Berlin, G.L. 1980. *Earthquakes and the Urban Environment.* Boca Raton, FL. CRC Publishing Co., 3 volumes.
Besant, Sir Walter. 1903. *London in the Time of the Stuarts.* London. A&C Back. 384 pp.
Bibby, G. 1961. *Four Thousand Years Ago.* New York. Knopf. 398 pp. + index.
Bolt, B.A., W.L. Horn, G.A. Macdonald and R.F. Scott. 1975. *Geologic Hazards.* New York, Springer-Verlag. 302 pp. + 6 appendices, index.

Busch, N.F. 1962. *Two Minutes to Noon*. New York. Simon and Schuster. 191 pp.

Ceram, C.W. 1952. *Gods, Graves and Scholars*. New York. Knopf. 415 pp. + chronology, bibliography, index.

Chandler, C. *et al*. 1983. *Fire in Forestry*. New York. John Wiley. 2 vols.

Churchill, Sir W.S. 1953. *The Second World War*. New York, Houghton-Mifflin. 6 vols.

Colbert, E. & E. Chamberlin. 1871. *Chicago and the Great Conflagration*. Chicago. 278 pp.

Collins S.L. & L.L. Wallace, eds. 1990. *Fire in North American Tallgrass Prairies*. Norman, OK. University of Oklahoma Press. 175 pp.

Erickson, J. 1988. *Volcanoes and Earthquake*. Blue Ridge Summit, PA. TAB Books. 286 + appendix, index.

Hall, J.R. jr., *et al*. 1979(?). *Fire Code Inspections and Fire Prevention . . .* Boston. National Fire Protection Association. 122 pp. (NFPA Series, MSS-3).

Himmelwright, A.L.A. 1906. *The San Francisco Earthquake and Fire . . .* New York. The Roebling Construction Co., 270 pp.

Jacobs, H. 1965. *Frank Lloyd Wright: America's Greatest Architect*. New York. Harcourt-Brace.

Leet, L.D. 1948. *Causes of Catastrophe*. New York. McGraw-Hill. 227 pp. + index.

Legget, R.F. 1973. *Cities and Geology*. New York. McGraw-Hill. 552 pp. + bibliography, indices.

Leasor, J. 1961. *The Plague and the Fire*. New York. McGraw-Hill. 280 pp.

Miller, R. 1990. *American Apocapalypse; The Great Fire and Myth of Chicago*. Chicago. University of Chicago Press. 287 pp. + index.

Reddaway, T.F. 1940. *The Rebuilding of London after the Great Fire*. London. Jonathan Cape. 333 pp. + bibliography.

Shirer, W.L. 1960. *The Rise and Fall of the Third Reich*. New York. Simon & Schuster. 1143 pp. + notes, index.

Wilson, J.R. 1906. *San Francisco's Horror of Earthquake and Fire . . .* New York. Memorial Publishing Co. 416 pp.

Natural and Technological Disasters: Causes, Effects and Preventive Measures. Edited by .
S.K. Majumdar, G.S. Forbes, E.W. Miller, and R.F. Schmalz. © 1992, The Pennsylvania Academy
of Science.

Chapter Seven

HAZARDS ASSOCIATED WITH VOLCANOES AND VOLCANIC ERUPTIONS

DRU GERMANOSKI
and
LAWRENCE L. MALINCONICO, JR.
Department of Geology
Lafayette College
Easton, PA 18042

INTRODUCTION

The Nature of Volcanic Eruptions and the Associated Hazards

In the recorded history of man, it is estimated that more than 200,000 people have lost their lives as a result of volcanic activity (Coates, 1985; MacDonald *et al.* 1983). However, the advantages of living around a volcano, including the majestic beauty as well agricultural benefits, apparently outweigh the significant hazards associated with volcanic eruptions. In this paper we will examine some of the hazards associated with different types of volcanoes and volcanic eruptions.

Volcanoes are the surficial expression of the earth's internal heat. A volcano forms when melted rock, magma, makes its way through the earth's crust to the surface.

The products of volcanism may be divided into two major categories: lava, which is the general term for molten rock that solidifies at the surface; and pyroclastic debris, the term for materials that are ejected (usually into the air) from the vent. The type of volcano, the morphology, and the nature of the volcanic eruption, i.e. the explosivity of the eruption, is very strongly related to the character of the magma.

The general property that controls the nature of an eruption is the viscosity of the magma, a measure of the resistance of the magma to flow. All magmas contain a certain amount of gas (H_2O, SO_2, HS, HCl, CO_2) dissolved in the melt. These gases are kept in solution in the magma by the extreme pressures that exist at the point where the magma melts. However, as the magma rises towards the surface, the confining pressure on the magma is reduced and the gases begin to come out of solution and form gas bubbles in the magma. Since a bubble of gas has a greater volume than when it is in the dissolved state, the pressure within the magma chamber is increased. The nature of a volcanic eruption is determined by the following:

1) How easily can the trapped gas escape from the magma;
2) How much gas is initially dissolved in the magma.

The viscosity of the magma controls the first variable. If the magma is very fluid (low viscosity) the gases can easily escape; however, if the magma is very viscous, the gas will be trapped in the magma chamber and the pressure will continue to build. The more gas the magma contains, and the more viscous the magma, the greater the explosivity of the volcanic eruption.

The two most important properties that control the viscosity of the magma are the temperature and the silica content of the magma. The hotter the magma and lower the silica content, the lower the viscosity will be. We can therefore make the generalization that, hot, low-silica magmas will erupt "quietly" while cooler, high-silica magmas will erupt explosively.

We must now look at where different combinations of temperature and silica content occur relative to the location of a volcano on the surface of the earth. Volcanoes occur in three different plate tectonic settings; 1) at divergent margins - spreading centers (e.g. Iceland), 2) over hot spots (e.g. Hawaii) and 3) at convergent margins - subduction zones (e.g. the Andes and Cascades) (Figure 1).

At spreading centers and hot spots, the source of the magma is from partial melting of the upper mantle (in the asthenosphere, probably at depths of 60 kilometers, see Figure 1). Melting probably occurs in these locations because of their association with convection cells or more confined mantle plumes bringing hotter material from the lower mantle up to the base of the lithosphere. Since the mantle is composed primarily of low-silica minerals (olivine and pyroxene), the melt is also very low in silica and the composition of the resulting lavas in these settings is generally basaltic. The temperatures of these melts is also very high, often in excess of 1200°C (Williams and McBirney, 1979). The result is that the magmas and resulting lavas are very fluid, allow gases to escape easily and generally produce "quiet" eruptions. The exception to this is hot-spot volcanism that occurs under continental crust. The Yellowstone caldera is an example of this type of setting. Since the magma has to ascend through an extremely thick section of lithosphere (mantle and continental crust) it is significantly cooler and, as a result of a variety of processes, has a much higher silica content. The magmas become very viscous and the resulting eruptions are extremely explosive.

The morphology of a volcano is also directly related to the viscosity of magma. The low viscosity magmas at spreading centers and hot spots flow very easily producing very thin lava flows. This results in a shield volcano; massive volcanic edifices that have broad, but gently sloping (2° to 10°) flanks constructed almost entirely by lava flowing from a central vent or often times from a vent on the flanks of the volcano.

Approximately 80% of the worlds volcanoes are located around the Pacific Ocean Basin in the "ring of fire" (Figure 2). This cirum-Pacific belt is the result of melting of rock at convergent plate boundaries in subduction zones (Figure 1). In these settings the descending oceanic lithosphere heats up as it encounters increasing temperatures with depth. Once it has reached depths of 100 to 200 kilometers, the temperatures are high enough to begin melting the upper portion of the descending plate. Since the melted material (the magma) is less dense than the surrounding rock, it will rise towards the surface. The composition of the melt ranges from low-silica (basalts with approximately 50% SiO_2) to very high-silica content (rhyolites with approximately 70% SiO_2). However, the most abundant composition and resulting rock type is an andesite (named after the Andes Mountains) with around 60% SiO_2. While the initial melt might start out at fairly high temperatures, it will cool significantly as it passes through the large section of over-riding lithosphere. While not all volcanoes at subduction zones are explosive, the combination of higher SiO_2 and lower temperatures produces more viscous magmas which do not allow the gases to escape as easily. This combination can produce very explosive eruptions.

The more viscous magmas associated with subduction zone volcanism produce the morphologies that we typically associate with volcanoes. Pyroclastic eruptions produce steep-sided cinder cones composed entirely of material ejected from a central vent. As the magma becomes more viscous the eruptions may include both

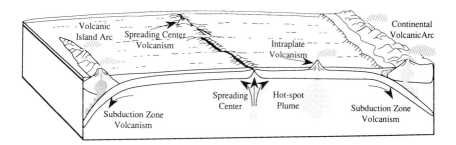

FIGURE 1. Block cross-section showing the relationship between volcanism and magma source to plate tectonic margins (modified from Levin, 1990).

pyroclastic material and lava flows. Volcanism with alternating layers of flows and pyroclastics forms composite cones, often with slopes approaching 30° to 35°. The hazards associated with different volcanoes are directly related to the style of eruption. When the volcano erupts "quietly", i.e. it has very fluid (low viscosity) magma, the primary concern will be for damage caused by lava flows. However, as the viscosity of the magma increases and eruptions become more explosive, the major hazards will involve pyroclastic flows and ashfall. Since more explosive eruptions also tend to produce volcanoes with steeper debris-mantled flanks, lahars (mud flows) and avalanches also occur.

HAZARDS ASSOCIATED WITH "QUIET" ERUPTIONS

Lava Flows

In settings where the magmas tend to be very fluid, the eruptions tend to be "quiet" and the greatest hazard is from damage caused by lava flows. These lava flows tend not to endanger human life, but are a significant threat to property. Eruptions on the island of Hawaii and the island of Iceland will serve to illustrate these problems.

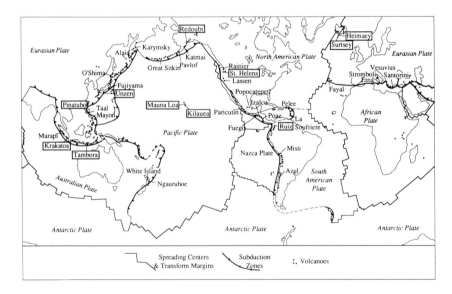

FIGURE 2. Map showing the location of some of the active volcanoes in the world and their relationship to plate tectonic margins (modified from Press and Siever, 1986 with additional data from Simkin *et al.*, 1981).

Kilauea, Hawaii

Eruptions from Kilauea volcano are characterized by spectacular fire-fountaining episodes followed by extended periods of lava flow activity. A "typical" lava flow on the island of Hawaii might be 10 kilometers long, 200 meters wide and 1 to 3 meters thick. Lava can flow at speeds of 5 to 50 kilometers per hour depending upon the viscosity and the slope over which it flows (Decker and Decker, 1989).

The recent eruption (1983 - 1991) of Kilauea volcano on the island of Hawaii is the longest and largest since records began in 1823. The eruptions have produced over 850 million cubic meters of lava, covering over 80 square kilometers and creating over 400,000 square meters of new land (Heliker and Wright, 1991; Decker and Decker, 1989). As of 1991 over 100 homes, the National Park Visitors Center and several sites along the Kalapana coast, including the famous Kalapana Black Sand Beach, had been destroyed (Heliker and Wright, 1991). While no lives have been lost, the cost estimates of the damage exceed $10 million (Decker and Decker, 1989) and, as of this writing (1991), the eruptions are continuing (Figure 3).

While the eruptions from Kilauea have proved costly during the past eight years, there is even greater concern for eruptions from the much larger volcano, Mauna Loa. Mauna Loa, in the mature stage of volcano growth (Decker and Decker, 1988), is much larger than Kilauea, and an eruption can generally produce a much larger volume of magma in a shorter period of time. As an example, the 1984 eruption of Mauna Loa covered 42 square kilometers in only three weeks time (Heliker and Wright, 1991).

FIGURE 3. View looking northwest towards the area covered by the 1983 - 1991 eruptions from the east rift zone of Kilauea volcano. The gas is coming from the active vent in the center-left of the picture. (Photo by Germanoski)

Surtsey and Heimay, Iceland

The island of Iceland was born and continues to grow as a result of its position directly over the spreading center known as the Mid-Atlantic Ridge (Figures 1 and 2). In mid-November, 1963, submarine eruptions began in the ocean off the south coast of Iceland. The eruptions, which lasted for almost 4 years, created the new island of Surtsey, almost 3 square kilometers in area, where there had previously been ocean (Decker and Decker, 1989). Ten years later (1973), new eruptive activity began. This time it was located on the island of Heimay, 15 kilometers to the northeast of Surtsey. The island of Heimay had formed in prehistoric time by the same processes that had created the island of Surtsey. However, volcanic activity had been relatively light since the island had been inhabited. The new activity threatened the existence of the town of Vestmannaeyjar, one of the most prosperous fishing villages in Iceland. There had been sufficient warning to evacuate the citizens of the town so no lives were lost. However, the vent, which was located at the edge of the town, produced spatter and ash which destroyed many houses, and the relentless movement of the lava flows from the vent threatened to block the port, crucial to the town's livelihood. The response of the residents to this eruption proved to be one of the more successful events in mitigating the effects from volcanic eruptions (see the section on hazard mitigation below).

HAZARDS ASSOCIATED WITH EXPLOSIVE ERUPTIONS

Avalanches, Pyroclastic Flows, Lahars and Ashfall

While lava flows pose a significant hazard at relatively "quiet" spreading center and hot spot volcanoes, the hazards associated with explosive dome and composite-cone volcanoes found at subduction zones are significantly more dangerous. The principle threats to human life and property associated with explosive volcanoes are: 1) blast-generated avalanches, 2) pyroclastic flows or nuée ardentes, 3) lahars and floods, and 4) ashfall.

While the relative threat posed by each of these hazards will vary from volcano to volcano, the 1980 eruptions of Mount St. Helens volcano, located in southern Washington State, can serve as an appropriate case study illustrating some of these hazards because this series of eruptions was the most intensely monitored and studied in human history. Property damage and loss of life resulted from the effects of a debris avalanche and pyroclastic flow unleashed by the initial blast, followed by lahars, flooding, and ashfall damage. The 1980 eruptions of Mount St. Helens caused hundreds of millions of dollars in property damage and resulted in the loss of sixty-two lives (McGeary and Plummer, 1992). While the volcano exacted a heavy toll, the eruptions had the positive effect of reminding people living in the Pacific Northwest that the Cascade volcanoes pose a real threat to people living in the region. Moreover, the eruptions provided new insights into volcanic behavior which could be used to improve predictive techniques and allow geologists and officials to better assess and respond to volcanic hazards presented by other volcanoes, both locally and globally.

Mount St. Helens is part of the Cascade Range — a range of volcanic mountains extending from northern California to southern British Columbia (Figure 4). The Cascade Range consists of a series of explosive composite cone and dome volcanoes which have developed as the result of the subduction of the Juan de Fuca Plate beneath the North American Plate (Figure 4). The Cascades volcanic complex is part of a nearly continuous chain of volcanoes which circumscribes the Pacific Ocean Basin and includes the volcanoes Mount Unzen in Japan and Mount Pinatubo in the Philippines which are currently erupting (Figure 2).

The silica-rich, lower temperature magma is highly viscous, and the magma traps dissolved gases and water vapor causing gas pressures in the magma chamber to build to explosive levels. The morphology of these volcanoes, typical of the circum-Pacific region, reflects the silica-rich chemistry and viscous nature of the lava. These volcanoes are typically steep-sided composite cones formed from alternating layers

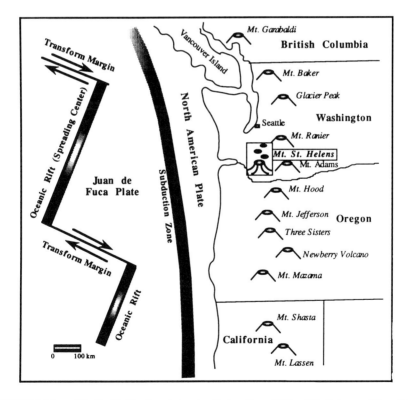

FIGURE 4. Map of the Pacific Northwest showing the location of Mount St. Helens and the relationship between the Juan de Fuca Plate and the Cascade volcanic chain (modified from Decker and Decker, 1981).

of viscous lava flows and pyroclastic material ejected during more explosive events, or steep-sided domes formed from the eruption of highly viscous lava.

Because the circum-Pacific volcanoes are all the result of similar geologic processes (subduction of the lithosphere), the chemistry of the magma and the eruptive behavior of many of the volcanoes (like Unzen and Pinatubo) are, in a general way, similar to that exhibited by Mount St. Helens. Likewise, because the hazards associated with a volcano are directly related to the eruptive style, the lessons learned from the eruption of Mount St. Helens can be applied to other explosive subduction zone volcanoes. These hazards include, but are not limited to, 1) blast-generated avalanches, 2) pyroclastic flows or nuée ardentes, 3) lahars and floods, and 4) ashfall.

Blast Generated Avalanches

Viscous magma can contain very high gas pressure in the magma chamber or feed conduit which, upon eruption, releases tremendous energy. For example, the total energy released during a nine hour period by the May 18, 1980 eruption of Mount St. Helens was nearly equivalent to the sequential detonation of 27,000 Hiroshima-size bombs (Decker and Decker, 1981). The initial eruption issued from the north-facing flank of the volcano and was directed laterally rather than upward, and therefore has been described as a directed-blast. Movement of magma into the northern flank of the volcano created a topographic bulge late in March, 1980 and minor eruptions began on March 27. The major eruption took place at 8:37 AM Pacific Daylight Time (PDT) on May 18, 1980. The catastrophic lateral blast, debris avalanche, and attendant pyroclastic flow was preceded by a magnitude 5.1 earthquake at 8:32 AM PDT (Christiansen and Petersen, 1981).

The main portion of the debris avalanche poured down the north flank of the volcano into the North Fork Toutle River, while one smaller lobe spilled into Spirit Lake and another smaller lobe flowed up and over a 380 meter ridge north of the mountain (Janda and Swanson, 1986). The debris avalanche and following explosion removed the upper 450 m of the mountain (Figures 5 and 6) and resulted in the deposition of over 2.5 km³ of debris spread over 60 km² to the north of the volcano (Janda and Swanson, 1986). The debris consisted of large blocks of rock, which formerly made up the flank of the mountain, mixed in a matrix of gravel, sand, and silt-sized volcanic debris and pyroclastic material (Figure 5 and 6).

Pyroclastic Surge or Nuée Ardente

The debris avalanche released the pressure which had been confined in the magma chamber on the flank of the mountain and a pyroclastic surge or nuée ardente followed immediately on the heels of the debris avalanche. A pyroclastic surge (nuée ardente) is a hot (up to 1000°C) mixture of gas, ash, cinders and other pyroclastic debris which may move at velocities exceeding the speed of sound. Because these hot clouds of gas and ash are more dense than air they sweep down the flanks of explosive volcanoes destroying virtually everything in their paths. At Mount St. Helens the pyroclastic surge mowed down mature stands of Douglas Fir trees and completely devastated an area of 600 km² north of the volcano (Christiansen and Petersen, 1981), (Figures 5 and 6). The debris avalanche combined with the pyroclastic surge were responsible for the majority of the 62 deaths caused by the blast including that of David Johnston, a U.S. Geological Survey (U.S.G.S.) geologist stationed on the ridge north of Mount St. Helens.

While the destruction wrought by this pyroclastic flow was complete, the damage and loss of life was greatly reduced because the area in the path of the blast was heavily forested with a very low population density. Moreover, many residents were evacuated from their homes and access to the area was restricted by officials following the advice of U.S.G.S. personnel. In other cases, nuée ardentes have exacted a much higher toll in terms of human lives. One of the most devastating nuée ardente killed up to 40,000 people on the island of Martinique in 1902 (Montgomery, 1992). The potential for the occurrence of similarly destructive nuée ardentes is quite high globally because, unlike Mount St. Helens, the flanks of many explosive volcanoes are heavily populated. Pyroclastic flows generated by the June 1991 eruptions of Mount Unzen in southwest Japan have killed 41 people, including a geologist with extensive research experience on Mount St. Helens, and two other geologists who were monitoring the volcano.

Lahars and Flooding

The term lahar is used to describe mudflows and/or debris flows associated with volcanic activity. Lahars are "dense, viscous slurries of poorly sorted gravel, sand,

FIGURE 5. Profile of Mount St. Helens five years after the catastrophic 1980 eruption. Note Douglas Fir logs in Spirit Lake in the left center, which has been dammed by debris avalanche material. (Photo by Malinconico)

mud and water" (Pierson, 1985) which often have the appearance of wet cement. Like most nonvolcanic debris flows and mudflows, lahars travel down valleys and through stream channels; however, the channels often fail to contain the large volume of material, which leads to property damage and perhaps loss of life.

The eruption of explosive volcanoes often leads to the development of lahars because a history of explosive behavior often provides the ingredients necessary for lahars to develop. The essential ingredients for lahar development are large volumes of unconsolidated debris and large volumes of water. The mixing of these components is further aided by steep slopes and explosive eruptions. Explosive volcanoes are typically mantled with unconsolidated or poorly consolidated pyroclastic debris from previous eruptions which is further augmented by pyroclastic debris ejected during the lahar forming event. The other ingredient necessary for lahar development is a large volume of water. Composite cone and dome volcanoes are often built to heights sufficient to maintain glaciers and significant snow fields on their summits. The heat associated with eruptive activity melts the ice and snow and provides the water which incorporates and mobilizes the pyroclastic debris into lahars. The Cascade volcanoes are typically mantled by glaciers and extensive snow fields as are many of the volcanoes located around the periphery of the Pacific basin including those in the Andes, Central America, Indonesia, Japan, and the coast of Alaska.

Lahars produced by the 1980 eruption of Mount St. Helens poured down virtually all of the major valleys draining the volcano (Janda *et al*. 1981). Debris from the initial avalanche and pyroclastic surge was transformed into a massive lahar which moved rapidly down the North Fork of the Toutle River into the Cowlitz River. Debris in this lahar included a logging truck fully loaded with logs, buildings, and

FIGURE 6. Debris avalanche deposits. Large dark blocks are pieces of the north flank of Mount St. Helens which were part of the initial slope failure. View is from the crater facing north. (Photo by Germanoski)

chunks of glacial ice (Cummans, 1981). Deposition of material derived from the North and South Forks of the Toutle River in the Columbia River decreased the navigational capacity of this river and blocked the passage of ocean-going vessels for a short time (Harris, 1990). Passage of lahars through the Toutle/Cowlitz River system altered the channel morphology through erosion and deposition, and destroyed vegetation, buildings, bridges, and personal property. Similarly, lahars wreaked havoc in the Pine Creek and Muddy River drainage systems on the east and south flanks of the volcano (Pierson, 1985). Fortunately, as a result of evacuation and warning, no lives were lost to the lahars.

Debris deposited by the debris avalanche and lahars continue to create problems in the river systems draining Mount St. Helens. Unconsolidated debris deposited in the drainage ways is continually being remobilized and redeposited downstream causing water quality problems and keeping the rivers in a steady state of flux (Figure 7). This situation was exacerbated by above average sediment delivery from the hillslopes in the region, which resulted from blast-induced devegetation, deposition of easily eroded ash, and slope failures.

Meltwater from glaciers and snowfields also generated flooding in all of the rivers draining the volcano. The flood hazard was further increased by the deposition of material in the channels which reduced channel cross-sectional area and reduced channel capacity to transmit discharge.

As the lahars flowed down the Toutle River Valley, into the Cowlitz River, and then into the Columbia River (Janda, *et al.* 1981), the impact was felt over 100 km away from the volcano. Lahars and flooding caused significant damage and prob-

FIGURE 7. Debris deposited in the North Fork Toutle River being incised and remobilized. In addition to the material deposited during the eruption, deforestation of the area around the volcano has exposed more surface material to the effects of erosion. The alluvial fans on the river terraces in the background have developed as a result of increased erosion and sediment availability. Note people for scale. (Photo by Germanoski)

lems on the east and south flanks of the volcano which had escaped the most serious damage caused by the eruption itself. Thus, lahars and flooding transfer the volcanic hazard to areas well beyond that directly influenced by the initial blast and pyroclastic surge. It is interesting to note that the lahars associated with the 1980 eruption were less voluminous and affected a smaller area than those generated by some previous eruptions (Janda *et al.* 1981).

The threat of lahars unleashed by the June 1991 eruptions of Mount Pinatubo in the Philippines along with passing tropical storms has forced the evacuation of thousands of Filipinos and American servicemen stationed at Clark Air Base. The death of over 20,000 people due to lahars roaring down the flanks of the Colombian volcano Nevado del Ruiz, during a 1985 eruption, reinforces the need for extensive mobilization and evacuation of people in the vicinity of Mount Pinatubo. Through early July 1991, lahars have destroyed villages and buildings over 40 km from Mount Pinatubo volcano and have severely damaged military facilities at Clark Air Base, northwest of Manila.

Ashfall Damage

The May 18, 1980 eruption of Mount St. Helens released a minimum of 1.1 km^3 of pyroclastic ash based on isopach maps of debris deposited down wind of the volcano (Sarna-Wojcicki *et al.* 1981). Within 10 hours the ash cloud, carried by westerly air flow, extended across the state of Washington into Idaho and Montana. Ash fallout created major problems throughout the region, damaging crops, automobiles and machinery, and accumulating to dangerous depths on rooftops and roadways. In addition, ash in the atmosphere disrupted air traffic in the Pacific Northwest. While the ash fallout did not result in any immediate fatalities, pyroclastic debris does present a true health hazard in the form of lung damage resulting from the respiration of fine-grained volcanic glass and ash. Ashfall damage exceeded the predictions of U.S.G.S. geologists, yet the total volume of ash emitted by the catastrophic May 18 eruptions of Mount St. Helens is quite small in comparison to other historic eruptions of volcanoes such as the 1815 eruption of Tambora and the 1883 eruption of Krakatoa in Indonesia (Montgomery, 1992).

Property damage and health hazards caused by ash fallout is a problem associated with virtually all explosive volcanoes around the Ring of Fire. For example, ash eruptions of Redoubt volcano have disrupted air traffic around Anchorage, Alaska several times since the volcano became active again in 1989, and much of the property damage effectuated by the current eruptions of Mount Pinatubo in the Philippines resulted from ashfall events.

HAZARD ASSESSMENT AND MITIGATION

Mitigation of volcanic hazards must begin with careful and detailed hazard assessment. Initial hazard assessment can be based in a very general way on the overall characteristics of the volcano in question. However, any serious attempts to reduce property damage and loss of life that could result from the eruption or activity of any individual volcano must be based upon detailed research of the volcano's history of eruptions and detailed examination of the effects of those eruptions. These records and observations can then be used to produce educated predictions of the potential for future activity at a specific volcano. Hazard assessment and mitigation ultimately depends on reliable predictions of the effect volcanic eruptions might have on the surrounding environment and estimates as to how often the volcano might erupt on both long- and short-term time scales.

Hazard Assessment

The first step in hazard assessment is the identification of volcanoes which have erupted in the past 10,000 years and then establishing the eruptive history of each specific volcano. Active volcanoes can be further subclassified on the basis of whether they have erupted during the past 1,000 years or during the past 300 years. In addition to determining when the most recent eruption of a volcano occurred, hazard assessment is also based upon the frequency of eruptions during recent geologic past. This eruption history can usually be reconstructed through the field mapping and dating of ashfall, lava flow, and lahar deposits around the periphery of the volcano.

Once a volcano has been identified as a threat, the next step in hazard assessment is to characterize the style of eruption and to determine the relative importance of various hazards. While the establishment of an understanding of eruptive style and past behavior is critical in predicting future behavior, predictions of future behavior and hazard assessment must also be based upon knowledge of magma and volcano evolution. In all cases, a certain degree of uncertainty will always remain.

Kilauea, Hawaii

Unfortunately, it often takes a significant disaster before hazard assessments are taken seriously. The geologic record of eruptions at Kilauea volcano had indicated an extreme likelihood that there would be future eruptions from the east rift zone of the volcano (Mullineaux *et al.* 1987). Despite this fact, developers had been allowed to build subdivisions in areas that were eventually over-run during the recent eruptive episode. It was only after the significant damage caused by this eruption (in 1990, President Bush issued a Federal Disaster Declaration for the Kalapana area) that plans were developed between the Federal Emergency Management Agency, state and county officials and the U.S. Geological Survey's Hawaiian Volcano Observatory to mitigate the effects of future eruptions on the Island of Hawaii (Heliker and Wright, 1991). This work has involved the reproduction of hazard maps for the Island of Hawaii identifying zones with high lava flow hazard probabilities (Heliker and Wright, 1991). These maps are now being used as the basis for recommendations that would limit development in many areas around Kilauea's east rift zone.

Mount St. Helens, Washington

The eruptive behavior of Mount St. Helens during its 40,000 year history had been pieced together (using field mapping techniques such as those described above) to assess the potential volcanic hazards in 1978 (Crandell and Mullineaux, 1978). The general approach to hazard assessment was given credibility by the correspondence between the predictions made in the hazard maps prepared before the 1980 eruption and the actual results of the 1980 eruption. It is also important to acknowledge that the hazard assessment maps were not perfect, and that important lessons were learned from the differences between the predictions and the realities of the 1980 eruptions.

The relative quality of hazard maps also can depend upon the type of hazard being mapped. Unfortunately, the greatest uncertainty is usually associated with the prediction of debris avalanches, blast directed surges, and nuée ardentes, which present the greatest threat to human life. Deposits of pyroclastic material and debris avalanche deposits may be used quite successfully to determine the likelihood of these phenomena, but much uncertainty exists regarding the prediction of the direction that such eruptions may take. For example, prior to the development of the bulge on the north flank of Mount St. Helens, it was virtually impossible to predict the northerly lateral blast and debris avalanche.

Predictions of the amount of damage associated with lahars and ash falls are generally more reliable because, in most cases, a more complete record exists. In the case of lahars; 1) topography exerts significant control on flow paths and the resultant distribution of damage, and; 2) the record of lahar development is often very well preserved in valleys radiating from volcanoes (Figure 8). Lahar stratigraphy

FIGURE 8. Lahar stratigraphy in the Toutle River drainage. The deposits from several lahars are well preserved and easily identified, and can be used to document potential hazards from future eruptions. (Photo by Germanoski)

can serve as an important record of eruptive history, and determining the distribution and extent of lahar deposits is an important part of hazard evaluation. Lahar hazard maps are extremely important because lahars extend the volcanic hazard well beyond the limits of the initial blast and associated pyroclastic surges.

In a similar manner, ash stratigraphy can be used to predict and establish procedures for coping with this volcanic hazard. Once again, although extreme variability will likely exist between eruptions, ashfall hazard maps illustrate the range of possibilities and allow officials to develop contingency plans on the basis of real data.

Hazard Mitigation

Hazard mitigation has two objectives: one goal is to minimize property damage, and the other, perhaps more important, objective is to reduce or eliminate the loss of life resulting from volcanic activity.

Minimization of property damage can best be achieved through detailed hazard mapping followed by land-use planning and the establishment and enforcement of strict zoning codes. Ostensibly, this objective appears to be quite easy to meet; however, reality proves otherwise (see the discussion of Kilauea volcano in the assessment section). The difficulties associated with successful land-management are many: a) careful hazard mapping requires financial support which is not always available; b) it is often impossible to convince the public that a real hazard exists; c) the public has difficulty dealing with the uncertainties associated with volcanic activity; d) scientists (volcanologists) have trouble clearly communicating their conclusions to the public (Peterson, 1988). Even with the catastrophic eruption of Mount St. Helens fresh in their minds, it is difficult to convince many people that future hazards remain. Moreover, in places where high population density places heavy demands on land resources, such as in Japan or Indonesia, it is virtually impossible to leave large portions of the landscape uninhabited, regardless of the consequences.

Reduction in human casualties is, to a large extent, a direct consequence of hazard mapping and effective land-use management. However, casualty reduction can be achieved even in situations where the flanks of the volcano are heavily populated. The death toll can be reduced significantly through successful short-term (weeks, days, hours) prediction of impending eruptions (Malinconico, 1987), effective communication of the threat, and the development and use of a well-coordinated evacuation plan. Similar to the problems associated with the enactment of land-use plans, completely successful short-term prediction of volcanic eruptions, and the development of a communication network and evacuation plan is easier said than done.

In addition to these problems, because short-term predictive techniques are not always 100% accurate, geologists often face credibility problems with the general public (Peterson, 1988). Casualty reduction would be easier to achieve if the general public had a better understanding of volcano behavior and the predictive techniques used by geologists and geophysicists. Thus, education must be another goal of geologists and officials attempting to mitigate volcanic hazards.

Long-term predictions of volcanic activity are useful for land-use planning and siting of dangerous facilities such as nuclear reactors, hazardous waste dumps, and power production facilities. However, short-term prediction is based upon so-called "precursor" activity — phenomena which have been observed to precede many eruptions.

Precursor phenomena include harmonic seismic activity generated by magma movement in the volcano, topographic deformation of the volcano, increase in heat flow, increase or change in gas chemistry emitted by the volcano, and other geophysical changes in the volcano such as a change in the magnetic signature or a change in seismic velocities through the volcano (Decker and Decker, 1989). Obviously such data require that various instruments such as seismometers, tiltmeters, and gas sampling apparatus be emplaced on and around the volcano. Typically, seismic activity originating in the area of an active volcano will draw the attention of volcanologists and geologists, and result in more detailed monitoring. In the United States active volcanoes in the Pacific Northwest Cascade Range and in the Coastal Range in Alaska are closely monitored by U.S.G.S. scientists stationed at the Cascades Volcanoes Observatory in Vancouver, Washington, and the Hawaiian Volcanoes are monitored by U.S.G.S. personnel stationed at the Hawaiian Volcanoes Observatory on Kilauea, Hawaii.

Kilauea and Mauna Loa, Hawaii and Heimay, Iceland

While prediction can play a very important role in reducing the effects of an eruption before it occurs, it is sometimes possible to mitigate the effects while the eruption is occurring. This is sometimes true for attempts to control the damage caused by lava flows. Attempts to control this sort of damage can take three forms; (1) the construction of barriers; (2) the use of explosives (bombs or placed charges) to block or divert flow; and (3) using water to cool and solidify the flow (MacDonald *et al.*, 1983; Mullineaux *et al.*, 1987). These methods have been attempted with limited success at

  a. Mauna Loa volcano, Hawaii (1935 and 1942): bombing the lava channels upslope from the threatened area;
  b. Kilauea volcano, Hawaii (1960): barriers built in attempts to contain the lava flows;
  c. Mt. Etna, Sicily: digging new channels and blasting the lava channel with placed charges.
  d. Heimay, Iceland (1973). The most successful mitigation effort occurred during the 1973 eruption on the island of Heimay. In addition to the destruction of homes by ash and spatter, lava flows threatened to block the harbor. In this eruption, the residents of Vestmannaeyer fought the flows in two ways. First they built barriers to divert the flow; then they sprayed the advancing flow front with seawater. The effect of the spray was to cool and solidify the front of the advancing flow thereby causing the still molten lava behind the front

to be diverted elsewhere. The effort, which cost approximately $1.5 million, successfully saved many of the houses in town and, most importantly, stopped the harbor from being blocked (Coates, 1985; Mullineaux *et al.*, 1987; McGeary and Plummer, 1992).

Mount St. Helens, Washington: Mount Unzen, Japan and Mount Pinatubo, Philippines

The lessons learned at Mount St. Helens have proved very instructive to volcanologists and geophysicists and their predictive 'track' record has become very successful in the past decade or so. For example, U.S.G.S. geologists have successfully predicted 19 of 22 eruptions which have occurred on Mount St. Helens since 1980 (Nash, 1991). In Japan and the Philippines, the death toll resulting from recent eruptions of Mount Unzen and Mount Pinatubo would have been much greater if officials had not have been warned of the impending eruptions and directed large scale evacuation.

Nevertheless, much work remains to be done. Geologists must continue to collect data and refine predictive techniques, characterize and map active volcanoes around the globe, create hazard maps for active volcanoes, and educate the general public. Officials and leaders must establish realistic land-use plans and develop contingency plans for evacuation and population mobilization based upon geological maps and reports. Of equal importance, the public must be made aware of volcanic hazards and educated in the techniques of prediction. Evacuation is very expensive and frustration builds and credibility is lost when false predictions are made. If people have some understanding of volcano behavior and predictive techniques, the almost inevitable false alarms will become a better accepted part of living in the vicinity of an active volcano.

REFERENCES

Christiansen, R.L. and D.W. Petersen. 1981. Chronology of the 1980 eruptive activity, pp. 17-30. In P.W. Lipman and D.R. Mullineaux, *The 1980 Eruptions of Mount St. Helens.* U.S. Geological Survey Professional Paper 1250. 844 p.

Coates, D.R. 1985. *Geology and Society;* Chapman and Hall, New York. 406 p.

Crandell, D.R. and D.R. Mullineaus. 1978. *Potential Hazards From Future Eruptions of Mount St. Helens volcano, Washington*; U.S. Geological Survey Bulletin. 1383-C, 26 p.

Cummans, J. 1981. Chronology of mudflows in the South Fork and North Fork Toutle River following the May 18 eruption; pp. 479-486. In P.W. Lipman and D.R. Mullineaux, *The 1980 Eruptions of Mount St. Helens.* U.S. Geological Survey Professional Paper 1250. 844 p.

Decker, R. and B. Decker. 1981. The eruptions of Mount St. Helens; Scientific American. v. 244, (3), pp. 68-80.

Decker, R. and B. Decker. 1988. Volcanology in Hawaii; Earthquakes and Volcanoes. v. 20, (1) pp. 4-30.

Decker, R. and B. Decker. 1989. *Volcanoes*; W.H. Freeman and Company, New York. 285 p.

Harris, S.L. 1990. *Agents of Chaos: Earthquakes, Volcanoes, and Other Natural Disasters*; Mountain Press Publishing Company, Missoula, MT. 260 p.

Heliker, C. and T.L. Wright. 1991. Lava hazards from Kilauea's current eruption; Geotimes. v. 36 (5), pp. 16-19.

Janda, R.J., K.M. Scott, K.M. Nolan and H.A. Martinson. 1981. Lahar movement, effects, and deposits; pp. 461-478. In P.W. Lipman and D.R. Mullineaux, *The 1980 Eruptions of Mount St. Helens*. U.S. Geological Survey Professional Paper 1250. 844 p.

Janda, R.J. and F.J. Swanson. 1986. Introduction: landscape disturbance — The Mount St. Helens example; In R.M. Iverson and H.A. Martinson (eds.) *Mount St. Helens*, 178 p. American Geomorphological Field Group Field trip guidebook and abstracts. September 3-6, 1986. Cispus Center, Washington.

Levin, H.L. 1990. *Contemporary Physical Geology*; Saunders College Publishing, Philadelphia. 623 p.

MacDonald, G.A., A.T. Abbott and F.L. Peterson. 1983. *Volcanoes in the Sea, The Geology of Hawaii*; University of Hawaii Press, Honolulu, 2nd edition. 517 p.

Malinconico, L.L. Jr. 1987. On the variation of SO2 emission from volcanoes; Jour. of Vol. and Geotherm. Res. v. 33, pp. 231-237.

McGeary, D. and C.C. Plummer. 1992. *Physical Geology, Earth Revealed*; Wm. C. Brown, Dubuque, Iowa. 550 p.

Montgomery, C.W. 1992. *Environmental Geology*; Wm. C. Brown, Dubuque, Iowa. 465 p.

Mullineaux, D.R., D.W. Peterson and D.R. Crandell. 1987. Volcanic hazards in the Hawaiian Islands; in *Volcanism in Hawaii*, edited by R.W. Decker, T.L. Wright and P.H. Stauffer, U.S. Geol. Sur Prof. Paper 1350, vol. 1. pp. 599-624.

Nash, M. 1991. What makes them blow; Time, June 24, 1991. pp. 42-44.

Peterson, Donald, W. 1988. Volcanic hazards and public response; Jour. Geo. Res. v. 93, n. B5. pp. 4161-4170.

Pierson, T.C. 1985. Initiation and flow behavior of the 1980 Pine Creek and Muddy River lahars, Mounts St. Helens. Washington; Geological Society of America Bulletin. v. 96. pp. 1056-1069.

Press, F. and R. Siever. 1986. *Earth*; 4th edition, W.H. Freeman and Company, New York. 656 p.

Sarna-Wojcicki, A.M., S. Shipley, R.B., Waitt, Jr., D. Dzurisin and S.H. Wood. 1981. Areal distribution, thickness, mass, volume, and grain size of air-fall ash from the six major eruptions of 1980; pp. 577-600. In P.W. Lipman and D.R. Mullineaux, *The 1980 Eruptions of Mount St. Helens*. U.S. Geological Survey Professional Paper 1250. 844 p.

Simkin, T.L. Siebert, L. McClelland, D. Bridge, C. Newhall and J.H. Latter.

Volcanoes of the World, A Regional Directory, Gazetteer, and Chronology of Volcanism During the Last 10,000 Years; 1981, Smithsonian Institution, Washington, DC. 233 p.
Williams, H. and A.R. McBirney. 1979. *Volcanology*; Freeman, Cooper and Co., San Francisco, CA. 397 p.

Natural and Technological Disasters: Causes, Effects and Preventive Measures. Edited by
S.K. Majumdar, G.S. Forbes, E.W. Miller, and R.F. Schmalz. © 1992, The Pennsylvania Academy
of Science.

Chapter Eight

VOLCANIC ERUPTIONS

ROBERT F. SCHMALZ

Department of Geosciences
The Pennsylvania State University
University Park, PA 16802

By turns hot embers from her entrails fly,
And flakes of mountain flame that arch the sky.

(Virgil)

INTRODUCTION

Volcanic eruptions are arguably the most spectacular of natural phenomena. Fifteen to twenty major volcanic eruptions occur each year around the world. Many of these, of course, take place in sparsely populated regions and cannot be considered "disasters" although their environmental effects may be quite devastating and some severe injuries or deaths may result. The eruptions themselves may be quiet or violent, beautiful, awesome or terrifying; their aftermath may be regional devestation and human tragedy on a massive scale, or a mountain peak of great beauty. Most of these characteristics occurred together in one of the most famous volcanic events of history: the eruption of Monte Somma (Vesuvius) which destroyed the Roman resort towns of Herculaneum, Pompeii and Stabiae in the summer of 79 A.D.

In late August, 79 A.D., a Roman fleet commanded by Gaius Plinius was at anchor in the Bay of Naples. The fleet was based at Misenum, where Pliny was living with his sister and nephew, Plinius Secundus. Monte Somma's flat-topped cone, fifteen kilometers to the east, overlooked the Bay and the coastal resorts. The mountain was known to be a volcano, but it was thought to be extinct, despite a series of earthquakes which had shaken the area around the mountain beginning in 63

A.D. Shortly after noon on August 24, 79 A.D., his sister and nephew called Pliny's attention to an unusual sight across the Bay. The events which followed are described in two letters written by the younger Pliny to the historian, Tacitus, after the event.

"A cloud was rising from one of the hills which took the form of a stone-pine, very nearly. It imitated the lofty trunk and the spreading branches. . . . It changed color, sometimes white, and sometimes when it carried up earth or ashes, dirty and streaked."

The elder Pliny set sail to observe the eruption more closely, but as he approached the port of Herculaneum, he was surprised to find that the water in the harbor was too shallow to permit his ships to enter. He therefore ordered several ships to sail along the coast as close as possible to the shore to rescue survivors, while he sailed south along the Sorrento Peninsula toward Stabiae where a friend, Pomponianus, had a house. The letter continues,

". . . ashes began to fall on his ships, thicker and hotter as they approached the land. Cinders and pumice, and also black fragments of rock cracked by the heat, fell around them."

Pomponianus had prepared to flee by ship, but an unfavorable wind made this impossible. Because the hour was late, and in an attempt to reassure Pomponianus, Pliny agreed to dine and spend the night with him, although,

". . . there began to break out from Monte Somma, in many spots, high and wide-shooting flames whose brilliancy was heightened by the darkness of approaching night."

Pliny did retire, but was awakened by his host in the early morning because cinders and ash were falling so heavily on the roof and in the *atrium* that it seemed he might be trapped.

"The house was tottering with frequent and heavy shocks of earthquake, and seemed to go to and fro as if moved from its foundations. But in the open air there were dangers of falling pumicestones, though to be sure they were light and porous. (Pliny and Pomponianus) tied pillows on their heads by way of defence against falling bodies and sallied out. (The dawn) was a blacker and denser night than they had ever seen, although torches and various lights made it less dreadful . . . the sea was as wild and appalling as ever. (As they fled toward the sea) a flame with a forerunner of sulfurous vapor drove off. . ." most of the party.

Pliny (a corpulent and asthmatic man) was overwhelmed by the dust and gases, and fell to the ground. He struggled briefly to rise, then fell back and died. Three days elapsed before a rescue party could return to seek his body (Leet, 1948; Bolt *et al*, 1975).

This account by the younger Pliny is one of the earliest detailed descriptions of a volcanic eruption and in a real sense marks the beginning of the science of volcanology.

Although perhaps the best known, Pliny the Elder was not the only victim of the eruption in 79 A.D. When the eruption was over, the entire top of Monte Somma, including the tree-covered "dormant" crater, was gone. In its place was a new crater (more properly a "caldera") more than 3 kilometers (1.9 miles) across. Quantities of molten lava blown out of the volcano by explosively expanding gases had fallen on the surrounding countryside as dust-size fragments, solidified chunks of frothy pumice, and blobs of once-liquid lava. The wind carried most of the ash and debris to the south and west where it buried the towns of Stabiae, Herculaneum and Pompeii beneath a layer of warm, gas-charged debris up to sixty feet deep. Scores of people were trapped in their houses (as Pliny very nearly was) and many more died as they tried to flee. A large group who sought shelter along the seawall at Herculaneum were trapped there quite literally, "between the devil and the deep blue sea." Scores of bodies have been discovered, preserved as moulds in the ash; many of them still in the positions of whatever activity occupied them on that summer afternoon almost two thousand years ago. The death toll is believed to have exceeded 16,000 persons, approximately ten percent of the population of the region at the time (Bolt *et al*, 1975; Erickson, 1988).

It is interesting to note that the shallow water which frustrated Pliny's attempt to sail into Herculaneum and the caldera from which modern Mount Vesuvius rises may be related. Rocks expand when heated, and molten rock ("magma") is appreciably bulkier than the solid rock from which it is derived. As a mass of magma forms beneath a volcano, therefore, the expansion causes the surface of the ground above to swell in a broad arch - a kind of gigantic blister. It was probably such arching or "inflation" of the volcano that caused the retreat of the shoreline reported in the letter to Tacitus. Similar changes in the shoreline have been observed prior to several more recent eruptions of Vesuvius. After the molten rock has erupted from the volcano, "deflation" occurs and the mountain may resume its original shape and height. If the volume of ejected lava is very great, however, as was the case in the eruption of Monte Somma, the strength of the crustal rock above the emptied magma chamber may be inadequate to support the overlying mountain mass. As a result, a large portion of the volcanic edifice may collapse into the empty magma chamber forming a caldera like that formed after the eruption of Monte Somma in 79 A.D. (Bullard, 1984; Gorshkov, 1970).

(The series of earthquakes which began in 63 A.D. may also have been related to the eruption, although they were not recognized as such at the time. This possibility will be examined in greater detail when we consider the recent eruptions of Kilauea on the island of Hawaii.)

Today, a new volvanic cone, Vesuvius, rises near the center of the Monte Somma caldera. An eruption in 172 A.D. began building the present "Gran Cone" and the mountain has continued to grow as eruptions at irregular intervals add lava and fragmental material. A major eruption in 1906 was particularly destructive, and a period of activity in 1944 played a minor but significant part in the Allied war effort. (Volcanic dust in the air and tephra falling on nearby runways used by Allied planes briefly disrupted aerial activity in the Allies' drive northward along the Italian peninsula.)

The three resort towns along the Bay of Naples were abandoned by the Romans after the great eruption of 79 A.D., but today after careful excavation, their ruins afford the visitor a beautifully preserved image of Roman life in the first century.

DISTRIBUTION OF VOLCANOES

Most volcanoes are concentrated along the margins of the great rigid plates which make up the crust of the earth. In particular, they are found in zones of tension where the plates are being pulled apart as new crustal rocks are formed, and in areas of convergence or subduction where compressional mountain ranges are forming or where older crustal rocks are being drawn downward into the mantle (Bullard, 1984; Williams & McBirney, 1979).

In areas of crustal tension like the Rift Valley of eastern Africa or the mid-ocean ridges, the rocks of the crust are stretched thin and weakened by faults and fractures. Convection currents in the viscous rock of the upper mantle rise beneath such spreading axes, then carry the brittle rocks of the crust laterally away like passengers on a "moving sidewalk." Several factors thus favor the development of volcanoes over the spreading axes. The rising convection current itself represents an anomalous source of heat at the bottom of the crust. The reduced pressure which results from the thinner crust lowers the melting point of the rock. Fluids derived from the mantle below or which invade the weakened crustal rocks from above further reduce the melting temperature. And finally, extension fractures in the brittle rocks of the crust afford the molten magma upward passage to intrude the crust or to erupt at the surface. Linear volcanic trends delineate the spreading axes of the mid-ocean ridges, and volcanoes characteristically mark both active and "failed" rift zones within the continents. Examples include the volcanic islands of the central Atlantic from Iceland to Tristan da Cunha, and snow-covered Mount Kilimanjaro on the (failed?) African rift (Gorshkov, 1970).

Volcanoes are also typical of convergent plate margins where one crustal plate is subducted beneath another. Along such plate boundaries, surficial rocks, often charged with fluids, are subjected to enormous compressive stresses and frictional heating. During subduction the rocks are heated further by the normal geothermal gradient as they are transported into the deeper crust or upper mantle. Where melting results, the buoyancy of the relatively low density magma carries it upward into the tectonically weakened overlying crust or farther upward to erupt on the surface. Classic examples of convergence zone volcanoes include the island arcs of the northwestern Pacific basin (Japan and the Aleutians, for example), the West Indies and the volcanic ranges of the western margin of South America (Williams & McBirney, 1979).

In a few locations around the world isolated mid-plate volcanoes appear to mark local "hot spots." These may be the result of melting caused by thermal "plumes" in the upper mantle, by local concentrations of fluids or radioactive materials in the crustal rocks, by locally reduced pressure or by a combination of related factors. The Hawaiian-Emperor seamount chain in the Pacific, the Yellowstone volcanic area on the North American continent and the Kelvin Seamounts and the Bermuda platform in the northwest Atlantic are examples of such probable "hot spots" (Bullard, 1984).

PROPERTIES OF MAGMAS

Whatever the cause(s), the melting which forms the magma occurs in most cases at depths of a few miles or a few tens of miles below the surface, in the mid- to lower-crust or near the top of the upper mantle. At these depths, the composition of crustal rocks is usually similar to that of basalt — relatively rich in iron and magnesium, and poor in silicon and aluminum. Rocks of this composition melt at temperatures on the order of 1,000° to 1,200°C and the molten magma is quite fluid compared to magma of more sialic composition. If the magma reaches the surface after contacting (and reacting with) only rocks of similar composition, the physical and chemical properties of the erupting lava will be unaltered. The lava erupting from a mid-ocean ridge volcano, for example, will have passed mainly through basaltic rock of the oceanic crust. Because granitic crust is very thin or missing entirely in most ocean basins, there would be little opportunity for the magma to assimilate sialic or alkaline constituents. Volcanoes associated with the mid-ocean ridges or mid-ocean "hot spots" are therefore characteristically basaltic. By contrast, magmas which must traverse thousands of feet of granitic continental crust or pass through thick sequences of surficial sediments or metamorphic rocks are likely to assimilate some constituents of those rocks and erupt as lavas of intermediate or sialic composition. It is not surprising, therefore that mid-ocean volcanoes are almost invariably basaltic, while andesitic and rhyolitic lavas are produced almost exclusively by volcanoes located within the margins of the continental plates (usually at convergent plate boundaries) (Williams & McBirney, 1979).

As magma moves upward from a deep crustal source, its progress may be accompanied by a series of minor earthquakes. We may presume that these tremors are caused by fracturing of the country rock as the magma, under intense pressure, forces its way toward the surface. Some fragments of the country rock may break free to be assimilated into the magma, contributing to the changes in composition. Elsewhere, the country rock must simply be broken and the fissures forced to allow the magma passage. In either case, minor earthquakes should precede and accompany volcanic activity, and might be used to provide forewarning of an impending eruption. Some investigators have suggested that the series of earthquakes which preceded the Monte Somma eruption were just such foreshocks. Inasmuch as the location of the earthquake events should be related to the advancing magma, a suitably designed seismometer array might be used to monitor the movement of magma in the subsurface and to predict (in broad terms, perhaps) both the time and location of an eruption. Studies in Japan and of Kilauea volcano in Hawaii have demonstrated the practicability of just such an approach (Finch & Macdonald, 1953).

ERUPTION TYPES

The differences in lava composition described above are critical to the discussion of volcanic disasters. Composition is one of three factors which determine the viscosity of a lava, and the nature of a volcanic eruption is determined in large measure by the lava viscosity. As a general rule, the viscosity of lava increases as the composition becomes more sialic, as its temperature is reduced, and as the concentration of dissolved volatiles (water vapor, carbon dioxide and other gases) decreases. Thus, a hot, volatile-rich basaltic lava is likely to be very fluid, whereas a cooler, andesitic lava poor in volatiles may flow only with difficulty, and a rhyolite may be extruded as a pasty or plastic mass which resists flow entirely. In an extreme case, volatile-rich, fluid lava may erupt in a series of regularly repeated degassing events in the volcanic vent, almost like a coffee percolator. Such a "Strombolian" eruptive pattern is in striking contrast to the extremely slow extrusion of a cool (700°-800°C) rhyolitic spine or dome which might most resemble toothpaste oozing from a tube.

The lavas of Mauna Loa and Kilauea on the island of Hawaii are representative of very fluid flows which lack the abundant volatiles characteristic of Strombolian eruptions. The name "Hawaiian" is given to the eruptive patterns they commonly exhibit. During the early eruptive phases of Mauna Loa or Kilauea, a lake of molten lava may fill the volcano's crater. Streams of escaping gas rising through the lava lake from time to time entrain the hot liquid, and may form spectacular fountains which sometimes jet upward as much as 1,500 feet above the lake surface. If the crater walls are breached as they were at Mauna Loa in 1881, 1935 and again in 1942, rapidly moving lava may flow down the mountain slopes, overwhelming and burning everything in its path. Such flows appear threatening and a flow in 1881 did, in fact, enter the city of Hilo. Despite their occasional very rapid movement (measured velocity of one Hawaiian flow exceeded 60 kilometers/hour) they rarely advance so swiftly that a person cannot avoid them, and ordinarily the movement is slow enough to permit an orderly evacuation of threatened property. Consequently eruptions of the "Hawaiian" type rarely lead to significant loss of life (Bole et al, 1975; Williams & McBirney, 1979). Such flows may spread over extensive areas, however, doing vast damage to land and property. The 1783 Laki fissure eruption in Iceland covered an area of 560 square kilometers (140,000 acres). Sequential flows of this type may accumulate to great thickness. The result is a volcanic mountain of great areal extent but rather gentle slopes, which resembles an inverted inner plate or classical Greek shield. Mauna Loa is an example of such a "shield" volcano. Approximately 60 miles in diameter at sea level, the mountain stands more than 13,600 feet above the sea, and the lava pile rises almost 20,000 feet from the seafloor to the surface. Its average (subaerial) slope is only slightly more than two degrees. Although an eruption of especially fluid lava from Kilauea destroyed a small coastal village in 1823, there was little or no loss of life, and characteristically, shield eruptions present little serious threat of disaster (Finch and Macdonald, 1950; Macdonald, 1958; Macdonald & Abbott, 1970).

Eruptions of more viscous lavas — cool, volatile-poor basalts or more sialic lavas — usually present a greater risk. The viscous lavas tend to plug volvanic vents, and by preventing the escape of either gases or lava, cause pressures to build in the sub-surface. A violent explosive eruption will occur if the pressure in the magma chamber exceeds the strength of the rock plugging the vent. Degassing of the magma follow-ing the sudden reduction of pressure may then give rise to additional explosions or frothy pumice flows. The volcano, in short, behaves very much like a bottle of warm champagne when the cork is loosened. After degassing, some very viscous lava may be extruded, but the eruptive activity usually stops quite soon as the vent again becomes obstructed. The sequence of explosion, degassing and viscous flow may be repeated at irregular intervals, gradually constructing the steep-sided cone of interlayered ash and flow material characteristic of a "composite" or "strato-volcano" (NRC/NAS, 1984; Bolt et al, 1975). Various forms of this basic eruptive pattern have been responsible for the great volcanic disasters of the past.

Viscous andesitic or rhyolitic lavas may erupt with explosive violence and have been responsible for many of the most disastrous volcanic events in history. Two general patterns of explosive activity have been observed. "Plinian" or "Krakatoan" eruptions resemble the eruption which cost Pliny the Elder his life; "Peléan" erup-tions follow the pattern of the eruption of Mount Pelée in 1902.

In a "Plinian" eruption, a powerful gas blast ejects a large volume of volcanic ash and pumice, followed (usually) by collapse of the volcanic peak to form a large caldera. Such an eruption destroyed the island of Thera (Santorini) about 1475 B.C. and may have inspired Plato's tale of the lost continent of Atlantis. Crater Lake, Oregon, was formed by a Plinian erupsiton of Mount Mazama about 5000 years ago. The extraordinary volume of ash produced by the (Plinian) eruption of Mount Pinatubo which began in June, 1991, illustrates the kind of problems which such eruptions may generate. A blanket of ash several tens of meters thick may cover the area adjacent to the volcano, its weight alone being sufficient to cause struc-tures to collapse. Rivers clogged with ash may flood, and unstable ash-covered slopes may be transformed into fast-flowing and very destructive mud flows by the first rain storm. Water supplies are contaminated, and transportation is disrupted by ash blocking highways, airports, rail lines and waterways. Crops buried beneath the ash will not mature and cannot be harvested; years may pass before the ash-covered land can return to productivity. In human terms, the 1991 eruption of Mount Pinatubo will certainly prove to be a disaster, even though the loss of life directly attributable to the eruption may be small.

"Peléan" eruptions are characterized by the extrusion of viscous lava domes and spines of intermediate or rhyolitic compositon accompanied by eruptions of effer-vescing lava and fast-moving "directed blasts" of glowing ash.

The spectacular eruption of Mount St. Helens in May, 1980, was of the "Peléan" type. A slowly expanding dome grew in the side of the crater, emitting occasional bursts of ash and steam. On May 18th, a cloud of black ash shot upward from the top of the dome, and simultaneously a "directed blast" of hot ash and gas exploded down the mountain flank. Fortunately, at Mount St. Helens there was no city in the path of the blast, and the loss of life was small and the damage was largely confined to felled timber (Keller, 1986; Carson, 1991; Swanson *et al*, 1989). The effects of the Mount St. Helens eruption are relatively mild compared to those of the directed blast which swept over the city of St. Pierre on Martinique in 1902.

THE ERUPTION OF MOUNT PELÉE, MAY 8, 1902

One of the most costly eruptions in recent history was that from which Peléan eruptions take their name. At the opening of the twentieth century, the island of Martinique was the capital of the French colonies in the West Indies. Its political capital was Fort de France, but its commercial and diplomatic center was the port city of St. Pierre at the foot of Mt. Pelée. The volcano had been quiet since 1851, and was considered "dormant" or "extinct." In mid-April, 1902, however, a series of mild eruptions of steam and ash began. The eruptions increased in frequency through the last weeks of April, and sulfurous gases and fine ash blown southwestward by the trade winds made residents of St. Pierre increasingly uneasy. Observers reported a dome of lava growing in the crater. In early May, jets of steam bursting through the forest floor on the mountain's flank caused several deaths, and many people living in small villages closer to the summit fled to St. Pierre for safety. Shortly before eight o'clock on the morning of May 8, a series of violent explosions rocked the summit and a large black cloud rose high in the air above the mountain. At the same time, another blast ejected a cloud of incandescent ash almost horizontally through a fracture in the crater wall. A glowing cloud, at a temperature of 1000°C as it burst from the crater rim, drove directly toward the city at a speed in excess of one hundred miles per hour. In a matter of just a few minutes it blanketed the city with ash and gases at a temperature still exceeding 700°C (it fused tableware into shapeless masses). At a distance of more than six kilometers from the summit, the force of the blast was sufficient to destroy masonry walls a meter thick. The cloud of ash continued across the bay, burning and capsizing seventeen of the eighteen ships at anchor, and continued out to sea. By ten minutes past eight, the disaster was essentially complete. We do not know just how many persons died in those few minutes, but the city was totally destroyed. The population of the city, normally 29,000, had been increased by as many as 10,000 refugees, and included the French Governor and his entire staff. Of those in the city that morning, just four survived, one of whom, ironically, was a condemned murderer. Photographs of the city taken several months after the disaster present a scene of desolation reminiscent of the urban ruins of Dresden or Hiroshima after World War II.

A series of similar glowing cloud ("nuée ardente") eruptions continued intermittently into the following year, and the later stages of the eruption were marked by the extrusion of spines of extremely viscous lava which slowly emerged from the mountain's summit (Lacroix, 1904; Perret, 1935).

The activity observed in 1991 at long-dormant Mount Unzen on the island of Kyushu follows the typical pattern of a Peléan eruption in its early phases. Beginning in late spring, a lava dome has grown in the crater and its growth has been accompanied by minor eruptions of ash and steam. Anticipating a moderate to heavy fall of ash and the possibility of one or more directed blasts and nuées ardentes, the Japanese government has evacuated the area below the growing dome. Volcanism elsewhere on Kyushu has been described by Kuno and by Kubotera (1981).

The explosive eruption of Krakatau in 1883 is a typical "Plinian" eruption, very similar to the Monte Somma eruption 1800 years earlier. It is noteworthy, however, for three reasons: it is one of the largest eruptions of any type in historic time, it contributed *indirectly* to a shocking loss of life, and it was certainly one of the noisiest natural events ever known.

THE ERUPTION OF KRAKATAU, AUGUST 27, 1883

The eruption which destroyed St. Pierre in 1902 was certainly among the most costly of human life in recent history. More than 30,000 persons died as a *direct* result of that eruption. A similar number died as an indirect result of the Plinian eruption of Krakatau in 1883 (Francis, 1985). The repeated and extremely violent explosions which marked the Krakatau eruption make it one of the noisiest natural events in history.

Krakatau was a volcanic island rising just 2,640 feet above sea level between Java and Sumatra, in the middle of the Sunda Strait. The volcano was known to have been active in the late 17th century, but had lain dormant since 1687. On May 20, 1883, a number of explosions were heard in Batavia (now Jakarta). The sounds were soon identified as a series of minor eruptions at Krakatau, more than 120 miles to the west. From that date, explosions were heard with increasing frequency, and ships arriving at Batavia reported seeing clouds of ash rising above the island, and encountering floating ash and pumice when passing through the Sunda Strait. The eruptive phase culminated in a series of extremely violent explosions on August 26-27. The explosions were clearly heard in communities throughout Indonesia, and were described as sounding "like distant cannon fire" as far away as Daily Waters and Alice Springs, Australia (2,017 and 2,225 miles from the source respectively) and on Rodriquez Island in the Indian Ocean, at a distance of 2,975 miles! The explosions threw quantities of volcanic ash high into the atmosphere, causing vividly colored sunsets around the world for more than two years. The dust may have contributed to temporary cooling of the world climate, as well. In the closing phases of the eruptive paroxysm, a major part of the volcanic island collapsed into the emptied magma chamber beneath, leaving a bay nearly 1,000 feet deep where previously a mountain had towered more than half a mile above the sea. The collapse generated a seismic seawave ("*tsunami*") which was detected in Panama, San Francisco and in France, more than 15,000 miles away. Along the coast of Java and Sumatra, the wave attained heights of at least 120 feet, and is believed to have been responsible for the deaths of no fewer than 36,000 persons (Furneaux, 1964; Simkin & Fiske, 1983; Francis, 1985).

VOLCANIC GASES

Volcanic eruptions are accompanied by the release of large volumes of volatile constituents. Water vapor and carbon dioxide predominate (usually at least 90%), but the gases may also include significant concentrations of HCl, H_2S, carbon monoxide, hydrogen fluoride and various oxides of sulfur. Meteoric water, transformed to steam by contact with hot magma as it approaches the surface, is probably the principal source of water vapor, but it may be augmented by vapor derived from the magma itself. Sulfur dioxide, sulfur trioxide, hydrogen chloride and hydrogen fluoride dissolved in the vapor form acid aerosols which may be widely dispersed and which are toxic to both animals and plants. Fluorine poisoning has been reported as a cause of death among domestic animals and perhaps humans as well in the proximity of an eruption (Einarsson *et al*, undated). Suffocation, however, may be the most common cause of death among victims of eruptive disasters. Heavy gases produced by the volcano hug the ground surface and displace essential oxygen. Victims already weakened by the heat, with metabolism accelerated by fear, are particularly vulnerable, and if they do not suffer asphyxiation, they may be poisoned by toxic gases or suffer massive heart attack.

The entire population of a small village on the flank of Mt. Pelée was killed by stream jets prior to the eruption of 1902. Some of the victims were undoubtedly scalded, but many more almost certainly died by asphyxiation.

In 1984, a lethal gas burst caused the deaths of at least thirty-seven persons in the African nation of Cameroun. The incident was clearly related to volcanism although it was not the result of an eruption in the ordinary sense. Lake Monoun is a deep volcanic crater with restricted circulation. The stagnant bottom water is charged with carbon dioxide derived from the dormant volcanic source beneath. During a minor earthquake on August 15, 1984, a portion of the crater rim collapsed into the lake, which disturbed the water column and released a large volume of gas. The carbon dioxide, being heavier than air, flowed downslope and settled in inhabited valleys on the mountain's lower flanks. Occupants of these "death valleys" suffocated before they could flee (Sigurdsson *et al*, 1987). Similar incidents have been reported elsewhere (Williams & McBirney, 1979; Latter, 1989; Bold *et al*, 1975).

PREDICTION, CONTROL AND MITIGATION

Obviously, the simplest means of minimizing the disastrous impact of volcanic eruptions would be to stay well away from volcanoes. In may cases, this is neither practical nor desirable. If we must live on or near volcanic mountains, it would be helpful if we could devise means to predict impending eruptions, to control and minimize their efforts (Tanaka, 1986; Bold *et al*, 1975).

The simplest attempts to predict eruptions rely upon an assumed periodicity of eruption. Study of historical records may reveal a quasi-regular recurrence of activity for a particular volcano and suggest the need for extra precautions as the close of an inferred period of quiescence approaches. Although there may be some theoretical justification for this approach (given a uniform heat source at depth a reasonably uniform period might be required to melt sufficient magma to erupt) historical data inspire little confidence in the method. More than a century of observation of Mauna Loa, for example, has shown that summit eruptions are followed by a flank eruption approximately 36 months later. Although it would be convenient to rely upon this sequence, the interval separating summit and flank events is observed to vary between 6 and 38 months, and flank eruptions are sometimes missing entirely. Vesuvius, during nearly two millennia, has shown no detectable periodicity (Bolt *et al*, 1975).

Inflation or tumescence of a volcano prior to eruption is easily measured. Changes in slope and vertical uplift of as much as one meter can be observed with ordinary surveying techniques, and post-eruptive deflation of comparable amount has also been observed in Hawaii. As mentioned earlier, the shoaling which frustrated Pliny's attempt to enter the harbor at Herculaneum in 79 A.D. was probably the result of pre-eruptive inflation, and the phenomenon has been observed along the shore of the Bay of Naples on several occasions since that time. Inflation, however, is not a certain indicator of an impending eruption; magma intruded into the volcanic edifice may solidify without erupting. Inflation or tumescence appears to be a common indicator of the presence of molten magma at depth, but it affords no guarantee that the magma will erupt at the surface.

Where suitable seismic arrays are in place, earthquake shocks may be used (under favorable conditions) to follow the movement of magma toward the surface. The Japanese volcanologist Minakami demonstrated such a pattern at Mount Asama, and observed that the beginning of the eruption itself was marked by the initiation of continuous high-frequency harmonic tremor. Three-dimensional analysis of seismic data on a real time scale can be used to predict both time and location of an eruption (Macdonald and Abbott, 1970). The moving mass of magma beneath the surface may also give rise to electrical or magnetic anomalies, but these have not yet been successfully used to predict eruptive activity. Finally, the presence of a body of magma beneath a volcano causes increased heat flow at the surface. Today such a heat flow anomaly can be detected on infrared images from orbiting satellites. Although the anomalies are not certain indicators of an imminent eruption they can serve to alert investigators to potential trouble spots.

If our ability to predict volcanic eruptions remains imperfect, our ability to control or mitigate such events is almost non-extant. The explosive power of a directed blast such as that which destroyed St. Pierre is so great that virtually nothing could be done to avert disaster. We have, however, achieved modest success in controlling lava flows — perhaps the least dangerous form of eruptive activity. In Hawaii, diversion barriers have been proposed to protect the city of Hilo (Macdonald, 1958). An older concept involves chilling the flank or snout of an advancing flow to slow its movement and thus to block or redirect its advance. The earliest known attempt to accomplish such diversion occurred on Mount Etna in 1669 when residents attempted to divert a flow which threatened to destroy the city of Catania. Dressed in hides, they threw water on the flank of the advancing flow. The effort was moderately successful, but the redirected flow threatened the village of Paterno, whose residents, understandably upset, set upon the Catanians. During the battle which ensued, the eruption ceased, and the ultimate effectiveness of the effort remains moot (Bolt *et al*, 1975). Presumably the Catanians and the Paternoans retired to resolve their differences over a bottle of chianti. More recently firefighting apparatus was used to spray water on the fronts of lava flows advancing into the village of Kapoho (Hawaii). The purpose was not to stop the advance, but to delay it sufficiently to allow orderly evacuation of houses and in some cases to permit the removal of furnishings. The technique proved effective as did a similar effort to protect a fish cannery at Heimaey (Iceland) in 1973.

Finally, efforts to stop or divert Hawaiian lava flows by bombing either the flow itself or the volcanic vent from which the lava was emerging have yielded mixed results (Bolt *et al*, 1975).

CONCLUSION

Volcanic eruptions have inspired both awe and dread in humankind since the earliest times. The passage of time and a growing understanding of the phenomena have done nothing to reduce their vast power. If anything, the human hazard that volcanoes present has increased as world population has grown, and as a greater and greater part of that population has settled in urban centers along the margins of continents.

Oceanic volcanoes are usually located along mid-ocean spreading axes or above "hot spots." The lavas erupting from them are usually fluid basalts, and their eruptions generally of the flow-dominated "Hawaiian" or "Strombolian" type. Although destructive of property, flow-dominated eruptions do not ordinarily present a grave threat to human lives.

Far more dangerous are the explosive eruptions typical of more viscous lavas of intermediate or rhyolitic composition. Volcanoes characterized by "Plinian" or "Peléan" eruptive style occur along "active" continental margins where crustal rocks of continental ("granitic") composition override a subduction zone. Unfortunately, such volcanoes lie around the entire perimeter of the Pacific Basin, putting many of the major seaport and commercial centers of the circum-Pacific region in jeopardy. Recent eruptions of Mount Pinatubo in the Philippines, Mount Unzen in Japan, Mount St. Helens in the United States and of a host of volcanoes in Central and South America serve to direct attention to the hazard. Consequent dangers, from pre-eruptive earthquakes, ash falls, mud-flows, flooding and tsunami make the danger even greater.

In the nineteen hundred years since the eruption of Monte Somma destroyed Pompeii, we have learned to recognize many of the warning signs which may precede a volcanic eruption, but we cannot predict an eruption with certainty, nor do we have any effective means of preventing or controlling an eruption. At this point, our best means of minimizing the disastrous consequences of a volcanic eruption are to avoid volcanic regions, especially those susceptible to explosive eruptions;

to heed whatever warning signs we can recognize; to encourage timely evacuation of threatened areas; and to keep residents of those regions adequately informed of the nature and immediacy of the risk they face (Tanaka, 1986; Fiske, 1984).

REFERENCES

Bolt, B.A., W.L. Horn, G.A. Macdonald and R.F. Scott. *Geological Hazards*. New York. Springer-Verlag, c1975. 302 pp. + 6 appendices, index.

Bullard, F.M. *Volcanoes of the Earth*. Austin. University of Texas Press, c1984. 576 pp. + 2 appendices, glossary, bibliography, index.

Carson, R. *Mount St. Helens: The Eruption and Recovery of a Volcano*. Seattle, WA. Sasquatch Books, c1990. 157 pp. + glossary.

Einarsson, T., G. Kjartansson and S. Porarinsson, Eds. Part III *in* S. Porarinsson, Ther Eruption of Hekla, 1947-1948, volume 2, pp. 1-67. (undated)

Erickson, J. *Volcanoes and Earthquakes*. Blue Ridge Summit, PA. TAB Books, c1988. 293 pp. + glossary, index.

Finch, R.H. and G.A. Macdonald. *Hawaiian Volcanoes During the 1950s*. Washington, D.C. U.S. Geological Survey Bulletin 996-B 1953. pp. 27-89.

Fiske, R.S. Volcanologists, Journalists and the Concerned Public: A Tale of Two Crises in the Eastern Caribbean. Chapter 13 *in* NRC/NAS *Explosive Volcanism*, 1984. pp. 170-176.

Francis, P.W. (1975). The origin of the 1883 Krakatau tsunamis. Jour. Volcanology & Geothermal Research, vol. 25, pp. 349-363.

Furneaux, R. *Krakotoa*. Englewood Cliffs, N.J. Prentice-Hall, c1964. 207 pp. + bibliography, index.

Gorshkov, G.S. *Volcanism and the Upper Mantle*. (Translated by C.P. Thornton). New York. Plenum Press, 1970. 348 + bibliography, index.

Keller, S.A.C. (ed.) *Mt. St. Helens: Five Years Later*. Cheney, WA. Eastern Washington University Press, c1986. 438 + appendix.

Kubotera, A. (ed.) *Field Excursion Guide to Sakurajima, Kirishima and Aso Volcanoes*. Hakone. Volcanological Society of Japan, 1981. 52 pp.

Lacroix, A. *La Montagne Pelée et ses Éruptions*. Paris. Masson & Cie., c1904. 662 pp.

Latter, J.H. (ed.) *Volcanic Hazards: Assessment and Monitoring*. New York. Springer-Verlag, c1989. 598 pp + index.

Leet, L.D. *Causes of Catastrophe*. New York. McGraw-Hill, c1948. 227 pp. + index.

Macdonald, G.A. (1958). Barriers to protect Hilo from lava flows. *Pacific Science*, volume 12, pp. 258-277.

Macdonald, G.A. and A.T. Abbott. *Volcanoes and the Sea: The Geology of Hawaii*. Honolulu. University of Hawaii Press, c1970. 441 pp.

NRC/NAS *Explosive Volcanism: Inception, Evolution and Hazards*. (Series, NRC/NAS Studies in Geophysics). Washington, D.C. National Academy Press, c1984, 176 pp.

Perret, F.A. *The Eruption of Mt. Pelée in 1929-1933*. Washington, D.C. The Carnegie Institution of Washington, 1937. 120 pp. + 2 appendices.

Porarinsson, S. *The Eruption of Hekla, 1947-1948.* Reykjavik. H.F. Leiftur, 2 volumes. (undated)

Sigurdsson, H., J.D. Devine, F.M. Tchoua, T.S. Presser, M.K.W. Pringle and W.C. Evans. 1987. Origin of the lethal gas burst from Lake Monoun, Cameroun. Jour. Volcanology & Geothermal Research, vol. 31, pp. 1-16.

Simkin, T. and R.E. Fiske. *Krakatau 1883: The Volcanic Eruption and its Effects.* Washington, D.C. The Smithsonian Institution Press, 1983. 439 pp. + bibliography, index.

Swanson, D.A., *et al.* Cenozoic Volcanism in the Cascade Range and Columbia Plateau, Southern Washington and Northernmost Oregon. *in* Hanshawe, P.M. (ed.) *Volcanism and Plutonism of Western North America.* Volume 1, Guidebook Series, 28th International Geological Congress, Washington, D.C. American Geophysical Union, c1989. pp. T106:1-60.

Tanaka, J.M.C. Where (or What) in the World is Volcanic Hazard Management. *in* Keller, S.A.C. (ed.), *Mount Saint Helens: Five Years Later.* pp. 395-398. 1986.

Williams, H. and A.R. McBirney. *Volcanology.* San Francisco. Freeman-Cooper, c1979. 365 pp. + bibliography, index.

Natural and Technological Disasters: Causes, Effects and Preventive Measures. Edited by
S.K. Majumdar, G.S. Forbes, E.W. Miller, and R.F. Schmalz. © 1992, The Pennsylvania Academy
of Science.

Chapter Nine

TSUNAMIS - SEISMIC SEA WAVES

GEORGE D. CURTIS*

Joint Institute for Marine and Atmospheric Research
University of Hawaii at Manoa
Honolulu, HI 96822

INTRODUCTION

Of all the water waves that occur in nature one of the most destructive is the
tsunami (tsoo-nah-mee). Literally, "harbor wave" in Japanese, the term was adopted
internationally for sea waves originating from underwater earthquakes. "Tidal
wave" is a historic misnomer; there is no connection with tides although these waves
may resemble fast rising tides.

Almost all tsunamis originate from earthquakes under the ocean with a Richter
scale magnitude of 7 or greater. A series of very long waves is generated which can
impact shores thousands of miles away. Because the wavelength is hundreds of
kilometers, the wave travels as a shallow water wave, at a speed equal to $\sqrt{gd}$ where
g is the acceleration of gravity and d is the depth. The resulting speed across the
deep ocean is around 750 km/hr, or about that of a jet airplane. At sea, the height
is less than a meter and cannot be detected aboard a ship. But the energy is tremendous due to the mass of water in the long waves, and when they reach the shallow
water near a coast, that energy causes the height to increase as the waves slow down.

Such waves, with periods of between 5 and 90 minutes (ordinary wind waves do
not exceed a period of 20 seconds) can impact a shoreline at heights up to 20 meters
and sweep inland for hundreds of meters. Because these waves can cause such extensive damage and can do it without warning from weather or sea conditions, they
have produced tragic losses, especially in the Pacific Rim. The National Geophysical

*Home address: Box 237, Honomu, HI 96728

Data Center estimates that in this century alone, over 51,000 lives have been lost from tsunamis.
As we will see later, much of this human loss is avoidable.

THE EXTENT OF THE HAZARD

Unlike hurricanes, the force of tsunami waves attacks from afar without any warning from nature (except in the special case of local tsunamis, where the earthquake itself may give warning). The sporadic nature of the event, combined with the need and desire of people to live and work at the edge of the ocean has caused recurring catastrophes from tsunamis. Table 1 shows the size and effects of some of the most significant of these in the last 100 years (adapted from Cox, 1964, 1, 10).

TABLE 1

Areas of Origin, Maximum Runup Heights, and Effects of
the Most Significant Tsunamis of the Last Century

Date	Source	Maximum Runup Height	Effects
1867 Nov. 18	Caribbean	60 ft. at Guadeloupe	Widespread damage throughout Caribbean.
1868 Apr. 2	Hawaii Island	60 ft. on southeast coast of Hawaii Island	81 deaths; 2 villages swept away. Local tsunami.
1868 Aug. 13	Arica, Peru	70 ft. at Concepcion	24 ft. drawdown at Iquique; extensive damage in Hawaii.
1871 Mar. 2	Tagulandang I., Dutch East Indies	84 ft. at town of Buhias	25 ft. wave, much damage.
1877 May 9	Chile	75 ft. at Arica	Widespread damage; vessel tossed 2 miles inland; 5 deaths; 37 houses destroyed in Hilo, Hawaii; damage in Japan.
1878 Jan. 10	New Hebrides	40 ft. at Tanna Island	Quake and eruption.
1883 Aug. 26	Sunda Strait	135 ft. at Mera, Java	Resulted from explosion of Krakatoa volcano; subsequent waves generated atmospheric pressure disturbances observed world wide; 36,000 deaths.
1896 June 15	Sanriku Coast, Japan	90 ft. at Ryori Bay	27,122 deaths; 10,617 houses swept away.
1899 Sept. 10	Yakutat Bay, Alaska	30 ft. in bay only	No wave at sea.
1908 Dec. 21	Messina Strait, Italy	30 ft.	3 deaths; moderate damage; turbidity currents noted.
1917 May 1	Kermadec Islands	40 ft. at Samoa	Wave recorded on west coast of U.S.
1918 Aug. 15	Mindanao, Philippine Islands	24 ft. at Mindanao	100 deaths.
1918 Sept. 7	Kuril Islands	40 ft. at Nemuro, Japan	24 deaths; 10 ft. Hawaii and San Francisco.

Table 1 *continued* . . .

Date	Source	Maximum Runup Height	Effects
1918 Oct. 11	Northwest coast, Puerto Rico	18 ft. at Point Jiguero	328 ft. inundation at Agua dilla, causing 30 deaths.
1922 Nov. 11	Coquimbo, Chile	30 ft. at Chanaral	1½ miles inundation at Coquimbo; 1,000 deaths; many homes destroyed.
1923 Feb. 3	East coast of Kamchatka	26 ft. in Kolygir Bay	26 ft. along southern coast of Kamchatka; 20 ft. in Hawaii; 6 deaths at Hilo, Hawaii.
1923 Apr. 13	Gulf of Kamchatka	65 ft. in gulf	18 deaths; many canneries and buildings destroyed.
1923 Sept. 1	Kwanto, Japan	35 ft. in Sagami Bay	868 houses swept away; 160 deaths.
1925 Nov. 16	Mexico	35 ft. at Zihautcanejos (west end of state of Guerrero)	Town inundated.
1933 Mar. 2	Sanriku coast, Japan	96 ft. in Ryori Bay	2,986 eaths; 4,086 houses swept away.
1944 Dec. 7	Tonankai, Japan	33 ft. in Owase	998 deaths; 3,059 houses swept away.
1945 Nov. 28	Pakistan	Little valid data	8.3 earthquake off coast; 4,100 deaths.
1946 Apr. 1	Aleutian Islands	25 ft. in Hawaii	173 deaths; 500 buildings destroyed; $27 million damage in Hawaii.
1946 Dec. 20	Nankaido, Japan	22 ft. on Kii Peninsula	1,500 deaths; 2,000 houses swept away.
1952 Nov. 4	Kamchatka	65 ft. along east coast of northern Kuril Islands	12 ft. at Talcahnano, Chile; $285,000 damage in Hawaii.
1956 July 9	Grecian Archipelago	100 ft. at Amorgos I.	
1957 Mar. 9	Aleutian Islands	52 ft. Kauai I., Hawaii	$3,000,000 damage in Hawaii.
1958 July 10	Lituya Bay, Alaska	1740 ft. in Lituya Bay	Resulted from rockslide triggered by earthquake; effects negligible outside bay.
1960 May 22	Chile	35 ft. at Hilo, Hawaii; 18 ft. at Japan	61 deaths, 537 buildings destroyed $22 million damage in Hilo; 33 ft. at Valdivia, Chile, 2000 killed.
1964 Mar. 28	Kodiak - Prince William Sound, Alaska	60 ft. on Kodiak Island	Damage severe and widespread along coastline; 119 deaths; severe damage at Seward, Valdez, Whittier and Kodiak.
1976 Aug. 23	Celebes Sea, Philippines	30 ft.	7,000 deaths; 90,000 homeless Local tsunami.
1983 May 26	Sea of Japan	30-40 ft. at coast	103 lives lost, thousands of homes and boats destroyed.

Note that tsunamis occur in all oceans, although most occur in the Pacific and originate in the Pacific Rim. Figure 1 shows the seismically active zones (the so-called "Rim of Fire") which produce this hazard. As the Hawaiian Islands are in the center of this area, the phenomenon has received much attention there, and most evaluation of effects and scientific study of causes has been done at the University of Hawaii and in Japan, because of their long and tragic experience with the hazard.

Why do people build, live and work in tsunami-prone areas? The oceans are of course a vital historic and present transportation artery and basic food source. All of these activities need facilities at sea level and people nearby. Thus the paradox — people need the ocean, but the ocean can be an enemy at times. Traditionally, people who use the ocean learn to live with it and to accept the risk in exchange for its benefits.

In recent decades, people have increasingly moved into coastal areas previously sparsely settled, for recreation — or just because they like it. And the density of seaport/harbor areas has increased with urbanization in both advanced and poorer countries. This urbanization has greatly increased the hazard we have to be concerned with, as the problem changes from a few or experienced people to large numbers of new people who don't have to be there — but are in an exposed area. And don't know what to do if they should get a warning.

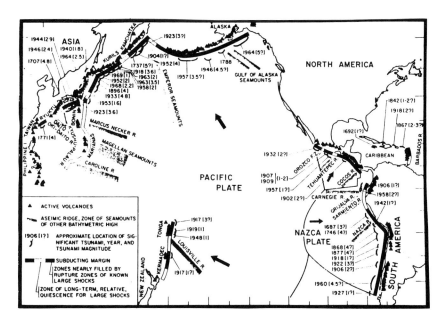

FIGURE 1. Map of the Pacific Region, showing the "Rim of Fire" (USGS).

FIGURE 2. A tsunami wave impacting port facilities, Sea of Japan, 1983 (NOAA/NGDS).

PRESENT MITIGATION MEASURES

Table 2 lists what can be done — and in some areas is done — to reduce the effects of the tsunami hazard. The human problem is far more complex than the structure problem. The latter can be worked out over a period of years; but public safety requires planning and procedures in place to ensure evacuation of danger areas in a couple of hours. A difficult task, but if properly done loss of life from a distant tsunami can be completely avoided.

Obviously, a warning system is essential. The seismic action that initiates the series of waves also provides the cue for warning systems. Starting in the 1920's, the seismographs at the Hawaii Volcano Observatory detected seismic signals from which observers were able to alert harbor users on the island of at least two tele (distant) tsunamis.[2] Unfortunately, communications in that era were not good enough to permit verification from tide gauges that a wave had actually developed — even only a few magnitude 7 earthquakes under the ocean produce a significant tsuanmi — and the false alarm rate was far too high. However, by 1941, the Japanese did start warning from seismic data when strong earthquakes were detected in areas around their islands which long experience showed would produce a tsunami. (This type seldom traveled far across the ocean.)

It took the April 1, 1946 tsunami in the Pacific, combined with communication systems and other factors evolved during World War II, to initiate the present tsunami warning systems. The 1946 event hit particularly hard at Hilo in the Hawaiian Islands. Competent scientists there were able to study this tsunami thoroughly, and they urged that a formal warning system be established to prevent future loss of life.

After much negotiating and effort, the Seismic Sea Wave warning system was established at the U.S. Geological Survey's Honolulu (magnetic) observatory in 1948.[3]

Starting with inputs from a few cooperating seismic stations, and ad hoc com-

TABLE 2

Mitigation of Tsunami Hazards

People	Structures
Warning + Evacuation + Education	Accurate Zonation Insurance Standards Building Codes

Improve Warning System By:
- Better evaluation of seismic event (long period, auto eval., etc.)
- Better, rapidly accessible data on conditions & history enroute to location (1984 paper)
- Deep ocean sensors (HIG/JTRE-PMEL)
- Quantitative predictions; lead time
- But - *never a miss of a damaging event*

Improve Evacuation By:
- Reduce size of evacuation areas; consider population increase & routes
- Prepare public & officials & procedures
- Consider priority and selected areas
- Improve lead time but reduce unnecessary evacuation
- Local tsunamis not involved

Programs:
- Monitor tsunami waves impacting Hawaii
- Prepare to evaluate runup after an event
- Propose projects to improve/resolve problems listed above
- Advise state and county civil defense agencies
- Educate and exchange info; publish journal
- Prepare better evacuation maps

munication arrangements, the system soon developed the capability to provide warning of tsunamis in the Pacific — and has never missed a damaging event since. Figure 3 depicts the essentials of operation of what is now the Pacific Tsunami Warning Center which is part of the National Weather Service.

It serves the entire Pacific and involves the cooperation of some 23 countries, most of whom provide some input from tide gauges. These inputs are important because although the earthquakes associated with tsunamis are always of a Richter magnitude of 7.5 or more, many such large earthquakes simply do not produce significant tsunamis. Therefore, the warning center queries observers at stations near the apparent source, advising them of the estimated time of arrival (ETA) of the first wave. More recently, a number of automatic telemetered gauges which also report wave activity have been connected to the system.

Thus, generation of a tsunami can be confirmed with reliability and enough warning time to allow authorities to evacuate coastal areas. The warning center, it should be noted, advises civil and military authorities; it does not warn the public directly.

The first notice given is a "watch": a Pacific-wide tsunami *may* have been generated; the ETA is also provided. When confirmed, a *warning* is issued, and transmitted to all civil authorities in coastal areas of the ocean. An ETA is calculated for each locality. The goal is to provide a 3 hours warning. In the case of an Aleutian tsunami impacting Hawaii, the sequence of events above had to be done in only 1.5 hours! Figure 4 is a map often used for estimating the ETA when the source location is known. These maps have been calculated for most locations which need warning, and simply represent the graphical solution of the $\sqrt{gd}$ formula mentioned earlier. In the warning center, the "map" is in a computer which centers it on the source; the result is the same. Obviously, it is easier to know where you *are* than where the next earthquake is going to be. (We do have a good idea of the areas, as shown in Figure 1, but not *when* they will happen.)

When the warning is given, people must promptly clear the "low-lying" coastal areas. Evacuation is difficult in the middle of the night, or at rush hour, or if the police and the public have not prepared ahead of time. In a few localities, such as the States of Hawaii and Alaska, and in Japan, procedures are already in place, and maps have been prepared with hazard areas delineated. Figure 5 is an evacuation map published in the phone directory for the island of Oahu.

Experts try to impress on the public that "a tsunami" is a series of waves; many people have been killed because they returned to the shore after a small wave, only to be smashed by the following larger one.

Figure 6 shows a tsunami as recorded at gauges in three locations. Note that the fourth wave is the largest at Honolulu, and also that the waves persist for hours. A large tsunami literally sets the whole ocean into a complex oscillation. Harbors

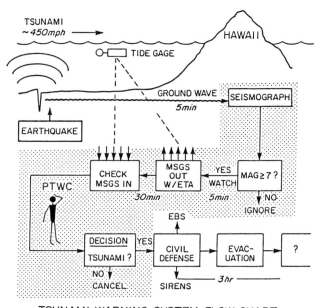

TSUNAMI WARNING SYSTEM FLOW CHART

FIGURE 3. Functional diagram of the Pacific Tsunami Warning System (JIMAR/Univ. of Hawaii).

can add their own resonance — Hilo Bay oscillates with a period of around 18 minutes — and can further amplify the effect of the waves as they steepen upon entering shallow water.[4]

Every tsunami is different and each one reacts differently at various coastlines. So, the warning center does not (at least publicly) predict the wave heights. Their decision, and the evacuation, is and must be "go" or "no-go". Yes or no. They dare not miss a real tsunami, yet cannot afford false alarms and expensive, troublesome evacuations very often without losing public confidence. Not an easy position!

The five geophysicists who are the round-the-clock staff of the Pacific Warning Center are now getting more help from newer computers and more seismic and sea level data, much of it by satellite telemetry from sensors maintained for other scientific purposes. Figure 7 shows those now available.

In Alaska and Japan, special, less elaborate warning centers are maintained because of the problem of local tsunamis from seismic disturbances under nearby ocean areas. These centers give an immediate warning when an earthquake occurs which might — and historically has — caused waves. There is no time for confirmation — the people must flee when the sirens sound. The public in most such locales is aware of the problem, often from tragic experience. And if the quake is nearby the warning system is via the feet as is the evacuation. However, technical aids to the near-local warning problem have been attempted. In 1978, seismic trigger devices were deployed at police stations in Hawaii for this purpose,[9] and recently,

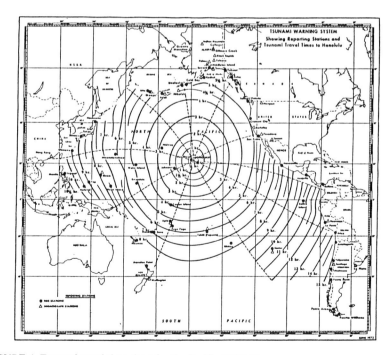

FIGURE 4. Tsunami travel time chart for the Pacific (NOAA).

a more elaborate system has been installed in Valparaiso, Chile, with NOAA aid. But, evacuation time remains a critical problem.

An interesting facet of evacuation is that boats must put to sea. The general rule is to clear the 100 fathom (200 m) line. The wave height is not significant there, and the wavelength is still fairly long. No ship at sea has ever detected a tsunami, but they have occasionally watched them cause havoc as they swept ashore.[5]

In several densely populated coastal communities of Japan, large seawalls have been constructed as tsunami barriers. Since these places are fishing ports, ready

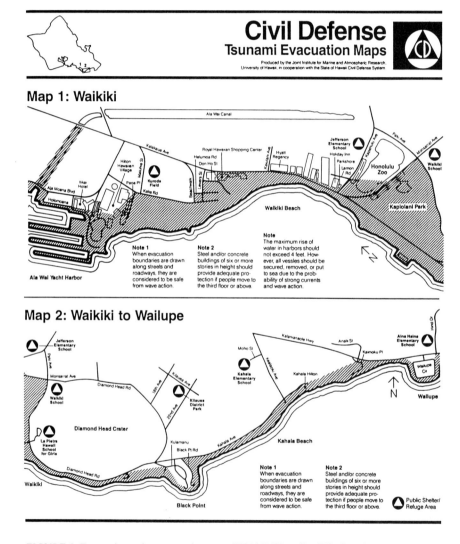

FIGURE 5. Tsunami warning evacuation map (JIMAR/Hawaiian Telephone).

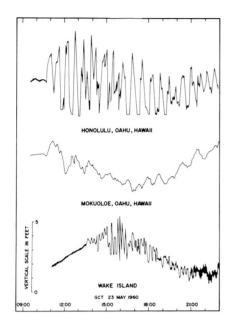

FIGURE 6. Tide gage records from three locations, showing the varied waves from the same event (NOAA/NSF).

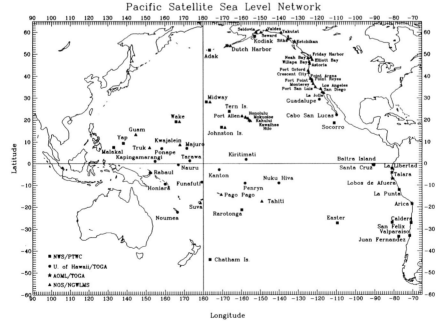

FIGURE 7. Sea level stations in the Pacific; most are for other purposes but can be read by the Warning Center when needed (Univ. of Hawaii).

access to the docks is necessary, and a large gate is provided for that purpose. The warning system tells the keeper to close the gates, so both are essential. This system has functioned on several occasions. But the primary means of protection of property is to keep it out of the hazard zone. Many coastal cities have adopted such zoning policies, allowing only "permitted uses" such as dockside facilities, marinas, etc. in the inundation zones.[6] Where some structures are just "desirable", such as restaurants, they are built on raised foundations or use breakaway walls to minimize the effects of the waves and resultant currents, which may be as great as 60 km/hr onshore.

FUTURE MEASURES

Mitigation measures not yet fully implemented may be divided into those to improve the warning and those to improve the response. Major research in Japan, the U.S., and in the U.S.S.R. in the last decades offers promise in both of these areas but progress seems slow simply because the primary problems are already solved.[7]

Although the warning system has never "missed" since 1948, the decision is increasingly harder. With much more information rapidly available there is a chance to improve the odds of a valid "yes", but the buildup of population mentioned earlier suggests a "no" unless the staff is certain. But the basic questions of which large earthquakes will result in a tsunami, and will it be a hazard to a specific shore, do not yet allow a sure answer.

Certainly, the number of telemetered tide/wave gauges in the Pacific now permits a much better confirmation of a significant wave, and often the reverse, but this does not help all locations, especially those relatively near the source. Therefore, work has been concentrated on rapid and useful analysis of seismic signals and, to a lesser extent, evaluation of expected runup.

The installation of several long period seismometers in the last decade allows fairly fast and accurate estimation of the size of the earthquake fault which usually correlates (along with magnitude) with tsunami generation. Although the Richter scale is "open ended" (has no upper limit), in fact the usual way of determining it begins to saturate around the level 8 — which is critical to tsunami generation. Using the newer instruments which can measure periods as long as 100 seconds, seismologists can estimate more meaningful magnitudes, based on the moment of the motion of the fault over the mantle of the earth. Of course, depth of the ocean in the area and orientation of the fault are factors which also affect the generation of the waves.

Other researchers are investigating various analytical methods to apply to the long period seismic data, to evaluate the area and the vertical motion ("dip") which affects tsunami generation. A renewed effort is being made to use sub-acoustic signals from hydrophones which sense the "T-phase" of a seismic event for detection of tsunami-generating quakes.[7]

All such methods are studied by "hindcasting" available recorded data from previous events, to see if a tsunami could have been reliably forecast. Of course, the careful researcher includes a few large but non-tsunamigenic events to check the real capability of his method!

Other work has been done or is planned using more unusual but scientifically useful phenomena. One which has shown promise is the effect of the earthquake on the ionization layer above our atmosphere; this is the top of the duct which propagates short wave radio waves. Its motion can be sensed with readily available instruments, and used to gain knowledge of the vertical component of the earthquake, especially if undersea. In addition, low-frequency sound waves appear to be generated in the atmosphere by such earthquakes (as well as by storms, large explosions, etc.). These can be detected by microbarographs although the signal travels slower than seismic data.

The goal of all such improvements is not only to improve the validity of a prompt analysis, but to make it quantitative. As noted, at present, warnings are purely binary: evacuate or cancel. In areas subject to near-local tsunamis, there is no choice — a strong earthquake in a generating area now means warning without further evaluation. But even with more time and more reports, there is no way to specify a degree of danger. If it were certain that a wave system at a coast was only 1 meter high, for example, evacuation could only be done in a few vulnerable areas. And the public confidence in the system — vital to any hazard warning — would greatly increase with accurate predictions. The ongoing research will eventually provide that. The great availability of fast, cheap computing technology is a major contributor to current advances.[8]

EVACUATION

Once a prompt and accurate warning is issued to the civil authorities, what can be done to improve the safe response of the affected public? In most coastal areas, the public — and even the police — do not have a clear idea of who may be affected. Unlike a hurricane, where whole districts are evacuated but a day or more is available to do so, a tsunami threatens a very limited area but with only two or three hours to evacuate. It is vital to have defined zones requiring evacuation, and plans to do so. Of the few localities where this has been done, the State of Hawaii was probably the first; the mapped evacuation zones were established after obvious problems with the devastating 1960 tsunami. Apparently, it takes a tsunami — or the threat of one — to produce such improvements. After a problem-laden evacuation for the small 1986 tsunami (costing an estimated $30 million), the State eventually authorized new maps and reworked their evacuation procedures. The record shows that for 20 years, there was not a tsunami warning; meanwhile the population increased 50%. One favorable consequence of the rework is that the new evacuation zones, based on careful inundation calculations, are smaller than before and therefore often have fewer people to evacuate. Figure 5 is an example of the evacuation zone maps which appear in all telephone books in Hawaii. Such aids are needed in other coasts at risk.

Much research, observation, and analysis has gone into the development of these evacuation zones. Present ones are based on delineating the maximum expectable inundation. This is usually estimated by compiling available historical wave heights (or runup heights) in the coastal areas involved and developing statistics to indicate how high they might be in the future. After defining the topography — the slopes and nature of the coastal land — the maximum wave is then "run up" on the land using hydrodynamic formulas. Thus, a line can be drawn along contours on a map to show how high the water might rise (high tide is added, to be sure).

To make this line into an *evacuation* line, it is moved inland to some physical feature, if possible, that the public can see. Usually a road is used. This is carefully noted on the maps; the inundation line is not shown. Often, signs are erected to show evacuation routes. In Japan the zones are sometimes marked on buildings and streets. All of these steps are taken because there is such a short time for evacuation. And, with warning of a distant tsunami, evacuation can reduce the hazard to humans to virtually zero.

Having such maps available in phone books for the public and on wall maps and plans for the police and other authorities is vital for an effective evacuation. So far, such maps exist for only a few areas in the U.S. and Japan. After the next major tsunami, they will doubtless be generated for other areas where lives were lost.

PROTECTION OF PROPERTY

As shown in Table 2, protection of property from the tsunami hazard is quite different from protection of life. Many structures simply must be "at risk" because of their nature — fishing and shipping facilities for example. As long as the people can be evacuated, this is certainly a risk to be accepted. Even restaurants, resorts, etc. may be reasonably located in a hazard zone; rebuilding, say, every 20 years is justifiable since people are very willing to pay for recreation at the edge of the ocean.

But what of the non-essential buildings, residents, and operations which appear in photos of areas damaged by tsunamis? Often, there is an "it won't happen to me" or a "we've never had a problem" philosophy at work, usually accompanied by short memories. Since 1970 in the U.S., a flood insurance law has severely limited the availability of insurance for structures in areas subject to flooding from storms and also tsunamis. Originally developed for stream flooding, where ample data are available, this zonation project has been extended to many coastal areas using methods akin to those used for the inundation work discussed above. However, some important differences are: wave effects are considered; flooding up to 4 feet is allowed; human risk is not considered; and hurricane surge, stream flooding, and tsunamis may (or may not) be considered in a coastal area, and are not differentiated.

In addition, many localities have building and planning codes which permit commercial structures in a flood zone, and allow others if built on a raised foundation or which have breakaway walls. The general intent is "acceptable risk". A good example is Hilo, Hawaii. After a series of destructive events of 1946, '52, '57, and '60, construction of a large breakwater was modeled and analyzed. It was concluded that it would be better to avoid reconstruction of buildings in the devastated areas. Most of the zone was given over to parks and other compatible uses; however, hotels are allowed with open parking garages at grade and the lobbies at the second story level, plus a reinforced structure. Businesses and residences were relocated to other areas. Offices begin in a region filled above the 20 ft. level. An example of the flood insurance map for that area is shown in Figure 8.

In Japan, clear zones heavily planted with low trees have been used in a few locations to minimize tsunami runup. In at least two densely populated harbor towns, barricades are in place to limit the impact of waves. Many tsunamis which strike Japan originate in the general area, and like Alaska, there is a very short time to warn and evacuate. Thus, protection of life and property tend to merge.

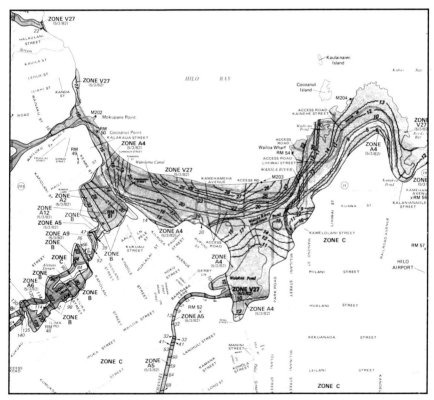

FIGURE 8. A Flood Insurance Rate Map; the shaded areas can only obtain flood insurance under special conditions and most of that land is now a park. (U.S. Flood Insurance Administration).

IN SUMMARY: THE FUTURE

As a hazard to public safety, tsunamis range from an infrequent, avoidable phenomenon (distant tsunamis in a region with warning and evacuation plans) to a dangerous surprise, deadly to a small area (local tsunami near any populated area).

FIGURE 9. Even one of the small, later, waves builds up as it rolls ashore; Hilo, 1946. (Univ. of California).

Worldwide, over 51,000 have died in the past century, virtually all in the Pacific. The rarity of the events, their variability, and their unpredictability add greatly to the hazard. And when a warning is provided — as it has been for all Pacific - wide tsunamis since 1948 — the short time for evacuation is a unique problem.

Scientific studies of the cause, propagation, and effects of these waves have provided the warning system for them, and a statistical understanding of their behavior. This knowledge has aided in the development of expected inundation limits, which facilitate the evacuation of people at risk when the waves are enroute, and zoning to control building in hazard areas.

Since most tsunamis are associated with earthquakes, the work on predicting earthquakes is of future interest. Analysis of "seismic gaps" — areas where seismic pressure has built up — indicates where the next major tsunami *might* come from. The Shumagin gap in the Aleutians is such a place, and scientists have emplaced special bottom pressure gauges near there to record a tsunami in the open ocean. Since that may entail a long wait, recordings of even minor events that have been observed are input to a numerical (computer) model which allows extrapolation to the effects of a large tsunami. Figure 10 is an example of the results.

These analyses eventually can be used, with other inputs, to quickly evaluate a real event and make a quantitative prediction. Satellite data links will continue to add to the real time capability of the warning system perhaps to improve the go/no-go limitations now in effect.[9]

Local tsunamis reemain a troublesome hazard in specific areas; even the best warning system can hardly ensure evacuation. The natural warning of shaking ground in a coast is hard to improve on. Education about this, as well as about nor-

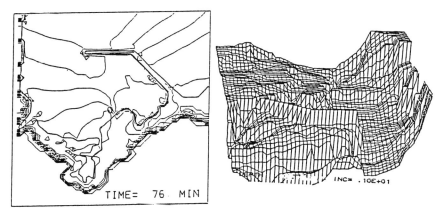

TIME= 76 MIN

FIGURE 10. The output of a computer model of a series of tsunami waves moving into a bay: plan view, top; perspective from the ocean, bottom. (JIMAR/Univ. of Hawaii).

mal evacuation for a distant source, is vital to public safety to reduce the historical tolls.[10] As with other infrequent hazards, maintaining public interest as well as procedures and training for officials, is a constant problem. We sometimes wish for a non-damaging tsunami, or a near-miss hurricane, to alert the populace to the problem and to ensure some funding for research and training. One worker summed it up as "prepare today for an event tomorrow which we hope won't even happen this decade".

That's good advice for any hazard.

For further reading, two readily available books are recommended:

• Tsunami!, by Dudley and Lee, University of Hawaii Press (1988)
• The Great Waves, by Douglas Myles, McGraw-Hill (1985)

REFERENCES

1. Cox, D.C. 1964. "Tsunami Forecasting". University of Hawaii. HIG-64-15.
2. Dudley, Walter and Min Lee. 1988. *Tsunami!*. University of Hawaii Press, Honolulu.
3. Bascom, Willard. 1964. *Waves and Beaches*. Doubleday-Anchor, Garden City, N.Y.
4. Murty, Tad. 1977. *Seismic Sea Waves-Tsunamis*. Fisheries and Marine Service Bulletin 198, Ottawa, Canada.
5. Van Dorn, William. 1974. *Oceanography and Seamanship*. Dodd, Mead & Co. New York.
6. Pruess, Jane. 1982. "Land Management Guidelines in Tsunami Hazard Zones". Urban Regional Research, Inc/NSF.

7. Bernard, Eddie and Richard Goulet, ed. 1981. "Tsunami Research Opportunities". NSF/NOAA. Washington, D.C.
8. Curtis, George D. and Charles Mader. 1987. "Real Time Monitoring and Modeling for Tsunami Threat Evaluation", Journal of the Tsunami Society, Vol. 5, No. 1.
9. Adams, Wm. M. and George D. Curtis. 1984. "Design and Development of an Intelligent Digital System for Computer-Aided Decision-Making During Natural Hazards". Journal of the Tsunami Society. Vol. 2, No. 2.
10. Iida, Kumize, Doak Cox and George Pararas-Carayaunis. 1967. *Preliminary Catalog of Tsunamis Occurring in the Pacific Ocean*. University of Hawaii Institute of Geophysics. HIG-67-10.

Natural and Technological Disasters: Causes, Effects and Preventive Measures. Edited by
S.K. Majumdar, G.S. Forbes, E.W. Miller, and R.F. Schmalz. © 1992, The Pennsylvania Academy
of Science.

Chapter Ten

THE HURRICANE HAZARD IN THE UNITED STATES

JOHN A. CROSS

Department of Geography
University of Wisconsin-Oshkosh
Oshkosh, WI 54901

INTRODUCTION

Hurricanes are one of the most destructive natural hazards which threaten our
nation's population. When we consider that a natural hazard is defined as "an interaction of man and nature, governed by the coexistent state of adjustment in the
human use system and the state of nature in the natural events system," (Kates, 1971)
this threat should engender even greater concern. Climatological conditions point
to more frequent and more severe hurricane occurrences within the next decade.
Population growth within low-lying coastal locations is proceeding far more rapidly
than the nation's overall growth rate. Now changes in both physical and social conditions are interacting to accentuate the hurricane hazard threat. This threat takes
on even greater urgency when we consider that 1989's Hurricane Hugo — which
was not the strongest category storm — caused $10 billion in damages, nearly twice
the damages caused by California's Loma Prieta earthquake, which shook San
Francisco just three weeks later. Thus, it is time to review the threat of hurricanes
along the United States shore and to discuss spatial variations in this threat along
our shore.

INCREASING POPULATION AT RISK

Rapid population growth along the U.S. Gulf and Atlantic shore has now placed
nearly a third of all Americans at risk from hurricanes. Sixty-three million persons
live in coastal counties from Texas through Maine (Culliton and others, 1990).

Population growth rates within coastal communities greatly exceed those of the nation as a whole. Preliminary 1990 census figures show that Florida grew by 33 percent during the 1980s. Both Georgia and Texas increased by 19 percent (U.S. Bureau of the Census, 1991). Areas along the shore grew faster than the coastal states as a whole, continuing a trend which was apparent even several decades ago. Indeed, between 1960 and 1970 the population of coastal counties grew 19 percent but the smaller coastal subdivisions increased 26 percent, and beach subdivisions gained 43 percent (Frank, 1974). Although the coastal growth rate slowed during the 1970s, it increased again in the 1980s, and these high rates are projected to continue (Culliton and others, 1990). Thousands of weekend visitors and vacationers swell the population of many coastal communities during the summer, the height of the hurricane season. Indeed, the population of Ocean City, Maryland often exceeds 200,000 on a summer weekend, far in excess of its 6,000 year-round population (Leatherman and Dubois, 1984).

Exacerbating the problems caused by population growth is the overall hurricane inexperience of most coastal inhabitants. For most of the American shoreline, the 1970s and most of the 1980s was a period of below average hurricane activity, particularly when considering the largest and most dangerous hurricanes (Saffir-Simpson category 3 and higher). In their studies of population trends and hurricane exposure, Hebert, Taylor and Case (1984) found that 78.2 percent of the residents of the U.S. coastal counties have never experienced a direct hit of a major hurricane. For Florida, they measured inexperience at 84.8 percent, for Virginia at 97.7 percent. In the decade since the completion of their previous study (Hebert and Taylor, 1975), the experienced coastal population grew by four million. Because of their inexperience, few coastal residents can visualize the magnitude of the risk from a great hurricane. Hazards experts have also expressed concerns about experiences which individuals may have had with either minor hurricanes or tropical storms or at the outer fringes of larger storms, causing residents to underestimate the actual threat (Drabek, 1986). Nevertheless, longitudinal research within the Florida Keys has demonstrated that hurricane awareness is high among its "inexperienced" population, and that overall perceptions that hurricane winds and flooding are problems facing residents have actually increased over a twelve year period. Experience with minimal Hurricane Floyd in 1987 had little effect upon most of the residents' concerns about potential hurricane damage, but nearly a fifth of the residents indicated heightened concern (Cross, 1990).

Simply evacuating certain barrier island communities is estimated to require a day or more — a process which must be completed hours before the eye of the storm moves onshore. Indeed, Robert Sheets (1985) director of the National Hurricane Center warns, "Evacuation of only the vulnerable residents of communities such as the Tampa Bay area, the Fort Myers area, the Florida Keys, and Miami and Ft. Lauderdale, Florida, as well as Galveston, Texas, and Hilton Head, South Carolina, require lead times of 20 or 30 hours or more." Evacuation of a metropolitan area such as New Orleans would require 72 hours (Sheets, 1990). Because of rapidly growing coastal population, not only does it become more difficult to evacuate vulnerable areas, often over highways and bridges whose capacities to handle such traffic are severely overtaxed, but such evacuations must be started in advance of precise forecasts of hurricane movements. Furthermore, "rates of improvement in forecast skills have been far outpaced by rates of population growth in areas vulnerable to hurricanes" (Sheets, 1990 A).

INCREASING FREQUENCY OF HURRICANES

Residents along the U.S. coast, particularly from peninsular Florida north along the Atlantic coast, may experience significantly greater hurricane activity during the 1990s if the trend of the 1980s continues. This may be particularly true considering hurricanes of Saffir-Simpson category 3 or higher (winds exceeding 110 miles per hour) (Gray, 1990). The U.S. experienced several major damaging hurricanes during the 1960s, including Hurricane Donna which devastated the Middle Florida Keys and the Lower Florida Gulf Coast in 1960, Hurricane Carla which struck near Corpus Cristi, Texas in 1961, and Hurricane Camille which inundated Southern Mississippi with a storm surge of 23 feet in 1969. All of these storms had sustained winds exceeding 130 miles per hours, with those of Hurricane Camille approaching 200 miles per hour.

No storm even approaching the severity of these storms had hit the U.S. for two decades until 1989's Hurricane Hugo. A total of five category 4 or 5 hurricanes occurred in 1988-89, the greatest number for a two year period since 1960-61, which had six such storms (Case and Mayfield, 1990). The fourteen tropical storms and hurricanes which occurred in 1990 were the most for any Atlantic hurricane season since 1969, although only one storm (Gustav) reached category 3 intensity. Sixteen hurricanes (and 20 tropical cyclones) developed within the Eastern Pacific during 1990, a new record number of hurricanes for a season. Two of these Eastern Pacific hurricanes (Hernan and Trudy) were among the strongest, if not the strongest, hurricanes ever recorded within the Eastern Pacific (Avilia, 1991).

Recent climatological research by William Gray (1990) not only provides an explanation for the relative inactivity of the previous two decades, but also indicates that the climatological conditions which reduced the hurricane activity have now abated, thus heralding a return to the increased frequency and severity of hurricanes which characterized the 1950s and 1960s. Gray has noted a strong correlation between drought conditions within the Western Sahel of West Africa and a reduction in the incidence of intense hurricanes within Florida, along the U.S. East Coast, and in the Caribbean Basin. Drought conditions persisted from 1970 through 1987 in the Sahel. Rainfall was above average within the Western Sahel in both 1988 and 1989, with the Caribbean suffering two severe hurricanes in 1988 (Hurricanes Gilbert and Joan) and Hurricane Hugo striking the U.S. Virgin Islands, Puerto Rico and South Carolina the following year. Hurricane Gilbert had the lowest barometric pressure ever recorded in the Western Hemisphere — 887 millibars or 26.19 inches (Lawrence and Gross, 1989) breaking the old record of 26.35 inches (892.5 mb) set by the Labor Day hurricane of 1935 which destroyed the railroad to Key West, Florida. Hurricane Hugo was the strongest hurricane to hit the U.S. since 1969's

Hurricane Camille, and caused the greatest monetary damages of any hurricane ($7 billion in the Carolinas and $3 billion in the Caribbean) (Case and Mayfield, 1990). These recent storms may well be the forerunners of other intense hurricanes which may occur during the 1990s and the first decade of the 21st Century (Gray, 1990).

Gray emphatically states, "The historical data imply that such an increase in intense hurricane activity should be viewed as a natural change and not as a result of man's influence on his climate" (Gray, 1990). Unfortunately, human-induced increases in the so-called Greenhouse gases, especially carbon dioxide and methane, are expected to result in significant warming of the earth's atmosphere. Such warming may well result in the increased frequency and severity of hurricane activity (Schneider, 1989). Climatologists have long recognized a correlation between sea surface temperatures and the frequency of hurricanes (Wendland, 1977). Warmer ocean waters would also permit hurricanes to attain significantly lower central pressures, thus resulting in hurricanes with stronger winds (Emanuel, 1987). Furthermore, hurricanes might form in areas farther north than present, as warm waters conducive to such formation became more extensive. Global warming is also expected to raise sea levels by 0.5 to 1.5 meters (1.6 to 4.9 feet) by the end of the 21st Century (Schneider, 1989 A). Any rise in sea level would increase the vulnerability of coastal communities to storm surge flooding, permit the surges to penetrate farther inland and intensify already serious problems of coastal erosion. Considering the effect of global warming on both hurricane frequency and sea level increases, Tirpak (1988) warns, "the overall impact of increased hurricane frequency would be small compared to the impact of sea level rise. While a doubling of hurricanes would convert 100-year floodplains to 50-year floodplains throughout much of the Southeast, a 1-m rise would convert them to 15-year floodplains."

DISTRIBUTION OF THE HURRICANE HAZARD

A map illustrating a century of hurricane tracks shows that no location along the nation's Atlantic or Gulf coasts is immune from hurricanes, although, the threat of hurricane destruction is not uniformly distributed along the U.S. coastline (Neumann and others, 1990). Distinct differences in the probability of hurricane occurrences, expected storm surge heights, overwash distance, and susceptibility of the beach to coastal erosion all determine the severity of the physical threat.

Nearly two-thirds of the hurricanes within the North Atlantic Basin have occurred during the months of August and September (Figure 1), although hurricanes have formed as early as March and as late as December. Early season (May and June) hurricanes and tropical storms have historically developed within the Gulf of Mexico, the far western Caribbean, or in waters off the Bahamas. In contrast, the Atlantic Ocean west of the Cape Verde Islands frequently spawns hurricanes during late summer, such as 1989's Hurricane Hugo. Late season hurricanes are again more likely to develop in the Gulf of Mexico or the Caribbean (Neumann and others, 1990). Although these seasonal shifts in tracks can be discerned, hurricane paths of one decade may often bear little resemblance with those of the next decade (Sheets, 1990 A).

Over the past century the North Atlantic has averaged 8.4 tropical cyclones annually, 4.9 which were of hurricane intensity. Approximately five hurricanes make landfall in the United States every three years, and a major hurricane crosses some portion of the U.S. coast "about twice every 3 years" (Neumann and others, 1990). The area just east of the Miami-Ft. Lauderdale area, including the northern portion of the Bahamas, has the greatest number of tropical cyclone occurrences, on average, of any location within the North Atlantic. Within an area measuring five degrees of longitude by five degrees of latitude (or roughly an area with a radius of 150 nautical miles) an average of 1.8 tropical cyclones will pass each year. At least one such storm a year can be expected to pass within 150 nautical miles of all of the southeastern United States south and east of a line extending from Port Arthur, Texas to Norfolk, Virginia. Even as far north as coastal Maine and Nova Scotia two tropical cyclones are expected to pass within 150 nautical miles every three years (Crutcher and Quayle, 1974).

Tropical cyclones along the Pacific coast of the United States are far rarer. Although the Eastern Pacific Ocean has averaged 15.6 hurricanes or tropical storms annually (Lawrence, 1990) and tropical cyclones are over three times as likely to

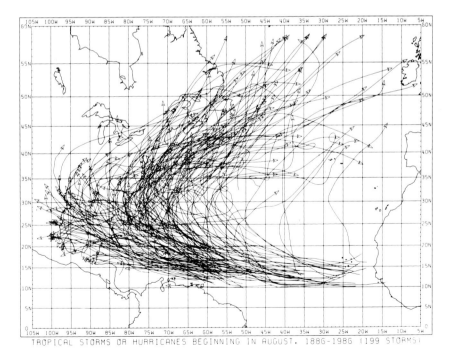

TROPICAL STORMS OR HURRICANES BEGINNING IN AUGUST, 1886-1986 (199 STORMS)

FIGURE 1. Tracks of all tropical cyclones (both hurricanes and tropical storms) occurring during the month of August between 1886 and 1986 (Neumann *et al*, 1990).

occur southwest of Acapulco, Mexico than in the Bahamas, they rarely move as far north as southern California. Indeed, a tropical cyclone moves within 150 nautical miles of Baja California Norte only about once every decade (Crutcher and Quayle, 1974). Most Pacific hurricanes lose strength as they move west across cooler water as Hurricane (then Tropical Storm) Marie did in 1990 when it threatened Hawaii. Hurricane Dot, which struck Kauai in August 1959, was the most recent damaging hurricane to develop west of Mexico and track westward to Hawaii. Hurricane Iwa, which caused $200 million in damages in Hawaii, particularly on Kauai, in November 1982, typified the late-season tropical cyclone, which develop to the south of the islands and move rapidly to the north or northeast (Rosendal, 1983). Overall, tropical storms pass within 150 miles of the Hawaiian Islands of average once every two to five years, with the greatest probability of occurrence in the easternmost islands (Crutcher and Quayle, 1974). Notwithstanding these Pacific examples, most attention about hurricanes within the U.S. has been directed towards the nation's east coast.

LANDFALL FREQUENCIES

The southern tip of the Florida peninsula and the Florida Keys have the greatest frequency of landfalling tropical cyclones (considering both tropical storms and hurricanes together) of any location in the nation. Ho and associates (1987) have calculated, based upon a 114 year record, that the frequency of landfalling tropical cyclones, per 10 nautical miles of coast, is an average of 2.2 tropical cyclones per century within that area, which is exposed to both Atlantic and Caribbean hurricanes. The northwest coast of Florida near St. Marks has a cyclone entry frequency nearly as high as the Florida Keys. Other areas of high landfalling frequencies include the upper Texas coast, just west of Galveston, and Cape Hatteras, North Carolina, where 1.9 and 1.6 cyclones per century, per ten nautical miles of shore, respectively, could be expected (Ho and others, 1987). Because hurricane force winds during a major hurricane often affect more than 100 miles of shoreline, the frequencies of landfalling storms for these short coastal segments are roughly indicative of the number of direct hurricane hits, in which the eye of a hurricane (or center of a large eye) passes over any specific location, and thus underestimate the number of episodes of hurricane damage which any location might experience.

The likelihood that either the center of a hurricane or the storm's most intense hurricane force windfield, to the right of the eye, would cross various 50 mile long (80 kilometer) segments of the Gulf and Atlantic coasts has been calculated by Simpson and Lawrence (1971) and is shown in Figure 2. The coast with the shortest return period — with a hurricane making landfall on average once every six years — is southeastern Florida, from Miami through West Palm Beach. Segments of coastal Texas and Louisiana, the shore from Mobile Bay to Panama City, Florida, and the Florida Everglades and the Lower Florida Keys can expect a hurricane on average every seven years. Thus, the probability that a hurricane would cross these shorelines during any given year would range from 13 to 16 percent (Simpson and Riehl, 1981). The Outer Banks of North Carolina will experience a hurricane in one of nine years.

In contrast, the 50 mile coastal segment extending north from Charleston, South Carolina has a 21 year return interval. Although several areas north of the Outer Banks have historically experienced few landfalling hurricanes, and thus have low probabilities, so does the coast stretching from near Daytona Beach, Florida to Cumberland Island, Georgia, with a reoccurrence interval of 85 years, an annual probability of one percent.

Landfalls of the most intense hurricanes, such as great hurricanes (winds exceeding 125 miles per hour), or Saffir-Simpson Category 4 or 5 storms, (with minimum wind speeds of 131 and 156 miles per hour, respectively) have a somewhat different spatial pattern (Simpson and Lawrence, 1971). For example, great hurricanes are most frequently expected along the southeast Florida coast (once every fourteen years — a 7 percent probability any given year), the same area which is most likely to experience hurricanes in general. Conversely, two segments of the Alabama coast and Florida Panhandle have not experienced a great hurricane in over a century, yet have almost as high a probability of experiencing a hurricane as does southeast Florida. The fact than an area has a low probability or that it has not experienced a major hurricane does not necessarily mean that it cannot

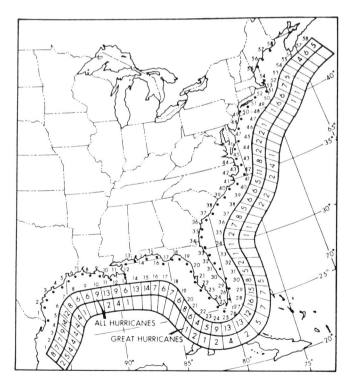

FIGURE 2. Probabilities that a hurricane or a great hurricane (with winds exceeding 125 miles per hour) will occur within 50 mile long segments of the U.S. coastline during any given year (Simpson and Lawrence, 1971).

or will not experience such a storm. Indeed, Hurricane Hugo struck an area of South Carolina which had not experienced a major hurricane in over a century, for which probabilities were less than one percent.

HURRICANE WIND PROBABILITIES

All of the U.S. coastline from Cape Charles, Virginia south to the Rio Grande experiences sustained hurricane force winds on average at least once every 25 years, with the Florida coast running from Fort Myers south through the Keys and north to Vero Beach expecting such winds at least once a decade (Batts and others, 1980; Georgiou and Davenport, 1988). The coastline extending from western Long Island, New York to near Glouchester, Massachusetts also experiences hurricane force winds every 25 years. Although only four segments of the coast — Mobile, Alabama to Cedar Key, Florida; Daytona Beach, Florida to Savannah, Georgia; Cape Charles, Virginia to eastern Long Island, New York; and north of Boston, Massachusetts do not experience winds exceeding 100 miles per hour at least once a century, the Florida coast between Tampa Bay and Vero Beach experiences such winds at least twice a century (Batts and others, 1980). Sustained winds exceeding 140 miles per hour could be expected throughout South Florida at least once every thousand years. (Georgiou and Davenport, 1988). Most locations even 200 kilometers (124 miles) inland of the Gulf or Atlantic experience hurricane force winds at least once every half century.

HURRICANE FLOODING

Destruction from storm surge flooding and wave action is confined to a much narrower zone than the area exposed to hurricane force winds. Flooding and wave action have historically been responsible for 90 percent of all hurricane fatalities (a percentage which is now falling in the United States because of better warning and evacuation). The size and intensity of a hurricane are only partly responsible for observed variations in storm flooding. The storm surge results from the transport and circulation of water put into motion by hurricane winds and because of the pressure gradient. For each 1 millibar drop in atmospheric pressure, sea level rises hydrostatically by 1 centimeter (.4 inch). Although even greater flooding comes from the accumulation of water driven shorewards by the winds, the severity of the flooding and flood height are substantially influenced by both regional and local topographic and bathymetric conditions (Simpson and Riehl, 1981).

Storm surge heights and overwash distances differ considerably along the U.S. coast. Three lengthy segments of the Gulf and Atlantic coasts are at very high risk from storm and wave damage: (1) the Gulf coast extending from west of Galveston, Texas through the Mississippi Delta of Louisiana, plus the Mobile Bay region of Alabama; (2) the barrier islands of Florida extending from Miami Beach to north of West Palm Beach; and (3) the shore of Long Island, New York through Cape

Cod, Massachusetts (Kimball and others, 1989). Within the first two segments, hurricanes are the greatest storm threat. Extratropical storms can cause damage similar to that of a hurricane, particularly along the east coast extending north of Cape Hatteras, North Carolina, and are the significant determinant of overall coastal hazard there.

The hundred year hurricane (a storm with a one percent probability any given year) would cause flooding ranging from six to 15 feet along the Atlantic coast, according to early flood insurance studies prepared for the Federal Insurance Administration (Brinkmann, 1975). Within the Florida peninsula, the 100-year storm surge levels range from a low of 7.5 feet between Fort Lauderdale and West Palm Beach to a maximum of 16.5 feet near Chokoloskee, southeast of Marco Island (Pilkey and others, 1984). Within the Florida Keys still water surge levels range from eight feet near Key West to 17 feet in the Upper Keys (Federal Emergency Management Agency, 1983-89). Wave action would raise these flood levels to 21 feet on Key Largo. Rare, extremely intense hurricanes, would cause flooding of far greater severity than the hundred-year storm. For most of the U.S. shoreline, no Category 5 hurricane has ocurred for over a century, but such a storm could occur. For example, flooding from a category 5 hurricane, such as Hurricane Camille, would result in flooding of 32 feet near Cedar Key, Florida versus the 100-year flood level of 16 feet (Pilkey and others, 1984).

Local topographic and bathymetric conditions cause considerable variation in storm surge levels within virtually every coastal community. For example, the seaward shore of barrier islands usually experiences lower flood levels than the landward sides of the lagoons behind barrier islands. Surge heights are maximized where shoals extend a fair distance offshore and where flood surges are funneled into bays or estuaries. Indeed, surge heights in bays and estuaries are often at least 50 percent higher than along the open coast (Simpson and Riehl, 1981). Thus, an island surrounded by deep water is far less vulnerable to extreme storm surge heights than a community located at the head of a narrow bay. Eroding beaches and subsidence place shorefront construction at greater risk from hurricane waves and flooding.

HURRICANE PRECIPITATION

Precipitation resulting from hurricanes and tropical storms can be either a curse or a blessing. When a hurricane stalls or when the clouds encounter topographic barriers, extremely heavy precipitation can occur. For example, the remnants of Hurricane Juan produced devastating flash flooding and downstream flooding within eastern West Virginia and western Virginia in November 1985. One location in Virginia recorded 19.8 inches from six days of rain. Similar high rainfall totals were recorded from Tropical Storm Agnes, which dumped eight to twelve inches on the Middle Susquehanna Valley of Pennsylvania during a twenty-four hour period in June 1972 *(Storm Data)*. Flooding from Hurricane Camille's rains of up to nearly 30 inches in six hours in Virginia killed 109 persons, nearly as many as the storm killed in the Gulfport-Biloxi areas of Mississippi (Pielke, 1990). Hurricane induced precipitation need not be so copious to cause significant damage. Moisture from remnants of Hurricane Olivia brought rains of 0.5 to 2.0 inches to much of California in September 1982, ruining over half the state's raisin crop and causing $325 million in agricultural losses (Gunther and others, 1983).

Precipitation from hurricanes can also be a "drought breaker". Hurricanes and tropical storms are responsible for at least ten percent of the total average precipitation which occurs between June and October for the entire Gulf and Atlantic coastal plain, running from the Rio Grande through the eastern tip of Long Island, and extending west to near the Blue Ridge (Cry, 1967). During September, the height of the hurricane season, tropical cyclone precipitation provides over 25 percent of the mean precipitation for eastern Louisiana, coastal Mississippi and Alabama, the Florida Panhandle and the northwestern half of the Florida Peninsula, plus the eastern halves of South Carolina, North Carolina, Virginia, and Maryland, and Delaware, New Jersey and Rhode Island, and portions of Maine. Nevertheless for South Florida, the contribution of hurricanes on average, over the entire year is "not all that much" (Brandes, 1982). However, seasonally, and during a drought, hurricane precipitation can be significant.

CONCLUSIONS

Hurricanes pose one of the greatest environmental threats facing Americans. Hurricanes pose a major threat to nearly a third of the nation's population and net annual dollar damages from hurricanes are expected to exceed those of all other natural hazards — even riverine flooding — in the nation by the end of the century (Petak and Atkisson, 1982). Advances in our ability to accurately track hurricanes by satellite, to provide timely communication of storm forecasts and warnings, including recently introduced probability forecasting, and to accurately model expected storm surge levels for any given storm along the coast using the SLOSH model which so accurately predicted flood levels within the Charleston, South Carolina area during Hurricane Hugo are all negated by other human actions which only accentuate the risk. Although most Americans have forgotten that a hurricane killed 6,000 persons in Galveston, Texas in 1900 and approximately 2,400 died during a 1928 hurricane in South Florida, hurricanes still pose a significant threat. Hurricane Camille was one of the nation's most destructive natural disasters ever when it occurred in 1969. Three years later the floods resulting from Tropical Storm Agnes claimed that distinction. Hurricane Hugo left $7 billion in damages stateside in 1989 — the greatest dollar losses of any American disaster in history. Although losses of life in the U.S. have been minimal in recent years, thanks to timely warnings and evacuation, our luck may not hold out. The American Meteorological Society (1986) has warned, "We are more vulnerable to hurricanes in the United States now than we have ever been in our history." They conclude, "If we do not move forward quickly in seeking solutions to the hurricane problem, we will pay a severe price. The price may be thousands of lives."

REFERENCES

American Meteorological Society. 1986. Is the United States Headed for Hurricane Disaster? *Bulletin American Meteorological Society.* 67:537-538.
Avilia, Lixion A. 1991. Eastern Pacific Hurricanes: A Record Year. *Weatherwise.* 44:39-43, 54.
Batts, Martin E., Martin R. Cordes, Larry R. Russell, James R. Shaver, and Emil Simiu. 1980. *Hurricane Wind Speeds in the United States* NBS Building Science Series 124. National Bureau of Standards, Washington.
Brandes, Donald, 1982. Hurricane Rainfall in South Florida. *The Florida Geographer.* 16:17-24.
Brinkmann, Waltraud A.R. 1975. *Hurricane Hazard in the United States: A Research Assessment,* Monograph 7, University of Colorado Institute of Behavioral Science, Boulder.
Case, Bob and Max Mayfield. 1990. Atlantic Hurricane Season of 1989. *Monthly Weather Review.* 118:1165-1177.
Cross, John A. 1990. Longitudinal Changes in Hurricane Hazard Perception. *International Journal of Mass Emergencies and Disasters.* 8:31-47.
Crutcher, H.L. and R.G. Quayle. 1974. *Mariners Worldwide Guide to Tropical Storms at Sea* NAVAIR 50-1C-61. Naval Weather Service, Asheville, NC.
Cry, George W. 1967. *Effects of Tropical Cyclone Rainfall on the Distribution of Precipitation over the Eastern and Southern United States* ESSA Professional Paper 1. U.S. Department of Commerce, Washington.
Culliton, Thomas J., Maureen A. Warren, Timothy Goodspeed, Davida G. Remer, Carol M. Blackwell and John J. McDonough III. 1990. *50 Years of Population Change along the Nation's Coasts: 1960-2010.* National Oceanic and Atmospheric Administration, National Ocean Service, Rockville, MD.
Drabek, Thomas E. 1986. *Human System Response to Disaster: An Inventory of Sociological Findings.* Springer-Verlag, New York.
Emanuel, Kerry A. 1987. The Dependence of Hurricane Intensity on Climate. *Nature.* 326:483-485.
Federal Emergency Management Agency. 1983-1989. *Flood Insurance Rate Maps* for Monroe County, Florida (Community No. 125129). FEMA, Washington.
Frank, Neil. 1974. The Hard Facts about Hurricanes. *NOAA.* 4, number 3:4-9.
Georgiou, Peter N. and Alan G. Davenport. 1988. Estimation of the Wind Hazard in Tropical Cyclone Regions. pp. 709-725. In: El-Sabh, M.I. and T.S. Murty, (editors), *Natural and Man-Made Hazards.* D. Reidel Publishing Co., Dordrecht.
Gray, William M. 1990. Strong Association Between West African Rainfall and U.S. Landfall of Intense Hurricanes. *Science.* 249:1251-1256.
Gunther, E.B., R.L. Cross, and R.A. Wagoner, 1983. Estern North Pacific Tropical Cyclones, 1982. *Mariners Weather Log.* 27, no. 2:67-76.
Hebert, Paul J. and Glenn Taylor. 1975. *Hurricane Experience Levels of Coastal County Populations – Texas to Maine.* National Oceanic and Atmospheric Administation, Miami.
Hebert, Paul J., Glenn Taylor, and Robert A. Case. 1984. *Hurricane Experience*

Levels of Coastal County Populations — Texas to Maine (Technical Memorandum NWS NHC 24). National Oceanic and Atmospheric Administration, Miami.

Ho, Francis P., James C. Su, Karen L. Hanevich, Rebecca J. Smith and Frank P. Richards. *Hurricane Climatology for the Atlantic and Gulf Coast of the United States Technical Report NWS 38,* National Oceanic and Atmospheric Administration, Washington.

Kates, Robert W. 1971. Natural Hazard in Human Ecological Perspective: Hypotheses and Models. *Economic Geography.* 47:438-451.

Kimball, Suzette, Fred Anders and Robert Dolan. 1989. Coastal Hazards. National Atlas Map 38077-AX-07M-00. U.S. Geological Survey, Reston, VA.

Lawrence, Miles B. 1990. Eastern North Pacific Tropical Cyclones, 1989. *Mariners Weather Log.* 34, no. 2:18-22.

Lawrence, Miles B. and James B. Gross. 1989. Atlantic Hurricane Season of 1988. *Monthly Weather Review.* 117:2248-2259.

Leatherman, Stephen P. and Roger Dubois. 1984. Coastal Environments of Maryland and Delaware. *Geography and Public Policy Field Trip Guide.* Association of American Geographers, Washington. pp. 22-35.

Neumann, Charles J., Brian R. Jarvinen and Arthur C. Pike. 1990. *Tropical Cyclones of the North Atlantic Ocean, 1871-1986 (with Storm Track Maps Updated through 1989)* Historical Climatology Series 6-2, National Climatic Data Center, Asheville, NC.

Petak, William J. and Arthur A. Atkisson. 1982. *Natural Risk Assessment and Public Policy.* Springer-Verlag, New York.

Pielke, Roger A. 1990. *The Hurricane.* Routledge, London.

Pilkey, Orrin H., Jr., Dinesh C. Sharma, Harold R. Wanless, Larry J. Doyle, Orrin H. Pilkey, Sr., William J. Neal and Barbara Gruver. 1984. *Living with the East Florida Shore.* Duke University Press, Durham, NC.

Rosendal, Hans E. 1983. Hurricane Iwa. *Mariners Weather Log.* 27:63-66.

Schneider, Stephen H. 1989. *Global Warming: Are We Entering the Greenhouse Century?* Sierra Club Books, San Francisco.

Schneider, Stephen H. 1989. The Greenhouse Effect: Science and Policy. *Science.* 243:771-781.

Sheets, Robert C. 1985. The National Weather Service Hurricane Probability Program. *Bulletin of the American Meteorological Society.* 66:4-13.

Sheets, Robert C. 1990. "Hugo and Loma Prieta: Preparedness, Response, and Response Lessons" presentation during 15th Annual Hazards Research Workshop, Boulder, Colorado, July 15-18.

Sheets, Robert C. 1990 A. The National Hurricane Center — Past, Present, and Future. *Weather and Forecasting.* 5:185-232.

Simpson, Robert H., and Herbert Riehl. 1981. *The Hurricane and Its Impact.* Louisiana State University Press, Baton Rouge.

Simpson, Robert H. and M.B. Lawrence. 1971. *Atlantic Hurricane Frequencies along the U.S. Coastline* Technical Memorandum NWS WM SR-58. National Oceanic and Atmospheric Administration.

Storm Data. National Oceanic and Atmospheric Administration, Washington. Various issues.

Tirpak, Dennis A. 1988. Southeast, Volume 1, pp. 6-1 — 6-68. In: Smith, Joel B. and Dennis A. Tirpak (editors). *The Potential Effects of Global Climate Change on the United States: Draft Report to Congress.* Washington.

U.S. Bureau of the Census. 1991. Census Bureau Press Release CB91-07, January 7, 1991. U.S. Dept. of Commerce, Washington.

Wendland, Wayne M. 1977. Tropical Storm Frequencies Related to Sea Surface Temperatures. *Journal of Applied Meteorology.* 16:477-481.

Natural and Technological Disasters: Causes, Effects and Preventive Measures. Edited by S.K. Majumdar, G.S. Forbes, E.W. Miller, and R.F. Schmalz. © 1992, The Pennsylvania Academy of Science.

Chapter Eleven

HURRICANE HUGO'S IMPACT ON THE SOUTH CAROLINA COAST

STEPHEN P. LEATHERMAN

Department of Geography &
Laboratory for Coastal Research
University of Maryland
College Park, Maryland 20742

INTRODUCTION

The incidence of landfall hurricanes along the South Carolina coast is low in comparison to the more exposed Florida and North Carolina coasts and especially with respect to the "hurricane alley" of the Gulf of Mexico. The actual impact of a hurricane on a coastal area depends upon the storm characteristics, coastal geomorphology, and human habitation. Hurricane Hugo, while not the largest hurricane to attack the U.S. coasts, was the most damaging because of its magnitude and the developed nature of this low-lying coastal area. However, the damage could have been far worse if the storm had made landfall just south rather than north of Charleston. Likewise, the geologic changes (e.g., inlet breaching) would have been much more severe and widespread if hurricane landfall occurred along the microtidal barrier islands constituting the Outer Banks of North Carolina.

The South Carolina coast represents a transition zone between that of North Carolina and Georgia. The North Carolina coast is dominated by long, thin (microtidal) barrier islands with few tidal inlets. By contrast, the Georgian coast to the south is comprised of short, stubby barrier separated by many large tidal inlets. The South Carolina coast is characterized by: (1) frequently spaced tidal inlets that can accommodate large tidal flows; (2) extensive salt marshes in adjacent bays and lagoons; and (3) large ebb-tidal deltas that absorb incoming open-ocean wave energy (Hayes, 1979). All three are stablizing influences for barrier islands, reducing the probability of inlet cutting and massive destruction during hurricane conditions.

The last major hurricane to affect the Charleston area occurred on August 28, 1893. While the records are poor, it is reported that perhaps as many as 2,000 people drowned in this storm tide of 8.9 feet. By contrast, there were only a few reported drownings associated with the much higher storm surge of 12 to 20 feet generated by Hurricane Hugo (Figure 1), and even these few deaths were preventable (NRC, 1991). Table 1 ranks the storm tidal elevations affecting South Carolina during the past century. Hurricane Hazel in 1954 did little damage along the coast, but caused widespread destruction along southeast North Carolina, destroying all the beachfront houses in some communities as it made landfall. Building codes were strengthened and upgraded in the wake of Hazel so that Hurricane Diana in 1984

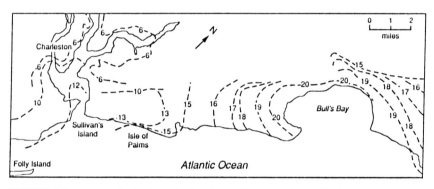

FIGURE 1. Storm surge levels along the South Carolina coast (from FEMA).

TABLE 1
Storm surge tidal elevation affecting the South Carolina coast (1893-1979)
(from Jordan et al., in press.)

Storm	Date	Area	Maximum Storm Tide (Ft)
27-28	Aug. 1893	St. Helena, Hilton Head	20
13	Oct. 1893	Georgetown	13
25-26	Sept. 1894	Charleston	10
2	Oct. 1898	Lower coast	14
27-28	Aug. 1911	Charleston, Beaufort	12
11-15	Aug. 1940	Entire coast	13
17	Sept. 1945	Parris Island	9
15	Oct. 1947	Parris Island	9-12
15	Oct. 1954	Upper coast ("Hazel")	17-18
9	July 1959	Bulls Bay ("Cindy")	10
29	Sept. 1959	Lower coast ("Gracie")	8-9
4-5	Sept. 1979	Charleston ("David")	8-9

caused relatively little damage by comparison (NRC, 1986). South Carolina did not have the "benefit" of realizing the ineptitude of their coastal building practices so that the damage inflicted by Hurricane Hugo was devastating. However, many of the newer houses showed markedly less damage where FEMA standards were adopted and adhered to (Wang, 1990).

STORM SURGE

Many of the tide gauges along the South Carolina coast were destroyed by storm waves during Hurricane Hugo's passage. Fortunately, the tide gauge at Charleston operated throughout the event, recording a maximum elevation of 12.9 feet. A plot of the predicted tide compared to the observed elevations graphically illustrates the pronounced rise of the water on the night of September 21 (Figure 2). The tide gauge data show that the storm surge rapidly increased as the hurricane moved onshore with the peak surge occurring to the right of the storm tract (Figure 1). In South Carolina a typical 100-year storm surge is in the range of 13 to 15 feet (see FEMA Flood Insurance Rate Maps), certainly qualifying Hurricane Hugo as such an event. There was little wave data available, but offshore deep-water readings at NOAA NDBC stations indicated a maximum height of 28 feet (E. Meindl, written comm., 1990).

The average elevation of the low country in coastal South Carolina is about 10 feet above mean sea level. The outer barrier islands had average elevations less than this amount, with only 5 feet or less elevations near the bayside. This means that

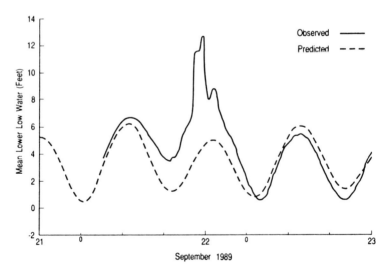

FIGURE 2. Observed and predicted tidal elevations at Charleston, S.C. on September 21-22, 1989 relative to mean lower low water (from NOAA-NOS, 1989).

most of the barrier surface was totally under water during the height of the storm surge. The mainland in this area is all part of the low-lying coastal plain, which gently slopes up to an elevation of approximately 20 feet near U.S. Route 17 (Figure 1). Driftlines of debris and floatables were found across this road just north of Bulls Bay, indicating the landward extent of saltwater flooding. The best data acquired by FEMA for the determination of surge heights for the plotting of isolines across the flooded area were the many houses on the developed barrier islands and inland mainland area. Inside water marks are considered good sources of water elevation information as the buildings act as stilling wells. There is an extensive amount of information on the storm surge level from which Figure 1 was compiled by FEMA personnel and contractors; this data set is available elsewhere (Gee and Jenson, 1989).

The large storm surge generated by Hurricane Hugo is due largely to the wind set-up (120 km sustained onshore winds aloft, which literally pushes and piles the water up onshore) and the low atmospheric pressure of the storm (934 mb) at landfall (termed the inverse barometer effect). Rainfall was rather light during the onslaught of this tropical storm so that flash floods and the normally higher water levels in rivers, such as the Cooper and Ashley that surround Charleston, were not a problem. Instead, the heavy rainfalls fell several days later causing extensive interior damage to houses that had their roofs sheared off by the high wind gusts or damage from tree fall.

The height of the storm surge, which varied along the South Carolina coast, is a good index of the damage wrought by this hurricane. The most southerly area to experience severe destruction was Folly Beach where the surge was 12 feet above MSL (Figure 1). Islands further south (Kiawah and Seabrook) experienced only minor surge-related damage although wind-inflicted losses on the backside of the storm were still significant. As previously mentioned, the highest surge and most intense waves and winds occurred to the right of the storm path. Fortunately, this immediate area (Bulls Bay) was largely undeveloped, but just to the north at Garden City and Pawleys Island damage was particularly severe to pre-FIRM houses of inadequate construction according to FEMA's standards for flood-prone areas (Wang, 1990). The surge continued to decrease northward toward southeastern coastal North Carolina — the northward limit of wave and surge damage. The degree of erosion also tapered off toward the Grand Stand where the most heavily developed portion of South Carolina exists at Myrtle Beach (Stauble et. al., 1990).

BEACH EROSION

Ground reconnaissance and aerial surveys were made of the South Carolina coast from the North Carolina border to Folly Island. The beaches receded markedly and complete dune lines were eroded away along much of the study area. The damage to beachfront houses was extensive on many of the barrier islands near the storm track (e.g., Pawleys, Sullivans, and Follys). It should be noted, however, that the true erosional potential of this Class IV hurricane was not realized because of the rapid forward motion of the storm (24 mph, which is over twice the normal rate of progression).

Further south at Garden City, the island was totally overwashed, resulting in massive destruction of houses along this critically low and narrow barrier beach. Overwash sand was transported 400 feet landward on average. Damage at nearby Pawley's Island was also catastrophic, particularly on the south end of the island where a temporary inlet was cut through the barrier. Houses were floated from the island across the marsh and onto the mainland in the 18 foot high storm surge (Figure 1). The two inlets generated by Hurricane Hugo were closed artificially by the U.S. Army Corps of Engineers.

Folly Beach experienced considerably more and extensive damage as compared to the other barrier island communities, in spite of the fact that it was on the weaker (south) side of the storm center. The beach at Folly has been subjected to long-term erosion, perhaps averaging 2 to 4 feet per year historically (Eiser and Jones, 1989), so that it was already critically narrow before storm occurrence. Folly Island is considered to be relatively stabilized, but subject to dramatic storm-induced erosion. A 1940 hurricane caused an average recession of 75 feet along the beachfront, and in 1959 hurricane erosion varied between 35 and 50 feet (U.S. Army Corps of Engineers, 1965). In the process a complete row of houses have been lost in the last 50 years.

Prior to the advent of Hurricane Hugo, there was essentially no beach along the developed portion of Folly Island (Figure 3). Residents had resorted to dumping

FIGURE 3. Pre-storm (July 1989) conditions at Folly Island, showing the limited dry beach area (courtesy of Mr. Tony Pratt).

large stones and concrete rubble on their beaches to form riprap revetments so that the shore was heavily armored. These preparations were largely ineffective as the high surge allowed the storm waves to overtop these coastal engineering structures and inflict heavy damages to the beachfront houses.

The Atlantic House, a local landmark and popular seafood restaurant on Folly Beach, was completely destroyed by Hurricane Hugo (Figure 4). In actuality, a much smaller hurricane could have claimed this building as the restaurant was sitting on piles fully in the ocean water during normal tides. The incessant erosion had gradually whittled away the beach so that a perched ramp over the water was necessary in order to even reach this restaurant. While the hurricane surely swept away the building, it was the long-term erosion that set it up for eventual destruction (Leatherman and Moller, 1990).

The importance of acquiring historical shoreline change data and applying this information to establish building setback lines was well illustrated by the relative damage to beachfront houses in the affected area. The differences in sustained damage at Isle of Palms (north of Charleston and eye of hurricane, maximum average storm surge of 12 feet) was striking. While there was extensive damage at Isle of Palms due to inundation of the island, beachfront houses were generally protected by a wide beach and sand dunes. This storm buffer zone serves its purpose well with damage concentrated where the beaches were narrow and dunes small to absent. The building practices at Isle of Palms were generally consistent with shoreline dynamics and most damage was inflicted upon pre-FIRM houses sitting on grade.

Unreinforced concrete block houses were particularly susceptible to destruction in the V-zone (floodplain subject to high velocity wave action) as often no more than a few blocks of the whole house could be found still attached after the storm. These ill-suited houses appeared to have been "blow-out" by the storm surge and superimposed hurricane-generated waves (Wang, 1990).

DISCUSSION

The post-storm field inspection revealed striking differences among the amount of destruction wrought by Hurricane Hugo to beachfront houses. The first requirement is that the houses be properly elevated on deep pilings above the storm surge to prevent flood damage. Secondly, proper construction and building standards must be utilized and enforced to prevent unnecessary damage. FEMA has done an excellent job in setting these standards through the Federal Insurance Administration (National Research Council, 1990) as evidenced by the high survivability of most new homes as compared to the pre-FIRM vintage houses.

The third requirement, which was not always adhered to, was establishment of a buffer zone of beach and dunes between the high energy surf and the beachfront buildings. Some residents, especially on Folly Beach, relied upon rubble and riprap for protection to no avail as the storm surge topped and hurricane-driven waves

FIGURE 4. Pre- and post-Hurricane Hugo photographs of the Atlantic House, a locally renowned seafood restaurant.

swept over the island, smashing the first line of houses. The generally better conditions on Sullivans Island by comparison largely reflected the setback of over 100 yards. Here the beach seems to be stable with a slight accretionary trend reported (Eiser and Jones, 1989).

The long-term annual erosion rate was a fairly good indication of the damage experienced when factoring in the overall surge levels. For example, the beaches at Pawley's Island and Garden City have been eroding at rates exceeding 1 foot per year (Kana, 1988); this factor of long-term erosion certainly contributed to the widespread destruction experienced on these barrier island communities. Lack of a sufficiently wide buffer zone coupled with severe storm-induced erosion resulted in catastrophic damage to beachfront homes.

Damage at Myrtle Beach was only moderate to light compared to that experienced further south. The downtown area was protected by a seawall, which although fractured, held in place. In general, the erosional scarp stopped short of the houses, and the debris line was clearly evident in the grassed yards and on the door steps.

The recent beach nourishment project at Myrtle Beach was actually a small-scale project, but this influx of sand was helpful to a degree in protecting the upland property. This sacrificial beach may have served its purpose, but now the town and state must contemplate a new beach nourishment and dune building project to restore adequate protection against future hurricanes.

The aftermath of Hurricane Hugo presents a good opportunity to reassess building practices. The general public has much difficulty in understanding *process* (the gradual, long-term erosion of beaches), and the total emphasis is placed on an *event* (hurricane) in terms of the resulting damage. Clearly, better data on long-term shoreline changes, public understanding and acceptance of this information, and the institutionalization of conformance standards for setbacks needs to be given top priority.

Only a year earlier (1988) the State of South Carolina passed the Beachfront Management Act to control unwise development along the open-ocean coast. Provisions of this new law included restrictions on new construction (must be setback at least 20 feet landward of the actual or estimated dune line) and redevelopment (if two-thirds of a beachfront building is damaged, it cannot be rebuilt). A quick survey of Folly Beach and some of the other barrier islands indicated that over 200 heavily damaged houses fell into this category, making lots valued up to $500,000 essentially worthless (non-buildable). The Mayor of Folly Beach claimed that 65 percent of the beachfront property has been lost as well as most of the town's tax base. Local citizens lamented that "we survived the storm, but can we survive the government"?

Following a disaster of this magnitude and extent, emotions run high and decisions based on stop-gap measures often supercede sound long-term planning. Millions of dollars were spent under emergency procedures to scrape sand off the beach to rebuild dunes with little consideration of sustainability. Perhaps more importantly, state legislators called for rescision of the Beachfront Management Act or at least a liberal interpretation of its provisions so that beachfront homes can be rebuilt in their pre-storm locations. Certainly this is a difficult time to enforce regulations that are viewed by the affected as "taking". The reality is that in many cases their property has been physically eroded away, and any reconstruction must be setback an appropriate distance based on the long-term erosion rate (Leatherman and Dean, 1991).

National attention is being focused on South Carolina in terms of their recovery from this devastating coastal storm and application of the Beachfront Management Act. Bowing to political pressure and lawsuits, the State legislators recently voted to allow some rebuilding in the zone of complete destruction, and new beachfront houses can be constructed in the location of storm-induced destruction. State officials claim that these changes represent a compromise between a complete ban on rebuilding and the overbuilding that would result if public choice was exercised. Clearly, the Beachfront Management Act as originally conceived was not implemented in the wake of Hurricane Hugo.

If we learned anything from this storm, it is that the hard decisions must be made before a catastrophe occurs and that the public must be aware of the consequences for post-storm construction. Delineation of an E(erosion) Zone and implementation of a new FEMA directive in utilizing building setback requirements (National Research Council, 1990) will go a long way to relieve the current dilemma and public misunderstandings.

CONCLUSIONS

Hurricane Hugo inflicted heavy damages along the South Carolina coast for three primary reasons. First, many of the outer barrier islands were subject to long-term, chronic beach erosion which set the stage for hurricane-driven waves to strike beachfront buildings directly with velocity. Secondly, many of the houses were built at ground level on these low-lying barrier islands; these pre-FIRM buildings were easily damaged by the waves (blown apart) and surge-induced currents (floated away). Finally, the high storm surge of 15 feet generated by this 100-year storm completely inundated the barrier islands, allowing the waves to overtop natural and artificially-constructed defensive structures. This deadly combination of hurricane processes and existing conditions caused massive destruction, but it is indeed fortunate that most coastal residents heeded the hurricane warning so that deaths were rare.

The response to hurricane landfall and resulting damage was fairly predictable — people could scarcely believe their eyes in terms of the destruction but in the same breath were ready to reoccupy their houses where still standing. Others less fortunate collected their house insurance from both the private and public sectors for wind and surge-related damage, respectively and were immediately ready to rebuild. The South Carolina Beachfront Management Act was eventually amended after considerable debate and political maneuvering so that "limited" rebuilding of beachfront houses in some totally devastated areas is being allowed. Clearly a hurricane of this magnitude is bound to inflict heavy damage, but States are yet to come to grips with the problem of beachfront development in highly vulnerable areas along receding shorelines.

The following general statements can be gleamed from this reconnaissance-level survey of the South Carolina coast in the aftermath of Hurricane Hugo:

1. Tourism is the number one source of State revenue, and coastal resources account for the lion's share of this income. Therefore, the State of South Carolina must be careful not to allow their beaches to be lost or compromised (despoiled) by unwise development practices.

2. Coastal erosion is a pervasive, on-going process along much of the South Carolina shore, and better long-term shoreline change data and public understanding of this information needs to be undertaken. The State should support FEMA's efforts to include erosion hazards (E-Zones) and building setbacks as a part of their National Flood Insurance Program (NFIP).

3. Shore protection devices installed by private property owners were shown in a dramatic fashion to be largely ineffective in preventing damage to their houses. Instead, this splay of rubble and riprap have essentially ruined the natural qualities of the beach and in some cases resulted in increased damage when projectiles were pushed into the adjacent structures (Figure 5). Well designed, engineered, and maintained seawalls, such as at Myrtle Beach and fronting the Holiday Inn on Folly Island, performed quite well. However, the high storm surge was able to sweep over the largely intact seawall on Folly Island, inflicting heavy damage on the first floor of the Holiday Inn.

FIGURE 5. Massive destruction of beachfront houses occurred at Folly Island in spite of emplacement of rubble and riprap.

4. The South Carolina Beachfront Management Act is based on the correct premise of disallowing development in damage-prone areas. It also addresses the difficult issue of redevelopment of lots where the previous house was destroyed or significantly damaged. These provisions need to be firmly based on long-term erosion rates and other technical and engineering requirements. However, some level of compensation should be made available to those property owners not allowed to rebuild, perhaps based on the fair-market value for the proportion of the remaining upland. Certainly the post-storm value will be considerably less than pre-storm assessments due to storm-induced land loss. This pro-active approach by the State will avoid expensive litigation with respect to the "taking" issue of private property and will allow the State to maintain an uncluttered public beach.

5. New construction within a designated zone, landward of the setback line, should be built on deep-seated pilings as movable structures. As erosion proceeds, these houses with the upgraded building standards will probably be able to survive future storms and eventually outcrop on the public beach. Texas has instituted on Open Beaches Act that forces homeowners to move their houses off the newly-declared public beach. While this prospect may seem to be several decades away, now is the time to set public policy, not when the problem is at hand.

6. South Carolina needs to come to grips with its current and possible future coastal development. Planning must be instituted on a community basis in terms of any protective action, such as beach nourishment. Also, a mutually agreed upon time frame of up to 50 years must be incorporated into planning efforts.

7. At the national level, FEMA needs to incorporate erosional trends into their flood insurance program as clearly stated in the 1990 National Research Council report "Managing Coastal Erosion". Failure to consider erosion as part of the natural flood hazard and overall shore vulnerability tends to undermine federal programs by allowing insurance rates to be set substantially below that for the actual risk and condoning inadequate construction regulations.

ACKNOWLEGEMENTS

This paper was supported by the U.S. National Academy of Sciences as part of the post-storm assessment of Hurricane Hugo's impact on the South Carolina coast. Dr. Leatherman was a member of the National Research Council team that surveyed the coast, and these findings will be incorporated into the forthcoming Academy report on Hurricane Hugo.

REFERENCES

Eiser, W.C. and C.P. Jones, 1989. Analysis of beach survey data along the South Carolina coast, South Carolina Coastal Council, Charleston, S.C., 56 pp.

Gee & Jenson, Inc., 1989. Preliminary post-storm survey report on Hurricane Hugo to FEMA, West Palm Beach, FL, 15 pp.

Hayes, M.O., 1979. Barrier island morphology as a function of tidal and wave regime, S. Leatherman, ed., Barrier Islands, Academic Press, N.Y., p. 1-27.

Jordan, L.W., R. Dukes, and T. Rosengarten, 1990. A history of storms on the South Carolina coast, South Carolina Sea Grant Consortium, Charleston, S.C., 143 pp.

Kana, T.W., 1988. Beach erosion in South Carolina, South Carolina Sea Grant Consortium, Charleston, S.C., 55 pp.

Leatherman, S.P. and R.G. Dean, 1991. Beach Erosion Rates and the National Flood Insurance Program, EOS Transactions, AGU, V. 72, p. 9.

Leatherman, S.P. and J.J. Moller, 1990. Hurricane Hugo's Impact on the South Carolina Beaches, Proceedings of the Skagen Symposium, Skagen, Denmark, p. 332-357.

National Ocean Service, 1989. Hurricane Hugo: Effects of water levels and storm surge recorded at NOAA-NOS level stations, NOAA, Rockville, MD.

National Research Council, 1986. Hurricane Diana, North Carolina, September 10-14, 1984, National Academy Press, Washington, D.C., 108 pp.

National Research Council, 1990. Managing Coastal Erosion, National Academy Press, Washington, D.C., 182 pp.

National Research Council, 1991. Hurricane Hugo, South Carolina, September 21, 1989, National Academy Press, Washington, D.C., in press.

Stauble, D.K., W.C. Eiser, W.A. Birkemeier, L.Z. Hales, W.C. Seabergh, 1990. Erosion Characteristics of Hurricane Hugo on the beaches of South Carolina, Shore and Beach, V. 58, p. 23-36.

U.S. Army Corps of Engineers, 1965, Interim hurricane survey of Folly Beach, South Carolina, House Document 302, 84th Congress.

Wang, H., 1990. Water and erosion damage to coastal structures — South Carolina coast, Hurricane Hugo, 1989. Shore and Beach, V. 58, p. 37-47.

Natural and Technological Disasters: Causes, Effects and Preventive Measures. Edited by
S.K. Majumdar, G.S. Forbes, E.W. Miller, and R.F. Schmalz. © 1992, The Pennsylvania Academy
of Science.

Chapter Twelve

FLOODS: A RIVER FORECAST CENTER PERSPECTIVE

WILLIAM B. REED[1]

Middle Atlantic River Forecast Center
228 Walnut Street
Harrisburg, PA 17108

INTRODUCTION

Flooding is a natural phenomenon that has helped shape the surface of our planet.
Essentially, flooding has created the low-lying areas adjacent to rivers and streams.
These areas historically are important for commerce, as sites for agriculture and
industry. As these areas developed, so did the need for accurate flood forecasting.
Forecasting is a difficult task because significant floods occur neither regularly (at
a set interval), nor frequently (compared to the average span of a human lifetime).

The National Weather Service's Middle Atlantic River Forecast Center (MARFC)
is responsible for preparing river forecasts (including flood forecasts) for twelve
major river basins in seven states. Additionally, with regard to floods, the MARFC
provides flash flood and headwater guidance, and technical support for local flood
warning systems.

Floods During Ancient and Modern Times

The shores of lakes and the low-lying lands adjacent to rivers and streams have
always been important to our species. It is no coincidence that the remains and arti-
facts of the first hominids and early peoples have been found along the shores of
ancient stream and lake beds. The floods that covered these primitive campsites
with sediment have preserved an important record of the past.

---

[1]Present address: National Weather Service Southern Region, Attn: Bill Reed, 819 Taylor
Street, Room 10A26, Fort Worth, TX 76102-6171

Later, at the dawn of civilization, two important centers of culture, Mesopotamia and Egypt, were located on and adjacent to the flood plains of major rivers. Here the sediments laid down by floods provided the fertile soils necessary for agriculture, and concurrently civilizations, to develop and flourish. Mesopotamia, literally the land between rivers, existed between the Tigris and Euphrates Rivers in what is present-day Iraq. As early as 3550 B.C., the plow was being used on the banks of the Euphrates and, subsequently, an elaborate system of canals was built for irrigation and to control floods *by a people who continuously lived in fear of the destructive force of flood waters.*[1] In Egypt, the annual floods of the Nile River enriched a long strip of land in an otherwise extremely arid region. It is this strip of land which fed the civilization of Egypt, including the builders of the pyramids and the pharaohs now buried within. However, the silts that once supplied the lower region during the late summer and autumn period of high flow are now trapped behind the Aswan High Dam.[2] (This dam was built in modern times to provide flood protection and to increase agricultural acreage through irrigation.)

During the founding of America, rivers and streams provided paths for exploration and commerce as well as water power for emerging industries. In Pennsylvania, Philadelphia was established on the banks of the tidal Delaware River, near the mouth of the Schuylkill River. Other major mid-Atlantic cities were established on the banks of rivers at the fall line, where free flowing rivers become tidal, e.g., Richmond on the James River, and Georgetown (now a part of Washington, D.C.) on the Potomac River. After a Revolutionary War, to aid the continued growth of our Nation, canal systems and improved waterways were constructed. By 1830, some 1,400 miles of canals were planned, under construction, or completed in Pennsylvania alone.[3]

It is this history of river and canal transportation, and the need for water power and supply, that led to a close association between early centers of commerce and the Nation's rivers. Unfortunately, this has also resulted in *a potential for loss of life and property* because of the developments on the rivers' flood plains. As the watersheds of our Nation's rivers and streams become more urban, flooding may become more frequent and severe.

The Role of the National Weather Service

The primary mission of the National Weather Service (NWS) is the protection of life and property. Hence, the basic functions of the NWS include:

1. the provision of forecasts and warnings of severe weather, flooding, hurricanes, and tsunami events;

2. the collection, exchange, and distribution of meteorologic, hydrologic, climatic, and oceanographic data and information; and

3. the preparation of hydro-meteorologic threshold values and other indices as guidance for determining when flooding might begin.

Flood mitigation strategies can be categorized as 1) structural techniques (e.g., dams and dikes) and 2) nonstructural techniques (e.g., local zoning ordinances to control development in flood plains and *flood forecasts and warnings).* Within the

Federal government, the NWS is the agency responsible for providing river and flood forecasts and warnings to the Nation. This mission is carried out by the NWS hydrologic service program. Within the NWS, hydrologic services are assigned to River Forecast Centers (RFCs), Weather Service Forecast Offices (WSFOs), and Weather Service Offices (WSOs) spread throughout the United States.

FLOODS IN PENNSYLVANIA

Floods in Pennsylvania are caused by several circumstances influenced by antecedent soil moisture conditions as well as physical setting (basin and channel characteristics). Usually, flooding is caused by rainfall associated with storm systems (large scale, localized, or tropical); but can also occur due to dam releases and failures, debris or ice jams, and high tides. In states with heavy winter snow packs, flooding can occur due to snow melt. In Pennsylvania, snow melt can contribute to the severity of a flood; however, flooding due to snow melt alone is unlikely.

The diverse geology and related topography of the Commonwealth of Pennsylvania provide a wide range of basin characteristics. Shape, slope, soil type, vegetative cover, and land use are a few of the basin characteristics that influence local rainfall-runoff relationships. *A change in these and other characteristics can cause a basin to respond differently than in the past; i.e., can cause flooding to occur more frequently or can cause areas to be inundated that historically have been safe.*

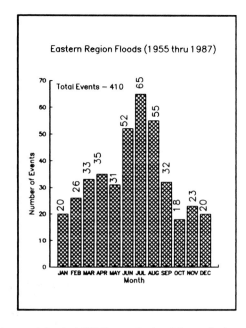

FIGURE 1. Floods by month for the NWS Eastern Region (16 states in the eastern United States).

Figure 1 presents the number of flood events within the NWS Eastern Region by month for the time period of 1955 through 1987. *Floods occur throughout the year, and can occur at any time — day or night — spring, summer, fall or winter. Flash floods can occur with little or no advanced warning.* A few severe mid-Atlantic floods that have occurred in modern times are:

The Johnstown Flood of May 1889. This western Pennsylvania flood, partially caused by the failure of a dam on the Little Conemaugh River, is generally considered *the worst flood disaster* to have occurred in the United States. A total of 2,209 people died.[4] River floods also occured at about the same time as the Johnstown Flood; e.g., the stage of the Susquehanna River at Harrisburg reached 26.8 feet on June 2, 1889. This is approximately 10 feet above the flood state of 17.0 feet.

The Floods of March 1936. Record-breaking flooding occurred throughout the northeastern United States caused by two storm systems (both with heavy rainfall) closely following one another — with snow melt also contributing to the runoff in the northernmost basins. A total of 80 people died in Pennsylvania alone.[5] As a result of the large-scale flooding throughout Pennsylvania (e.g., flooding within the Susquehanna River basin at Williamsport, Sunbury, and Harrisburg; and flooding within the Ohio River basin at the confluence of the Allegheny and Monogahela Rivers in Pittsburgh); the predecessor of the MARFC was established as a joint State and Federal endeavor 3 years later. The stage of the Susquehanna River at Harrisburg reached 30.3 feet on March 19, 1936. This is approximately 13 feet above flood stage. In the Eastern States, severe flooding also occurred within the Kennebec, Androscoggin, Saco, Merrimack, Thames, Connecticut, Housatonic, Delaware, Potomac, and James River basins.[5]

The Floods of May and July 1942. During May 1942, 3 weeks of frequent heavy rains in eastern Pennsylvania culminated in flooding within the Susquehanna (Lackawanna River) and Delaware River basins.[6] A total of 33 people died. The Lackawanna River basin (where 24 of the total 33 deaths occurred) was especially hard hit. (However, the Susquehanna River at Harrisburg reached only 16.3 feet on May 24, 1942; lower than the flood stage of 17.0 feet.)

During July 1942, a cloudburst caused severe flooding in the Susquehanna (Sinnemahoning Creek) and Ohio (Allegheny River) River basins. When the flooding in New York and Pennsylvania ended, a total of 15 people were dead.[7]

Agnes - The Floods of June and July 1972. Record-breaking flooding occurred in the middle Atlantic States caused predominately by Hurricane Agnes. A total of 117 deaths is attributed to the flooding, with 48 occurring in Pennsylvania.[8] To this day, Tropical Storm Agnes flooding is *the worst natural disaster* to have occurred in Pennsylvania.

The stage of the Susquehanna River at Harrisburg reached 32.6 feet on June 24, 1972. This is approximately 3 feet higher than 1936 and 6 feet higher than 1889. The peak flow (maximum discharge at flood crest) at Harrisburg was 1,020,000 cubic feet per second (cfs)[8], (Figure 2). Severe flooding also occurred within the Delaware, Potomac, James, and Ohio River basins[8].

Eloise - The Floods of September 1975. Several days of rainfall associated with

Tropical Storm Eloise resulted in flooding within the Susquehanna River basin. A total of 10 deaths is attributed to the flooding, with 6 occurring in Pennsylvania.[9] Record-breaking flooding (here exceeding Agnes) occurred within the upper Susquehanna River basin on the Chemung River in New York and northern Pennsylvania. The stage of Susquehanna River at Harrisburg reached 23.8 feet on September 27, 1975; a stage higher than in 1889, but lower than in 1936 and 1972.

The Johnstown Flood of July 1977. In July of 1977, the vicinity of Johnstown, Pennsylvania was once again the site of major flooding. This time at least 78 lives were lost; primarily along the Laurel and Solomon Runs and Conemaugh River.[10] Although rains associated with thunderstorms were widespread, a mesoscale quasi-stationary thunderstorm outflow boundary (due to subcloud evaporation) *and* regional topography is believed to have focused the heaviest rains in the vicinity of Johnstown.[10]

Juan - The Flood of November 1985. Several days of rainfall associated with Tropical Storm Juan resulted in flooding within the Potomac, James, and Ohio River basins. West Virginia was particularly hard hit with record-breaking flooding on the North and South Branches of the Potomac River. Within the Potomac River basin, a total of 43 people died.[11] However, the storm did not cause flooding within the Delaware and Susquehanna River basins. The water year (October 1, 1985 to September 30, 1986) extreme for the Susquehanna River at Harrisburg (a stage of 18.5 feet) occurred 4 months later on March 16, 1986.

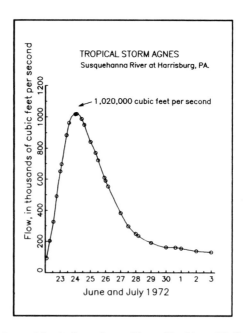

FIGURE 2. Flood Hydrograph for the Susquehanna River at Harrisburg, PA: Tropical Storm Agnes, June 20-25, 1972.

The Flash Flood of May 1986. Near Etna in western Pennsylvania, no flow occurs within Little Pine Creek (a tributary to the Allegheny River) on many days. However, on May 30, 1986 a flash flood caused the stage of the creek to be greater than 10 feet, corresponding to a maximum discharge of 7,190 cfs.[12] Nine deaths are attributed to this extreme localized event.

EFFECTS OF CHANGING LAND USE

Although considerable attention has been directed to the effects of urbanization on watershed runoff characteristics, a recent study by Reed[13] *illustrates the effects of changing land use over 300 years on the hydrology and flood potential of Valley Creek* (a watershed of 23 square miles — located approximately 20 miles west of Philadelphia). In this study, land use was divided into five major phases:

Phase I. Pre-1700s. When the watershed was heavily forested, the stream flow of Valley Creek was very different than it is today. Under these conditions, soil infiltration rates were high and watershed runoff was dominated by subsurface (interflow) processes. Overland flow, which conveys precipitation to stream channels more rapidly than subsurface flow, was probably less common. Thus, *peak discharges associated with precipitation were of lesser magnitude and severe flooding was less frequent than it is today.* In contrast, the base flow of Valley Creek was greater, being fed by larger soil moisture and ground water reserves during dry seasons. Because the magnitude of peak flows associated with precipitation were smaller, the stream channel was presumably neither as deep nor as wide as it is today. An estimate of the 2-year peak discharge (resulting from a 24-hour rainfall of 3.2 inches) for near the end of this phase is 350 cfs.

Phase II. 1700 to 1776. As the colonists moved into the watershed they cleared a small portion of the valley floor for agriculture. An estimate of this clearing could be as high as 20 percent[14] or as low as 4 percent[15] of all available land. Such a change in land use likely had a relatively mild impact upon watershed condition. This is because the areas cleared probably had very mild slopes and productive soils (well-drained, highly permeable loams), and were not major sources of runoff even after clearing. An estimate of the 2-year peak discharge for near the end of this phase is 400 cfs.

Phase III. 1800s. As deforestation continued over the next century, resulting in 40 to 50 percent of the watershed deforested[15], the hydrology and geomorphology of Valley Creek changed noticeably. For the first time, towns — as we know them — were founded[16]. The main factors causing the presumed change in the hydrology and geomorphology of Valley Creek was a significant loss in vegetative and soil cover. The reduced infiltration of impacted soils would favor overland flow. This change resulted in both a significant increase in peak flows and a significant decrease in base flows. *Initially, severe flooding occurred more frequently.* Eventually, the stream channel increased its capacity to convey larger flows by becoming wider and deeper. An estimate of the 2-year peak discharge for near the end of this phase is 800 cfs.

Phase IV. 1900 to 1985. During this phase, the effect of continued deforestation and the conversion of marginal agricultural lands to other purposes, began to severely threaten the natural and cultural resources of the watershed. The amount of developed land in Chester County doubled from 1970 to 1985[17].

At least one historically perennial tributary to Valley Creek lost its base flow due to the construction of a planned community. Base flow is the sustained or fair-weather runoff resulting from subsurface processes (groundwater runoff and delayed interflow). Such a severe response to changing land use occurs when a large percentage of the watershed becomes impervious. This change results in reduced infiltration and greater storm runoff. Also, peak flows associated with storms become larger than in the past as the watershed's response to rainfall becomes flashier due to a shortened time of concentration.

Even for moderately developed watersheds, runoff volumes may be increased by more than 50 percent and time of concentrations may be decreased by as much as 50 percent — particularly if extensive drainage "improvements" are made[18]. An estimate of the 2-year peak discharge for near the end of this phase is 1,450 cfs.

Phase V. 1985 to possibly the year 2000. In general, only the least productive soils and steeper slopes are still forested[16]. Although agriculture and woodlands are the two largest land use categories in Chester County, these land uses have decreased the most since 1970[17]. The conversion of marginal and prime agricultural lands to corporate parks and isolated estates may actually improve the previous watershed

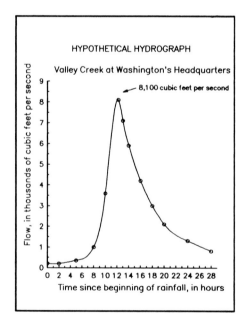

FIGURE 3. Hypothetical Flood Hydrograph for Valley Creek at George Washington's Headquarters: 100-year storm.

condition by reducing peak flows and sediment loads through best management practices (BMPs). However, the watershed's true potential will likely only be achieved through the establishment of a watershed committee or advisory board. *Without proper stormwater management, peak discharges will increase as the impervious area within the watershed increases.*[9] An estimate of the 2-year peak discharge for near the end of this period is 1,350 cfs (assuming that BMPs are implemented). Without proper stormwater management, an estimate of the 2-year peak discharge is 2,800 cfs; almost twice the discharging of the previous phase.

The hydrograph in Figure 3 illustrates the response of Valley Creek watershed to 7.2 inches of rainfall in 24-hours at the end of Phase V. This hydrograph "shape" is typical of flash floods, i.e., the peak occurs "abruptly" after the beginning of the storm, i.e., the peak occurs within hours after the beginning of the precipitation (Figure 3) instead of days after (Figure 2).

Whereas during this phase hydrologic conditions may improve (assuming that stormwater runoff will be better managed), channel conditions (unless otherwise altered) will decline. This decline is because the stream channel is still adjusting to previous changes in watershed conditions (i.e., the channel is just beginning to respond to increased flows resulting from changes that occurred during the previous phase). Unfortunately, in the East, urbanization following years of previous land use changes often results in fluvial systems that resemble those of the desert Southwest.

RIVER FORECASTING

As mentioned earlier, providing accurate flood forecasts is a difficult task because significant floods occur neither regularly nor frequently. However, recent advances in data collection, transmittal, and management, and in radar and computer technology, have made the completion of this formidable task more timely and easier for hydrologists and other professionals.

In general, modern river (and flood) forecasting requires the sequential completion of several tasks:

1. the collecting of data, e.g., air temperature, precipitation amounts, and river stages,

2. the transmittal of data from observers, data loggers, or data platforms,

3. the quality control of received data,

4. an estimate of future precipitation, e.g., quantitative precipitation forecasts (QPFs),

5. an evaluation of this information by using river forecast models of empirical and theoretical methods to collectively simulate past, present, and future hydrologic conditions,

6. an adjusting of selected values and parameters by the forecaster (based on physical processes) to improve the modeling of existing and future conditions; step 5 is then repeated (step 5 and 6 may be repeated several times),

7. an evaluation by the forecaster of all available information, including the final results of step 5,

8. the preparation of quantitative and narrative forecast statements, and

9. the distribution of these statements.

This sophisticated process may be completed once or several times per day depending on the frequency of data collection, the limitations imposed by the various techniques used within the river forecast system, and the needs of the user. Additionally, if supplemental river forecasts are required, manual procedures can be used to circumvent data requirements and other restrictions imposed by computerized river forecast systems. However, forecasts prepared by manual procedures can be unreliable and imprecise.

MARFC Precipitation and River Gaging Network

The precipitation and river gaging network currently used by the MARFC consists of more than 700 precipitation and 200 river stage reports. The reports include manual observations (NWS personnel, volunteers, and others), automated data loggers (DARDCs, LARCs, Telemarks, etc.), radio telemetry gages (ALERT and IFLOWS), and satellite-relayed data collection platforms (GOES). Redundancy is intentionally a part of the river gaging network with approximately a third of the stations monitored by more than one means. Such redundancy insures that crucial data are received in the event of equipment failure, and simplifies quality control.

National Weather Service River Forecast System

The National Weather Service River Forecast System (NWSRFS) is used by the MARFC to evaluate the influx of data from the precipitation and river gaging network and to prepare river forecasts for twelve major river basins in seven states. The NWSRFS is a nationally supported system of computer programs, data bases, and documentation that provides the forecaster with the techniques needed to produce river forecasts. The forecaster can pick and choose among the available techniques to adapt the system for local hydrologic and climatic conditions.

Generally, runoff based on actual and forecast rainfall is estimated for local watersheds by using rainfall-runoff models, and supplementary runoff due to snow melt is estimated from snow models. Then the flows from headwater points and local watersheds are estimated based on unit hydrographs, and future headwater stages are determined from stage-discharged relationships. The unit hydrograph is the signature of a watershed based on 1 unit of runoff (resulting from 1 inch of effective rainfall, "unit depth," uniformly distributed over the basin during the specified time period). The time period of the unit hydrograph is the time in which the 1 unit of runoff occurs. Next, future downstream flows are estimated by using hydrologic or hydraulic routing, and future downstream stages are determined from stage-discharge or crest-stage relationships. These future stages are then evaluated by the forecaster and a forecast is prepared. Prior to modern computers, these computations were extremely time consuming. However, *the entire river forecasting process (from data collection to forecast statement) can now be accomplished in less than 4 hours.*

The NWS has also developed a dam-break model to assist in forecasting downstream flooding (time and inundation) due to dam failure. However, the simplified version of this model for desk-top and hand-held microcomputers is used autonomously, i.e., the dam-break model is not currently a component of the NWSRFS.

Forecast Products and Their Dissemination

Generally, each forecast statement prepared by a RFC is transmitted to the appropriate Hydrologic Service Area (HSA) — assigned to a WSFO or WSO — by using the Automation of Field Operations and Services (AFOS) network. One of the principle roles of the HSA is to distribute these forecasts to the public. To avoid confusion, strict adherence to NWS policy is followed by the RFC and HSA when selecting a heading to identify the type of product being transmitted or issued.

Once a forecast is prepared, it is distributed to the public or other users. *Within the Federal Government, the NWS has the exclusive responsibility for providing flood forecasts and warnings to the general public.* Other Federal agencies may prepare forecasts for their own needs.

Depending on current and developing hydro-meteorologic conditions, the NWS may release a *Watch* (an event is possible but not certain), *Warning* (an event is forecast or in progress at a specific location), or *Statement* (with regard to floods, a statement follows a watch or warning to provide the most recent information) for the following types of events:

Flash Floods. This type of flooding occurs quickly (generally in less than 6 hours) after the *beginning* of the causative event, e.g., heavy rainfall, dam failure, or sudden release from an ice jam.

Small Stream Floods. Flooding of small streams can also occur quickly — so quickly as to preclude specific stage forecasts. The NWS issues Flood Watches / Warnings for county-level zones when small stream flooding is a threat, or forecast to occur.

Urban Floods. The flooding of streets, underpasses, or low-lying areas from other than rivers or streams (e.g., flooding caused by clogged storm drains). This type of flooding should not be confused with other types of flooding in urban areas.

Headwater Floods. This term is used to indicate flooding at the headwater of major rivers or their tributaries. Usually for these locations, specific stage forecasts are prepared with limited knowledge of upstream river or stream conditions. Accurate headwater forecasting requires an accurate description of ambient watershed conditions and an accurate description of the expected areal distribution, duration, intensity, and timing of forecast precipitation.

Main Stem Floods. This term is used to describe flooding along major rivers far downstream of headwater and tributary forecast points. Here the forecaster has the advantage of knowing previous and current conditions upstream, and usually has the time to change the forecast after conditions evolve. For these sites it is also possible to provide more forecast lead time, the time from the causative event (e.g., heavy rainfall) to when flooding begins. Traditionally, the accuracy of these types of forecasts has been better than the accuracy of the "one shot" forecasts for head-water points.

OTHER FLOOD-RELATED NATIONAL WEATHER SERVICE ACTIVITIES

Other flood-related NWS activities include:
1. local flood warning system (e.g., ALERT and IFLOWS) technical support (advice on system design including software, equipment, and site selection, data availability, radio path analysis, and the calibration of models), and
2. the preparation of flash flood and headwater guidance.
These self help projects provide local communities and other political entities with the assistance and information required to provide site-specific forecasts and warnings (in real-time) for situations where more standard flood forecasting techniques may be inadequate (e.g., small watersheds or headwater areas subject to flash floods).

Local flood warning systems can be either simple or complex. An example of a simple system is one consisting of an automatic stream gage that sets off an alarm when a preset water level is exceeded. An example of a more complex system is one consisting of a network of automatic self-reporting river and precipitation gages that is evaluated in real-time by a system operator using computer models on a microcomputer.

Local warning systems can also be manual; i.e., after data is collected manually and transmitted by telephone, it is evaluated by using manual procedures such as tables, graphs, and charts. Such procedures often require the use of flash flood and headwater guidance products (e.g., advisory rainfalls, final indexes, and average antecedent precipitation indexes) produced by the appropriate RFC. At the MARFC, the flash flood guidance is updated daily and the headwater guidance is updated twice a week.

MODERNIZATION OF THE NATIONAL WEATHER SERVICE AND FLOOD FORECASTING

The National Weather Service is currently undergoing a modernization and restructuring that — by the end of this decade — will result in the United States having *indisputably* the most advanced weather and flood forecasting system in the world. In the near future, highly trained NWS personnel will have a versatile array of advanced technologies readily available for rapid observation, analysis, and communication of information relating to hydrologic and meteorologic events. The Next Generation Weather Radar (WSR-88D), which combines Doppler radar with advanced computer processing, is only one of the new technologies that will result in earlier, more reliable warnings of flash floods, the number one cause of weather-related deaths. The Automatic Surface Observing Systems (ASOS),

WSR-88D, and the Advanced Weather Interactive Processing System (AWIPS) will greatly enhance the NWS hydrologic service program. The precipitation data provided by ASOS (an envisioned modern network of approximately 1000 automatic ground-based sensor sites) and WSR-88D will allow an almost instantaneous analysis of developing hydro-meteorologic events by using the powerful computational and interactive capabilities of AWIPS.[20]

After modernization and restructuring, the RFCs will be collocated with Weather Forecast Offices (WFOs). The WFOs will handle the releases to the public of all forecast products, including flood forecasts and warnings. Primarily, this will be accomplished, as it is today, through the use of NOAA Weather Radio, NOAA Weather Wire, Commercial Radio, TV and Cable.

An integral component of the RFCs will be Hydrometeorological Analysis and Support (HAS) groups that will serve as a bridge between the RFC and the WFO collocated at each facility. The HAS group can be viewed as the catalyst for improved hydro-meteorologic services and products.[20] An important HAS function will be to facilitate and refine the QPF provided to the RFC by the WFO. It is anticipated that these improved basin-specific precipitation forecasts will provide the forecaster with better lead times for the issuance of flood forecasts and warnings.

DISCUSSION / CONCLUSION

Population growth, urbanization, suburban sprawl, and other population trends and land use changes will cause an increased demand for accurate flood and flash-flood forecasts in the near future. Utilized effectively, recent advances in data collection, transmittal, and management — and recent advances in radar and computer technology — will provide a modern weather service with the tools to meet these and other hydro-meteorologic needs.

ACRONYMS

ALERT	Automated Local Evaluation in Real Time
AFOS	Automation of Field Operations and Services
ASOS	Automatic Surface Observing Systems
AWIPS	Advanced Weather Interactive Processing System
BMP	Best Management Practice
DARDC	Device for Automatic Remote Data Collection
GOES	Geostationary Operational Environmental Satellite
HAS	Hydrometeorological Analysis and Support
HSA	Hydrologic Service Area

IFLOWS   Integrated Flood Observing and Warning System
LARC   Limited Automatic Remote Collection System
MARFC   Middle Atlantic River Forecast Center
NOAA   National Oceanic and Atmospheric Administration
NWS   National Weather Service
NWSRFS   National Weather Service River Forecast System
QPF   Quantitative Precipitation Forecast
RFC   River Forecast Center
WFO   Weather Forecast Office
WSFO   Weather Service Forecast Office
WSO   Weather Service Office
WSR-88D   Next Generation Weather Radar (Doppler)

REFERENCES

1. Brinton, C., J.B. Christopher, and R.L. Wolf. 1971. *A History of Civilization, Prehistory to 1300, Fourth Edition.* Prentice-Hall, Inc., Englewood Cliifs, NJ, 383 pp.
2. Goudie, A. 1982. *The Human Impact, Man's Role in Environmental Change.* The MIT Press, Cambridge, MA, 316 pp.
3. Shank, W.H., T.F. Hahn, T.G. Hobbs, and R.S. Mayo. 1982. *Towpaths to Tugboats, A History of American Canal Engineering.* The American Canal and Transportation Center, York, PA, 72 pp.
4. U.S. Department of the Interior. 1985. *The National Parks: Index 1985.* U.S. Government Printing Office, Washington, DC, 111 pp.
5. Grover, N.C. 1937. *The Floods of March 1936, Part 3. Potomac, James, and Upper Ohio Rivers.* U.S. Geological Survey Water-Supply Paper 800. U.S. Government Printing Office, Washington, DC, 351 pp.
6. PA Department of Forest and Waters. 1942. *The Floods of May 1942 in the Delaware and Lackawanna River Basins.* Commonwealth of Pennsylvania, Harrisburg, PA, 29 pp.
7. PA Department of Forest and Waters. 1943. *A Flood of July 1942 in the Upper Allegheny River and Sinnemahoning Creek Basins.* Commonwealth of Pennsylvania, Harrisburg, PA, 35 pp.
8. Bailey, J.F. and J.L. Patterson. 1975. *Hurricane Agnes Rainfall and Floods, June-July 1972.* U.S. Geological Survey Professional Paper 924. U.S. Government Printing Office, Washington, DC, 403 pp.
9. U.S. Department of the Army. 1976. *Tropical Storm Eloise, 23-27 September 1975; Post Flood Report.* Baltimore District Corps of Engineers, Baltimore, MD, 40 pp.

10. Hoxit, L.R., R.A. Maddox, C.F. Chappell, and S.A. Brua. 1982. *Johnstown-Western Pennsylvania Storm and Floods of July 19-20, 1977.* U.S. Geological Survey Professional Paper 1211. U.S. Government Printing Office, Washington, DC, 68 pp.

11. Scatena, F.N. 1986. *Floodplain Reconnaissance Study, November 1985 Flood, Potomac River Basin.* Interstate Commission on the Potomac River Basin, Rockville, MD, 20 pp.

12. Lescinsky, J.B., M.B. Coll, Jr., and R.W. Siwicki. 1989. *Water Resources Data, Pennsylvania, Water Year 1988, Volume 3. Ohio River and St. Lawrence River Basins.* U.S. Geological Survey Water-Data Report PA-88-3. U.S. Department of Interior, Harrisburg, PA, 217 pp.

13. Reed, W.B. 1990. *Qualitative Evaluation of the Effects of Changing Watershed Land Uses on the Hydrology, Channel Morphology and Historical Uses of Valley Creek, Valley Forge National Historical Park, Pennsylvania.* U.S. National Park Service Technical Report NPS / NRWRD / NRTR-90 / 08. U.S. Department of Interior, Fort Collins, CO, 48 pp.

14. Brush, G.S. 1989. Abstract: A history of sediment and metal influxes in some Mid-Atlantic estuaries. *Eos,* October 24, 1989.

15. Defries, R.S. 1986. *Effects of Land-Use History on Sedimentation in the Potomac Estuary, Maryland: A Water-Quality Study of the Tidal Potomac River and Estuary.* U.S. Geological Survey Water-Supply Paper 2234-K. U.S. Government Printing Office, Washington, DC, 23 pp.

16. Chester County. 1982. *Chester County Open Space and Recreation Study.* Chester County Planning Commission, and Chester County Parks and Recreation Department, West Chester, PA, 364 pp.

17. Chester County. 1988. *Chester County Land Use Plan.* Chester County Planning Commission, West Chester, PA, 107 pp.

18. Schueler, T.R. 1987. *Controlling Urban Runoff: A Practical Manual for Planning and Designing Urban BMPs.* Metropolitan Washington Council of Governments, Washington, DC, 201 pp.

19. Sloto, R.A. 1988. *Effects of Urbanization on Storm-Runoff Volume and Peak Discharge of Valley Creek, Eastern Chster County, Pennsylvania.* U.S. Geological Survey Water-Resources Investigations Report 87-4196. U.S. Government Printing Office, Washington, DC, 32 pp.

20. NOAA. 1989. *Hydrometeorological Service Operations for the 1990's.* Office of Hydrology Document. National Weather Service, Silver Spring, MD, 166 pp.

Natural and Technological Disasters: Causes, Effects and Preventive Measures. Edited by
S.K. Majumdar, G.S. Forbes, E.W. Miller, and R.F. Schmalz. © 1992, The Pennsylvania Academy
of Science.

Chapter Thirteen

NATURAL CALAMITIES DUE TO FLOODING AND CYCLONIC STORMS: BANGLADESH

NAZRUL I. KHANDAKER

Geology Department
Lafayette College
Easton, PA 18042-1768

INTRODUCTION

Bangladesh, meaning land of Bangladeshis, is a small country with an area of 88,000 square kilometers and home for 110 million people. Bangladesh, formerly known as East Pakistan, became an independent and sovereign country on December 16, 1971. It is surrounded by India to the east, north, and west. Burma fringes a narrow tip of the southeast border while the south is open to the Bay of Bengal (Figure 1). Bangladesh is located between 20° 35′ N to 26° 40′ N latitudes and forms a part of the subtropical Asia with semihumid climate. The annual rainfall ranges from 130 cm to 575 cm; however it can reach up to 800 cm in the northeastern region of the country. Most of the precipitation occurs during the monsoon season, May to October.

Bangladesh is a riverine country and forms a major portion of the Bengal Delta, one of the largest deltaic complexes in the world. The mighty Ganges-Brahmaputra drainage system, one of the largest in the world, is responsible for the delta-building activity. It is one of the most-densely populated countries in the world and, similar to other developing nations in southeast Asia, is overburdened with complex socioeconomic problems. In addition, Bangladesh is particularly frequently subjected to natural calamities due to flooding and cyclonic storms.

Currently, the country is constantly experiencing frequent catastrophic and high-magnitude flooding and cyclonic storm events. Warm, moist, maritime, airmasses associated with excessive precipitation cause severe local flooding. Sometimes daily precipitation can reach up to 50 cm and make it impossible for adequate drainage in an otherwise flat terrain. The total inability of the large rivers to contain very rapid and extremely high discharge from the upstream region causes severe flooding in this region. *Besides the rapidly growing demographic trend (almost 2 percent every year since 1970) and food shortage, these floods and cyclonic storms constitute the major national problem.* Nowadays, flood and cyclonic storm-induced disasters are becoming international crises since the country is unable to effective-

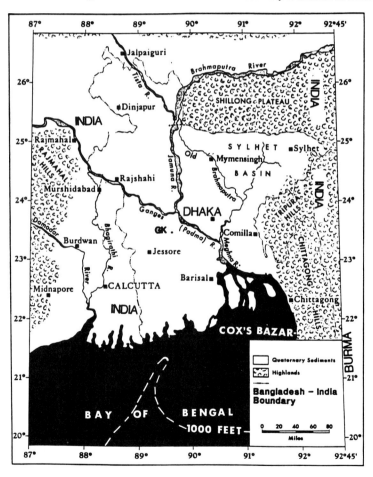

FIGURE 1. Physiographic map of Bangladesh and adjacent countries. Quaternary Sediments: mostly deltaic-floodplain sediments (younger than 1.5 million years); Highlands: composed of pre-Quaternary and older rocks. GK: Ganges-Kobadak Project. (With permission from Morgan & McIntire, 1959)

ly respond to these natural calamities alone. About 1/3 of the total country is annually flooded. Excessive and long-term flooding events, sometimes lasting for
several weeks, inundate almost 3/4 of the country (1973 and 1988). Similar flooding
happens in several regions in South Asia, but the effects are not always disastrous.
Ironically, without the annual deposition of organic-rich silts from the Ganges and
Brahmaputra Rivers, intensive rice and jute cultivation characteristic of the country would be impossible.[1]

CAUSES

The primary causes for excessive flooding and cyclonic storms in Bangladesh
can be attributed to several factors including, *climatic, geological, geomorphological, deforestation in the high Himalayas, and global warming trends.*

CLIMATOLOGICAL

The unique geographic situation of Bangladesh with respect to warm ocean water
of the Bay of Bengal in the south and Himalayan Mountain belt in the north provides a critical control on the monsoonal precipitation in the country. This monsoonal precipitation is largely due to the effect of excessive heating over the higher
Himalayas and inland deserts which force a strong onshore monsoon flow during
the summer. The fundamental driving mechanism of this circulation is differential heating. The inland temperature attains a maximum compared to the surface
ocean, which is relatively cooler and denser. The heated continental airmass having a lower density than cool ocean airmass results in an ascending current over
the land and an onshore flow in which denser ocean airmass pushes against the
lighter air inland. The magnitude of the ascending and onshore circulation of airmass is determined by the degree of heating of the higher Himalayas and inland
deserts. In addition, the close proximity of the region to the very warm surface waters
of the Bay of Bengal contributes very high moisture content to the onshore airmass.
As the warm moist air rushes inland it is forced to rise where it encounters the
topographic barrier posed by the mountains. The rising air mass cools, which results
in condensation, cloud development, and heavy rainfall. Orographic lifting coupled
with the development of cyclonic storms, produces tremendous rainfall intensity
which ultimately leads to flash flooding. Hence, flooding is an integral part of the
climate of Bangladesh largely because of its characteristic geography and
topography[2,3,4]

GEOLOGICAL

Geologically, Bangladesh is a very recent landform, emergent since Holocene
(10,000 years ago) time. Bangladesh constitutes about 80 percent of the Ganges-
Brahmaputra delta. It is generally a featureless plain with elevation ranging from
near sea-level to 10 m for most of the country. The southeastern and northern part

is dominated by an elevated region (175 m above mean sea-level). An enormous accumulation of deltaic to floodplain sediments, mostly less than 3.5 million years old, and on the order of 15,000 to 17,000 m thick, constitutes the basin-fill.

Geologically, most of the northwestern and southeastern regions of Bangladesh are neotectonically active (indicating current tectonic activity). Recent structural modification of these deltaic and floodplain sediments are expressed in the form of raised stream terraces, shifting stream courses, unique drainage patterns, and seismic activity (Figure 1). Two meters of Holocene uplift over an extent of more than 2000 km^2 in the northcentral region of Bangladesh has been documented by recent study.[5,6] This northcentral region is situated within the previously documented geologically active zone (Figure 1) which roughly follows the trend of the Jamuna-Padma-Meghna river system. This evidence points either to a subsiding basin or to a single major fault at depth.[5]

GEOMORPHOLOGICAL CONSTRAINTS

Drainage patterns and behavior

The present Brahmaputra River, west of the Madhupur Tract (Figure 1), now known as the Jamuna River, has shifted course dramatically during the recent history. During 1792 and about 1830, the Brahmaputra River, now known as the old Brahmaputra River, shifted westward about 100 km from the east of the Madhupur Tract. During higher flood events, overflow is still diverted into the old Brahmaputra and enables the two rivers to flow at the same level. Changes in the courses of the Ganges and Brahmaputra rivers across the northcentral region of Bangladesh during the last few hundred years can be attributed to faulting and resultant tilting of fault blocks. This remarkable channel shifting is accentuated by lateral migration with some minor channel switching and a prominent avulsion in the last 200 years.[5,7] Coleman (1969) concluded that the change in course took place gradually due to increased flood discharge, faulting, or a combination of both.[8] The avulsion (shifting) resulted in a maximum channel displacement of 100 km westward.

The unique nature of drainage patterns, especially complex braiding (characterized by extremely variable discharge, high width-depth ratio, easily erodible banks, and formation of sandbars within or across the main channel which results in the development of a network of interlacing channels separated by bars or islands) associated with most of the rivers in northcentral Bangladesh directly influence the flooding phenomenon. The characteristic channel pattern in the Brahmaputra River reflects the interaction of the hydrologic regime, sediment supply, grain size, and slope.[9]

Variable discharge

The Brahmaputra River is 2840 km long and drains an area of some 380,000 km^2

from Tibet to the Bay of Bengal. The maximum discharge recorded in 1984 (September 18) was 75,700 m^3/sec; the minimum discharge also in 1984 (February 20) was 3,950 m^3/sec.[9] The large variability in discharge results from the variable seasonal monsoon rains. High discharge condition may last for six to eight weeks and could cause prolonged overbank flooding. The overbank flood in 1973 had lasted for eight weeks. The Ganges-Brahmaputra river systems carry about 2 billion tons of sediments denuded from the higher Himalayas over Bangladesh.[9,10] Very high suspended sediment loads (4,544 ppm) characterize the Brahmaputra River.[11,12] High-sediment yield coupled with shifting courses and frequent bank collapse also trigger major flooding.

Formation of sandbars

Formation of sandbars, the large width and depth of the channel, and higher rate of bottom siltation exacerbates to the flood event during the monsoon periods. The unique development of sand bars due to high sediment-load and bank collapse along and within the channel provide an additional constraint on the flow-path. Morphologically, these sandbars constitute around 53 percent of all deposition within the main river.[9] Development of sandbars within the main channel drastically reduces the depth of the main channel, decreases the stream velocity, and promotes overbank flooding.

In addition, bottom siltation and clogging of city sewage or underground drainage networks by plastic bags or nondecomposible garbage were one of the reasons the city of Dhaka (Figure 1) was severely flooded in 1988.

DEFORESTATION

Extensive deforestation in the upstream areas is considered to be an integral factor in increasing the frequency and magnitude of flood events in Bangladesh.[13] Deforestation decreases infiltration and increases the runoff generated by any precipitation event, and therefore may lead to unprecedented flooding. Deforestation enhances loss of topsoil which in turn promotes siltation in riverbeds. Large-scale deforestation in Nepal (source of the Ganges) and Assam (upstream Brahmaputra) has been going on for several decades. In addition, within the territorial limit of Bangladesh, total forest area rapidly declined from 25 percent to a mere six percent in the last several decades.

Rapid urbanization, demand for more ploughable land, and reliance on wood as a convenient source for energy, all pose a dangerous threat on the rapidly perishing forest resources of the country. The adverse effect of deforestation on the ecology, particularly the declining population of the Royal Bengal Tiger in the Sunderban mangrove forest is well-known, and has been cited as one of the primary causes for the diminishing population of this royal beast.

GLOBAL WARMING

A very significant factor pertaining to frequent flooding in Bangladesh may be attributed to the global-warming connected with the greenhouse effect. A gradual warming trend is believed to be global in character, based on the average temperature records from 1800 to the present.[13] This warming trend, seems to be compatible with greenhouse scenarios predicted by computer simulations. The effect of global warming on the existing air-circulation and precipitation patterns, and characteristic vegetation zones could be far-reaching and can easily disrupt a wide range of human and natural systems. Other effects, especially rise in sealevel due to increased melting rates of glaciers in the mountainous region, can inundate a large portion of the low-lying areas. This would definitely be devastating for coastal regions of Bangladesh and Maldives[13].

A sea-level rise of ten meters would leave three quarters of Bangladesh permanently under water[1]. Furthermore, its effect could be devastating on crops and human settlement on low-lying coastal regions. Melting of glaciers in the high Himalayas coupled with unusual precipitation and rapid deforestation rates are believed to be the primary causes of unprecedented flooding in Bangladesh during late monsoon of 1988. This late monsoonal flood inundated almost the entire country for six weeks, caused loss of human lives (officially 2000 people died), and heavy damage to roads and highways, houses, autumn crops, and livestock. It is quite apparent that the recurrence interval of higher magnitude flood events is being shortened considering eight of the world's ten worst floods severely affected Bangladesh in the last century.[14]

CYCLONIC STORMS AND CAUSES

The most dramatic natural disasters in South Asia have been associated with cyclonic storms[1]. These cyclonic storms originate in the late summer over the oceans of southeast Asia when water temperatures considerably exceed 27°C, the critical minimum for tropical cyclones to form. Once formed, the storms travel across the Bay of Bengal, guided by the Upper Air Easterlies. The Bay of Bengal acts as a funnel, and if the curved path of the storm brings it across the coast of Bangladesh, the most populated parts of the flat islands, large-scale catastrophic disaster can occur[1]. Some of the flooding in Bangladesh owes its origin to the sea. Bangladesh is particularly susceptible to such floods because much of the terrain is less than 10 m in elevation above sea level.

Storm surges, associated with cyclones, are capable of raising sea level temporarily by three meters or more[1]. In 1970, 1988 and 1991, for example, this led to the inundation of coastal regions. This effect, known locally as *Gorki* or tidal bore, caused not only loss of life on a colossal scale but also long-term damage to agricultural land through salinization, The recent cyclonic storm happened on April 30, 1991, severely destroyed the seaside town of Cox's Bazar and nearby islands, where 95% of the houses were completely destroyed (Figure 1). These islands and cyclone-affected continental region, are home to ten million people. The cyclone had struck during a full moon and high tide. 100,000 fishermen had been out in the sea and became the victims of the voracious tidal bore. Official estimates put the death toll around 125,000. Ten million people remain homeless. Of the ten million people, four million are classified as "in immediate risk".[4]

Fishermen lost their precious and hard-earned fishing fleets. Nearly one-tenth of the country's population live in the area and helplessly experienced the merciless effects of the storm. Cyclonic winds reaching up to 230 km/hour levelled most of the mud and straw huts. Prior warning systems in the form of megaphones and beating drums were sounded. Fortunately, hours before the cyclone hit, several thousand people took shelter in some of the sophisticated cyclone shelters built on three-story-high columns.

Similar tidal-storm surges have also wreaked havoc in other parts of South Asia. Some of the atolls of the Maldives, situated in the southern Indian Ocean, have been completely inundated, resulting in total loss of life and destruction of the island habitat.[4] This recent crisis compares closely with the 1970 cyclone in Bangladesh that claimed 0.5 million lives. The catastrophic disaster of November 12, 1970 will long be remembered. Sea level rose by over two meters in close proximity to the low pressure zone and where onshore winds pile up water against the shore. The sea surge coincided with very heavy rain and hurricane winds. Cyclonic storm-induced wind speeds reaching up to 240 km/hour triggered a tidal wave of up to nine meters in height. This tidal wave approached the nearby densely populated, low-lying, coastal islands situated near the mouth of the Ganges delta. The early warning system for cyclones was largely ineffective, and, without the protection of a sea wall or shelter, tens of thousands of people had nowhere to flee. Official estimates put the death toll as high as half a million.[1]

CONSEQUENCES OF FLOODING

The disastrous effects of flooding on the country's economy, human lives, agriculture, communications, livestock, and properties are numerous. Encroachment of salt water associated with the 1970 and 1991 cyclonic storms into the coastal surface and subsurface water ruined drinking supplies and thousands of acres of rice crops which were almost ready for harvest. These coastal areas are well known for their shrimp farms, seafish, and salt industry. Contamination due to seabrine on these coastal sites is long-ranging and it might take several years before these areas can be profitably utilized again. Frequent failures to harvest or raise crops due to flood damage place the country on a tremendous hardship when there is not enough food to support the entire population in the first place. Very often, food grains stored in private sectors are damaged due to excessive flooding. Disruption of communications further worsens the situation. Most of the roads especially semi-paved or unpaved village roads which are the major link to the nearby towns or markets, are washed away and even make it extremely difficult to distribute relief goods to the outlying areas of the country. Diseases such as cholera, typhoid, and dysentery spread as epidemics and take a heavy toll on human lives. Extreme shortages of safe drinking water during flood stages also add to the epidemics.

LONG TERM SOLUTION

Flooding and cyclonic events and their resultant consequences in Bangladesh are clearly connected to several factors including *climatic, physiographic, geologic, demographic, global climatic change, and international situations*. Any long-range planning to address these natural hazards requires complete understanding of each of these critical components. Educating people about the havoc of cyclonic and flooding events, building sophisticated shelters, creating emergency food storage to circumvent any catastrophic situation, establishing a well-organized relief force, and implementing effective warning systems through radio and television, will perhaps, substantially reduce the loss of human life and livestock. Damage to drinking water, crops, shrimp cultivation, and salt pan are more difficult to overcome.

Currently, large-scale flood-prevention measures include the Ganges-Kobadak project (see Figure 1) situated in the north-central part of the country. The project is designed for flood control, irrigation, and drainage[15,16] This project, built in the 1960's in the Kushtia District, is fed by the water drawn from the Ganges River, the second largest river flowing into Bangladesh (the Brahmaputra being the largest). An intake channel receives pumped water from the Ganges River.

The Ganges-Kobadak project is also designed to partially help irrigate land during the drier months of February and March when the discharge through the Brahmaputra-Ganges system is the lowest (3,950 m^3/sec compared to 75,700 m^3/sec in September).[9] During the months of February - April, the north-central portion of Bangladesh faces a near drought condition when the surface runoff as well as precipitation is the lowest. Without adequate precipitation, aquifers in this region are not properly recharged. Groundwater pumping to meet the demand for water results in excessive drawdown and further worsens the situation. Eventually the underground water table drops deeper into the aquifer.

The initiation of this project has greatly improved the agricultural practices in the project area. Rice production, especially from high yield varieties (HYV) of rice, developed in the early 1960s, has been extremely fruitful. Other cash crops such as sugar cane, tobacco, wheat, and dal (lentils) also showed similar improved yields[17]

A successful implementation of this project will have a tremendous impact on the socioeconomic situation of the country. However, like some other waterprojects in Bangladesh, the Ganges-Kobadak project has its engineering as well as bottom-siltation problems. Nedeco (1983) estimated a net 30 percent water loss since its initiation and ascribed this to infiltration and ineffective operational procedures[15] Other significant geotechnical problems related to the projects are uneven distribution of water to the adjacent agricultural plots and rapid siltation within the intake channel. Creation of several secondary intake channels and building of earth dams along the channels have been recommended to overcome these geotechnical problems.[8] In addition, the expensive year round dredging will be a necessity for the successful implementation of this project.

Regional Water and Forestry Management Policy

Regional problems pertaining to waterpolicy and deforestation require effective participation of Bangladesh, Bhutan, China, India, and Nepal. This could be augmented by setting up a *multinational commission* to impose forestry management and water-flow regulations.[3,19] Bangladesh is trying to establish a regional water policy involving India, China, and Nepal. Complete participation and establishment of a multinational commission has yet to take place. So far, China has expressed its willingness for bilateral cooperation. In the interim, frequent dialogues between Bangladesh and India during the past several years have helped to ease the situation and a more congeniel water-treaty between the two countries seems very likely in the near future.

According to World Watch Paper 89, "an estimated 40 percent of the world's population depends for drinking water, irrigation, or hydropower on the 214 major river systems shared by two or more countries; 12 of these waterways are shared by five or more nations".[13] Since the Ganges-Brahmaputra waterways are primarily shared by India, Nepal, and Bangladesh, the downstream users, particularly Bangladesh, have no effective means to solve flood problems alone and have to depend on cooperation of the upstream countries. Political disputes pertaining to water use rights have long been a traditional problem and exist in virtually all parts of the world. Some of the critical components of these water disputes involve reduced water flow through dams constructed by upstream countries, water diversion, siltation of rivers, and flooding aggravated by deforestation and soil erosion.[13]

Any long-term measures directed towards preventing flood-induced calamities require utmost cooperation among the neighboring countries within a particular drainage basin. Equitable distribution of this precious water resource is extremely crucial in terms of developing agricultural products, and in the transporting and proper marketing of these goods.

Local preventive measures

Local preventive measures include detailed morphometric analyses of the major and tributary river systems draining the entire country. Channel shifting, intricate braiding patterns, high sediment load, rapid growth of sandbars along or within the channels, and easily erodible banks contribute much to the flood problem. Understanding the river evolutionary pattern and providing a long-term solution to this problem requires close interaction between disciplines such as geology, meteorology, and water engineering.

Currently, the first phase of a detailed *Quaternary Geology Project* on Bangladesh has been completed under the joint sponsorship of the United States Geological Survey and Bangladesh Geological Survey. Preliminary published data strongly indicate neotectonic activity along the north-central part of Bangladesh where the major river systems enter the country.[6] Incorporation of this geological data into the climatological and water engineering data will improve efforts to predict flash floods and to cope with the incoming flood situation. However, an absolute solution to this problem has to be of *bilateral or multilateral nature considering the unique geographic entities of Bangladesh.*

Rapid population growth, often cited as one of the primary causes in excessive loss of human lives, must also be considered in this context. In the last two decades, the population of Bangladesh has increased from 75 million in 1970 to 110 million in 1990. An increase of 35 million people over a period of 20 years has not only exerted tremendous pressure on the national economy, it has forced the farmers to utilize all the available land for rice production, irrespective of soil condition. Farmers lacking the knowledge regarding *crop patterns* and still using traditional agricultural practices are rendering some of the farmland *less productive.* This trend will be detrimental for the future food production in the country. Farmers need to be educated and made aware of this situation.

Increased rice production has not been able to keep up with rapidly changing demographic patterns. Current birth-control measures are semi-effective and a very strong birth-control campaign must be undertaken as a positive step towards minimizing untold human suffering.

Discouraging people from living on recent floodplains will be a *futile exercise* considering the present agro- and-socio-political system in Bangladesh. Building houses above the maximum flood event, construction of several reservoirs in the north-central part of Bangladesh, year round dredging of the major river systems and erecting earthen dams along the frequently threatened flood-prone regions will minimize the impact of flooding on the people. However, acquisition of land and availability of substantial amount of resources for the purpose of building reservoirs in the north-central part of Bangladesh remains a critical factor. External funding might improve the situation, yet relocation of thousands of people from the reservoir site to another locality will be an extremely difficult task to accomplish since there is hardly any uninhabited land in the country.

CONCLUSIONS

Any long-term efforts towards solving the present flooding problem in Bangladesh will certainly be a *monumental task* for the people and the government. Domestic steps including birth control, building several reservoirs in the north-central part of the country, creating earthen dams adjacent to potential flood-prone areas, establishing emergency food and medical supply, building temporary shelter on concrete structures, and implementing an effective flash flood warning system will certainly minimize the colossal effect of this critical national problem on the economy and social-infrastructure of the country. However, any effective long-term policy to cope with the flooding problem in Bangladesh has to be of *bilateral or multilateral dimension.*

Creating a *Flood Data Bank* and allowing free exchange of climatological, geological, and Landsat data among India, Bhutan, Bangladesh, Nepal, and China will help these countries to formulate a multilateral water policy, and understand individual problems and needs. With the current change in attitude toward and ease in initiating frequent political dialogues between these countries, especially China and India, Bangladesh should be highly optimistic for close participation of the neighboring countries in establishing a coherent and long-term water policy to prevent the negative outcome of the recurrent flooding situation. Finally, a sustainable long-term solution to this traditional national problem in Bangladesh will depend on the sincerity of the government, continued and amiable co-existence with the neighboring countries, and a stable political system.

REFERENCES

1. Robinson, F. 1989. The Cambridge Encyclopedia of INDIA, PAKISTAN, BANGLADESH, SRI LANKA. pp. 12-35.
2. Webster, P.J. 1987. The Elementary Monsoons, pp. 3-33. In: J.S. Fein and P.L. Stephens (Ed.) *Monsoons.* John Wiely & Sons, pp. 632.
3. J. Shukla. 1987. Interannual Variability of Monsoons, pp. 399-461. In: J.S. Fein and P.L. Stephens (Ed.) *Monsoons.* John Wiely & Sons, pp. 632.
4. Y.P. Rao. 1981. The Climate of the Indian Subcontinent. pp. 67-70. In: K. Takahashi and H. Arakawa (Ed.) *Climates of Southern and Western Asia.* World Survey of Climatology Volume 9. Elsevier Scientific Publication Company, New York, pp. 333.
5. Morgan, J.P., and McIntire, W.G. 1959. Quaternary Geology of the Bengal Basin, East Pakistan and India. *Geol. Soc. Am. Bull.* 70: 319-342.
6. Coates, D.A., and Alam, A.K.M. Khorshed, 1990. The Mymensingh Terrace: Evidence of Holocene deformation in the delta of the Brahmaputra River, central Bangladesh. *Geol. Soc. Am. Bull.* Abstracts with Programs 22: A310.
7. Rennell, J.J. 1781. The Ganges and Brahmaputra Rivers. *Royal Soc. London. Phil. Trans.* LXXI: 91-103.
8. Coleman, J.M. 1969. Brahmaputra River channel processes and sedimentation. *Sed. Geol.* 3: 129-239.
9. Bristow, C.S. 1987. Brahmaputra River: Channel migration and deposition, pp. 63-74. In: F.G. Ethridge, R.M. Flores, and M.D. Harvey (Ed.) *Recent Development In Fluvial Sedimentology.* Contributions from the Third International Fluvial Sedimentology Conference. Society of Economic Paleontologists and Mineralogists Special Publications No. 39, 389 pp.
10. Curry, J.R., and Moore, D.G. 1971. Growth of the Bengal deep-sea fan and basin denudation in the Himalayas. *Geol. Soc. Am. Bull.* 82: 563-572.
11. Goswami, D.C. 1983. Brahmaputra River (Assam, India) suspended sediment transport, valley aggradation and basin denudation. Unpublished Ph.D. Thesis, Johns Hopkins University, Maryland, 199 pp.
12. Latif, A. 1969. Investigation of the Brahmaputra River. *J. Hydraulics Division. Am. Soc. Civil Eng.* 95, HY5: 1687-1698.

13. Renner, M. 1989. Worldwatch Paper 89. National Security: The Economic and Environmental Dimensions. pp. 33, 35-36.
14. New York Times. May 3, 1991.
15. Nedeco. 1983. Feasibility study of the Ganges-Kobadak Rehabilitation and Improvement Project. Draft Final Report. Arnhem. The Netherlands.
16. Rahman, M.L. 1982. Ganges-Kobadak Project, Phase - 1, Agro-Economic Evaluation. Bangladesh Water Development Board (BWDB), Dhaka, Bangladesh.
17. Manalo, E.B. 1976. Agro-climatic survey of Bangladesh. Published jointly by the Bangladesh Rice Research Institute (BRRI) and the International Rice Research Institute (IRRI), Los Banos, Laguna, Philippines.
18. Ahmed, M., and Khandaker, N.I. 1987. Sedimentation problem in the Ganges-Kobadak Irrigation Project in Bangladesh: A field and laboratory approach. *EOS, Trans. Am. Geophys. Union* 68: 1267.
19. Stepanek, J.F. 1978. Bangladesh. Equitable Growth? Pergamon Press, New York.

ACKNOWLEDGEMENTS

I thank Dr. Dru Germanoski, Geology Department, Lafayette College, for critically reading this paper and providing constructive criticisms towards the improvement of the manuscript. Critical reviews by an anonymous reviewer are also acknowledged. I am indebted to Dr. Mushtaque Ahmed, Bangladesh Engineering University for introducing me to the Ganges-Kobadak Project and collaborating with this paper. Finally, I would like to thank Dr. S.K. Majumdar, Biology Department, Lafayette College, for inviting me to write on this topic.

Natural and Technological Disasters: Causes, Effects and Preventive Measures. Edited by S.K. Majumdar, G.S. Forbes, E.W. Miller, and R.F. Schmalz. © 1992, The Pennsylvania Academy of Science.

Chapter Fourteen

AVIATION DISASTERS: MICROBURSTS AND OTHER CAUSES

GREGORY S. FORBES

Associate Professor of Meteorology
The Pennsylvania State University
University Park, PA 16802

24 June 1975 near John F. Kennedy International Airport[1]:
1559 E.D.T., FAA controller to all aircraft:
Eastern Flight 902 aborted its landing due to
"a severe wind shift" on final approach.
1600 E.D.T., Eastern Air Lines Flight 66 (cockpit voice recorder):
Captain: "You know this is asinine."
Crew member: "I wonder if they're covering for themselves."
1605 E.D.T., Eastern Flight 66 struck an approach light tower,
caught fire, and came to rest on Rockaway Boulevard,
killing 113 of 124 on board.

INTRODUCTION

Relatively Safe Transportation

An unfortunate fact of life is that hazards cannot be completely avoided. The costs would be far too great, both in terms of lifestyle and monetary expense. The

---

[1]Excerpts from the cockpit voice recorder recovered from the wreckage of Eastern Air Lines Flight 66, which crashed at New York's John F. Kennedy International Airport on 24 June 1975 in a microburst! Microbursts and their hazard to aviation are discussed in a section later.

tradeoffs betwen risk, convenience, cost of safety measures/features, and afford-ability are inherent in many human decisions, though not always recognized. One type of decision concerns form of transportation, and this section will show that no one should have a fear of flying due to a belief that commercial aviation is less safe than other forms of transportation.

A fortunate characteristic of disasters is that they are rare events, at least at any one location. Most individuals will never experience one within a time span of 70 years, the typical life expectancy. In fact, for many natural disasters, the probabil-ity of the hazardous phenomenon occurring at any individual site during a specific year is about 1 in one million. The rarity of occurrence of disasters has human psychological ramifications, however. It is very easy for individuals to develop an attitude of "it can't happen here" or "it can't happen to me", even to the extent that specific warnings may be ignored. When combined with the fact that many hazard-ous phenomena strike suddenly, without any advance circumstances that can be recognized by ordinary citizens, the individual's feelings of immunity can lead to fatality.

Pilots, perhaps, tend to develop a special sense of immunity, fostered by a tremen-dous sense of self-confidence engendered by years of flying and dozens or hun-dreds of successful maneuvers out of difficult situations. Nevertheless, accidents do occur. Many of them are determined to have been caused by pilot error. Others, such as when major mechanical problems arise, are beyond the control of the pilot. The range of factors involved in fatal accidents is discussed in the second section below.

A particular form of aviation hazard, the microburst, is discussed in detail in the fourth section. The existence of this type of weather phenomenon was not known prior to the mid-1970s, so that pilots had not been trained to recognize an encounter with one and had not learned the special set of responses needed to maximize the chances of avoiding a microburst-caused accident. The incident cited in the quota-tion beginning this chapter spawned more than a decade of research, leading to changes in pilot training and to improved weather-detection instrumentation that have already been credited with saving lives.

Deaths in Transportation Accidents Versus Other Causes

Table 1 shows that, by far, more people die per year due to diseases (93%) than from all other causes combined, limiting the extent to which risks can be avoided (except through altering eating habits and activities that enhance the risk of heart disease and cancer). Of the accidental causes of death, slightly more than half are associated with modes of transportation, and automobile accidents are by far the most common. While major commercial airline crashes gain national media attention, these accidents are not at all common. It should be noted, however, that the statistics of Table 1 give only a crude measure of relative risks, since far more people use automobiles than any other form of transportation.

TABLE 1

Estimated death rates[a,b] in the United States, 1989, by cause, per 100,000 persons[2]

DISEASES		802.7
Heart, arteries		396.2[c]
Cancer		199.2
Other		207.3[c]
ACCIDENTS		37.2
Motor vehicles		18.9
Automobiles	(18.9)	
Bus	(0.02)	
Railroad	(<0.001)	
Falls		5.0
Poison (solid, liquid)		2.3
Drowning		1.9
Fires, burns		1.8
Choking, suffocation		1.6
Firearms		0.6
Poison (gas)		0.4
Bicycle, motorcycle		0.4
Other		4.3
Commercial Aviation (0.07)		
General Aviation (0.3)		
SUICIDE		12.3
HOMICIDE		8.8
OTHER		1.0
TOTAL		862.0

[a]Number of deaths in the United States, divided by the total population.
[b]It should be noted that this table does not truly reflect the risk associated with certain types of
  activity, since not every person in the United States participates in each type of activity.
[c]Includes deaths often termed "due to natural causes".

Comparison of Risks from Various Forms of Transportation

A more realistic comparison of the relative risks of various forms of transportation is obtained by computing fatalities per passenger mile. The average numbers
of fatalities per 100 million passenger miles in 1986 to 1988 were: automobiles and
taxis, 1.23; passenger trains, 0.06; buses, 0.03; scheduled airlines, 0.03.[2] *On a per-
passenger-mile basis, no form of transportation is safer than by commercial airlines.*
Since the number of passengers varies among the various forms of transportation,
another way of assessing risk is through the number of fatal accidents per 100 million
vehicle miles (in 1989): automobiles and taxis, 1.98; large airlines, 0.18; commuter
airlines, 1.3.[3] Hence, it is ironic that when it comes time to decide on mode of

transportation, some people avoid air travel because they perceive it to be unsafe. Aviation accident statistics are kept in categories, according to the nature of the flights. Air travel is commonly subdivided into two categories: general and commercial aviation. The latter involves airlines operating scheduled flight service available to the public (large commercial airlines and commuter airlines). General (i.e., "private") aviation includes transportation involving corporate and individually owned aircraft being operated for non-public transportation.

Table 2 shows the rates of fatal accidents and fatalities for various types of air transportation[4], per million aircraft hours. Travel on large commercial airliners is much less risky than other types of air transportation. Travel via non-commercial aircraft is considerably more hazardous. Related statistics on the number of fatal accidents per 100 million general aviation aircraft miles flown in 1989 (estimated from Reference 3) show a fatal accident rate of approximately 7.0, which indicates that general aviation is more risky than automobile transportation (1.98, as cited above).

AVIATION DISASTERS AND THEIR CAUSES

Commercial Airline Accidents

Table 3 shows the accident rates for major jet airline transportation for 1970-78 and 1979-85, by principal causes[5]. About 9-10% of the accidents were fatal in each period, involving about 0.4 and 0.3 fatalities per million enplanements, respectively.[5] The comparable fatality rates for commuter airlines are 4-6 times higher: 2.65 and 1.27, shown in Table 4.[5]

Also shown in Table 4 are the principal causes of the fatal commuter airline accidents. *Equipment failures, weather, general aviation interference, and pilot error*

TABLE 2

Average Number of Fatal Accidents and Fatalities in the United States, 1980-1989
per Million Aircraft Hours

	Fatal Accidents	Fatalities
Commercial Aviation:	3.1	19.6
Large commercial airline	0.3	13.1
Cargo and non-scheduled	2.2	110.2[a]
Commuter airline	3.7	18.0
On-demand air taxi	10.5	24.5
General aviation:	16.5	31.9

[a]The unrepresentative, large fatality rate for cargo and non-scheduled airlines appears to be due to several accidents where, due to unusual circumstances, passengers were being transported by airlines not normally operating as charter passenger carriers.

are the leading causes of fatal accidents (also true of major jet airliner transportation), with miscellaneous other factors making up more than a third of the causes.
"General aviation interference" typically refers to collisions where a general aviation aircraft inadvertently strays into the path of a commercial airliner.

An issue in the media in recent years has been the *maintenance* of aircraft
mechanical safety. A thorough examination of this topic could easily command
a chapter of its own. All that will be noted here is that the accident rates and fatality rates due to equipment failures decreased significantly between the periods

TABLE 3

*Number of Accidents (Fatal and Non-Fatal) per Million Aircraft Departures, by Principal
Contributing Factor, Domestic Scheduled Service*

Contributing Factor	Major Airlines (Jets)	
	1970-78	1979-85
Equipment failure	1.49	0.43[a]
Seatbelt not fastened[c]	1.49	0.68[a]
Weather	0.82	0.33[a]
Pilot error	0.54	0.21[a]
Air traffic control	0.26	0.11[b]
Ground crew error	0.23	0.11
General aviation interference	0.10	0.04
Other	0.39	0.50
TOTAL	5.28	2.42[a]

[a]Significantly lower in 1979-1985, at the 95% confidence level.
[b]Significantly lower in 1979-1985, at the 90% confidence level.
[c]Virtually never principal cause of accidents involving fatalities.

TABLE 4

Passenger Fatalities per Million Enplanements, by Cause, Commuter Airlines

Principal contributing factor	1970-78	1979-85
Equipment failure	1.07	0.35*
Seatbelt not fastened	0.00	0.00
Weather	0.61	0.27
Pilot error	0.46	0.05
Air traffic control	0.04	0.00
Ground crew error	0.00	0.01
General aviation interference	0.22	0.20
Other	0.24	0.39
TOTAL	2.65	1.27*

*Significantly lower in 1979-85, at the 90% confidence level.

1970-78 and 1979-85. However, statistics reported by the International Air Transport Association[6], whose members perform 66% of the total world air transport operations, indicate that the number of maintenance and overhaul employees increased by only 0.5% between 1979 and 1989. During the same period the number of passengers carried increased by 4%, and the number of passenger miles, number of tons of freight, and number of ton-miles each increased by 5%. It remains to be seen whether this imbalance has safety repercussions.

In actuality, *there are usually several factors that contribute* to a fatal accident. Many readers will have seen the movie "Crash" on television, the true story of Eastern Airlines Flight 401 which crashed in the Everglades shortly before midnight on 29 December 1972, killing 103 of the 176 persons on board. The flight originated at New York's John F. Kennedy International Airport and diverted from its approach to Miami International Airport moments before landing when one of the indicator lights in the cockpit did not illuminate to indicate that the nose landing gear had locked in the down position. The aircraft then climbed to 2000 feet above sea level (MSL) and headed west while the crew attempted to determine whether or not the landing gear was extended and if the nose gear indicator light was defective. The first officer, who was flying the Lockheed L-1011, put the jet on autopilot while he worked on the nose gear indicator, the second officer and a maintenance specialist riding in the jump seat went below to the electronics bay to visually check the position of the nose gear, and the captain communicated with the Miami Airport Air Traffic Controller and collaborated with his crew. Though the weather was clear, it was a moonless night and the crew could not visually determine the condition of the nose gear. During the preoccupation with the perceived mechanical problem, the pilot or first officer inadvertently and unknowingly bumped the aircraft control "wheel" forward, causing the aircraft to begin a steady descent rather than a level flight, and then did not hear the audio warning signal emitted when the radar altimeter detected a descent through 1750 feet MSL. Seven seconds before the crash the first officer noticed "We did something to the altitude." The last words on the "black box" were from the captain: "Hey, what's happening here?" National Transportation Safety Board investigators ascertained that the nose landing gear was in a locked down position. The cause of the crash was a combination of two burned-out 30-cent light bulbs, a moonless night, an accidental bump, and a distracted crew that failed to ensure that someone was monitoring the flight instruments.[7]

General Aviation

Table 5 lists causes of and factors in fatal accidents involving general aviation aircraft.[8] *Pilot error* is the leading cause of these accidents, and is either the cause or a factor in nearly all accidents. An archetypical example of a person at risk in general aviation is a businessman and amateur pilot who flies his own plane to out-of-town meetings. Cost factors dictate that private aircraft typically do not have the range of safety features standard on commercial airliners, and maintenance may sometimes be sub-standard. More importantly, however, the pilot does not typi-

have the degree of experience of a commercial pilot and there is generally no copilot to reduce the chances of a fatal mistake.

Weather is the leading factor in general aviation fatal accidents. A substantial portion of general aviation accidents occur in adverse weather conditions, especially when encountered by pilots and aircraft certified only for VFR (visual flight rules) conditions: i.e., for flying outside clouds in high visibility conditions where near-by aircraft are sighted visually and navigation is assisted by sighting of ground land-marks (and lights, at night). The archetypical casualty, faced with the conflict be-tween economic loss from a cancelled trip and safety risk when weather is marginal, proceeds with the trip and encounters weather-related IFR (instrument flight rules) conditions. Often the added stress of facing a situation for which he is unprepared and ill-equipped, combined with the fatigue of flying after getting ready for the business meeting, leads to fatal errors in these situations.

Weather factors often contributing to aviation accidents include (1) reduced visibility in clouds and fog that may result in disorientation, vertigo, and possibly a collision with other aircraft, obstructions, or mountains; (2) snow, freezing rain, freezing drizzle, and supercooled cloud droplets (liquid at temperatures slightly below freezing) that cause aircraft icing and can lead to an inability to maintain altitude or carburetor icing that can lead to engine stoppage; (3) thunderstorm; (4) severe clear-air turbulence sometimes found in portions of the jet stream can also occasionally lead to fatal mechanical problems for private jet aircraft, but more typically (though rarely) causes minor injuries on commercial flights. Thunderstorms pose a range of hazards, including (i) extreme updrafts that can carry a plane to low-oxygen altitudes, leading to pilot blackout; (ii) large hail that damages the engine or causes loss of lift or control, (iii) turbulence so strong that

TABLE 5

Percentages of Fatal Accidents Having Various Causes and Factors, General Aviation, 1979

Cause/Factor	Cause*	Factor	Cause or Factor*
Pilot error	83	19	85
Other personnel error(s)	7	5	12
Airframe flaw	1	2	4
Landing gear flaw	0	0	0
Powerplant flaw	8	1	8
Systems	1	<1	2
Instruments, Equipment, Accessories	<1	<1	1
Rotorcraft interference	2	0	2
Airport/airways/facilities	0	2	2
Weather	1	40	41
Terrain	<1	14	14
Miscellaneous	3	1	3
Undetermined	8	0	8

*Some accidents have more than one cause and/or more than one factor, so it is meaningless to add numbers in a column.

the airplane is structurally damaged; (iv) lightning that causes loss of navigation capabilities; (v) intense downdrafts, called microbursts, that cause loss of altitude or reduce airspeed below that necessary to maintain altitude; (vi) tornadoes that destroy the aircraft or send it out of control. Microbursts are discussed further in a later section. Incidentally, lightning rarely poses a direct threat to aircraft passengers, as the metal airframe surrounding the cabin protects the occupants much the same as does an automobile body. Further, since the fuel supply is enclosed, and cannot readily mix with oxygen, a lightning strike rarely causes an aircraft to explode.

Aircraft icing is a problem because the ice coating accumulated on the aircraft not only adds gross weight to the vehicle, but also roughens the surface of the airplane and changes the shape of the wing (airfoil) surface. Thus, icing not only increases the force of gravity, but also tends to reduce the efficiency of the airfoil, which reduces the amount of lift attained for a particular airspeed. Further, the roughened aircraft requires additional work by the engine to maintain airspeed. In such situations, the pilot will change altitudes to try to avoid the hazard. Furthermore, all commercial aircraft have heating elements and/or mechanical devices that act to reduce or eliminate icing buildup, whereas many aircraft used in general aviation do not. The operators of such aircraft do not intend to fly under icing conditions, and when such conditions are inadvertently encountered, accidents can result because altitude cannot be maintained.

Icing is particularly dangerous during the takeoff and climb stage of a flight, when altitudes are low and power is already fully used in attempting to gain altitude with a full weight of fuel. For this reason, aircraft on the ground that have picked up coatings of frost, snow, or ice from freezing rain falling at the airport are normally sprayed with a de-icing solution prior to takeoff. Otherwise, the aircraft may run of out runway before a sufficient speed can be attained for takeoff. If such an aircraft was able to take off, further in-flight icing could mean that the aircraft, already at full power during ascent, would begin to descend in a manner beyond the control of the pilot. This situation caused a notable crash into a bridge by an Air Florida commercial airliner that took off from Washington, DC, National Airport without properly de-icing in 1982.

Particularly dangerous en-route icing situations sometimes occur over mountainous regions. Under the critical temperature and wind conditions, strong updrafts generated where air is being forced to ascend over mountains can produce zones of concentrated supercooled water that can yield rapid icing build-ups when penetrated by aircraft. The mountainous region offers less space to descend in search of warmer temperatures, is too rough for safe crash landings, and tends to be sufficiently remote that the descending airplane may crash before reaching a safe landing site.

Clear air turbulence develops in layers having very large vertical wind shear, i.e., large variation in horizontal wind velocity over a short vertical distance. In such cases, a series of disturbances can develop in the layer, each having a rolling motion about a horizontal axis (oriented like a log rolling along the ground). In these disturbances, air is rapidly rising along one side of the roll and descending along the other side, giving rise to sudden jolts (referred to as turbulence) as the aircraft flies through the roll circulation. Another type of turbulence, called wake turbulence, is due to roll circulations generated by and left behind aircraft. Wake turbulence is usually avoided through air traffic control procedures which maintain appropriate distance and temporal separations between aircraft.

Mechanical problems are another source of aviation accidents. Various types of problems can arise, including: loss of power, loss of control, and fire or explosion. Loss of power due to engine failures typically dictates a change of destination because, in order to maintain a stable flight, a minimum airspeed (i.e., one faster than the stall velocity) must be maintained. To do this during total engine failure, the pilot must place the aircraft on a gradual glider-type descent in which airspeed can be maintained and descent is at a constant rather than accelerated rate. Small aircraft are often able to select an emergency landing site in a field or on a road, whereas the size of a large aircraft dictates that an airport should be found. The angle of descent and aircraft height at the time of engine failure determine the distance the aircraft can travel before reaching ground. Though there have been heroic efforts by pilots trying to land commercial airliners on roadways when faced with these circumstances and unable to reach an airport, they have usually been fatal. One notable example occurred in 1977, when a Southern Airways jet encountered a hailstorm over Georgia, damaging its turbines and causing total loss of power. The air traffic controller who inadvertently directed the aircraft into the hailstorm reportedly committed suicide as a result of the incident.

AVIATION SYSTEM SAFEGUARDS

Aircraft are very complicated machines, and discussing the range of catastrophic *mechanical difficulties* that could be (and occassionally have been) encountered is beyond the scope of this chapter. It may suffice to note that the relatively low risk associated with air transportation must be partly due to the considerable *redundancy built into the electrical and hydraulic systems* of commercial airliners, so that electrical control of the aircraft is rarely lost. Similarly, sufficient reserve power exists in the power systems (except, perhaps, during takeoff) of airliners to allow stable flight even if half of the engines fail. Maintenance schedules are followed that seek to replace parts vulnerable to prolonged use before they are expected to fail. For example, it is known that repeated minor flexings of the wings can lead to metal fatigue in certain parts, much like a wire clothes hanger can ultimately be snapped by repeatedly bending it back and forth about the same pivot point.

Mid-air and runway collisions are minimized by thorough monitoring and guidance by *air traffic controllers*. The air space surrounding all major airports is constantly monitored by radar, which enables air traffic controllers to assist pilots in maintaining sufficient separation between various aircraft taking off, landing, and entering or departing the region. All commercial and some other aircraft are equipped with transponders that help the controllers to locate and identify them and more readily establish radio communication with the pilots. Some transponders indicate altitude information that helps controllers maintain vertical separation of aircraft. Though much of the tracking is computerized, the stress on the controllers is considerable. Nevertheless, controller errors are few. Rare misunderstandings between controller and pilot, improper instructions given to pilots, and failure to follow controller instructions have led to accidents. Enhanced hazard potential occurs when there is congestion at an airport for some reason, and controllers must direct incoming aircraft to circle in "holding areas" while waiting to land. Aircraft are directed to fly at a specified altitude in a stack of levels 1000 feet apart. As one airplane is cleared to land, the other aircraft in the stack are directed to descend to the next lowest level. Accidents can occur if two airplanes in the stack mistakenly wind up at the same level, or if an outside aircraft travelling through the area unknowingly wanders into the stack. The latter could occur if the "intruder" was experiencing radio failure, had set the communications radio at the wrong frequency, or had failed to hear (or turned off) the communications equipment for some reason and could not be contacted by the air traffic controller (and is more likely if the aircraft did not have an altitude-transmitting transponder).

A great *many services are available* to pilots from the Federal Aviation Administration, though not always used in general aviation. *Pre-flight briefings* can be obtained in person or via telephone, through which the pilot can learn of weather and other potential hazards. Pilots can file flight plans, enabling *Air Route Traffic Controllers* to monitor their en-route progress using radar. Networks of several forms of electronic transmitters are operated which assist pilots in navigation. *In-flight weather briefings* can be obtained from Air Traffic Controllers, who also attempt to notify pilots of significant weather problems to be avoided. Once a flight nears a major airport, *Airport Traffic Controllers* maintain contact with pilots to control their altitude, heading, and airspeed in order to ensure a safe separation between aircraft in a "densely" occupied air space, and to ensure safe and orderly takeoffs and landings. Most commercial aircraft are equipped with *instrument landing systems* that enable the pilot to follow a signal broadcast from the airport down a specified landing glide path. Once on the ground, the movement of the aircraft on and off of runways, taxiways, and gates is dictated by FAA personnel known as *ground controllers*. These and other factors make air travel safe and dependable.

MICROBURSTS

There can be a tragic feedback between disaster infrequency, sudden hazard occurrence without advance signals, lack of knowledge of safety procedures for avoiding or escaping hazardous natural situations, and human feelings of immunity. This is perhaps illustrated best from the situation on 24 June 1975 at John F. Kennedy International Airport in New York (JFK) which was referenced at the opening of this chapter. The pilot of Eastern Airlines Flight 66 had his Boeing 727 jet aircraft on a normal final approach for landing when he received a radio report that another Eastern aircraft (Flight 902) moments before had a very difficult time when it encountered strong wind shear—sudden variations of the wind—during attempted landing. The Eastern 66 Captain's reaction was captured by the cockpit voice recorder: "This is asinine!" Probably inferring that the pilots of the other aircraft had botched the approach and were using weather as an excuse, an Eastern 66 crew member added "I wonder if they're trying to cover for themselves." The implicit attitude is "it can't happen to us."

For the next 4.5 minutes, it looked as if the Captain was right, as the descent was proceeding normally. At 4:05 PM and 6 seconds all must still have appeared normal to the flight crew, who noted that the "runway is in sight". Five seconds later the sound of impact was recorded on the cockpit voice record.

Post-crash investigation revealed that the strong shear encountered by the two Eastern aircraft, and by several other aircraft attempting to land during this time period, was due to several small but intense downdrafts or "downbursts"[9,10], now referred to as "microbursts", which occurred along the approach to JFK that day. Until the time of the accident, few (if any) meteorologists or pilots knew of the existence of this type of downdraft. Broader, gentler downdrafts are more normally encountered. It is now known that microbursts occur in both dry and moist climates, in the tropics and mid-latitudes, on several continents and over mid-oceanic islands.[11] Other notorious accidents caused by microbursts occurred near New Orleans on July 9, 1982 and at Dallas-Fort Worth, Texas on August 2, 1985.[11,12]

Circumstances of the JFK crash were similar to all others during encounters with microbursts during final approach to landing. The microburst along the approach to JFK was encountered so suddenly and at such a critical stage of the flight—the plane was less than 150 meters (500 feet) above ground—that it drove the aircraft into the ground before the flight crew could take actions to prevent the crash. This is depicted in Figure 1. Similarly, the microburst is also a hazard when encountered at a low altitude during takeoff.

Perhaps if the JFK microburst had been encountered 2 seconds earlier the crew could have reacted in time to pull up the aircraft and avoid the crash. After flying for decades, the pilot met his fate in an incident in which 2 seconds were crucial; 113 of the 124 on the aircraft were killed.

As a result of this crash and the research it has spawned since then, hazards due to microbursts, or more generically due to "wind shear", have gained notoriety among pilots. Commercial airlines now include microbursts among the situations on the flight simulators used to train pilots. These efforts have already been credited with saving lives, as pilots trained to recognize and respond quickly to the microburst have been able to pull their aircraft out of the potentially deadly descent. The meteorologist credited with the discovery of and pioneering research on the microburst, Professor T. Theodore Fujita of the University of Chicago, has been honored by airlines, flight safety foundations, and other agencies in the United States and abroad, including Japan and France.

The microburst is a narrow and short-lived but intense downdraft and outflow of air, having diameter of about 4 km (2.5 miles) or less and duration of about 10 minutes or less. Most, but not all, are produced by thunderstorms.

Most microbursts are associated with a shaft of precipitation emerging beneath cloud base, where the raindrops begin to evaporate in the unsaturated air. The evaporation cools the air immediately surrounding the raindrops, making it cooler than the air outside the rainshaft where evaporative cooling is not taking place. The chilled air is denser than in the rain-free portions of the air layer beneath cloud base, and begins to accelerate downward, much like objects heavier than water sink to the bottom of a pond. Downward speeds of the airflow in the microburst typically exceed 5 m/s (11 mph) and may exceed 20 m/s (45 mph).

Evaporation occurs whenever precipitation falls into the air beneath cloud base, but the important distinction in the case of the microburst is that there is a relatively narrow shaft of precipitation. When widespread precipitation falls into the sub-cloud layer, a more gentle downdraft of air develops. Melting of small hail may also sometimes contribute to the cooling that creates the microburst. In some microbursts, called "dry" microbursts, the precipitation may fully evaporate before reaching the ground. Others, called "wet" microbursts, are accompanied by a driving rainfall.

As the chilled, descending bubble or column of air within the microburst rapidly approaches the ground, it forces aside the sub-cloud air previously occupying its route. Upon reaching the ground, the cool air is deflected into a quasi-horizontal

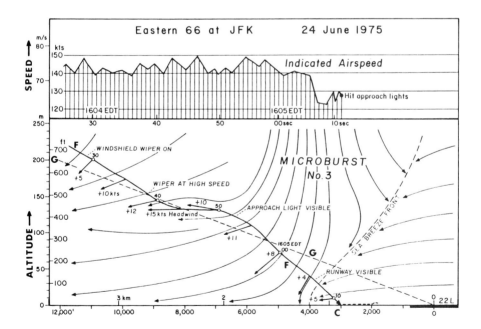

FIGURE 1. Schematic diagram of the final 3.5 km of the approach of Eastern Flight 66 from the northeast (left) to southwest (right) to John F. Kennedy International Airport on 24 June 1975. Bottom portion of the diagram shows path of the aircraft as a solid line labelled F; intended glide slope, labelled G; and streamlines of the microburst downdraft and outflow. Distance from intended point of touch down on runway 22L (0) is shown along the x axis; altitude along the y axis. Top portion of the diagram shows indicated airspeed and time. Adapted from Reference 12. Crash location shown by letter C.

outflow away from the microburst center. Horizontal outflow speeds typically exceed 10 m/s and can reach 75 m/s (168 mph).

Fig. 1 shows a schematic diagram of the airflow in the JFK microburst, reconstructed from the Eastern 66 flight recorder data and from surface weather data at JFK.[10,11,12] The deadly microburst was the third one produced by the storm in the vicinity of JFK airport. Because temperatures over the airport inland were warmer than the waters of the Atlantic Ocean immediately offshore, a cool sea breeze had drifted onshore, yielding wind from the south-southwest at the airport. Accordingly, aircraft were landing on runway 22L (i.e., heading toward 220 degrees, the southwest). The sea breeze front indicates the leading edge of the onshore flow, where it meets the microburst, which was located about 1 km northeast of the runway. The streamlines there depict the downward flow within the microburst, fanning out toward both the northeast (left) and southwest (right) as it approached the ground.

The need to detect microbursts and prevent airplanes from flying into them has helped motivate the National Weather Service to begin to deploy a network of Doppler weather radars, as described in the chapter "Modelling, Remote Sensing, and Prediction of Natural Disasters: An Overview." The Doppler radar measures the radial velocity (i.e., the component of velocity directly toward or away from the radar) of precipitation and other tracers in the air (such as insects) which drift horizontally approximately with the wind. Since the radar is not typically pointing vertically, it is not the downdraft but rather the outflow which reveals the presence of a microburst in the Doppler velocity data. The microburst's outflow pattern yields a tell-tale "divergence signature" on displays of Doppler radial velocity: a large positive value (velocity away from the radar) on the side of the microburst farthest from the radar and a large negative value (velocity toward the radar) on the side of the microburst nearest the radar. Thus, the Doppler radar data can be monitored for the existence of hazardous microbursts near airports. When this occurs, the airport can be closed until the microburst-producing storm dissipates or moves away from the airport.

Research has shown the divergence signature accompanying microbursts typically develops aloft and descends toward the surface within a few minutes. Detection of the divergence signature aloft, particularly when it is accompanied by other radar-detected clues, can allow air traffic controllers to warn approaching aircraft to abort their landings rather than encounter the microburst. Similarly, aircraft preparing to take off can be held on the taxiways.

The other clues which suggest that a divergence signature aloft might be due to a developing microburst are: (1) a core of radar-detected heavy precipitation accompanying and above the location of the divergence signature; (2) a convergence signature near the top of the heavy precipitation area, suggesting an inflow into the top of the accelerating downdraft; (3) particularly when the convergence center is near the edge of the radar echo. The latter condition increases the likelihood that dry air from the flanks of the storm is being drawn into the top of the downdraft. This would enhance evaporation and the associated cooling, yielding stronger downdrafts.

AERODYNAMICS OF FLIGHT AND
AIRCRAFT RESPONSE TO MICROBURSTS

The details of the way that a microburst causes an airplane to crash merit special attention, which requires a digression to explain the aerodynamics of flight. The essential factor in level air flight is to maintain a zero net balance of forces on the aircraft, especially in the vertical. The vertical forces acting on the aircraft are gravity (downward) and lift force (upward).

The lift force of an aircraft arises because the wing has been designed as an airfoil. The shape of the wing causes a horizontal air flow encountering it to be deflected into two branches, one flowing above and the other below the wing, as shown in Figure 2. The upper branch of the deflected air current flows faster over the curved top surface of the wing than the air beneath the wing. In fact, because the wing is angled slightly upward from the horizontal, there is typically a point along the bottom surface of the wing, labelled S in Fig. 2, where the air speed diminishes to zero. In Fig. 2, the streamlines are of the velocity relative to the wing of the moving aircraft.

The difference in speeds of the air in the two branches of flow straddling the wing determines the magnitude of the lift force, according to the "Bernoulli Principle." Where the relative air speed is slow beneath the wing, the air pressure is increased above its ambient value. Where the air speed is fast above the wing, air pressure is decreased below its ambient value. The vertical difference in air pressure across the wing results in an upward-directed pressure or "lift force" on the wing and, hence, on the aircraft.

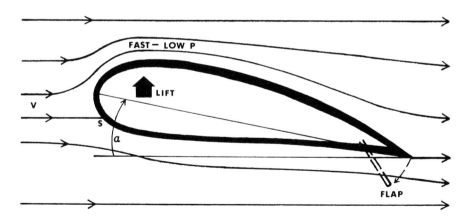

FIGURE 2. Schematic diagram of the cross-section through an aircraft wing. Streamlines are of air flow relative to the wing. Relative air speed is fastest above the wing, and is zero at spot S beneath the wing surface. The overall orientation of the wing is tilted slightly upward from horizontal, and the attack angle a is the angle with respect to the relative wind. The dashed projection pivoting downward beneath the wing depicts the lowering of a flap to increase lift, as is done during takeoff and landing.

The air speed difference across the wing transforms to an air pressure difference because the total energy in a stream of air, representing the sum of kinetic and potential energies, is conserved. The kinetic energy is proportional to the square of the speed of flow approaching the wing multiplied by the air density, and the potential energy is proportional to the air pressure. Thus, in the upper branch where air is accelerated, since the kinetic energy increases the potential energy (air pressure) must decrease. Quantitatively, the lift force (L) per unit area of wing surface is L = 0.5 ϱ V^2 C_L, where ϱ is the air density, V is the indicated air speed (magnitude of vector difference, ambient wind velocity minus aircraft velocity with respect to the ground), and C_L is the coefficient of lift. This coefficient is variable, and for a particular airplane is largely a function of the angle of the aircraft wing with respect to the ambient wind velocity, referred to as the attack angle in Fig. 2. As the attack angle increases (up to a limit), the coefficient and lift force increase.[12, 13]

For a particular air density, the lift force on the aircraft increases as the indicated air speed increases. Increasing engine thrust will increase lift by causing the indicated air speed to increase. The pilot can also increase lift by lowering the movable flaps on the wings, as shown by the dashed position in Fig. 2. By pointing the nose of the airplane upward or downward, the attack angle (and coefficient of lift) of the wing is increased or decreased, which also affects the magnitude of the lift force.

An airplane in a microburst responds according the same aerodynamic principles, but not in a way that results in level, stable flight. Referring to Fig. 1, as the aircraft approaches the microburst it encounters an increased headwind within the outflow of the microburst. This results in increased lift and the plane rises above the intended glide slope. The normal response of the pilot would be to lower the nose of the airplane to head back toward the proper path of descent. This response lowers the angle of attack at a time when the microburst airflow is beginning to change into a downdraft, reducing the indicated airspeed and further reducing the angle of attack. These factors combine to reduce the lift force while there is an increasing downward force on the aircraft due to the microburst's downdraft. A net downward force results and the aircraft steeply descends to levels below the intended glide slope, unless the pilot takes prompt counteractive measures. Eastern 66 crashed at this stage of the microburst encounter. Had it remained airborne a few seconds longer, it would have encountered the southeast (right) side of the microburst, where the outflow would have been a tailwind, resulting in a still slower indicated airspeed and reduced lift.

Radical shifts from headwinds to crosswinds are also dangerous at low levels, as they can cause the aircraft to drift laterally off course or off the runway. They can also tip the aircraft from horizontal and cause a wing to strike runway lights, telephone poles, or other obstacles beyond the end of the runway, or even the runway. This type of situation occurs when aircraft travel through the flanks of a microburst, rather than travelling directly through its center.

Pilots are now taught to apply power and pull up rather than point down the nose of the aircraft if increased headwinds are suddenly encountered while landing in showery weather. Airports have been equipped with low-level wind shear alert systems (LLWAS) to detect dangerous shifts in low-level wind speed and/or direction that could lead to drastic changes from headwinds to tailwinds as aircraft land or take off. Pilots are alerted to low-level wind shear conditions indicated by LLWAS, and to reports from other pilots of strong low-level shear. The deployment of Doppler radars promises to greatly reduce the chance that aircraft, crew, and passengers will encounter microbursts.

REFERENCES

1. National Transportation Safety Board, 1976: Aircraft Accident Report, Eastern Air Lines, Inc., Boeing 727-225, John F. Kennedy International Airport, Jamaica, New York, June 24, 1975. Nat'l. Transp. Safety Board, Washington, D.C., 52 pp.
2. Hoffman, M.S., ed., 1991: *World Almanac and Book of Facts*. Pharos Books, NY, 960pp.
.3 National Safety Council, 1990: Accident Facts, 1990 Edition. National Safety Council, Chicago, IL, 108pp.
4. Federal Aviation Administration, 1989: *F.A.A. Statistical Handbook of Aviation*. Government Printing Office, Washington, DC, 132pp.
5. Aviation Safety Commission, 1988: *Aviation Safety Commission Report, Volume II: Staff Background Papers*. Government Printing Office, Washington, DC, 140pp.
6. International Air Transport Association, 1990: *IATA Members' Air Transport Operations, 44th Edition, 1979-1989*. Int'l. Air Transport Assoc., Geneva, Switzerland, 97pp.
7. National Transportation Safety Board, 1973: *Aircraft Accident Report, NTSB-AAR-73-14*. Nat'l. Transp. Safety Board, Washington, DC, 45pp.
8. National Transportation Safety Board, 1981: *Aircraft Accident/Incident Reports, Brief Format, Suppl. Issue, 1979 accidents. NTSB-BA-81-4*. Nat'l. Transp. Safety Board, Washington, DC.
9. Fujita, T.T. 1976: Spearhead echo and downburst near the approach end of a John F. Kennedy Airport runway, New York City. SMRP Res. Paper. 137, The University of Chicago, 51pp.
10. Fujita, T.T. and H.R. Byers, 1977: Spearhead echo and downbursts in the crash of an airliner. *Mon. Wea. Rev., 105,* 129-146.
11. Fujita, T.T., 1985: *The Downburst: Microburst and Macroburst*. Satellite and Mesometeorology Research Project, The University of Chicago, 122pp.
12. Fujita, T.T., 1986: *DFW Microburst on August 2, 1985*. Satellite and Mesometeorology Research Project, The University of Chicago, 154pp.
13. Kundu, P.K., 1990: *Fluid Mechanics*. Academic Press, New York, 638pp.

Natural and Technological Disasters: Causes, Effects and Preventive Measures. Edited by S.K. Majumdar, G.S. Forbes, E.W. Miller, and R.F. Schmalz. © 1992, The Pennsylvania Academy of Science.

Chapter Fifteen

TORNADOES

GREGORY S. FORBES

Associate Professor of Meteorology
The Pennsylvania State University
University Park, PA 16802

INTRODUCTION

Defining and Investigating Tornadoes

Once known to many only from the movie *The Wizard of Oz*, home videos and cable television have brought the real image of tornadoes in progress to nearly all Americans. Fortunately, few tornadoes are as strong as those typically seen on television, and none contain wind speeds of 500 mph (233 m/s) or that approach the speed of sound, as some encyclopedias once reported. Nevertheless, a few tornadoes per year have wind speeds of 200-318 mph (90-142 m/s), and enough tornadoes have the potential for death and destruction, to warrant cautious respect, as well as considerable research to identify their causes.

The tornado is a violently rotating column of air, usually associated with a funnel-shaped cloud pendant from a thundertorm (or one of the rapidly growing clouds on the flank of a thunderstorm), which produces damage when it encounters objects protruding vertically from the earth's surface. more than 99% of tornadoes rotate counterclockwise in the Northern Hemisphere. The rotating column of the tornado is typically made visible mainly by dust and debris at low levels, giving way to primarily cloud further aloft. A typical appearance of a well-defined tornado is shown in Figure 1.

The definition of tornado given above is necessarily somewhat vague because, in fact, not all tornadoes are created equal! Most tornadoes are not as strong as the ones which make the television news, are not strong enough to totally demolish a home, nor large and persistent enough to cause a disaster. In fact, the author has seen cases where the obstacles encountered by these weak "mini" tornadoes have destroyed the tornado circulation, rather than vice versa. Hence, the term "violent" does not always apply. A weak tornado generally does not have a well-defined funnel cloud that reaches all the way from cloud base to the ground, but instead has a dust and debris whirl near the surface and a funnel-shaped cloud extending only part way to the ground. However, the appearance of a tornado can be deceiving, changing rapidly as the tornado moves across a varied countryside. The tornado becomes highly visible over plowed fields (where it whips up dust), forests (leaves and branches), and residential areas (debris) and hardly visible over grassy fields (where very little short grass is pulled up). Hence, when faced with any approaching whirlwind, it is safest to assume it is life-threatening.

Tornadoes are commonly referred to as twisters, and are sometimes mistakenly referred to as cyclones or hurricanes. The two latter storms also have winds that rotate counterclockwise in the Northern Hemisphere, but are many times larger in size— having radii of about 1000 km, compared to a tornado diameter of about 100 m. The tornado is also much smaller than its "parent" thunderstorm which, in turn, is a tiny disturbance embedded in the flow of the cyclone or hurricane. Similarly, the tornado is not the same as a dust devil or waterspout. These are typically weaker, smaller vortices (or whirlwinds; generic names for rotating atmospheric phenomena) which do not form in association with thunderstorms. Fortunately, only approximately 1 thunderstorm in 1000 produces a tornado.

FIGURE 1. Photograph of a well-defined debris-filled tornado, near Wheatland, PA, on 31 May 1985, by Richard M. Cione of Farrell—the strongest recorded tornado in Pennsylvania history.

The dust devil forms over land on a sunny day and develops its rotation, either counterclockwise or clockwise with about equal frequency, from some whirl generated by a localized gust interacting with a topographic feature, or even by a farmer plowing a field. The initial whirl is concentrated by the updraft of a thermal rising from the heated surface. Wind speeds occasionally become strong enough to damage trees (>20 m/s). Waterspouts form over warm water bodies, typically near the Gulf Stream (and occasionally over the unfrozen Great Lakes during a cold-air outbreak), in the updrafts of a developing cloud. Most rotate counterclockwise. In fact, waterspouts occasionally move onto the adjacent shore and produce minor damage for less than 1 km, but wind speeds rarely reach 30 m/s. Of course, thunderstorms sometimes spawn actual tornadoes over water, capable of strong winds and considerable destruction.

Because of their small size, relative rarity, and concentrated violence, the study of tornadoes using direct measurements has had limited success. In a few instances, conventional meteorological instruments—barometers, which measure atmospheric pressure; anemometers, which measure wind speed; and wind vanes, which measure wind direction—have survived at least an indirect hit or have given data until they were blown away. The peak gust measured during a tornado was 67 m/s at Tecumseh, MI in 1965. The largest drop in pressure was recorded in 1904 from an unofficial (citizen's) barometer reading in Minneapolis: 19.2 kPa (192 millibars, 5.67 inches of mercury or 19% of normal sea-level pressure), a dubios value. It is quite likely that the response times of the instruments and their recording devices are inadequate to measure the full range (and, hence, the maximum and minimum values) of the extremely rapid variations of wind and pressure during a tornado passage, and the jostling of the instruments may lead to false spikes on the recording strips. Recently there have been coordinated efforts by teams of meteorologists chasing tornadoes in the Midwest to deploy a portable instrument package in the path of a tornado. Some interesting data have been collected. Attempts have also been made to fly instrumented rockets and remote-controlled airplanes through tornadoes.

Most tornado wind speed measurements have come from indirect methods: tornado movie photogrammetry, damage-based estimation, and Doppler lidar and Doppler radar remote sensing. Wind speeds are computed from movies of tornadoes by tracking the movement of portions of the funnel cloud or debris within the tornado circulation. Like measuring by anemometer, there is no guarantee that photogrammetric calculations reveal the maximum winds. Nevertheless, wind speeds as high as 127 m/s (at 386 m above ground) and 118 m/s (at 20 m AGL) have been measured by this technique, within a tornado that contained multiple internal rotating funnels, called "suction vortices". Maximum wind speed measured in a tornado without suction vortices has been 99 m/s (at 110 m AGL).

Structural and civil engineers make estimates of the wind speeds experienced by engineered structures (schools, factories, hospitals, storage tanks, etc.) that were destroyed by the wind or withstood it. This involves making calculations of the forces needed to blow down walls, lift off roofs, allow objects to become airborne, etc. Simplified rules have been generated based upon these calculations and upon intercomparison with residential, crop, and tree damage nearby and in other cases when tornado winds could be measured or estimated. This classification system couples six wind speed ranges, F0 to F5, with the types of damage normally encountered. The numerical "ratings", related to wind speeds and damage intensity in Table 1, are called Fujita-scale assessments, after the scientist[1] who proposed adopting them. All tornadoes in the United States are now officially classified by this method in *Storm Data*[2], and F-scale estimates have been assigned to all tornadoes since 1916 using recorded summaries of the damages they produced. Engineers argue that such broad applications are reasonable for scales F0 to F3, but that at higher wind speeds the construction idiosyncracies of individual buildings become increasingly impor-tant, and that the appearance of F4 or F5 damage does not necessarily imply winds quite as high as in Table 1. On the whole, F-Scale wind estimates are thought to be accurate to within 15-20 m/s.

Characteristics and Structure of Tornadoes

Tornadoes come in a variety of intensities, shapes, and diameters and have greatly varying lifetimes, as summarized in Table 2. Tornadoes are often grouped into three

TABLE 1
The Fujita Scale of Wind Speed and Damage

Scale	Wind Speed (m/s)	Damage Class; Character of Damage
F0	17 - 32	LIGHT. Some damage to chimneys and television antennae; branches break off trees; crops heavily damaged; billboards badly damaged; some shallow-rooted trees uprooted; old trees with hollow insides break or fall.
F1	33 - 49	MODERATE. Mobile homes overturned; outbuildings blown down; trees uprooted; shingles and parts of roofs peeled off; windows broken; many trees on soft ground uprooted; some trees snapped; moving autos pushed off road.
F2	50 - 69	CONSIDERABLE. Roofs torn off houses, leaving strong walls standing; weak structures and outbuildings destroyed; mobile homes demolished; rail-road boxcars pushed over; large trees snapped or uprooted; autos blown off highways; block structures and walls badly damaged; light missiles generated.
F3	70 - 92	SEVERE. Walls torn off well-constructed frame houses; outbuildings flat-tened or demolished; steel-framed warehouse-type structures badly torn; most trees in a forest uprooted, snapped, or levelled; block structures often levelled; homes with weak foundations slide off and begin to crumble; trains overturned; autos lift off ground and roll some distance.
F4	93 - 116	DEVASTATING. Well-constructed frame houses levelled, leaving piles of debris; structures on weak foundations blown, disintegrated; cars thrown some distance, rolled considerable distances, disintegrate; trees debarked by flying debris; sandy soil eroded, gravel flies in wind; heavy missiles generated.
F5	117 - 142	INCREDIBLE. Strong frame houses lifted clear off foundations, disintegrate over considerable distances; steel-reinforced concrete structures badly damaged; automobile-sized missiles fly distances of 100 m; trees completely debarked.

classes: mini tornadoes (F0, F1) moderate tornadoes (F2, F3) and maxi tornadoes (F4, F5). The F-scale of a tornado is assigned according to its *strongest* damage (i.e., fastest winds) *at any point* along the path.

Mini tornadoes, weakest in intensity, are also typically the smallest in diameter and have the shortest paths of damage (lifetimes). Mini tornadoes usually have a path a few kilometers or less (mean is 3 km) in length, 70 m in width, and lasting for only about 4-5 minutes. The mini tornado sometimes has appearance like that of a dust devil or ropey waterspout, with minimal funnel cloud aloft. Mini tornadoes have wind speeds of 17-49 m/s and can demolish mobile homes, autos, barns, trees, and crops, but normally do no worse than damage the roofs of well-constructed homes.

The moderate tornado has wind speeds of 50-92 m/s, a diameter typically 100 m or more, and a path of 10 km or more. The mean damage path is about 11 km long and 180 m wide. Its funnel is usually a cylinder or elongated cone. The moderate tornado usually causes extensive damage to all but engineered structures made of steel or reinforced concrete, shreds mobile homes and blows down most of the walls of frame or brick homes.

The maxi tornado possesses the strongest winds on earth, 93-142 m/s. The strongest hurricane and typhoon, at best, can match the wind speeds of a marginal maxi tornado; similarly, the near-surface winds of a maxi tornado exceed those of the strongest jet streams found 10-12 km aloft. In addition to the strong horizontal winds, the maxi tornado may contain upward velocities of 50 m/s or more, which assist the tornado in its work of total destruction. The maxi tornado often appears as a broad cylinder or cone, but often has multiple suction vortices, sometimes visible and sometimes hidden within an outer curtain of dust and debris. Construction

TABLE 2

Characteristics of Tornadoes of the United States

Feature	Average or Typical Value	Range	Feature	Average or Typical Value	Range
F-Scale	F1	0 - 5	Pressure deficit, kPa	2	3 - 20
Maximum damaging wind speed, m/s	45	18 - 142	Length of damage path, km	8	0.1 - 470
Maximum tangential velocity, m/s	35	10 - 120	Translation speed, m/s	15	0 - 30
Maximum radial velocity, m/s	20	10 - 60	Duration of tornado, min	9	< 1 - 440
Maximum vertical velocity, m/s	15	5 - 100	Maximum local duration of damaging winds, sec	20	1 - 400 +
Width of damage path, m	120	1 - 3000	Level of maximum winds, m	30	20 - 100
Radius of maximum winds, m	60	1 - 500 +			

1 kPa = 10 mb = 10,000 dynes per sq. cm. = 0.2953 in. Hg

costs make it impractical to build most structures to withstand the maxi tornado; even engineered structures like hospitals, schools, stadiums, and bridges can be severely damaged by the maxi tornado. The only structure regularly built to withstand a maxi tornado is the inner core of a nuclear reactor facility, which in the heart of the Mid-western tornado belt is designed to withstand about 160 m/s, giving a margin of safety in even the strongest maxi tornado.

The structure of tornadoes has been examined using the measurement techniques previously described, has been inferred through measurements of waterspout and dust devil circulations, and has been examined by laboratory models, numerical models, and theoretical models. The tornado contains (1) a strong tangential velocity (wind rotating horizontally about the tornado axis) that reaches a maximum at a radius usually just inside the edge of the dust cloud and several tens of meters above ground, (2) a radial (inward/outward) velocity that is inward in the lowest few tens of meters and weakly outward above that level (at least in the outer portion of the tornado), (3) a strong upward vertical velocity that is maximum near the radius of maximum tangential winds and the top of the inflow layer, (4) a pressure field that reaches a minimum at the center of the vortex, and possibly (5) a slight warm core. The decrease of tornado wind speed near the surface is a natural consequence of friction and the roughness of the earth's surface due to topography, trees, and buildings. Little is known, however, about the typical level of maximum winds in a tornado and whether or not this elevation is variable. Figure 2 illustrates the location of the maximum velocity components for a well-studied tornado.

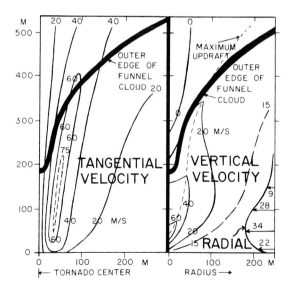

FIGURE 2. Illustration of the maximium velocity components in the Dallas, TX tornado of April 2, 1957, after Hoecker.[3] Left section shows tangential velocities as a function of height and radius from the tornado center. Right section shows vertical velocities and a profile of radial (toward tornado center) velocities at a radius of 150 m. Heavy solid line denotes outer edge of funnel cloud.

The total velocity field of a tornado is the vector combination of tangential, radial, vertical, translation, and suction vortex contributions. The ratio of these components can vary considerably between tornadoes and there have not been a great number of detailed studies separating the component wind speeds. Table 2 gives estimated ranges of the various component speeds.

All evidence suggests that as a first-approximation the tornado can be approximated as a Rankine-combined vortex: having a core of constant angular velocity extending to the radius of maximum winds, and an exterior that has constant angular momentum. This formulation can be written

$$V = V_{max} R \cdot R_{max}^{-1}, \ R \leq R_{max} \ ; \ V = V_{max} R_{max} R^{-1}, \ R \geq R_{max} \ , \tag{1}$$

where V is the tangential velocity in m/s and V_{max} is the maximum tangential velocity (m/s) at the radius of maximum winds, R_{max} (in m).

Another generally accepted first approximation is that the pressure distribution of the tornado is specified by the cyclostrophic approximation, commonly described as a balance between lateral pressure force and centrifugal force. The left-hand side represents the change of pressure with radius,

$$\frac{\partial P}{\partial R} = \varrho V^2 R^{-1} , \tag{2}$$

where P is the atmospheric pressure in kPA and ϱ is the density of the air in kgm^{-3}. Integrating this equation with respect to radius from infinity, where the pressure takes the ambient value P_∞, to r = 0, the vortex center, gives a measure of the deficit pressure $\Delta P_\infty - P_0$. This is the reduction of the pressure experienced as the tornado passes over a point:

$$\Delta P = \varrho V_{max}^2 . \tag{3}$$

Since the atmospheric density is about 1 kg/m^3, the maximum deficit pressure of the weakest F0 tornado (about 20 m/s) is about 0.4 kPa, only enough to lower cloud base by about 40 m—hence, there may really be a tornadic wind field near the surface but only a short funnel cloud aloft. This tornado would only be visible by its surface wind-generated dust cloud. As the tornado intensifies, say to tangential velocity of 70 m/s, pressure at the vortex center decreases by 4.9 kPa. This is enough to lower cloud base by about 500 m, and generally allow a funnel cloud to extend most or all of the way to the ground. It should be emphasized that the tornado would cause damage long before the funnel cloud "touched down", and that the funnel cloud is not a material surface: it descends while air is continually flowing rapidly upward through it. Finally, note that even the strongest maxi tornado (142 m/s) would reduce the pressure by only 19 kPa, approximately 20% of the ambient pressure. Thus, there is never a vacuum in the center of a tornado—merely reduced pressure.

A suction vortex is called that because its inflow often gathers in small debris (such as corn stubble) toward the low pressure at its center. The debris is left behind because the updraft near the ground is not strong enough to pick it up, forming a debris path called a suction swath. The suction vortex orbits about the tornado center under the influence of the tornado's tangential velocity. At the same time, the tornado is translating across the countryside. Hence, the actual track taken by a suction vortex is not a circle but a looping path or "cycloid". Because the suction vortex has its own counterclockwise wind circulation of 20-40 m/s, which adds to that of the parent tornado, the strongest winds are experienced along the suction swath, and especially when the suction vortex is rounding the right side of the tornado (facing in the same direction as the tornado movement). The suction vortex diameter is usually 10-40 m, much smaller than that of the parent tornado, such that only a fraction of the area affected by the tornado is hit by a suction vortex. Structures in the way of a suction vortex (see Figure 3) may be wholly destroyed, yet the adjacent house may suffer only minor damage due to the weaker winds of the parent tornado.

Tornado Climatology and Risk

Tornadoes occur at a rate of several per year in many countries of the world, as shown in Figure 4. Violent tornadoes occasionally strike India, Bangladesh, and Uruguay, for example. Moderate tornadoes are experienced in many low-lying portions of the middle-latitudes, such as Europe and western U.S.S.R., Israel, Japan, Australia, New Zealand and South Africa. In coastal regions of Japan, New Zealand, and Australia, some occurrences are from waterspouts moving onshore. Of all the countries in the world, however, the United States has the greatest area exposed to above-normal tornado risk. Tornadoes occur most frequently over the Midwest of the United States, though every State has experienced at least one in the last 15 years. Typically, the United States now experiences between 700 and 1100 tornadoes per year (average was about 850 during the years 1980-1990).

 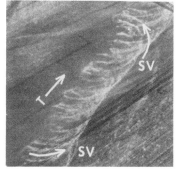

FIGURE 3. Photographs of suction swaths: piles of corn stubble (lighter than dark, "undisturbed" field) left behind by multiple subsidiary "suction" vortices (SV) revolving about the tornado (T). Arrows are drawn parallel to the direction of movement of the tornado and suction vortices.

The annual reported tornado frequency in the United States is shown in Figure 5. The "tornado alley" from Texas, through Oklahoma, to Nebraska is easily noted. If mapped by tornado intensity, however, that alley would shift. Violent tornadoes are more prevalent in the States straddling the Mississippi River. Fatal tornadoes and especially killer outbreaks primarily occur between the Mississippi River and the west slopes of the Appalachians.

In the United States, the area of maximum tornado frequency shifts seasonally: from the Gulf Coast States during the months of January and February, to the States

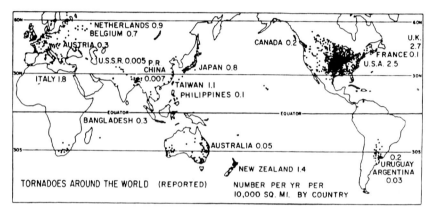

FIGURE 4. Diagram depicting countries of the world that typically experience several or more tornadoes per year, revised from an original by Fujita, and showing reported annual tornado occurrences per 10,000 square miles, by country where available.

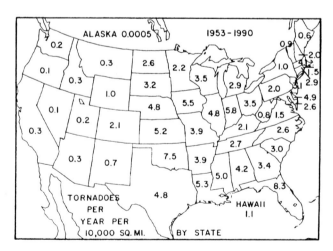

FIGURE 5. Diagram depicting reported annual tornado frequency per 10,000 square miles in the United States, by State, 1953-1990.

straddling the Mississippi River during March and April, to the Central Plains during May and June, to the Northern Plains in July and August, and shifts back toward the Gulf States by December. Tornado frequency in autumn is considerably less than that in the spring.

Tornadoes in the United States occur primarily during the late afternoon. About 60% occur between local noon and sunset; only 19% occur between midnight and noon, with minor seasonal and regional variations. Tornadoes in the West have an early afternoon maximum. When tornadoes occur after sunset, they will most likely be over the Central Plains, and tornadoes after midnight are typically found in the South.

Tornado frequency, however, is only one factor in computing tornado risk. In terms of human safety, tornado intensity is a crucial factor. Table 3 shows a breakdown of the number of tornadoes reported per year since 1920, the intensities of these tornadoes, and the fatalities produced by intensity class. It is clear that most tornadoes (about 700 per year) are mini tornadoes. In an averge year there are only about 10 maxi tornadoes in the United States. Although comprising only about 1-2% of the tornadoes each year, maxi tornadoes are responsible for about 66% of the annual tornado-related fatalities, averaging almost 6 per tornado in the period 1950-1979, versus 1 death per moderate tornado and only 3 deaths per 424 mini tornadoes during the same period. It can also be seen that the number of fatalities due to mini tornadoes is small (3 per year) and not varying with time, and that deaths due to moderate tornadoes are also fairly constant per year.

It can easily be seen that the trend of increasing tornado frequency has largely been due to increased numbers of moderate and, especially, mini tornadoes. It is probable that there has not really been any increase in occurrence, but rather a greater awareness and reporting of these events. The number of maxi tornadoes has remained essentially constant. Also striking is that the number of deaths due to maxi tornadoes has been decreasing, indicative of improving ability to detect and predict their occurrences. It must be noted that tornadoes become a part of the official NWS record only if their occurrences become known to the NWS. In regions far from NWS offices where NWS personnel cannot do post-storm surveys, tornadoes often become "official" on the basis of whether or not the storms are described in local newspapers and whether or not clipping services forward the stories to the NWS. The net result is that tornadoes are underreported almost everywhere, but especially in low population density areas far from NWS offices.

TABLE 3

Annual Frequency of Tornadoes and Fatalities by Intensity

Intensity	1920-1949		1950-1979		1980-1990	
	Number	Deaths	Number	Deaths	Number	Deaths
Mini	54 (33%)	5 (2%)	424 (63%)	3 (6%)	685 (81%)	3 (6%)
Moderate	96 (60%)	97 (3%)	236 (35%)	32 (239%)	154 (18%)	22 (46%)
Maxi	11 (7%)	144 (58%)	13 (2%)	76 (68%)	7 (1%)	23 (48%)
Total	161 (100%)	246 (100%)	673 (100%)	111 (100%)	846 (100%)	48 (100%)

Statistical computations for rare events can be difficult, especially when dealing with short periods of record, as in the case of tornadoes. The presence or absence of one sizeable tornado outbreak can appreciably alter the statistics of the entire period of record; especially the fatality statistics! Such an event occurred on 31 May 1985 when 76 people were killed in Pennsylvania and eastern Ohio during a tornado outbreak that was the worst ever in those regions. A better appreciation of the mismatch between tornado risk and the period of record can be gained by the following note: in the heart of the Midwestern tornado belt the chances of 120 m/s tornado winds making a direct hit on an individual structure are estimated to be only about one in a million per year; about one in ten million per year in the Northeast, Rockies, and West.[4]

Most tornado statistics are in the form of frequencies or frequency densities; i.e., total number of events in some fixed area or number per unit area, respectively, for some time period. Given the strong evidence that fatality rates are a function of tornado intensity (Table 3), frequency statistics are not a good measure of tornado risk unless F-scales are taken into consideration. Further, not all tornadoes affect the same area; path length and width should be used to compute climatological values of tornado-affected area. In addition, only a small fraction of the total tornado area is affected by the fastest winds. Lower F-scale winds are experienced on the fringes of the tornado. An empirical formula to estimate damage area per mile of path length (DAPPLE) for each F-scale class has been developed.[5]

Tornadoes in Pennsylvania

Figure 6 shows the annual frequency of tornadoes in Pennsylvania, normalized to units of number per 10,000 sq. mi. per year. The reporting bias factors discussed previously are evident, as maxima of tornado frequency density correlate highly with population density. In fact, if the units are converted to frequency per million people, the maxima in southwestern and southeastern Pennsylvania disappear, and the pockets of maxima approximately follow I-80 across the north-central part of the State. Thus, Figure 6 represents *reported* tornado occurrence, not necessarily the true atmospheric tornado distribution.

Seventy percent of reported Pennsylvania tornadoes occur from May-August, and 66% occur from 4-10 PM EDT. They move toward the northeast, east or southeast on most occasions. Maxi tornadoes, though only 3.4% by number, have accounted for 75% of the fatalities; 56% are mini tornadoes, which account for only 1.4% of the fatalities. In the last 75 years, only two people in Pennsylvania are known to have died from mini tornadoes (out of 142). It should be noted, however, that 77% of the fatalities occurred on just two days: May 31, 1985 and June 23, 1944. Thus, the fatality statistics are much more heavily influenced by outbreak days than is tornado frequency density, as there were 498 total tornadoes in the 75-year sample.

Causes of Tornadoes

The tornadic regions of the world (especially those regions having F3 and stronger tornadoes) are basically found where three ingredients occasionally occur simultaneously: (1) warm, moist air at low levels that has typically originated over a warm ocean or sea, (2) approach of a low-pressure system, cold front, and jet stream aloft, and (3) dry air at levels of about 3 km. These factors affect the geographical and seasonal frequency of tornadoes primarily by controlling the occurrence of severe thunderstorms. The need for low-level warmth and moisture favor the spring, summer, and fall seasons and the low-lying areas, which can receive flows of moisture from the oceanic sources at sea level. The need for travelling weather systems which trigger and enhance the severity of thunderstorms favors the mid-latitudes, where the frequency of cyclones is maximum, and the spring (storm systems are weaker in summer and early fall). As a result, many regions of the world have spring and summer tornado maxima. Dry air aloft helps to suppress small thunderstorms, but favors the development of large thunderstorms on days when travelling weather systems are present. Hence, moist regions adjacent to deserts or barren mountains are favored for tornado outbreaks. Weak tornadoes can occur under somewhat different conditions, such as in association with typhoons (in the autumn near Japan), when waterspouts move inland, and when cold pockets aloft move over humid air at low levels (United Kingdom and Pacific Coast of the United States, for example).

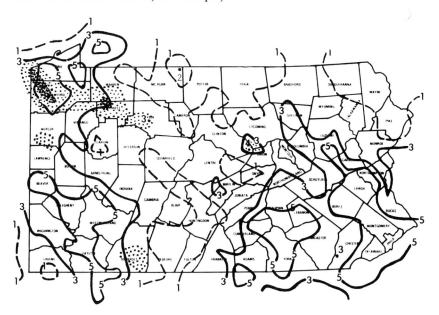

FIGURE 6. Reported tornado frequency in Pennsylvania, April, 1916 - March, 1990, in number of tornadoes per 10,000 square miles per year. Shaded regions have greater than 1 or 3 deaths per 10,000 persons per 75 years (expected lifespan).

Although the exact circumstances which allow individual tornadoes to form when and where they do on any particular occasion are likely to be quite complex and rather difficult to diagnose, it is generally recognized that tornadoes can be separated into at least two rather different groups with regard to the manner in which they are formed. One group of tornadoes, tending to include almost all maxi tornadoes and many of the moderate and mini tornadoes, forms within the circulation of a counterclockwise-rotating thunderstorm; basically forming by further concentrating the rotation already present in the thunderstorm. This type of thunderstorm is called a supercell and its circulation, usually 5-10 km in diameter, is called a mesocyclone.

The other type of tornado, generally relatively weak, forms along the gust front of the thunderstorm: the interface between warm ambient air and evaporatively cooled downdraft air flowing outward from the thunderstorm. These tornadoes, sometimes referred to as "gustnadoes", apparently derive their rotation by concentrating weak transient circulations that form within the zone of strong convergence and horizontal wind shear at and across the gust front.

The equations representing the processes by which rotation develops or weakens can be found in any textbook about atmospheric dynamics.[6] The rate of rotation is generally expressed as "vorticity", which for atmospheric vortices like tornadoes is twice the angular velocity. Vorticity increases/decreases by four processes, termed for simplicity: stretching, tilting, thermal, and frictional. The later process, caused by friction and obstacles in the flow, generally slows down the rate of rotation. Thermal processes, sometimes called solenoidal or baroclinic processes, allow for the general development of circulations where there are horizontal temperature variations, such as at the interface between warm thunderstorm inflow and cool outflow.

The stretching process is commonly known as the law of conservation of angular momentum, $r^2\omega$, where ω is the angular velocity and r is the radius of the point being traced during the stretching/contraction. This is the means by which a skater can spin faster by contracting his/her arms. In the thunderstorm, the contraction is done by inflow air converging toward the center of the updraft. Since most rotating thunderstorms form within the slow counterclockwise circulation of a cyclone, a contracting ring of inflow air that conserves this angular momentum will have an increase in angular velocity to compensate the decrease in r. The process is called stretching because the ring of inflow is stretched upward by the accelerating updraft as it contracts horizontally toward the center of the updraft. This process may be the most important for the formation of gustnadoes.

The tilting process is thought to be critically important in the formation of rotating thunderstorms. These supercells typically form on occasions when there is a large wind shear (i.e., vector difference) between the surface and about 3 km. This shear represents a form of vorticity or rotation about a horizontal axis, that can be thought of as inducing a rolling motion in a tube inserted into the midst of the shear layer, as depicted in Figure 7. In the region between the south edge of the thunderstorm and the center of the updraft—where the vertical velocity goes from 0 to as much as 30 m/s upward, the tube will be tilted into a more vertical orientation, such that the rolling is converted to a counterclockwise rotation about a vertical axis. In this portion of the thunderstorm the tilting, stretching, and thermal processes all act to generate the mesocyclone. A clockwise circulation is generated on the north side of the updraft, but is usually offset by other processes. The mesocyclone of the supercell thunderstorm forms in this environment in about 30-60 minutes, a rate consistent with the processes acting on the cyclone-scale vorticity sources.

The formation of maxi tornadoes is still under investigation, but is now thought to involve a two-step process first involving the formation of the mesocyclone (largely by tilting) and then a stretching of the mesoscylone-scale vorticity to tornadic magnitudes. Doppler radars, which can detect the movement of precipitation particles and, hence, the horizontal winds in which they are embedded, reveal that the mesocyclone forms first near 5-6 km, and descends toward the ground prior to tornado formation. This not only indicates that the mesocyclone is intensifying, but also suggests that some of the circulation aloft is being transported toward the surface by downdrafts on the flanks of the updraft. If this air is drawn back into the inflow, in this stretching cycle the angular velocity is roughly 100 times greater than that of the cyclone scale, and a tornado can be generated.

The supercell thunderstorm, because of its rotating wind field, develops a distorted precipitation pattern where curtains of precipitation are drawn into a counterclockwise filament about the periphery of the mesocyclone. This shows up on radar as a hook echo, Figure 8. Not all such storms are tornadic, however, and not all tornadic storms take on such a classic shape. Doppler weather radars, now being installed across the United States, promise to greatly improve the detection of the dangerous mesocyclones and—as never before—to allow warnings based on the occasional mesocyclone descents that usually anticipate the occurrences of potentially deadly moderate or maxi tornadoes.

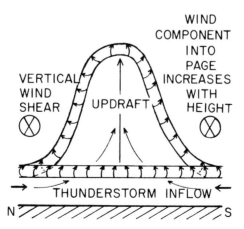

FIGURE 7. Schematic diagram of the tilting process that forms a rotating thunderstorm where an updraft develops within a strong pre-existing vertical wind shear. A once-horizontal tube becomes distorted, and gains a component of rotation about a vertical axis.

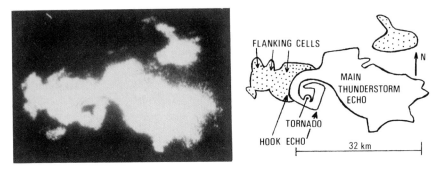

FIGURE 8. Radar image of a hook echo over the Moshannon State Forest on 31 May 1985, accompanying an F4 tornado. Debris from the forest is making the large tornado also visible in the "dot".

Tornado Myths; Safety Facts

A phrase commonly heard is: "the tornado skipped over my house and hit the one next door." In general, this perception is false. In surveys of the damage paths left by more than 150 tornadoes, the author has seen little evidence that tornadoes proceed in a discontinuous or random manner. Instead, two regular aspects of tornado "behavior" can explain most cases of tornado "skips". One explanation is the existence of suction vortices, which have been discussed previously. Being hit or missed by a suction vortex can mean the difference between minor damage and total destruction over a distance of 10 meters in some cases.

The other explanation deals with tornado "skips" of several kilometers. Many tornadoes occur in families; i.e., as part of a sequence produced by the same parent thunderstorm. This is common of supercell thunderstorms, and on days when there is a severe thunderstorm outbreak over a several-State region. Often the dissipating tornado makes a turn 20 degrees or more to the left or right and becomes ropey in these cases. Occasionally the next tornado in the sequence touches down before the previous one has totally lifted off.

Another myth deals with pressure effects in tornadoes: "the whole house just exploded outward." Structural engineers indicate that virtually all houses are sufficiently porous that houses do not explode because of air trapped inside expanding outward as the lowered pressure in the tornado core passes overhead. Common sense dictates that in a tornado filled with debris, windows will be the first part of the house to be destroyed, thereby allowing any such pressure buildup to equilibrate. Accordingly, if faced with the imminent danger of an approaching tornado, do not waste precious seconds opening windows! If the tornado strikes, its winds will open the windows for you. Also, remember that it rains and hails near the tornado, and these fall nearly horizontally in a strong wind. If the tornado passes a couple blocks away, by opening the window you will have saved nothing and possibly cost yourself new carpeting! Follow the safety rules of Table 4.

TABLE 4

Safety Rules When a Tornado is Imminent

In HIGH-RISE OFFICE OR APARTMENT BUILDINGS: Go to the basement or a small interior room preferably on a lower floor and avoid windows. Protect yourself under a sturdy object.

In BRICK or FRAME HOMES: Take shelter in the basement under sturdy items—such as laundry tubs, work benches, pool tables, desks, staircases, or adjacent to furnaces or water heaters—that will break the fall of debris. If there is no basement, take cover in an interior bathroom or closet (do not lock the doors) or under heavy stuffed furniture in the center of the house. Keep away from windows and outside walls.

In SCHOOLS and CHURCHES: Avoid rooms with large ceiling areas, such as auditoriums, gymnasiums, and churches. Go to an underground shelter, or a small interior room. Avoid windows and long hallways open to the southwest, west or northwest unless they have baffled entrances.

In FACTORIES, SHOPPING CENTERS: Take shelter in a basement or a small room in the interior. Avoid windows, hallways exposed to the southwest, west or northwest, and rooms or covered walkways with large roof areas. If there is only one large room, take cover under heavy objects away from walls and preferably in the northeast portion of the room.

In MOBILE HOMES: Leave the mobile home and take shelter in a shelter area or well-constructed building. If there are no buildings nearby, seek shelter in a ditch southwest or west of the mobile home and protect your head as well as possible.

In a MOTOR VEHICLE: Leave the vehicle and seek shelter in a ditch to the west or southwest (where the tornado is least likely to blow the vehicle onto you). Protect your head as well as possible.

In OPEN AREAS: Seek shelter in a nearby building or in a ditch, preferably to the west or southwest of any objects that might be blown by the tornado. Protect your head as well as possible.

Communities that plan ahead can lessen the magnitude of weather-related disasters. Preparedness planning includes establishing a network of spotters to be on the lookout after watches are issued; implementing a warning distribution system (such as sirens); designating school and hospital shelter areas; conducting school, hospital, and community drills; and conducting public education programs. A subsequent chapter lists additional measures that can minimize risk.

REFERENCES

1. Fujita, T.T. 1973. Tornadoes around the world. *Weatherwise* 26(2), pp. 56-62, 78-83.
2. U.S. Dept. of Commerce. Storm Data. Nat'l Climatic Data Center, Asheville, NC. [monthly; May 1990 is Vol. 32, No. 5]
3. Hoecker, W.H., Jr. 1960. Wind speed and air flow patterns in the Dallas tornado of April 2, 1957. *Mon. Wea. Rev.* 88(5), pp. 167-180.
4. Fujita, T.T. 1987. *U.S. Tornadoes, Part 1: 70-Year Statistics.* Satellite and Meso-meteorology Res. Proj. The University of Chicago, IL. 122 pp.
5. Abbey, R.F., Jr. and T.T. Fujita. 1975. Use of tornado path lengths and gradations of damage to assess tornado intensity probabilities. Preprints, 8th Conf. Severe Local Storms. Amer. Meteor. Soc. Boston. pp. 286-293.
6. Dutton, J. 1986. *The Ceaseless Wind.* Dover, NY. 617 pp.

Natural and Technological Disasters: Causes, Effects and Preventive Measures. Edited by S.K. Majumdar, G.S. Forbes, E.W. Miller, and R.F. Schmalz. © 1992, The Pennsylvania Academy of Science.

Chapter Sixteen

SNOWSTORMS AND BLIZZARDS

PAUL J. KOCIN

National Meteorological Center
NOAA / National Weather Service
5200 Auth Road, Room 410
Camp Springs, MD 20746

INTRODUCTION

Modern society often regards snowstorms with a considerable degree of ambivalence. On one hand, many people who have grown up in regions that experience at least occasional episodes of snowfall view it as a phenomenon that occasions memories of pleasurable childhood experiences, such as sledding, snowball fights, first attempts at skiing and perhaps, days off from school. There probably aren't many children that you'd hear making the statement "I hate snow"! While other atmospheric phenomena such as tornadoes, hurricanes, thunderstorms and lightning are often feared as a menace meriting protection of life and property, snow is often viewed as benign, and at worst, as a nuisance that limits mobility (Figure 1).

While snow can be a nuisance, impeding travel and the daily routine, there are occasions when snowstorms and blizzards can become natural disasters with high personal, social and economic costs. In this chapter, the human and economic consequences of such disasters will be described, including some brief accounts of some famous (or infamous) historical disasters, followed by a brief discussion of some of the physical processes that contribute to their development, and our ability to predict such storms. Some steps that are taken to minimize the impact of snowstorms, both from predictive and logistical viewpoints, are presented. A perspective on how our ability to cope with such natural disasters has evolved and will need to evolve concludes the chapter.

HUMAN AND ECONOMIC CONSEQUENCES

The impact of snowstorms is felt in many ways. Light snowfall with temperatures near or above freezing normally presents little or no concern. However, a light dusting of snow accompanied by temperatures falling from above to below freezing can quickly become an urban nightmare as wet roads freeze and cars begin to slide. Major urban areas that are unable to treat roadways, such as those in the southern United States, where snowstorms are too rare to justify dedicated crews of personnel and equipment, are often paralyzed in such situations. While these snowfalls are rarely catastrophic, they can have high costs in injuries and fatalities and a considerable economic cost, in terms of road cleanup and car repairs.

Perhaps the most debilitating of snowstorms are the widespread storms that produce accumulations in excess of 25 cm accompanied by high winds and, sometimes, bitterly cold temperatures, especially in highly populated regions. In general, the term "blizzard" is applied to such storms but the term generally applies to any form of cold, windy snowstorm, whether or *not* snow is falling. Blizzards are any storm accompanied by high winds, low temperatures and reduced visibilities due to falling or blowing snow. Blizzard conditions may exist without snow actually falling. For example, the Northern Plains states are notorious for "ground blizzards" that follow the cessation of snowfall, when high winds, blowing snow and rapidly falling temperatures create life-threatening conditions. However, the worst storms are those in which cold temperatures and high winds combine with heavy falling snow.

Conversely, some hazardous snowstorms do occur with surface temperatures near or slightly above freezing. In these conditions, snow will adhere to many surfaces such as tree limbs and overhead wiring and the resultant weight of the snow can lead to falling trees, widespread power outages and collapsed roofs.

In an assessment of the hazard of snow in the United States, Cochrane *et al.* (1975) estimated that the greatest impact of heavy snowfalls appears to occur in the northeastern United States, where occasional episodes of major storms affect the greatest concentration of people. The impact of snow on rural states is less due to relatively low urban populations. In the southern United States, the threat of snowfall is not as great as further north, but the combination of large concentrations of population in urban centers and relatively small allocation of resources to the infrequent snowfall problem occasionally results in extremely disruptive snow events.

The major social consequences of snowstorms and blizzards are disruption and inconvenience, but conditions can become life-threatening in some situations. Snowfall is often accompanied by high winds and cold temperatures that add to human suffering. Death and injuries result from increased susceptibility to traffic accidents due to poor traction and reduced visibility. Deaths may also result from heart attacks due to overexertion from shoveling. Injuries related to use of snowplows are common during major storms. In the worst cases, people can become disoriented, lost and can collapse from exertion if shelter is not found quickly. Delays in medical treatment also heighten the human impact of snowstorms.

In urban areas, a common sight following heavy snowfall is the stream of abandoned cars on major roadways. Many people are often stranded and must seek serv-

FIGURE 1. Two residents of Syosset, NY clear snow from a residence following the storm of 6-7 February 1978.

ices from police and fire departments and lodging for shelter. The positive social impact of snowstorms is the tendency for communities to band together when digging out. The effect on crime can be two-fold. In some cases, crime diminishes because most normal patterns of human activity are disrupted (even a thief can't get out of the house). However, there have been instances of increased crime, such as looting following a major snowfall, since police services are curtailed.

The economic consequences of snowstorms can be staggering. With increased urbanization, a snowstorm yielding only moderate accumulations can bring an entire metropolitan area to a halt for a day, costing millions of dollars in cleanup and lost revenue and services. In highly urbanized centers such as the northeastern United States, one storm can impact tens of millions of people for several days. A snowstorm in February 1983 virtually shut down the cities of New York, Philadelphia, Washington, D.C., Boston, Baltimore and a host of smaller urban centers for a period of 2 to 3 days. The economic costs, in which 20 million people are affected, are monumental. Lost business, transportation shutdowns, snow removal, repairs and school closings are all greatly affected during these events. There are, however, some economic beneficiaries of such storms, including hotel industries, car towing and repair services. Unfortunately, the economic benefits pale when the costs are added up.

One example of the high human and economic costs of a major snowstorm is demonstrated by the 6-7 February 1978 snowstorm in the Middle Atlantic States and New England. As reported in a National Oceanographic and Atmospheric

Administration National Disaster Survey report (NOAA 1978), this one storm was responsible for 99 deaths, 4587 injuries and illnesses, more than 500 hospitalizations, 339 dwellings destroyed, 7000 more damaged (from wind, wave and snow loading), and more than 39,000 people in need of shelter. Total economic losses exceeded 650 million dollars (1978 figures), well over a billion dollars in 1991 figures. Clearly, such storms can result in as much personal and economic ruin as most major hurricane landfalls, which are probably perceived to have greater costs. Given the relative frequency in which these storms can occur during the course of the winter across many sections of the United States, their health and economic costs can be staggering.

SNOWFALL AND SNOWSTORM DISTRIBUTION

The annual distribution of snowfall across the coterminous United States is shown in Figure 2. Annual measurable snowfall occurs across practically the entire country with the exception of portions of Florida and southern California. Therefore, snow and the problems associated with it are a concern, to a varying degree, to nearly all parts of the United States. Certainly, in those areas averaging a few cm of snow per year, such as in the Gulf Coast region and Texas, the problems are infrequent but typically, the few events that actually occur may have a tremendous impact because the region may not be prepared for its consequences. While major snowfalls

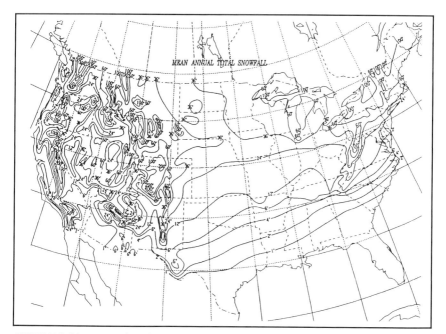

FIGURE 2. Mean annual total snowfall in the United States (in inches).

are nearly nonexistent, the light snowfalls can produce severe short-term disruptions. With regions that average greater than 10 inches (25 cm) per year, anywhere north of a region from Oklahoma eastward across the Tennessee Valley into the Middle Atlantic States, we begin to see areas that become susceptible to occasional crippling storms. For example, Washington, D.C. may average only 42 cm per winter season but some of that average is made up of the few major snowstorms that can paralyze the region for several days. Back-to-back snowstorms in January 1987 exceeded the annual mean snowfall and led to a week of business and school shutdowns. As annual snowfalls increase above 75 to 100 cm per year, we begin to see areas that are used to disruptions from occasional winter storms. In these locales, such as Buffalo, Chicago and Denver, the occasional moderate snowfall will not have much effect on the local economies since the economies take into account such disruptions, but major single events will still have the potential to bring these centers to a standstill, although relatively infrequently.

It is in those regions that only occasionally experience heavy snowfall that such occurrences can cause the greatest disruptions. In general, these are regions that experience 100 cm of snow per season or less. Many years can pass in these areas with no crippling storm occurrence and yet the local economies must factor in the possibility that such a storm may occur, although in any given year it may be unlikely. However, the infrequent occurence of heavy snowfall may catch these regions entirely off guard and their consequences can be disastrous in terms of lives lost, economic loss and uncertainty and frayed nerves when necessary services are not provided. For example, snowstorms have been known to topple local city governments when municipal services don't respond promptly and effectively. Major snowstorms and problems with the city's response to the storms in Chicago in 1979 and in New York City in 1969 severely undermined the legitimacy of the local governments at the time.

EXAMPLES OF MAJOR SNOWSTORMS AND THEIR IMPACT

One of the most legendary examples of a snowstorm that had a catastrophic impact was the March 1888 "Blizzard of '88" (see Caplovich 1987 and Kocin 1988 for pictorial and meteorological summaries of the storm). This unexpected storm in the waning days of winter produced an estimated 400 casualties, many in the New York City area, when a major snowstorm combined with record-setting cold temperatures and very high winds. Many casualties resulted when people were stranded outdoors, became disoriented and were quickly overcome by life-threatening cold and wind. Fifty to as many as 125 cm of snow fell over a 3-day period. While this is a notoriously infamous storm whose severity is not typical of many snowstorms, it serves as a reminder of how severe some storms can become.

More recent examples of severe snowstorms abound, although few were as lethal as the Blizzard of '88. The northeastern United States, including the Commonwealth of Pennsylvania, is occasionally prone to very disruptive snowstorms. One of the most famous storms is the Thanksgiving storm of 1950 that brought perhaps the most severe combination of snow, high winds and heavy rain to Pennsylvania. While the eastern half of the state received heavy rainfall and winds gusting in excess of 50 m s⁻¹ at some locations, the western half of the state was influenced by perhaps its greatest snowstorm on record, where amounts of 50 to 75 cm were common, accompanied by high winds and temperatures that fell to near 0°F, very similar to the Blizzard of '88. In Pittsburgh, the storm dropped 56 cm of snow and brought the city to a halt. Another storm in late March 1958 was poorly forecast to be a rainstorm because of the time of the year and because temperatures prior to the storm were marginal for snowfall. One of the more notable storms for Pennsylvania, it lasted for several days and while yielding generally 25 to 50 cm across much of eastern Pennsylvania, it locally produced snowfall totals as high as 100 to 125 cm in portions of southeastern Pennsylvania, the greatest snow amounts ever measured in Pennsylvania.

More recent storms in February 1983 and February 1987 were particularly severe in eastern Pennsylvania. In February 1983, a storm left accumulations of 50 to 63 cm across the southeastern half of the State, closing schools and businesses for several days to a week. A surprisingly intense snowstorm in February 1987 resulted in widespread power outages when wet snow accompanied by temperatures near or slightly above freezing caused many wires and trees to collapse under the weight of 25 to as much as 60 cm of snow.

FACTORS THAT PRODUCE SNOWSTORMS

There are many factors that produce snowstorms. While there are a variety of mechanisms that can result in snow, only those that contribute to the widespread, urban snowstorms common to the northeastern United States (e.g., see Kocin and Uccellini 1990) will be discussed here.

Most of the major heavy snow events in the Northeast United States are associated with midlatitude extratropical cyclogenesis. Since midlatitude cyclogenesis is common in wintertime and produces a wide variety of precipitation elements, there are processes and features that allow certain cyclones to be more conducive as heavy snow producers.

For heavy snowfall, there must be a source of cold air at low levels of the earth's atmosphere that allows the snow to remain in that form when it reaches the earth's surface. Cold air is usually supplied by high pressure systems or anticyclones that form over Canada or further north above the Arctic Circle. In general, these anticyclones that move equatorward across Canada must interact with the developing cyclones to allow cold low-level air to flow toward the developing anticyclone at the same time that warmer, moist air off the Atlantic Ocean, in association with the cyclone, can ascend over the cold air. A deep layer of east winds from off the Atlantic Ocean is a prerequisite for major East Coast snowstorms. The ascent of the relatively warm, moist air above the surface cold airflow, depicted schematically in Figure 3, occurs in conjunction with a complex series of processes. First, the northward transport of warm, moist air is associated with the development of a cyclone, which is typically associated with an upper-level disturbance or trough and upper-level wind maximum or jet streak (Uccellini and Kocin 1987). The cyclone develops downwind of the axis of the upper-level trough in the "exit region" of the jet streak, a region downwind of the maximum winds of the jet streak. Air parcels passing through the jet streak decelerate downwind of the maximum winds, promoting a favorable environment for cyclogenesis. At the same time, a cold anticyclone to the north is also associated with a separate upper-level trough/jet system. Vertical circulations about the upper-level jet associated with the anticyclone allow cold air to flow southward toward the cyclone at the same time that warm, moist air is transported northward in association with the cyclone. The ascent of the warm,

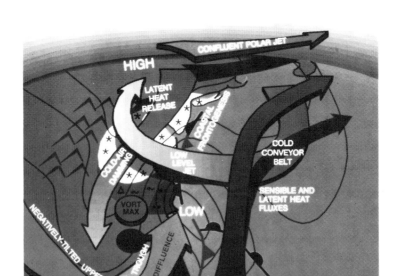

FIGURE 3. Schematic of the important airflows, features and processes common to major Northeast Snowstorms (from Kocin and Uccellini 1990).

moist air produces clouds and precipitation while cold air is maintained near the earth's surface that allows precipitation to remain as snow.

While the above scenario is a general description of how snowstorms develop, the severity of the storm will be dictated by other factors, such as the relative strengths or intensities of the surface cyclones and anticyclones (which will influence the magnitude of the resulting moisture influx into the storm) and of the intensities of the upper-level trough/jet systems that influence the development of the surface cyclones and anticyclones. For the East Coast, the intensity of the storms will be influenced by a number of factors including the interaction of upper-level jet streaks (Uccellini *et al.* 1984; 1985; 1987), land-sea temperature enhancements associated with the entrapment or "damming" of cold air between the Appalachian mountains and the coastline (Forbes *et al.* 1987; Stauffer and Warner 1987), the development of intense frontal zones near the coastline termed "coastal fronto-genesis" (Bosart 1975), fluxes of latent and sensible heat off the Atlantic Ocean surface (i.e., evaporation and modification of cold polar airflow over the warm western Atlantic Ocean; Sanders and Gyakum 1980; Gyakum 1983a, b) and the enhanced moisture and thermal effects provided by low-level wind maxima or jet streaks (Uccellini *et al.* 1987). The cold air supplied by the numerous high pressure systems that invade the United States during winter and the precipitation-generating capacities of developing cyclones can lead to many instances of snowfall during the winter months. However, only a few systems gain enough energy to produce truly significant snowstorms or blizzards.

An example of the evolution of a classic midwinter Northeast snowstorm in February 1983 is shown in Figure 4. The snowfall distribution for this storm is shown in Figure 5 and illustrates the relatively narrow width of the heavy snow band commonly found in many storms. In a given winter, few storms may affect any given region of the United States, while in other winters, many storms may affect different regions of the country or one region may experience several major snowstorms.

While the above scenario is a gross simplification of the complex interactions that occur to generate major snowstorms over one part of the country, there are other mechanisms that are also responsible for heavy snowfall. Near large bodies of water, such as the Great Lakes, heavy snowfall may result from cold air that passes across the warm water surface, picking up heat and moisture, and then producing localized heavy snow amounts on the leeward sides of the water bodies. Mountainous terrain is also prone to heavy snowstorms since the mountains themselves will force air to ascend.

THE ABILITY TO PREDICT SNOWSTORMS

Much of the ability to cope with natural hazards such as snowstorms depends on whether one has the ability to foresee it. Without warning, the impact of snowstorms can catch the public off guard. Therefore, the ability to predict snowstorms is crucial to minimize the effects of such disasters.

SURFACE

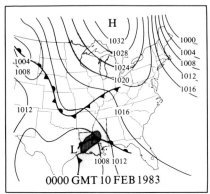

0000 GMT 10 FEB 1983

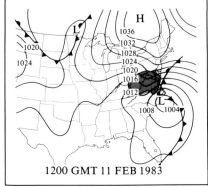

1200 GMT 11 FEB 1983

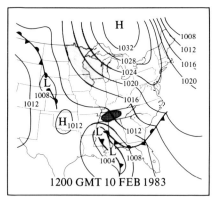

1200 GMT 10 FEB 1983

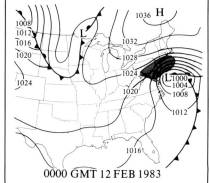

0000 GMT 12 FEB 1983

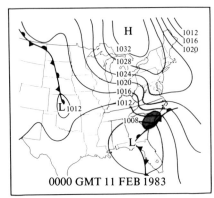

0000 GMT 11 FEB 1983

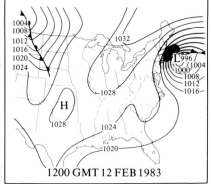

1200 GMT 12 FEB 1983

FIGURE 4. Evolution of the February 1983 snowstorm utilizing surface weather analysis. Solid contours are isobars (in mb) and shading represents current precipitation (from Kocin and Uccellini 1990).

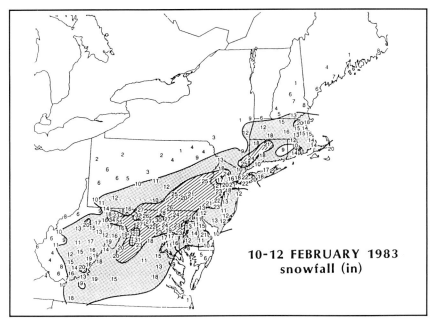

10-12 FEBRUARY 1983
snowfall (in)

FIGURE 5. Snowfall distribution (in inches) for the 10-12 February 1983 snowstorm. Shading depicts amounts greater than 10 inches (25 cm); hatching depicts amounts greater than 20 inches (50 cm) (from Kocin and Uccellini 1990).

Historically, the United States, through the U.S. Signal Service and later the Weather Bureau and Weather Service, has provided warnings of impending storms since the late 19th century. These warnings were based on the extrapolation of weather systems as depicted by a network of surface weather observations that showed various surface low and high pressure systems. Unfortunately, the data network was incapable of detecting the many subtle changes through the depth of the atmosphere that influence the development of the weather systems that are crucial for a successful prediction of snowstorms. Eventually, devices were developed to monitor information above the earth's surface. Empirical forecast rules based on the surface and upper-air information were derived in the first 50 years of the 20th century and 1 to 2-day forecasts of weather systems and snowstorms were developed but met mixed results. Unfortunately, many snowstorms are associated with rapidly changing surface and upper-level conditions, which the empirical rules were often incapable of detecting.

By the 1950's, the mechanisms responsible for cyclogenesis were receiving vigorous treatment from the research community. At the same time, mathematical models of the atmosphere were being applied on computers and weather prediction become more objective (see Shuman, 1989, for a history of numerical weather prediction). In the years since the 1950's, rapid changes in computer technology and in the understanding of atmospheric processes have greatly increased the reliability of forecasts (for example, see Bonner 1989; Junker *et al*. 1989; and Caplan and White 1989). Weather forecasts are routinely made 3-4 days in advance that have the accuracy of the 1-2 day forecasts just 20 years ago. Forecasts out to 7 days are now believable in many instances, at least on a large atmospheric scale of motion.

With regard to the specific problem of forecasting snowstorms, there has only been limited attention focused on improvements in their prediction (Stokols *et al* 1990). As a measure of depicting the skill of both model-derived and human-interpreted forecasts, the Anomaly Correlation Scores for the Winter Season (December through February) during the 13-year period between 1977 and 1990 are shown in Figure 6. The anomaly correlation score is an area-averaged correlation between the forecast and observed sea-level pressure fields with climatological values subtracted. The scores were computed for the global spectral forecast model. What is clearly shown in Figure 6 is that there has been a steady improvement in the model 3, 4 and 5-day predictions throughout the late 1970's and 1980's during winter. The 5-day forecast score is now approaching the skill of the 3-day forecast just over a decade ago. The improvements in skill have been attributed to the improved resolution and parameterizations introduced into the models.

One can argue that along with the general improvements in forecasting during the winter season, snowstorm forecasting has also improved. While that is not to say that there haven't been recent occurrences of very poor forecasts, there are greater numbers of successes than have occurred in the past. For example, despite the enormous losses incurred by the February 1978 storm in New England, this particular storm was considered at the time a rare "successful" forecast of a major winter storm

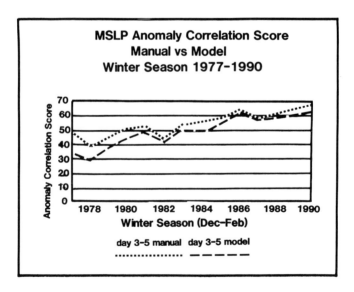

FIGURE 6. The mean sea-level pressure (MSLP) anomaly correlation score for the 3-5 day winter season forecasts 1977-1990: model versus man (from Stokols *et al.* 1990).

several days in advance (Brown and Olson 1978). While meteorologists were pat-
ting themselves on the back for the excellent forecast, a major snowstorm the following year was missed by the same operational model. Much research has gone into
understanding the reasons behind the model failure (Bosart 1981, Uccellini *et al.*
1984; 1985; 1987, and others) and the identification of model deficiencies has led
to improvements in current model formulations. While there have not been many
major Northeast snowstorms since the middle to late 1980's, the numerical weather
prediction models appear to be more reliable in their forecasts of the evolution of
cyclones and anticyclones, but it still can be difficult to distinguish locally varying
conditions that may mean the difference between 20 inches (50 cm) of snow or
merely 2 inches (5 cm) of rain.

The techniques presently used to forecast the storms involve the interpretation
of numerical model output supplied primarily by national forecast centers. In
general, the models provide fields of atmospheric variables over a period of time
in the future, typically 12-hour forecasts up to 48 hours. Some models now provide forecasts 10 days into the future but reliability drops off rapidly past 5 days.
Meteorologists will examine a variety of fields, including charts of surface variables
such as temperature, humidity and winds and examine many parameters at various
levels of the atmosphere and try to diagnose how those fields are changing with
time. They will also examine vertical slices of the atmosphere, termed cross sections,
to determine if the vertical structure of the atmosphere is conducive for snow.
Crucial factors that meteorologists examine during snowstorms are the evolution
of cyclones and anticyclones, whether or not they are forecast to intensify, their
paths, how patterns of moisture, winds and ascending and sinking motions evolve,
and critical temperatures in the lower atmosphere.

Twenty years ago, weather forecasters were beginning to utilize a state-of-the-art
numerical prediction model based on the full equations of atmospheric motion,
but had only a limited ability in simulating real atmospheric features. While that
model is currently still in existence, it will be discontinued shortly and has been
replaced by 2 working operational models with greater horizontal and vertical
resolution (that can capture more atmospheric detail) and much improved physical
parameterizations. These models have provided improved forecasts both in the
short-term (1-2 days) and in the medium- to long-terms (3-7 days; see Hoke *et al.*,
1989, and Kanamitsu, 1989). An experimental model (see Mesinger *et al.*, 1990) and
numerous research models hold the promise that improvements in snowstorm
forecasting will be seen in the near future. While none of these systems can be viewed
as close to perfect, they may allow more reliable forecasts that could minimize the
skepticism with which winter storm forecasting is now greeted by the public.

DISCUSSION — REDUCING THE THREAT OF FUTURE DISASTERS

While improvement in the science of weather prediction is the major step
necessary toward reducing the hazards imposed by snowstorms, one must recognize

that snowstorms can be more hazardous than other perceived disasters, such as hurricanes and tornadoes, particularly in heavily urbanized areas. It is conceivable that a major snowstorm in the northeastern United States could result in dozens of lives lost and economic losses exceeding one billion dollars.

Our ability to cope with natural disasters such as snowstorms depends on improvements in prediction and warning and the ability for highly populated regions to assess the risk of snowstorms and react to the situation, as described in Cochrane *et al*. (1975). Since weather modification has had only very limited success in modifying precipitation over very small regions, is no longer actively studied and is not a practical solution to diminishing the impact of snowstorms, communities must set strategies to minimize losses accrued during these storms. Communities react to major snowstorms by closing schools and businesses that can't function during storms to ease cleanup, alter normal commuting patterns, encourage alternate forms of transportation, and set design standards for buildings to withstand the weight of snow (Cochrane *et al.*, 1975). Since snowstorms can not be prevented, losses must be handled through insurance, supplying aid in terms of food and shelter to stranded motorists, and public and private assistance. These strategies require that snow be removed as efficiently as possible, requiring early mobilization. It is critical that false alarms from erroneous forecasts be minimized because they waste resources and erode public confidence.

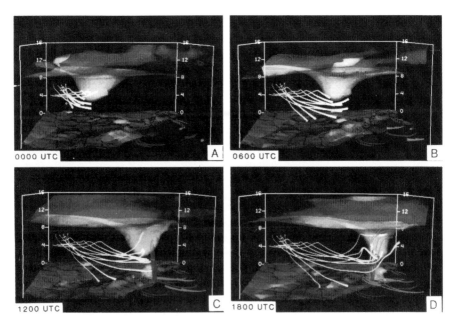

FIGURE 7. A 3-dimensional perspective of meteorological processes derived from the application of the University of Wisconsin's MCIDAS system to a numerical simulation of the Presidents' Day Cyclone (from Hibbard *et al.* 1989).

With regard to weather forecasting, mathematical models that presently forecast the larger-scale aspects of the storms quite well must be able to forecast the small scale structures that can occasionally produce localized havoc. An excellent example of a case that went undetected by the operational models and local forecasters was a small region of heavy snows that fell in the Washington D.C. area on November 11, 1987. While surrounding suburbs received light snow of 8 cm or less, the immediate city received 30 cm of snow with some nearby suburbs receiving as much as 43 cm. Such localized storms are very difficult to diagnose and predict at the current time. It is still questionable if models will be able to detect such systems in the near future.

Weather forecasts must provide better accuracy and lead time. Four-dimensional visualization (see Figure 7) now afforded by the introduction of computer workstation technology may allow meteorologists to examine far greater detail from numerical weather prediction models than at present that would allow them to understand processes in snowstorms that could only be inferred from limited 2-dimensional displays (Hibbard *et al.* 1989). Animated numerical output will allow a much greater understanding of the mechanisms that generate these storms and allow forecasters greater confidence and lead time in warning the public.

REFERENCES

1. Cochrane, H.C., B.A. Knowles, B.S. Dunn and O.W. Untermann. 1975. Urban snow hazard in the United States: A research assessment. Program on Technology, Environment and Man, NTIS NSF-RA-E-75-018, 60 pp.
2. NOAA. 1978. Northeast Blizzard of '78 February 5-7, 1978. A report to the administrator. Natural Disaster Survey Report 78-1.
3. Caplovich, J. 1987. Blizzard! The Great Storm of '88. Vero Publishing Co., 242 pp.
4. Kocin, P.J. 1983. An analysis of the "Blizzard of '88". Bull. Amer. Meteor. Soc. 64, 1258-1272.
5. Kocin, P.J. and L.W. Uccellini. 1990. Snowstorms along the northeastern coast of the United States, 1955-1985. Meteor. Monogr., no. 44, 280 pp.
6. Uccellini, L.W. and P.J. Kocin. 1987. An examination of vertical circulation associated with heavy snow events along the East Coast of the United States. Wea. Forecasting, 2, 289-308.
7. Uccellini, L.W., P.J. Kocin, R.A. Petersen, C.G. Wash and K.F. Brill. 1984. The Presidents' Day cyclone of 18-19 February 1979. Synoptic overview and analysis of the subtropical jet streak influencing the precyclogenetic period. Mon. Wea. Rev., 112, 31-55.
8. Uccellini, L.W., D. Keyser, K.F. Brill and C.H. Wash. 1985. The Presidents' Day cyclone of 18-19 February 1979: Influence of upstream trough amplification and associated tropopause folding on rapid cyclogenesis. Mon. Wea. Rev., 113, 962-988.

9. Uccellini, L.W., R.A. Petersen, K.F. Brill, P.J. Kocin and J.J. Tuccillo. 1987. Synergistic interactions between an upper-level jet streak and diabatic processes that influence the development of a low-level jet and a secondary coastal cyclone. Mon. Wea. Rev., 115, 2227-2261.

10. Forbes, G.S., R.A. Anthes and D.W. Thompson. 1987. Synoptic and mesoscale aspects of an Appalachian ice storm associated with cold-air damming. Mon. Wea. Rev., 115, 564-591.

11. Stauffer, D. R. and T.T. Warner. 1987. A numerical study of Appalachian cold-air damming and coastal frontogenesis. Mon. Wea. Rev., 115, 799-821.

12. Bosart, L.F. 1975. New England coastal frontogenesis. Quart. J. Roy. Meteor. Soc., 101, 957-978.

13. Sanders, F. and J.R. Gyakum. 1980. Synoptic dynamic climatology of the bomb. Mon. Wea. Rev., 108, 1589-1606.

14. Gyakum, J.R. 1983a. On the evolution of the QE II storm. Part I: Synoptic aspects. Mon. Wea. Rev., 111, 1137-1155.

15. Gyakum, J.R., 1983b. On the evolution of the QE II storm. Part II: Dynamic and thermodynamic structure. Mon. Wea. Rev., 111, 1156-1173.

16. Shuman, F.G. 1989. History of numerical weather prediction at the National Meteorological Center. Wea. Forecasting, 4, 286-296.

17. Bonner, W.D. 1989. NMC Overview: Recent progress and future plans. Wea. Forecasting, 4, 275-285.

18. Junker, N.W., J.E. Hoke and R.H. Grumm. 1989. Performance of NMC's regional models. Wea Forecasting, 4, 368-390.

19. Caplan, P.M. and G.H. White. 1989. Performance of the National Meteorological Center's Medium-Range Model. Wea. Forecasting, 4, 391-400.

20. Stokols, P.M., J.P. Gerrity and P.J. Kocin. 1990. Improvements at NMC in numerical weather prediction and their effect on winter storm forecasts. First International Symposium on Winter Storms, New Orleans, La, 15-19.

21. Brown, H.W. and D.A. Olson. 1978. Performance of NMC in forecasting a record-breaking winter storm. 6-7 February 1978. Bull Amer. Meteor. Soc., 59, 562-575.

22. Bosart, L.F. 1981. The Presidents Day snowstorm of 18-19 February 1979: A subsynoptic-scale event. Mon. Wea. Rev., 109, 1542-1566.

23. Hoke, J.E., N.A. Phillips, G.J. DiMego, J.J. Tuccillo and J.G. Sela. 1989. The Regional Analysis and Forecast System of the National Meteorological Center. Wea. and Forecasting, 4, 323-334.

24. Kanamitsu, M. 1989. Description of the NMC Global Data Assimilation and Forecast System. Wea. and Forecasting, 4, 335-342.

25. Mesinger, F., T.L. Black, D.W. Plummer and J.H. Ward. 1990. Eta model precipitation forecasts for a period including Tropical Storm Allison. Wea. Forecasting, 5, 484-493.

26. Hibbard, W.L., L.W. Uccellini, D. Santek and K.F. Brill. Applications of the 4-D McIDAS to a model diagnostic study of the Presidents' Day Cyclone. Bull. Amer. Meteor. Soc., 70, 1394-1403.

Natural and Technological Disasters: Causes, Effects and Preventive Measures. Edited by
S.K. Majumdar, G.S. Forbes, E.W. Miller, and R.F. Schmalz. © 1992, The Pennsylvania Academy
of Science.

Chapter Seventeen

EL NIÑO AND PERU: A NATION'S RESPONSE TO INTERANNUAL CLIMATE VARIABILITY

PABLO LAGOS[A] and JAMES BUIZER

NOAA, Office of Global Programs
1335 East-West Highway
Silver Spring, MD 20910

INTRODUCTION

For at least one century, local fishermen along the northern coast of Peru have
observed that, generally near the end of each calendar year, a warm ocean current
would extend southward along the coast. As it occurred around Christmastime,
they termed this current "Corriente del Niño", or "El Niño Current", referring to
the Christ child. In recent decades, however, the term "El Niño" has become popularly used in reference to an incidence of exceptionally warm water appearing every
2-9 years along the equator and extending down the west coast of South America.
The intrusion of this warm surface water suppressed the upwelling of colder,
nutrient-rich water from below, inhibiting productivity. It has been blamed for the
death and displacement of countless species of fauna and flora along the west coast
of South America, as well as for having contributed to the collapse of the once-
thriving Peruvian anchoveta fishery. Climate scientists link this oceanographic
phenomenon with a related atmospheric event referred to as the "Southern Oscillation", arriving at the term El Niño-Southern Oscillation (ENSO). The Southern
Oscillation is, as described by Trenberth (1991), "a see-saw in atmospheric mass
involving exchanges of air between eastern and western hemispheres in tropical and
subtropical latitudes with centers of action located over Indonesia and the tropical

APermanent affiliation: Instituto Geofisico del Peru, Lima, Peru

South Pacific Ocean." Evidence suggests that the ENSO phenomenon contributes to, or is responsible for, anomalous weather patterns throughout the world, sometimes of disasterous proportions. For example, the 1982/83 ENSO, the strongest event of the century, has been held responsible for widespread incidents of drought, flooding and severe storms in 5 continents, resulting in several hundred deaths, and damages estimated at $8.65 Billion (Canby, 1984).[2] Peru was one of the countries most severely impacted by this event having suffered hundreds of deaths, and an estimated $2 Billion in damages to agriculture, fisheries, transportation, housing and other sectors of the economy.

The tremendous societal consequences related to ENSO have prompted 18 nations to support hundreds of scientists in a coordinated research effort to gain an understanding of the dynamics of this phenomenon in order to ultimately be capable of predicting its occurrence months in advance. Our understanding of ENSO has improved a great deal in recent years. It now appears that in some regions of the world the occurrence of an ENSO is closely related to local climatic variability; that is, to the timing and magnitude of seasonal rainfall. Scientists in a few countries, such as Peru, Brazil, Ethiopia, Australia and India, have begun applying knowledge of the dynamics of ENSO to forecast the associated climatic consequences. Effectively applied, these forecasts can be used to mitigate the socio-economic impacts of interannual climate variability on the local population. The best example of a nation applying recent scientific findings about ENSO in an effort to mitigate the socio-economic impacts associated with this natural phenomenon can be found in Peru.

This chapter describes the anomalous precipitation and temperature patterns observed in the agricultural, northwestern region of Peru during the 1982/83 ENSO, and analyzes the subsequent efforts by the Peruvian Government to mitigate the adverse socio-economic impacts due to variability in their climate. Finally, some actions which need to be taken in order to improve our ability to predict interannual climate variability, and to better prepare policy-makers throughout the world in the use of these predictions, are suggested.

EL NIÑO - SOUTHERN OSCILLATION (ENSO)

The mean annual climate cycle in the Pacific is determined by a complicated interplay between the temperature of the ocean water at the surface, or sea surface temperature (SST) patterns, featuring an extensive warm pool in the west, and a cold tongue of water just south of the equator in the east, and atmospheric circulation patterns, dominated by relatively light winds in the west and strong trade winds further east. The cold water along the coast of South America can be attributed to upwelling of deeper waters, rising to replace surface waters being pushed westward and equatorward by the prevailing winds, and affected by the rotation of the earth. These patterns determine, in great part, the light precipitation generally observed along the west coast of South America during non-ENSO, or "normal" years.[B]

Although no two ENSO events are exactly alike in their intensity (defined by the size of departure from average SSTs), geographic manifestation, duration or impacts, some general statements can be made to characterize the phenomenon. During ENSO years, a weakening or collapse of the predominant easterly winds in the central and eastern tropical Pacific, along with associated anomalous SST warmings, result in a shift in precipitation patterns throughout the region. The low pressure area which normally sits over eastern Indonesia shifts eastward, taking with it the associated atmospheric convection, and hence precipitation, into the central Pacific. ENSOs have been characterized as consisting of four phases: a precursory phase, an onset phase, a phase when the anomalous conditions grow and mature, and a phase during which anomalous conditions decay, lasting anywhere between 6 and 24 months (Nicholls, 1987).[3]

Understanding of the dynamics of this recurring climate phenomenon has evolved over the decades. Sir Gilbert Walker observed interannual fluctuations in atmospheric pressure over the low pressure region in the western Pacific and high pressure region in the eastern south Pacific. (Walker, 1923).[4] This recurring fluctuation became known as the Southern Oscillation (SO). The Southern Oscillation Index (SOI), defined as the atmospheric pressure at Tahiti minus the pressure at Darwin, Australia has been a useful indicator for the monitoring of ENSO. Walker and Bliss (1932)[5] recognized the relationship of the SO to tropical and subtropical weather phenomena. Berlage (1957)[6] was the first to show the strong correlation between the SOI and SST fluctuations along the coast of Peru. Bjerknes (1966a, 1966b)[7,8] proposed a mechanism connecting the SO to El Niño, arguing that the coastal winds, weakened as a response to the weakened trade winds, reduce coastal upwelling, thus causing the anomalously warm El Niño Current. Wyrtki (1975)[9] proposed that, in fact, the warm waters appearing off the coast of Peru were in direct response to the weakening of the trade winds in the central and western equatorial Pacific, and not due to lighter-than-normal coastal winds. Normally, the easterly winds push the upper ocean water toward the western Pacific, deepening the thermocline and causing a rise in sea level in the west relative to the east. During an ENSO, when the winds relax, the warm water is displaced toward South America in a wavelike fashion, reversing the state; that is, causing the thermocline in the east to deepen, and the sea level to rise. For Peru, this marks the onset of an ENSO.

Although efforts to model the behavior of both the ocean and the atmosphere began as early as 1976, it is the occurrence of the very strong 1982/83 event that motivated unprecedented amounts of research directed toward predicting these episodes. Most of our current understanding of the dynamics of ENSO are as a result of models. These include physical-statistical methods (Barnett, 1984; Barnett et al., 1988);[10,11] linear dynamical models (Inoue and O'Brien, 1984);[12] and coupled

---

[B]There is another recurring climatic phenomenon which is quite opposite to ENSO. These so-called "Cold Events" (which have also been referred to as "anti-ENSO" or 'La Niña") are characterized by generally opposite oceanographic and atmospheric manifestations (and climatic variations) as in the "warm" ENSO. A detailed description of this "cold" phenomenon is beyond the scope of this chapter, but it is worth mentioning that, generally, the climatic impacts in Peru during a Cold Event are opposite to those during ENSO. That is, instead of high precipitation, there is very light precipitation in the northeastern region.

ocean-atmosphere models (Cane, 1986).[13] In 1983, the ICSU Scientific Committee on Oceanic Research (SCOR) defined El Nino as the appearance of anomalously warm water along the coast of Ecuador and Peru as far south as Lima (12° S), during which a normalized SST anomaly exceeding one standard deviation occurs for at least four consecutive months at three or more of five coastal stations (Talara, Puerto Chicama Chimbote, Isla Don Martin and Callao.)

The current understanding is that the SO is caused by interannual SST variations in the tropical Pacific (Philander, 1990)[14] and that El Niño events are characterized by positive SST anomalies along the coasts of Ecuador and Peru and along the equator eastward of 130°W, and by an equatorward expansion and intensification of the Inter-Tropical Convergence Zone (ITCZ)[C] over the eastern Pacific (Deser & Wallace, 1990).[15]

THE SCIENTIFIC RESPONSE

In the 1970's, the World Climate Research Program (WCRP) was developed under the World Meteorological Organization (WMO) and the International Council of Scientific Unions (ICSU). Prediction of climate fluctuations emerged as one of its major objectives, and in the early 1980's a series of scientific workshops were convened to develop a comprehensive program for the study of interannual variability in the Tropical Ocean and Global Atmosphere (TOGA). The international TOGA Program officially began January 1985, and is scheduled to continue through December 1994. The scientific objectives of the research program, as defined within the International Scientific Plan (WCRP, 1985),[16] are: a) to gain a description of the tropical oceans and the global atmosphere as a time dependent system, in order to determine the extent to which this sytem is predictable on time scales of months to years; b) to study the feasibility of modeling the coupled ocean-atmosphere system for the purpose of predicting its variations on time scales of months to years; and c) to provide the scientific background for designing an observing and data transmission system for operational prediction, if this capability is demonstrated by coupled ocean-atmosphere models. The 10-year research program encompasses four major elements: a) *long term observations,* to define the time-dependent structure of the tropical oceans and the global atmosphere and the interactions at the ocean-atmosphere interface; b) *empirical studies,* essential for estimating the predictability of the coupled climate system and for understanding the processes that control the system; c) *process studies,* focussed on specific processes identified as critically important for an understanding of large-scale ocean-atmosphere interaction; and d) *modeling* efforts guided by the long-range goal of operational prediction (NRC, 1986).[17]

In 1990, the National Academy of Sciences commissioned a mid-term review of the TOGA Program, and concluded that a remarkable degree of progress has been made toward meeting the objectives of the program. The coupled ocean-atmosphere

---

[C]The ITCZ is defined as the band of atmospheric convergence which circulates the globe, parallel to, and north of, the equator. This is an area of high atmospheric convection, cloudiness and precipitation.

system over the Pacific is now being monitored in near real time using both *in situ* and satellite remote sensing techniques, and an ocean observing system adequate for initialization and verification of prediction models is near completion. A modest ability to simulate the ENSO cycle with computer models has been demonstrated, and a plausible hypothesis has been proposed to explain the physical basis for the predictive nature of ENSO. Hence, the initial elements of an observational and prediction system are in place. However, a great deal of work remains if the full potential of prediction of the behavior of the tropical oceans and their relationship with the circulation of the global atmosphere is to be realized (NRC, 1990).[18]

ENSO-RELATED PRECIPITATION PATTERNS IN PERU

The west coast of South America, from the northern coast of Chile toward the northern coast of Peru, is characterized climatalogically by light precipitation, resulting in a semi-arid to arid climate. Along the northwestern coast and in the Andean highland region seasonal rainfall patterns prevail. East of the Andes mountain range, in the Peruvian Amazon basin, precipitation occurs year-round, but is greatest during a September to April "rainy season." A rainy season is also experienced between September and April in the highland region, as contrasted with the northern coastal region where precipitation begins in January and ends in April of each year. Total precipitation generally decreases as we move away from the equator, and south of 7°S practically no precipitation falls. At the same time there is a general increase in total rainfall as a function of altitude. From time to time, the northern coastal region is subjected to intensive precipitation and flash floods, while other regions in the Andean highland are experiencing intensive droughts, resulting in severe social and economic hardship.

Two meteorological mechanisms determine the precipitation patterns in the northwestern region during a normal rainy season. First, there are convective processes associated with the seasonal peak of SST in the eastern equatorial Pacific. During austral summer, the ITCZ shifts equatorward until, the average, its southern boundary is located near northern Peru. Secondly, there is a westward displacement of convective processes and precipitation crossing over the Western Andean mountain range, providing much of the precipitation at higher altitudes along the coast.

The climatological precipitation averages recorded during the rainy season at representative sites along the northern coast of Peru are presented in Table 1. Note that the precipitation decreases with latitude but increases with altitude, as stated above.

During ENSO events, the ITCZ is observed to shift further south, even crossing the equator when the episodes are strongest. Furthermore, SST values off the coast reach 2°12°C above normal, depending on the strength of the event. As a result of this southward shift of the ITCZ, atmospheric convection becomes more intense. This, combined with increased evaporation associated with higher SSRs, lead to relatively large increases in precipitation initially near the coast and then moving eastward. These increase are most pronounced at altitudes up to 300 meters, with more modest increases above that height. The dramatic increase in rainfall often results in flooding and mud slides along the western flank of the Andean mountain range.

Increases in precipitation in the northern coastal region of Peru during ENSO events are reflected in Fig. 1, which shows the relationship between anomalies observed in the SOI, the Puerto Chicama SST anomalies and the precipitation observed at Chulucanas during the rainy season. Due to the unique terrain around Chulucanas, which is located at an altitude of 95 meters, the moisture moving inland from the coast is more efficiently intercepted. As convective processes reach the Andean foothills, they become amplified, due to the regional topography, resulting in the development of large storm systems which then spread back across the desert areas.

A number of theories have been postulated to explain the precipitation patterns observed in Peru during the 1982/83 ENSO. For example, Horel and Cornejo-Garrido (1986)[19] suggested that atmospheric processes in the Amazon basin migrate westward and are responsible for the intensification of the storm systems in the northwestern region. On the other hand, Goldberg et al. (1987)[20] observed that storms originate near the coast and move eastward, reaching maximum intensity during evening and nighttime, and lasting 6 to 12 hours, or more. Satellite images of this event provide evidence that both processes contribute to the development of the storm systems.

SOCIO-ECONOMIC IMPACTS TO PERU

Historically, droughts and floods have been the greatest natural causes of famine in Peru, while earthquake-induced landslides have been among the most destructive throughout the Andean region. During ENSO events, heavy and repetitive convective rain storms have been the main cause for the devastating flash floods at the western Andean foothills and in the coastal plains region, whereas during Cold Events a lack of precipitation leads to droughts. The effects of droughts and floods on total food production have caused much human suffering and stress to society. Crop failures have lead to shortages of food and loss of employment, causing great social and political concern.

The most thorough compilation of the ocurrence of ENSO episodes during recorded history is given by Quinn et al. (1987),[21] whose analysis included the

TABLE 1.
Normal Precipitation (mm/month) along the northwestern coast of Peru

Name (Lat., Altitude)	Jan	Feb	Mar	April
Tumbes (3.5°S, 25m)	25	55	51	27
Talara (4.5°S, 50m)	3	8	7	3
Chulucanas (5.1°S, 95m)	21	59	109	27
Huarmaca (5.6°S, 2100m)	125	173	248	153
Chiclayo (6.5°S, 27m)	3	2	6	2

accounts of ENSOs found in documents related to the Spanish conquest. They identified the 1925/26 and 1982/83 events as the most severe of the 20th century. Evidence of historical catastrophic floods in Peru resulted from a study by Nials et al. (1979)[22] of the early irrigation system used in the coastal region. They found evidence that an ENSO 2-4 times the intensity of the very strong 1925/26 event occurred sometime within a century of 1100 A.D. Paleoclimatalogical records allow us to identify prehistorical events using proxy data such as cadmium content in tropical corals (Shen et al., 1987),[23] and oxygen isotope content in ice cores (Thompson et al., 1984).[24] These, and other proxy data related to climate change, are undergoing further study in Peru. Stratigraphic studies of the Casma floodplain, about 300 km north of Lima, have resulted in the identification of at least eighteen floods which have occurred over the past 7,000 years (Wells, 1990).[25]

The compilation of quantitative information on the impact of ENSO phenomena in Peru began after the 1972/73 event, when the Peruvian anchoveta fisheries collapsed. For this reason, impact studies originally focussed on the fisheries sector, and not on agriculture and other sectors. However, during the 1982/83 event, damage to the agricultural sector due to floods and drought exceeded that to

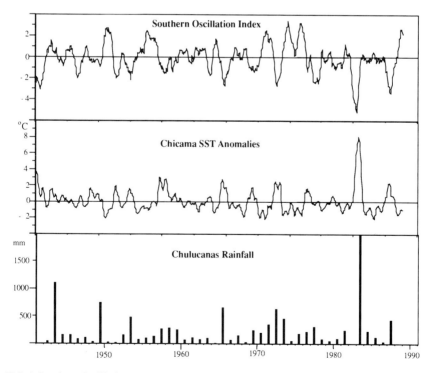

FIG. 1. Southern Oscillation Index, SST at Chicama, and rainfall at Chulucanas. The SOI is the five-month running mean of the difference between the standardized sea level pressure anomalies at Tahiti and Darwin (Tahiti-Darwin). The SST at Chicama is of the five-month running monthly means. The rainfall at Chulucanas is the accumulated seasonal (Jan-Apr) precipitation of each year.

fisheries. As a consequence, detailed information regarding impacts on land-based resources during this event are now more readily available.

During the 1982/83 event, flash floods and mud slides destroyed bridges, highways and farmland and killed hundreds of people. The nature, strength, extent and impacts of this event have been well documented in the scientific literature (Barber and Chavez, 1983; Cane, 1983; Halpern et. al., 1983; Lukas et. al., 1984; and Glynn, 1988)[26,27,28,29,30] as well as in popular magazines. Table 2 provides a breakdown of the estimated $2 billion in economic losses suffered by Peru due to the 1982/83 ENSO, based in the reports by CEPAL (1983)[31] and INP (1983).[32] These do not include other societal effects, such as malnutrition and disease, loss of employment and personal belongings, which are difficult to quantify. Social stresses and restoration of the physical infrastructure lasted for many years after the event.

GOVERNMENT RESPONSE TO INTERANNUAL CLIMATE VARIABILITY

Like other disastrous natural phenomena, the occurrence of ENSO's cannot be prevented; societies must adjust to cope with their impacts. Over the centuries, the people of Peru have been forced to endure ENSO-related reductions in agriculture and fisheries production. The strongest events have impacted the nation's capacity to produce food so severely that famine has resulted, along with the associated ills such as malnutrition, disease, etc. Until recently, the Government of Peru has had no option but to "mop up" after the event. For example, the well-documented collapse of the Peruvian anchoveta fishery associated with the 1972/73 event (CPPS, 1987; Glantz, 1990; Jordan, 1991)[33,34,35] resulted in the enactment of governmental decrees regulating further exploitation of the damaged resource. During 1983, the Government reacted in a similar manner. They declared the fishery, agriculture and transportation sectors "in emergency" and followed with a series of decrees and regulations, mostly related to fisheries. Fishing fleets were relocated to other areas, and refitted to target other species such as shrimp. Also, the Government

TABLE 2.
Estimated economic losses (in $ million) due to floods and droughts during the 1982/83 ENSO in Peru

Agribusiness (reduced agricultural and livestock production)	649.0
Fishing (reduced landings)	105.9
Industry (reduced production of consumer goods and oil products)	479.3
Electric Energy (damage to power plants and infrastructure)	16.1
Mining (reduced production)	310.4
Transportation and Communication (damage to infrastructure)	303.1
Housing (damage due to flooding)	70.0
Health (contamination of water, damage to sewage systems, health care centers and hospitals)	57.1
Education (damage to schools)	5.9
TOTAL	1,996.8

undertook a number of unscheduled oceanographic research cruises in order to assess the composition and quantity of coastal marine resources. Furthermore, as a result of the reduced agricultural production, the Government approved increased rice imports. Finally, in an effort to contend with the budget deficit resulting from the disastrous ENSO, the Government issued "Reconstruction Bonds" to be purchased by the population.

In Peru, as in most developing countries in the tropical region, the nature of economic activities is highly sensitive to the variability of climate, particularly in the agriculture sector. Therefore, these countries potentially have the most to gain from an ability to forecast seasonal variations in precipitation, especially as it relates to the growing season. To be useful, any forecast must be accompanied by an effective communication network so that the information will reach the affected communities. After all, a climate forecast has economic value only if it affects Governmental action and societal behavior.

For example, if upcoming precipitation patterns were predicted with reasonable accuracy one to two months before the growing season begins, farmers could be advised with greater confidence on the optimal crop which should be planted for the projected amount of rain and ambient temperature, hence increasing their yields. To a farmer, knowledge of the timing of the onset of the rainy season is critical, as it determines the timing of the planting of his crops. Quantitative forecasts of the amount and temporal distribution of precipitation and the range of ambient temperature during the growing season is important for planning purposes, but more difficult to forecast. Furthermore, in the fisheries sector, a forecast of future physical oceanic conditions in general, and anomalous events like ENSO in particular, would allow for strategic planning and adjustments in fishery practices, which should result in reduced capital losses and reduced unemployment.

Prior to the 1982/83 ENSO event, citizens and policy-makers in the Peruvian agricultural sector were unaware of the availability of climate data, collected outside the region, that could be used in national economic planning and mitigation of impacts of anomalous climate. They became aware of the potential benefits of proper application of available information only after the 1982/83 event, when a series of experimental forecasts were attempted, based on an improved understanding of the dynamics of ENSO.

The example presented here refers to the application of the climate forecast to crop productivity in the northern region of Peru, a region where precipitation and ambient temperature are known to be well correlated with ENSO events (see Figure 2).

In Peru, economic development is based on a set of interrelated national plans for each social and economic sector. The agricultural plan is, by constitutional law, a component of utmost priority within the national economic plan. Its purpose is to promote the efficient development of the sector. It sets forth the basic actions and general goals to be followed by the various public and commercial agencies involved. Specifically, the program establishes annual guidelines and goals for production. The execution of the program is subjected to continuous evaluation which allows for pertinent corrections and for the improvement of the formulation of future plans. The Government, through the Ministry of Agriculture, and the national committees of nongovernmental agrarian organizations together play a critical role in achieving the agricultural production goals, through a consensus-building process. The issues debated include regulation of water distribution in the irrigated areas, prices of fertilizer, interest rates for loans from the agrarian bank and prices of agricultural products. They also discuss the provision of subsidies for particular goods as well as the availability of technical assistance in certain areas.

Once the 1982/83 event ended and the rains ceased (late June 1983) the entire population along the northern coastal region as well as the industries related to agriculture and the agrarian organizations and the Government itself shared a deep concern about what would happen during the subsequent rainy season. Based on knowledge of the behavior of some previous events, there was local speculation that the heavy rains would return late 1983 and early 1984. The need for scientific advice was imperative. Peruvian scientists attempted to explain what had happened and proposed to develop a program to forecast future events. The first task was to forecast the climate conditions for the upcoming rainy season. A network of communication to receive extra-regional climate-related information was set up in September 1983 and analysis of the data began.

The results, based on the analysis of current global ocean-atmosphere observations, indicated that the event would not be repeated in the following rainy season, and were presented early November 1983 to the heads of the agrarian organizations, banking officials, and to the Minister of Agriculture. This information was incorporated into national planning for the 1983-84 agrarian campaign, as well as in the ongoing reconstruction program, and plans of other government and private agencies. The 1983-84 agrarian campaign was a successful one.

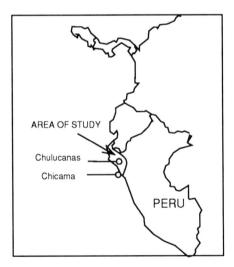

FIG. 2. Location of area of study and observational sites referred to in Figs. 1 and 3.

From this point on, in early November of each year, a forecast of the character of the upcoming rainy season has been incorporated into national planning for the agricultural sector. The scenario can be described as follows: in September of each year, scientists at the Peruvian Geophysical Institute (IGP) analyze the pertinent oceanographic and meteorological data, consult with modelers in the U.S. and elsewhere, and prepare a November forecast based on the current understanding of the evolution of ENSOs and Cold Events, and their impacts to the climate in the northwestern region of Peru. This forecast is presented as one of four possibilities: (i) normal or average condition, (ii) slightly warmer and wetter than normal, (iii) ENSO condition, and (iv) Cold Event - cooler and drier than normal. Once the forecast is made, on behalf of the farming community, the Head of the nongovernmental agrarian organization and Governmental officials meet to arrive at a production strategy. Decisions are made, based on the outlook for the coming rainy season, regarding the appropriate combination of crops to be sown, in order to maximize the yield of the area planted. For example, rice and cotton, which are two of the primary crops sown in the northeastern region, are highly influenced by the quantities and timing of rainfall. For maximum yields, rice needs large

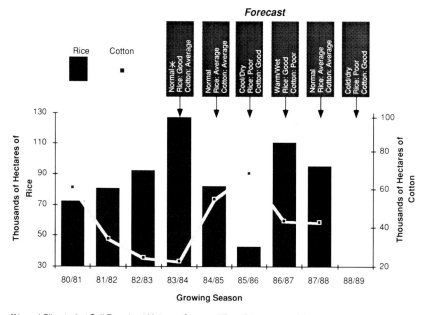

FIG. 3. Pre and post-ENSO 1982-83 agricultural area sowed in the northern coastal region of Peru. Forecast was issued at least one month before the beginning of each crop season.

volumes of water and relatively warm ambient temperatures throughout the growing season combined with relatively dry and cooler nighttime temperatures during the ripening phase. Rainfall is, by far, the most limiting climatic constraint to the growth of rice. On the other hand, cotton, with its deeper root structure, is capable of thriving, hence yielding greater production, during years of light precipitation. Once a forecast is made, farmers can chose the optimal combination of crops to sow. Fig. 3 shows the area sowed with rice and cotton in the northern coastal region between 1980 and 1987. Notice the areal increase or decrease depending on the forecast beginning in the 1983-84 growing season.

Of particular interest is the 1987 ENSO forecast. This forecast, issued late September 1986, was based on results of models developed in the U.S. combined with oceanographic and atmospheric data collected in the tropical Pacific. It looked as though an ENSO event of moderate intensity was developing. The information circulated throughout the scientific community as well as throughout Government agencies and even by the popular media. The President of Peru called his experts together, and after much debate he issued an official announcement of the forecast in late December 1986. Again, the forecast was used in the formulation of national agricultural planning and in other sectors, as early as October 1986.

DISCUSSION AND FUTURE DIRECTIONS

Societies learn to conduct daily affairs and economic activity according to the climatic regimes in which they exist, and are often unprepared to adjust as quickly as desirable to dramatic deviations from this expected state. The ENSO phenomenon provides us with an interesting example of how populations are affected by dramatic changes in climate, and how they can organize to react, adjust and (most recently) anticipate and prepare for anomalous behavior.

Future Research

There are a number of tasks remaining as we continue our quest to understand the coupled ocean-atmosphere climate system, and to model and predict its anomalous meteorological manifestations in order to prepare society for its impacts. Recognizing that, the TOGA scientific community plans to undertake a large experiment, the Coupled Ocean-Atmosphere Response Experiment (TOGA-COARE) in the western tropical Pacific region, in order to improve our understanding of the physical processes taking place at the ocean-atmosphere interface. This multinational experiment is aimed at understanding the principal processes responsible for the coupling of the ocean and the atmosphere in the western Pacific region (which exhibits the warmest SSTs on earth), the principal atmospheric processes that organize convection in the region, the oceanic response to combined buoyancy and wind stress forcing in the western Pacific, and the multiple-scale interactions that extend the oceanic and atmospheric influence of this warm region to other regions and vice versa. It is anticipated that achievement of these goals will lead to improved simulations of the coupled ocean-atmosphere system, and improved operational capability aimed at the prediction of coupled ocean-atmosphere phenomena such as ENSO and Cold Events on the time scale of months to years (WCRP, 1990).[36]

It should be recognized that although much work remains in improving the predictive skill of coupled General Circulation Models, great progress has been made in making predictions of ENSO as a result of improved understanding of the dynamic ocean and atmospheric systems in the tropics. The TOGA community feels it is time to pursue a more systematic investigation of the predictability of the tropical climate system and to begin planning for routine and regular predictions of the atmospheric and oceanic fields connected with the phases of ENSO. To this end, the TOGA Program on Seasonal to Interannual Prediction is being developed (NOAA, 1991).[37]

Finally, an improved understanding of the climatic teleconnections, or the relationship between the traditional TOGA domain and other regions, is highly desirable. Relationships have been suggested between ENSO and climate variability outside the tropical Pacific region, such as fluctuations in the annual monsoon cycle in the Indian Ocean and Western Pacific region (Shukla and Paulino, 1983),[38] reduced precipitation in northeast Brazil (Moura and Shukla, 1981),[39] Southern Africa (Ogallo, 1987)[40] and the USSR (Pitavranov, 1987),[41] as well as between Cold Events and drought in the north central United States (Trenberth, et al, 1988).[42] Although these anomalous climate patterns have been observed in conjunction with ENSO and Cold Events, the physical atmospheric teleconnections are not well understood. Regional models should be developed to document the effects of ENSO to specific regions, within and outside the tropical Pacific.

ENSO-Related Climate Impacts

Interpretation of the results shown in Fig. 3 is very encouraging in terms of societal responses. As the skill of climate prediction improves, the economic benefit associated with the applicability of this information will increase. The Peruvian experience can provide insights into how societies in other countries might become prepared to benefit from such climate forecasts in the future. In order that individual nations can benefit from ENSO predictions, however, they must have a good understanding of their mean and anomalous climate and precipitation patterns. Nations must organize themselves to benefit from the effort of the global scientific community in providing reliable predictions. This means analysis of existing historical data sets as well as improved systematic data collection efforts. Statistical studies of relationships between regional precipitation patterns and specific ENSO and Cold Events will assist nations in characterizing the differing manifestations of the various ENSO "types".

Socio-Economic Impacts

Predicting ENSOs and understanding the related fluctuations in temperature and precipitation patterns is not enough. Economists and social scientists must be encouraged to join their physical and natural science colleagues in studying the impacts of this phenomenon on society. Unless we have specific evidence on how society will be affected by a particular change in climate, decision-makers will be unprepared to act, either to minimize adverse impacts, or maximize positive impacts. Studies of the economic benefits of societal and governmental responses to climate forecasts should be encouraged.

Public Sector Response

We have established that, in Peru, advanced knowledge of climate conditions can play an important role in the decision-making process, particularly on the use of agricultural lands in order to maximize the yield. It is especially interesting to note the experience during the 1983-84 growing season. Decision-makers were about to act according to their best knowledge as they prepared for the upcoming growing season. Everything they knew was leading them to plan for another ENSO, and sow only the area which would not be damaged by the expected inundation. Scientists came forward and forecasted "normal conditions", and although this was the first attempt to forecast, policy-makers acted on the advice of the scientists and developed a production plan whch resulted in excellent rice crop yields. Thus, a climate forecast—properly applied—made a great difference in the total crop production that year.

Other nations affected by ENSO should be encouraged to formalize a policy-making infrastructure capable of utilizing ENSO forecasts. The experience in Peru which we have provided should be viewed as a model with elements of relevance to each of the interested nations.

REFERENCES

1. Trenberth, K.E. 1991. General characteristics of El Niño, pp. 13-42. In: M. Glants, R.W. Katz and N. Nicholls (Ed.) *Teleconnections Linking Worldwide Climate Anomalies.* Cambridge University Press, New York, N.Y., 371 pp.
2. Canby, T.Y. 1984. El Niño's ill wind. *Nat. Geogr.* 165 (2): 144-183.
3. Nicholls, N. 1987. The El Niño/Southern Oscillation Phenomenon. In: M. Glantz, R.W. Katz and M. Krenz (Ed.) *The Societal Impacts Associated with the 1982-83 Worldwide Climate Anomalies.* UNEP Report, 105 pp.
4. Walker, G.T. 1923. World weather. I. *Mem Indian Meteorol. Dep.* 24: 75-131.
5. Walker, G.T. and E.W. Bliss. 1932. World weather V. *Mem R. Met. Soc.* 4: 53-84.
6. Berlage, H.P. 1957. Fluctuations of the general atmospheric circulation of more than one year, their nature and prognostic value. *K. Ned. Meteorol. Inst. Meded. Verh.* 69: 152 pp.
7. Bjerknes, J. 1966a. Survey of El Niño 1957-58 in its relation to tropical Pacific meteorology. *Inter. Am. Trop. Tuna Comm. Bull.* 12: 1-62.

8. Bjerknes, J. 1966b. A possible response of the atmospheric Hadley circulation to equatorial anomalies of ocean temperature. *Tellus.* 18: 820-829.
9. Wyrtki, K. 1975. El Niño - The dynamic response of the equatorial Pacific Ocean to atmospheric forcing. *J. Phys. Oceanogr.* 5: 572-584.
10. Barnett, T.P. 1984. Prediction of El Niño of 1982-83. *Mon. Weather Rev.* 112: 1403-1407.
11. Barnett, T.P., N. Graham, M. Cane, S. Zebiak, S. Dolan, J. O'Brien, and D. Legler. 1988. On the prediction of El Niño of 1986-1987. *Science.* 241: 192-196.
12. Inoue, M. and J.J. O'Brien. 1984. A forecast model for the onset on a major El Niño. *Mon. Weather Rev.* 112: 2326-2337.
13. Cane, M.A. 1986. El Niño. *Annu. Rev. Earth Planet Sci.* 14: 43-70.
14. Philander, S.G. 1990. *El Niño, La Niña, and the Southern Oscillation.* Academic Press, Inc., 289 pp.
15. Deser, C. and J.M. Wallace. 1990. Large-scale atmospheric circulation features of warm and cold episodes in the tropical Pacific. *J. Climate.* 3: 1254-1281.
16. World Climate Research Program Publication Series No. 3. 1985. *Scientific Plan for the Tropical Ocean and Global Atmosphere Programme.* World Meteorological Organization, 146 pp.
17. National Research Council. 1986. *US Participation in the TOGA Program: A Research Strategy.* National Academy Press.
18. National Research Council. 1990. *TOGA: A Review of Progress and Future Opportunities.* National Academy Press, 66 pp.
19. Horel, J.D. and A.G. Cornejo-Garrido. 1986. Convection along the coast of northern Peru during 1983: spatial and temporal variation of clouds and rainfall. *Mon. Weather Rev.* 114: 2091-2105.
20. Goldberg, R.A., G. Tisnado and R.A. Scofield. 1987. Characteristics of extreme rainfall events in northwestern Peru during the 1982-83 El Niño period. *J. Geophys. Res.* 92: 14, 225-14, 241.
21. Quinn, W.H., V.T. Neal and S.E. Antunez de Mayolo. 1987. El Niño occurrences over the past four and a half centuries. *J. Geophys. Res.* 92: 14, 449-14, 461.
22. Nials, F.L., E.E. Deeds, M.E. Mosley, S.G. Pozorski, T.G. Pozorski and R. Feldman. 1979. El Niño: the catastrophic flooding of coastal Peru. *Field Mus. Nat. Hist. Bull.* 50(8): 4-10.
23. Shen, G.T., E.A. Boyle and D.W. Lea. 1987. Cadmium in corals as a tracer of historical upwelling and industrial fallout. *Nature.* 328: 794-796.
24. Thompson, L.G., E. Moseley-Thompson and B. Morales-Arnao. El Niño-Southern Oscillation events recorded in the stratigraphy of the tropical Quelccaya ice cap, Peru. *Science.* 226: 50-53.
25. Wells, L.E. 1990. Holocene history of the El Niño phenomenon as recorded in flood sediments of northern coastal Peru. *Geology.* 18: 1134-1137.
26. Barber, R.T. and F.P. Chavez. 1983. Biological consequences of El Niño. *Science.* 222: 1203-1210.
27. Cane, M.A. 1983. Oceanographic events during El Niño. *Science.* 222: 1189-1195.
28. Halpern, D., S.P. Hayes, A. Leetma, D.V. Hansen and S.G. H. Philander. 1983.

Oceanographics observations of the 1982 warming of the tropical eastern Pacific. *Science.* 221: 1173-1175.
29. Lukas, R., S.P. Hayes and K. Wyrtki. 1984. Equatorial sea level response during the 1982-1983 El Niño. *J. Geophys. Res.* 89: 10, 425-10, 430.
30. Glynn, P.W. 1988. El Niño-Southern Oscillation 1982-83: nearshore population community and ecosystem responses. *Annu. Rev. Ecol. Sys.* 19: 309-345.
31. CEPAL (UN Economic Commission for Latin America). 1983. Los desastres naturales de 1982-83 en Bolivia, Ecuador y Peru. E/CEPAL/G 1274. New York: United Nations.
32. INP (Instituto Nacional de Planificacion) 1983. Programa integral de rehabilitacion y reconstruccion de las zonas afectadas por los desastres de la naturaleza. Vol. I: Evaluacion de daños en las zonas afectadas. Lima, Peru: INP.
33. Pacifico Sur (Comision Permanente del Pacifico Sur). 1987. Fenomeno de El Niño 1982-1983 con particular referencia a sus efectos sobre los recursos pesqueros y las pesquerias en el Pacifico sudeste. 16: pp. 278.
34. Glantz, M.H. 1990. Does history have a future? forecasting climate change effects on fisheries by analogy. *Fisheries.* 15(6): 39-44.
35. Jordan, R. 1991. Impact of ENSO events on the southeastern Pacific region with special reference to the interaction of fishing and climate variability, pp. 401-430. In: M. Glantz, R.W. Katz and N. Nicholls (Ed.) *Teleconnections Linking Worldwide Climate Anomalies.* Cambridge University Press, New York, N.Y. 371 pp.
36. World Climate Research Program Report No. 3. Addendum. 1990. *Scientific Plan for the TOGA Couple Ocean Atmosphere Research Experiment.* World Meteorological Organization, 118 pp.
37. NOAA Climate and Global Change Special Report No. 4. 1991. *Prospectus for a Tropical Ocean Global Atmosphere (TOGA) Program on Seasonal to Interannual Prediction,* 46 pp.
38. Shukla, J. and D.A. Paolino. 1983. The Southern Oscillation and long-range forecasting of the summer monsoon rainfall over India. *Mon. Weather Rev.* 111: 1830-1837.
39. Moura, A.D. and J. Shukla. 1981. On the dynamics of droughts in Northeast Brazil: Observations, theory and numerical experiment with a general circulation model. *J. Atmos. Sci.* 38: 2653-2675.
40. Ogallo, L. 1987. Impacts of the 1982-83 ENSO event on Eastern and South Africa. In: M. Glantz, R.W. Katz and M. Krenz (Ed.) *The Societal Impacts Associated with the 1982-83 Worldwide Climate Anomalies.* UNEP Report, 105 pp.
41. Pitovranov, S.E. 1987. The impact of the 1982-83 weather anomalies on some branches of the economy of the USSR. In: M. Glantz, R.W. Katz and M. Krenz (Ed.) *The Societal Impacts Associated with the 1982-83 Worldwide Climate Anomalies.* UNEP Report, 105 pp.
42. Trenberth, K.E., G.W. Branstator and P.A. Arkin. 1988. Origin of the 1988 North American drought. *Science.* 242: 1640-1645.

Natural and Technological Disasters: Causes, Effects and Preventive Measures. Edited by
S.K. Majumdar, G.S. Forbes, E.W. Miller, and R.F. Schmalz. © 1992, The Pennsylvania Academy
of Science.

Chapter Eighteen

DROUGHT: ITS PHYSICAL AND SOCIAL DIMENSIONS

DONALD A. WILHITE
Associate Professor
Department of Agricultural Meteorology and
Director, International Drought Information Center
University of Nebraska
Lincoln, NE 68583-0728

INTRODUCTION

Drought has been a threat to human existence throughout history. Today, as in the past, drought alters the course of civilizations. It is not merely a physical phenomenon, but the result of an interplay between a natural event (precipitation deficiencies due to natural climatic variability on varying timescales) and the demand placed on water supply by human-use systems. Extended periods of drought have resulted in significant economic, environmental, and social impacts, including food supply disruptions, famine, massive soil erosion, migrations of people, and wars.

Human activities often exacerbate the impacts of drought (e.g., the Dust Bowl in the Great Plains, the Sahelian drought of the early 1970s). This trend appears to be accelerating because of the increasing demand being placed on local and regional water resources as a result of the earth's rapidly expanding population. Recent droughts in developing and developed countries and the concomitant impacts and personal hardships that resulted have underscored the vulnerability of all societies to this natural hazard. It is difficult to determine whether it is the frequency of drought that is increasing, or simply societal vulnerability to it.

DROUGHT AS NATURAL HAZARD

Drought differs from other natural hazards (such as floods, hurricanes, and earth-quakes) in several ways. First, since the effects of drought accumulate slowly over a considerable period of time, and may linger for years after the termination of the event, its onset and end are difficult to determine. Because of this, drought has been described as a "creeping phenomenon". [1] Second, the absence of a precise and universally accepted definition of drought adds to the confusion about whether or not a drought exists and, if it does, its severity.[2] Third, drought impacts are less obvious and are spread over a larger geographical area than are damages that result from other natural hazards. Drought seldom results in structural damage. For these reasons the quantification of impacts and the provision of disaster relief are far more difficult tasks for drought than they are for other natural hazards.

Drought is a normal part of climate for virtually all climatic regimes. It is a tem-porary aberration that occurs in high as well as low rainfall areas. Drought therefore differs from aridity since the latter is restricted to low rainfall regions and is a per-manent feature of climate. The character of drought is distinctly regional, reflect-ing unique meteorological, hydrological, and socioeconomic characteristics. Many people associate the occurrence of drought with the Great Plains of North America, Africa's Sahelian region, India, or Australia; they may have difficulty visualizing drought in Southeast Asia, Brazil, Western Europe, or the eastern United States, regions normally considered to have a surplus of water.

Drought should be considered relative to some long-term average condition of balance between precipitation and evapotranspiration in a particular area, a con-dition often perceived as "normal". It is the consequence of a natural reduction in the amount of precipitation received over an extended period of time, usually a season or more in length, although other climatic factors (such as high temperatures, high winds, and low relative humidity) are often associated with it in many regions of the world and can significantly aggravate the severity of the event. Drought is also related to the timing (i.e., principal season of occurrence, delays in the start of the rainy season, occurrence of rains in relation to principal crop growth stages) and the effectiveness of the rains (i.e., rainfall intensity, number of rainfall events).

Drought Types and Definitions

Because drought affects so many economic and social sectors, scores of defini-tions have been developed by a variety of disciplines. Each discipline incorporates different physical, biological, and/or socioeconomic factors in its definition of drought. Because of these numerous and diverse disciplinary views, considerable confusion often exists over exactly what constitutes a drought. Research has shown that the lack of a precise and objective definition in specific situations has been an obstacle to understanding drought, which has led to indecision and/or inaction on the part of managers, policy makers, and others.[2] It must be accepted that the importance of drought lies in its impacts. Thus definitions should be impact and region specific in order to be used in an operational mode by decision makers. A universal definition of drought is an unrealistic expectation.

Drought can be grouped by type as follows: meteorological, hydrological, agricultural, and socioeconomic. *Meteorological* drought is expressed solely on the basis of the degree of dryness (often in comparison to some "normal" or average amount) and the duration of the dry period. Definitions of meteorological drought must be considered as region specific since the atmospheric conditions that result in deficiencies of precipitation are highly variable from region to region. *Hydrological* droughts are concerned more with the effects of periods of precipitation shortfalls on surface or subsurface water supply (stream flow, reservoir and lake levels, ground water) rather than with precipitation shortfalls. Hydrological droughts are usually out-of-phase or lag the occurrence of meteorological and agricultural droughts. The frequency and severity of hydrological drought is often defined on the basis of its influence on river basins. *Agricultural* drought links various characteristics of meteorological drought to agricultural impacts, focusing on precipitation shortages, differences between actual and potential evapotranspiration, soil water deficits, and so forth. An operational definition of agricultural drought should account for the variable susceptibility of crops at different stages of crop development. *Socioeconomic* drought associates the supply and demand of some economic good with elements of meteorological, hydrological, and agricultural drought. This concept of drought supports the strong symbiosis that exists between drought and human activities. For example, poor land use practices such as overgrazing can reduce vegetative quality and increase soil erosion. Ultimately, this practice will lead to a reduction in animal carrying capacity, exacerbating the impacts of and vulnerability to future droughts.

Drought Charcteristics and Severity

Droughts differ in three essential characteristics—intensity, duration, and spatial coverage. *Intensity* refers to the degree of the precipitation shortfall and/or the severity of impacts associated with the shortfall. It is generally measured by the departure of some climatic index from normal and is closely linked to duration in the determination of impact. The simplest index in widespread use is the percent of normal precipitation. With this index, actual precipitation is compared to "normal" or average precipitation (defined as the most recent 30-year mean) for time periods ranging from one to twelve or more months. Numerous other precipitation-based indices exist, such as the decile-based system used operationally in Australia for monitoring meteorological/climatological drought.[3]

The most widely used method for determining drought severity in the United States is the Palmer Drought Severity Index (PDSI).[4] The PDSI evaluates prolonged periods of abnormally wet or abnormally dry weather. It relates accumulated differences of actual precipitation to average precipitation for individual climatic regions, taking into account evapotranspiration, runoff, and soil infiltration. PDSI values generally range from +4 (extreme wetness) to −4 (extreme drought), although values above or below these thresholds are not unusual. The PDSI, which was developed in the mid-1960s, is used operationally to track moisture conditions and anomalies in the United States. It has also been used to classify and compare historical drought periods from 1895 to the present.[5]

Another distinguishing feature of drought is its *duration*. Droughts usually require a minimum of two or three months to become established but then can continue for several consecutive years. The magnitude of drought impact is closely related to the timing of the onset of the precipitation shortage, its intensity, and the duration of the event.

Each drought has unique spatial characteristics. The percent of the total area of the contiguous United States affected by severe to extreme drought has been highly variable over the past century (Figure 1). The largest area affected by drought occurred during the 1930s—particularly 1934, when more than 65 percent of the

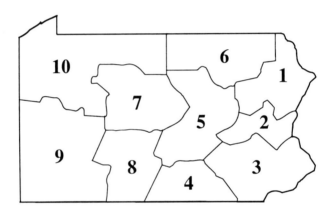

PDSI Value	District										
	1	2	3	4	5	6	7	8	9	10	Avg.
< -2.00	17.3	18.9	15.7	16.9	19.4	19.1	17.1	16.1	18.1	18.7	17.7
-2.00 to -2.99	1.5	1.3	0.8	1.8	4.3	3.6	3.9	2.9	2.8	3.2	2.6
-3.00 to -3.99	10.9	11.1	10.1	10.4	9.0	11.0	9.3	8.0	11.4	9.6	10.1
≤ -4.00	4.9	6.5	5.0	5.0	6.1	4.7	3.9	5.3	3.9	6.0	5.1

FIGURE 1. PDSI values for Pennsylvania, 1895-1989, for the state's ten climatic divisions.

country was experiencing severe or extreme drought. Significant areas of the United States experienced severe to extreme drought in the 1890s, 1910, 1925-26, 1953-57, 1964-65, 1976-77, 1983, and 1988-91.

From a historical perspective, the frequency of drought occurrence varies by region according to climatic regime. Wilhite and Wood[6] have shown that the greatest frequency of extreme drought (4 to 10%), according to the PDSI, occurs in the interior portion of the country, particularly states in the Great Plains, Rocky Mountains, Great Basin, and Upper Midwest.

An analysis of PDSI values for Pennsylvania for the period 1895-1989 reveals only a minor degree of east-west variation in drought frequency for the ten climatic divisions (Figure 1). For moderate to extreme drought (PDSI $\leq$ – 2.00), PDSI values range from 19.4% in division 5 to 15.7% in division 3. The average for the state is 17.7%. Moderate (– 2.00 to – 2.99), severe (– 3.00 to – 3.99), and extreme ($\leq$ – 4.00) droughts average 2.6%, 10.1%, and 5.1%, respectively, across the State.

Figure 2 depicts a historical time series of PDSI values for the Pocono Climatic Division in northeastern Pennsylvania for the period of 1895-1989. The length of the bar above or below the zero (normal) line indicates the magnitude of dry or wet periods during this period. This time series has several noteworthy characteristics. First, wet and dry years are often clustered, such as in the years from about 1962 to current. Second, the duration of wet and dry periods in this climatic division was less from 1895 until the early 1960s. Since the early 1960s there has

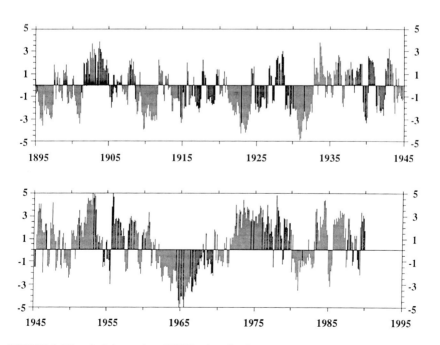

FIGURE 2. Historical time series of PDSI values for the Pocono Climatic Division, 1895-1989.

occurred one extended drought and one extended wet period. Since 1980, drought and wet periods have been of short duration and moderate intensity. Third, the drought of record for this climatic division is the period of years in the mid-1960s. Drought conditions persisted between 1962 until about 1968 with PDSI values less than − 4.00 (extreme drought) during 1964-1965. The drought of record is an important concept for engineering design purposes. For most of the country, the 1930s represents the drought of record, although this will vary from one region to another.

CAUSES AND PREDICTABILITY

Empirical studies conducted over the past century have shown that drought is the result of many causes, and these are often synergistic in nature. Some of the causes may be the result of influences that originate far from the drought-affected area. In recent years, research on the role of interacting systems, or *teleconnections*, has helped explain regional and even global patterns of climatic variability. These patterns tend to recur periodically with enough frequency and with similar characteristics over a sufficient length of time that they offer opportunities to improve our ability for long-range climate prediction, particularly in the tropics. One such teleconnection is the El Niño/Southern Oscillation (ENSO).

The immediate cause of drought is the predominant sinking motion of air (subsidence) that results in compressional warming or high pressure, thus inhibiting cloud formation and resulting in a lowered relative humidity and less precipitation. Most climatic regions experience varying degrees of dominance by high pressure, often depending on the season. Prolonged droughts occur when large-scale anomalies in atmospheric circulation patterns become established and persist for periods of months, seasons, or longer.

The underlying causes for these disruptions in large-scale atmospheric circulation patterns are not well understood. The principal causal mechanisms that have been identified are the El Niño/Southern Oscillation (ENSO), abnormal sea-surface temperature patterns, soil moisture desiccation, and nonlinear behavior of the climate system.[7] Although the occurrence of an ENSO event is principally associated with disruptions in atmospheric circulation patterns in the tropical and southern hemispheric areas of the Pacific Ocean and changes in sea-surface temperatures in the eastern and central equatorial Pacific, weather patterns are disrupted for regions well outside of the Pacific region. The recent severe ENSO event of 1982-83, for example, resulted in floods and drought worldwide. ENSO events have been related to droughts in Australia, Indonesia, India, and the United States, to name just a few locations.

The extreme drought that affected the United States and Canada during 1988 is a good example of a large-scale atmospheric circulation anomaly. This drought was one of the most extensive droughts to occur in North America in many years. A common explanation for the drought, which set up quickly in the spring and continued through most of the summer months, was the displacement of the jet stream to the north of its normal position so that storm tracks were similarly displaced.

However, to fully understand the origins of the drought, one must investigate the reasons for the displacement of the jet stream. Several years of drought for portions of the United States preceded the extremely dry conditions of 1988. Drought conditions in the southeastern United States, along the West Coast, and in the Pacific Northwest persisted into the spring of 1988, spreading across the Prairie Provinces and the northern and midwestern portions of the United States during the spring and summer months. The West Coast drought of 1987 had been associated with the occurrence of El Niño conditions in the tropical Pacific Ocean. Associated with an El Niño event are major alterations in atmospheric circulation, which in turn result in conditions favorable to the development of an unusually strong high pressure ridge near the West Coast of the United States and lower pressure over the north Pacific Ocean. In 1987, this resulted in a split of the jet stream into two branches. The southern branch was not very active and did not result in much precipitation in southern California; the northern branch was displaced far to the north. The end product of this pattern was that the high pressure ridge blocked the passage of precipitation-producing low-pressure systems and cold fronts into the western states and the northern Great Plains states. The establishment and persistent recurrence of an atmospheric system such as a ridge of high pressure can dominate a region for a month, season, year, or period of years and thus set the stage for the persistent subsidence of air and drought.

Very little skill currently exists to predict drought for a month or more in advance. What are the prospects that these predictions can be improved significantly in the near future? The potential predictability differs by region, season, and climatic regime. Recent technological advancements make prospects somewhat better today than a decade ago for some regions, such as the tropics. Meteorologists in this area now know that a major portion of the atmospheric variability that occurs on time scales of months to several years is associated with variations in tropical sea surface temperatures. But significant advancements beyond what has been achieved will require major breakthroughs in the use of dynamical models that couple the ocean-atmosphere systems. Meteorologists do not believe that highly skilled forecasts are attainable for all regions a season or more in advance.

THE IMPACTS OF DROUGHT

Drought impacts are often referred to as direct or indirect, or they are assigned an order of propagation (i.e., first-, second-, or third-order). Conceptually speaking, the more removed the impact from the cause, the more complex the link to the cause. In other words, a loss of yield resulting from drought is a direct or first-order impact of drought, but the consequences of that impact, such as loss of income, farm foreclosures, outmigration, and government relief programs, are secondary or tertiary impacts. First-order impacts are usually of a biophysical nature; higher-order impacts are usually associated with socioeconomic valuation, adjustment responses, and long-term "change". The impacts of drought can be classified into three principal types: economic, environmental, and social (Table 1). Economic impacts range from direct losses in the broad agricultural and agriculturally related sectors, including forestry and fishing, to losses in recreation, transportation, banking, and energy sectors. Other economic impacts include added unemployment and loss of revenue to local, state, and federal government. Environmental losses are the result of damages to plant and animal species, wildlife habitat, and air and water quality; forest and range

TABLE 1.

Economic, environmental, and social impacts of drought.

Problem Sectors	Impacts
Economic	• loss from dairy and livestock production 　reduced productivity of range land 　forced reduction of foundation stock 　closure/limitation of public lands to grazing 　high cost/unavailability of water for livestock 　high cost/unavailability of feed for livestock 　increased predation 　range fires • loss from crop production 　damage to perennial crops; crop loss 　reduced productivity of crop land (wind erosion, etc.) 　insect infestation 　plant disease 　wildlife damage to crops • loss from timber production 　forest fires 　tree disease 　insect infestation 　impaired productivity of forest land • loss from fishery production 　damage to fish habitat 　loss of young fish due to decreased flows • loss from recreational businesses • loss to manufacturers and sellers of recreational equipment • loss to energy industries affected by drought-related power curtailments • loss to industries directly dependent on agricultural production (e.g., fertilizer manufacturers, food processors, etc.) • unemployment from drought-related production declines • strain on financial institutions (foreclosures, greater credit risks, capital shortfalls, etc.) • revenue losses to State and local governments (from reduced tax base) • revenues to water supply firms 　revenue shortfalls 　windfall profits • loss from impaired navigability of streams, rivers and canals • cost of water transport or transfer • cost of new or supplemental water source development

TABLE 1 *(continued)*

Problem Sectors	Impacts

Environmental	• damage to animal species
	    wildlife habitat
	    lack of feed and drinking water
	    disease
	    vulnerability to predation (e.g., from species concentration near water)
	• damage to fish species
	• damage to plant species
	• water quality effects (e.g., salt concentration)
	• air quality effects (dust, pollutants)
	• visual and landscape quality (dust, vegetative cover, etc.)

Social	• public safety from forest and range fires • health-related low flow problems (e.g., diminished sewage flows, increased pollutant concentrations, etc.) • inequity in the distribution of drought impacts/relief

fires; degradation of landscape quality; and soil erosion. These losses are difficult to quantify, but growing public awareness and concern for environmental quality has forced public officials to focus greater attention on these effects. Social impacts involve public safety, health, conflicts between water users, and inequities in the distribution of impacts and disaster relief programs.

Because of the number of affected groups and sectors associated with drought, the geographic size of the area affected, and the problems associated with quantifying environmental damages and personal hardships, the precise determination of the financial costs of drought is difficult. Although drought occurs somewhere in the country each year, *significant* or *major* episodes often occur in clusters. Therefore, direct and indirect losses may be extremely large for one or two consecutive years and then negligible for several years. The impacts of the 1988 drought in the United States have been estimated at nearly $40 billion.[8]

DROUGHT RESPONSE AND PREPAREDNESS

With the occurrence of any natural disaster come appeals for disaster assistance from the affected area. During the twentieth century, governments have typically responded to drought by providing emergency, short-term, and long-term assistance to distressed areas. Emergency and short-term assistance programs are often reactive, a kind of "Band-Aid" approach to more serious land and water management problems. Scientists, government officials, and recipients of relief have long criticized this approach as inefficient and ineffective. Long-term assistance programs are far fewer in number, but they are proactive. They attempt to lessen a region's vulnerability to drought through improved management and planning.

Governmental response to drought includes a wide range of potential actions to deal with the impacts of water shortages on people and various economic sectors. In the United States, agencies of the federal government and Congress typically respond by making massive amounts of relief available to the affected areas, mostly in the form of short-term emergency measures to agricultural producers, such as feed assistance for livestock, drilling of new wells, and low-interest farm operating loans. This reactive approach to natural disasters is commonly referred to as crisis management. In crisis management the time to act is perceived by decision makers to be short. Emergency relief programs do little if anything to reduce vulnerability to drought and may in fact increase vulnerability in the long term.

Research has demonstrated that reaction to crisis often results in the implementation of hastily prepared assessment and response procedures that lead to ineffective, poorly coordinated, and untimely response. An alternative approach is to initiate planning between periods of drought, thus developing a more coordinated response that might more effectively address longer-term issues and specific problem areas. Also, the limited resources available to government to mitigate the effects of drought could be allocated in a more beneficial manner. But because drought is not as well-defined as other natural disasters, governments have been less inclined to invest resources to develop well-conceived mitigation programs and contingency plans. Until recently, States have traditionally played a passive role in drought assessment and response efforts, relying largely on the federal government to come to their rescue during periods of severe water shortages.

Drought Planning

To improve society's level of preparedness to future droughts, contingency plans can be developed by governments to improve the efficiency of assessment and response efforts. Drought planning is defined as actions taken by individual citizens, industry, government, and others in advance of drought for the purpose of mitigating some of the impacts and conflicts associated with its occurrence. From an institutional or governmental perspective, drought planning should include, but is not limited to, the following activities:

1. Creation of a monitoring/early warning system to provide decision makers at all levels with information about the onset, continuation, and termination of drought conditions and their severity.
2. Establishing operational assessment programs to reliably determine the likely impact of the drought event in a timely manner.
3. Formulate an institutional structure for coordinating governmental actions, including information flow within and between levels of government, and criteria and procedures for drought declaration and revocation.
4. Establish appropriate drought assistance programs (both technical and relief) with predetermined eligibility and implementation criteria.
5. Allocate financial resources to maintain operational programs and to initiate research required to support drought assessment and response activities.

6. Initiate educational and public awareness programs designed to promote an understanding and adoption of appropriate drought mitigation and water conservation strategies among the various economic sectors most affected by drought.

To be successful, drought planning must be integrated between levels of government, involving regional organizations and the private sector as appropriate.

Drought Policy and Planning Objectives

Before a drought contingency plan is prepared, government officals should formulate a drought policy to define what they hope to achieve with that plan.[9] The objectives of a drought *policy* differ from those of a drought *plan*. A drought *policy* will be broadly stated and should express the purpose of government involvement in drought assessment, mitigation, and assistance programs. Drought *plan* objectives are more specific and action-oriented.

The objectives of drought policy should encourage or provide incentives for agricultural producers, municipalities, and other water-dependent sectors or groups to adopt appropriate and efficient management practices that help to alleviate the effects of drought. Past relief measures have, at times, discouraged the adoption of appropriate management techniques. Assistance should also be provided in an equitable, consistent, and predictable manner to all without regard to economic circumstances, industry, or geographic region. Assistance can be provided in the form of technical aid or relief measures. Whatever the form, those at risk would know what to expect from government during drought and thus would be better prepared to manage risks. At least one objective should also seek to protect the natural and agricultural resource base. Degradation of these resources can result in spiraling economic, environmental, and social costs.

One question that government officials must address is the purpose and role of government involvement in drought mitigation efforts. Other questions should address the scope of the plan and identify geographic areas, economic sectors, and population groups that are most at risk; principal environmental concerns; and potential human and financial resources to invest in the planning process. Answers to these and other questions should help to determine the objectives of drought policy and therefore provide a focus for the drought planning process.

IMPEDIMENTS TO DROUGHT PLANNING

As a first step, government officials may have to identify the principal obstacles or impediments to drought planning. Some common impediments include an inadequate understanding of drought, uncertainty about the economics of preparedness, lack of skill in drought prediction, variability in societal vulnerability to drought, information gaps and insufficient human resources, inadequate scientific base for water management, and difficulties in identifying drought impact sensitivities and adaptations.

In the United States, the most significant impediments to drought planning are an inadequate understanding of drought and uncertainty about the economics of preparedness.[9,10] Drought is often viewed by government officials as an extreme event that is, implicitly, rare and of random occurrence, and they may not be convinced that the expense of planning is justified. But officials must understand that droughts, like floods, are a normal feature of climate, and their recurrence is inevitable. Planning, if undertaken properly and implemented during nondrought periods, can improve governmental ability to respond in a timely and effective manner during periods of water shortage. Thus, planning can mitigate and, in some cases, prevent some impacts while reducing physical and emotional hardship. Planning should also be a dynamic process that reflects socioeconomic, agricultural, and political trends. Conversely, post-drought evaluations have shown assessment and response efforts of state and federal governments with a low level of preparedness to be largely ineffective, poorly coordinated, untimely, and economically inefficient. Unanticipated expenditures for drought relief programs can also be devastating to State and national budgets. For example, during the droughts of the mid-1970s in the United States, specifically 1974, 1976, and 1977, the federal government spent more than $7 billion on drought relief programs.[11] The federal government has expended similar amounts during subsequent drought periods.

Drought plans should be incorporated into general natural disaster and/or water management plans wherever possible. This would reduce the cost of drought preparedness substantially. Politicians and many other decision makers simply must be better informed about drought, its impacts, and alternative management approaches and how existing information and technology can be used more effectively to reduce the impact of drought at a relatively modest cost.

STATUS OF DROUGHT PLANNING IN THE UNITED STATES

Governments worldwide have shown increased interest in drought planning since the early 1980s. Several factors have contributed to this interest. First, the widespread occurrence of severe drought over the past several decades and, specifically, the years during and following the extreme ENSO event of 1982-83 focused attention on the vulnerability of all nations to drought. Second, the costs associated with drought are now better understood by government. These costs include not only the direct impacts of drought, but also the indirect costs (i.e., personal hardship, the costs of response programs, and accelerated environmental degradation). Nations can no longer afford to allocate scarce financial resources to short-sighted response programs that do nothing to mitigate the effects of future droughts. Finally, the intensity and frequency of extreme meteorological events such as drought are likely to increase, given projected changes in climate associated with increasing concentrations of CO_2 and other atmospheric trace gases.

Governmental interest in and progress toward the development of drought plans has increased significantly in the United States in the past decade. The greatest progress has been made at the State level, although contingency plans are also being prepared at the local level by municipalities and at the regional level for river basins by the U.S. Army Corps of Engineers and other organizations such as the Delaware River Basin Commission.[2] In 1982, three States had developed drought plans: South Dakota, Colorado, and New York. At present, twenty-three States have drought plans (Figure 3). These plans differ considerably in their structure and comprehensiveness, but at least these States have taken a first step to address the unique and complicated assessment and response problems associated with drought. The goal of these plans is to reduce the direct and indirect impacts of drought, lessen the need for government relief programs, and ultimately minimize societal vulnerability.

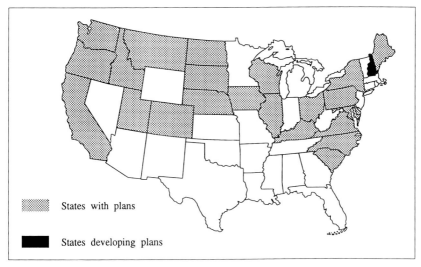

States with plans

States developing plans

FIGURE 3. Status of drought planning. 1991.

CONCLUSIONS

Drought is a pervasive natural hazard that is a normal part of the climate of virtually all regions. It should not be viewed as merely a physical phenomenon. Rather, drought is the result of an interplay between a natural event and the demand placed on water supply by human-use systems. Drought should be considered relative to some long-term average condition of balance between precipitation and evapotranspiration.

Many definitions of drought exist; it is unrealistic to expect a universal definition to be derived. Drought can be grouped by type or disciplinary perspective as follows: meteorological, hydrological, agricultural, and socioeconomic. Each discipline incorporates different physical, biological, and/or socioeconomic factors in its definition. It must be accepted that the importance of drought lies in its impacts. Thus, definitions should be impact- and region-specific in order to be used in an operational mode by decision makers.

The three characteristics that differentiate one drought from another are intensity, duration, and spatial extent. Intensity refers to the degree of precipitation shortfall and/or the severity of impacts associated with the departure. Intensity is closely linked with the duration of the event. Droughts normally take two to three months to become established but may then persist for months or years, although the intensity and spatial character of the event will change from month to month or season to season.

Drought is the result of many causes, which may be synergistic in nature. Some of the causes may be the result of influences that originate far from the drought-affected area. Prolonged droughts occur when large-scale anomalies in atmospheric circulation patterns become established and persist for periods of months, seasons, or longer. Recent droughts in the United States (1988-90) are a good example.

The skill to predict meteorological drought for a month or season in advance is very limited. The potential for improved forecasts differs by region, season, and climatic regime. Significant advances have been made in understanding the climate system in the tropics. Much of this improvement is the result of a better understanding of the fact that a major portion of atmospheric variability which occurs on time scales of months to several years is associated with variations in tropical sea surface temperatures. In the extratropical regions, current long-range meteorological forecasts are of very limited skill and are not likely to improve significantly in the next decade.

The impacts of drought are diverse; they ripple through the economy and may linger for years after the termination of the period of deficient precipitation. Impacts are often referred to as direct or indirect. Because of the number of groups and economic sectors affected by drought, its geographic extent, and the difficulties in quantifying environmental damages and personal hardships, the precise calculation of the financial costs of drought is difficult. Drought years frequently occur in clusters, and thus the costs of drought are not evenly distributed between years. Drought impacts are classified as economic, environmental, and social.

Government response to drought includes a wide range of potential actions to deal with the impacts of water shortages on people and various economic sectors. The types of actions taken will vary considerably between developed and developing countries and from one region to another. Few, if any, actions of government attempt to reduce long-term vulnerability to the hazard. Rather, assistance or relief programs are reactive and address only short-term, emergency needs; they are intended to reduce the impacts and hardships of the present drought.

Developing a drought policy and contingency plan is one way that governments can improve the effectiveness of future response efforts. A drought policy will be broadly stated and should express the purpose of government involvement in drought assessment, mitigation, and response programs. Drought plan objectives are more specific and action oriented and will differ between levels of government. The development of a drought contingency plan results in a higher level of preparedness that can mitigate and, in some cases, prevent some impacts while reducing physical and emotional hardship. An increasing number of governments in the United States and elsewhere are now developing policies and plans to reduce the impacts of future periods of water shortage associated with drought.

REFERENCES CITED

1. Tannehill, I.R. 1947. *Drought, Its Causes and Effects.* Princeton University Press, Princeton, New Jersey.
2. Wilhite, D.A. and M.H. Glantz. 1985. Understanding the drought phenomenon: The role of definitions. *Water International.* 10:111-120.
3. Coughlan, M.J. 1987. Monitoring drought in Australia. In: D.A. Whilhite and W.E. Easterling (Eds.). *Planning for Drought: Toward a Reduction of Societal Vulnerability.* Westview Press, Boulder, CO, pp. 131-144.
4. Palmer, W.C. 1965. *Meteorological Drought.* Research Monograph 45, U.S. Weather Bureau, Washington, D.C.
5. Karl, T.R. and R.W. Knight. 1985. *Atlas of Monthly Palmer Hydrological Drought Indices for the Contiguous United States.* Historical Climatology Series 3-6 (1895-1930) and 3-7 (1931-1983). National Climatic Data Center, Asheville, North Carolina.
6. Wilhite, D.A. and D.A. Wood. 1985. Planning for drought: The role of state government. *Water Resources Bulletin.* 21:31-38.
7. Orville, H.D. 1990. AMS statement on meteorological dought. *Bulletin American Meteorological Society.* 71:1021-1023.
8. Riebsame, W.E., S.A. Changnon and T.R. Karl. 1990. *Drought and Natural Resources Management in the United States: Impacts and Implications of the 1987-90 Drought.* Westview Press, Boulder, CO.
9. Wilhite, D.A. 1990. *Planning for Drought: A Process for State Government.* IDIC Technical Report Series 90-1. International Drought Information Center, Department of Agricultural Meteorology, University of Nebraska-Lincoln.
10. Wilhite, D.A. and W.E. Easterling, eds. 1987. *Planning for Drought: Toward a Reduction of Societal Vulnerability.* Westview Press, Boulder, Colorado.
11. Wilhite, D.A., N.J. Rosenberg and M.H. Glantz. 1986. Improving federal response to drought. *Journal of Climate and Applied Meteorology.* 25:332-342.
12. Hansler, G.M. 1991. Drought planning and response experience in the Delaware River Basin. In: D.A. Wilhite, D.A. Wood and P.A. Kay (Eds.) *Proceedings of the Seminar and Workshop: Drought Management and Planning.* IDIC Technical Report Series 91-1. International Drought Information Center, Department of Agricultural Meteorology, University of Nebraska-Lincoln, pp. 179-183.

Natural and Technological Disasters: Causes, Effects and Preventive Measures. Edited by
S.K. Majumdar, G.S. Forbes, E.W. Miller, and R.F. Schmalz. © 1992, The Pennsylvania Academy
of Science.

Chapter Nineteen

WILDFIRE
IN THE UNITED STATES

JAMES B. DAVIS*

1106 LeConte Drive
Riverside, CA 92507

INTRODUCTION

Wildland fire has always been with us. It has periodically burned forests and
grassland as long as flammable vegetation has existed on earth. A visitor to nearly
any forested area can find the scars of past fires at the base of most old trees—in
fact the type of vegetation present has largely been determined by the frequency
and intensity of past fires. Vegetation types as disparate as prairie grassland,
southwestern chaparral, and the Douglas fir forests of the Pacific Northwest have
developed because of fire. Many forms of vegetation have made adaptations to cope
with fire. These include the ability to sprout, produce seeds that can survive the
heat of a fire (in fact may even require the heat for germination), and the ability
to quickly take advantage of the fire's temporary removal of other competing vegetation. For example, chaparral sprout and produce heat-tolerant seeds. Douglas fir
seedlings will not grow under the dense shade of a mature forest but thrive in the
bare open space provided by a fire, thus getting a head start on their competitors
(cedar, hemlock, and spruce).

Fire has been part of our folklore and legend from earliest times. In the Iliad,
Homer describes the sun glinting off the bronze armor of the Greek soliders
advancing on Troy as "the color of a forest fire sweeping up a slope."

*Retired from U.S.D.A. Forest Service, Riverside, CA.

Man's role as both a cause of and victim from wildland fire has varied from time to time and society to society. Native Americans and European arrivals alike used fire as a tool for land clearing and hunting. However, as early settlers built their homes and villages in forested land, they soon learned that uncontrolled forest fires could result in serious loss of life and property.

RELATIVE IMPORTANCE OF WILDLAND FIRE AS A NATURAL DISASTER

Today in the United States, on the average, 250,000 wildfires burn over almost 5 million acres of forest, brush, and grass-covered lands each year. Protection services cost about one-half billion dollars annually. Losses approach two billion dollars. These costs do not include the services of thousands of volunteer fire departments, nor do they include the expenses of many city fire departments that fight fires on undeveloped lands within or near their jurisdictions.

Comparisons between wildland fire and other natural and technical disasters are difficult to acquire and may be misleading—partly because of the large difference between the number of people and property at risk in "urban" hazards such as structural fire and earthquakes and the potential loss from "rural" disasters such as flood or wildland fire. However, there are some clues. It has been estimated that about 1700 persons have lost their lives in earthquakes in the United States during the last two centuries[1,2] During this same period more than 2400 people were killed as forest fires swept over lumbering and mining towns—mostly during the last half of the 19th century.[3] Refer to Table 1.

Most people are unaware of this loss of life. However, almost everyone has heard of Mrs. O'Leary's cow. According to legend, on the evening of October 8, 1871, the cow kicked over a lantern that started the "Great Chicago Fire." The fire burned for more than 24 hours, consumed about 2000 acres on both sides of the Chicago River and destroyed nearly 18,000 buildings. At least 300 people lost their lives.

On the same day, a fire started in the Wisconsin back woods near the town of Peshtigo. The Peshtigo fire burned for about two weeks, swept 1,280,000 acres, destroyed Peshtigo and several other small towns—and killed more than 1500 people, many of them trapped in a train during a futile effort to escape the flames.[4] Yet, relatively few people have heard of Peshtigo, in most respects a much greater disaster

TABLE 1
Loss of Life In Selected Forest Fires In The United States

Fire Name, State	Date	Acres Burned	Lives Lost
Peshtigo, Wisconsin	1871	1,280,000	1,500
Michigan, Michigan	1881	1,000,000	169
Hinkley, Minnesota	1894	Undetermined	418
Yacoult, Washington	1902	Undetermined	38
Great Idaho, Idaho	1910	3,000,000	85
Maine Fires, Maine	1947	250,000	16

than the Chicago Fire. Because of the much greater media coverage given to the Chicago Fire the governor of Wisconsin had to appeal to the citizens of his own State to send aid to Peshtigo, rather to adjacent Illinois.

So far, the most serious single civilian fire loss this century occurred during the Maine fires of 1947. In a series of late fall fires, 16 persons lost their lives, 2500 were made homeless, 9 communities were leveled or practically wiped out, and 4 other communities suffered extensive damage. One witness described the roads as "crowded with people, livestock, cars, teams, and wheelbarrows fleeing before the fire." At one town—Bar Harbor—fleeing residents had to be rescued by Coast Guard, Navy, and private boats in a Dunkerque-like operation.[5]

Although most of the loss of life occurred during the last century, wildfires are still a threat to life and property. For example, during 1985, a somewhat worse than average year, wildfires destroyed or damaged 1,400 homes and other structures, killed 44 people and cost over 400 million dollars in firefighting operations.[6]

Wildland fires can be killers to those who fight them. Possibly the greatest number of firefighter casualties in a single fire of any kind in the United States occurred during the 1933 Los Angeles Griffith Park Fire in which 25 firefighters were killed and another 128 injured.[7]

SUCCESS STORY

Despite the loss of life and property, few activities, public or private, have had such a degree of success as forest and woodland fire prevention, control, and management. There are basically two reasons:

• During the past 75 years, almost all of the forested land in the United States has been brought under some form of organized fire protection (Figure 1). Most of this protection is provided by various State and Federal agencies. Measured in terms of the number of personnel and fire equipment, the U.S. Forest Service, a bureau of the United States Department of Agriculture, maintains the nation's (perhaps the world's) largest fire protection organization.

• Fire protection effectiveness increased many fold from 1925 to 1970, much of it due to the tools and methodology developed by forestry research (Figure 2). While the number of fires per thousand acres protected throughout the nation has remained about the same since 1925, the average fire size on protected land has been reduced from 120 acres in 1925 to about 20 acres in 1970. These years saw the introduction of organized suppression crews and the construction of extensive road systems into remote areas, allowing the use of fire trucks and bulldozers. The U.S. Forest Service now has more miles of roads, much of it for fire protection, under its control than any other governmental entity. This was also the period when air attack on forest fires started with smokejumpers in the late 1930's and air tankers beginning in the 1950's.

This relative success should not imply that the fire protection job cannot be done better. Fire protection agencies need to do the job more efficiently and economically. Fig. 2 also shows that there has been no decrease in area burned per 1000 acres protected during the past 20 years. While air tankers and heavy bulldozers are effective firefighting tools, they are also expensive. The solution is not just one of throwing more men and equipment at fires. Congress, State legislatures, and the fire protection agencies are very concerned about the high cost of wildland fire protection. Even a moderate-sized fire can cost more than a million dollars to suppress.

The U.S. Forest Service, some other Federal agencies, and some State agencies are using a computer simulation model called the National Fire Management Analysis System (NFMAS) to determine the most cost effective level and mix of firefighting assets—both people and equipment. The NFMAS outputs, expressed in least cost plus loss terms, have been accepted by Congress in its budgetary process.

As effective as NFMAS is, it is driven by commodity or market place values such as timber and range livestock in the trade-off between firefighting costs and potential resource losses. Intangible or difficult-to-measure forest products such as recreation, wildlife, and water are also considered in the system. However, NFMAS does not properly consider factors such as air quality, ecological diversity, and political issues such as public perceptions of natural resources and private property protection trade-offs.

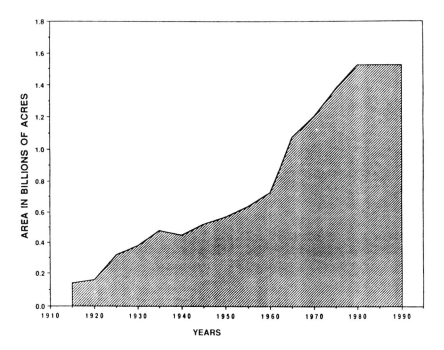

FIGURE 1. Area receiving fire protection in the United States.

While these "perceptions" may be difficult to measure, in many cases they determine firefighting decisions at the time of a fire. "Political" factors not accounted
for in the NFMAS model may determine the tactics and strategy that are actually
used. An example is fire protection in the urban-wildland interface. Over much of
this century there has been a flow of people from urban to rural or forested areas.
The critical boundary between wildland and more settled communities comprises
an area of between 1 million and 1½ million acres nationwide.[8]

Many wildland fire managers are surprised that they must cope with the fire protection for the most rapidly changing geographic area in our nation. Although the
increase in rural population has slowed somewhat since the 1970's, when rural counties were growing three times as fast as the urban counties, population growth in
many of the Nation's forest and range counties continues to exceed urban population growth and will probably continue to do so past the turn of the century.[9] For
example, in Virginia, the number of homes exposed to the threat of ignition from
wildfire is increasing four-fold every five years.

California, state-wide, will not double its 1970 population until at least 2020, a
period of 50 years. Yet, the population of 14 of its counties—all forested—will double in 20 years or less; the areas that are increasing in population most rapidly are
those most prone to wildfires.[10,11] The 1400 homes burned in wildfires in 1985 testify
to the fact that the associated fire protection problems are nationwide.[12]

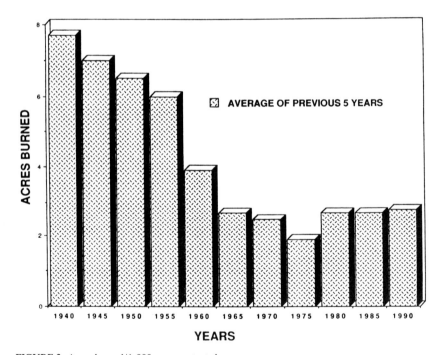

FIGURE 2. Acres burned/1,000 acres protected.

Efforts to introduce fire-safe planning in these rapidly growing rural areas have been hampered by an inadequate understanding of the relation between land use and fire risk by local community planners and political leaders. Increasing rural population and dispersed housing vastly raise the probability of fire loss and necessitate extensive and costly fire suppression efforts.[13]

An additional vexing problem for fire managers is that Federal agencies generally do not have the legal responsibility for protecting structures on nonfederal lands. Among State forestry agencies, the scope of responsibility varies considerably. Urban fire departments and fire protection districts may or may not be responsible for wildland protection in and adjacent to their city boundaries. Many agencies do not train and equip their personnel for both urban and wildland firefighting. However, responsibility and training frequently become moot points during an interface fire. Most forest fire protection agencies have found that there is a political necessity to protect structures at the expense of the forest. This can result in serious natural resource losses when wildland protection forces are assigned to structures, allowing the wildland fire to continue to burn unimpeded.

The lack of proper training and equipment can lead to a very dangerous situation for firefighters. In many respects, the urban-wildland interface is an artificial environment where structures and introduced vegetation, such as ornamental vegetation, are placed in a wildland setting. Neither foresters nor urban firefighters are trained and equipped to cope with fire behavior in this environment. Consequently, interface fires (along with wildland fires in general) can be killers. One-third of all firefighter fatalities caused directly by fire (as opposed to building collapse or smoke inhalation) occurred in wildland fires.[14]

While the specter of the raging forest fire sweeping into communities like Florida's Palm Coast or Maine's Bar Harbor is dramatic, it is only part of the problem.[15] With the increasing number of homes and other buildings exposed, an "average" fire can involve structures. In California, for example, the number of wildland fires involving structures each year has increased from 4 in 1950 to about 50 by 1985 and the trend appears to be increasing exponentially (Figure 3).

So far there have been few civilian casualties this century—although they do occur, as in the 1947 Maine fires. However, with the rapidly increasing percentage of wildland fires that involve homes, firefighters fear that it is possible in the not-too-distant future that loss of life may equal that of the last century.

There is another cost of success. Today one of the most important problems facing forest land managers is the build-up of forest fuels consisting of dead branches and even whole dead trees that would normally have burned in frequent naturally occurring low-intensity fires. These fuels have been allowed to accumulate because of effective fire protection; consequently, many fires burn with a higher intensity than they might have prior to organized protection.[16] Good examples were the 1988 Yellowstone fires. While the National Park Service and adjacent National Forests have had a policy beginning in the 1960's of allowing wilderness of "back country" fires started by natural causes to burn themselves out under proper weather conditions, the accumulation of 50 years of fuel prior to the policy change coupled with drought and strong wind conditions was too much for any combination of firefighters and their equipment[7]

DISCUSSION/CONCLUSION: SOLVING THE PROBLEMS

During the past 65 years, the average size of wildland fires has been reduced from 120 acres in 1925 to about 20 today. This has been accomplished in spite of the fact that the risk of fires starting, as determined by various types of land use, has increased more than ten times. Research has played an important part in this success. At the beginning of this century, foresters found themselves managing a wild remote area in which the causes, behavior, and effects of fire were poorly understood, if at all.

Early fire research was essentially engaged in management science—trying to determine the needs of a fledgling fire control organization and developing a policy for its activities. Since World War II, fire research has expanded to include the physical, biological, and social sciences. Current programs draw heavily on the fields of meteorology, engineering, administration, operations research, and computer science.

Fire Management in the Urban-Wildland Interface

The task of protecting lives and property from fire in the urban-wildland interface poses several of the most critical and elusive problems for fire managers and

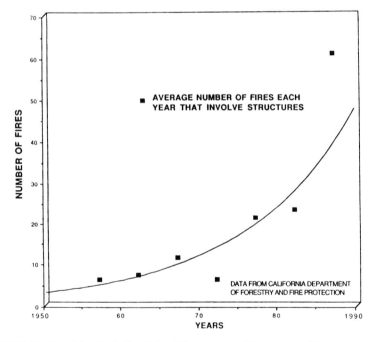

FIGURE 3. Number of fires in California involving structures (five year periods).

researchers today. If fire managers are to save lives and property, they need better knowledge and information on how to help homeowners, community planners, and builders design fire-safe communities. Fire managers believe that they possess the technical knowledge about fire resistant building materials, how to replace native vegetation with less flammable vegetation, and how to develop better road access and water systems—but they have failed in the process of persuading others—particularly when a fire-safe community may cost slightly more than a fire-prone one.[18,19]

Research is being conducted on two fronts:

- Studies are being conducted to find more effective methods to communicate with a very diverse, newly arrived, rural public who may have developed their attitudes toward fire safety while living within an urban environment. For example, it frequently comes as a shock to homeowners to find that protection for their homes may be provided by a forestry fire crew that is only available during the wildland fire season. Attitudes, general awareness, and communication paths are all being studied in an effort to find more effective strategies for dealing with people prone to loss from wildland fire.
- A second research effort is to develop a more effective way of communicating with the public through their policy makers and public leaders—persons who influence development in the urban-wildland interface. By influencing this group we can, in effect, "leverage" the promotion and adoption of fire-safe innovations for the millions of people who are at fire risk in the urban-wildland interface. For example, through research we are attempting to identify groups (architects, home lending organizations, community planners) whose opinions and actions could influence the character of housing developments and individual homes in a way that would reduce wildfire loss.

Prescribed Fire For Wilderness Management

Current policies of the National Park Service, Bureau of Land Management, and the Forest Service allow fire to resume a more natural role in those areas set aside as part of the National Wilderness System. More than 75 years of fire protection, however, have materially changed some wilderness ecosystems and allowed an accumulation of forest fuel that is difficult to manage. Land managers look to research to define the natural role of fire in wilderness and criteria for deciding when planned (prescribed fire) or unplanned ignitions (such as lightning fires) are appropriate. Not only must the ecological role of fire be considered, but also the accumulation of fuel and the weather at the time of the fire.

Social, Political, and Economic Values in Fire Management

How do you measure the worth of a scenic vista or a recreation experience? Difficult, perhaps, but not impossible.[20] Over the past decade, major progress has been made in developing economic analysis methods that relate investments in fire protection to the anticipated changes in resource values resulting from wildfires. In spite of this progress it is still difficult to incorporate political and social considerations into fire-management planning processes. As a result, decision makers have limited ability to evaluate alternatives in terms other than economic efficiency. Social and political attributes are still treated qualitatively, often resulting in inconsistent programs that sometimes are unacceptable to the public. An example is a fire protection organization, designed, staffed, and budgeted solely for wildland protection located in a rapidly developing urban-wildland interface.[21] Improved understanding is needed of the relationships among social, political, regulatory, and other factors with respect to decisions about fire-management investments.[22]

Fire Suppression: Productivity and Effectiveness

Foresters have been fighting fire for about 100 years; yet, they still do not have all the answers they need about how fast or well they do their job—partly because the job is much more complex than it used to be.

The most important reason for measuring productivity is that almost every task must be evaluated in terms of cost effectiveness. Fire research must provide an improved understanding of the factors governing fireline building and holding success, trade-offs and interactions among different fire control actions, and a better understanding of human physiology and motivation. In addition, many of the options once available to fire managers no longer exist. This is particularly true in the urban wildland interface. The use of heavy bulldozers may not be possible in subdivided areas nor is the option of retreating to a strong point such as a road or ridge top and starting a controlled low intensity fire to burn out the intervening flammable vegetation ahead of the approaching wildfire. This "burning out" or "backfiring" may not be possible if homes are in the area where such tactics would take place.

Effects of Atmospheric Change on Forest Health and Productivity

Planning, budgeting, and operating a fire protection organization involving thousands of people and pieces of equipment requires a thorough understanding of fire behavior. However, the effects of changes in the atmosphere on forest health, productivity, and flammability are not always known.

There are many atmospheric effects that result in a rapid accumulation of dead and dying vegetation—fuel for a wildland fire. Some weather impacts are sudden and dramatic such as the uprooting or snapping off of trees in a storm. Effects of drought or excessive moisture also are readily observable. For example, trees are much more vulnerable to pest attacks such as insect infections when they are stressed by drought. Some effects caused by gradual changes in normal conditions are not as obvious but are generally understood. Examples are early and late frosts and the impacts of recurring severe winters.

Yet another category of atmospheric effect involves climatic changes because of increasing levels of pollutants, including particulates, carbon dioxide, and acid rain. The effect may include reduced tree growth and increased mortality—all resulting in significant effects on fire behavior. We can only make an educated guess about the effects of global warming and the climatic changes that might accompany it. Forest vegetation is very dependent upon temperature and precipitation patterns and amount. The ecological consequences and the subsequent role of fire could be profound.

The opportunity for managers to deal with these effects is restricted by a lack of knowledge about the processes which translate long-term atmospheric change into ecological change and subsequent change in fire occurrence and behavior.

Allocation of Firefighting Assets

Fire management depends on maximum mobility of firefighting resources to provide satisfactory forest fire protection while keeping costs within budgetary constraints, prudently achieving a balance between need and cost. The effectiveness of mobility is directly related to the ability to determine where and when resources will be needed. However, this is made difficult because agencies must be prepared to adequately cope with a partially unpredictable "rare event." This is because, unlike urban structural fires, wildland fire rate of spread and burning intensity is highly dependent upon weather conditions at the time of the fire and to a lesser extent upon the weather during the previous week or two depending upon the type of forest or wildland. Those weather elements—strong wind, high temperatures, and low humidities—that contribute to "blow up" fire conditions occur only rarely, perhaps five to ten percent of the time depending upon the forest type and climatic regime.

Consequently, fire agencies must staff and budget for such comparatively rare events, keeping trained men and women and expensive equipment on standby or at least on call. In many fire protection agencies this results in a potential "overkill" on most fires provided all available equipment was used.

On the other hand, few organizations can afford to staff and equip for all eventualities. Most will have inadequate forces available part of the time even if everything available were utilized. Consequently, fire agencies are only rarely able to exactly match resources to the fire.

Research is being conducted in both the United States and Canada on two interrelated approaches to the problem:

- Research is developing reliable weekly, monthly, and seasonal fire severity forecasts. Systems under development will provide information on geographic variation of fire severity potential for resource allocation purposes. Some of these include imagery from geostationary satellites that detects seasonal changes in vegetation moisture content occurring over extensive forest and range areas.

- Other research includes the development of fast reliable computer allocation systems that can monitor firefighting assets and suggest movement strategies that would make the wisest use of those that can be shared between agencies.

The two research efforts, linked together, will allow long term weather projections to drive information and allocation systems that will enable managers to share firefighting assets and move them over broad geographical areas to keep ahead of the anticipated need.

Research Into the 21st Century

While much of the ongoing research is aimed at today's problems, fire scientists are also directing their efforts toward solving the problems of the early part of the 21st century. Fire scientists don't do this alone, but in cooperation with others in the scientific community and with what is called the "user group." The latter includes Federal, State, and local fire management officials: essentially those people who must put the results of research to practical use. Scientists and users, applying futuring techniques—a structured procedure for predicting several possible futures, determining the most likely, and then developing a management strategy to deal with it—have jointly identified high priority areas where both current and future research must be concentrated. While most wildland fire research and management effort is directed toward protecting natural resources, there is a growing concern for more research aimed at preventing loss of life or injury to the public.

REFERENCES

1. Rossi, Peter H., James D. Wright, Eleanor Webe-Burdin and Joseph Pereira. 1983. Victims of the environment, Plenum Press, NY, 238 pp.
2. Scott, Stanley, 1979. What decision makers need to know: policy and social science research on seismic safety, Institute of Governmental Studies, Univ. of California, Berkeley, CA, 38 pp.
3. Davis, Kenneth P. 1959. Forest fire: control and use, McGraw Hill Book Co., New York, 584 pp.
4. Pyne, Stephen J. 1982. Fire in America, Princeton University Press, Princeton, NJ, 654 pp.
5. Wilkins, Auston H. 1948. The story of the Maine forest fire disaster. *J. Soc. American Foresters* 46: 568-573.
6. NW/UPFC. 1987. Wildfire strikes home. Report of the National Wildland/Urban Fire Protection Conference, National Fire Protection Association. Quincy, MA, 90 pp.
7. Wilson, Carl C. 1977. Fatal and near fatal forest fires: the common denominators. *International Fire Chief.* 43(9): 9-15.
8. Schapiro, Morton Owen. 1980. Filling up America: an economic-demographic model of population growth and distribution in the nineteenth-century United States. JAI Press Inc. Greenwich, CN, 521 pp.
9. Bogue, R.J. 1985. The population of the United States: historical trends and future projections. The Free Press, New York, 350 pp.

10. Rice, Carol L. 1987. What will the western wildlands be like in the year 2000? future perfect or future imperfect. In: *Proceedings of the Symposium on Wildland Fire 2000, Gen. Tech. Rep. PSW-101.* Pacific Southwest Forest and Range Experiment Station, Forest Service, U.S. Department of Agriculture, Berkeley, CA, pp. 26-31.

11. Bradshaw, T.K. 1987. The intrusion of human population into forest and rangelands of California. In: *Proceedings of the Symposium on Wildland Fire 2000, Gen. Tech. Rep. PSW-101.* Pacific Southwest Forest and Range Experiment Station, Forest Service, U.S. Department of Agriculture, Berkeley, CA, pp. 15-21.

12. Davis, J.B. 1986. Danger zone: the wildland/urban interface. *Fire Management Notes* 47(3): pp. 3-5.

13. Rice, Carol L. and James B. Davis. 1991. Land use planning may reduce fire damage in the urban-wildland intermix. Gen. Tech. Rep. PSW-127. Pacific Southwest Forest and Range Experiment Station, Forest Service, U.S. Department of Agriculture, Berkeley, CA, 14 pp.

14. Statistical record on file. National Fire Protection Association. Quincy, MA.

15. Abt, R., D. Kelly, and M. Kuypers. 1987. The Florida Palm Coast Fire: an analysis of fire incidence and residence characteristics. *Fire Tech.* 23(3): 186-197.

16. Albini, F.A. 1976. Estimating wildfire behavior and effects. Gen. Tech. Rep. INT-30. Intermountain Forest and Range Experiment Station, Forest Service, U.S. Department of Agriculture, Missoula, MT, 92 pp.

17. Rothermel, R.C. 1991. Predicting the behavior of the 1988 Yellowstone fires: projections versus reality. *The Int. J. of Wildland Fire* 1(1): 1-10.

18. East Bay Regional Park District. 1982. 1982 report of the blue ribbon urban interface fire prevention committee. Oakland, CA, 98 pp.

19. Gardner, Philip D., Earl B. Anderson, and Mary E. Huddleston. 1986. Evaluating structural damage from wildland fires. *Fire Management Notes* 46(4): 15-18.

20. Shafer, Elwood L., and James Mietz. 1969. Aesthetic and emotional experience rate high with Northwest wilderness hikers. *Environment and Behavior* 1: 187-197.

21. USDA Forest Service. 1981. Criteria for deciding about forestry research programs. General Technical Report, WO-29 Washington DC, 30 pp.

22. Davis, J.B., and E.L. Shafer, 1984. The use of paired comparison techniques for evaluating forest research. In: *Proceedings of Society of American Foresters, Portland, Or,* pp. 4-8.

EPILOGUE

On Sunday, October 20, 1991, during the time this paper was being set in print, a major wildland-urban interface fire swept about 2000 acres of the Oakland-Berkeley Hills in California. Driven by strong, dry, northeast winds, the fire can be counted among the 10 worst in our nation's history. At the last count, 25 people were known dead, another 17 missing, and 150 injured. About 3,000 dwelling units, including single family homes and major apartment buildings were destroyed. Estimated damage varied between 1.5 and 2.0 billions of dollars (about the same as the Great Chicago fire in terms of 1991 dollars).

Although a surprise to many home owners, the fire was not unexpected by fire agencies. Serious fires have swept these hills about every 25 years. In spite of repeated warnings by fire and forestry agencies about flammable construction methods, narrow dead end streets, and inadequate water supplies, the area developed into a classic wildland-urban interface fire-prone community.

Perhaps more ominous is that California fire officials are calling this disaster the "fire of the future."

Natural and Technological Disasters: Causes, Effects and Preventive Measures. Edited by
S.K. Majumdar, G.S. Forbes, E.W. Miller, and R.F. Schmalz. © 1992, The Pennsylvania Academy
of Science.

Chapter Twenty

HISTORIC SHORELINE CHANGE ALONG THE NORTHERN GULF OF MEXICO

GREGORY W. STONE[1] and SHEA PENLAND[2]
[1]Department of Geography and Anthropology
Louisiana State University
Baton Rouge, LA 70803
and
[2]Louisiana Geological Survey

INTRODUCTION

A voluminous body of literature published during the past few decades provides irrevocable evidence that more than 70% of the world's sandy coastline has experienced net erosion historically (Bird, 1985). Unfortunately, it appears inevitable that his problem will worsen in the near future due to an accelerated rate of rise in eustatic sea-level in response to global warming of the earth's atmosphere (Titus, 1986; NRC, 1987; 1990). Along some sandy coastlines, however, there is evidence indicating that an adequate supply of sediment to the nearshore zone can effectively offset coastal erosion during long-term periods of sea-level rise, thereby maintaining conditions of stability or progradation/accretion. Sea-level in the northern Gulf of Mexico, measured relative to the land, is rising but at highly variable rates (Figure 1). According to tide gage records dating back to the early 1900's, relative sea-level is rising approximately ten times faster in Louisiana when compared with much of the remainder of the world. Consequently, Louisiana is experiencing the most severe land loss and coastal erosion when compared to the remainder of North

America. Yet, less than 150 kilometers to the east, the coastline of Northwest Florida and Southeast Alabama although experiencing relative sea-level rise, ranks among the most stable barrier coast in North America.

It is the objective of this chapter to demonstrate the highly variable response of these neighboring coastal segments to an historic rise in relative sea-level over the past century as well as a comparison of respective implications for coastal management and policy formulation.

MECHANISMS RESPONSIBLE FOR COASTAL EROSION

Beach erosion occurs when the quantity of sediment removed, through either natural or anthropogenically-induced processes, exceeds the quantity supplied. Thus, a variety of factors may be responsible for the initiation and maintenance of coastal erosion (cf. Walker, 1988; Bird, 1985; Bruun and Schwartz, 1985; NRC 1987; 1990; Carter, 1988) and include the following:

1. Anthropogenic — artificial structures, beach sand mining, offshore dredging, river damming, reduction in fluvial discharge;
2. Loss of beach sediment — onshore through overwash/foredune breaching and aeolian transport, offshore during return flow/rip current development, alongshore to shoals and inlets, and attrition, weathering and solution;
3. Sediment Supply — reduction due to deflation of the source of supply from either alongshore (headland) or offshore (shoal);

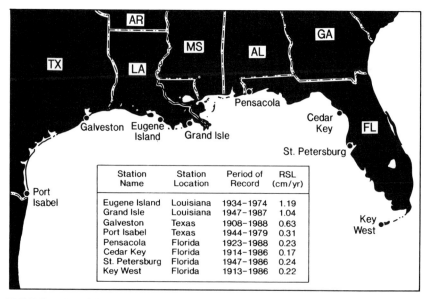

Station Name	Station Location	Period of Record	RSL (cm/yr)
Eugene Island	Louisiana	1934–1974	1.19
Grand Isle	Louisiana	1947–1987	1.04
Galveston	Texas	1908–1988	0.63
Port Isabel	Texas	1944–1979	0.31
Pensacola	Florida	1923–1988	0.23
Cedar Key	Florida	1914–1986	0.17
St. Petersburg	Florida	1947–1986	0.24
Key West	Florida	1913–1986	0.22

FIGURE 1. Map of the Northern Gulf of Mexico illustrating the location of the National Ocean Survey tide gages and rates of historic relative sea-level rise.

4. Increase in incident breaker wave angle and/or wave energy;
5. Increase in beach saturation due to a higher water table or increase in precipitation (Bryant, 1985);
6. Relative sea-level rise (Bruun, 1962; Schwartz, 1965; 1967; Bruun and Schwartz, 1985).

To determine the effectiveness of these elements in either initiating, maintaining or accelerating coastal erosion remains a difficult task when viewed over the long-term (100-150 years). However, progress is being made (cf. Everts, 1987; Dean, 1988; Walker, 1988; NRC, 1990; Stone, 1991). An evaluation of the relative importance associated with many of these parameters is discussed along the northern Gulf coast in the remainder of this chapter.

SHORELINE CHANGE ALONG THE FLORIDA-ALABAMA COAST

General Geomorphology

The 225 km-long section of coast under discussion here stretches from Morgan Point (Alabama) to Grayton Beach (Florida) (Figure 2). Late Quaternary deposits along the coast consist of a Pleistocene "headland" from Grayton Beach to Destin East Pass and a series of mid-to-late Holocene barrier and beach ridge deposits. Santa Rosa Island and Perdido Key are the main barrier island features along this coast, whereas to the west, well defined, concave seaward beach ridge sets occur between Gulf Beach and Morgan Point. Beaches are composed of 99%, medium quartz-sand, and approximately 1% heavy minerals (staurolite, rutile, ilmenite and kyanite). Breaker wave heights are typically less than 1 m and tides are diurnal with an average range of 0.4 m. Three inlets (Destin East, Pensacola and Perdido Passes)

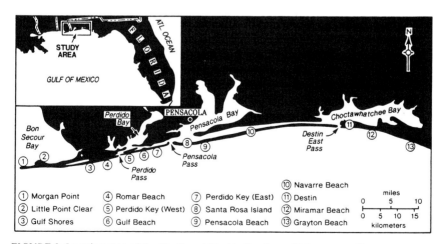

FIGURE 2. Location map of the Northwest Florida-Southeast Alabama coastline.

facilitate the exchange of waters from the Gulf of Mexico and the adjacent bays of Choctawhatchee, Pensacola and Perdido. Longshore sediment transport is predominantly westward along the entire coast increasing from some 50,000 m³/yr. to 150,000 m³/yr. west of Pensacola Pass (Stone, 1991, Stone *et al.*, in press). Sediment supply to the beach originates from two discrete sources: (1) from the Pleistocene "headland" prior to deposition along Santa Rosa Island; (2) from the inner shelf prior to deposition along Perdido Key and the Alabama coast.

Historic Shoreline Change

Over the past 125 years, data indicate that approximately 90% of the 185 km-long stretch of Holocene coast from Destin to Morgan Point has remained stable to accretionary (Stapor, 1975; Stone, 1991) as shown on Figure 3 for the general period 1856-1985. Long-term net erosion is apparent along the Pleistocene "headland" east of Destin, west of Pensacola Beach on Santa Rosa Island and the eastern half of Perdido Key. Whereas the vast majority of Santa Rosa Island has maintained net long-term stability the propensity towards accretion is apparent along western Perdido Key to Morgan Point.

The stability and accretion noted along the majority of this Holocene stretch of coast indicates that the erosional potential associated with relative sea-level rise recorded at the Pensacola tide gage (Figure 1) is being offset by other factors. In particular, an equilibrated and mature longshore transport system has been established along Santa Rosa Island, supplied by sediment from the eroding Pleistocene "headland" at Grayton Beach. Because there is no apparent supply of sediment to the "headland", long-term erosion is expected. The quantity of sediment transported along Santa Rosa Island from Grayton Beach decreases gradually to the Navarre-Pensacola Beach region prior to increasing to a maximum of 150,000 m³/yr. along the western end of Santa Rosa Island. Since the volume of sediment removed from this section of beach where transport rates begin increasing is not

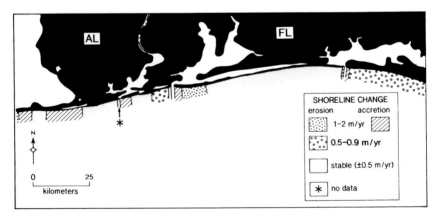

FIGURE 3. Historic shoreline change along the Northwest Florida-Southeast Alabama coast over the period 1856-1985.

replaced long-term erosion occurs. An analysis of historic aerial photography since 1940 also suggests that this localized zone of erosion west of Pensacola Beach, is in part due to overwash losses during repetitious breaching during storms and hurricanes because of significantly lower foredune elevations—typically 2 m above National Geodetic Vertical Datum—when compared with 4-6 m elsewhere along this coast (Stone *et al.*, 1985; Stone, 1991).

West of Santa Rosa Island, the coast appears more accretional with the exception of localized erosion along eastern Perdido Key (Figure 3). Low foredune elevations (3 m above NGVD) results in this area being susceptible to storm wave inundation and damage (Stone *et al.*, 1985; Stone and Salmon, 1988; Stone, 1991). To the west, however, an abundant supply of sediment from the low profile adjacent shelf has maintained stability and accretion. The occurrence of beach ridge sets, oriented concave seaward, indicates the accretional nature and the importance of sediment supply from the shelf during the last 4-5,000 years. Diminution in the supply of sediment from offshore in the last few thousand years has resulted in cessation in beach ridge growth. However, the amount of sediment supplied from offshore is significant enough to maintain stability and accretion along this coast.

The significance of the inner shelf as a sediment source is also apparent during high wave energy events during hurricanes. For example during Hurricane Elena Santa Rosa Island, from Navarre to Pensacola Pass, experienced net erosion of $5.8 m^3/m$ (882,000 m^3). Eastern Perdido, however, lost 3.9 m^3/m (160,000 m^3), the remainder of the island experienced deposition of material from the shelf approximating 0.8 m^3/m (22,000 m^3). The prevalence of overwash along the eastern half of Perdido Key and the progradational/accretional nature of its western counterpart is equally evident in a sediment budget constructed for the period 1890-1965 (Figure 4). A depositional volume of some 2 x 10^6 m^3 of sediment that accumulated along the western half of the island supports the idea of a dominant supply from the inner shelf.

Implications for Coastal Management

Relative to other barrier/beach ridge type coasts around the United States, the Holocene coast from Destin to Morgan Point presents few coastal management problems. This is due primarily to low density coastal development, historic shoreline stability along 90% of the coast and relatively few navigation inlets. In contrast to the many coastal areas, the most severe shoreline loss is being experienced along the north shore of Santa Rosa Island at Pensacola Beach (Figure 2). Between 1940 and 1989, episodic erosion has occurred and in some locations exceeded 60 m (Dr. James P. Morgan, personal communication, April 10, 1991). There is, however, no apparent relationship between periods of increased relative sea-level rise and increased erosion. Shoreline loss is most noted during cold front passage over the northern Gulf. The construction of sea walls and bulkheads to help protect coastal property has almost certainly exacerbated the erosion problem by causing reflection of incident waves offshore where sediment is transported and deposited on a series of actively prograding shoals. Studies are currently underway to establish

the possibility of pumping shoal sediment back to the eroding beach.
If the rate of relative sea-level rise does accelerate in the near future as predicted,
how might the Northwest Florida-Alabama coast respond? It would seem that at
least during the initial period of accelerated sea-level rise, the adjacent sources of
sediment supply would perhaps continue to maintain stability along this coast. The
Pleistocene "headland" at Grayton Beach houses an almost "inexhaustible" source
of sediment that would, assuming no significant changes in channel maintenance
practices currently undertaken at Destin East Pass, continue to furnish material
to Santa Rosa Island thereby maintaining stability. Similarly, along the beach ridges
in Alabama, sediment will probably continue to be supplied from the inner shelf.
At some time, however, diminution in the offshore source will occur similar to a
period of cessation in beach ridge growth a few thousand years ago. It is conceivable
that should this cessation occur, the beach ridge plains will then act as "headland"
sources supplying sediment to the longshore transport system.

Although coastline erosion is not a widespread problem along the Northwest
Florida and Southeast Alabama coast, coastal managers should be concerned with
the potential impacts of hurricanes. Since 1900, 16 hurricanes have variously impacted this area, the most severe of which occurred in 1906, 1916, 1926 and 1979.
It has been established that approximately 23% of the foredunes from Navarre
Beach to western Perdido Key lie well below the average elevation of 4.3 m (NGVD),
50% of which are located at Pensacola Beach (Morgan and Stone, 1987). It has

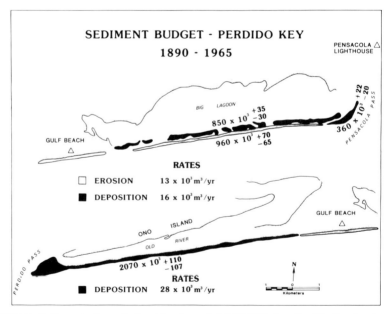

FIGURE 4. Sediment budget calculated for the period 1890-1965 along Perdido Key showing the
overwash-dominated, retrogradational eastern half of the island and the accretional section to the
west.

also been established that the major overwash and breach sites that occur during hurricanes are located in historic breach sites, repetitiously overwashed during earlier hurricanes (Morgan and Stone, 1987; Stone *et al.*, 1985; Stone and Salmon, 1988; Stone, 1991). Recommendations have been made to local governmental agencies explicitly detailing approaches to help ameliorate this problem including a dune stabilization and revegetation program (Morgan and Stone, 1987).

From a coastal management perspective, the apparent stability of the Northwest Florida-Alabama coastline is the exception rather than the norm. This will become apparent to the reader in the remainder of this chapter where we discuss the problems facing the rapidly subsiding coast of Louisiana.

SHORELINE CHANGE ALONG THE LOUISIANA COASTLINE

General Geomorphology

The coastline of the northern Gulf of Mexico is dominated by the Mississippi River. Since about 7,000 yr. B.P., the Mississippi River has built a deltaic platform comprising numerous individual delta lobes and groups of unrelated lobes known as delta complexes (Russell 1936; Fisk 1944; Kolb and Van Lopik 1958; Scruton 1960; Frazier 1967; Coleman 1988). The delta-building process consists of prodelta platform establishment, followed by distributary progradation and bifurcation, that results in delta plain consolidation. This process continues until the distributary course is no longer hydraulically efficient. Abandonment occurs, initiating the transgressive phase of the delta cycle. The abandoned delta subsides, and coastal processes rework the seaward margin, generating a sandy barrier shoreline backed by bays and lagoons (Kwon 1969; Penland *et al.*, 1981). Coastal land loss occurs naturally during this stage. Transgression occur repeatedly, both for delta complexes and delta lobes.

As a delta is abandoned, marine processes begin to dominate the system. Coastal land loss occurs and deltaic sand bodies supply coarse sediment to the nearshore current field. An erosional headland with flanking barrier spits develops, and an evolutionary process of barrier island formation begins (Penland *et al.*, 1988). The abandoned Bayou Lafourche delta headland is the most recent example of this landform. Erosion rates on the central headland average as much as 20 m annually, reaching over 50 m in hurricane years (Ritchie and Penland 1988). The Timbalier Islands to the west of the Bayou Lafourche headland and Grand Isle to the east, represent a Stage 1 barrier system. The Plaquemines barrier shoreline associated with the Modern delta complex also represent a Stage 1 barrier system (Ritchie *et al.*, 1990). With continued subsidence, marine waters intrude into the backbarrier marshes, resulting in the formation of a saline lagoon, separating the barrier from the mainland marshes and forming Stage 2, the barrier island arc. The best examples of this are the Isles Dernieres derived from the Lafourche delta complex and the Chandeleur Islands derived from the St. Bernard delta complex (Penland *et al.*, 1985; Ritchie *et al.*, 1989). Additional subsidence removes the coarser-grained distributary mouth bar and channel deposits from the nearshore wave field, resulting in a cessation of sediment supply to the barrier islands. Continued reworking by waves and storms begins degradation of the barrier islands. The subaerial island area decreases greatly as sediment is lost seaward to an inner shelf sand sheet, landward by overwash, and captured in tidal-inlet sinks. This process is well illustrated by the evolution of the Isles Dernieres. Ultimately the barrier system loses its subaerial integrity and forms Stage 3, and inner-shelf shoal (Penland *et al.*, 1989a).

Historic Shoreline Change

Louisiana is experiencing the highest rates of coastal erosion in the United States (Morgan and Larimore 1957; Adams *et al.*, 1978; Penland and Boyd 1981; van Beek and Meyer-Arendt 1982; Morgan and Morgan 1983; McBride *et al.*, 1989). Rates of coastal erosion in Louisiana average 4.2 m/yr. (+ / − 0.5 m/yr.) (Figure 5) and range between 3.4 m/yr. and 15.3 m/yr. The average Gulf of Mexico shoreline change rate is − 1.8 m/yr., the highest in the U.S. By comparison, the Atlantic erodes at an average rate of − 0.8 m/yr., while the Pacific coast is relatively stable at an average rate of + / − 0.00 m/yr. In Louisiana, the majority of the coastal erosion is concentrated in the barrier shoreline that front the Mississippi river delta plain. The average coastal erosion rate of 4.2 m/yr. represents the long-term conditions exceeding 50 years, averaged together by per unit length of shoreline for 600 km of coast. This number is not representative of the individual storm events that contribute to the long-term average. Episodic erosion associated with the passage of major cold fronts, tropical storms, and hurricanes is clearly apparent along this

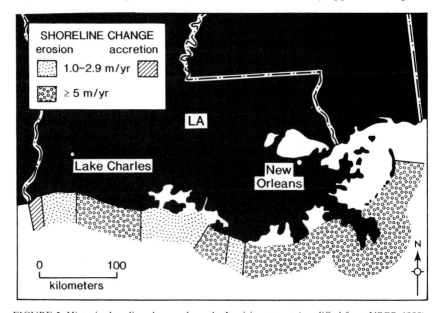

FIGURE 5. Historic shoreline change along the Louisiana coast (modified from USGS, 1988).

coast (Harper 1977; Penland and Ritchie 1979; Boyd and Penland 1981; Dingler and Reiss 1988; Ritchie and Penland 1988; Dingler and Reiss 1990). Field measurements have documented 20-30 m of coastal erosion during a single storm event lasting 3-4 days. These major storm events produce energetic overwash conditions that erode the beach and reduce the barrier landscape to lower relief landforms (Penland *et al.*, 1989b). In addition to beach erosion, the total area of Louisiana's barrier shoreline is decreasing rapidly. In 1880, the total barrier island area in Louisiana approximated 98.6 km². In 1980 the total area had decreased to 57.8 km². This represents a 41% decrease in area at a rate of 0.41 km²/yr. (Penland and Boyd 1982).

The barrier shoreline system experiencing the highest rate of coastal erosion in Louisiana is the Isles Dernieres located in Terrebonne Parish (Penland and Boyd 1981; McBride *et al.*, 1989). From 1890 to 1988, the Isles Dernieres shoreline eroded at an average rate of 12.2 m/yr. (+ / − 0.5 m/yr.) (Figure 6). The most significant beach erosion was measured in the central barrier island arc at Whiskey Island where a total of 2573 m of beach retreat took place at an average rate of − 19.1 m/yr. In 1890, the total area of the Isles Dernieres approximated 3360 ha, and by 1988 the island area was reduced to 771 ha, a total decrease of 2589 ha or 77% over 135 years (26.4 ha/yr.). Based on the above data, it is conceivable that the barrier island arc will experience complete erosion between the later part of this century (1998) and early next century (2007). Of immediate threat to Louisiana, particularly Terrebonne and Lafourche parishes, is the predicted loss of the isles Dernieres by the early 21st century. The destruction of the Isles Dernieres will dramatically impact the stability and quality of the Terrebonne Bay barrier-built estuary and the associated coastal wetlands.

IMPLICATIONS FOR COASTAL MANAGEMENT

As discussed earlier in this chapter, coastal erosion and land loss is a function of a variety of factors. Human impacts are secondary, but often serve to drastically increase coastal deterioration. To effectively manage this coastal problem, a consistent strategy must be developed and proper tactics applied. In Louisiana, two management options have been applied. The first centers on building coastal structures to combat natural processes and hold the remaining habitats in place, while the second involves replacing the material lost from the barrier island system and to hold it in place by planting dune and backbarrier marsh habitats. Of these options, the latter using sediment and vegetation has proven the most cost-effective of techniques capable of preserving and restoring Louisiana barrier shoreline habitats. Consequently, the strategy of any comprehensive management plan to preserve Louisiana's barrier shorelines must be to pursue sediment and vegetation as well as mitigation projects in an attempt to reverse deleterious anthropogenic influences. The tactics of this strategy will include beach nourishment, barrier restoration, shoreface nourishment, vegetation, and coastal structure modification. In order for this approach to be successful, a regularly scheduled maintenance program must be developed for each barrier-built estuary.

Understanding the coastal geomorphological processes, both natural and anthropogenically-induced, that control barrier island erosion, estuary deterioration, and salt marsh loss in the Mississippi River delta plain, is essential in evaluating the performance of the various coastal protection methods currently envisioned or being employed. Previous attempts at coastal preservation and restoration have shown that an integrated approach designed to enhancing natural processes, rather than combatting them, is the most effective. Highways are built with regularly scheduled maintenance programs and this same concept should be applied to the coastal zone. Preservation and restoration of our coastal environments requires a dynamic landscape maintenance program of regularly scheduled beach nourishment, barrier restoration, shoreface nourishment, vegetation, and coastal modification projects.

SUMMARY

The coasts of Louisiana and Northwest Florida-Alabama contrast markedly in their geomorphology and their response to an historic rise in relative sea-level. The effects of a continued rise in relative sea-level in the Gulf of Mexico will likely result in the reduction of significant portions of the Louisiana coast to subaqueous shoals by early next century unless significant remedial measures are taken. Along Northwest Florida and Alabama, however, stability of the coast will likely prevail during the near future assuming the current condition of equilibrium evident in the nearshore transport system remains unchanged.

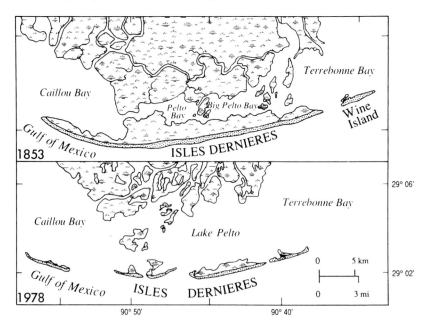

FIGURE 6. Historic shoreline migration along Isles Dernieres between 1853 and 1978.

REFERENCES

Bird, E.C. 1985. The study of coastline change. *Z. Geomorph. N.F. Suppl.-Bd.* 57:1-9.

Titus, J.G. 1986. Greenhouse effect, sea level rise, and coastal zone managment. *Coastal Zone Man. J.* 14(3):147-171.

NRC. 1987. *Responding to Changes in Sea Level: Engineering Implications.* Committee on Engineering Implications of Changes in Relative Sea Level, Marine Board, National Research Council, National Academy Press, Washington, D.C., 148 pp.

NRC. 1990. *Sea-Level Change.* Commission on Physical Sciences, Mathematics and Resources, National Research Council, National Academy Press, Washington, D.C., 234 pp.

Walker, H.J. (ed.) 1988. *Artificial Structures and Shorelines.* Kluwer Academic Press, Boston, MA. 708 pp.

Bruun, P. and M.L. Schwartz. 1985. Analytical predictions of beach profile change in response to a sea level rise. *Z. Geomorph. N.F. Suppl.-Bd.* 57:33-50.

Carter, R.W.G. 1988. *Coastal Environments.* Academic Press, New York, NY. 617 pp.

Bryant, E.A. 1985. Rainfall and beach erosion relationships, Stanwell Park, Australia, 1895-1980: worldwise implications for coastal erosion. *Z. Geomorph. N.F. Suppl.-Bd.* 57:51-65.

Bruun, P. 1962. Sea level rise as a cause of shore erosion. *Amer. Soc. Civil Eng. Proc., J. Waterways & Harbors Div.* 88:117-130.

Schwartz, M.L. 1965. Laboratory study of sea level rise as a cause of shore erosion. *J. Geol.*75:76-92.

Schwartz, M.L. 1967. The BRUUN theory of sea level rise as a cause of shore erosion. *J. Geol.* 75:76-92.

Everts, C.H. 1987. Continental shelf evolution in response to a rise in sea level, pp. 49-57. In D. Nummedal, O.H. Pilkey and J.D. Howard (Ed.) *Sea-Level Fluctuation and Coastal Evolution.* Soc. Econ. Paleontol and Mineralog. Spec. Pub 41: Tulsa, OK. pp. 267.

Dean, R.G. 1988. Sediment interaction at modified coastal inlets: Processes and policies, pp. 412-439. In: D.G. Aubrey and L. Weishar (Eds.) *Hydrodynamics and Sediment Dynamics of Tidal Inlets.* Lectures Notes in Coastal and Estuarine Studies 29; Springer Verlag, New York, NY. pp. 456.

Stone, G.W. 1991. *Differential Sediment Supply and the Cellular Nature of Coastal Northwest Florida and Southeast Alabama since the Late Holocene.* Ph.D. dissertation, University of Maryland, College Park, MD. pp. 365.

Stone, G.W., F.W. Stapor, J.P. May and J.P. Morgan. (in press). Multiple sediment sources and a cellular, non-integrated, longshore drift system: Northwest Florida and Southeast Alabama coast. *Mar. Geol.*

Stapor, F.W. 1975 Shoreline changes between Phillips Inlet and Pensacola Inlet, Northwest Florida Coast. *Trans. Gulf Coast Assoc. Geol. Soc.* XXV:373-378.

Stone, G.W., D.W. Fischer, and J.P. Morgan. 1985. The variability of Florida's coasts to storm wave susceptibility. *J. Shoreline Man.* 1:81-104.

Stone, G.W. and J.D. Salmon. 1988. Hurricane-related morphodynamics and implications for hazard mitigation, Perdido Key, Florida, U.S.A. *Coastal Man.* 16:245-270.

Morgan, J.P. and G.W. Stone. 1987. *A Dune Restoration and Protection Program for Escambia County Florida.* Coastal Studies Paper Series 1-87, Univ. West FL. Pensacola, FL. 2 vols., 75 pp.

Russell, R.J. 1936. Physiography of the lower Mississippi River delta. pp. 3-199 in R.J. Russell, H.V. Howe, J.H. McGuert, C.F. Dohm, Wade Hadley, Jr., F.B. Kniffen and C.A. Brown, *Lower Mississippi delta: reports on the geology of Plaquemines and St. Bernard parishes.* Geological bulletin no. 8. New Orleans: Department of Conservation.

Fisk, H.N. 1944. *Geolocial investigations of the alluvial valley of the Lower Mississippi River Comm.* U.S. Army Corps of Engineers, Vicksburg, Mississippi, 69 pp.

Kolb, C.R. and J.R. Van Lopik. 1958. *Geology of the Mississippi River deltaic plain, southeastern Louisiana.* Vicksburg, Mississippi: U.S. Army Corps of Engineers Waterways Experiment Station, technical report no. 3-483.

Scruton, P.C. 1960. Delta building and the deltaic sequence. pp. 82-102 in F.P. Shepard, F.B. Phleger and T.H. van Andel, eds., *Recent Sediments, Northwest Gulf of Mexico.* Tulsa, Okla.: American Association of Petroleum Geologists.

Frazier, D.E. 1967. Recent deposits of the Mississippi River, their development and chronology. *Transactions of the Gulf Coast Association of Geological Societies.* v. 17:287-311.

Coleman, J.M. 1988. Dynamic changes and processes in the Mississippi River delta. *GSA Bulletin.* v. 100:999-1015.

Kwon, H.J. 1969. *Barrier islands of the northern Gulf of Mexico coast: sediment source and development.* Louisiana State University Press, CSI Series November 15, 51 p.

Penland, S., R. Boyd and J.R. Suter. 1988. The transgressive depositional systems of the Mississippi River delta plain: a model for barrier shoreline and shelf sand development. *J. Sed. Pet.* v. 58(6):932-949.

Ritchie, W. and S. Penland. 1988. Rapid dune changes associated with overwash processes on the deltaic coast of south Louisiana. Mar. Geol. v. 81:97-122.

Ritchie, W., K.A. Westphal, R.A. McBride and S. Penland. 1990. *Coastal sand dunes of Louisiana: the Plaquemines shoreline.* Louisiana Geological Survey, Coastal Geology Technical Report No. 6, 90 pp.

Penland, S., J.R. Suter and R. Boyd. 1985. Barrier island areas along abandoned Mississippi River deltas. *Mar. Geol.* v. 63:197-233.

Ritchie, W., K.A. Westphal, R.A. McBride and S. Penland. 1989. *Coastal sand dunes of Louisiana: the Isles Dernieres.* Louisiana Geological Survey, Coastal Geology Technical Report No. 5, 60 pp.

Penland, S., J.R. Suter, R.A. McBride, S.J. Williams, J.L. Kindinger and R. Boyd, 1989a. Holocene sand shoals offshore of the Mississippi River deltaic plain. *Gulf Coast Assoc. Geo. Soc. Trans.* v. 39:471-480.

Morgan, J.P. and P.B. Larimore. 1957. Changes in the Louisiana shoreline. *Trans-*

actions of the Gulf Coast Association of Geological Societies. 7:303-10.

Adams, R.D., R.J. Banas, R.H. Bauman, J.H. Blackmon and W.G. McIntire. 1978. *Shoreline erosion in coastal Louisiana; inventory and assessment.* Baton Rouge: Louisiana Department of Natural Resources. 103 p.

Penland, S. and R. Boyd. 1981. Shoreline changes on the Louisiana barrier coast. *Oceans.* 81:209-19.

van Beek, J.L. and K.J. Meyer-Arendt. 1982. *Louisiana's eroding coastline: recommendations for protection.* Louisiana Department of Natural Resources, Baton Rouge, 49 p.

Morgan, J.P. and D.J. Morgan. 1983. *Accelerating retreat rates along Louisiana's coast.* Louisiana Sea Grant College Program, Louisiana State University, 41 p.

U.S. Geological Survey. 1988. Map of coastal erosion and accretion. *In National Atlas of the U.S.A.* The Department of the Interior, U.S. Geological Survey, Reston, Va.

Harper, J. 1977. Sediment disposal trends of the Caminada-Moreau beach ridge system. *Trans. Gulf Coast Association of Geological Societies.* v. 27:283-289.

Penland, S. and W. Ritchie. 1979. Short-term morphological changes along the Caminada-Moreau coast, Louisiana. *Trans. of the Gulf Coast Association of Geological Societies.* 29:342-246.

Boyd, R. and S. Penland. 1981. Washover of delaic barriers on the Louisiana coast. *Trans. of the Gulf Coast Association of Geological Societies.* v. 31:243-248.

Dingler, J.R. and T.E. Reiss. 1988. *Louisiana barrier island study: Isles Dernieres beach profiles August 1986 to September 1987.* U.S. Geol. Survey Open-File Rep. 88-7; 27 p.

Dingler, J.R. and T.E. Reiss. 1990. Cold-front driven storm erosion and overwash in the central part of the Isles Dernieres, a Louisiana barrier arc. *Mar. Geol.* v. 91:195-206.

Penland, S., K. Debusschere, K.A. Westphal, J.R. Suter, R.A. McBride and P.D. Reimer, 1989b. The 1985 hurricane impacts on the Isles Dernieres: a temporal and spatial analysis of the coastal geomorphic changes. *Trans. of the Gulf Coast Assoc. Geo. Soc.* v. 39:455-470.

Penland, S. and R. Boyd. 1982. Assessment of geological and human factors responsible for Louisiana coastal barrier erosion. In D.F. Boesch, ed., *Proceedings of the conference on coastal erosion and wetland modification in Louisiana: causes, consequences and options.* Joint publication FWS/OBS82159. Baton Rouge: Louisiana Universities Marine Consortium/U.S. Fish and Wildlife Service. pp. 20-59.

Natural and Technological Disasters: Causes, Effects and Preventive Measures. Edited by
S.K. Majumdar, G.S. Forbes, E.W. Miller, and R.F. Schmalz. © 1992, The Pennsylvania Academy
of Science.

Chapter Twenty-One

SINKHOLES AND SINKHOLE COLLAPSES

WILLIAM B. WHITE and ELIZABETH L. WHITE
Department of Geosciences and
Department of Civil Engineering
The Pennsylvania State University
University Park, PA 16802

INTRODUCTION

The term "sinkhole" is used to refer to any closed depression in the land surface.
It is synonymous with the term "doline", widely used in European karst literature.
The size of sinkholes ranges from small shallow depressions only a few meters in
diameter and less than a meter deep to depressions with diameters measured in
kilometers and depths of hundreds of meters. The present discussion is limited to
the smaller end of the size scale because these are the ones which commonly occur
in Pennsylvania. For discussion of large closed depression features such as valley
sinks, cockpits, poljes, and related features, see any textbook on karst geomorphology: Sweeting,[1] Jennings,[2] White,[3] or Ford and Williams.[4]

In addition to a range in size and depth, however, there is also a range in the
characteristic time scales for the creation of sinkholes. Some sinkholes, on a human
time scale, are permanent features of the landscape because they are depressions
in the bedrock surface itself formed by solution over very long periods of time.
Others of the soil-piping variety are features which literally form overnight which
also disappear on a time scale of months or years.

From a hydrological point of view, sinkholes are the inlets or recharge points of the karst groundwater system. Some closed depressions occur at the swallow points of sinking streams that rise on adjacent non-carbonate rocks or adjacent mountain slopes and pass underground where streams reach the limestone. All sinkholes have characteristic catchment areas and carry surface runoff underground rather than allowing it to reach surface streams as overland flow. The role of moving water is central to the transport of dissolved bedrock and for the transport of soil and other clastic materials in the excavation of the closed depressions.

THE TAXONOMY OF SINKHOLES

Figure 1 shows the principal components of a sinkhole. There is the closed depression in the bedrock surface itself although a bedrock depression is not an absolutely essential feature. The essential feature is the drain which allows water from the bottom of the basin to drain into the subsurface. One also assumes the existence of cave passages at depth which are necessary to transmit both water and clastic sediment out of the system although the caves are only rarely observed. An important fourth component is a mantle of soil, glacial moraine, volcanic ash, or other unconsolidated material covering the bedrock depression. The draping of soils across the bedrock depression results in a characteristic parabolic shape for sinkholes so that many sinkholes tend to look more or less alike when all one sees is the soil mantle.

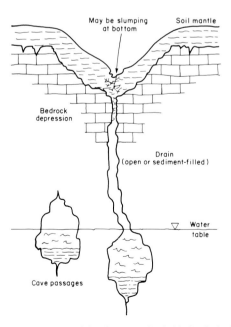

FIGURE 1. Sketch showing the characterizing features of a sinkhole: the bedrock depression, the drain, the underlying cave passages, and the soil mantle.

There are three processes which operate in sinkhole genesis (Fig. 2). One of these is the chemical solution of the bedrock by reaction of limestone, dolomite, or other soluble rock with the CO_2-containing runoff which flows into the sinkhole. The second process is one of bedrock stoping and collapse. In some cases, the depression results from shallow collapse of an underlying cave roof. In other cases voids deep in the subsurface provide an instability which can stope upward by collapse of the bedrock, ultimately reaching the surface to form a closed depression. Third, and from an environmental view the most important, is a process of piping of soils into the subsurface. Depending on the relative contribution of each of the three processes, one gets immediately the three main categories of sinkholes that have been widely discussed in the literature. Each of these three main categories of sinkholes then can be divided into several subcategories.

If the bulk of the dissolution takes place at the bedrock surface, the end result is a bowl shaped basin with a relatively small drain. Typical small sinkhole drains range from fractures a few centimeters wide to irregular solution chimneys tens of centimeters in aperture although generally not of the proportions that would admit to human exploration. If the solution attack is focused on the drain, the drain is enlarged to considerable depths and appears as a solution chimney or vertical shaft. Whereas the bowl-shaped basins typically have depths comparable to, or less than, their widths, the solution chimneys and vertical shafts can be tens or even hundreds of meters deep and only meters to tens of meters in diameter.

PROCESSES

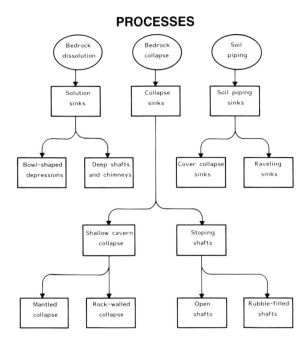

FIGURE 2. Classification scheme for sinkholes and related features based on the predominant process of their formation.

If the process of stoping and collapse takes place at shallow depths, such as, for example, the collapse of a cave roof, there is formed a relatively shallow depression which, when draped with soil, may be indistinguishable from a solution sink. However, if the cavity which initiates collapse is at depth either in fractured rock or in poorly consolidated rock, the opening can stope its way upward and if some mechanism at depth removes fallen blocks, the shaft can stope its way tens to hundreds of meters before it intersects the surface and can indeed stope its way through overlying non-soluble rocks. The end product of this process is the stoping shaft. These are frequently much deeper than they are wide.

The behavior of the soil-piping sink depends to a great extent on the cohesive character of the soils. If the soil is cohesive, its piping into the bedrock creates a void which enlarges, roofed by a soil arch, until it reaches a size where the ceiling becomes unstable. The final breakthrough of the soil-piping sink to the surface takes place essentially instantaneously as the soil arch collapses. If the soils are loose and non-cohesive, the transport of soil into the subsurface is by a continuous, or raveling, process of sand going down through a crack and the sinkhole forms more or less continuously without the formation of the void arch which can abruptly collapse.

MECHANISMS OF SINKHOLE FORMATION

The Solution Process

The dissolution of carbonate rocks is by the action of carbonic acid reacting with calcite or dolomite. The carbonic acid is derived from CO_2 in the atmosphere, decay of organic material, the action of microorganisms, and exhalation from the roots of plants. Concentrations of CO_2 in the soil range up to a few volume percent. Infiltrating water dissolves the carbon dioxide to form carbonic acid. There is a partitioning between the CO_2 which diffuses upward through the soil and is lost to the atmosphere and CO_2 which is carried downward in solution in the infiltrating water. The chemical reactions are shown below:

$$CO_2 \text{ (gas)} \rightarrow CO_2 \text{ (aqueous)}$$
$$CO_2 \text{ (aqueous)} + H_2O \rightarrow H_2CO_3$$
$$H_2CO_3 \rightarrow H^+ + HCO_3^-$$
$$HCO_3^- \rightarrow H^+ + CO_3^{-2}$$

The equilibrium chemistry for these reactions has been studied intensively (5-7). When the carbonic acid comes into contact with carbonate rock, the carbonate is dissolved by reaction with hydrogen ions, by direct reaction with dissolved CO_2, or by reaction with the water molecule itself:

$$CaCO_3 + H^+ \rightarrow Ca^{2+} + HCO_3^-$$
$$CaCO_3 + CO_2 + H_2O \rightarrow Ca^{2+} + 2\,HCO_3^-$$
$$CaCO_3 + H_2O \rightarrow Ca^{2+} + HCO_3^- + OH^-$$

The end result for all three reactions is the same. Solid limestone is taken away in solution as calcium ions and bicarbonate ions.

The equilibrium chemistry of carbonate dissolution, however, is not the critical factor is determining the rate of sinkhole development and sinkhole morphology. The kinetics of the dissolution of carbonates is relatively sluggish and both limestone and dolomite dissolve much more rapidly in highly undersaturated water than they do in waters that approach saturation. The characteristic time for the calcite reaction to approach saturation is on the order of 1 to 2 days. Water percolating slowly down the wall of the sinkhole at the soil / bedrock contact may approach saturation by the time it reaches the sinkhole drain. During storms, overland flow on top of the soil flows rapidly down the sink, may pond briefly at the bottom, then infiltrates rapidly through the soil and down the drain with very little contact with the soil itself. However, these rapid infiltration waters have very low carbon dioxide partial pressures and therefore very low carrying capacity for dissolved carbonates. The result from both kinds of input is a continuous enlargement of the bedrock basin but a very slow enlargement of the drain accounting for the observation that most sinkhole drains are quite small compared with the size of the sinkhole itself.

There appears to be a critical threshold which must be exceeded in the initial development of a solution sink. When water percolates through the soil and into the bedrock through joints and fractures, the rate of movement is sufficiently slow that the water reacts to saturation at the soil / rock contact producing a continuous lowering of the bedrock surface. The fracture enlarges slowly until it reaches a size on the order of a few millimeters to a centimeter at which time the velocity of flow through the fracture increases to the point where undersaturated water can be carried into the subsurface. Solution attack on the sinkhole drain at depth is then possible. At about the same aperture, the drain can carry sediment and begin to transmit a clastic load as well as a dissolved load. The onset of deep dissolution within the drain is a threshold or crossover between vadose water moving through fractures and incipient sinkhole development.

Processes of Bedrock Collapse, Stoping, and Subsidence

The creation of sinkholes by shallow bedrock collapse requires a preexisting cavity within the rock. This is usually a cave passage which formed in the limestone at some far earlier time and is now close to the land surface because of the gradual lowering of the landscape. Figure 3 shows the basic process for the simplest case of horizontally bedded limestones.

The limestone beds that form the roof of the cavity act as fixed beams and have a certain critical breaking strength. The sag of these beams produces a zone of stress in the overlying bedrock which is dome shaped as shown in the sketch. The fixed beams are stable and cave passage survives for a long time. If infiltrating water, enlarging joints by solution converts fixed beams to cantilevers, the ceiling can be weakened to the point where it can no longer support it own weight. Then follows a sequence of collapse which cascades upward through overlying beds, reaching the land surface to form a collapse sink.

In some cases the underlying cave passage is accessible from both sides of the sink and the origin of the collapse is perfectly obvious. Many times as least one side of the cave passage will be blocked by the breakdown and in many cases both sides will be blocked. The fallen rock becomes in time draped with soil and the superficial appearance of the sinkhole, as viewed from the land surface, no longer reveals its collapse origin.

Solution cavities at depth in fully consolidated rocks are usually stable unless there is some zone of structural weakness, such as a fracture zone, which allows access of surface water or unless they enlarge to a size where the primary strength of the ceiling beds is exceeded. Some ceiling collapse tends to be self-limiting with the formation of a breakout dome, a breakdown-enlarged chamber in the cave passage.[8] In other cases, deep seated collapse migrates upward through successively more and more intensively weathered rock, until the point is reached where the entire roof falls in (Fig. 4). If the overlying rocks are poorly consolidated and have a low mechanical strength, deep solution cavities can also migrate upward over distances of hundreds of meters without any structural weakness. Cavities which

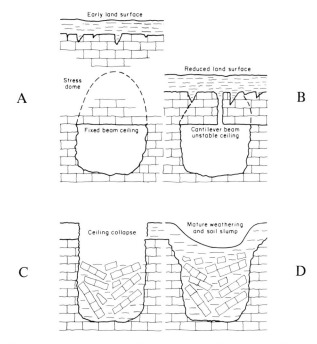

FIGURE 3. Sketch showing the stages in the development of a bedrock collapse sink. A. Stable cavity at depth in the bedrock. Stress pattern in cave roof shown by dashed line. B. Lowering land surface allows solutional attack by surface waters, disrupting beds and converting fixed beams into cantilevers thus placing the cavity in an unstable state. C. Cavity collapse by gravity slumping exposing bedrock walls of the resulting sinkhole. D. Final stage when continued rock weathering and soil slumping has masked the breakdown leaving only a shallow bowl-shaped depression visible on the surface.

may have formed at times of Pleistocene sea-level minima have become the activating mechanism for upward stoping processes that caused many of the catastrophic sinkhole collapses in the Florida peninsula.

If the fallen rock is simply stored in the underlying solution cavity, the stoping blocks also accumulate in the shaft. Simple mass balance considerations lead to the relationship between the volume of the constructed shaft

$$V_s = [(1 - \theta) / \theta] \, V_c$$

Where θ is the porosity of the breccia pile and V_c is the volume of the initiating cavity. It is possible for the entire shaft to be filled, leaving only a shallow collapse sink at the surface, but one with a deep breccia zone below it. If the fallen blocks are removed by solution, for example by a flowing stream in the cave passage, the upward migrating shaft remains open and when it breaks through to the surface a deep subsidence shaft results. Subsidence or stoping shafts are quite spectacular features in some karst areas; Sotano de las Golondrinas, San Luis Potosi, Mexico is more than 400 m deep and more than 200 m in diameter at the base.[9]

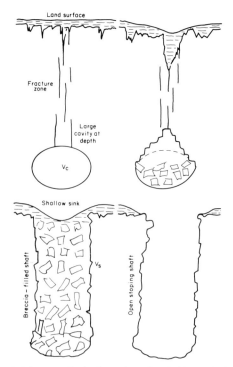

FIGURE 4. Sketch showing the stages in the formation of a subsidence shaft. If the breccia formed by the upward stoping shaft is not removed, only a shallow sink may be visible at the surface. If the rubble is removed by dissolution at the bottom of the shaft, a deep open shaft may be formed.

Soil Piping and Cover Collapse Sinkholes

From the perspective of environmental hazards, soil piping sinkholes are by far the most serious because they are formed on time scales which are short compared with human activities. They are also most susceptible to initiation or change by human land use practices. Figure 5 illustrates the stages in the formation of a cover collapse sinkhole. There must be a fracture system sufficiently enlarged by solution to transmit soil and other clastic material and there must be a subsurface drainage system capable of flushing the clastic material away. The infiltration water soaks through the soil and has to focus towards the open fracture which is the only route to the subsurface through the otherwise impermeable carbonate bedrock. The characteristics of the flow net are such that there will be a substantial increase in the flow velocity as the water is channeled into the fracture. The high velocity of storm runoff at the top of the fracture is capable of moving soil particles and this is the initiation point for the cover collapse sink.

The soils are flushed into the subsurface creating a small void directly above the fracture. A combination of continued inflow of water combined with gravitational collapse and spalling causes the arch to enlarge bit by bit. As time goes on a void chamber in the soil is formed with a floor on the carbonate bedrock and a ceiling formed by the soil arch. This cavity enlarges laterally and migrates upward. A point will be reached where the soil arch can barely support its own weight

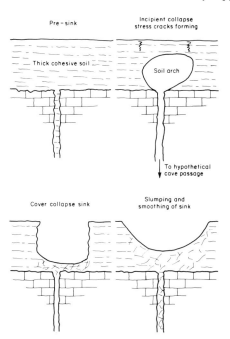

FIGURE 5. Sketch showing the stages in the formation of a cover collapse sink by piping of soils into the subsurface.

and circular stress cracks may be observed on the land surface as the soil begins to sag into the void space. In certain situations the void develops slowly enough that the circular stress cracks and associated shallow depression can be observed forming over a period of days. In other cases the final stages of the collapse take place so rapidly that they are essentially instantaneous. Usually the originating fracture and other bedrock features are buried under the pile of soil that drops into the hole when the ceiling collapses.

These are sharp-rimmed sinks usually with vertical walls entirely in soil and the bottom entirely in soil. Many variations on the basic concept are possible depending on the arrangement of the solution cavities in the underlying bedrock and on the thickness and cohesive character of the soil. A soil-choked solution chimney can be slowly opened up by an upward piping process and if there are intermediate level cavities that can act as storage spaces for the soils, quite large solution voids can be formed in the soil. This is apparently the mechanism for the formation of the huge catastrophic collapse sinks that have swallowed entire houses and mining plants in the South African gold fields.[10]

It appears that the abruptness with which the collapse occurs increases with increased soil cohesion. Loose, sandy soils, ravel continuously into the underlying limestone and there is a continuous settling and subsidence on the surface, whereas in cohesive soils there is little indication of void formation until final collapse occurs. The cover over the soil can act as a roof and support the soil arch thus allowing the ceiling to become much thinner before the ultimate collapse occurs. Grass and sod often assume this role and the final stages of collapse is a tearing away of the sod and forming a sharp rim. Concrete, or blacktop pavement can also serve this role so it is entirely possible for large void spaces to be excavated underneath roads, parking lots, sidewalks, or basements before the mechanical strength of the pavement is exceeded and collapse occurs.

ENVIRONMENTAL ASPECTS OF SINKHOLES

Sinkholes as Injection Points for Solid and Liquid Pollutants

Because of the intimate connection between sinkhole drains and the underlying karst drainage system, anything which introduces contamination into the sinkhole injects contamination into the groundwater as well.

Obviously, anything which contaminates a sinking stream not only is contaminating surface water but it is contaminating the associated groundwater. Less obvious is the contamination injected into the groundwater system through sinkholes. Because many sinkholes have no flowing water, they have always seemed convenient receptacles for the disposal of waste. Included here is the practice of disposing of dead and diseased farm animals by dumping the carcasses into convenient sinkholes. Individual farms and sometimes entire muncipalities use sinkholes as dumps and also as injection points for sewage and industrial wastewater. EPA classifies sinkholes as Class 5 injection wells.

Infiltrating water percolates through the garbage layer where it becomes a leachate which then flows down the drain and into the ground water system. In addition, processes of soil piping, stoping, collapse, and inwash of material often carries the wastes to substantial depths within the cave system. Once emplaced underground, these materials act as sources of pollution which can continue to function for long periods of time, even long after remedial measures have been taken on the sinkhole itself.

In addition to deliberate introduction of pollutants into sinkholes, there is a long list of what might be called inadvertent introduction of pollutants into sinkholes. Runoff from highways passing through carbonate areas frequently discharges into sinkholes carrying roadsalt and miscellaneous hydrocarbon contaminants from automobiles. In some carbonate areas, sinkholes provide a convenient discharge for stormwater. Stormwater drain systems are directed into sinkholes and this carries all the washoff from parking lots, streets, roofs and other pavements and flushes them directly into the groundwater sytem.

Sinkhole Flooding

Sinkhole terrains, especially in regions of shallow water table, are frequently flood prone areas. As such they may require special zoning restrictions or other controls on development such as are often applied to the alluvial flood plains of surface streams. The soil mantles in the sinkholes are often highly impermeable clays. As a result sinkholes (at the simplest level) collect surface runoff to form a temporary pond perched well above the local water table. Sinkhole ponds may take days or weeks to drain.

Because sinkholes are connected by their drains into the underlying groundwater system, rising water tables force water back up through the drain to spill out and pond in the sinkhole. Although it is certainly not obvious from casual inspection, the standing water level in a sinkhole can be the surface expression of the water table and the flooded sinkhole could be truly referred to as a sinkhole lake. One such occurs in central Pennsylvania where it is known locally as Phantom Lake[1]. The Phantom Lake depression is more than a kilometer in diameter, although relatively shallow. During the Hurricane Agnes storm of 1972, intense runoff from the surrounding mountain slopes forced water up through the drains in the small secondary sinkholes and filled the entire depression with a lake which reached depths of 10 meters and was nearly a kilometer in diameter.

There is a rather more subtle but more dangerous environmental hazard aspect of sinkhole flooding which has been most extensively studied in the Bowling Green area of southcentral Kentucky[2]. A shallow cave system carries the entire drainage from the region as the large underground stream known as Lost River. The Lost River has been contaminated with hydrocarbons and toxic organic chemicals from a variety of sources. These materials are insoluble in water and so they tend to collect where the underground river is ponded. When the river floods, the water rises, the entire conduit becomes water filled, and the water surface forces its way up through fractures and small solution chimneys which are the sinkhole drains. So although the sinkholes on the surface may or may not actually flood, toxic materials forced up through the sinkhole drains either collect on the surface or are forced into the basements of homes and schools.

ENGINEERING ASPECTS OF SINKHOLES

Foundation Engineering

Although cover collapse sinks form in natural environment, they can be exacerbated by human activities. Modifications of the landscape that accelerate sinkhole development usually involve either excessive lowering of water levels or excessive injection of water at the surface.

If water tables are lowered, for example by overpumping, hydraulic gradients are increased, increasing the ability of underground streams to carry sediment. Clays and soils that occupy solution chimneys and other cavities in the limestone above the water table have an opportunity to drain and dry out, become more friable, and then during storms infiltrating water can flush these materials into the subsurface, open up the chimneys, and provide initiation points for soil piping activity.

Whenever water is concentrated at a particular point of infiltration there is enhanced flow velocity at the top of the limestone and transport of soils and initiation of sinkholes. For this latter and more common type of situation, the way to avoid sinkhole formation is to make sure that storm water runoff is dispersed over as wide an area as possible. This means avoiding situations where all the water from an entire driveway or parking lot is emptied out on the ground at a single point. It means carrying roof runoff away from buildings, and dispersing it over an area rather than letting it go into the ground at the corner of a building where it can initiate soil piping directly under the structure. The existing sinkhole prone areas in urban regions can be most easily dealt with simply by using them as green areas, open land, or park land and allowing large portions of the area to grow up in thick grass and brush. The plant roots offer one of the most effective methods of keeping soils in place and allowing infiltrating water to be dispersed. Plants also slow down the velocity of overland flow.

Solutions to sinkhole problems come in two categories: (i) what can one do after sinkholes happen and (ii) what can one do to prevent sinkholes before they happen? Sinkhole engineering has received a tremendous amount of attention as sinkhole problems have become recognized as an universal land management problem in karst areas. For much of the recent literature on this see the Proceedings of the various sinkhole conferences that have been held at the University of Central Florida.[13-15] Sinkhole prevention is far more cost-effective than sinkhole repair.

The most common response to sinkholes is simply to fill them up again. This is often a futile operation because the filled sinkhole develops a new soil arch and collapses again or a new sinkhole develops somewhere in the immediate neighborhood. A sinkhole filling needs to allow for the infiltration of runoff water without concurrent movement of soil. Researchers have proposed inserting a filling of coarse stone followed by a filling of small stone and gravel, perhaps topped off with soil or sod[16] This arrangement permits surface runoff to percolate easily to the bedrock drain at the base of the sinkhole without carrying away large quantities of soil.

The sinkholes and soil voids that develop under structures or that undermine structures are a special problem. A whole range of engineering techniques have been developed to prop-up, bridge, grout, and reinstall structures. Often what is done is to jack the structures back into alignment, if necessary installing supporting pillars, and then either grout the solution cavities if they occur in bedrock or backfill appropriately for structures in loose soils. In new construction, pilings, caissons, or other structures that extend downward into solid bedrock can be installed to provide the needed load support. Any engineering solution to sinkhole problems is very expensive but there appears to be no alternative.

A special category of sinkhole problem is the loss of surface water through sinkhole collapse in stream beds. If it is necessary to maintain surface flows or reduce loss to groundwater, these holes must be sealed. A technique of filling the sinkhole with a layer of fine stone topped over with a layer of coarse stone, essentially replacing the normal stream bed stream armoring, has been effective.

Stormwater Management in Sinkhole Terrain

Stormwater management is an increasingly important problem in the limestone valleys throughout Pennsylvania. As the state becomes urbanized and more populated, it becomes more necessary to control stormwater, a difficult problem in areas underlain by carbonate rocks. Sinkholes and wide, shallow swale areas are prone to develop piping failure (cover collapse) sinkholes because of the runoff modifications that are installed for storm water management in urban areas.

Typical stormwater detention basins, usually earthen, are located at points where stormwater runoff has been concentrated by storm sewers, drainage swales, or ditches. Although engineers sometimes encourage the design of facilities which would always contain water (retention basins), detention basins have been more common. It is rare for storm sewers to be specified by ordinance as the only means of conveyance, since the cost of storm sewers to accommodate a 100-year storm would be prohibitive. Throughout Pennsylvania, a 25- or 50-year design is often the maximum criterion for storm sewers. This means that high runoff must be carried by the natural watercourses, drainage swales, or concerete drainage ditches. This can be a serious problem in areas of steep slopes, karstic bedrock, and landslide-prone or other easily eroded soils. Most municipalities require inside slopes of 2:1 or 3:1 for all detention or retention basins to insure that a child could safely walk out of a full basin. The outside slopes are usually 3:1.

If, during the course of development, existing natural sinkholes are allowed to serve as detention ponds, the ponded water saturates the soil filling the sinkhole and increases the seepage pressure at the base of the soil. Conditions are then optimum for soil piping and sinkhole failure may occur in the modified situation of a development project that would not have occurred under natural circumstances.

Detention and retention ponds built in karst areas have the same hydrologic characteristics as natural sinkholes.

SINKHOLE PRECURSORS AND SINKHOLE PREDICTION

Throughout most of Pennsylvania soils are not thick enough for cover collapse sinks to form a life threatening hazard but they can cause an immense amount of property damage and they are an expensive nuisance to developers, contractors, and home owners. From the property owner's point of view it could be very important to be able to recognize the beginning of a sinkhole problem before the actual sinkhole collapse takes place. Because of the mechanism for cover collapse sinkhole development, there is very little advance surface indication that a sinkhole might be forming. The following list are some predictors.
- The settling of buildings causes them to become slightly out of true. Doors do not close properly; windows do not slide smoothly in their frames; cracks appear in plaster and cinder block walls. (All are indications that the building is shifting slightly and going out of true.)
- Places where water puddles after rainstorms, particularly if the puddle areas are circular, can indicate slight subsidence of the ground where the soil arch is beginning to weaken. In the final stage of the process arcuate shear cracks may appear in the grass, although these are often an immediate precursor to collapse.
- The presence of a soil void in the subsurface drains water from the soils and circular patches of stressed vegetation, (grass or plants, that appear not to be as green or as hardy as in surrounding areas) may indicate the presence of a developing void beneath.

CONCLUSIONS

Sinkholes are a complex collection of phenomena involving processes of bedrock dissolution, bedrock collapse and stoping, and soil-piping. Solution sinkholes are permanent features of the landscape and are either visible at the surface or can be revealed by shallow test borings. Land use planning simply has to allow for them. Solution sinks do provide easy access pathways for pollutants to enter the groundwater system and this must be taken into account in the planning. Bedrock collapse sinks likewise tend to be permanent landscape features because the processes that lead to bedrock collapse occur naturally over long periods of time. However, deep excavations that remove bedrock may trigger bedrock collapses that would not have happened for many years under natural conditions.

Most of the concern with sinkholes as a land-use hazard refers only to soil-piping sinkholes. They pose the greatest threat to streets, buildings, and other structures. Cover collapse sinkholes formed by soil piping are ephemeral features, usually involving formation of large void spaces at shallow depths in thick soils since void development and sinkhole collapse are rapid processes on human time scales. They are also the type of sinkhole most responsive to human intrusion.

REFERENCES

1. Sweeting, M.M. 1972. *Karst Landforms.* Macmillan, London. pp. 362.
2. Jennings, J.N. 1985. *Karst Geomorphology.* Basil Blackwell, Oxford, pp. 293.
3. White, W.B. 1988. *Geomorphology and Hydrology of Karst Terrains.* Oxford University Press, New York, NY, pp. 464.
4. Ford, D., P.W. Williams. 1989. *Karst Geomorphology and Hydrology.* Unwin Hyman, London, Great Britain, pp. 601.
5. Busenberg, E., L.N. Plummer. 1982. The kinetics of dissolution of dolomite in CO_2-H_2O systems at 1.5 to 65 C and 0 to 1 atm P_{CO_2}. *Amer. J. Sci.* 282: 45-78.
6. Loewenthal, R.E. and G. v.R. Marais. 1978. *Carbonate Chemistry of Aquatic Systems: Theory and Application.* Ann Arbor Science, Ann Arbor, MI pp. 433.
7. Stumm, W., and J.J. Morgan. 1981. *Aquatic Chemistry,* 2nd Ed. John Wiley, New York, NY, pp. 780.
8. White, E.L. and W.B. White. 1969. Processes of cavern breakdown. *Natl. Spel. Soc. Bull.* 31: 83-96.
9. Raines, T.W. 1968. Sotano de las Golodrinas. *Bull. Assoc. Mexican Cave Studies* 2: 1-20.
10. Jennings, J.E. 1966. Building on dolomites in the Transvaal. *The Civil Engineer in South Africa* 8:41-62.
11. White, E.L. and W.B. White. 1984. Flood hazards in karst terrain: Lessons from the hurricane Agnes storm. *Internatl. Contr. Hydrogeol.* 1:261-264.
12. Crawford, N.C. 1984. Sinkhole flooding associated with urban development upon karst terrain: Bowling Green, Kentucky, In: B.F. Beck (Ed.) *Sinkholes: Their Geology, Engineering, and Environmental Impact.* A.A. Balkema, Rotterdam. 297-304.
13. Beck, B.F. 1984. *Sinkholes: Their Geology, Engineering, and Environmental Impact.* A.A. Balkema, Rotterdam. pp. 429.
14. Beck, B.F. and W.L. Wilson. 1987. *Karst Hydrologeology: Engineering and Environmental Applications.* A.A. Balkema, Rotterdam. pp. 467.
15. Beck, B.F. 1989. *Engineering and Environmental Impacts of Sinkholes and Karst.* A.A. Balkema, Rotterdam. pp. 384.
16. White, E.L., G. Aron, and W.B. White. 1984. The influence of urbanization on sinkhole development in central Pennsylvania. *Environ. Geol. Water Sci.* 8: 91-97.

Natural and Technological Disasters: Causes, Effects and Preventive Measures. Edited by
S.K. Majumdar, G.S. Forbes, E.W. Miller, and R.F. Schmalz. © 1992, The Pennsylvania Academy
of Science.

Chapter Twenty-Two

HAZARDOUS AND TOXIC WASTE SITES: STRATEGIES OF CONTROL

E. WILLARD MILLER

Professor of Geography and
Associate Dean for Resident Instruction (Emeritus)
College of Earth and Mineral Sciences
The Pennsylvania State University
University Park, PA 16802

INTRODUCTION

For many years the disposition of toxic and hazardous chemicals and biological
by-products of our technological society was largely ignored. Abandoned dump-
sites and polluted streams were prominent features of these practices. By the 1970s
it was becoming evident that the environment was becoming contaminated (Lave,
Upton, 1987). This chapter presents an overview of these problems and some of
the control strategies that are evolving to create a livable environment in the future.

MAJOR HAZARDOUS AND TOXIC WASTE SITES

The public became aware of the massive problem of environmental contamination when massive hazardous and toxic waste sites were revealed to have possible
adverse health effects (Schnell, Monmonier, 1984). These sites were widely
distributed in the nation so that national attention was soon focussed on the
problem.

Love Canal, Niagara Falls, New York

Of these sites, Love Canal in Niagara Falls was the first to receive national attention. The saga of this waste site began in 1892 when William T. Love proposed to build a power canal along the Niagara River starting about eight miles above Niagara Falls. The canal would carry water to the edge of the precipice where it would drop several hundred feet providing electricity. Part of the canal was constructed, but then abandoned. The canal filled with water and was long used as a recreational facility.

In the 1940s the Hooker Chemical Company (In 1968 it became affiliated with the Occidental Petroleum Company) purchased the canal and until 1953 used it to dispose of toxic waste materials. It was considered an excellent disposal site for the canal was about 10 feet deep and 60 feet wide and was dug into a clay layer, a material through which liquid flowed slowly. It is estimated that 20,000 metric tons of waste in metal drums were buried and covered with clay. The clay was to create a 'vault' to hold the chemicals securely in place.

By 1953 a large portion of the canal was filled with chemical wastes when the Hooker Chemical Company sold the land to the Niagara Falls School Board for $1.00. In the deed it was stated that the property was filled with waste products, but no warning was given that a potential health problem existed. A school was built on the rim of the canal and the remainder of the land was sold for the construction of one-family houses.

The first evidence of health problems emerged in 1958 when children received chemical burns while playing along a road building operation. A few drums had ruptured. The waste material was removed and the area refilled, apparently solving the problem.

The modern day Love Canal problem can be traced to 1976 when residents adjacent to the canal began to complain of chemical odors and claimed that their discomfort was related to the seepage of water from the Love Canal landfill. To emphasize the health problems a reporter, Michael Brown, of the *Niagara Gazette* began a series of articles about suspected cases of toxic waste induced illnesses among people living in the Love Canal area. The *Courier Express-Niagara News* also created an atmosphere of concern.

In 1978 Love Canal began to receive national publicity when the New York State Commissioner of Health began to investigate the situation. Eventually, over 400 chemicals were identified, including a number of carcinogens, teratogens and mutagens. Some were measured at 5,000 times the maximum safe concentrations. Health problems began to be reported. Women located in the Canal area suffered miscarriages at the rate of fifty percent higher than normal. In one section 4 of 24 children had birth defects. Many adults began to suffer liver damage. In August 1978 pregnant women and children under two years of age were encouraged to leave the area.

President Jimmy Carter declared Love Canal a disaster area, which made federal aid available to the residents. In addition the Federal government purchased 237 homes and removed the inhabitants. The school was closed and a chain fence put around the area. In May 1980 President Carter declared a second emergency and an additional 710 families were offered the opportunity to sell their homes to the government (Landers, 1988).

The Environmental Protection Agency began a cleanup program to remove all chemical wastes. It thus provided a test-area to develop new clean-up procedures. Tens of millions of dollars have been spent. Lawsuits totalling billions of dollars have been filed by Love Canal residents against Hooker, the Niagara Falls Board of Education and the city of Niagara Falls. Both New York State and the Environmental Protection Agency have sued Hooker. The lawsuits will not be settled for decades.

The Love Canal incident alerted the nation to the problems created by toxic chemical dumps as no other incident had done. The pioneering efforts to defuse Love Canal's 'ticking time bomb' initiated the investigations of other waste sites that were buried and forgotten, but potentially health hazards to a population.

In May 1990 the Environmental Protection Agency declared that the toxic chemicals had been removed and the area was safe for habitation. The houses that had stood vacant for years are now being sold at reduced prices to private citizens. These new home owners believe that the health hazards have been removed. However, this does not conclude the saga of the Love Canal for environmental groups are protesting the decision of the EPA in the courts believing that a potential health problem still exists in the area.

Times Beach, Missouri

In the early 1970s some 2,000 gallons of a combination of oil and industrial waste were sprayed on an open field near Times Beach, Missouri. The waste was contaminated with dioxin. Soon after the spraying, birds, rodents, and horses died in the area, and two children playing in the area required hospitalization. By 1975 it was apparent the area was contaminated. To complicate the problem, the citizens of Times Beach were concerned that flooding would spread the toxic substances throughout the town.

The U.S. Center for Disease Control recommended lifetime human exposure limit of 1 ppb of dioxin was exceeded in some soil samples by as much as 100 ppb. The CDC officials recommended evacuation. The Environmental Protection Agency agreed to spend some $30 million to purchase all of the homes of Times Beach.

In the years since the evacuation of the population of Times Beach there is no evidence that the health of the people has been permanently affected. The Missouri director of the Division of Health has stated, "We have seen nothing to alarm us or make us believe that Missourians are feeling acute health effects." In June 1983, the American Medical Association passed a resolution at its Chicago convention that there is no scientific evidence that small quantities of dioxin in the environment poses a direct threat to health (*Washington Post,* June 23, 1983). The AMA further voted to "adopt an active public information campaign...to prevent irrational reaction and unjustified public fright and to prevent the dissemination of possibly erroneous information about the health hazards of dioxin."

Times Beach illustrates the hysteria that a community suffers when it becomes known that a toxic substance is located in a populated area. Times Beach also illustrates that reliable information is not always available to the public. However, when it is believed that the toxic substances contaminate an area it must be remedied quickly so that human health will not be adversely affected.

In July 1990 the Environmental Protection Agency announced a plan to clean up the Times Beach abandoned area. An incinerator, at a cost of $118 million, will be built to burn the waste material. After the cleanup is completed, Times Beach will once again become a habitable community.

Other Major Toxic Sites

Other examples of massive toxic waste sites gained attention in the 1970s. These were widely distributed throughout the nation. For example, in Bayou Sorrel, Louisiana, millions of gallons of toxic wastes were dumped in huge open pits. The air currents contaminated nearby areas. In Saltville, Virginia a chemical plant used open pits for more than three quarters of a century to deposit mercury toxicants that not only contaminated the soil but the ground water that flowed into the North Fork of the Halston River. In Byron, Illinois more than 1,500 containers of such industrial wastes as cyanide, chromium, arsenic and heavy metals were buried on farmland. As the containers deteriorated the substances entered the soil and ground water. At Shepardville, Kentucky, an area that came to be known as the "Valley of the Drums," had about 100,000 drums of waste deposited illegally on farmlands. The drums were abandoned by the company and gradually contaminated the soil and water supplies. As the public became aware of the dangers of hazardous and toxic waste sites, a major problem has arisen in finding sites for these materials. The viewpoint "not in my backyard" has become nationwide (Freudenberg, 1984).

NATIONAL LEGISLATION

By the mid-1970s it became evident that a national program was needed to focus on the cleanup of hazardous waste sites (Mallow, 1981). The Resources Conservation and Recovery Act of 1976 provided the basic framework to initiate and accelerate a national research and development program for new and improved methods for economic solid waste disposal. In the passage of this Act, Congress recognized that continuing technological progress and modern methods of manufacturing, packaging, and marketing of consumer products had resulted in an ever-mounting increase in the mass of waste materials. As this degradation of the land occurred it was becoming increasingly evident that land was too valuable a national resource to be needlessly polluted by waste materials disposed of in open dumps and sanitary landfills. To implement the environmental legislation Congress passsed the Comprehensive Environmental Response, Compensation and Liability Act of 1980, known as the Superfund Act (Shortreed, Stewart, 1988).

In 1986 the Superfund Amendment and Reauthorization Act (SARA) was passed to strengthen the 1980 Act. A major addition defined "pollutants and contaminants" to:

Include, but is not limited to, an element, substance, compound, or mixture including disease-causing agents, which after release into the environment and upon exposure, ingestion, inhalation or assimilation into any organism, either directly from the environment or indirectly by ingestion through food chains, will or may reasonably be anticipated to cause death, disease, behavioral abnormalities, cancer, genetic mutations, physiological malfunctions, or physical deformations, in such organisms or their offspring.

The Superfund Amendment provided an elaboration of the provision relating primarily to response and liability. These include response authorities, national contingency plan, reimbursements, liability, penalties, use of funds, health-related authorities, claim procedures, public participation, cleanup standards, regulations and relativity to other laws (Jones, McSlarrow, 1989).

Federal Superfund

To implement the Comprehensive Environmental Response Compensation and Liability Act, the Superfund, a National Contingency Plan was developed by the Environmental Protection Agency. This plan included: (a) methods for discovering sites where hazardous wastes had been disposed of, (b) procedures for evaluating the extent of the hazardous wastes including an estimation of the cost of removal, (c) methods and criteria determining the appropriate extent of removal and remedy of the site, (d) appropriate roles and responsibilities of the Federal, state and local governments and for interstate and nongovernmental entities in implementing the plan, (e) provisions for identification, procurement, maintenance, and storage of response equipment and supplies, (f) method of assignment and responsibility for assigning facilities, (g) criteria for determining toxic releases or threatened releases throughout the United States for the purposes of taking remedial action, and (h) a plan to establish national priorities (Skinner, Bassin, 1988 and Majumdar, Miller, 1989).

Scope of the Problem

The first task of the Environmental Protection Agency with the cooperation of the states was to determine the number of hazardous and toxic waste sites. The number and wide spread distribution of hazardous and toxic waste sites discovered dwarfed the scope of the problem originally visualized. As of 1989 more then 31,000 hazardous waste sites had been identified, with 27,0000 having undergone preliminary field review and classification. Of these, nearly 1,200 have been assigned high priority for immediate action by EPA. An average of 2,000 new sites have been added annually. Because remediation of the most dangerous sites involves years of painstaking treatment, new sites continue to be placed on the National Priorities List much faster than existing sites can be removed.

Assessment and Implementation

The assessment of a hazardous site includes size of the site, contaminating possibilities, type and quantities of waste, local hydrological and meteorological conditions, and the environmental impact. At the site, evidence is gathered as to immediate contamination including effects on vegetation and quality of the water supply.

After the evaluation, the sites are ranked according to type, quantity and toxicity of waste, the number of people potentially exposed, the possible pathways for exposure, the vulnerability of local aquifers, and possible other factors. The sites are ranked by the Hazard Ranking System (HRS) to determine the eligibility for placement on the National Priorities List. This ranking system does not determine if cleanup is possible or the amount of cleanup needed. Rather, it measures the severity of the problem and the likelihood and potential magnitude of exposure to hazardous substances for humans and the contamination of the environment. This scoring system allows priorities to be made among the many thousands of hazardous waste sites (Wu, Hilger, 1984).

The initial assessment and site evaluation provides basic data. From this data three scores are obtained that measure the possibility of (1) hazardous substance spreading from the site through ground water, surface water or air and reaching populated regions, (2) people coming in direct contact with hazardous substances, or (3) fire and explosions caused by hazardous substances. The first score is used to place sites on the National Priorities List and is called the HRS score. Sites are placed on the NPL only if they receive a ranking score of 28.5 or more (on a scale of 0 to 100), except when designated by a state or priority site by the EPA regardless of the score. The second and third scores are used to identify sites that need removal actions.

As the hazardous sites were identified, the NPL has grown steadily. In October 1981, the EPA published an interim priority list of 115 sites and followed it with an expanded list of 45 additional sites in July 1982. In December 1982 EPA published a list of 418 sites. This list grew to 747 by 1989 (Table 1). According to present estimates, the NPL is expected to grow to at least 2,100 sites by the year 2000.

Evaluation of Success

By 1989 the Superfund had removed 26 hazardous waste sites from the National Priorities List, with another 10 sites nearly completed. This does not appear to be an impressive record, but evaluating the work of the Superfund by tallying completed sites is inherently misleading. At each site years of work must first be done in multi-stages before the program is completed. EPA must monitor sites long after cleanup has been achieved to ensure that the standards remain in effect (Acton, 1989 and Yang, Tracy, 1986).

Success of the Superfund is more appropriately measured in terms of the success of interim steps that quickly provide a margin of safety for local residents. For example, the EPA has conducted emergency removal of waste to attack the most immediate sources of toxic exposure at more than 1,300 sites in communities across the nation. This program has cost over $400 million. In addition, EPA has used its enforcement authorities to get responsible parties to take removal action in another 200 sites. In addition, long term cleanup work is currently underway to neutralize the sources, contain the spread and systematically reduce or eliminate toxic pollution at over 675 sites under Superfund's remedial program.

TABLE 1
National Priorities List Sites

	Selected for List	Proposed for List	Total
REGION I			
Connecticut	8	6	14
Maine	6	2	8
Massachusetts	22	1	23
New Hampshire	15	0	15
Rhode Island	8	3	11
Vermont	4	4	8
REGION II			
New Jersey	100	7	107
New York	73	3	76
REGION III			
Delaware	12	8	20
Maryland	7	3	10
Pennsylvania	71	24	95
Virginia	12	9	21
West Virginia	5	1	6
REGION IV			
Alabama	10	2	12
Florida	32	15	47
Georgia	7	6	13
Kentucky	12	5	17
Mississippi	2	1	3
North Carolina	15	7	22
South Carolina	14	7	21
Tennessee	10	3	13
REGION V			
Illinois	23	16	39
Indiana	30	7	37
Michigan	65	15	80
Minnesota	40	0	40
Ohio	29	3	32
Wisconsin	35	4	39

TABLE 1 *continued*

REGION VI			
Arkansas	10	0	10
Louisiana	9	2	11
New Mexico	6	4	10
Oklahoma	8	3	11
Texas	24	4	28
REGION VII			
Iowa	9	15	24
Kansas	9	2	11
Missouri	14	7	21
Nebraska	3	2	5
REGION VIII			
Colorado	13	3	16
Montana	8	2	10
North Dakota	2	0	2
South Dakota	1	0	1
Utah	5	7	12
Wyoming	1	2	3
REGION IX			
Arizona	5	4	9
California	52	36	88
Hawaii	0	6	6
Nevada	0	0	0
REGION X			
Alaska	1	0	1
Idaho	4	0	4
Oregon	6	1	7
Washington	25	17	42

Source: U.S. Environmental Protection Agency, *An Analysis of State Superfund Programs: 50-State Study,* Office of Emergency and Remedial Response, Washington, DC, 1989, pp. 49-52.

STATE LEGISLATION

Since the passage of the Comprehensive, Environmental Response, Compensation and Liability Act of 1980, cooperation has developed between the federal and state governments in the cleanup of hazardous waste sites. A vast number of known and important sites are not eligible for inclusion on the National Priorities List and states are now responsible for enforcing and/or funding cleanup at non-NPL sites. The prospect for increasing state involvement at both NPL and non-NPL sites depends on the willingness and capacity of states to develop effective programs, to secure adequate resources to fund cleanup, to obtain private funds for cleanups, and to conduct oversight activities. Under the Superfund Amendments and Reauthorization Act (SARA) of 1986, Congress required the EPA to involve states in the Superfund program in a "substantial and meaningful" way. The State and

(Environmental Protection Agency, 1989).

Of the 50 states, at least 20 have compiled a priority listing of hazardous waste sites. A uniform system of priority listing has, however, not been used by the states. Eleven of the states follow a formal ranking system using the federal Hazard Rank-Some of the states also manage cleanups at NPL sites as well. Fourteen of the 39 states have funds replenished at specific times resulting in high and low periods of activity.

The remaining eleven states have limited cleanup capabilities or enforcement authorities. Of these, six states have removal or emergency response programs, but limited remedial action authorities or capabilities. Waste removal action may be needed in a variety of situations, including accidents during transport and at active hazardous waste facilities. In contrast, remedial action is intended to effect permanent or long-term solutions that consider two vital aspects of site remediation—source controls and waste migration mangement—and meet legally applicable and appropriate requirements. The remaining five states do not have superfund programs per se, yet each addresses the problem of hazardous waste sites in some fashion. Nebraska uses it groundwater regulations. Oklahoma and Georgia use RCRA laws to order cleanups of hazardous sites and Colorado has a fund but limits it use to CERCLA cost-share and related administrative cost at NPL sites.

The statutes of the states vary considerably (Environmental Protection Agency, 1989). Fifteen states have citizen suit provisions. These provisions allow persons who are or will be adversely affected by a release or threat of a release of hazardous substance to file a civil action requiring that the responsible parties prevent further damage or, take corrective actions. Courts may also assess penalties in civil actions filed by citizens. Citizen suits and property transfer programs provide alternative methods for cleanups outside the Superfund process. The object of a property transfer program is to ensure that contaminated property does not pose health or environmental risks related to hazardous waste releases. In this procedure, property owners must file a declaration concerning past or present storage, disposal or release of hazardous waste at their property site. Four states—New Jersey, Illinois, Connecticut, and Iowa—have mandatory property transfer programs. Minnesota has a voluntary program.

Eleven states have provisions for compensating victims of hazardous waste releases. In six of the states, the compensation is limited to reimbursement for costs of securing temporary or permanent alternative water supplies. In the other five states, compensation is authorized for a broader array of release-related expenses.

Scope of the Problem

The number of total waste sites is unknown in the United States. The number of sites reported in a state is largely a response to the level of the state's program. The number of reported sites varies from none in Nevada to over 25,000 in California (Table 2). Sites needing attention in states range from zero to 6,654 in California. Eleven states have 100 or fewer sites needing attention, 16 have 100 to 300, 16 have 300 to 1,000 and seven states have over 1,000 sites needing remedial attention

Local Coordination Branch (SLCB) of the EPA is responsible for developing regulations, guidance and policies related to this congressional mandate (Rabie, 1986). At the present time 39 states have funded enforcement authorities of which 25 are actively involved in managing removal and remedial actions at non-NPL sites. ing System (HRS) or another scoring system. Ten states use a modified HRS or a non-quantitative ranking system.

TABLE 2
State Hazardous Waste Sites

EPA	Total Identified* Hazardous Waste Sites	Sites Needing* Attention	Priority List	Inventory or Registry
REGION I				
Connecticut	560	560		567[1]
Maine	237	117		317[1,2]
Massachusetts	1,800	1,725	1,152[3]	1,634[2]
New Hampshire	400	400		150-175[2]
Rhode Island	280	280		
Vermont	260	241	130[4]	50[2]
REGION II				
New Jersey	3,225	3,000		336
New York	1,167	1,039	1,091	615[2]
REGION III				
Delaware	200	160	48	200[3]
Maryland	304	254	25[1]	300[2]
Pennsylvania	1,100	1,100		2,295[2]
Virginia	450	150		
West Virginia	299	299		
REGION IV				
Alabama	500	500		500 + [2]
Florida	821	821		500 + [3]
Georgia	753	628		
Kentucky	450	250		500[2]
Mississippi	319	300		
North Carolina	799	758	85	781
South Carolina	44	42	42	
Tennessee	1,000	755	281[1]	800-900[2]
REGION V				
Illinois	224	224	29	1,325[2]
Indiana	1,400	1,400		
Michigan	1,667	1,667	2,019	
Minnesota	117	117	157[1]	300[2]
Ohio	1,000	700	430[1]	1,074[2]
Wisconsin	223	223	60[1]	173[2]

TABLE 2 continued

REGION VI				
Arkansas	296	108	7[1]	26[2]
Louisiana	499	257		
New Mexico	510	495		
Oklahoma	30	30		
Texas	88	88	29[1]	over 1,000[2]
REGION VII				
Iowa	370	164	19(37)[1]	384[2]
Kansas	328	314		489[2]
Missouri	1,070	446	54	
Nebraska	40	38		
REGION VIII				
Colorado	361	361	159[1]	
Montana	134	132		about 151[2]
North Dakota	47	21		
South Dakota	1	1	56	
Utah	164	164		
Wyoming	100	86		
REGION IX				
Arizona	503	453	23	
California	25,000	6,654	328	about 5,000[2]
Hawaii				
Nevada	0	0		
REGION X				
Alaska			1[1]	277[2]
Idaho	164	164		
Oregon	750			
Washington	506	506		700[1,2]

Code:
1   Includes some or all NPL sites
2   Includes unconfirmed sites/potential sites
3   Investigated/confirmed
4   Includes all types of hazardous waste sites
5   High or medium priority

Source: *General Accounting Office, Survey of States' Cleanups of Non-NPL Hazardous Waste Sites, 1989, Washington, D.C.
    U.S. Environmental Protection Agency, An Analysis of State Superfund Programs: 50 State Study, Office of Emergency and Remedial Response, Washington, D.C., 1989, pp. 49-52.

Twenty-eight of the states have developed an inventory or registry of sites. This listing is usually broader than a priority list, and includes unconfirmed sites. Connecticut's statute, for example, requires that a site be listed on the state inventory before funds are provided to investigate the site. Ohio's informal list contains sites categorized after a preliminary assessment as high, medium or low priority. Iowa uses a five tiered system of evaluating sites ranging from imminent threat to closed with no management needed.

Program Organization

The states' administrative programs for cleanup of hazardous waste sites are located in state agencies with primary responsibility for environmental matters. The focus of the program may be on the environment and/or health considerations. Many of the cleanup programs are divided into several units. To illustrate, Pennsylvania has a staff of over 100 people, of which 30 are located in the Department of Environmental Resource's (DER) Hazardous Sites Cleanup Program, which has four sections: site assessment, federally-funded cleanup, enforcement, and state-funded cleanup. This headquarter's staff is assisted by 42 technical personnel in six regional offices. In addition, the DER's Bureau of Laboratories has seven persons engaged in state Superfund work, and the Office of Engineering, which is responsible for remedial action contracting, also has seven positions. The DER's Office of Chief Counsel has 15 lawyers assigned to the cleanup programs. Finally, emergency responses are handled by a separate program within the DER—each of the six regions as a separate emergency response team of 6 to 12 DER employees. The staffing level of each state varies greatly from more than 600 in New Jersey's Hazardous Waste Management Division to the lack of a staff in South Dakota and Wyoming.

Legal Support

State Superfund programs obtain legal support from within the state agency, from the state's attorney general's office, and/or a combination of these. Twenty-three states report to the state attorney general's office as the sole source of legal support for the cleanup program. Ten states rely on their agency's personnel for legal support, and sixteen states rely on a combination of these two for legal support.

When the legal support is divided between the attorney general's office and the state agency, the agency's legal staff generally provides support for the administration of enforcement issues. When a case requires a lawsuit, such as in court action for cost recovery, the attorney general's office is normally responsible.

Funding

The availability of a fund or funding mechanisms is an essential element of a state's hazardous waste cleanup program. Typically a fund is characterized by a depletion and a revolving expenditure. A continuing fund allows a state to control

306 Natural and Technological Disasters: Causes, Effects and Preventive Measures

the pace of cleanup. If the persons responsible for the waste problems do not cooperate, the state can proceed and later seek punitive damages.

State funds are authorized and/or used in 48 states for one or more uses relating to mitigation of hazardous waste risks. Fifteen of the states have more than one fund. The only states without funds are Delaware and Nebraska.

There are ten types of activities for which funds are provided: remedial activities, CERCLA match, disposal at or development of hazardous waste facilities, emergency response, grants to municipalities and local governments, site investigation, operations and maintenance, removal of wastes, studies and design, and victim compensation. Table 3 shows the number of funds and the number of states having at least one fund whose monies are or may be applied to a specific activity.

Emergency responses are the most common activity for which funds have been authorized. Removal of hazardous waste sites is also widely authorized. Studies and design for remedial action are slightly more frequently authorized than complete remedial action, most likely because of the limited resources of many states. In six of the 11 states, authorizing victim compensation is limited to providing alternative drinking water supplies.

A number of these funds have broad provisions for their uses. For example, Pennsylvania Hazardous Cleanup Fund is used to develop recycling and the development of alternative types of land disposal.

Enforcement

Enforcement authorities enacted by 37 states vary significantly under the state laws. Within those states where superfund programs include enforcement provisions, most have been able to reach the generators and transporters of the hazardous materials. Consequently there is generally no reason for these states to show the existence of the violation of the law. Rather, the issue is the scope of the liability.

TABLE 3
State Uses of Funds

	Number of States	Number of Funds
Emergency Response	47	55
Removals	46	51
Studies and Design	42	47
Remedial Actions	41	41
CERCLA Match	41	47
Operation and Maintenance	36	40
Victim Compensation	11	11
Site Investigation	8	8
Disposal at or Development or Hazardous Waste Facilities	4	4
Grants to Municipalities and Local Governments	3	3

Source: U.S. Environmental Protection Agency. *An Analysis of State Superfund Programs - 50 State Study,* Office of Emergency and Remedial Response, Washington, DC., 1989, p. 24.

For the 13 states that rely on non-superfund authorities there is sometimes difficulty in reaching the original generators of the waste materials. For the most part, these states have cleanup provisions that require proof of a Resource Conservation and Recovery Act type of violation.

Cleanup Guidelines

Cleanup policies are key elements in state superfund programs. Twenty-two states use the Environmental Protection Agency's guidelines of federal standards either as their role source of cleanup standards or in conjunction with other standards. Standards set by RCRA or CERCLA are important. Six of the 22 states use Maximum Containment Levels (MCL's) set by the Safe Drinking Water Act as minimum standards for surface and groundwater remediation.

Eighteen states have established their own standards for cleanup of water, soil and air. Groundwater is of particular concern in a number of states. For example, in California the potential effect of remedial action on groundwater must be specifically evaluated, and in Minnesota, guidelines for determining site specific groundwater cleanup goals must be consistent with the state's groundwater protection strategy.

Risk standards for carcinogens are used by at least seven states. A risk standard is applied as an alternative standard to be used when applicable or relevant and appropriate requirements do not exist or as a standard to be achieved at each cleanup. Of the 7 states, Arizona, Indiana and Minnesota, invoke risk standards only in the absence of applicable standards and California, Virginia, Maine, and Ohio have risk standards that apply generally.

Five states—Florida, Kentucky, Oregon, Pennsylvania, and South Carolina—use ambient quality as the cleanup standard.

Public Participation

The degree of public participation varies greatly from state to state. In 22 states public participation is required under state statute or regulation. In 14 others, the state agency seeks public input while 14 states do not request public input. In some of the states public concern has created some participation.

Eleven states require public notice at one or more points in the site handling process. Most of these states require notification regarding either site listing or remedial action plans. At least 4 states—Minnesota, Wisconsin, Oregon, and Washington—require notification at several stages during the site remedial actions. In addition, Washington publishes notices of compliance and enforcement orders and violations.

Twelve states solicit public comments on site listing or remedial plans. Seven of these states have a designated comment period ranging from 30 to 60 days. Public meetings or hearings are required by 8 states. In 2 of these—Michigan and Missouri—only an annual meeting is required, either to update a site list or revise the state program. In 4 states a public meeting must be held upon petition or request.

In 12 of the states meetings are held as a matter of policy at the discretion of program officials.

Community relations are a developing feature of state public participation activities. Only 3 states—Illinois, Louisiana, and Minnesota—have developed extensive community relations efforts with regard to hazardous waste sites. In Minnesota each site is assigned a public relations officer and in Louisiana the Department of Environmental Quality conducts a community relations program at its waste sites. Illinois maintains an active community relations program designed to fine-tune remedy selections using information provided by the local residents. The development of public participation will be increasingly important as the removal of hazardous wastes sites advances.

REFLECTIONS

The federal program to cleanup hazardous waste sites began with high expectations of great success. This assumption appeared reasonable with public and congressional support and a growing network of state, local, and private authorities. Further, the Environmental Protection Agency had led the nation in progress for clean air and water. With an initial appropriation of $1.6 billion the task appeared relatively simple to cleanup what was assumed to be a few hundred discrete toxic sites.

Regrettably the program has been far more complex than originally visualized. To begin with, there was no proven technology on how to manage waste sites. The EPA has had to devise may ad hoc control strategies to deal with hundreds of emerging problems. Progress has been slow. A 1989 report of EPA states, "As a consequence, the nation is now beginning to confront the real dilemma: how to reduce environmental risks from a growing list of sites presenting ever new complexities, in a situation characterized by incomplete knowlege, immature technology, and relentless pressure on a limited pool of resources." (Management Review of the Superfund Program, Environmental Protection Agency, 1989, p.2).

The scope of the problem of the cleanup of hazardous and toxic waste sites has now been defined. Because it is a far greater problem than originally visualized it will require years, if not decades to solve. In order to be successful in such a massive endeavor a long-range strategy must be developed. Fundamental to the ultimate success is the coordination of Federal, State and local agencies in order to clarify commitments and gain broad acceptance of the fundamental strategies from the public.

SELECTED REFERENCES

Acton, Jon Paul, 1989. *Understanding Superfund: A Progress Report,* Santa Monica, CA: Rand Corporation, 65 pp.

Environmental Protection Agency, 1989. *An Analysis of State Superfund Programs: 50 State Study,* Washington, DC: Office of Emergency and Remedial Response.

Freudenberg, Nicholas, 1984. *Not In Our Backyards,* New York: Monthly Review Press, 304 pp.

Jones, David E. and Kyle E. McSlarrow, 1989. "But Were Afraid to Ask: Superfund Case Law, 1981-1989," *Environmental Law Reporter* 19 (October): 10430-10457.

Landers, Robert K., 1988. "Living with Hazardous Waste: The Evacuation of Hundreds of Families from Love Canal in August 1978 Dramatized the Hazardous Waste Threat; Congress Responded by Creating the 'Superfund,' But Relatively Few Hazardous Waste Sites Have Actually Been Cleaned Up Despite Efforts to Strengthen the Program" *Editorial Research Reports* (July 29): 378-387.

Lave, Lester B. and Arthur C. Upton, eds., 1987. *Toxic Chemicals, Health and the Environment,* Baltimore, MD: John Hopkins University, 304 pp.

Majumdar, Shyamal K., E. Willard Miller and Robert F. Schmalz, eds., 1989. *Management of Hazardous Materials and Wastes: Treatment, Minimization, and Environmental Impacts,* Easton, PA: The Pennsylvania Academy of Science, 473 pp.

Mallow, Alex, 1981. *Hazardous Waste Regulations: An Interpretive Guide,* New York: Van Nostrand Reinhold, 403 pp.

Office of Technology Assessment, 1983. *Technologies and Management Strategies for Hazardous Waste Control,* Washington, DC: GPO, 407 pp.

Rabie, Barry G., 1986. *Fragmentation and Integration in State Environmental Management,* Washington, DC: Conservation Foundation, 174 pp.

Schnell, George A. and Mark Stephen Monmonier, 1984, in Majumdar, Shyamal K., E. Willard Miller and Robert F. Schmalz, eds., *Hazardous and Toxic Wastes: Technology, Management and Health Effects,* Easton, PA: The Pennsylvania Academy of Science, 106-123.

Shortreed, J.H. and A. Stewart, 1988. "Risk Assessment and Legislation," *Journal of Hazardous Materials,* 20 (December): 315-334.

Skinner, J.H. and N.J. Bassin, 1988. "The Environmental Protection Agency's Hazardous Waste Research and Development Programs," *JAPCA,* 28 (April): 377-387.

Wu, J.S. and H. Hilger, 1984. "Evaluation of EPA's Hazard Ranking System," *Journal of Environmental Engineering,* 110 (August): 797-807.

Yang, Edward and James Tracy, 1986. "Superfund Technology: A Long-Run Perspective," *Environmental Forum,* 4 (January): 40-46.

Natural and Technological Disasters: Causes, Effects and Preventive Measures. Edited by
S.K. Majumdar, G.S. Forbes, E.W. Miller, and R.F. Schmalz. © 1992, The Pennsylvania Academy
of Science.

Chapter Twenty-Three

INDUSTRIAL DISASTERS: LESSONS FROM BHOPAL

CURTIS C. DAEHLER*
and
SHYAMAL K. MAJUMDAR
¹Department of Biology
Lafayette College
Easton, PA 18042

INTRODUCTION

Late in the night of December 2, 1984, water mysteriously entered a tank of methyl
isocyanate at the Union Carbide India (Ltd.) insecticide plant in Bhopal, India
(population, approx. 800,000).[1] The ensuing uncontrollable exothermic reaction
resulted in the release of 41 metric tons of deadly methyl isocyanate gas through
a pressure release valve, past three ineffective safety systems, and directly into the
atmosphere above Bhopal.[2] The cream-colored gas, being heavier than air, fell over
the sleeping city of Bhopal with little warning.[3] Many people did not wake at all.
Others were aroused with watery, burning eyes. The streets became crowded with
bodies; those people still conscious were choking and vomiting as they ran.[4] The
gas acted rapidly on its victims, most commonly causing asphyxiation by pulmonary
edema.[3] The final outcome of the disaster has been a reported 3,600 deaths and
some 500,000 affected.[5,40] Many surviving victims remain affected today by chronic
health problems in breathing, vision and sleeping.[6] Physical handicaps, spontaneous
abortions, still births and even human chromosome alterations have also been
reported.[6,7] How could a seemingly careless accident of such magnitude have
occurred in our modern industrial world? How can such disasters be prevented or
minimized in the future? These issues will be cursorily addressed in the following
analysis.

---

*Present address: Department of Zoology, University of California, Davis, CA 95616

Aggravating Factors

There were several factors and events which aggravated the Bhopal gas leak, escalating the incident from a simple gas leak to a major disaster. If these aggravating factors, which ranged from technological to human, had not been present, many lives would have been saved. At the plant, the first safety system, a vent-gas scrubber which uses caustic soda to neutralize the gas, was not operational[10] The second system, a flare tower designed to neutralize by burning any remaining gas escaping the release valve, had been shut down, awaiting replacement of a part and, even if operational, would have been unable to handle the rapid rate of gas release which resulted from the extremely high pressure within the tank[!] The third system, a series of water spraying hoses, was ineffective because water pressure in the hoses was insufficient to reach the top of the 30 meter stack where the gas was billowing out[10] In addition to these safety systems, there was also a refrigeration unit which was designed to keep the tank cool on hot summer days. Had the coolant not been drained from this refrigeration system for use in another part of the plant, it may have been used to help lower the pressure within the tank.[8]

Besides these technological aggravating factors, there were also human aggravating factors involved. Supervisors at the Bhopal plant did not take immediate action when an employee noticed the pressure gauge rising and other employees reported a leak.[8] Apparently, small leaks were common at the Bhopal plant, and pressures gauges were known to be temperamental, inaccurate or nonfunctional[!] As a result, supervisors did not act on the reports until after a half hour tea break.[8] At that point, it was too late since pressure in the tank had built past controllable levels, triggering the safety release valve to open. By the time the supervisor sounded the alarm to warn the city of Bhopal, the gas was already leaking uncontrollably. Many people of Bhopal did not know what the alarm meant or could not hear the alarm.[9] Furthermore, the alarm was shut off after a few minutes[10] Most waking people of Bhopal did not know which way to run and evacuation transportation was inadequate.[9] Bhopal's hospitals and doctors were ill-prepared to handle and treat so many victims. Most doctors did not even know the nature of the gas, let alone a treatment for poisoning.[3] Doctors could only treat victims symptomatically but not at the rate which the victims were appearing. It was not until much later that doctors realized that sodium thiosulfate could be used effectively to treat many victims[11] Even then, there was an insufficient supply of medicine and hospital space.

Who Was Responsible?

According to the "accidental introduction" hypothesis, supported by the Indian Government, water was accidentally introduced into the tank during a routine purging of pipes when removal of a slip-joint accompanied by other piping system malfunctions and human errors allowed water to enter a pipe leading to the tank.[8] On the other hand, the "saboteur hypothesis" brought forth by an Arthur W. Little,

Inc. investigation supported by Union Carbide, proposes that a disgruntled employee, intending to spoil the batch of chemical, maliciously contaminated the tank of methyl isocyanate with water through a direct hose connection.[2] In this scenario, it is overly simplistic to blame the disaster on a saboteur. Rather, a saboteur acted only as a catalyst. For if one examines the situation at the Bhopal plant prior to the leak, one can see that at Bhopal, a disaster was just waiting to happen.

Private industry, namely Union Carbide, must take some blame for its contribution to aggravating factors and the accident in general. Immediately after the accident, Union Carbide's president, Warren Anderson, insisted that the Bhopal plant was maintained and operated by the same standards as similar U.S. plants. However, as the investigations of the plant carried on, Mr. Anderson was forced to concede that his previous statement was not true.[12] The Bhopal plant was inferior to U.S. plants in management, employee training, employee safety, equipment, maintenance, and emergency systems. Many personnel at Bhopal were inadequately trained. Employees often carried out routines, without knowing what exactly they were doing or why.[13] One reason for this may have been the rapid rate of turnover in employees and managers at the Bhopal plant. For example, over 15 years, the Bhopal plant had a change in head manager eight times and many of these managers did not have chemical-industry backgrounds.[14] The dangers of methyl isocyanate were not clear to many employees.[14] In 1981, one worker died and three others were injured from gas exposure at the Bhopal plant.[1] Equipment and maintenance were unsatisfactory, as demonstrated by the undependable pressure gauges and nonfunctional scrubber, flare tower, and refrigeration unit. All safety systems at the Bhopal plant, including leak detection systems and emergency systems, were manually operated, while similar U.S. plants were computer assisted. The most common way of detecting gas leaks at the Bhopal plant was through employees' complaints of watering eyes.[15] Many of these safety and training problems were detected in a safety audit conducted by Union Carbide in May 1982;[14] however, they weren't sufficiently acted on.[15] Clearly, when established industry standards are not followed or are lax, the chances of an industrial disaster increase substantially.

While private industry has been shown to be at fault in the Bhopal disaster, some blame for the Bhopal disaster can be carried over to the Indian government as well. In 1969, Union Carbide offered to bring capital to an economically depressed area of India by building a multi-million dollar pesticide plant in Bhopal and employing several hundred workers.[16] The Indian government found the proposal impossible to resist. The land was bought by Union Carbide India (Ltd.) at a low price.[16] Between 1970 and 1984, the Bhopal plant expanded from a $1 million dollar pesticide packaging plant to a $25 million dollar pesticide synthesizing plant.[16] The problem was that, at the same time, the human population of Bhopal was also increasing nearly exponentially. Shanty town slums were appearing all around the Bhopal plant. Two such heavily populated areas were located right across the street from the plant.[17] Most people living in these areas were squatters, simply looking for a place to live. Most did not know of the potential dangers within the Bhopal plant. The area around the plant was not designated as residential[17] and at the same time, the plant's location was not zoned for hazardous industries.[18] Had the government taken steps to either remove the squatters or relocate the industry, many lives could have been saved.

Another policy of the Indian government, the "local use" policy, may have contributed partially to the industrial disaster. The government required the use of local labor, equipment, and material in the construction and operation of the Bhopal plant[.] This policy, designed to stimulate the local economy, is questionable when involving dangerous, "high technology" industrial plants where higher quality parts, engineers, or technicians are available from foreign countries[.] The design, construction, and maintenance of a hazardous industrial plant such as the one at Bhopal should be of the highest quality possible to ensure safety, even if some local economic development must be sacrificed. The appropriate infrastructure necessary to support safe operation and maintenance of a hazardous industrial plant simply did not exist in the city of Bhopal[.][7]

The Indian government's final flaw was it inadequate Department of Environment, which was supposed to inspect plants for safety[.][7] In some states of India, inspectors were able to visit less than 15% of the targeted plants each month[.][9] Even when inspections were made, industrial polluters were given fines ranging from only $40 to $400[.][7] The government did not want to sacrifice potential jobs by discouraging industrial developers with stiff fines for violations. These actions of the Indian government compromised the safety of the Indian people.

Lessons from Bhopal

Population centers and industrial centers are simply incompatible environments. Today, there are still many hazardous industries located amidst dense population centers throughout the world[.] Governments worldwide must act to relocate either populations or industries by initiating strong zoning laws. In addition to the risk of all out disasters, industrial plants are prone to creating waste products which affect local air, soil and water. The long term effects of even trace amounts of many of these environmental contaminants on people may range from increased incidence of cancers to birth defects. Unfortunately, studies of these effects are insufficient since so many potential environmental contaminants exist, and it is difficult to prove that specific human health problems have resulted from specific industrial waste products.[3] In any case, it is unquestionable that when the human population surrounding an industrial area is minimized, the potential for deaths due to industrial accidents is minimized as well. Ideally, the human populations which surround hazardous industrial plants should be relocated and replaced by a "green belt" consisting of a zone of dense plant growth containing species which have a high tolerance to the types of hazardous chemicals being produced at the site.[3] In third world countries, the problem is worse. Often, only the population centers have established electricity and water supplies necessary for industrial plant operations. Even when electricity and water can be routed away from population centers, transportation for workers is often unavailable or expensive, so workers must live in close proximity to the plant. The economic needs of these workers can then cause the area to blossom into a population center. When a government does not have the means to control such industry-related population problems, the government must acknowledge that it is not in the best interest of the people to promote rapid hazardous industry development in their country, even though it may mean temporary loss of economic opportunity.

A second element which will help to minimize industrial disasters is improved education of people at all levels. "About 75% of the people in the United States live in proximity to a chemical plant". Everybody should know where hazardous industries are located in their communities, what these industries are producing, what the potential hazards of the products are, and what to do in case of an emergency. The dissemination of these facts can be carried out by public service messages, educational pamphlets, community mini-workshops, and even tours of the plants. Local school systems are powerful tools in educating children; for example the American Chemcial Society's Chem Com curriculum program is designed to teach high schoolers about the impact of chemicals on their lives.[20] These steps make communities more prepared to cope with an industrial accident thus preventing a disaster. At the same time, education of communities helps to put some control on hazardous industries. When people are educated on local issues, they may decide that the risks involved in a particular industry are too great and community protests and rallies may help prevent disasters by pressuring installation of improved safety systems or preventing a potentially dangerous expansion of an industrial plant. Specific community members require special education and training to minimize the effects of an industrial accident. These community members, including doctors, emergency medical technicians, firemen and police should be trained by industry officials or city/county emergency management coordinators to deal with different types of potential disasters from local plants. Organizations such as the National Chemical Response and Information Center (NCRIC), Federal Emergency Management Association (FEMA) and the Chemical Manufacturers Association (CMA), with its emergency hotline, can also help to provide information and training in dealing with specific community disasters. In other countries, government environmental regulation agencies, and the World Health Organization (WHO), an international organization, can disseminate information to help cope with and minimize industrial disasters.[17]

At the industrial plant itself, it is essential that workers understand the hazards of the plant and their particular jobs. There should always be a manager on duty who knows all the potential hazards and can supply technical information to authorities in the event of an accident. These steps will simply require improved training and perhaps even testing, through graded examinations, of employees. Every plant should undergo a yearly "environmental and safety audit," with funds being reserved and required for use in implementation of safety/environment improvements.[17] Frequent testing of safety systems and emergency procedures is essential for continued safety. The tests should be carried out independently by both private industry and government officials at random times. When maintenance is required for a safety system, the plant operation must stop. Safety systems should have automatic controls with the option of manual operation as well, since even the most modern computer controlled systems can be faulty.[1] Government inspectors must have the authority to shut down plants on site and hit companies with stiff fines when regulations are not being followed or standards are not being met.

Low employee morale may increase the likelihood of an accident at an industrial plant. Prior to the disaster at the Bhopal plant, the plant had been losing money for several years and workers were being laid off.[7] There was also talk of Union Carbide selling or closing the plant.[7] When working under such low-confidence or cost-pressured conditions, employees may be more likely to make mistakes or ignore potential problems.[8] To minimize the risk of accidents, employees in hazardous industries should be well paid and rewarded for good work. Employees must have pride in their work and trust in their company. For example, if an employee observes something that does not meet regulations, that employee must feel free to speak out, tell the supervisor, or fix the problem without fear of losing his/her job. Employees must be highly concerned with both their own safety and the safety of their co-workers. Many large American companies, including the American automobile industry, have recently restructured their employee programs to create this type of working environment.[21,22] Chemical and other hazardous industries must follow suit to improve safety.

Another deficiency which becomes clear from the Bhopal disaster is the general lack of chemical knowledge. For example, physiological effects of methyl isocyanate on man were not available prior to the disaster.[23] In addition, a 1983 study by the National Academy of Sciences found that the United States Environmental Protection Agency (EPA) held adequate information on the health hazards of only 10% of 3,350 pesticides and their ingredients.[24] Our lack of understanding of chemcial intermediates during processing is even more disturbing. The EPA and private industry scientists around the world must step-up toxicity, teratogenicity and mutagenicity research on common industrial chemicals. Scientists must make a priority of seeking better understandings of the chemical reactions and intermediates formed in industrial processes so that potential hazards of contaminants and incomplete reactions can be identified and minimized.

One obvious way to decrease the risk of unanticipated chemical reactions is to avoid storing hazardous chemicals in large batches. At Bhopal, methyl isocyanate was stored in huge 60 metric ton tanks for long periods of time.[3] Often, the tanks were fuller than the recommended capacity.[7] An alternate method for pesticide production is used by many companies. In this "closed loop system", only as much methyl isocyanate as is immediately needed is synthesized, thus cutting substantially the risk of a large-scale disaster.[1]

Improved techniques for accident clean-up are also needed. For example, recent research has led to a new method for the clean-up of mercury-contaminated sites by increasing the frequency of a naturally occurring bacteria with mercury reduction capabilities in endemic microorganism populations.[25] Bacteria were also used experimentally for mitigation of the Exxon Valdez oil spill in 1989.[26] Funding for research on environmental remediation of such industrial contaminants must be increased to enable new approaches to be explored.

Third World Issues

Many underdeveloped countries are a special attraction for hazardous industries. These countries are a source of low-cost labor since unemployment tends to be high. In addition, governments of these countries may provide special incentives to attract industries, such as subsidized building costs or tax exemptions.[6] Superficially, it would appear that rapid construction by large multi-national industries would benefit any third world nation by boosting the economy and improving the nation's world market reputation. These benefits, however, are in reality not as clear-cut as they appear. Often, more of the profit leaves the underdeveloped country than is put in by the multi-national companies. For example, in 1984 a large Swiss bank reported that third world countries input twice as much capital into international banks as they received, resulting in a large net export of profits.[27] In addition to low returns from industry, underdeveloped countries are prone to other problems which make rapid industrial development a dangerous prospect. Underdeveloped countries tend to already have water and air pollution problems which are only compounded by industrial wastes and by-products. The infrastructure to support hazardous industry is not in place,[17] which makes individual industries self-dependent for equipment, supplies, technicians and emergency systems and makes the local people more vulnerable to the effects of industrial accidents. Finally, the governments of many third world countries simply do not have the resources (technical or monetary) to monitor private industries to ensure safety standards, which may result in corporations cutting corners in plant design or operation in these countries.[1]

Large chemical corporations may intimidate the governments of small, underdeveloped countries. Many such countries have smaller annual GNP's than the corporations' annual profits.[28] Under these circumstances, the chemical industries can use their leverage to affect government policies. For example, government officials may recommend to farmers increased use of particular pesticides or herbicides due to pressure or even rewards from private industry representatives.[1] This scenario may not seem unjust from a purely capitalist viewpoint as the corporations are merely trying to sell their products; however, in underdeveloped countries where government controls are malleable by the corporations themselves, the people stand to be harmed. It is known that certain third world countries are used as testing sites by chemical industries for many pesticides not used in the United States due to insufficient information as to the potential hazards of the chemicals.[1] In addition, farmers may not be properly instructed on proper dosages and hazards of pesticides and herbicides. As a result, more than 10,000 deaths each year may occur in third world countries alone due to pesticide poisoning.[29] For many people in underdeveloped countries, life may consist of a daily struggle for food. These millions of people do not have the time to picket for clean water, or the resources to sue industries for their health problems. They depend on their government to protect them from exploitation by multi-national corporations producing and selling hazardous products; otherwise the economic boosts provided by such industries may only result in national disasters. Those corporations doing business in underdeveloped countries have an ethical duty to take on some responsibilities of the government (protection of the people) where the official government lacks sufficient resources.[17]

To help promote consistent industrial safety in third world countries, an international set of standards could be developed for use as a guideline for hazardous industry development, operation, and maintenance.[17] Some corporations are already voluntarily setting international standards within their own plants.[17] Although some countries may have more stringent standards than those being enforced by these corporations internationally, voluntary standards are a positive first step towards prevention of exploitation in underdeveloped countries. In addition, the United States government must do its part to raise industry standards by preventing U.S. industries from exporting such hazards as pesticides banned in the U.S., to underdeveloped countries where regulation of these hazards has not been established.[30]

Risk vs. Benefit

We must accept the fact that, no matter how much money we spend on the design and implementation of safety features, we will never be able to cut the risk of an industrial disaster to zero. However, it is unreasonable to say that because of this inherent risk, we should ban all hazardous industries. Instead, we must weigh carefully the risks and benefits of particular hazardous industries in our society. In particular, risk/benefit evaluations of industries should focus on: benefit of the product to society, types of environmental or health problems involved, and our understanding of and capability to remedy potential problems which may arise from the industrial processes involved in the manufacturing of the product. The chemical industry generally, when subjected to such an evaluation, proves to be unsatisfactory. Since the variety of chemicals being synthesized has increased so drastically in recent years, regulatory agencies, such as the EPA and National Toxicology Program (NTP), have been unable to adequately evaluate the safety of many new chemicals, especially in long-term, low dosage studies.[31] As a result, our understanding of how many chemicals interact with the environment and our bodies is severely lacking.[3] We must examine our use of chemicals in society and limit the production of unessential chemicals whose hazards have been poorly researched. At the same time, we must minimize our use of the chemicals which are deemed essential to our society. For example, the recently developed Microscale kits designed for use in chemistry laboratory classes and research, cut the volume of chemicals necessary to perform laboratory experiments to fractions of a milliliter, as opposed to the 10s or 100s of milliliters of chemicals previously required with conventional glassware. Reductions in our use of chemicals can decrease the likelihood of an industrial accident by reducing the frequency of production and the number of sites needed for manufacture of these chemicals.

The pesticide/herbicide branch of the chemical industry holds special dangers, since chemicals are generally produced on a large scale and are either directly applied to our food or indirectly enter our bodies through contaminated water or the food chain. Do the benefits of the use of such chemicals outweigh the risks? In some cases, the answer is clearly "no". For example, the widespread use of organo-chlorides like DDT as pesticides has caused water contamination, resulting in highly publicized health and environmental problems on a worldwide scale. A more general case, where agricultural chemical use had been identified as detrimental to people, is the use of herbicides in many third world countries. Where labor is cheap and plentiful, the obvious benefits of hand-weeding are far greater than the risky benefits of herbicide use.[32] In many instances, the potential outcome of regular chemical use is not carefully examined nor are the potential alternatives sufficiently explored.

Alternatives to Agricultural Chemicals

A simple way to reduce industrial accidents is to eliminate or cut down the number of hazardous industries which are non-essential. Non-chemical strategies for pest reduction, such as crop rotation, removal of old crop residues, physical traps for pests, and interplanting crops with plant species which repel pests, can be used in concert to reduce pesticide use. These practices have been termed "integrated pest management" (IPM).[33] A government study found that by using IPM strategies, pesticide use on 4 major U.S. crops could be cut by 70-80% over 10 years.[33] Recent studies indicate that the cost of reducing pesticide use substantially would be low.[34] Additional research must emphasize alternative biological controls for agricultural pests. Relatively recent research efforts focusing on the use of natural occurring nematodes, fungi, and bacteria have given promising results for chemical-free or chemical-reduced pest control.[35,36,37] Also, pest-resistant crop varieties are being developed through cross-breeding and genetic engineering. All of these alternatives are available for implementation in farming practices on a worldwide basis, and offer reduced risks over agricultural chemical production and use.

CONCLUSIONS

Immediately following the Bhopal disaster, many hazardous industrial plants around the world were inspected for safety by government agencies and private inspectors. At many plants, suggestions were made for improving safety, such as more frequent testing of safety systems, updating of safety system operations and increased employee safety precautions. At some plants these plans were implemented. However, other than drastic cuts in the availability of industrial accident insurance coverage,[38] no serious modification or restructuring of hazardous industry operations or hazardous industry policy took place on a worldwide scale. In 1989, five years after the Bhopal disaster, the Indian government settled the Bhopal legal case in the Indian Supreme Court with a $470 million suit, about $200 million of which was covered by insurance.[39] Union Carbide's financial status was not seriously harmed by the settlement. The Indian government encountered many problems in distributing the money to the victims.[4] Overall, the $470 million did little to relieve victim's suffering and poverty in the densely populated city.[4]

As with any tragedy, when Bhopal faded from the press in the weeks following the disaster, the public in general lost immediate fear of future industrial accidents, and once again public pressure for expensive safety measures and the condemnation of hazardous industries due to their inherent risks returned to an occasionally publicized protest by concerned environmentalists. Today the risks of another industrial disaster are far higher than they should be due to several factors. These factors include rapid growth of hazardous industries in underdeveloped countries; a high worldwide demand for potentially hazardous chemicals which continues despite the existence of possible alternatives; and a lack of understanding by the public of the dangers of chemicals and hazardous industries due to poor community education. Reduction of risks due to hazardous industries will require a substantial cooperative effort by the scientific community, government agencies, and the hazardous industries. Such a cooperative effort will possibly be hindered by the fact that the hazardous industries may have much to lose. To speed essential industry changes, the public must actively show its support for those companies which are voluntarily making serious efforts to improve industry safety and minimize pollution. Such voluntary improvements by industries and manufacturers have become increasingly common in the wake of Earth Day 1990. The 1990's has been designated the International Decade for Natural Disaster Reduction. The recent introduction of two international journals: *Disaster Management* and *Natural Hazards* is evidence of increasing concern among the scientific community for world hazard and disaster reduction. We hope continued awareness and concern for hazardous industry safety, by all interest groups on a worldwide scale, will work to reduce the risk of future industrial disasters.

REFERENCES

1. Weir, David. 1987. *The Bhopal Syndrome*. Sierra Club Books, San Francisco, CA. pp. 210.
2. Kalelkar, Ashok S. 1988. Investigation of large-magnitude incidents: Bhopal as a case study. Arthur D. Little, Inc., Cambridge, MA. pp. 37.
3. Talukder, Geeta and Archana Sharma. 1989. The Bhopal Accident,: its after-effects. pp. 409-417. *In: Management of Hazardous Materials and Wastes*. eds. S.K. Majumdar, E.W. Miller and R.F. Schmalz. The Pennsylvania Academy of Science, Easton, PA. pp. 474.
4. Hazarika, Sanjoy. 1990. Payouts in Bhopal are going slowly. *NY Times* (July 23).
5. Fineman, Mark and Mark Wagenveld. 1984. The horror that crept over Bhopal. *Philadelphia Inquirer* (December 9).
6. Wiesman, Steven R. 1985. Disabling and incurable ailments still afflict thousands in Bhopal. *NY Times* (March 3).
7. Talukder, G. 1987. Unpublished data in: Three year survey of cytogentic effects in exposed populations in Bhopal. ICMR project.
8. Diamond, Stuart. 1985. The Bhopal disaster: how it happened. *NY Times* (January 28).

9. Diamond, Stuart. 1984. The pain of progress racks the third world. *NY Times* (December 9).
10. Union Carbide Corporation. 1985. Bhopal methylisocyanate incident investigation team report. (March) Danbury, CT.
11. Indian Council of Medical Research. 1985. Report on health effects of exposure to toxic gas at Bhopal (December).
12. Diamond, Stuart. 1985. Warren Anderson: A public crisis, a personal ordeal. *NY Times* (May 19).
13. Winslow, Ron. 1984. Union Carbide confirms that problems with tanks in India were found in '82 *Wall Street Journal* (December 11).
14. Union Carbide Corporation. 1982. Operating safety survey CO/MIC/Sevin units Union Carbide Ltd. Bhopal plant. (May), Danbury, CT.
15. Winslow, Ron. 1985. Union Carbide moved to bar accident at U.S. plant before Bhopal tragedy. *Wall Street Journal* (January 28).
16. Annon. 1985. Pesticide plant started as a showpiece but ran into problems. *NY Times* (February 3).
17. Shrivastava, Paul. 1987. *Bhopal: Anatomy of a Crisis.* Ballinger Publishing Co., Cambridge, MA. pp. 184.
18. Town and Country Planning Department. 1975. Bhopal development plan. Bhopal Municipal Corporation.
19. Mathai, P.G. 1985. Belated Awakening. *India Today.* (January 31) pp. 112-3.
20. Chiapetta, Euguene L. 1991. School science education in the U.S.: a historical overview. pp. 75-91. *In: Science education in the United States: issues, crises and priorities.* eds. S.K. Majumdar, L.M. Rosenfeld, P.A. Rubba, E.W. Miller and R.F. Schmalz. Pennsylvania Academy of Science. Easton, PA. pp. 542.
21. Saddler, Jeanne. 1990. GM agrees to fight repetitive motion woes of employees. *The Wall Street Journal* (November 21).
22. Gawronski, Francis J. 1990. The Cunningham challenge: customer satisfaction, parts and training head Chrysler's priority list. *Automotive News* (July 23).
23. Dangani, Ron. 1985. Data on MIC's toxicity are scant, leave much to be learned. *Chem. Eng. News.* 63:37-41.
24. Wasserstrom, Robert F. and Richard Wiles. 1985. Field duty: U.S. farmworkers and pesticide safety. World Resources Institute, Study 3. Washington, DC. pp. 24.
25. Goldstein, R. and D. Porcella. 1990. Application of genetic ecology to bioremediation. *EPRI Journal.* v. 15, no. 1. pp. 38-41.
26. Annon. 1989. EPA, Exxon plans microorganism test with spill. *The Oil Daily.* (June 6).
27. Agence France Presse. 1985. More $$ flow out of third world than in. *Star,* Malaysia. (March 4).
28. Annon. 1974. Union Carbide: a study in corporate power and the case for union power. Oil, Chemical and Atomic Workers International Union (June).
29. Bull, David. 1982. A growing problem: pesticides and the third world poor. Oxfam. Oxford, U.K.

30. Weir, David and Mark Shapiro. 1981. *Circle of Poison: Pesticides and People in a Hungary World.* Institute for Food and Development Policy, San Francisco.
31. National Toxicology Program. 1990. National Toxicology Program fiscal year 1990 annual plan. U.S. Department of Health and Human Services. NTP-90-152.
32. Lipton, Michael and Richard Longhurst. 1989. *New Seeds and Poor People.* John Hopkins Univ. Pres. Baltimore, MD.
33. Brownstein, Ralph and Ralph Nader. 1981. *Who's poisoning America?* Sierra Club Books. San Francisco, CA. pp. 317.
34. Pimentel, D.L. McLaughlin, A. Zepp, B. Lakitan, T. Kraus, P. Kleinman, F. Vancini, W.J. Roach, E. Graap, W. Keeton, G. Selig. 1991. Environmental and economic effects of reducing pesticide use. *Bioscience.* 41:(6)402-409.
35. Nothhall, P. 1988. Revolutionary methods to control Nicaragua's pests. *New Sci.* 119:51.
36. Hochberg, M.E. 1989. The potential role of pathogens in biological control. *Nature.* 37:262-265.
37. Miller, J.A. 1989. Microbes to aid plants from within. *Bioscience.* 39:227-228.
38. Walsh, Mary William. 1985. Risky business: insurers are shunning coverage of chemical and other pollution. *Wall Street Journal* (March 19).
39. Hazarika, Sanjoy. 1990. The Bhopal case: seeking new Bhopal pact. *India Abroad.* (November 30).
40. Majupuria, Sanjeev. 1991. Gas victims still feel helpless. *India Abroad.* (December).

Natural and Technological Disasters: Causes, Effects and Preventive Measures. Edited by
S.K. Majumdar, G.S. Forbes, E.W. Miller, and R.F. Schmalz. © 1992, The Pennsylvania Academy
of Science.

Chapter Twenty-Four

THE VALDEZ OIL SPILL: ENVIRONMENTAL, ECONOMIC AND SOCIAL IMPACTS

E. WILLARD MILLER

Professor of Geography and
Associate Dean for Resident Instruction (Emeritus)
College of Earth and Mineral Sciences
The Pennsylvania State University
University Park, PA 16802

INTRODUCTION

The occurrence of accidental oil spills in the ocean became significant when ocean transportation grew due to the development of the oil fields in the non-consuming countries of the world. In order to market the oil for such regions in the Middle East, Venezuela, North Africa, and Nigeria great tanker fleets have been built. As demand for oil grew, the world movement of oil grew from a little less than 3,500 million barrels of oil in 1960, to 12,500 million barrels in the early 1970s, to about 15,000 million barrels in recent years.

The first major oil spill from a supertanker occurred on March 18, 1967 when the Torrey Canyon grounded on Seven Stones Shoal about 21 miles off Cornwall's Land End. The tanker spilled 840,000 barrels of Kuwait oil into the sea. Since then there have been scores of accidents of vessels creating spills of oil in the oceans. The most recent one occurred on March 24, 1989 when the Exxon Valdez ran aground on Bligh Reef in Prince William Sound, shortly after leaving Valdez, Alaska. This chapter describes and analyzes the Exxon Valdez oil spill as to its environmental impact, economic effects, and social disruptions of the area and concludes with some recommendations for management of future oil spills.

Technology

Although massive oil spills have been occurring for more than two decades, there is still no acceptable technology to protect the environment. It is now recognized that many of the remedial measures taken in Prince William Sound to clean the beaches may have actually had a negative impact on the environment. The technologies used to clean the beaches were adapted from techniques used for other purposes. Many questions have been raised about the process that used high temperatures and high pressure sprays, repeated 10 to 20 times to clean the oil from the beach. In the cool waters of the Sound the hot waters have a tendency to kill all animal life thus destroying the natural ecosystem.

The oil that was collected was in general biodegradable and placed in plastic bags. Because of the quantity there was no place to deposit the oil in Alaska and most was transported to a hazardous waste landfill in Arlington, Oregon, one of two hazardous waste landfills in the Pacific northwest. At the time of the spill there were no facilities available for ocean incineration. By late summer the Environmental Protection Agency allowed small quantitites to be burned on ocean barges. Out of this experience it is hoped that federal guidelines will be developed for disposal of emulsified oils. The development of biodegradable bags and the determination of the affect of salt water on the oily waste could aid the cleanup process.

Control of the Spill

At the time of the Valdez accident there had been little planning to manage a major oil spill. Prior to this spill the general attitude had been that such an event could not occur. As a result a computer system to teach spill movement, location of vulnerable areas, availability of personnel, and a clean-up program were not in place.

After the oil spill there was a "window of response" that lasted about 72 hours during which effective mechanical removal of oil from the surface of the water was possible. Dispersants and burning techniques would have been effective, particularly to control movement of the spill, during this period. The initial "window" ended when the oil was emulsified during a stormy day. After the storm, there was a second window of lessor opportunity of about one week during which a significant portion of the emulsified oil could have been recovered by mechanical pick up. This period also represented the optimal time for preventive booming of sensitive beaches (Harrald, Marcus, Wallace, 1989).

During this 10-day period, however, resources were not available at the scene of the accident to remove the oil effectively. In addition, there was a lack of coordination between industry, state and federal agencies. In this period, less than 5 percent of the oil was contained, removed, dispersed or burned. With an optimal response another 10 to 20 percent of the oil may have been prevented from reaching shore. After the first 10 days, little else could have been done to reduce the amount of oil impacting on the beach, although protective booming could still have influenced where the oil reached the beach. During severe weather in Prince William Sound, no amount of equipment or dispersants could have kept the oil from the beaches.

In spite of an ineffective system of oil removal, an inventory by the U.S. Forest service of the Sound four weeks after the spill, indicated that about 35 percent of the oil had evaporated, 17 percent recovered, 8 percent burned, 5 percent biodegraded, and 5 percent was dispersed. Another 18 percent of the oil had been deposited on the beaches, and 10 percent was contained in oil slicks. To clean the more than 300 miles of beaches more than 4,000 persons worked in the area in this early recovery period.

Environmental Impact

The effects of the oil spill on the ecosystem will be difficult to evaluate until years have gone by. The spill occurred in one of the world's richest biological areas. Within one week after the oil spill a U.S. Fish and Wildlife Service biologist estimated that more then 15,000 seabirds had been exposed to oil. There was also concern about the safety of the area's 5,000 sea otters. They are especially vulnerable to oil because it reduces their insolation and buoyancy of their fur. In an attempt to survive they can ingest fatal doses of oil while licking if off their coats. Of the dozens of otters that were cleaned of oil in the weeks after the spill, only a few survived. Hundreds died in the first days after the spill on remote oil-fouled shores.

The evidence is still outstanding of the effects of the oil spill on a wide variety of plants and animals. Such questions remain, what is the effect on the plankton that are the foundation of the food chain in the sound; can the spawning habits of herring and salmon survive the oilspill; what will be the effect on the bears of the region from eating polluted animals, will whales and sea lions be able to pass through the Sound?

By Fall 1989 an initial evaluation of damage to the ecosystem could be made. It was conservatively estimated that in the Prince William Sound area 33,000 birds, 980 otters, 30 harbor seals, 17 gray whales and 14 sealions had died. In addition an observer of aberrant bird behavior indicted that 75 percent of the bald eagles of the area failed to nest.

Economic Costs

Fishing is the major economic activity in the towns of the Prince William Sound. In 1988 these waters yielded $131 million worth of salmon, herring, halibut, and shellfish. The spill occurred just prior to the herring season. As a result the herring season was canceled with a loss to local fisherman of about $12 million. The oil spill also occurred just prior to the scheduled release of millions of salmon fry to the ocean.

The long-term economic impact on the fishing industry can not be evaluated until the 1992 to 1994 fishing seasons. Clayton McAuliffee of Chevron Oil indicates that "extensive studies show it is highly unlikely that the crude oil spill or the chemical dispersion used to control the spill will cause mortality of marine organisms in the water column or in bottom sediments." In opposition a study by the National Oceanic and Atmospheric Administration states that oil remains toxic to sea life in subarctic waters at least 12 months after an oil spill and fish will suffer during this period.

The economic cost to Exxon two years after the accident exceeded $500 million, but the ultimate cost will not be determined for many years. In 1991 Exxon was initially fined $100 million, but the courts have contested this amount as being far too low. There is also a court decision that Exxon pay Alaska $1.2 billion for damages. This decision is also being contested. Besides the major costs, there are scores of smaller claims that will be adjudicated by the courts in the next decade. The court cases will continue for many years.

Social Disruption

The Valdez oil spill occurred in a region of sparse population. To measure the social impact on a community, the team of Picou, Gill, Dyer and Curry (1990) surveyed the people of Cordova as to how the spill changed their lives. Cordova on Prince William Sound is isolated from other settlements by mountains, glaciers and the sea. The single road to the rest of Alaska was destroyed in the 1964 earthquake. The economy of Cordova is dominated by the fishing industry. Cordova fishermen hold 55 percent of the salmon and 44 percent of herring licenses of the Prince William Sound area. The town people have a history of subsistence practices stemming directly from a Native-Alaskan heritage. About 20 percent of the residents of Cordova are Native-Alaskans. Although the oil spill did not reach the Cordova beaches, it impacted critical fishing grounds used by local fishermen.

In the disaster assessment two towns were selected, one that was directly affected by the spill, Cordova, and a control town, Petersburg, that was not affected by the spill. The research design included the collection of data in a stratified random sample of households, an ethnographic sample of native Alaskans, and a random telephone survey of the inhabitants.

Four questions were asked of residents in Cordova and Petersburg. The first question was have you noticed any changes in the way your family gets along together. In the control area (Petersburg) 91 percent responded no change and 9 percent a change, while in the impact (Cordova) area the response was 61 percent no change and 39 percent a change in family relationships. Of the question, have you made any changes in the plans for the future, the families of the control area responded 86 percent no and 14 percent yes, but in the impact area 51 percent answered yes and 49 percent no. To add to the information the question, have other family members changed their future plans, was asked. The impact area families indicated 70 percent no and 30 percent yes, and in the control area, 83 percent no and only 17 percent yes. Finally, the question was asked, have things changed for you at work. The Cordova residents responded 68 percent yes and 32 percent no, while the Petersburg residents indicated 81 percent no change and only 19 percent a work change (Picou and others, 1990).

These results indicate that the spill had a significantly greater social disruption in Cordova than in the Petersburg area. These disruptions included family relations and future plans of the community members. The four researchers who conducted this study felt that the general uncertainty that characterized Cordova residents was directly related to the threat posed by the spill for future economic viability in the community.

In another survey, measuring post-traumatic stress disorders, there were also significant different responses between the residents of Cordova and Petersburg. The majority of the residents of Cordova had such intrusive recollections of the spill such as inadverted thoughts, unexpected negative pictures and thoughts that would result in an emotionally upset. Other contrasts in the emotions between the residents of the two communities included stress behavior in Cordova in the avoidance and recollection of the traumatic aspects of the spill. In summation the results of this research report clearly documented the existence of significantly more social disruption and post-traumatic stress disorders in Cordova.

Management Planning

The technology to control oil spills is still in an initial stage of development. In 1979 a report of the National Research Council of the National Academy of Sciences stated that, "Little attention has been paid to how government and industry would respond to a major maritime casualty involving hazardous cargo…(and)…the technical community…is not concerned about the capability to do so." In a 1984 *Management Science* article, it concluded, "The problem of providing an immediate response (to an oil spill) in areas where major environmental damage may be done in less than 6-12 hours has not been solved or extensively studied."

The difficulty in preparing for and responding to oil spills stems from the fact that there are extremely rare events (Harrald, 1989). Society has not learned how to deal effectively with low probability, high consequence events, particularly when the risk is due to technological failure. The attitude of the public and governmental officials toward these events tends to be polarized. When there is low probability the normal reaction is that the event will never occur and therefore any response plan is wasteful. In contrast, others recognize the consequences of the possible disaster, and would totally prohibit the activity. In the latter situation the catastrophe develops high initial interest, but if it does not reoccur, interest quickly diminishes. A system has been developed to handle small accidents that occur routinely, but a procedure has not been developed to deal rationally with catastrophic and rare events (Wenk, 1986).

The Exxon Valdez oil spill has demonstrated, however, that these catastrophic accidents cannot be ignored. A system must be developed that can effectively control the environmental and economic damages and keep social disruptions at a minimum. This involves a number of steps.

In retrospect, it has become apparent that determination of the ecological impact of the Valdez oil spill on the environment was hampered by a lack of scientific information on birds, fish and other wildlife in the area. Basic information needed to assess the impact on the ecosystem was found to be sorely lacking. A hodgepodge of scientific studies have been completed, but no one has developed a comprehensive analysis.

To correct this deficiency the U.S. Environmental Protection Agency in 1990 began a long term project known as EMAP—The Environmental Monitoring and Assessment Program. The program will collect basic scientific data on the nation as a whole. When this information, is placed on a gird it can provide basic environmental and ecological information for any ocean area around the United States. If, for example, a tanker ran aground in the Delaware Bay area, scientists could immediately secure information about the environment of that area. EMAP will provide a geographic information system that will be vital for decision making in oceanic disasters.

From a technological viewpoint an initial step is to reduce the risk of the accident. These procedures include the making of the port facilities and the harbor channel safer, the control of vessel traffic in the harbor, and the establishment of personnel standards. All oil tankers must be constructed to reduce spills. Of those modifications, the use of the double hull is crucial. In these vessels if the outer hull is penetrated no oil will escape (Harrald, 1989).

Beyond these initial endeavors there must be contingency planning in the high risk areas so that an immediate response can be mounted at the time of the accident. Necessary equipment must be present including computer based aids to allocate resources, provide information on spill movement, and clean-up progress, and allocate key personnel to strategic areas.

REFLECTIONS

The control of major oil spills has not received high priority by either industry or government in the past in spite of the fact that the environmental, economic, and social impacts have been significant in the areas of the oil spills. Although these catastrophes have been infrequent and are geographically widely distributed in the world, there must be the establishment of the organizational, financial, and technological resources required to minimize the impact of these incidences.

SELECTED REFERENCES

Davidson, A., 1990. "Valdez Reflections." *Sierra* 75(May-June):42-49 + .

Gibson, T. December, 1989. "Impacts of an Environmental Disaster on a Small Local Government: The Valdez, Alaska, Oil Spill." *Public Management* 71:18-19.

Harrald, John, Henry Marcus, and William A. Wallace, 1989. *The Management of a Maritime Crisis: The Integration of Planning, Prevention and Response.* Boulder, CO: The Natural Hazards Research and Information Center, Quick Response Report, #34.

Lewis, Thomas A., 1979. "Tragedy in Alaska." *National Wildlife* 23:(June-July):5-9.

Mason, Rachel, 1989. *Community Preparation and Response to the Exxon Oil Spill in Kodiak, Alaska.* Boulder, CO: The Natural Hazards Research and Information Center, Quick Response Report #36

Niering, Frank E. May, 1989. "Implications of Alaskan Oil Spill." *Petroleum Economist* 56:149-151.

Nulty, Peter. 1989. "The Future of Big Oil: Is Exxon's Muck-up at Valdez a Reason to Bar Drilling in One of the Industry's Hottest Prospects? Not According to Those Closest to the Scene: The Alaskans." *Fortune* 119(May 8):46-49.

Picou, Steven, Duane A. Gill, Christopher L. Dyer and Evans W. Curry, 1990. *Social Disruption and Psychological Stress in an Alaskan Fishing Community: The Impact of the Exxon Valdez Oil Spill.* Boulder, CO: The National Hazards Research and Information Center, Quick Response Report #35.

"Special Report: Troubled Waters." 1989. *Amicus Journal* 11(Summer):10-31. (Five articles assessing the aftermath of the Valdez oil spill).

U.S. Congress. House. Committee on Interior and Insular Affairs. Subcommittee on Water, Power and Offshore Energy Resources, 1989-1990. *Investigation of the Exxon Valdez Oil Spill, Prince William Sound, Alaska: Oversight Hearings: Pts 1-3, May 5-July 28, 1989.* 101st Cong, 1st sess. Washington, DC: GPO, 3 pts.

Wenk, Edward, Jr., 1986. *Tradeoffs: Imperatives of Chance in a High-Tech World.* Baltimore, MD: Johns Hopkins University Press.

Natural and Technological Disasters: Causes, Effects and Preventive Measures. Edited by
S.K. Majumdar, G.S. Forbes, E.W. Miller, and R.F. Schmalz. © 1992, The Pennsylvania Academy
of Science.

Chapter Twenty-Five

ENVIRONMENTAL IMPACTS OF THE PERSIAN GULF WAR

CURTIS C. DAEHLER*
and
SHYAMAL K. MAJUMDAR
Department of Biology
Lafayette College, Easton, PA 18042

INTRODUCTION

The technological revolution of the twentieth century has enabled us to alter our environment on a scale never before possible. One inherent danger of living with twentieth century technology is that it may be abused, resulting in rapid, large scale damage to both human populations and remaining natural ecosystems of the Earth. Abuse of nuclear technology is a major source of concern; however, equally formidable environmental disasters may also result from abuse of modern industrial technologies. Three scenarios which may precipitate large-scale environmental damage are war, terrorism, and technological accidents.

This chapter examines significant man-made environmental damage which has resulted and which potentially may result from the Persian Gulf War of 1991. The intent of this chapter is not to belittle the tragedy of lost human lives during fighting of the war, but to point out some environmental problems associated with the war. Such environmental problems are often discounted at the time of war, in the wake of immediate loss of lives; however, in the long term, it may be the environmental problems which accrue the most substantial economic and human costs, including continued loss of lives long after commencement of the war.

Oil Spills

During the week of January 20, 1991, about 1.5 million barrels of oil (63 million gallons) were spilled in the Persian Gulf offshore of Kuwait. The spill was more

---

*Present address: Department of Zoology, University of California at Davis, CA 95616

than five times larger than the 11 million gallon Exxon Valdez spill of 1989.[2] The 1991 Persian Gulf spill originated from at least two sources. The major source was a pipeline leading from Port Mina al Ahamari, Kuwait, to the Sea Island filling station 10 miles offshore.[3] The other, lesser source of spilled oil was 5 leaking super-tankers off the coast of Kuwait. Oil from the supertankers may have been due to damage from Coalition force attacks, while oil from the pipeline is believed to have been deliberately spilled by Iraq.[3] On January 26, 1991, Coalition forces were able to reduce the flow of oil from the pipeline to a trickle through precision bombing, but not before a massive slick had formed.[3] Several possible motives for the deliberate spillage of this oil by Iraq included: discouragement of an amphibious invasion of Kuwait by Coalition forces with the potential damage to motors of am-phibious landing vehicles and the potential for lighting beaches afire during an invasion[4]; damage of offshore naval vessels from oil drawn through water intakes of ships, resulting in contamination of the ships' drinking water and damage to steam turbines[5]; fouling of desalination plants in Saudi Arabia, depriving civilians and soldiers there of drinking water, and also possibly generation of electricity.[4,6]

While these tactical motives for the oil spill were largely unsuccessful, the en-vironmental effects have been significant, with the full extent of these effects not yet known. In comparison to the oil spilled from the Exxon Valdez in Prince William Sound, the oil spilled in the Persian Gulf was a "light" crude, meaning that it con-tained a higher proportion of highly aromatic volatile compounds, which evaporate rapidly, especially in the warm Gulf waters, which range from $10°C$ to over $30°C$.[3,7] However, it is the volatile compounds, which include benzene and toluidine, which are most toxic.[3] It has been estimated that 15% of the spill initially evaporated from the water surface, while eventually, after weathering, only 10% of this "light" crude will remain to contaminate beaches and sediments (as compared to 20-50% which remained from the Exxon Valdez spill).[3,8,9] Ecological effects of the spilled oil have been exacerbated however, by the conditions under which the spill took place, the water flow characteristics of the Persian Gulf basin, and the high diversity of marine organisms native to the Gulf.

Since the oil spill took place within the war zone, dangers of artillery fire and floating mines severely hindered both evaluation of the extent of the spill and remediation efforts.[2,3] This led to an original ambiguity as to the size and location of the spill and prevented many conventional clean-up measures such as contain-ment of the spill within booms, skimming of the water by cleanup vessels and ap-plication of chemical dispersants.[3] While 5.4 million gallons of the spill have reportedly been recovered by an internationally-aided cleanup, the vast majority of the oil has been left for nature to disperse.[10]

The Persian Gulf basin is a nearly land locked body of water and has a low rate of mixing with the Indian Ocean.[7] Three to five years are required to flush surface waters of the Gulf to the Indian Ocean, as compared to only 28 days required to flush the water of the Prince William Sound, the site of the Valdez spill, into the Pacific.[7] A second basin-related factor is the depth of the Persian Gulf, which averages only 35 meters.[7] This shallow depth gives the Persian Gulf a relatively low water column volume available for dispersion of the oil and associated toxic compounds. In addition, the relatively low wave action within the Persian Gulf will slow dispersion of the oil onto the shore line and may result in deposition of thick oil mats and tar balls over large areas of beach where the slick hits shore.[6] These thick deposits, especially tar balls, can release toxic compounds over long time periods.[3]

The flow of water within the Gulf is generally counter-clockwise, which will cause the slick to move south, past Saudi Arabia and eventually towards India.[10,11] In Saudi Arabia, much of the peoples' water supply is derived from desalination plants along the coast. The desalination plant at Jubail uses about 3 billion gallons of water per day from the Persian Gulf to provide 270 million gallons of fresh water to the people of Riyadh and surrounding communities.[12] Although the slick itself has not clogged the plant's intake pipes, the plant may take in water which has been contaminated with trace amounts of dissolved toxic compounds from the oil, which could affect the safety of the water for drinking.[10] By the time the oil reaches India, it is likely to be well dispersed, however, the possibility remains that the oil could affect shrimp, lobster, oyster and scallop harvests, which provide a large source of income to many people.[11]

The Persian Gulf contains a high diversity of ecosystems, which include coral reefs, mangroves, and sea grass communities.[3] There are 450 animal species associated with coral reefs alone.[10] Also, 180 species of mollusks, 106 species of fish, 5 species of dolphins, 113 species of overwintering birds, 3 species of whales and numerous sea turtles, dugongs, and sea snakes have been scored in the Gulf.[6,10,13] The effects of oil on sea birds may be most devastating. During the first six months after the spill, 20,000 avian casualties have been reported.[14] Oil can coat the birds' feathers, hindering flight and causing loss of the feather's insulating properties. At the same time, birds ingest oil from contaminated food or while cleaning their feathers.[15] This oil is then delivered to young hatchlings as food, which, even in trace amounts, greatly increases hatchling mortality.[16] The oil-soaked cormorant has become symbolic of the ecological damage caused by the spill.[7]

The Gulf War oil spill was probably not the largest spill on record (that notoriety belongs to the Ixtoc spill of 1979-1980 during which 140 million gallons were released into the Gulf of Mexico[6]). Neither was the Gulf War spill the only recent spill in the Persian Gulf, as there have been 125 major spills in the Persian Gulf since 1978.[6] However, the Gulf War spill was unique in that it was a deliberate act. This act resulted in immediate threats to human lives through loss of drinking water, and may continue to threaten humans if water from desalination plants becomes tainted with trace hydrocarbons or other oil pollutants, or if marine food harvests are affected.[10,11] At the same time, many marine animals were lost and delicate ecosystems may have been altered, perhaps forever.

Oil Well Fires

Over 700 of Kuwait's approximately 800 oil wells were set ablaze by Iraqi invaders.[18,19] As a result, heavy smoke clouds covering most of Kuwait have been observed by satellite. On some days, smoke clouds were visible over a 42,000 km^2 area including parts of Iraq, Iran, Qatar, Pakistan, Turkey, Sri Lanka, India,

Bulgaria and even the Soviet Union.[10,20,21] While the consensus among atmospheric scientists is that no measurable global effect will result, local effects have been severe and regional damage is a threat. Prior to the Gulf War, there had been a record of 3 simultaneous oil well fires in Kuwait.[22] The Gulf War oil fire disaster was two to three orders of magnitude higher than this record and was compounded by Iraqi placement of mines around wells and the destruction of well depth and configuration plans.[23]

Since most of Kuwait's wells are under natural pressure, extinguishing by explosives and/or capping is required to put out each fire.[24] Globally, eight teams have had experience in the dangerous art of extinguising oil well blazes and they have been working in Kuwait since the end of the war.[25] One blaze can take up to two weeks to extinguish at a cost of up to 10 million dollars.[18,25] Approximately 1-3 years will be required to extinguish all fires.[10] Estimates of the amount of oil burning in Kuwait in 1991 range from 1.5 to 6 million barrels per day.[26] Assuming the lower rate of burning, the cost of the fires in oil loss alone exceeds 10 billion dollars annually, assuming 1991 oil values.

Oil well fires release large amounts of hydrocarbons and particulates which are most likely to have local effects. On many afternoons, it has been common to see pitch black skies over large areas of Kuwait, including Kuwait City.[10] The smoke particulates absorb and/or reflect much of the sun's radiation to outer space, which has resulted in decreases in average peak daily temperatures to as much as 10°C below normal over areas of Kuwait and Iraq.[26] In Baharain, for example, 400 km from the fires, the averge temperature in May 1991 was 7.5°C below normal, making it the coldest May in 35 years.[27] Although it is difficult to establish an absolute cause and effect relationship between the fires and the unusually cool weather, the observed temperature changes are consistent with atmospheric models, which have predicted temperature reductions of 5-8°C at 250 km from the smoke source and reduction of 1-2°C at distances as far as 750 km.[26]

Children and eldery are most susceptible to respiratory problems due to inhalation of smoke components.[10] Days with low wind and high barometric pressure are worst for all since smoke dispersion is decreased and concentrations of air pollutants become dangerously high.[18] Included in the smoke particulates are hydrocarbons and traces of lead, arsenic, and copper, which are known to be carcinogenic or neurotoxic through chronic inhalation or ingestion.[28,29] Tens of millions of people are expected to ingest toxic residue from smoke and, over the next generation, some are likely to develop chronic respiratory problems. The incidence of cancers may increase due to both inhalation and ingestion.[14,22,30] Various other effects also prevail. While fires continue to burn, people and animals cannot drink rainwater in Kuwait.[31] Persistent fumes of burning diesel and burning rubber have been reported throughout Kuwait, and an oil film covers buildings and automobiles.[30,32] Black and white cows have been reported to appear gray.[23] The effects of the oily film on vegetation is unknown, however a decrease in temperature of as little as 2°C is known to reduce crop growth rates, possibly affecting fruit and agriculture production in Iraq and Iran.[7,33] Since most particulates in the smoke are hygroscopic and have short atmospheric half lives (4-6 days), the major health and environmental threats of smoke particulates are limited to local and small regional effects.[26,27]

On a larger regional scale, acid precipitation, at a pH of 3.0-3.6, is predicted as far as 2000 km downwind from the oil fires.[26] This acid precipitation is likely to affect at least Iraq, Saudi Arabia, Bulgaria, Afghanistan, and Pakistan.[26,32] Acidic precipitation may cause damage to crops, although alkaline soils in some areas may reduce this effect.[18,26] In higher areas where snow falls, such as mountains in south Iran and the Himalayas, snow has been reported to be gray with acidic soot.[4,22,26] During the spring, snow melt may be more rapid than usual due to higher radiation absorbance of the darkened snow, resulting in flooding and acid shock in certain streams and irrigation systems, possibly causing death of sensitive aquatic species and crop damage.

Global effects due to the oil fires have not been observed yet, primarily because the majority of the smoke has been confined to the troposphere (the average smoke injection height has been below 2 km[26]). Although there was reported a 20-times-normal carbon soot reading over Hawaii in April 1991,[34] it appears that most smoke did not reach the stratosphere, where its atmospheric effects would have been much more pronounced. If smoke had been ejected with sufficient force, or had a great degree of lofting occurred, then a longer atmospheric retention time of particulates, a larger and more rapid distribution of smoke, and a greater effect of blocking incoming solar radiation could have had disastrous global implications.[3] Fortunately, smoke from the oil fires is not ejected nearly as forcefully as that from volcanoes or nuclear explosions, and the stratosphere remained largely unaffected.[26] Effects of the fires on the summer monsoon over the Indian subcontinent are expected to be negligible.[26,34]

In terms of global increases of atmospheric pollutants in the troposphere, the Kuwaiti oil fires are expected to increase the world carbon dioxide output by about 1% in 1991, and the sulfur dioxide output of the fires is predicted to be the equivalent to output of the United Kingdom in 1991.[26] While these atmospheric inputs are minor on a global scale, the small region from which they originate has suffered high local concentrations of atmospheric pollutants on scales not before caused by man, with the possible exception of burning of tropical rainforests in the Amazon.[26]

Desert Disruption and Damage

The desert of Kuwait harbors its own unique ecosystem which has been affected detrimentally by the war. The ecosystem consists of animals such as snakes, camels, gazelles, spiders, scorpions and sheep, and is stabilized by an upper layer of sand, pebbles and microorganisms which has been referred to as the "desert shield".[18,35] Pebbles ranging in size from about 0.5 cm to 2 cm in diameter form the natural upper layer of the ecosystem and are large enough to resist movement during most wind storms, thus holding in place the smaller grains below.[35] In addition, a network of microorganisms including bacteria form an interlocking mesh among the smaller upper sand grains, which allows resistance to wind disturbances.[18]

Military fortifications and massive-scale vehicle movements have disrupted this "desert shield" in Kuwait, and it may require decades to recover.[8,35] The result may be increased sand storms, as have been documented after the Iran-Iraq wars of the 1980's. Dunes may move, most likely to the south, where they may engulf agriculture areas, cities, or airports.[35] To prevent such disasters, it may be necessary to construct large windbreaks and funneling systems to direct sand around sensitive areas.[35]

Another problem in most of Kuwait may be ground water contamination. Hydrocarbon deposition from oil well smoke and deliberate spilling of oil in trenches and irrigation channels throughout Kuwait is expected to contaminate ground water, making water from natural wells unsafe to drink.[32] Finally, mines left buried throughout the desert will pose a hazard to travelers for years to come, however, it has been suggested that the mine threat may be beneficial to nature in that it may allow the desert ecosystem to recover more rapidly by discouraging further human disruption.[8]

Hazardous Debris

A final environmental threat lies in the debris and wreckage left by Coalition attacks on Iraq. Coalition forces bombed all known chemical factories and chemical weapons storage depots throughout Iraq. Hazardous chemicals have been released into the areas surrounding many chemical factories and storage sites.[36] These chemicals may pose a threat to any habitants nearby. While dismantling Iraq's nuclear, biological and chemical capabilities is required by U.N. Security Council Resolution 687, cleanup of such contaminated sites can be extremely expensive and is probably not a priority for Iraq at this point in time.[36] As a result, persistent chemicals may have time to spread in the environment, contaminating both humans and animals. In addition, it has been reported that an Iraqi nuclear reactor was bombed by Coalition forces, and it is possible that radioactivity has been, or is being, released.[4] If such a situation is a reality, then we may expect further casualties for many years to come.

Call for International Policy

Death and destruction are inherent elements of war; however, non-strategic, non-essential destruction of the environment is not an acceptable action by any party in any situation. Iraq has not been the first country to use a "scorched Earth" policy. In fact, in the United States, "scorched Earth" policies were used by Union generals against southern cities, and by Confederate generals against Pennsylvania towns during the Civil War.[21,37] The problem, however, has become most dire in the twentieth century due to technological developments. While one could argue that an unwritten rule has never been sufficient and a firm policy against "scorched Earth" should have been made long ago, it has been only during the twentieth century that such a stringent policy has become absolutely essential for global security. Prior to the twentieth century, human-induced violent destruction has been limited to local areas of unrest. Today, the actions of one party against the Earth can potentially be felt globally. When the Earth becomes violently damaged by one party, we all now pay, whether it is through loss of life, health, or the burden of remediation costs. The United Nations must develop a policy which makes "environmental terrorism" an international crime with severe penalties which will be upheld and supported by all Organization members. The wording of such a policy must be straightforward and understood by all parties, such as with the existing policy for treatment of prisoners of war (POWs).

In a sense, during the Gulf War the Earth was lucky. Many worse scenarios can be imagined than the present reality. It should be obvious, however, that we cannot depend solely on the technology of our defenses to protect the Earth. The governments of the world must mutually agree to spare the environment as far as is possible in future confrontations and in the future development of weapons and war strategies, with an understanding of internationally enforced penalties for failure to oblige.

REFERENCES

1. Radwan, S. 1991. Gulf oil spill. *Nature.* 350:465.
2. Washington Post. 1991. Gulf oil spill cleanup can be handled in time. *The Express.* Easton, PA. March 1.
3. Raloff, J. and Monastersky, R. 1991. Gulf oil threatens ecology, maybe climate. *Sci. News.* 139:71-73.
4. Shenon, P. 1991. Huge slick still a threat to Saudi water plants. *NY Times.* January 28.
5. Washington Post. 1991. Oil may be used as military weapon. *The Express.* Easton, PA. January 27.
6. Annon. 1991. Persian Gulf falls victim to war. *Chemecology.* 20(2):4-5.
7. Pearce, F. 1991. Wildlife choked by world's worst oil slick. *New Sci.* February 2:24.
8. Ford, P. 1991. Vital Saudi water plant prepares for oil slick. *Chr. Sci. Mon.* February 1:2
9. Miller, E.W. 1991. The Valdex Oil Spill: environmental, economic and social impacts. In:*Natural and Technological Disasters.* eds. S.K. Majumdar, *et al.,* The Pennsylvania Academy of Science, Easton, PA. pp. 322-328
10. Schmitt, E. 1991. Fouled region is casualty of war. *NY Times.* March 1.
11. Nayar, K. 1991. Effects of Monsoon Discounted. *India Abroad.* March 8.
12. Holusha, J. 1991. U.S. companies join bid to minimize Gulf oil spill. *NY Times.* January 29.
13. Schneider, K. 1991. Saudis seek U.S. help with oil spill. *NY Times.* January 27.
14. Warner, F. 1991. The environmental consequences of the Gulf War. *Environment.* 33(5):7-9
15. Nybakken, J.W. 1982. *Marine Biology, an ecological approach.* Harper and Row. New York. 446 p.
16. Carefoot, T.H. 1977. *Pacific Seashores: a guide to intertidal ecology.* University of Washington Press. Seattle. 208 p.
17. Goodman, E. 1991. Deliberate oil spill in Persian Gulf is a crime against

humanity. *The Express.* Easton, PA. February 1.

18. Elmer-Dewitt, P. 1991. A man-made hell on Earth. *Time.* March 18.

19. Hoffman, H. 1991. Taking stock of Saddam's fiery legacy in Kuwait. *Science.* 253:971.

20. Limaye, S. *et al.* 1991. Satellite observations of smoke from oil fires in Kuwait. *Science.* 252:1536-1539.

21. Emerson, S. 1991. When Earth takes a hit. *Int. Wildlife.* 21(4):38-41.

22. Zuckerman, M. 1991. When it's dark at high noon. *US News & World Rept.* April 1.

23. Lorch, D. 1991. Burning wells turn Kuwait into land of oily blackness. *NY Times.* March 6.

24. Edmonds, P. 1991. Burning oil could be environmental disaster. *The Express.* Easton, PA. January 23.

25. Wald, M. 1991. Damage to Kuwait oil production requires a close and expert look. *NY Times.* February 23.

26. Browning, K. *et al.* 1991. Environmental effects from burning oil wells in Kuwait. *Nature.* 351:363-367.

27. Irby, R. and J. Snow. 1991. The scientific team in Kuwait. *UCAR Newsletter.* 15(3):3-5.

28. Leerhsen, C. *et al.* 1991. Hellfighters to the rescue. *News Week.* March 25.

29. Molholt, B. and R. Nilsson. 1991. Inhalation carcinogenesis by metals. In: *Air Pollution: Environmental Issues and Health Effects.* Eds. S.K. Majumdar, E.W. Miller and J.J. Cahir. The Pennsylvania Academy of Science. Easton, PA. pp. 379-395.

30. Green, M. 1991. Health experts arrive in Kuwait. *USA Today.* March 15.

31. Seitz, R. 1991. Black skies or pale fire? *Nature.* March 21.

32. Ibrahim, Y. 1991. Another war begins as burning oil wells threaten a region's ecology. *NY Times.* March 16.

33. Schneider, S. 1991. Smoke Alarm. *World Monitor.* March: 50-51.

34. Tyson, R. 1991. Soot from Kuwait fires settles on Hawaii. *USA Today.* May 1.

35. Holden, C. 1991. Kuwait's unjust deserts: damage to its desert. *Science.* 251:1175.

36. Associated Press. 1991. Chemical arms pose problem. *The Express.* Easton, PA. June 9.

37. Jacobs, M. 1864. *The Rebel Invasion of Maryland and Pennsylvania.* J. Lippincot and Co. pp. 9-11.

EPILOGUE

By the first week of November 1991, all oil well fires in Kuwait had been extinguished. This accomplishment was achieved much sooner than expected, due in large part to the intense efforts of some 28 teams assembled to fight the fires (Wald, 1991).

Wald, M.L. 1991. Amid ceremony and ingenuity, Kuwait's oil-well fires are declared out. *NY Times.* November 7.

Natural and Technological Disasters: Causes, Effects and Preventive Measures. Edited by
S.K. Majumdar, G.S. Forbes, E.W. Miller, and R.F. Schmalz. © 1992, The Pennsylvania Academy
of Science.

Chapter Twenty-Six

CONTROLLABILITY, SOCIAL BREAKDOWN AND TECHNOLOGICAL DISASTERS: THE CASE OF THE CENTRALIA COAL MINE FIRE

STEPHEN R. COUCH[1] and J. STEPHEN KROLL-SMITH[2]

[1]Schuylkill Campus
The Pennsylvania State University
Schuylkill Haven, PA 17972
and
[2]Hazleton Campus
The Pennsylvania State University
Hazleton, PA 18201

INTRODUCTION

In contrast to the relatively constant number of natural catastrophes, technological disasters are increasing both in number and in the amount of financial, social and human devastation they cause. The increased capacity of societies to understand natural disasters contrasts sharply with their bewilderment over a variety of complex issues posed by technological disasters and hazards. Just as societies have developed some capacity to mitigate the consequences of natural disasters, so we are in the midst of trying to develop such capacities in relation to technological disasters and hazards.

Recent studies of technological disasters document the comparatively greater amount of psychological stress in these types of calamities. Natural disasters in developed countries are frequently experienced as emotional shocks, but only rarely do they result in long-term psychological impairment.[2,3,4] The trauma of technological calamities, however, frequently lasts for years, impeding the psychological development of victims.[5,6]

What is it about technological disasters that creates adaptational demands that frequently exceed the demands made by natural disasters and often exceed the capabilities of individuals and communities to cope effectively with the stress?

While our research indicates a number of possible answers, this paper will discuss one of them: the problem of controllability. Behind the idea of controllability is the relationship between technological disasters and human agency. Human activity—willful, negligent, or otherwise—is responsible for creating the disaster, and human intervention into the environment is required to abate, extinguish or otherwise control the disaster agent. The often extreme difficulties in detecting and measuring aversive agents that are invisible to the senses, and in developing and implementing mitigation plans that stop their advance, creates the problem of controllability. And this problem, in turn, is a principle source of psychosocial stress in technological disasters.

The case of the Centralia coal mine fire will be used to illustrate the problem of controllability and suggest its relationship to the destructive levels of psychosocial stress experienced by the residents of this northern Appalachian village. The Centralia case is a particularly good one to use, as efforts to control the fire continued for twenty years, creating the types of problems that are likely to follow repeated efforts to stop the advance of a technological disaster agent. In addition, the response of the community to both the fire and the efforts of government agencies to contain it are well documented through newspaper accounts and through correspondence of the various parties involved.

The Centralia Mine Fire

From the founding of the town in 1866, life in Centralia revolved around the mining of anthracite coal. With the decline of the anthracite industry during the first half of this century, Centralia lost population and importance. By mid-century, the thousand-or-so people living in the borough were largely aged, poor and working class. According to a 1983 survey, forty percent of the residents were over sixty-five years of age, forty-two percent earned less than $10,000 a year, and fifty-two percent have lived in Centralia for twenty-five years or longer.[6]

In 1962, fire was discovered in a garbage dump on an abandoned mine stripping at the southeastern edge of the borough. Initial efforts to extinguish the blaze were ineffectual, and the fire ignited an outcropping of coal. The blaze spread underground into the abandoned mine shafts which honeycomb the ground under the area. Over five million dollars were expended be state and federal governments over the following two decades, with no control of the fire being achieved. Instead, the fire continued its underground march.

As time went on and no degree of control was achieved over the fire, the social fabric of the community disintegrated. Public meetings increased in number and became occasions for the expression of bitter hostility of residents against the government and against one another. Fist fights, a fire bombing, slashed tires and telephone threats were indicators that Centralians had turned their anger, fear and frustration inward, expressing it interpersonally among neighbors and friends. Our interview data indicate that the primary stressor in Centralia, from the point of view of the residents, was not the fire but the pervasive intramural conflict separating neighbor from neighbor. It is reasonable to assume that had the engineering attempts to extinguish the mine fire been successful, it is possible that Centralians would have, in time, resolved their anger and worked towards a revitalization of neighborliness. The mine fire, however, was beyond the control of the experts.

The seriousness of the situation was driven home in July of 1983, when a government-sponsored engineering study reported that the fire was worse than anyone had thought. The study concluded that if left to burn itself out, all of Centralia would be made uninhabitable, and if continued efforts were made to control or extinguish the blaze, life in Centralia would become intolerable. The solution: Centralia must go. In October of 1983 a bill authorizing forty-two million dollars to purchase Centralians' property was passed by Congress. The vast majority of residents accepted the government's offer to buy their homes. Only about three dozen families remain in Centralia.

Why was controllability impossible to achieve? And what effects did it have on community residents? We will approach these questions by briefly highlighting efforts to control the fire during the first twenty years of its existence.[7,8]

1962-1971

It was in May of 1962 that refuse material was discovered to be on fire in an illegal garbage dump just southeast of the Borough limits near the Odd Fellows Cemetery. Borough workmen flooded the fire with water and installed a clay seal. Despite these initial efforts, by July, the fire had spread to an outcrop of coal in the Buck Mountain vein.

Control was clearly beyond the means of the borough, and the Pennsylvania Department of Mines and Mineral Industries was called in to for help. The state designated the fire as an emergency and suspended the usual bidding procedures. State agencies budgeted $30,000 for a project to excavate the burning material. Unfortunately, two months after excavation began, borehole temperatures showed that the fire had advanced beyond the area being excavated.

In November, a new state contract was awarded. This one involved the drilling of 80 boreholes and the flushing of 10,000 cubic yards of fine breaker refuse material separated from usable coal during the processing. In March of the following year, funds were depleted and the project was terminated. Then in July, the state awarded a contract of $36,225 to dig a trench to limit the fire's eastward advance. Once again, the contractor's efforts did not stop the fire. In October, fire was discovered on both sides of the incomplete trench. By then, the state had spent over $106,000 and had achieved no degree of control.

Frustrated in its piecemeal attempt to battle the blaze with severely limited funds, the state made no new moves to curtail the fire for a year and a half. But then, in March of 1965, the 89th Congress passed the Appalachian Redevelopment Act. Designed "to provide public works and economic development of the Appalachian Region," the law gave the Secretary of the Interior authority for projects which rehabilitated land damaged by previous mining practices. This rehabilitation included the extinguishing of mine fires. A new source of funding, this time of major proportions, had become available.

In June of 1965, the state, in cooperation with the Bureau of Mines, submitted a proposal to the Appalachian Regional Commission to stop the fire once and for all. The first phase of the project would cost $300,000 and would involve efforts to stop the air flow to the fire and to discover its exact location. During the second phase a permanent isolation trench would be dug, beyond which the fire could never burn. The cost of phase two: $2.2 million.

The Appalachian Regional Commission approved the project and agreed to pay 75 percent of the cost (the maximum allowable under the law). The state would pay most of the remainder. In November of 1967, phase 1 was completed at a cost of $326,123.

Early the following year, the BOM analyzed the data collected during phase 1. It was discovered that to carry out phase 2 effectively would not cost 2.2 million as originally thought, but $4.5 million. This was considered too costly, and plans for phase 2 were abandoned. Instead, the BOM decided to construct barriers of fly-ash through which the fire could not burn, at a much reduced cost of $519,000. Work finally began in May of 1969.

In the meantime, the fire was having an increased impact upon the borough's population. Families near the fire were becoming more and more concerned about the possible health effects of gases caused by the blaze. Some complained of increased headaches and other problems. On May 22, three families were evacuated from their homes after a state mine inspector found trace readings of carbon monoxide in the basement of one of the dwellings.

Other evidence of danger began to flow in. One family in the impact zone found its pet canary dead. Since canaries are very sensitive to carbon monoxide, the family concluded that the gases caused by the fire had killed their pet. Some people who lived near the fire reported having trouble breathing. After investigating the situation at one home, a state mine inspector stated: "I would not sleep in that house if it were mine." But the inspector had no authority to order people to leave their dwellings. Indeed, confusion reigned as to who, if anyone, had the authority to help people who left their homes due to the fire.

This illustrates a general problem in chronic technological disasters—there is a lack of legislation and precedent for dealing with them. The lack of precedent is exacerbated by the fact that, as with environmental issues in general, authority for response is decentralized, located in a myriad of agencies at different levels of government. There is liable to be an appearance, at least, of buck-passing and confusion about who is in charge of what.

Perhaps as an outgrowth of increasing disenchantment with the government's efforts, residents became increasingly alarmed and were dissatisfied with the fly ash project which had just begun. Some residents feared that the technology would not be adequate and demanded that a trench be dug to protect them and their homes. Indeed, the fly-ash barrier was considered a demonstration project at the time, and not a few residents were unhappy about the use of an experimental technology where their health and perhaps their lives seemed to be at stake. Help from elected officials was solicited and apparently was forthcoming. In June, the Bureau of Mines approved an emergency change in the contract in order to allow excavation to take place, in addition to the fly-ash barrier.

But still more work needed to be done. Borehole data indicated that the fire presently had crossed an anticline in the southeast portion of the impact zone. A contract was awarded to construct an eastern barrier, at a cost of $1,352,125. The project was to take over three years to complete.

In the meantime, during 1971, the Bureau of Mines sponsored an excavation to the east of Locust Avenue, the main north-south street in the borough. Burning coal was discovered about 500-800 feet east of Locust Avenue. The actual fire had been located. The Bureau of Mines had some funds with which to continue excavating, but asked Columbia County to contribute $25,000, one half of the cost of completing the excavation. The County could not come up with the money. Consequently the digging ceased and the excavation was backfilled, leaving the coal burn. Many believe that the expenditure of this $50,000 would have solved the mine fire problem forever.

In assessing government agency response to the fire from 1962 to 1971, it is easy to see how controllability became a political issue. Technical uncertainty leading to escalating costs and a policy vacuum in the area of chronic technological disasters assured that considerable legislative intrigue and debate surrounded the engineering projects. For not a few people, both in and out of town, the first decade of government's management of the crisis left little doubt that technical decisions only imperfectly masked political choices.

1971-1981

During the early 1970's, the fire continued to burn and to become ever more troublesome and costly. The eastern fly-ash barrier project was completed in December of 1973, at a total cost of a whopping $1.8 million. Over the seven years of the joint federal-state venture, 1635 boreholes had been dug; 122,556 tons of fly ash injected; 117,220 cubic yards of sand flushed; 60,000 cubic yards of material excavated; 19,000 cubic yards of clay seals installed; and $2,768,208 spent. Everyone hoped that the Centralia mine fire had been controlled at last.

Unfortunately, this was not the case. In August of 1976, the Bureau determined that more money was needed to reinforce the existing fly ash barriers. The following month the state Department of Environmental Resources (DER) requested funds from the Appalachian Regional Commission. What followed was a bureaucratic nightmare which provides an excellent illustration of the kinds of delays which continually thwarted fire control efforts.

The proposal to reinforce the existing barriers outlined two phases. The first involved the drilling of boreholes to determine the extent of the problem. During the second phase, flushing would take place to reinforce the existing barrier or create new barriers. $385,000 was approved for the project in the spring of 1977.

At this point, a dispute arose over the cooperative funding agreement between the federal Bureau of Mines and the state Department of Environmental Resources, holding up the awarding of a contract. In September, the problem was resolved, and a low bid was accepted. However the low bid was for $429,550. Since this was higher than the amount of funds which had been approved for the project, additional money had to be sought from the federal, state and county governments. This meant still more delays.

Finally in January of 1978, a year and a half after the original funding request for the project, the funding was approved and the contract awarded.

In November of 1978, the flusing project was completed at a cost even higher than anticipated ($498,138). But even before its completion, the Bureau of Mines had realized that more work was needed and had developed yet another final solution to the Centralia problem. This plan would involve isolating the fire by digging a trench. One major problem with this alternative, however, was that it required the acquisition of residential property, a point of heated controversy within Centralia. This also posed legal difficulties, as the Bureau of Mines lacked the authority to purchase homes. Nevertheless, the plan was presented to the Centralia Borough Council. At a public meeting attended by between 350 and 500 citizens, Borough Council approved plans for the project. Subsequently, the Bureau of Mines approved the plans, and the Appalachian Regional Commission committed some funds. However, as the plans continued to be worked out, cost estimates skyrocketed to $10 million, with much of the funding coming from state and local sources. At this point, the state and county withdrew, killing the proposed trench. After generating a great deal of controversy, the project was dropped, and no other options were on the table. Naturally, Centralians' confidence in the Bureau of Mines was undermined further, with many feeling that the Bureau could not make up its mine.

Apparently, changes within the federal bureaucracy were behind a lack of alternative plans during 1978-1979. In August, 1977, Congress passed the Surface Mining and Reclamation Act. It provided "for the cooperation between the Secretary of the Interior and the States with respect to the regulation of surface coal mining operations, and the acquisition and reclamation of abandoned mines, and for other purposes." The Office of Surface Mining and Reclamation (OSM) was created and given a reclamation fund contributed by active mining operations, to be used to reclaim abandoned coal mine lands. The OSM's authority included the ability to purchase private land as part of its reclamation efforts. It seems that the Bureau of Mines was waiting for the OSM to become involved before developing any new projects. Again, bureaucratic machinations caused significant delays.

While offering a new source of funding to combat the mine fire, the advent of the OSM also presented a new source of confusion and delay, even after it became active in Centralia. This confusion is made painfully evident by the events of 1979 and 1980.

During 1979, BOM and state officials developed a cheaper alternative to the abandoned trench idea. Slated to cost $6 million, it involved filling a 35-acre tract of land with noncombustible material and fly ash slurry, and sealing with cement grouting. It was to take four or five years to complete, and again was touted as a final solution to the problem.

However, while BOM experts believed this option would work, OSM experts disagreed. A memo to the director of the OSM from the Director of the OSM's Region 1 stated that "the proposed project would neither extinguish nor confine the fire." Indeed, it was argued that previous "boreholes have increased the air circulation in the underground fire area," thereby aiding, not abating, the fire. The memo notes a difficulty in obtaining information from the BOM. The summary of Region 1's position even betrays a concern that the fire may be beyond control:

"Until adequate analytical information is made available, and pending appropriate analysis, no further drilling should be undertaken. The technology for extinguishing the fire may not be available. Extinguishing the fire by known techniques could be impossible and at the very least prohibitively expensive. After we have reviewed all the documents which we need from the Bureau of Mines we may recommend a minimal program of sealing entries and other sources of air which feed the fire."

This memo, which was to have been "administratively restricted," became public in August, 1979. As expected, it generated great concern among Centralians, with many viewing Centralia as being caught in the middle of a bureaucratic power struggle between the OSM and the BOM. Finally, at month's end, the two agencies entered into an agreement by which the OSM would provide the BOM with $137,400 to drill boreholes, map the status of the fire, and develop alternative strategies for final abatement.

As time wore on, the fire caused increasing short-term problems with which people had to deal. In 1980, the OSM facilitated the removal of several families because of rising subsurface temperatures. The events around the acquisition of these endangered properties provides an additional illustration of problems arising from a lack of clear legislative authority concerning chronic technological disasters.

In January of 1980, an OSM document on the proposed relocation stated: "The potential for carbon monoxide and other gases seeping into homes above the fire area is an extreme danger to the public health and safety." The following month, the OSM announced that appraisals of eight properties would be made. In April, the OSM began making offers to acquire the properties. By the end of June, all but one family had accepted the government's relocation offer.

However, problems of law and precedent began to be perceived. A memo from an OSM official concerning the acquisition of the eight properties expressed concern about the wording used by one OSM official. Specifically, objection was raised to:

"OSM's PA Department's use of words 'potentially dangerous area.' The words are inflammatory, provocative and designed to give rise to fear. If this is a dangerous area, and if this is the only criteria for acquisition then everyone in the fire area can sue us and ask that OSM acquire their homes."

By the fall of 1980, such problems had not been resolved. It became apparent that the emergency flushing activities had not solved gas problems for three other Locust Avenue residents. At a public meeting in Centralia on September 29 and 30, according to an OSM memo, OSM officials "did state conclusively that as a part of the over-all plan at Centralia, upon a finding by the Pennsylvania Health Department that a given residence was no longer suitable for human habitation due to levels of toxic gases from the mine fire, OSM would immediately relocate or dislocate residents to temporary quarters until some permanent remedial action could be taken. Failing any successful remedial action, the affected residence would then be acquired or moved." One of the affected residents was granted OSM permission to move to a temporary residence.

However, when the OSM legal office became aware of this action, it raised objections. In an October 31 memo, a Region 1 Field Solicitor stated:

"We are of the opinion that Title IV does not envision or authorize such relocation expenses unless the property in question must be taken or vacated as an actual integral part of the reclamation and/or abatement process. The fact that the dwellings may have been declared uninhabitable would not in itself give us the authority to purchase the property or pick up the relocation expenses of the occupants."

Frustration was clearly expressed by OSM's Region 1 director over the situation: "We are faced with a very serious dilemma. Based on the authority which was passed on to us verbally...we did, in fact, make several statements in Centralia which charted our course of action...Now there is a very serious question as to whether or not the assumed authority is in fact real. We must have some relief."

In the end, under dubious legal authority, the OSM did acquire the three properties. Nevertheless, this incident illustrates how questionable information was often passed on to Centralia residents as fact, only later to be questioned, modified, or retracted. The decentralized nature of decision making over such issues, and the lack of clear legislative precedent, was largely to blame. Understandably, Centralians became increasingly frustrated and suspicious of governmental activities.

In September of 1980, the long-awaited BOM report on the condition of the fire and on eleven possible solutions was issued. It was discussed at a public meeting of over 300 people on September 29-30. The option which the BOM seemed to favor involved excavating part of the fire and constructing two isolation trenches, at a proposed cost of $32.4 million. At that meeting people were told that the OSM was evaluating the data, and that the Secretary of the Interior would make a decision on a final mine fire abatement plan by January 1, 1981. Many were optimistic that a final solution was close at hand.

However, once again, the optimism was unfounded. By early December, the OSM was backing away from its commitment to come up with a plan by January 1. One OSM official stated, "I've got no idea when a decision on an option will be made. It depends. I can't speculate." In the end, the trenching project was never carried out.

Centralians were far from oblivious to the government's decision-making problems. Residents came to see themselves as caught in the middle of a political whirlwind over which they had no control. On the one hand, residents accepted the government's technical definition of the problem, which meant that the extremely elusive issue of controllability became the issue upon which action concerning the mine fire was based. On the other hand, the lack of technical know-how and the competing interests of different sectors of government led to increased conflict within the town and failure to produce an adequate solution to the technical or the social problems with which Centralia was confronted. The situation in Centralia parallels that of other cases where, as Gephart points out, managerial activity itself caused an environmental disaster or aggravated an existing one.[9]

As with most situations of prolonged threat, tensions and stress increased, and the ability to cope was lessened.[10] The fire was spreading and seemingly could not be controlled. But how dangerous was it or could it become? Nobody seemed to know. Diffused feelings of anxiety and demoralization were rampant as Centralians experienced the kind of threat with which it is most difficult to cope, "the generalized dread of the unknown."[11]

Discussion

The plethora of engineering plans gone awry and the anger, hostility and demoralization of the residents of Centralia lead to two questions. How are we to interpret the inability of technical agencies to bring the Centralia fire under control? And what model of disaster impact can account for the stress-related response of the fire's victims?

First, let us consider the nature of a mine fire as a disaster agent. A mine fire is a very different sort of disaster than a tsunami (tidal wave), an earthquake, or a tornado. A tsunami hits a shoreline and recedes. The aftermath is frequently devastating, but survivors and relief workers can proceed to rebuild unencumbered with the need to abate the disaster agent itself. While it may be possible to predict a tsunami, nobody is expected to stop it. On the other hand, the Centralia mine fire, like the dioxin contamination of Times Beach, Missouri, was caused by human error, and human/technical intervention was required if control over the agent was to be achieved. Human beings started the Centralia mine fire, and human intervention was expected to control or abate the hazard.

Because a mine fire does not strike and recede, but continues to burn, advancing slowly but steadily through coal seams, the first and foremost problem for emergency response personnel is to control the fire. The official response, in other words, is less concerned with community relief and rehabilitation, and more intent on mitigating the hazardous conditions. Since advanced and expensive technological methods are needed to attempt to ameliorate the disaster agent, there is an unusually great reliance on state and federal governmental agencies to provide assistance.

Moreover, because the paramount issue is controllability, there is the tendency for the government to define chronic technological disasters as engineering puzzles rather than human (or social) problems, and to assign to technical agencies the lead role in managing the crisis. These agencies are staffed by engineers and other specialists who are used to tackling technological, not human, problems. Because mining engineers and geologists are likely to focus on definitions of situations that call for the skills and authority they possess, the personal, social and economic dimensions of the crises are likely to be underestimated.

This underestimation of the human toll of the mine fire is reflected in the fact that Centralia was never officially declared a disaster site. Nor were residents officially responded to as if they were victims. While the community may have been at a loss to collectively define its crisis, there was a consensus among state and federal officials that this was an engineering riddle, not a disaster, and was to be managed by technical, rather than social service, agencies. Ironically, however, a final technical solution to the fire eluded the specialists and assured that official information regarding the presence, extent and severity of the hazard was sufficiently vague or contradictory to legitimate (or at least not refute) the competing definitions of the crisis among residents.

Mainly, then, it was state and federal technical agencies which assumed responsibility for controlling the underground fire. There are three characteristics of these agencies which exacerbated the controlability problem and helped to produce the ineffective response and engender social conflict.

First, they are remote from Centralia. This is true in terms of geography, culture and power. Spatially distant, with norms, values and worldviews divergent from those of small coal towns, and with relatively enormous (but not unlimited) power, government agencies are unlikely to be sensitive to the needs and desires of small, politically weak communities. They are also liable to be perceived by community residents as uncaring and insensitive, thereby generating conflict between themselves and the communities they are mandated to assist.

These agencies are also bureaucratic. While a bureaucracy is governed by written rules and regulations, there are no laws or regulations, and few precedents, for dealing with chronic technological disasters. Therefore, the agencies are called upon to innovate, something bureacracies are not well suited to do. In following procedures designed for use in other types of situations, these agencies are even more prone than usual to be stifled by red tape and internal disagreements.

Finally, extra-local government power is decentralized, with a multitude of agencies at different governmental levels holding legislative responsibility in different policy areas. This decentralization greatly lessens governmental ability to implement policies effectively. In addition, the policies themselves are frequently unclear and conflicting concerning environmental issues. Given diffused power and authority, and adding to this the considerable expense involved in ameliorating a chronic technological disaster and aiding the affected population, agencies can be expected to differ among themselves concerning where responsibilities should lie.

Moreover, confronted with a technological problem containing many competing potential solutions, none of them certain, all of them expensive and with a hostile community, the agency response is liable to favor short-term problem management and containment, rather than long-term problem solution. Indeed, a primary agency goal might be to miminize political damage to the agency itself and to keep the outlay of public expenditures to a minimum.

These characteristics of the responding agencies, along with the fact that their focus is on attempting to control the fire through technical means, led to much hostility and lack of trust of the government by Centralia residents. A conceptual tool which helps us to understand the relationship between the problem of controllability and the intense psychosocial stresses experienced by Centralia residents is the disaster stage model.

When natural disasters are the cause of extreme environments, the unstructuring of routines and common coping modes typically begins with the warning stage, the apprehension that a calamity may occur.[2] By the threat stage, when there are unequivocal signs of the approaching disaster force, the extreme situation is under way. During impact, a maelstrom of flying debris or raging floods or towering walls of fire rip apart the last vestiges of "business as usual" in the full force of nature's wrath. The impact stage is temporally significant because it marks the most intense point in the disaster sequence, after which there may be considerable pain and grief but the destruction is over.

During the inventory and rescue stages immediately following impact, survivors begin to assess their losses and gradually piece together a picture of what has happened. Survivor groups emerge spontaneously—small, altruistic communities whose goals include treating the wounded, extinguishing fires, and freeing trapped victims. With the onset of the remedy stage, the extreme situation begins to subside, as outside relief agencies take control of the disaster scene and impose a formal structure (not always with the approval of the survivors) on the inventory and rescue stages. During the recovery stage, the extreme environment is replaced with either a reconstitution of the old structure or a modified pattern of personal and collective life.

Note that in this stage model, the time lapse between the warning, threat, impact, and inventory and rescue stages may be very brief—in some cases, only several minutes. The period most likely to be extended in time is the warning stage. The eruption of Washington State's Mount St. Helen's volcano in 1980, for example, had been anticipated for several weeks. The time lapse between the threat stage and the inventory-rescue, however, was less than an hour. The extreme environment created by natural disasters is typically short-lived, a horrendous moment in time bounded by two periods of stability—one historical, the other emergent. The customary sequence of stages in a natural disaster moves a community from order, to chaos, to the reconstitution of order. At that point, the disaster enters the collective memory, recalled only on those occasions deemed appropriate for remembering a shared experience of horror.

The type of extreme environment created by a chronic technological disaster (CTD) differs considerably from this description. The Centralia study and work on Love Canal[13] speak of a protracted, seemingly endless period of time between the discovery of the aversive agent and the realization that its worst consequences are past. There is no brief moment of terror, to be followed by an easily defined sequence of inventory, rescue, remedy, and recovery. Indeed, for many Centralians and residents of Love Canal, relief from fear came only when they were permanently removed from their homes and towns, a process that took several years.

CTD's tend to trap at least some of the population in the warning and threat stages of the model, freezing them in extended periods of apprehension and dread. A mine fire that moves slowly through accessible veins, or toxic chemicals that leach invisibly through underground swales, may at times give signals that danger is near, but the signals are frequently vague and open to dispute. Long-term exposure to warning and threat, particularly when distributed unevenly through the population, places severe demands on the coping resources of a settlement.

Occasionally, individuals or families feel the impact of the agent, in the form of subsidence, a chronic cough, or lassitude. But since the experience rarely extends beyond the person or the family, it is not likely to become the occasion for communal action. Indeed, the source of the threat—the reason that a family is always tired or a child or grandparent has upper respiratory trouble—is itself frequently vague to the point of inviting multiple interpretations. In other words, the impact of the CTD, to borrow a distinction from C.W. Mills, is more likely to remain a "trouble," a personal problem, than to become an "issue," a socially recognized occasion for communal response.[14]

Trapped by a CTD in the first two stages of the disaster cycle, a population is prevented from progressing to the point of reassembling itself into a complementary distribution of understandings and tasks. Any attempt at what we might call remedy and recovery are not humanistic efforts directed toward the affected population but technical activities aimed at disposing of the aversive agent. More likely than not, as we witnessed at Times Beach, Centralia, and Love Canal, remedial and recovery technology, however confounded by political game playing, will be unable to stop the advance of the disaster agent. Residents are rescued only be relocation, which does not allow the settlement to reestablish itself. The web of social positions woven by common understandings is ripped apart before there is an end to the severe social and ecological disruption.

The more the stages of warning and threat become institutionalized—that is, the more these normally temporary stages take on the character of permanence—the greater will be the toll on affected populations. A CTD does not create a moment between points of stability; rather, it imposes a fixed, seemingly permanent period of instability, a time within which conventional patterns of behavior no longer seem to work. Extended periods of ambiguous warning and threat cues destabilize a human settlement by rearranging the traditional pattern of social relationships.

In the end, it appears that the focus on controlability exacerbates a community's problems when dealing with a chronic technological disaster. It heightens the difficulties a community faces as it tries to move toward a resolution of the human and social disaster it confronts. By recognizing this problem, we hope that increasing attention will be given to non-technical dimensions of technological disasters and, in so doing, the social responses can lessen rather than increase human suffering in these unfortunate situations.

ACKNOWLEDGEMENT

This chapter is adapted from J. Stephen Kroll-Smith and Stephen R. Couch, 1991, *The Real Disaster Is Above Ground: A Mine Fire and Social Conflict*. The University Press of Kentucky, Lexington, KY.

REFERENCES

1. Kates, R.W. (Ed.) 1977. *Managing Technological Hazards: Research Needs and Opportunities*. University of Colorado, Institute of Behavioral Science, Boulder, CO, p. 250.
2. Mileti, Dennis S., Thomas E. Drabek and J. Eugene Haas. 1975. *Human Systems in Extreme Environments: A Sociological Perspective*. University of Colorado, Institute of Behavioral Science, Boulder, CO.
3. Smith, Elizabeth, Carol S. North and Paul C. Price. 1988. Response to Technological Accidents, pp. 52-95. In: Mary Lystad (Ed.) *Mental Health Response to Mass Emergencies*. Brunner/Mazel, New York, p. 60.
4. Baum, Andrew. 1987. Toxins, Technology and Natural Disasters, pp. 5-54. In: Gary Van den Bos and Brenda Bryant (Ed.) *Cataclysms, Crises and Catastrophes*. The American Psychological Association, Washington, DC.
5. Erikson, Kai T. 1976. Everything in its Path: Destruction of Community in the Buffalo Creek Flood. Simon and Schuster, New York.

6. Department of Community Affairs. 1983. *Acquisition/Relocation Survey: The Centralia Report.* The Commonwealth of Pennsylvania, Harrisburg, PA.
7. After 1981, technical efforts became centered on implementing an $850,000 borehole study, the results of which were presented in 1983 and led to the relocation of most of Centralia's residents.
8. The chronology of events is drawn mainly from issues of *The Shamokin News-Item* and from government reports and memoranda. A fully referenced chronology can be found in J. Stephen Kroll-Smith and Stephen Robert Couch. 1991. *The Real Disaster Is Above Ground: A Mine Fire and Social Conflict.* The University Press of Kentucky, Lexington, KY, pp. 29-42.
9. Gephart, Robert P. 1984. Making Sense of Organizationally Based Environmental Disasters. *Journal of Management* 19:205-225.
10. Baum, Andrew, Jerome E. Singer and Carlene S. Baum. 1981. Stress and Environment. *Journal of Social Issues* 37:25-26.
11. Lang, Kurt, and Gladys Engel Lang. 1964. Collective Responses to the Threat of Disaster, pp. 58-75. In: George H. Grosser, Henry Wechsler and Milton Greenblatt (Ed.) *The Threat of Impending Disaster.* MIT Press, Cambridge.
12. Chapman, Dwight A. 1962. A Brief Introduction to Contemporary Disaster Research, pp. 3-22. In: George W. Baker and Dwight W. Chapman (Ed.) *Man and Society in Disaster.* Basic Books, New York.
13. Levine, Adeline G. 1982. *Love Canal: Science, Politics and People.* Lexington Books, Lexington, MA.
14. C. Wright Mills. 1959. The Sociological Imagination. Oxford University Press, New York.

Natural and Technological Disasters: Causes, Effects and Preventive Measures. Edited by S.K. Majumdar, G.S. Forbes, E.W. Miller, and R.F. Schmalz. © 1992, The Pennsylvania Academy of Science.

Chapter Twenty-Seven

SAFER STUFF: NASA RESPONDS TO AEROSPACE ACCIDENTS

GREGORY S. FORBES

Department of Meteorology
The Pennsylvania State University
University Park, PA 16802

"On every flight there is a chance that something will go wrong."—Space Shuttle Operator's Manual [1]

INTRODUCTION

Virtually everyone in the United States has seen video or photographs of the explosion of the Space Shuttle Challenger on 28 January 1986 and has heard of the notorious O-rings which precipitated the catastrophe. This section, then, is not merely a case study of the Challenger accident. Rather, it is an overview of the problems in the Space Progam leading to, and in the aftermath of, the Challenger tragedy, and a presentation of various steps that have been taken to avoid future accidents in the space program. Additional detail is given regarding weather factors. Some might argue that the Challenger accident was not a disaster in that, unlike other disasters in this book, it did not directly affect the public welfare. However, an equally valid argument can be made that immeasurable damage was done to the United States' collective scientific and technological self-esteem by the event.

COMPONENTS OF THE SPACE SHUTTLE VEHICLE
AND THEIR FUNCTIONS

The Space Shuttle is a marvel of technology, comprised of seemingly countless numbers of individual parts forming three main components, as shown in Figure 1: orbiter, external tank (ET), and two solid rocket boosters (SRBs). The orbiter is an airplane-like vehicle consisting of three main engines (numbered 1-3 in Figure 1) and two reaction control and orbital maneuvering systems (RC) at the rear, the cargo bay at the center, and the crew compartment at the front. For launch, the orbiter is connected to the external tank which fuels the main engines with liquid oxygen (LOX, in front part of ET) and liquid hydrogen (LH, in rear). The SRBs attach to the sides of the ET and use a solid propellant (i.e., fuel). Together, the main engines and SRBs accelerate the vehicle upward during launch. The main engines can be controlled through regulation of the flow of LOX and LH to them. Once ignited, the SRBs burn until the fuel is all consumed. The reaction control and orbital maneuvering engines are smaller and provide thrust for attitude (orientation) corrections during flight and for orbital changes once the launch is complete.[2]

Once the SRBs have completed their task, small explosive charges disconnect them from the ET. The SRBs then drop on parachutes into the Atlantic Ocean, where they are picked up and prepared for use on a subsequent launch. Just before orbit is achieved, the main engines shut down and the ET is jettisoned away from the orbiter. The ET falls back toward earth and breaks into pieces upon re-entry. The orbital maneuvering engines then boost the Shuttle into its proper orbit and, after completion of the mission, nudge the Shuttle out of orbit and back toward earth. After re-entry, the orbiter follows a gliding path and lands like an airplane, normally on a dry lakebed at Edwards Air Force Base in California (EDW), or on a runway at EDW or Kennedy Space Center (KSC), Florida. There are a number of emergency landing sites around the world. Unless the orbiter lands at KSC, it is flown back to the KSC launch facility piggy-back-style atop a Shuttle Carrier jet aircraft.[2]

The ET is filled on the launch pad. The SRBs are built from a stack of individual "canisters" filled with solid propellant at a manufacturing plant and shipped on railroad cars to KSC, where they are stacked atop one another and bolted together. An individual canister is shaped much like a roll of toilet paper—except for solid propellant in place of paper. The hot combustion gases flow down the hollow central tube and provide upward thrust as they exit the aft (rear) portion of the SRB. "Cans" made of 3/4-inch-thick metal surround the propellant to form the outer sides of the canisters. The top and bottom edges of the sides of the SRB canisters are designed to fit together in a tang and clevis (male-female) configuration (Figure 2), comprising the metal parts of a "field" joint. Bolt-like "pins" are inserted through the field joint (i.e., a joint assembled at KSC rather than at the factory) at 2.6-inch intervals around the circumference of the joint to connect adjacent canisters of the SRB.

The field joint also contains a pair of O-rings. A cross section of a small portion of the right SRB field joint is shown in Figure 3, representing the side of the SRB facing the ET. The O-rings look like small circles in the cross section, 0.28 inches in diameter, but are three-dimensional basketball hoop-shaped rings that encircle the SRB within the field joint. Their function is to block any narow gap (typically 0.004 inches wide at the time of ignition) resulting from imperfect fits of the tang of one canister into the clevis of the adjacent canister, thereby preventing leakage of hot or burning gases. Putty is used to fill gaps between insulation materials with the joints.[3]

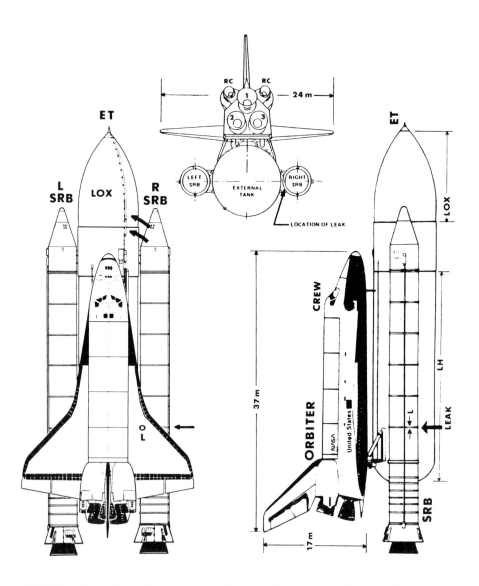

FIGURE 1. Views of the major components of the Space Shuttle at time of launch, when vehicle is pointed upward. At left, view from orbiter side; center, from below; right, from right side. "L" on right diagram depicts position of leak in a joint of the right solid rocket booster (SRB), on the side of the SRB facing the external tank (center diagram) near the location of the lower strut connection, and beneath the orbiter at position "o" of the left diagram. LOX and LH indicate liquid oxygen and liquid hydrogen portions of the external tank, respectively. Pair of curved arrows on left diagram indicate collision of SRB with external tank during Challenger accident. On center diagram, numbers indicate main engines on orbiter; RC indicates reaction control and orbital maneuvering systems.[3,7]

THE CHALLENGER EXPLOSION AND OTHER ACCIDENTS

The immediate cause of the Challenger accident was that two O-rings in the right solid rocket booster (SRB; Figure 1 center) did not perform their intended function. The details of the failure may not be as well known. During ignition, the SRB joints are flexed, causing the gaps to widen to about 0.029". The O-rings have diameter large enough that under normal conditions they are still wide enough to block the widened gap and prevent escape of hot gases further into the joint. The implication of this design is that prior to ignition the O-rings are compressed (flattened between tang and clevis parts), and must "rebound" to a more circular diameter as the gap widens (Figure 3). However, temperatures on 28 January were much colder (by almost 13 °C) than on any previous launch, and engineers at Morton Thiokol, the joint manufacturer, were concerned that the O-rings and putty would be too stiff to react properly. Their concern was heightened because they knew that on 7 of the previous 24 launches there had been detectable O-ring ero-

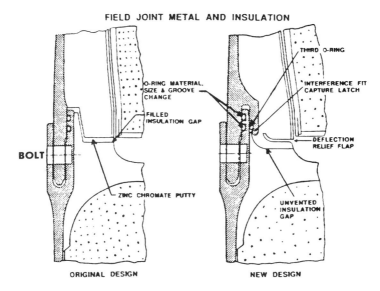

FIELD JOINT METAL AND INSULATION

THIRD O-RING

O-RING MATERIAL,
SIZE & GROOVE
CHANGE

INTERFERENCE FIT
CAPTURE LATCH

FILLED
INSULATION GAP

DEFLECTION
RELIEF FLAP

BOLT

ZINC CHROMATE PUTTY

UNVENTED
INSULATION
GAP

ORIGINAL DESIGN   NEW DESIGN

FIGURE 2. Cross-section through the field joint at the location shown in Figure 1 (center diagram): design before accident (left) and post-Challenger improved design (right). Shaded areas are metal parts of joint, where side "walls" of adjacent canisters of the SRB are bolted together in a tang (upper canister) and clevis (lower canister, horeshoe shape) connection. Dotted regions represent propellant inside SRB. Unshaded areas are insulation material. Small circles are O-rings intended to block narrow gap between metal pieces; putty originally filled gap between insulation materials of upper and lower canisters. In new design, both canister walls have horseshoe shape in connecting region, putty has been eliminated, and a third O-ring added![1]

sion indicative of hot gases blowing by them, reflecting joint design problems that might be worsened by unprecedentedly cold temperatures. Unfortunately, the engineering concerns were not passed along to higher-level NASA officials making the launch decision.[3]

The leak developed about 30 cm away from one of the struts which connect the right SRB to the external tank, a position where flexing of the joint, and gap widening, would be maximized. In combination, this position was one where the pre-ignition gap was likely to have been minimized, and the metal tang and clevis could have been touching. The latter situation arose because on this occasion the sides of the SRB canisters were not perfectly circular, so that in fitting the tang and clevis parts together there were larger-than-average gaps at some locations and smaller gaps at others. Further, the leak developed at a shadowed spot, where the lack of sunlight may have kept the joint colder than elsewhere around the SRB. Initially compressed to a near-zero gap, the cold-stiffened O-rings did not "rebound" fast enough to seal the widened gap, allowing hot combustion gases to blow through the joint. Investigators felt that ice in the joint may have contributed to the failure of the second O-ring, as there had been about 7 inches of rain at KSC since the spacecraft had been moved to the launch pad on 21 December 1985, and temperatures were below freezing. There was considerable ice on the mobile launch structure on the morning of 28 January 1986, and a team was dispatched to inspect the vehicle and remove ice that could potentially have broken free and damaged the spacecraft.[3]

As a consequence of the failed O-rings, a jet of hot gases emerged through the joint 0.678 seconds after ignition. This was evidenced by a plume of smoke in film records of the launch, visible until 3.375 sec. No further evidence of a leak could be seen (though the leak was sometimes hidden from view), or detected in data measuring SRB performance, for about 55 seconds. Investigators feel that the gap may have temporarily been plugged by the damaged O-rings or with soot from the O-rings or putty. Between 37 and 62 seconds after ignition, the spacecraft underwent attitude (heading and orientation) excursions, some a planned part of the launch and some in response to strong sudden variations in the wind. Wind-induced stresses at about 55-59 and 66-68 seconds exceeded those previously encountered, but were less than the spacecraft was built to withstand and, hence, did not directly cause the SRB or external tank to crack or develop a leak. However, investigators felt that the maneuvers in response to sudden wind variations may have further widened the gap in the joint and enhanced gas blow-by. Maximum stresses were experienced at about 59 seconds.[3]

At about 58.8 seconds a flame emerged from the leaking SRB joint. The flame is believed to have had a blow torch effect on the external tank (ET) at the location where the SRB strut connected to the ET (Figure 1), breaching the side of the ET (64.66 sec), causing a hydrogen leak and allowing the strut and rear portion of the right SRB to break free from the ET (72.2 sec). These events precipitated the ultimate explosion.[3]

The succeeding events, as concluded by examination of flight data, photographic records, and recovered Shuttle debris,[3] included an uncontrolled release of hyrdogen

(66.8-72.6 sec) which created forward accelerations that tended to crush and weaken the portions of the ET ahead of the leak. The freed right SRB was thrust against the upper portion of the ET (Figure 1), triggering an oxygen leak (73 sec) and initiating a fireball of uncontrolled, explosive combustion of oxygen and hydrogen (73.2 sec). The freed right SRB also struck the underside of the right wing of the orbiter, perhaps contributing to the breakup of the orbiter. Finally, the fuel in the reaction control and orbital maneuvering systems was ignited (74.5 sec), accelerating the orbiter and breaking it free of the fireball surrounding the ET. The crew compartment broke away from the orbiter and began a fatal plunge to the ocean below. The capsule is believed to have struck the water 3-4 minutes later while travelling at a speed of 333 km/h, resulting in forces that were about 200 g in magnitude, and killing any of the 7 astronauts who survived the explosion and crew compartment depressurization.[3]

The only other astronaut fatalities in the United States' space program occurred during a launch pad fire on 27 January 1967, killing all 3 aboard the Apollo spacecraft. Following the Challenger accident, however, a series of accidents compounded the crisis to include the United States unmanned space program. A Titan 340 rocket exploded during launch in April, 1986, followed a month later by a Delta rocket that veered off course and had to be destroyed by range safety officials (by triggering explosive devices on the spacecraft, to protect nearby population). In March, 1987 an Atlas Centaur rocket was launched into clouds and rain, and triggered lightning strokes which caused the spacecraft to veer off course, requiring its destruction. Until the causes of these accidents could be determined and eliminated, the United States was left temporarily with no operational space launch capabilities. In May, 1988, the Pacific Engineering and Production Company suffered a fire and explosion, reducing by half the world's capability to manufacture SRB propellants. A number of other problems, notably those which delayed subsequent Shuttle launches, further focused media scrutiny on the space program.

It should be pointed out that other space agencies have also experienced accidents. The Soviet space program has had fatalities. The European Space Agency endured the 1990 explosion of an Ariane rocket. Several commercial launch attempts have failed since that industry began in the United States in 1989.

THE AFTERMATH OF THE ACCIDENTS

Following the Challenger tragedy, numerous expert panels were empowered to review and assess various aspects of the space program. The author served as a member of the National Research Council Panel on Meteorological Support for the Space Program, and is currently a member of an interagency Joint Working Group for Weather Support to NASA. A great deal of the material dealing with meteorological support problems and needs has been covered in the NRC Panel report.[4] However, this chapter is not being written under the auspices of those panels, and addresses issues beyond their purviews. In regard to these other topics, heavy reference above has been made to the Report of the President's Commission on the Space Shuttle Challenger Accident[3] (generally cited in the media as the "Rogers

Commission"; named after its chairman) and, in the material to follow, to NASA reports to Congress, and to NASA press releases (not specifically cited).

Following numerous Space Shuttle modifications and tests, launches resumed in September, 1988, and there have been 16 successful post-Challenger Shuttle missions through early June 1991. However, the space program is one in which there

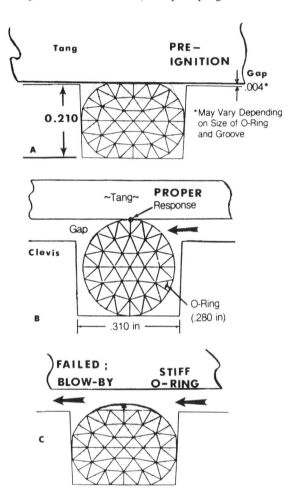

FIGURE 3. Detailed examination of the field joint of Figure 2, demonstrating (A) the pre-ignition and (B) proper post-gap-widening configurations of the O-rings following ignition, and (C) the nature of the O-ring failure thought to have occurred during the launch of Space Shuttle Challenger on 28 January 1986. A non-circularity of the SRB canisters forced the tang-clevis gap to narrow to nearly zero width prior to ignition (i.e., even narrower than in A), and caused maximum compression of the O-rings. As the tang-clevis gap widened following ignition, cold-stiffened O-rings did not return to circularity quickly enough to close the gap, allowing hot gases to penetrate the joint (arrows in C).[3]

are clearly great risks. Manned United States spacecraft have spent a total of about 25,000 hours in space from 1961 through early June 1991, with one fatal accident and 7 fatalities (excluding the Apollo pre-launch accident). If this accident rate were to continue, the number of fatal accidents per million spacecraft hours would be 40, about 2.5 times that of general aviation, 10 times that of commuter airlines, an 130 times that of major airlines.[5]

Space flight risk can be minimized but not eliminated, and added safety measures mean increased costs. Such costs must be weighed against available resources and the need to complete a mission. In this age of robotics, decisions to use manned or unmanned space vehicles must also be made, though it must be pointed out that astronauts are volunteers, aware from the start (see the quote commencing this chapter) that they could face the dire consequences of becoming lost in space or killed in an accident. To put these issues in context, it is necessary to briefly review the history of the space program.

FACTORS IN THE EVOLUTION OF THE SPACE SHUTTLE PROGRAM

The origins of the space program which put Americans on the moon were part scientific adventuresome spirit and partly cold-war era competitiveness, pride and patriotism. The Space Shuttle has grown up in quite a different climate. Rather than a scientific showcase in a competitive space race, the Shuttle was billed as the routine transportation system of the future. Thus, NASA's world became far more cruel, as its mission became one of economic enterprise rather than scientific and engineering challenge. With this change of emphasis, a conflict between economic cost and astronaut safety became more likely.[3]

At the time of its conception, the Space Shuttle was not intended to be a scientific showpiece. NASA considered the real showpiece a Space Station community, with the Shuttle merely a vehicle by which humans and material would be transported to and from the Space Station. Funding decisions, however, delayed the showpiece Space Station and NASA proceeded with the Shuttle component, referred to officially (until 1990) as the National Space Transportation System. As the default showpiece, the Shuttle has not enjoyed unbridled support from the scientific community.[6]

Perhaps to recent Presidents and Congress, the Space Program had become little more than just another Federal program, as NASA's fractional share of tax dollars decreased nearly each year from 1964 to 1986, despite NASA's commitment to an increasing flight rate. Demands to meet schedules in the face of procurement delays reduced the number of test flights as new systems were acquired or changes made. Increased flight rate meant heavier demands on a fixed number of flight simulators and, hence, a decreased amount of simulator training time per astronaut. Spare parts became a luxury, and engineers resorted to cannibalizing one Shuttle vehicle in order to equip another. Reusable vehicles necessitated complicated landing systems continually in need of maintenance or repair. Between launches, the 30,000 thermal tiles (each different) had to be inspected and possibly replaced. Manpower did not expand to meet the accelerated launch schedule, and long hours ensued. To meet the schedule, employees had to work in a frenzy between launches; job fatigue became a major problem. Federal salary caps meant attrition of top managers, aggravating the problem. This was the cold reality of the Space Program in January, 1986, enmeshed in political, economic, and scientific compromise.[3]

In such an austere setting, the safety program suffered. Most personnel with safety-related responsibilities at KSC and at the Johnson and Marshall Space Centers reported to supervisors in charge of Shuttle processing (who, therefore, had vested interests in meeting deadlines), so that inspections were not truly independent. The Chief Engineer at NASA headquarters, with a staff of 20, dedicated two persons part-time to safety matters. One of them worked quarter-time on quality control, and the other spent 10% of his time on flight safety matters.[3] Considering that a single flawed part on the Shuttle could prove catastrophic, they must have been overwhelmed. Using NASA's terminology for this type of part, there were over 700 parts on the Shuttle that were criticality 1 at the time of the Challenger tragedy,[7] and more than 2300[7,8] that were either criticality 1 or 1R (the latter meaning that a redundant part was built into the system, but that if both the primary and backup systems failed, the Shuttle could be destroyed).

From a risk standpoint, it could be argued that if ever a machine was designed to verify Murphy's Law, the Shuttle was it. That 40 flights prior to and after the Challenger accident have resulted in only a few really worrisome situations is probably a testament to how carefully the inherently dangerous Shuttles are built. In the pre-Challenger era, some NASA officials felt the chance of a catastrophic failure was as low as 1 in 100,000.[3] A post-Challenger study estimated it was more like 1/70 to 1/80.[9] As a result of critical item reviews following the Challenger accident, the number of criticality 1 and 1R items rose to more than 4600 by late 1987.[8]

The information-flow and decision-making processes at NASA came under intense scrutiny following the Challenger tragedy. Besides the O-ring problems that were not communicated far enough up the chain of command, the Challenger was launched despite other adverse conditions on 28 January 1986. Ice on the vehicle and launch platform were concerns that have already been described. The "go" decision was made while the ships that recover the SRBs were in a battle for survival in gale conditions over the western Atlantic. Procedures at the time allowed program component managers or the launch director to issue "waivers" to negate automatic delays that would have been imposed due to certain constraints, and waivers were not infrequent.

STEPS TO RECOVERY

NASA has conscientiously addressed the various concerns raised by the numerous panels, and has made many improvements in a relatively short period of time. The Rogers Commission[3] made 9 recommendations to the President, concerning: (1) solid rocket motor joint redesign, (2) Shuttle management, (3) critical item review and hazard analysis, (4) safety, (5) improved communication, (6) landing safety, (7) launch abort and crew escape, (8) flight rate, (9) maintenance safegurds. Even before the recommendations were delivered to the President on 9 June, NASA had in most cases taken steps toward remedying the problems, and steps were taken to

address each recommendation by late 1986. Initial steps typically involved creating an expert team to study the problem and recommend actions to be taken.[10]
It is beyond the scope of this article to indicate each of the actions taken. However, the NASA commitment to improved safety is extremely evident. Based upon known concerns and others uncovered during the recommended critical item review, more than 400 changes were made to the Shuttle. These included 145 to the solid rocket boosters, 39 changes to the Space Shuttle main engines (including new high-pressure oxidizer turbopumps), and 220 changes to the orbiter, including improved thermal tiles. SRB changes included a redesign of the shape and components of the field joints (Figure 2), eliminating the putty and adding a third O-ring, a deflection relief flap that will help force the joint gaps closed, and a heating strip around the outside of the joint. Orders have been placed for an advanced solid rocket motor (delivery 1994), designed to eliminate about 175 criticality 1 or 1R failure modes and allow an increased payload. New computers were acquired for the orbiter and main engine units, along with new portable lap-top computers used in scientific tasks. (Citations for each change described will not be given, as these were normally in the form of NASA press releases. A general reference is [9].)
Landing is generally conceded to be a risky part of a Shuttle mission. Changes to improve braking and control include new landing gears, new carbon brakes, and a drag shute to take some of the load off the braking system. A new orbiter transport vehicle has been acquired to carry the orbiter from the orbiter processing facility to the vehicle assembly building where it is connected to the external tank and SRBs, thus avoiding the wear on the tires when the orbiter is moved on its own wheels. The runway at the KSC landing facility has been ground down and regrooved to reduce tire wear.
A crew escape package has been developed. An escape pole has been added to the orbiter, so that if a critical situation occurs while the orbiter is in (or can quickly be placed in) a gliding flight the crew can bail out and parachute to the surface. The astronauts receive in-orbit medical consultation. New extra-vehicular activity suits have been obtained. Weather protection systems have been installed at both Shuttle launch pads (39A and 39B), that offer protection against lightning and stabilize the spacecraft against winds. Both pads are now equipped with an emergency escape system, consisting of baskets on each of 7 cables in which the crew can slide from the orbiter to the ground in case of a launch pad emergency, and take refuge in one of 3 underground bunkers. A safety net beneath the cables protects against falls, and a lightning arrestor wire above offers a cone of protection during the slide. A sound suppression water system has been installed at the launch pads to protect the orbiter and adjacent areas from acoustic energy and rocket exhaust during blast-off. An engine deluge system is intended to prevent fires on the launch pad. At least 138 modifications were made to pad 39A to bring it back to operational status.
Many other changes have been made, or are in progress. A fourth orbiter, Endeavor, has been assembled to replace Challenger, easing schedule pressures. A second Shuttle carrier aircraft has been acquired for transport of the orbiters from their normal landing site at Edwards Air Force Base to KSC. Had an accident

befallen the single carrier, the Shuttle fleet could have been forced to land at KSC or be stranded at EDW. Two additional trans-Atlantic emergency landing sites have been acquired, at Ben Guerir, Morocco, and Banjul, the Gambia (augmenting Zaragoza and Moron, Spain). Personnel have been reassigned and new positions have been created to enhance safety and improve management.

One of the specific aspects of recommendation 3 above was the creation of a National Research Council Committee on Shuttle Criticality Review and Hazard Analysis Audit. One of the findings of that committee was that qualitative information was often used in NASA decision making and that there was a need for determination of *quantitative* measures of risk. A similar finding was made with regard to weather factors.[4] NASA managers make a valid point, however, when they indicate that statistical analyses are not necessarily straightforward. While it would seem that the total risk would be the sum of the probabilities of failure of each of the 700-plus (independent) criticality 1 parts, the probabilities of failure of the individual parts are hard to define accurately without extensive testing, since their failure rate is expected to be on the order of 1/100,000. Second, 40-50% of the motor defects, for example, are due to workmanship flaws, which are not necessary random. Further, the probability of triggering a fatal accident is not equal for each criticality 1 item. In fact, 56 criticality 1 items failed without loss of life on flights prior to the Challenger accident![8]

Given the inaccuracies of risk assessment, it is difficult to be sure that the priority list for making improvements to the Space Shuttle system is in the proper sequence. Hence, some managers and observers felt that modifications to the Space Shuttle main engine should take precedence over development of an advanced solid rocket motor, for example. Those problems generally felt most urgent have been addressed, as cited above. With regard to weather factors, as discussed subsequently, the post-Challenger response has been to increase the number of launch constraints so that launches are prevented in virtually any potentially catastrophic weather situation. That approach could not be taken with regard to criticality 1 parts, for it would take years before they all could be eliminated through redesign. Thus, considerable risk remains. However, the launch decision process is now more cautious, and steps have been taken to formalize into launch constraints a number of factors which were previously not quantified. These involve several atmospheric factors, including electric field strength, discussed subsequently.

WEATHER AND THE SPACE PROGRAM

One facet of space operations acknowledged as an operational problem by all astronauts is the weather at Cape Canaveral, which can change rapidly and seemingly unpredictably due to its immediate proximity to the ocean. The paragraphs below indicate weather elements of concern to various aspects of the space program, problems in dealing with these elements during launch decision making, and steps that have been taken to reduce or eliminate risk associated with these weather factors. Weather rules for launch have been upgraded (Table 1). Perhaps as a consequence, there have been 15 delays or scrubs (rescheduling to subsequent day) in

18 launches following the Challenger accident, as opposed to 9 in the 25 missions up to and including the final Challenger launch.

During thunderstorms, but also in some non-thunderstorm situations, clouds develop a net charge different from that of the ground. Normally the atmosphere is a poor electrical conductor, and no electrical current is able to pass between cloud and ground. If the rate of charge generation in the cloud is great enough, however, the air ceases to be an insulator and lightning (a tremendous electrical current passing through the atmosphere) results. Since KSC is in one of the areas of the world most frequently struck by lightning, steps must be taken to ground and shield sophisticated electronic equipment from lightning and power surges. Because of the presence of highly volatile fuels, lightning poses a serious safety hazard at the launch site at all times, not merely on launch days. When lightning threatens, personnel must move to shelter.

The problem of cloud electrification goes beyond the cloud-to-ground lightning threat. During launch in an electric field insufficient to yield natural cloud-to-ground lightning, the rocket carries a surface-type net change upward toward the in-cloud charge center. As the separation of the cloud and rocket charge centers decreases, the insulation capacity of the air (technically called the "breakdown potential") may be exceeded. The ensuing lightning stroke between cloud and rocket is called *triggered* lightning, and poses a range of hazards to the rocket and its contents. An unmanned Atlas-Centaur spacecraft was struck by triggered lightning in March, 1987. The lightning current damaged the on-board computer system, initiating a change of heading by the spacecraft which sent it toward a populated area. In such situations, as in this case, authorities must explode the spacecraft before it can harm the community.

To address the problem of triggered lightning, NASA has taken a number of steps. Several types of measurement systems were already in existence at Kennedy Space Center (KSC) at the time of the Challenger tragedy which made various measurements of lightning and electric field strength. However, readings from these systems were not a part of the launch decision process. Readings from a network of electric field mills, which measure the electric field strength at the surface, are now used in the launch decision, and manned launches are postponed if unusually large readings are occurring. Several networks of lightning sensors operate over and surrounding KSC, that detect electromagnetic emissions from lightning and use triangulation methods to determine the location of the stroke. A launch is now postponed if there is lightning detected in or moving toward the vicinity of KSC. In addition, NASA has conducted tests using instrumented small rockets to try to determine minimum values of surface electric field strength in which a launched rocket will trigger lightning, and has conducted an airborne field mill program to investigate the safety of the new lightning-related launch constraint criteria. An advanced field mill network is to be acquired and installed in 1992 to improve measurements of the electric field values.

Strong winds and especially strong wind shears (i.e., vertical variations of wind direction or speed) potentially pose a hazard to launched spacecraft. Unexpected wind conditions could send the rocket and spacecraft off course during launch or, far worse, cause sufficient torque on the rockets or spacecraft to cause structural failure. The torque experienced by the Challenger as it encountered a strong shear layer may have aggravated or accelerated the structural problems initiated by the failed O-ring.[3] The on-board computer of the Space Shuttle is programmed for a flight through a climatological mean wind profile, and the space vehicle (Shuttle plus rockets and fuel tanks) is designed to withstand the stresses and torques exerted by winds and wind shears within an expected range of departures from the climatological profile. When unexpected wind conditions are encountered, the on-board computer initiates an attitude (heading or orientation) adjustment that will reduce stress on the space vehicle. Thus, the computerized navigation of the spacecraft does not formally take into consideration winds measured in real time just before launch. Instead, the spacecraft senses and is able to adjust for, within limits, the winds and shears it encounters. [Note added in proof: system upgrades in 1991 now allow use of day-of-launch winds in the on-board computer.]

Measurements are taken to try to ensure that the winds and wind shears along the flight path do not exceed the range of expected values in which the space vehicle can "self-adjust". Weather balloons are sent aloft a few hours prior to launch, and their winds used in a computer program to determine the "loads" (stresses, torques) that would be experienced by the space vehicle. If the program indicates excessive load, then the launch is delayed. Recognizing that weather systems move, and that observations taken 3h earlier above KSC might not be representative of conditions overhead during launch, the NRC Panel[4] recommended that winds be measured immediately before the launch and worked into the launch constraint criteria. A Doppler wind profiler was recommended: a device that can "continuously" and remotely monitor wind conditions overhead (by tracking the drift of small eddies having variations of refractive index along their edges). A wind profiling system designed specially for the needs of the space program was acquired and installed and is being worked into the constraint procedure. A Doppler weather radar is being installed at Melbourne, Florida that will monitor wind and precipitation in the region surrounding KSC.

Table 1 lists the launch constraints posed by various weather phenomena. Further, because the spacecraft might encounter problems and need to return to launch site or land at one of the Trans-Atlantic sites, launches cannot proceed unless *landing* conditions are satisfactory at several sites. Lists similar to Table 1 also exist for landings, in which emphasis is also placed upon having sufficiently high visibility and ceiling (cloud base height) for the commander to land the orbiter safely. In addition to factors similar to those for launch, excessive surface wind speeds, cross-runway wind components, and turbulent gusts must be avoided in order to minimize landing difficulties. Rain must be avoided to prevent damage to thermal tiles on the orbiter. Standing water, slush, snow, and ice on runways must also be avoided. Short-term forecasts (90 minutes prior to landing) are the basis for deciding whether to land, to continue in orbit, or select an alternate landing site if adverse conditions are predicted at the primary landing site.

Weather observations and forecasts are also a factor in determining whether or not the orbiter can be flown back to KSC from a landing at EDW. Thunderstorms,

TABLE 1

Weather constraints to Space Shuttle Launch from Kennedy Space Center[1]

Ambient Temperature:
(1) Loading of cryogenic propellants into the External Tank shall not be initiated if the average temperature for the preceding 24 hours has been below 41°F.
(2) The countdown shall not be continued nor the Shuttle launched if the ambient temperature exceeds certain criteria for a period of more than 30 minutes: (a) greater than 99°F, (b) below 37°F when wind speeds are at least 5 knots, or (c) below 47°F when wind speeds are below 5 knots.

Precipitation:
(1) The Shuttle will not be launched if precipitation (visible rain, virga, or radar precipitation echo) exists in the flight path. (Virga is precipitation not reaching the ground.)
(2) The Shuttle will not be launched if there is a sufficiently thick ice buildup on certain areas of the External Tank (where ice that broke off would impact and possibly damage the Orbiter thermal protection system).

Surface (20m) Winds:
(1) Sustained winds must not be more than 22 kts.
(2) Peak gust must not be more than 34 kts.

Winds Aloft: the Shuttle will not be launched into wind conditions that would yield loads (stresses on the Shuttle) exceeding those the Shuttle was designed to withstand.

Natural and Triggered Lightning:
(1) The Shuttle will not be launched if any type of lightning is detected within 10 nautical miles of the launch site or planned flight path within 30 minutes prior to launch, unless the meteorological condition that produced the lightning has moved more than 10 nautical miles away from the launch site and planned flight path.
(2) The Shuttle will not be launched into (a) cumulus clouds with tops at altitudes where temperatures are colder than 5°C, (b) through or within 5 n. mi. of cumulus clouds with tops at altitudes where temperatures are colder than $-10°C$, (c) through or within 10 n. mi. of cumulus clouds with tops at altitudes where temperatures are colder than $-20°C$, or (d) through or within 10 n. mi. of the nearest edge of any cumulonimbus or thunderstorm cloud or associated anvil.
(3) The Shuttle will not be launched if, within the 15 minutes prior to launch, the one-minute average of absolute electric field intensity at the ground exceeds 1 kilovolt per m within 5 n. mi. of the launch site unless: (a) there are no clouds within 10 n. mi. of the launch site or (b) smoke or ground fog is causing the abnormal readings.
(4) The Shuttle will not be launched if the planned flight path is through a vertically continuous layer of clouds[2] at least 4500 feet thick that intercepts the layer where temperatures are between 0 and $-20°C$.
(5) The Shuttle will not be launched if the planned flight path is into or within 5 n. mi. of clouds having temperatures at or below 0°C and associated with disturbed weather.
(6) The Shuttle will not be launched into thunderstorm debris clouds, or within 5 nautical miles of thunderstorm debris clouds unless a field mill network shows they have low electric field intensity or radar shows they have reflectivity factor less than 10 dbZ.

[1]As of March, 1991; these constraints shall not be waived. (paraphrased from "NASA Launch Commit Criteria and Background")
[2]*Definitions:*
Cloud layer: any broken or overcast cloud layer or layers connected by cloud elements, e.g. turrets from one cloud layer to another.
Disturbed weather: any meteorological phenomenon producing precipitation of at least moderate intensity.
Planned flight path: trajectory of the flight vehicle from the launch pad through its flight until at least 100,000 feet, varying by up to $+/-0.5$ n. mi. horizontally up to an altitude of 25,000 feet.

TABLE 1 *(continued)*

---

[2]*Definitions:*

Cumulonimbus cloud: any convective cloud having top at level where temperature is $< -20°C$

Debris cloud: any cloud layer other than a thin fibrous layer that has become detached from the parent cumulonimbus within 3 hours prior to launch.

Anvil: stratiform or fibrous cloud produced by the upper-level outflow from thunderstorms. Anvil debris does not meet the definition if it is optically transparent.

---

turbulence, clouds and rain must be avoided both during daytime flight and on overnight stays. In addition, weather plays a role in various daily decisions. In addition to lightning, high winds prevent many operations involving work on scaffolding or movement of the upright space vehicle. Low-level wind forecasts and observations are needed to plan evacuations in the event of a toxic release. Thus, accurate forecasts enhance safety, but over-cautious forecasts yield lost man-hours.

An Applied Meteorology Unit has been established at KSC to try to improve the process of observing, monitoring and predicting the weather elements critical to the space program. Thunderstorm forecasting studies were initiated with the National Severe Storms Laboratory of the National Oceanic and Atmospheric Administration (parent agency of the National Weather Service). Buoys have been added offshore of KSC to collect surface observations there, including optical measurement of rainfall. A local-area small-scale numerical forecast model has been investigated for use in forecasting for the KSC area. A Joint Working Group for Weather Support to NASA has been formed to advise NASA on evolving technological and meteorological capabilities of potential benefit to KSC and the space program that could be implemented in the future.

CONCLUDING REMARKS

In conclusion, NASA (and other agencies involved) have made a tremendous effort to improve the safety and quality of the space program. Hundreds of changes have already been enacted, and others are ongoing. A major change of policy has arisen, dictating that NASA will continue with manned and unmanned (expendable) launch programs rather than relying solely on the Space Shuttle. The Teacher-in-Space program, put on hold after the Challenger tragedy, has been postponed through at least the end of 1991. At present the United States space program is again fully operational, with 8-12 Shuttle flights planned for 1992. As for the future, the progress toward absolute spaceflight safety and full exploitation of space depends largely on the priority and resources which the United States, and other countries, assign to their space programs.

Despite the improvements, the Space Shuttle is still acknowledged to be a very risky form of space transportation.[9] Many criticality 1 items have yet to be eliminated, due to a combination of funding, manpower, and facility limitations, in conjunction with a need to, first, resume launches and then accelerate the rate of launches. The launch schedule still requires that three vehicles be worked on simultaneously, and there is concern that a fourth vehicle and accelerated launch schedule will deteriorate safety and maintenance measures to their pre-Challenger levels. However, indications are that NASA Space Shuttle program managers are now more attuned than before to the problems and are more informed about the safety ramifications of operational and longer-term planning decisions. The can-do spirit typified in the movie "The Right Stuff" has, perhaps, given way to a more realistic and cautious approach, that might be termed the "safer stuff."

REFERENCES

1. Joels, K.M., G.P. Kennedy and D. Larkin. 1982. *The Space Shuttle Operator's Manual*. Ballantine Books, NY. Citation lists the opening words of Chapter 4, "Emergency Procedures."
2. NASA. 1989. *Countdown! NASA Launch Vehicles and Facilities, Information Summaries PMS 018-A* (KSC). July 1989, 25 pp.
3. Rogers, W.P., Chairman, Presidential Commission on the Space Shuttle Challenger Accident. 1986. *Report of the Presidential Commission on the Space Shuttle Challenger Accident*, 5 volumes. Washington, DC, 1702 pp.
4. Hosler, C.L. Chairman, Panel on Meteorological Support for Space Operations. 1988. *Meteorological Support for Space Operations: Review and Recommendations*. National Research Council, National Academy Press, Washington, DC, 77 pp.
5. Federal Aviation Administration. 1989. *F.A.A. Statistical Handbook of Aviation*. Gov't. Printing Off. Washington, DC, 132 pp.
6. Logsdon, J.M. 1986. The Space Shuttle program: A policy failure? *Science, 232*, 30 May 1986, 1099-1105.
7. Committee on Science and Technology, House of Representatives, June 10-25. 1986. *Investigation of the Challenger Accident, Hearings, Volume 1* (No. 137). Gov't. Printing Off. Washington, DC, 774 pp.
8. Slay, A.D., Chairman, Committee on Shuttle Criticality Review and Hazard Analysis Audit. 1988. *Post-Challenger Evaluation of Space Shuttle Risk Assessment and Management*. National Academy Press. Washington, DC, 144 pp.
9. U.S. House of Representatives. 1989. *Review of the Aerospace Safety Advisory Panel Report for NASA Fiscal Year 1990 Authorization*. Hearing before the Subcommittee on Space Science and Applications of the Committee on Science, Space, and Technology, 101st Congress, First Session, September 28, 1989 (No. 69). Gov't Printing Off. Washington, DC, 110 pp.
10. Fletcher, J.C., Administrator. 1986. *Report to the President: Actions to Implement the Recommendations of the Presidential Commission on the Space Shuttle Accident*. National Aeronautics and Space Administration. Washington, DC, 51 pp.
11. Committee on Commerce, Science, and Transportation, United States Senate, January 22, 1987: *Space Shuttle Oversight Hearing*. Govt. Printing Off. Washington, DC, 167 pp.

Natural and Technological Disasters: Causes, Effects and Preventive Measures. Edited by S.K. Majumdar, G.S. Forbes, E.W. Miller, and R.F. Schmalz. © 1992, The Pennsylvania Academy of Science.

Chapter Twenty-Eight

THE NUCLEAR ENERGY INDUSTRY: CATASTROPHE OR SALVATION?

E. WILLARD MILLER

Professor of Geography and
Associate Dean for Resident Instruction (Emeritus)
The Pennsylvania State University
University Park, PA 16802

INTRODUCTION

The use of nuclear raw materials to produce energy began in 1957 when the first reactor at Shippingport, Pennsylvania, began operation. At that time nuclear power was hailed as a cheap, clean, efficient and safe energy source in the world. It was thought that nuclear power would replace the traditional fossil fuels in the production of electricity in a few years. As a consequence, the 1960s and early 1970s witnessed rapid development of nuclear energy throughout the world.

As the general public became aware of the potential health hazards from radiation, the acceptance of nuclear power in the United States has dwindled over the years. The opposition crystallized with the Three Mile Island incident of 1979 and the Chernobyl Accident of 1986. Many doubts have been raised about the safety of using radioactive materials to produce power.

NUCLEAR FUEL CYCLE

There are numerous processes in the nuclear fuel cycle. The main steps involve:
Mining of the Ore
Milling
Conversion
Enrichment
Fuel fabrication
Power production (nuclear energy)
Fuel reprocessing
Waste management
In all of these steps there is some danger of exposing the public to harmful radiation. The greatest danger stems from the possibility of a reactor accident during energy production and the problem of nuclear waste disposal after energy production.

Mining

As early as the sixteenth century it was recognized that many of the miners, who worked in the pitchblend mines of the Erz Mountains of Germany and in Joachimsthal in Czechosolvakia, died in middle age of a pulmonary disease known as Bergkrankbeit, or mountain sickness (Union, 1975).

An early study of the Schneeberg miners in Germany conducted between 1869 and 1877 revealed that the 650 miners working during that period had a life expectancy of 20 years after entering the mines. About 75 percent of the deaths were due to lung cancer. The death rate was higher for underground workers than for workers on the surface. The doctors incorrectly assumed that the high mortality rate was due to breathing arsenic. Further studies between 1900 and 1940 provided statistical evidence that the high incidence of lung cancer was due to the presence of radioactive substances in the mines.

Prior to 1945, uranium ore was mined for radium in Arizona, Nevada, Utah, Colorado, and New Mexico. Beginning in 1946, large scale uranium mining began, first for atomic weapons and later for electricity. Intensive mining continued through 1968, when the existence of adequate stockpiles of uranium led to a reduction in activities.

In the mining process, natural decay of uranium 238 results in the formation of the various radioactive products in ore bodies. Of these, radon 222 is a noble gas that escapes from rock surfaces within the mine. Radon has a half-life of 3.8 days and decays through a set of short-lived nuclides, which as a group exhibit a half-life of about one-half hour before reaching lead 210.

Radon daughters, either as free ions or absorbed in water or dust particles, are inhaled, deposited and retained in the respiratory system. Consequently, the respiratory system can be exposed to high concentrations of radioactive radon. When lung tissues are exposed to radon, the major tissue damage is attributed to alpha particles, which have short range and high linear energy transfer. Lung damage from radon daughters appears normally in the hilar region of the lung. This is an area that is ciliated and covered with a sheet of mucous. Because this surface layer of cells develops from a layer of basal cells attached to the basement membrane, the integrity of the epithelium depends on the continued integrity of the basal cells. Thus, the basal cells become the relevant biological target for the alpha rays.

Radon measurements were first made in U.S. uranium mines in 1951. By this date at least 6,000 miners had been exposed to radon. During most of the 1950s the surveys were spotty and carried out to collect information rather than to control radio-activity in mining operations. Finally in 1957 the U.S. Public Health Service published the results of radon daughter surveys and predicted a significant mortality rate from lung cancer among miners. As a result, in 1961 major control programs were initiated in underground mines. Advances in ventilation technology have continually improved the situation. Prior to 1952 it was common for miners to operate at 5-10 WL, with a few operating at 20-200 WL. (A working level, WL, is defined as any combination of short-lived radon daughters in one liter of air that would result in the ultimate emission of 1.3×10^5 MeV of potential alpha energy). By 1968 a majority of the mines showed values of 0.5 - 2 WL, with about 20 percent less than 0.5 WL and none greater than 5 WL. Although the risk of acquiring lung cancer has not been eliminated for miners, it has been greatly reduced.

Milling of Uranium

In the milling of uranium ore, 99 percent of the product is considered as waste. Consequently, huge piles of tailings are accumulated at the mill sites. For many years the danger from radioactivity was not recognized. Because of the sheer volume, the Environmental Protection Agency believes that mill tainings will have a major environmental impact for decades. The extraction of a few pounds of uranium to fuel a single 1,000 megawatt reactor for a year requires the generation of at least 106 tons of tailings.

By the late 1950s it was recognized that a number of streams near uranium mill sites had been badly polluted with radioactive materials and that water for human consumption and irrigation was endangered. Further, for many years the fine-grained tailings were used for many purposes by the public. The use of tailings at construction sites in Grand Junction, Colorado illustrates the early use of this material. In 1958, the AEC discovered that radon originating in the piles created a high level of airborne radioactivity in the immediate vicinity of the tailings. In addition, there was a high level of gamma rays near the surface of the tailings. By 1959 the U.S. Public Health Service recognized the seriousness of the problem, and new regulations by the Atomic Energy Commission were gradually established.

The solution of the mill tailings problem is not an easy one. The ultimate solution to the problem is the complete removal of the tailings, but because they are widely scattered over southwestern United States the cost is prohibitive. Several measures can be taken to minimize the radiation hazard from the tailings. The simplest procedure is to flatten the piles and cover them with earth. One problem here is that the half-life of radium 226 is 1,630 years. Thus, the radium is likely to outlive the protection of a thin earth covering. The best procedure is to return the tailings to the mill and recover the radium content. The tailings could then be mixed with cement to ensure the entrapment of radon. The most sophisticated solution is to chemically recover the radium, incorporate it with the reactor fuel, and finally destroy it by transmutation and fission. Because of the relatively small quantity of radium these recovery procedures are expensive.

Conversion

The next step in the cycle is the production of semi-refined uranium oxide (U_3O_8), known as yellowcake. Historically, the size of the uranium industry has been measured by the amount of uranium concentrate produced. This is because only about 0.002 percent of the concentrate becomes uranium oxide. In 1960, 8 million tons of uranium concentrate produced 17,637 tons of U_3O_8. The quantity of waste rock has many radioactive materials, thus presenting a major environmental problem.

The second stage in the conversion process is to change U_3O_8 to UF_6. In this process, there are small radioactive and air emissions from the plant. The Environmental Protection Agency has indicated that conversion plant emissions produce an average dose of much less than 1 million/year to individuals within 50 miles of the plant. The five UF_6 conversion plants in the United States are located at Metropolis, Illinois; Sequoyah, Oklahoma; Barnwell, South Carolina; Apollo, Pennsylvania, and West Valley, New York. The conversion of U_3O_8 to UF_6 has little possibility of environmental contamination.

Enrichment

The next step in the cycle is the enrichment of the hexafluoride UF_6. The enrichment is accompanied by a gaseous diffusion process. The UF_6 is passed through about 1,700 barriers in which the U 235 concentration is increased from the natural 0.7 percent to a level of 3 to 4 percent, the balance being U 238. The amount of U 235 produced is determined by technical and economic considerations. In this process large quantities of heat, water, and electricity are required. The enriched fuel for one year's operation of a 1,000-million-watt (MW) light water reactor (LWR) requires about 11 billion gallons of water and 310 million kilowatt-hour of electricity. This is about 4 percent of the energy generated in a plant.

The large amount of cooling water required has a major environmental impact in the enrichment process. Cooling towers are required to reduce the temperature of the water. Other environmental impacts are minimal. The radiation dose to an individual living at the plant boundary would only be about 2 millrems/year. (A rem is defined as a dose of a particular type of radiation to produce the same biological effects as one roentgen of gamma radiation).

Fuel Fabrication

The final step before the fuel is used in the nuclear reactor takes place when the enriched UF_6 is converted into uranium dioxide (UO_2). The UO_2 is formed into small ceramic pellets and enclosed in a thin tube made of suitable material, usually zircaloy, to form fuel rods. The fuel is then transported to the power facility in bundles called fuel assemblies. The number and arrangement of the fuel rods in the fuel assemblies are determined by the specification of the reactor core design.

The fabrication of fuel elements is a well established technology and unlike the enrichment process, fuel element fabrication plants operate on a commercial basis. In fuel fabrication plants, extensive tests and inspections are carried out during all stages of the operation to ensure safety. The Environmental Protection Agency has indicated that the process has little or no impact on the environment. At the plant boundary of a typical facility, an individual might receive a maximum of 10 mrem/year in the lungs from normal breathing, but the average dose within 50 miles of the plant would be less than 0.1 mrem/year.

Energy Production

One of the most controversial issues in the use of nuclear fuel to produce energy is the fission of atoms in the nuclear reactor. In all nuclear power plants, radioactive materials are produced in the nuclear reactor. The fissioning of the uranium and the neutron activation of the coolant produces many radioactive isotopes. These radioactive isotopes, particularly the gaseous ones, can escape from the fuel rods through pinhole defects to contaminate the coolant water or gases.

Technical specifications limit the amount and rate of release of these radioactive materials into the environment. Plants must report all "potentially significant safety accidents" ranging from a tool improperly left in an electric cabinet to a flawed reactor. In the four-year-period from 1984 to 1987, 11,410 incidents were reported of which 8,400 were personnel errors. Another measure of efficiency is the number of automatic shutdowns that occur at a plant during a year's operation. In 1984 there were 487 automatic shutdowns or an average of 5.24 per plant. By 1987 this number had been reduced to 347 or only 3.25 shutdowns per plant. While the number of automatic shutdowns has been reduced, it still remains quite high.

REACTOR PLANT ACCIDENTS

Although there have been hundreds of small accidents in the production of electricity using nuclear fuel, there have been only two major recorded accidents. In 1979 the reactor accident at Three Mile Island was controlled before a meltdown occurred. In constrast, in 1986 at Chernobyl, in the Soviet Union, a major meltdown occurred resulting in a massive explosion.

Three Mile Island

The Three Mile Island plant was dedicated on September 12, 1978. At the ceremony Deputy Secretary of Energy, John E. O'Leary, a leading advocate of nuclear power, commented, "It is fair to conclude...that nuclear (power) is a bright and shining option for this country." For more than a decade, three reactors produced electricity. On March 28, 1979 a maintenance crew accidentally stopped the flow of water in the main feedwater system of one reactor. Within seconds as the pressure rose, an accident was in progress. Although fission was stopped immediately, the decaying radioactive materials left from the fission process continued to heat the reactor's coolant water. Because a coolant was not available to control the temperature, the reactor was on its way to eruption.

Although there was a minor explosion of hydrogen at 1:50 p.m., the reactor was not destroyed. In retrospect, only great "good luck" prevented a massive explosion. In the next few weeks, a major effort was extended to control the accident. The principal concern was a hydrogen bubble that developed in the reactor. However, the bubble gradually disappeared with the gas being distributed through the system. The accident of Three Mile Island did not end with the lowering of the pressure and heat in the system and the disappearance of the gas bubble. It was several months before the danger of an explosion completely disappeared. The long process of cleaning up the Three Mile Island accident then began – a process that was not completed by 1991 and one that will continue for years to come (Stephens, 1980).

After the Three Mile Island accident, President Jimmy Carter appointed a commission to "make recommendations to enable us to prevent any future nuclear accidents." The commission investigated such aspects as the causes and severity of the accident, handling of the emergency, public and workers' health and safety, the right to information, the role of the Nuclear Regulatory Commission and the role of the electric utilities." (The material quoted is from the Report of the President's *Commission on the Accident at Three Mile Island: The Need for Change: The Legacy of TMI,* 1979, New York: Pergamon Press.)

The most fundamental findings on the technical aspects of the operation were:

The accident at Three Mile Island (TMI) occurred as a result of a series of human, institutional and mechanical failures. Equipment failure initiated the event and contributed to the failure of operational personnel to recognize the actual conditions of the plant. Their training was deficient and left them unprepared for the events that took place. These operating personnel made some improper decisions, took some improper actions, causing what should have been a minor accident to develop into the TMI-2 accident.

On training operating personnel, the commission report found:

Training of Met Ed operators and supervisors was inadequate and contributed significantly to the seriousness of the accident. The training program gave insufficient emphasis to the principles of reactor safety.

There is no scientific evidence, according to Dr. George Tokuhata, director of the Division in Epidemiology Research of the Pennsylvania Department of Health, that cancer incidents increased due to the accident. Post-accident studies revealed that the most radiation any individual within 50 miles of Three Mile Island could have received was about 70 mrems, less than what a person receives in a year from natural background radiation. The commission report stated:

> The major health effect of the accident appears to have been on the mental health of the people living in the region of Three Mile Island and of the workers at TMI. There were immediate, short-lived mental distress produced by the accident among certain groups of the general population living within 20 miles of TMI.

The Commission also considered the function of the Nuclear Regulatory Commission. It's basic findings were:

> We find that the NRC is so preoccupied with the licensing of plants that it has not given primary consideration to overall safety issues. NRC labels safety problems of plants as "generic". Once a problem is labeled "generic" the licensing of the individual plant can be completed without resolving the problem.

Chernobyl Nuclear Explosion

On Saturday, April 25, 1986, at 1:23 a.m., the number 4 reactor of the nuclear power station at Chernobyl exploded, blowing the roof off the reactor. A few seconds later, a second explosion ejected graphite blocks and radioactive fuel material. The hot graphite created a holocaust that threatened to engulf the power plant's three other reactors. After herculean efforts, the fire was contained to the reactor that had exploded. The release of radioactivity was equal to all the atomic bombs tested above ground, or more than one million times the omission from the Three Mile Island accident.

The radioactive plume of materials and gases - including iodine 131, cesium 137, and strontium 90 - was spewed into the stratosphere. The emissions reached a peak on April 26, when about 13 million curies (the amount of any radioactive substance that emits the same number of alpha rays per unit of time as 1 gram of radium) were released from the reactor. Between April 27 and May 1 the emissions ranged from 1 to 4 million curies daily. From May 1 to May 5 the emissions built up daily to about 7 million curies. The second build up was caused when a large amount of materials dropping on the core caused it to grow hotter and release more radioactive isotopes. Finally, on the eleventh day after the accident, May 6, liquid nitrogen was placed under the reactor, cooling it. The reactor fire was thus controlled and the emission of radioactive materials stopped.

The Soviet authorities did not report the accident immediately. The first evidence outside the Soviet Union that a nuclear accident occurred was at 2 p.m. on Sunday, April 27 when the Chernobyl radioactive cloud crossed the Swedish border. The next morning at the Fosmark nuclear power station north of Stockholm, workers undergoing routine daily radiation examination registered ten times the normal level of radioactivity on their shoe soles. By the afternoon at 3 p.m., Swedish radio reported "10,000 times the normal amount" of cesium 137 in the air. Within one week after the accident, the nuclear contamination covered an amazingly large area covering at least 20 countries and extending 1,200 to 1,300 miles from the point of the accident. The spatial pattern was complex due to the shifting wind patterns. For example, on the first day the radioactive cloud spread northward over the Soviet Republic of Byelrussia, Latvia, and Lithuania, across northern Poland, and then across the Baltic Sea to the Scandinavian countries. But, on the second to fourth days, the wind shifted to a west and southwesterly flow, blanketing the Ukraine, northern Poland, Austria, Czechoslovakia, southern Germany, Switzerland, northern Italy and eastern France. The fallout was extremely uneven. Some parts of Europe directly under the plume received little fallout, and other portions received large amounts. The amount of deposition was influenced by rainfall, which washed radioactive particles out of the air. Local topography played a role, concentrating radioactive materials and "hot" spots at certain places and dispersing them in others.

The effects of the accident must be viewed from two aspects: from within the Soviet Union and from beyond the Soviet borders. The effects of the accident were felt immediately at the plant site. Several plant workers were killed and about 116,000 people from the nuclear city, Pripyat, and neighboring villages, were immediately evacuated.

In July 1986 the Soviet government revealed that about 600 square miles had been affected by radioactive fallout in Ukraine. It was also revealed that 28 people had died and 203 people were being treated for radiation exposure.

By 1989 the Soviet government reported that a much larger area had been contaminated than previously acknowledged. Contamination at unsafe levels — over 20 curies per square mile — was present over 6,500 square miles, including about 4,500 square miles in Byelrussia, 1,200 square miles in Russia, and 1,000 square miles in the Ukraine. Pockets of radioactivity were found at Orel, about 300 miles from the plant.

The health danger to the 230,000 people living in the contaminated area is still not clear. Uncontaminated food must be imported and safety checks are continually carried out. Crude estimates indicate that between 5,000 and 100,000 fatalities may result from the Chernobyl accident. Reports from Soviet Scientists and foreign journalists suggest that there is growing frustration and anxiety among the people living in the contaminated area and bitterness about the government's initial reluctance to disclose the extent of the problem (Hawher, 1987).

The reaction of European countries to the Chernobyl accident varied. Many countries protested the long delay by the Soviets in announcing the magnitude of the accident. By the middle of May more than 20 countries had imposed restrictions on the consumption of fresh vegetables because of the level of radioactivity. Nevertheless, most governments were not prepared to deal with the rapid contamination of the environment. The international agencies did little to provide standards of safety. For example, the International Atomic Energy Agency provided no recommendations on food or health and the World Health Organization provided only a broad warning.

Fuel Reprocessing

The fuel cells in a reactor must be replaced when they are spent. Because the spent rods are highly radioactive, the normal procedure is to store them about a year underwater, during which time the most intense short-lived and intermediate half-life radioactive fission products have reduced their radioactivity. Although the United States has reprocessing laboratories, the only industrial scale plants are located at Marcoule, France, The Hague, Netherlands, and Windscale in the United Kingdom. The environmental impact of these plants varies considerably. Marcoule, which has tight environmental controls, discharges its waste into the Rhine River; the other two discharge their waste into the ocean.

The Environmental Protection Agency has attempted to predict the health effects at a reprocessing plant. It is estimated that a plant with a capacity of 5 metric tons per day serving 45 nuclear plants of 1,000-MW size would emit long-lived radioactive gases such as krypton 85 and tritium at a rate that would produce about 2.5 health effects annually in the United States and about 100 health effects annually worldwide. If the processing plants were increased in numbers to service 1,000 nuclear power plants, the health effects would increase to about 200 annually worldwide, of which there would be 130 cancer deaths.

Radioactive Waste Management

The final step in the nuclear fuel cycle is management and disposal of radioactive waste, some of which may have a radioactive half-life of tens of thousands of years. Although the nuclear power industry is more than 30 years old in the United States, all nuclear waste has been placed in temporary depositories. These depositories contain more than 99.8 percent of the nongaseous fission products produced in the reactor. At the present time these liquid wastes are usually concentrated by evaporation and stored as an aqueous nitric acid solution in high-integrity, stainless steel tanks. There is now general agreement in the nuclear industry that these wastes should be solidified and then placed in a permanent depository.

Since the development of the nuclear industry, spent fuel inventories have grown rapidly. Statistics are only available for the market economies and are missing for the nonmarket ones, primarily the Soviet Union. For the market economies the cumulative metric tons of heavy metals in the spent fuel inventories increased from 6,205 in 1970 to 16,714 in 1975, to 34,913 in 1980, and to 76,800 in 1986. Of this total the United Kingdom had 27,400 metric tons in 1986; the United States, 14,000; France, 10,800; Canada, 8,700; Japan, 4,300; and West Germany, 2,500 tons.

Numerous studies of the types of permanent disposal of nuclear wastes have been conducted. No universal agreement has been reached. One of the major problems in choosing and identifying suitable sites is the vocal objections of the general public. Although there is universal recognition that the waste products must be disposed of, there is also the viewpoint, "not in my backyard." The problem is thus not only a technical one but also one with wide political and social implications.

A number of suggestions for disposal of the waste include disposal in the ocean, sub-seabed burial, transporting the waste into outer space, and burial on land. Of these, land burial has been selected. In 1984 the U.S. Department of Energy constructed a Waste Isolation Pilot Plant near Carlsbad, New Mexico. This plant will store high-level waste temporarily until a permanent disposal site is located. In 1984 the DOE proposed three sites for permanent disposal facilities. These were Hanford, Washington; Hereford, Texas; and the Nevada Atomic Test Site, Yucca Mountains, in the desert of southern Nevada. In spite of opposition from Nevada's governor, the Yucca Mountain site was chosen.

At the Nevada site, geologists and engineers are beginning the task of preparing an underground depository to isolate high-level radioactive waste. The estimated cost is over $2 billion and the date of completion is 2003. Although work has begun, opposition is growing. Teams of geologists and engineers are attempting to predict whether the area is safe for depositing high-level waste. Although some of the waste would be hazardous for millions of years, predictions are limited to 10,000 years. Beyond this limit, questions of safety are simply unanswerable. There is conflict between engineers and geologists. Whereas engineers complain that the geologists' predictions reach beyond the limits of their expertise, geologists contest that the engineers sacrifice scientific rigor for adherence to procedure used to ensure satisfactory present-day engineering practices. These clashes between geologists and engineers reveal the difficulty of prediction. Because no one has even attempted to predict what a situation will be 100 centuries from now, an entirely new concept of thinking must be devised.

The disposal of high-level radioactive waste is one of the most difficult and perplexing problems found by mankind today. Completely rational decisions are not possible. Nevertheless, scientists and engineers must reach the best possible solution for it is a problem that is fundamental for all peoples.

Future of Nuclear Energy

Nuclear energy, once hailed as a source of energy "too cheap to meter", has nearly ceased to grow in many countries. Since 1979, 116 plants were cancelled in the United States and only 109 completed. There are a number of reasons for the decline of the importance of nuclear power. The Three Mile Island, and later the Chernobyl accident, created a massive public concern about the safety of atomic energy. In a 1989 survey most people did not approve nuclear power and 82 percent would be concerned if they lived near a nuclear plant.

In order to improve its image the nuclear industry has focused attention on improvements in nuclear technology that will make the reactors easier to build and safer to operate. The traditional light-water reactor was extremely complex. A typical conventional reactor may have as many as 40,000 valves, while a coal-fired plant of the same capacity will have 4,000 valves. A nuclear reactor is not only much more expensive but is more difficult to maintain and operate but with an increased possibility of an accident. A nuclear plant has had to be very large in production capacity in order to recover investments.

The new generation of reactors, still under development, will rely upon "passive" safety systems which substitute natural forces such as gravity and convection for the vast network of pumps, control systems and other complex components that protect the traditional nuclear plant. The new reactors may prove more reliable and easier to operate and maintain. Several new reactor concepts are being pursued in a number of countries. These include advanced versions of light-water reactors that include passive emergency cooling features. These cooling systems are intended to prevent damage to the core, in case of an accident, by quickly and automatically flooding it with enough water to dissipate its heat for at least three days. A number of other advances are being considered. A fundamentally difficult strategy being explored is to use liquid metal rather than water as the reactor coolant. Yet another innovative design is the modular high-temperature gas-cooled reactor using helium as the coolant gas.

These new reactor designs are still unproven in a full-scale prototype. Not all engineers accept the new concepts and opinions and are sharply divided as to whether advances are sufficient to make nuclear power an attractive alternative to fossil fuels. Some people maintain that present-day light-water reactors do not need replacing for they have proved safe in many countries. Others are skeptical of the safety claims of the new designs, and still others feel that nuclear power of any type is not acceptable due to accidents, unsolved problems of disposal of nuclear waste and the potential for nuclear bomb proliferation.

The future of nuclear power is still not determined. It remains not only a technical problem but a moral issue.

SELECTED REFERENCES

Cantelon, Philip L., and Robert C. Williams, 1982, *Crisis Contained: The Department of Energy at Three Mile Island,* Social Science and International Affairs Series, Carbondale, IL: Southern Illinois University Press, 213p.

Ford, Daniel E., 1982, *Three Mile Island: Thirty Minutes to Meltdown,* New York: Viking Press, 271p.

Gale, Robert Peter, 1988, *Final Warning: The Legacy of Chernobyl,* New York: Warner Books, 230p.

Gould, P., 1990, *Fire in the Rain: The Democratic Consequences of Chernobyl,* Baltimore, MD: Johns Hopkins University Press, 163p.

Gubaryev, V., 1987, *Sarcophagus,* Hammondsworth: Penguin Books, 81p.

Hawher, N. et al., 1987, *Chernobyl: The End of the Nuclear Dream,* New York: Vintage Books, 246p.

Martin, Daniel, 1980, *Three Mile Island: Prologue or Epilogue?* Cambridge, MA: Ballinger Publishing Company, 251p.

Report of the President's Commission on the Accident at Three Mile Island: The Need for Change: The Legacy of TMI, 1979, New York: Pergamon Press, 199p.

Stephens, Mark, 1990, *Three Mile Island,* New York: Random House, 245p.

Union of Concerned Scientists, 1975, *The Nuclear Fuel Cycle,* Environmental Studies Series, Cambridge, MA: MIT Press, 291p.

Natural and Technological Disasters: Causes, Effects and Preventive Measures. Edited by S.K. Majumdar, G.S. Forbes, E.W. Miller, and R.F. Schmalz. © 1992, The Pennsylvania Academy of Science.

Chapter Twenty-Nine

DISASTER-RELATED INSURANCE PROBLEMS AND SOLUTIONS

FRANKLIN W. NUTTER

President, Reinsurance Association of America
1819 L. Street, N.W. 7th Floor
Washington, DC 20036

INTRODUCTION

The property/casualty insurance industry has always insured homes, businesses, and automobiles against the risk of natural catastrophies. In recent years, concerns have been raised that most homeowners who are at risk due to an earthquake are uninsured, and that in the event of a major earthquake, many of our financial institutions, particularly the property/casualty insurance industry, are at grave risk for their continued financial viability. Insurers believe that a program is needed involving a partnership between the private sector, the federal government, and state and local governments in providing for loss mitigation and other preventive measures, together with insurance and reinsurance programs to promote financial security arising from earthquake risks.

The Impact of Earthquakes in the United States

The United States Geological Survey has determined that 39 states have a major or moderate exposure to damaging earthquakes. Although most people perceive earthquakes as a "California only problem," many other sections of the United States are at risk or have experienced major earthquakes. Indeed, the largest earthquake in recorded American history occurred in the central United States. The New Madrid fault earthquakes of 1811-1812 were thirty times more powerful than the 1989 San Francisco earthquake. These fault lines run through seven states: Tennessee, Missouri, Kentucky, Illinois, Arkansas, Indiana, and Mississippi. In addition, major fault lines exist in the southeast, particularly in South Carolina, and in New England and throughout northern New York State and Massachusetts. These known fault lines have been identified because of the occurrence of earthquakes. With the exception of California, where scientists have for years seismically tracked earthquakes and therefore identified fault lines, few fault lines beyond major ones completely related to known occurrences have been identified in most other sections of the United States.

Damage due to a major earthquake are not always obvious. While most attention following an earthquake is centered on damaged homes and commercial building structures, the fact is the true cost of a major earthquake extends to a myriad of subjects, including:

Infrastructure: Since few mitigation measures have been taken to protect them, pipelines, electric power lines and facilities, telecommunications networks, river traffic and highways and bridges are all highly susceptible to earthquake damage.

Financial Markets: An earthquake of major proportions would cause the sudden sale of bonds and securities by insurers and self-insurers to pay for repair and rebuilding. In addition, any economic activity (e.g., businesses and government) which supported the issuance of securities and bonds and which was destroyed as the result of an earthquake, would severely deplete the value of those obligations.

Taxpayers: All taxpayers, both federal and state, would be assessed the cost of disaster relief through higher taxes or government borrowing. For examples, analysts have estimated that each taxpayer contributed $17.00 for Hurricane Hugo disaster assistance.

Insurers/Policymakers: The depletion of insurers' surplus and other assets to meet contractual obligations could impair the ability of the industry to maintain, renew or extend new coverages in the affected disaster area, as well as in other parts of the country. The industry's basis for writing coverages is a function of its capital and surplus, which, if depleted, would restrict its ability to write those coverages.

The Insurance Research Council estimates that a major earthquake in the Los Angeles basin or San Fancisco Bay area, could cause insured losses of $40 to $60 billion, including shake damage, fires resulting from an earthquake, and commercial losses under such coverages as workers' compensation and business interruption. Probable maximum loss estimates developed by the California Insurance Department support these dramatic scenarios.

Population centers and related economic activity have increased dramatically in the last twenty years along the following or near the following fault lines: San Andreas, California; Newport/Englewood, Maywood, California; Wasatch, Utah; New Madrid, Central United States; Charleston, South Carolina; and Cape Ann, Massachusetts. While California has recently developed seismic building codes, in most areas of the United States outside of California, cities and states have done little to minimize the effect a major earthquake would have on property damage and loss of life. Yet, scientists predict that a major earthquake is not only inevitable, but will likely strike the United States by the year 2020. The question is not if, but when.

Underwriting the Earthquake Risk

Insurance to protect earthquake losses is generally available to homeowners and small businesses. Yet, even in high risk areas, no more than one-quarter of all homes have earthquake insurance protection. The nationwide average is probably under five percent of all such homes at risk. While insurers currently make this coverage available, there are several deterrents to widespread coverage:

- The acceptance of the risk by those who know their exposure.
- The lack of knowledge of the exposure due to inadequate seismic assessment or publicity about it.
- The high cost of insurance for those at greatest risk because of a lack of a sufficiently large policyholder base to provide a sufficient spread of risk.
- Deductibles set at amounts which may exceed the probable loss for most homeowners.

The "insurance industry" comprises over 2,000 individual companies of various sizes, each operating in a specific market niche with a different management style and goals. Each insurer establishes its own marketing, pricing, underwriting, and claims philosophies. Each determines the coverages it will write, the line and risk limits, its underwriting standards and devices, and the rates it will use for the risk assumed. The exposures to losses due to earthquake vary among companies based on these factors.

Insurers are strictly regulated by the states, particularly as relates to issues of solvency. In setting their respective courses, each insurer evaluates its current and future financial position to assure compliance with applicable state regulatory guidelines.

Generally, insurers are required to maintain "minimum levels" of surplus in relation to premiums written. Because insurers may not reserve funds for losses which have not yet occurred, an insurer's surplus becomes its cushion against catastrophic events such as a major earthquake. If an insurer's surplus drops below the "minimum level," a state regulatory authority could prohibit or restrict that insurer from writing new business. If several insurers experienced significant depletion of surplus, at the same time, and state regulators were to order them to suspend writing new business—in an effort to maintain solvency standards—an insurance availability crisis ("market failure") of unparalleled dimensions could result. This is the scenario which might evolve if a catastrophic earthquake were to occur.

Insurance functions most effectively only when the "cause of loss" to be insured meets defined "standards of insurability." To be insurable, a "cause of loss" must meet each of the following "standards":

- It must be identifiable in terms of time and place;
- It must be manageable—will not affect a great number of insured properties at once;
- It must be measurable in effect—in monetary terms; and
- It must be actuarially predictable—subject to "the law of large numbers."

Potentially catastrophic earthquakes do not meet all of the "standards of insurability." Earthquakes are different from most other "causes of loss" (e.g., fire, theft, auto). These are not predictable, a reasonable estimation of total loss is problematic, and they recur with insufficient frequency to permit the development of actuarial data.

Simply stated, insurers could write earthquake insurance as long as:

- They could be selective, i.e., not take all comers.
- They could avoid adverse selection (i.e., insuring only those at imminent and foreseeable risk).
- They could establish diversity of risk classification, for instance, between frame and masonry structures.
- There were adequate reinsurance capacity available.
- The premium were adequate to offset the exposure.

With respect to a catastrophic earthquake, these conditions do not exist.

A Partnership to Address the Problem

The lack of insurance coverge nationwide, the failure of many local governments to impose loss mitigation techniques through building codes and zoning, and the economic impact upon securities market and financial institutions, has focused many on the need for a solution involving government and the private sector. The elements of a solution have been directed at the following objectives:

- The development of a program which would significantly reduce the number of deaths and injuries ensuing from earthquakes while concurrently lessening property damage.
- The development of a prefunded program which could take the place of disaster relief while making earthquake insurance available, at an affordable price, to the majority of homeowners.
- The establishment of a program which would provide for the continued viability of the property/casualty insurance business at no ultimate cost to the federal government.

- The forging of a partnership between the federal, state, and local governments and the private insurance industry which would accomplish the foregoing goals and simultaneously protect the nation's economic fabric from the impact of a catastrophic earthquake.

Legislation has now been introduced in Congress to provide a two-part program. The first part being a program of hazard reduction, providing incentives and phased-in requirements to ensure that earthquake-prone states and local communities adopt and enforce cost-effective measures to reduce the damage from future earthquakes. The second part of the program provides for two separate but parallel insurance programs underwritten by the federal government, but which operate in partnership with the private insurance industry. These programs would prefund natural disaster assistance by making affordable earthquake insurance coverage universally available to homeowners, and protect the national economy from a catastrophic earthquake.

The state-oriented earthquake hazard reduction program includes:

- *Development of Federal Criteria.* The Federal Emergency Management Agency would develop federal loss reduction criteria that must be workable, practical, and cost-effective. The specific loss reduction measures included in the criteria could consist of building codes, land use planning, and seismic strengthening of existing structures.
- *States Adopt Criteria.* Earthquake-prone states would have two years to comply with the relevant mitigation measures of the federal criteria. States would receive financial assistance from a self-sustaining mitigation fund (which consists of insurance premiums).
- *Enforcement Encouraged.* If an earthquake-prone state fails to certify compliance, residential property in that state could not qualify for federally backed mortgages, unless the homeowner voluntarily takes steps to mitigate damages from future earthquakes. Reward-based insurance incentives (e.g., lower deductibles and premiums) are also provided to those who meet the seismic standards.

The insurance program includes two parts:

1. a primary insurance program supported by homeowner-paid premiums to cover shake damage to residential property; and
2. an excess reinsurance program supported by industry-paid premiums which is triggered to cover damages resulting from a catastrophic earthquake.

Primary Insurance Program

Under the Primary Program, insurance coverage against direct damages from earthquakes and volcanic eruptions would be available for nearly all homeowners. The important features include:

- *Covers primarily residential property.* It applied to residential property and the personal contents of rented properties. The coverge could be expanded later to include other properties, such as small businesses.

- *Insurance participation.* All insurers participating would attach, on behalf of the federal government, an earthquake endorsement to their standard homeowner's policy.
- *Applies to federally backed mortgages.* Owners of residential property in earthquake prone states who acquire new or refinance existing mortgages backed or insured by the federal government would be required to purchase coverage for earthquakes.
- *Federal government sets the rates.* Rates would be actuarial to cover the frequency and severity of the earthquake risk over an extended period. The rates would vary by geographic zones. The government would also set coverge limits and variable deductibles.
- *Insurers collect premiums and service claims.* The premiums collected would be remitted to a federal trust fund. When the earthquake occurs, the insurers would process the claims and pay the losses to be reimbursed by the trust fund.
- *Payments still made if insufficiency.* To the extent that the trust fund is insufficient to pay all losses, the shortfall would be made up by borrowing from the U.S. Treasury and industry cost-sharing. The borrowing would be repaid with interest from future premiums.

Excess Reinsurance Program

Under the excess reinsurance program, the federal government would offer to all insurers and reinsurers excess reinsurance coverage against most losses resulting from a catastrophic earthquake.

Features of the excess program include:

- *Insurers purchase the reinsurance.* Insurance companies would pay premiums which are set by the federal government based on actuarial principles.
- *Most perils are covered.* The reinsurance would be available for many lines of coverage, including fire, workers compensations, business interruption, and most other liabilites.
- *Separate trust fund.* The premiums would be remitted to a second trust fund where they would be accumulated and used to pay losses following a catastrophic earthquake. Much like the primary program, there would be federal borrowing if the fund is insufficient to pay claims. The borrowing, however, is to be repaid with interest.
- *Only a major earthquake triggers the reinsurance program.* For an insurer to qualify for reinsurance payments, a catastrophic earthquake must result in at least $10 billion of insured losses for the industry. For example, the last U.S. earthquake which would have triggered federal reinsurance (and potential federal borrowing) under this program was the great 1906 San Francisco earthquake. There is also a separate eligibility trigger for each company and for small companies.

Dr. Robert Litan of The Brookings Institute foresees and describes the benefits to be derived from a national earthquake mitigation and insurance plan as follows:

A national cost-effective mitigation effort that takes account of differential risks of earthquakes throughout the nation would lower the physical and human costs of a future earthquake and, in the process, lower the cost of earthquake insurance. A national earthquake insurance program would cure the market failures that now prevent the supply of affordable insurance. And a self-financing federal reinsurance program for the property/casualty insurance industry to protect it from financial devastation would prevent all consumers from having to pay much higher insurance premiums or to face significant cutbacks in coverge in the aftermath of a catastrophic earthquake.

CONCLUSION

The high risk which many homeowners are taking, knowingly or unknowingly, and the contingent liability with the federal, state, and local governments have for disaster assistance, make a partnership among these entities the only realistic solution. Encouraging and requiring seismically safe structures and providing homeowners and business with affordable insurance protection would justify a program of this nature on its own. When you couple these advantages with the value of maintaining the future viability of the property/casualty insurance industry following a major earthquake, and the elimination of the government's contingent liability for assistance make a partnership a win-win proposal. Certainly, the securities community and the municipal bond market have much to gain by the stability which this program can provide. Mortgage, banking and other interest will suffer fewer defaults on residential property mortgages as a result of the financial protection the program offers homeowners and the financial community will suffer fewer dislocations since federal reserve funds will help cushion the economic blow of a truly catastrophic earthquake.

Natural and Technological Disasters: Causes, Effects and Preventive Measures. Edited by
S.K. Majumdar, G.S. Forbes, E.W. Miller, and R.F. Schmalz. © 1992, The Pennsylvania Academy
of Science.

Chapter Thirty

INDIVIDUAL PREPAREDNESS PLANNING FOR SAFETY AND WINDSTORM DAMAGE MITIGATION

JAMES R. McDONALD
Director, Institute for Disaster Research
and
Professor of Civil Engineering
Texas Tech University
Lubbock, TX 79409

INTRODUCTION

Each year, windstorms in the form of tornadoes, hurricanes and other extreme winds cause widespread damage, deaths and injuries. People normally look to the National Weather Service for advisories and warnings when severe weather threatens. After a windstorm event, the responsibility for aid and comfort rests with agencies of the local, State and Federal government, as well as other private groups. Despite all the help from these agencies, there are a number of preparedness and mitigation steps an individual can take on his own. The purpose of this chapter is to discuss and illustrate measures of protecting one's family and property from adverse effects of extreme windstorms. The discussion covers the protection of people and property. Finally, the elements of a personal preparedness plan are outlined.

Potential Windstorm Threats

In the United States, most severe windstorms are associated with either severe thunderstorms or hurricanes. Tornadoes, downbursts, and strong outflow winds are associated with thunderstorms. High winds, storm surge, waves, and flooding accompany hurricanes. Thunderstorms associated with the hurricane structure sometimes spawn tornadoes. Tornadoes are common in a large section of the U.S., primarily east of the Rocky Mountains. Figure 1 shows the distribution of tornado occurrences in the U.S. from 1950-79.[1] While almost 1000 tornadoes occur each year, the possibility of a strike at any one location is a relatively rare event. For this reason, there tends to be complacency among the population regarding the threat of tornadoes, even in areas where the frequency is relatively high. Even though people think tornadoes are relatively rare, they also believe they are very intense and that essentially nothing can be done to prepare for them.

Tornado intensity is rated by a subjective scale called the Fujita-Scale (F-Scale).[2] Tornadoes are classified by appearance of damage. The six classifications range from F0 to F5. Table 1 gives a description of the most intense damage in each F-Scale classification. Table 2 lists the number of reported tornadoes in the United States by F-Scale classification during the period of 1916-1978. The estimated peak gust wind speeds in each classification are also listed in Table 2. The cumulative percentages in the table are very significant: 50 percent of all tornadoes have wind speeds less than 112 mph, 85 percent have wind speeds less than 158 mph, and 95 percent have wind speeds less than 207 mph. The upper two classifications (F4 and F5), with wind speeds greater than 207 mph, account for only five percent of all tornadoes. The point of this discussion is that, with precautions and preparation,

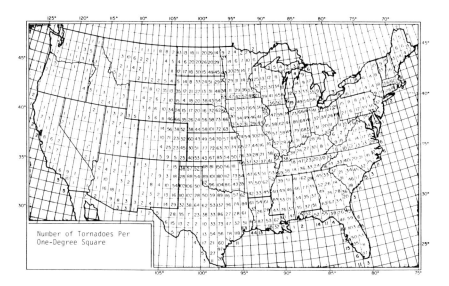

FIGURE 1. Distribution of tornado occurrences in the U.S. (1950-79)

chances of survival can be improved and the extent of damage can be reduced. Nontornadic thunderstorm winds and other "straight" winds (such as downslope winds), pose some danger, but are generally less threatening than tornadic winds. The greatest danger from severe winds is experienced in automobiles or mobile homes.

High winds are not the only danger from hurricanes. Waves, storm surge, and flooding also pose potential danger.[3] Because the time between hurricanes in a given location along the Gulf of Mexico or Atlantic coasts is relatively long, people tend to become complacent about hurricane danger. When a hurricane threatens, it is important to follow the advice of the local authorities. If they recommend evacuation, individuals should immediately respond, even though false alarms occasionally occur. The relatively long lead time in hurricane warnings usually gives time to protect property and to evacuate the threatened area.

TABLE 1

Fujita-Scale Classification of Tornadoes Based on Appearance of Damage

(F0)	LIGHT DAMAGE	40-72 mph

This speed range corresponds to Beaufort 9 through 11. Some damage to chimneys or TV antennae occurs; branches broken off trees; shallow-rooted trees pushed over; old trees with hollow insides break or fall; sign boards are damaged.

(F1)	MODERATE DAMAGE	73-112 mph

73 mph is the beginning of hurricane wind speed or Beaufort 12. Surfaces of roofs peeled off; windows broken; trailer houses are pushed or overturned; trees on soft ground are uprooted; some trees snapped; moving autos pushed off road.

(F2)	CONSIDERABLE DAMAGE	113-157 mph

Roofs torn off of frame houses, leaving strong upright walls standing; weak structures or outbuildings are demolished; trailer houses are demolished; railroad boxcars are pushed over; large trees snapped or uprooted; light-object missiles generated; cars blown off highway; block structures and walls badly damaged.

(F3)	SEVERE DAMAGE	158-206 mph

Roofs and some walls torn off well-constructed frame houses; some rural buildings completely demolished or flattened; trains overturned; steel frame hangar-warehouse type structures torn; cars lifted off the ground and may roll some distance; most trees in a forest uprooted, snapped or leveled; block structures often leveled.

(F4)	DEVASTATING DAMAGE	207-260 mph

Well-constructed frame houses leveled, leaving piles of debris; structures with weak foundations lifted, torn, and blown off some distance; trees debarked by small flying debris; sandy soil eroded and gravel flies in high winds; cars thrown some distance or rolled considerable distance, finally to disintegrate; large missiles generated.

(F5)	INCREDIBLE DAMAGE	261-318 mph

Strong frame houses lifted clear off foundation and carried considerable distance to disintegrate; steel-reinforced concrete structures badly damaged; automobile-sized missiles fly distances of 100 yards or more; trees debarked completely; incredible phenomena can occur.

Incentives for Precautions

Many people believe that because they have wind and flood insurance, there is nothing further they can do to prepare for a windstorm event. If their property is damaged, the insurance will cover the loss, so why bother to take further precautions or incur additional expense? The answer to this question can be quickly found by talking with someone who has gone through a severe windstorm event. The trauma, the loss of personal items, heirlooms, momentos and valuables, and the inconvenience and disruption of lives and families are but a few of the difficulties encountered in addition to the financial losses. Any precautionary steps to alleviate these problems are well worth the effort.

PROTECTING PEOPLE IN WINDSTORMS

Many people are injured or killed in severe windstorms by collapsing structures or building components, or by impact of flying debris.[4] Storm shelters provide the best protection, but protection areas identified by a knowledgeable engineer are the best places to be if no shelter is available.

Storm Shelters

Storm shelters are usually thought to provide protection from tornadoes. In the past, the storm cellar was the standard form of protection in rural areas of "tornado alley" in the midwestern part of the United States. These dugouts served a dual purpose of providing cool storage for foodstuffs, as well as protection from severe storms (and, in the early days of the Cold War, were perceived as useful nuclear fallout shelters). Basements have served adequately as storm shelters in those areas where basements are common.

A major drawback to a storm cellar is that the family must go outdoors and risk the danger of lightning strike or flying debris. When storms threaten at night, children must be awakened and carried outdoors to a musty cellar.

TABLE 2

Number of Reported Tornadoes by Fujita-Scale Classification (1916-78)

Fujita Scale	Wind Speed Range, mph	No. of Tornadoes	Percent	Cumulative Percent
F0	40 - 72	5,718	22.9	22.9
F1	73 - 112	8,645	34.7	57.6
F2	113 - 157	7,102	28.5	86.1
F3	158 - 206	2,665	10.7	96.8
F4	207 - 260	673	2.7	99.5
F5	261 - 318	127	0.5	100.0
Total:		24,930	100.0	

Engineers at Texas Tech University (TTU) in the early 1970s observed that even when a single-family residence was almost totally destroyed, a small interior room or closet nearly always remained standing, as illustrated in Figure 2. Intersecting walls provide the support needed to resist the high winds. The engineers reasoned that if small interior rooms are naturally wind resistant, a very good shelter could be obtained by providing engineering principles to the design of the room. Thus, the concept of an in-residence storm shelter was born.[5]

In-residence Shelter

The advantages of an in-residence shelter are (1) shelter is readily available from any location in the house, (2) the family is not required to go outdoors, and (3) the room can be used for other purposes when severe weather is not threatening. After studying the concept, the TTU engineers found that the shelter is relatively inexpensive, compared to the cost of an outdoor underground cellar.

The criteria for design was established to provide protection against 99% of all tornadoes recorded in the United States (F4 or less). The design criteria, which was established in a study for the Defense Civil Preparedness Agency,[6] requires the in-residence shelter to withstand 260 mph winds, even if the rest of the house is totally blown away. Winds blowing over and around a rectangular building create very high external pressures at wall corners, eaves and roof corners. Table 3 summarizes the wind pressures acting on an 8 ft. x 8 ft. shelter with an 8 ft. ceiling height, based

TABLE 3

Tornado Shelter Design Criteria

	Location	Pressure, psf	Direction
Wind-Induced External Pressures	Windward Wall	138	Inward
	Leeward Wall	87	Outward
	Side Walls	121	Outward
	Flat Roof	121	Outward
Local Pressures*	Wall Corner	347	Outward
	Eave	415	Outward
	Roof Corner	865	Outward
Atmospheric Pressure	Sealed Room	205	Outward
	Vented Room	0	—
	Venting Area, sq. ft. = 0.00098 x volume (cu. ft.)		

Missile Impact
    2 in. x 4 in. x 12 ft. long timber plank, weighs approximately 15 lbs. and impacts on end at 100 mph.

Load Combination
    These loads are considered to be ultimate loads; each can be assumed to act separately. Ultimate strength concepts may be used.

*Act on strips 0.1w wide, where w is least width of the shelter. External and local pressures should not be combined.

on the DCPA criteria. Wind pressures acting on a shelter tend to slide the structure off its foundation and to rotate it about the leeward edge. The shelter must be securely attached to a foundation to prevent sliding and rotation.

Tornadoes have a lower-than-ambient pressure at the center of the vortex.[7] If the in-residence shelter is tightly sealed, the atmospheric pressure change (APC) produces large, outward-acting pressures on the walls and roof that combine with the external pressures to cause a more severe loading condition than the external pressures alone. The effect of the APC can be relieved by providing vents in the walls or roof with sufficient area to allow air to flow from the room and equalize the pressure. Vending requirements are listed in Table 3.

The wind pressure and APC can be easily dealt with in the shelter design. The controlling criterion is the potential perforation of the shelter walls or roof by tornado-generated missiles. Documentation of missiles in tornado damage paths and computer simulation of tornado missile trajectories suggest that a 2 x 4 in. timber plank weighing 15 lbs. and traveling at 100 mph could be airborne in a tornado having wind and pressure within the limits of the in-residence shelter.[8] Comparable missiles are found in the damage paths where tornadoes have passed through a residential area and have destroyed roofs and strong walls. Figure 3 is an aerial view of tornado damage in Sweetwater, Texas (1986). The large collection of missiles are comparable to the 2 x 4 in. timber plank.

Studies were conducted at Texas Tech to determine what kind of walls would resist the impact of the design missile.[9,10] The tornado missile cannon shown in Figure 4 was designed and constructed to test various wall configurations found in normal house construction. Two-by-four stud walls with wood or metal siding and those with brick veneer were not capable of stopping the design missile.

FIGURE 2. Small room remains intact even though house is totally destroyed

A number of other wall configurations were considered in the in-residence shelter. Two concepts emerged: one for existing houses and one for new construction. Construction of an in-residence shelter in an existing house requires four layers of ¾ in. plywood on walls and ceiling to stop the design missile. For new construction, 8 in. concrete block walls with each vertical cell filled with grout and one ⅜ in. dia. reinforcing bar are recommended for the shelter. The four layers of plywood or a 3.5 in. reinforced concrete slab is recommended for the roof of the block wall shelter.

FIGURE 3. Aerial view of tornado damage in Sweetwater, Texas (1986) showing tornado missiles from damaged residence

FIGURE 4. Air-actuated cannon for testing tornado missile impact resistance of wall and roof configurations

The general concepts for the two in-residence shelters are shown in Figures 5 and 6. Construction plans are available from the author.

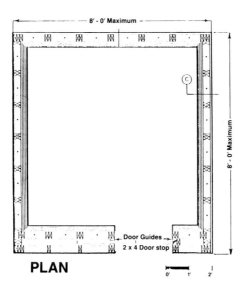

PLAN

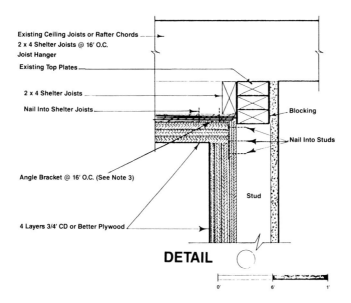

DETAIL

FIGURE 5. In-residence shelter concept for existing houses

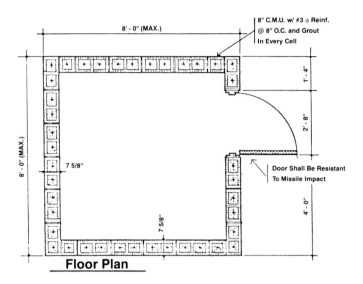

Floor Plan

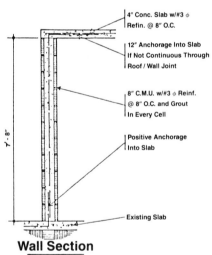

Wall Section

FIGURE 6. In-residence shelter concept for new construction

Protective Areas

People are not always at home when severe weather threatens. They may be at school, at work, shopping, or at play. For personal safety, it is imperative to know what actions to take when severe weather threatens. In some cases, authorities will direct persons to protective areas of safety. In other cases, an individual must determine the best course of personal action.

Certain principles of windstorm safety are discussed in this section. The first rule of personal safety is to seek shelter in a substantial structure, if available.[11] Being caught outdoors or in an automobile is the worst possible situation. Flying debris, broken power lines and lightning threaten persons outdoors. Automobiles easily roll and tumble in high winds. If no structure is immediately available, a person should find a ditch or depression and stay low to the ground. The face and head should be covered with clothing, books, or other material.

Buildings designed by an architect or engineer perform well in windstorms.[12] These buildings are required to meet building code requirements and are not likely to collapse under high wind loads. Government buildings, fire stations, hospitals, city halls, courthouses, and jails are examples of buildings that receive a high degree of professional attention. One should go to the basement or small interior room on the first floor to find an acceptable protective area. School buildings, light industrial buildings, or commercial buildings provide adequate protective areas, but caution should be observed. The rule "put as many walls between you and the outdoors" is a good one. However, other factors must be considered. Large open areas such as a gym or auditorium should be avoided. Areas immediately below tall walls or chimneys that could collapse are dangerous. One should stay away from exterior brick or concrete block walls. These walls may be supporting the roof or floor above. If unreinforced, they could suddenly collapse and crush persons next to the wall.

Broken glass can be transported by the wind. Because small pieces of glass become lethal projectiles, shelter should be sought away from windows and glass doors.[13] Again, small interior rooms, closets, or bathrooms are the best choices. Interior hallways also provide good protection. The belief that tornadoes always come from the southwest is a myth. Because tornado winds are rotational, the winds can blow from any direction.

Opening a window does nothing to mitigate tornado loads on a building. The loading can actually become worse if the winds blow directly into the open window. Doors should be closed, if time permits, including interior doors that open into hallways.

Tiles in hanging acoustical ceilings may become dislodged, if wind circulates through the building. Light fixtures, which are suspended from the hanging ceiling, may fall down along with the ceiling tiles (see Figure 7). To protect from such debris, it is a good idea to cover the face and head with books or clothing, or to crawl under a desk or other heavy furniture.

Mechanical equipment rooms that contain heating, ventilation and air conditioning equipment should be avoided. These rooms may be structurally sound, but should be avoided because of high voltage electricity, hot water, natural gas or toxic chemicals. Janitorial closets are also dangerous, because of the chemicals stored inside.

When severe weather suddenly threatens, there may not be time to look for protective areas. All public and private buildings should have floor plans posted that identify protective areas. Protective areas should not be represented as "shelters" unless the buildings have been designed to meet the DCPA criteria.[14] Protective areas simply identify the best places of safety in a particular building.

FIGURE 7. Ceiling tiles have become dislodged by wind circulating through building

PROTECTING PROPERTY

Few incentives are available to encourage an owner to invest money in windstorm protection[15] Reduction of discomforts and inconveniences mentioned previously are the main motivations. Fortunately, there are a number of steps that can improve wind resistance at little or no cost. Suggestions presented here relate to building a new home, retrofitting an existing home, or simply taking a few precautions around your home that will mitigate wind damage.

Building a New Home

Many concepts and ideas are available to increase the wind resistance of a new home for very little additional cost. Building a new home is the best opportunity to incorporate these measures. The two most important factors are site location and builder selection.

The location of the property can drastically influence wind effects. Homes located on the shore of a large body of water, at the crest of a hill, or in a valley where the wind can channel through will experience higher wind forces than those placed in more sheltered locations. Exposed locations are often the most desirable because of the panoramic view. They need not be ruled out, but the owner and builder should be aware of the higher potential for wind damage.

Trees surrounding a home can be both an advantage and a disadvantage. Tall, closely spaced trees provide shelter from the wind by drastically reducing the wind loads. On the other hand, significant damage can occur if a tree falls on a struc-

FIGURE 8. Collapsed tree has heavily damaged roof of a home in Louisville, KY

ture (see Figure 8). Thus, the location of trees around a building is important. They should be located a safe distance from houses and driveways to prevent damage should they collapse.

A house with a low profile is less susceptible to wind forces. Berms, strengthened fences and landscaping can serve as the first line of defense against wind, thus reducing loads on the house itself.[6]

It is important to select a builder/designer who is knowledgeable of wind loading concepts and who is willing to incorporate wind-resistant practices in the facility. Many inexperienced builders will charge excessive rates for incorporating wind-resistant concepts in a design because the process may deviate from normal construction practice. Contractors with this attitude should be avoided. Figure 9 shows a house under construction which has several wind-resistant features.

One easy way to assure wind-resistance in a house is to insist that the design follow a deemed-to-comply standard. A *Deemed-to-Comply Standard for Single and Multifamily Dwellings in High Wind Regions*, published by the Southern Building Code Congress International, is an example of a well conceived wind resistant design.[6] Although primarily intended for homes in areas threatened by hurricanes, a home designed by the criteria will perform very well if struck by a weak tornado (Fujita-scale F0 or F1). The Uniform Building Code[17] contains prescriptive requirements which, when conscientiously followed, will lead to a suitable wind resistant design. In tornado-prone areas, consider including an in-residence shelter if the home does not have a basement.

Simple Retrofit

Retrofitting an existing home to make it more wind resistant is an expensive and

FIGURE 9. Wind-resistant features of this house include: (1) laterally braced piles, (2) floor joist anchors, (3) wall anchors, (4) roof anchors, and (5) hip roof.

disruptive proposition. However, there are a few things that can be done.

Berms, strengthened fences and landscaping, as mentioned previously will reduce wind loads on an existing house. When reroofing, have an engineer/designer check adequacy of the roof deck, and the joist or truss connections, consider changing the roof geometry and/or install a highly wind resistant roofing system. Have an engineer/designer check the anchorage and support of canopies, carports, or roof overhangs. Provide operable shutters over windows, replace lightweight garage doors with heavy duty doors and tracks. Inward collapse of garage doors results in higher uplift pressures on the roof. Replace annealed window glass with heat-strengthened or tempered glass. Replace sliding glass doors in lightweight frames with more substantial ones.

Other Precautions

Restrain loose items stored on your property to prevent them from becoming air-borne. Tie down trailers, boats and RVs when not in use. Anchor storage buildings to a permanent foundation or use strap ties similar to those for mobile homes. Be sure radio and TV antennas are guyed to prevent collapse. Be sure elevated air conditioning equipment is well anchored, especially if it is placed on the roof. All of these precautions tend to minimize flying debris, which will reduce danger to people and property damage.

A PERSONAL PREPAREDNESS PLAN

A personal preparedness plan involves personal safety precautions and damage mitigation, through near-term and long-term planning.

Personal Safety Plan

The following steps are recommended to initiate a personal preparedness plan:

1) Identify weather information sources, including public radio and TV stations, community sirens, and NOAA weather radio* (with or without alarms).
2) Identify protective areas in your home. Choices are basement, small room, hallway or closet in interior of house.
3) Train and practice with family at home. Be sure everyone in the family, including children, understand the watches and warnings issued by the National Weather Service.
4) Instruct family members on how to find protective areas when they are away from home, no matter where they might be when severe weather threatens. Seminars and lectures produced by the National Weather Service each year are extremely useful for this purpose.

Long term plans should include an evaluation of the wind resistance of your home. Consider installing an in-residence shelter if family members are apprehensive about severe weather protection. If you live in a manufactured (mobile) home, provide a nearby underground shelter, above ground shelter (similar to in-residence shelter), or urge the manufactured home park owners to provide adequate shelter for all residents.

Damage Mitigation Plan

Steps for damage mitigation have been discussed previously. The damage mitigation plan should implement both the near-term and long-term steps. The near-term steps should include:

1) Pick up or restrain loose objects.
2) Tie down trailers, boats, RVs and storage sheds.
3) Remove trees that could collapse onto the house and cause bodily injury.

Long-term steps include:

1) Construct an in-residence shelter.
2) Replace roofing system, strengthen roof deck, anchor roof to top of wall, or change roof geometry.
3) Replace weak doors and windows.
4) Utilize berms, reinforced fences, and landscaping to reduce wind loads on the house.
5) Anchor mechanical equipment and guy antennas on the roof.

---

*Public Weather advisories and alarms broadcast by the National Weather Service, which is a bureau of the National Oceanic and Atmospheric Administration (NOAA).

CONCLUSION

Persons cannot simply rely on the news media and public authorities to protect them when severe weather threatens. The well prepared person has developed an individual preparedness plan for himself/herself and the family. Such a plan includes aspects for personal safety, as well as mitigation of property damage. By following a few simple rules, the potential for safety can be improved considerably at very little cost. Everyone living in areas where severe windstorms are a threat should be urged to follow the guidelines presented in this chapter.

REFERENCES

1. NSSFC. 1979. Tornado data set (1950-1979). National Severe Storms Forecasting Center, NOAA. U.S. Dept. of Commerce, Kansas City, MO.
2. Fujita, T.T. 1971. Proposed characterization of tornadoes and hurricanes by area and intensity. SMRP research paper no. 91. University of Chicago, Chicago, IL.
3. Dunn, G.E. and B.I. Miller. 1960. *Atlantic Hurricanes.* Louisiana State University Press, Baton Rouge, LA.
4. Minor, J.E., K.C. Mehta and J.R. McDonald. 1972. Failures of structures due to extreme winds. *J. Struct. Div.*, ASCE. 98:ST11, 2455-2471.
5. Kiesling, E.W. and D.E. Goolsby. 1974. In-home shelters from extreme winds. *Civil Engineering.* 44:9, 105-107.
6. DCPA. 1975. *Interim Guidelines for Building Occupant Protection from Extreme Winds,* TR-83A. Defense Civil Preparedness Agency, U.S. Dept. of Defense, Washington, DC.
7. McDonald, J.R., K.C. Mehta and J.E. Minor. 1974. Tornado resistant design of nuclear power plant structures. *Nuclear Safety.* 15:4, 432-439.
8. Kennedy, R.P., S.A. Short, J.R. McDonald, M.W. McCann, Jr., R.C. Murray and J.R. Hill. 1990. Design and evaluation guidelines for Department of Energy facilities subjected to natural phenomena hazards, UCRL 15910. U.S. Department of Energy, Washington, DC.
9. McDonald, J.R. and J.R. Bailey. 1985. Impact resistance of masonry walls to tornado-generated missiles. *Proceedings,* Third North American Masonry Conference, Arlington, TX.
10. McDonald, J.R. and E.W. Kiesling. 1988. Impact resistance of wood and wood products subjected to simulated tornado missiles. *Proceedings,* International Conference on Timber Engineering, Seattle, WA, Vol. 2.
11. Harris, H.W. and K.C. Mehta. 1991. Design of tornado protective areas in schools. Ninth Structures Congress, ASCE, Indianapolis, IN, April 29-May 1.
12. Minor, J.E., J.R. McDonald and K.C. Mehta. 1977. The tornado: an engineering-oriented perspective. NOAA Technical Memorandum ERL NSSL-82.

13. Minor, J.E. 1984. Window glass performance and hurricane effects. *Proceedings*, ASCE Specialty Conference: Hurricane Alicia - One Year Later. Galveston, TX, August 16-17.

14. McDonald, J.R. 1991. Damage mitigation and occupant safety. *Proceedings*, Tornado Symposium III. Norman, OK, April 2-5.

15. Mehta, K.C., R.H. Cheshire and J.R. McDonald. 1991. Wind resistance categorization of buildings for insurance. *Proceedings*, Eighth International Conference on Wind Engineering. London, Ontario, July 8-12.

16. SBCCI. 1990. A deemed-to-comply standard for single and multifamily dwellings in high wind regions. Southern Building Code Congress International, Inc. Birmingham, AL.

17. ICBO. 1991. *Uniform Building Code*. International Conference of Building Officials, 1991 Ed. Whittier, CA.

Natural and Technological Disasters: Causes, Effects and Preventive Measures. Edited by S.K. Majumdar, G.S. Forbes, E.W. Miller, and R.F. Schmalz. © 1992, The Pennsylvania Academy of Science.

Chapter Thirty-One

RISK COMMUNICATION AND THE TECHNICAL EXPERT

JOSEPH R. HERKERT

Department of Civil Engineering
Lafayette College
Easton, PA 18042

INTRODUCTION

In their book, *Powerline: The First Battle of America's Energy War,* Casper and Wellstone[1] paint a vivid picture of how, fifteen years ago, a group of Minnesota farmers were driven to civil disobedience and violence as a result of their opposition to the construction of a high-voltage powerline through their fields. The farmers opposed the line, which was supported by 180 feet tall towers at intervals of roughly one quarter mile, because they questioned the need for the electric power the line would provide, and because they were concerned about the health and safety risks due to the electromagnetic fields produced by the line, the obstruction the towers would create for their farm operations and the aesthetic impact of the line on the countryside.

The farmers were given various opportunities to air their concerns at county and state hearings, and filed several unsuccessful lawsuits, but they were unable to provide scientific evidence that the line represented a health and safety risk and the utilities and government simply refused to pay much attention to their other claims. The farmers felt systematically excluded from the decision processes relating to construction of the line and, as a last resort, took to their fields in an effort to halt construction, even going so far as to knock some of the towers down after the line was energized. While many of the protesters fell victim to the farm crises of the mid-1980s, the powerline remains in operation today, a symbol of the triumph of scientific rationality over public fear and anxiety.

Over the past several decades, the techniques used by engineers and scientists to measure and assess risks have matured.[2] Within the past few years, for example, research has begun to indicate that electromagnetic fields may indeed constitute a public health risk.[3] As the Minnesota powerline struggle, and other controversies involving questions of technological risk—Three Mile Island, Love Canal, Times Beach, etc.—clearly illustrate, however, risk *assessment* is only the first stage in attempting to balance the benefits and risks of technology. Like other value-laden issues, questions concerning risk are ultimately political in nature and thus, in a democratic society, require for their resolution satisfactory means for public discourse.[4,5,6]

In order to address this aspect of the problem, a new field has recently emerged which focuses on *communicating* risk information. *Improving Risk Communication*, a 1989 study conducted by the National Research Council, defined risk communication as:

> ... an *interactive process* of exchange of information and opinion among individuals, groups and institutions. It involves multiple messages about the nature of risk and other messages, not strictly about risk, that express concerns, opinions, or reactions to risk messages or to legal and institutional arrangements for risk management [emphasis added].[6]

This broad conception of risk communication has only recently gained favor. A more conventional view, still held by many engineers and applied scientists, is that risk communication consists merely of "educating" the public to endorse expert judgement concerning which risks are acceptable and which are not; put another way, teaching the public to think like the experts. The conventional view formed the basis of attempts throughout the past two decades to increase public understanding of science and public acceptance of technology.[7,8] For example, Harold Finger[9], an engineer who served as President of the industry-sponsored U.S. Committee for Energy Awareness, in explaining his confidence in the future of nuclear energy, noted:

> When they are informed, Americans will recognize that electric power is an essential element of their day-to-day lives, that a growing supply is necessary for a growing economy, and that there are few options available to provide that supply. Our message is not a theoretical one: It is a thesis that is confirmed month after month as our economy evolves.

Note that it is the expert who has possession of the truth; the only problem is to see that the public is properly informed. Under the conventional model of risk communication, then, success is measured by how well the message gets across to the public, and whether or not the public accepts the views of the experts.[6,7]

The emerging view of risk communication, on the other hand, recognizes that non-experts are also in possession of relevant risk information, thus necessitating an exchange of information between experts and the public if effective communication about risk is to occur.[7,8] Under this broader definition of risk communication, success is measured by the level of increase in understanding of risk problems by all of the involved parties.[6]

In this paper, I review the research in the behavioral and social sciences which supports the need for the emerging view of risk communication as a two-way process between expert and public, and suggest some attitudinal changes required of engineers and applied scientists who wish to become meaningful participants in such risk communication efforts. As an example of the shortcomings of the conventional model of risk communication, I will conclude with a brief case study of "inherently safe" nuclear reactors.

Risk Perception Research in the Behavioral and Social Sciences

The two-way, interactive model of risk communication follows from research in the behavioral and social sciences which has indicated that while experts and the public view risk in fundamentally different ways, each has something unique to offer to the understanding of risk.

To date, most of the work on the perception of risk has been done by psychologists. Psychological research has determined that people employ mental strategies, known as heuristics, as aids in decision making in the face of uncertainty. While the use of heuristics is essential to avoiding a life frozen with indecision, they also introduce systematic biases in the way we evaluate risks. Such factors as difficulties in judging probabilities, sensational media coverage, and personal experiences often lead us to underestimate or overestimate risks.[10] The well-known gambler's fallacy (the longer I play a game of chance, the more likely I am to win) is an example of a heuristic which would cause one to underestimate risk. Television coverage of an airline crash and a close relative suffering from a rare disease are events which could lead to overestimation of risk. Significantly, experts can also fall victim to the same sort of biases, particularly when they are in the realm of applying intuition as opposed to dealing with available data.[10]

Using a technique known as the psychometric paradigm, psychologists have also determined that the concept of risk has a different meaning to experts, who usually focus on the probability of fatality from a given activity, than it does to members of the lay public, who tend to factor in other characteristics of hazards such as catastrophic potential, lack of control, delayed harm, etc.[5,10] Psychometric research has also indicated that the risks that are least understood and most dreaded by the public—such as those posed by nuclear power and other potentially catastrophic technologies—often have a very high "signal potential" regarding the indirect impacts of environmental pollution or technological accidents.[10]

Many scientists and engineers, for example, view the Three Mile Island nuclear accident, in which there were no apparent deaths, as testament to the *safety* of nuclear power. The impacts of the accident, however, have rippled throughout the industry and the economy. As will be discussed later, the industry has yet to recover from its effects. Had more attention been paid by industry and government experts to the public's perception of the risks involved, the accident and its costly indirect impacts may have been prevented.[10]

Some psychologists and risk analysts have viewed these findings as justification for the conventional model of risk communication. The public perception of risk is viewed as irrational, as compared to the rational judgement of experts. In order to close this gap, the experts' information must be transferred to the public.[7,11] Paul Slovic,[10] on the other hand, argues that psychometric research implies a broader conception of the risk communication process:

> . . . there is wisdom as well as error in public attitudes and perceptions. Lay people sometimes lack certain information about hazards. However, their basic conceptualization of risk is much richer than that of the experts and reflects legitimate concerns that are typically omitted from expert risk assessments. As a result, risk communication and risk management efforts are destined to fail unless they are structured as a two-way process. Each side, expert and public, has something valid to contribute. Each side must respect the insights and intelligence of the other.

Social scientists have begun to take exception to the amount of emphasis placed upon the cognitive aspects of risk perception, arguing that the way in which people perceive risk cannot be completely understood until more is known about the social and cultural determinants of risk perception.[7,12] For example, Mary Douglas, an anthropologist, and Aaron Wildavsky, a political scientist, have argued[13] that the risks people are most concerned about are selected on the basis of the cultural preferences associated with the particular social insitutions to which they belong. Cultural explanations of differences in risk perception have also been advocated by sociologists. Perrow,[14] for example, has argued for a social and cultural model of risk perception which emphasizes "diversity and social bonding." And Clarke[12] has suggested that closer attention be paid to the role of organizations in risk assessment.

It should be noted that the principal emphasis in most arguments for a broader conception of risk communication is on expanding the decision process rather than on limiting the role of the expert. As Plough and Krimsky[7] note:

> Cultural reason does not deny the role of technical reason. The former branches out, while the latter branches in. Cultural rationality does not separate the context from the content of risk analysis. Technical rationality operates as if it can act independently of popular culture in constructing the risk analysis, whereas cultural rationality seeks technical knowledge but incorporates it within a broader decision framework.

The Engineer and Scientist as Risk Communicators

As the definition of risk communication as a two-way process has grown in favor, research efforts have increased concerning the process of risk communication and the content of risk messages.[6,15,16,17] I would argue, however, that meaningful participation in risk communication efforts on the part of technical specialists first requires significant attitude changes on their part with respect to the relationship between expert and public.

First and foremost, engineers and scientists should value, on an equal footing with scientific and technical rationality, other ways of knowing and expressing. More than ever, we need creative and efficient technological solutions to problems. But we also need more than ever the perspectives humanists and social scientists can bring to bear on these problems.

Acknowledging that technical rationality is not the only valid frame of reference, and that it is not necessarily superior to other viewpoints, is only the first step toward more effective risk communication. Engineers and applied scientists should also have a commitment to *listening* to others,[5] and to incorporating alternative points of view into the search for technical solutions to problems. "Public participation" has long been a buzz phrase in the literature of technology and public policy. More often that not, however, as in the Minnesota powerline case,[1] public participation amounts to mere window dressing for decisions made by government and/or industry experts.[4,18]

It is a frequent contention of technical experts that the public wants absolute safety. For example, Granger Morgan,[19] a distinguished researcher in the field of engineering and public policy, has argued that ". . . we have done so well in reducing risks that now many seem to forget that no activity or technology can be absolutely safe." My experience, however, has been that few, if any, people expect a risk-free world. For example, the last four times I have taught my senior seminar for liberal arts majors on Technological Catastrophes, I have given the students a questionnaire to fill out during the first class session. One of the questions asks, "Is a zero-risk society achievable?" Of more than seventy respondents, not a single student has answered in the affirmative. While it is clear that these students are not a representative sample of the American public, I think most would agree that their level of "technological literacy" is not very high.

Even those engineers and applied scientists who acknowledge that the public is prepared to take risks, typically tend to claim that they are unwilling to spend money on risk reduction. Florman,[20] for example, has argued:

> It would be a lot easier for engineers if their fellow citizens would clearly stipulate that safety should be the paramount concern, whatever the cost. But people do not say this. They want automobiles that are affordable and attractive; they want airplanes that are light enough to conserve fuel, and power plants that will turn out cheap electricity. They appear willing to pay for relatively foolproof backup systems for space vehicles, but precious little else. In other words, people are willing to take risks, but, naturally, do not want to pay the penalty for taking those risks.

Such statements also misconstrue public views on risk. Opinion polls and surveys, for example, have consistently indicated that the public is willing to pay for increased safety and a cleaner environment. In a recent survey conducted by Opinion Dynamics Corporation, for example, 74 percent of those surveyed said they would choose "environmental cleanup and slower growth over economic growth".[21]

Perhaps the biggest obstacle in persuading engineers and applied scientists to listen more carefully to the concerns of the public is the overwhelming bias toward quantification in the work of technical specialists. For example, the route of the Minnesota powerline was originally planned by engineers who overlaid a grid on U.S. Geological Survey topographical maps and then assigned to each square in the grid an avoidance rating based upon land use and other factors. While incorporated areas, highways, state and federal lands, water resources and forests were given avoidance numbers ranging from one through nine, farm land was rated zero, thus virtually guaranteeing where the powerline would be constructed. In the words of one of the farmers:

> They assigned farmers zero. The computer routed it on farmers assigned zero only, and it did this . . . without any knowledge of anybody here. They sat around with their plastic suits and their white shoes around the table back in Michigan and destroyed these people's lives in secret two years before it was ever sprung out here where the route was going to be, without asking anybody, without ever seeing it, with no sense of values of the rural people or no human consideration on what they were doing.

As this example illustrates, merely assigning numbers to the decision parameters in a technological problem, doesn't mask the fact that value choices are often made by experts at the expense of the people affected by technology. Closing the gap between expert and public perception of risk thus implies closing the gap between the quantitative and the qualitative. And, as previously noted, it is both unproductive and unrealistic to think that the gap can and should only be closed in one direction; that is by educating the public in the understanding and use of quantitative methods.

Valuing other ways of knowing and expressing, as well as listening to the views of others, are essential prerequisites if engineers and applied scientists are to become effective risk communicators. Risk communication efforts will not go very far if technologists persist in dismissing public perceptions of risk, responding to oversimplified notions of what the public wants, and utilizing quantitative methods to camouflage their own value judgements.

"Inherently Safe" Nuclear Reactors

A classic example of how conventional attitudes about the role of expert and public can undermine risk communication can be found in the case of "inherently safe" nuclear reactors, which have been promoted as means of revitalizing the nuclear power enterprise in the United States.

Forbes magazine has described the domestic nuclear power industry as the "largest managerial disaster in business history," surpassing the Vietnam War and the space program in money spent. There have been no new orders of nuclear plants since before the 1979 Three Mile Island accident, and over 75 cancellations in that same period, including some plants in the advanced stages of construction. Faced with huge investments for unfinished plants or billion dollar write offs for canceled plants, several U.S. utilities approached bankruptcy in the mid-1980s.[22] Joining the financial woes of the nuclear industry at center stage, the 1986 accident at the Chernobyl nuclear plant in the Soviet Union, despite differences in the designs of Soviet and U.S. reactors, resulted in reappraisals of the safety of nuclear power. In demonstrating for the first time the reality of a "worst-case" accident, Chernobyl renewed concern over the adequacy of: containment structures and other design features, procedures to minimize human factors contributing to accidents, and evacuation and medical treatment capabilities in the event of an accident.[23,24] Following Chernobyl, public opposition to expansion of nuclear power in the U.S. increased from 67 to 78 percent.[25] A 1989 Louis Harris poll revealed that 62 percent of Americans remain opposed to expansion of nuclear power, and that concern over accidents is among the most important issues.[26]

Conventional explanations of the collapse of the nuclear power industry fall within the following categories: 1) mismanagement on the part of the industry, including overly optimistic cost estimation and imprudent rate of scale-up in reactor size; 2) self-interest of industry and government elites; 3) rising costs due to increased safety regulations; 4) construction delays and cost increases resulting from widespread public opposition; and 5) decreased demand for electricity.[27]

Two recent studies in the policy arena have contributed new insights to this question, with particular emphasis upon decision-making in a democratic society. Tomain[28] concluded that the nuclear power industry cut itself off from the market and was not sensitive enough to public input. Morone and Woodhouse[29] agree, and postulate that an industry more attuned to the public's concern for safety would have turned toward safer reactor designs early on in the development of nuclear power. Interestingly, both conclusions call to mind the "signal potential" of unknown and dread risks predicted by psychometric research on risk perception.[10]

In 1981, physicist Alvin Weinberg and colleagues at the Institute for Energy Analysis, Oak Ridge Associated Universities, began work on a study of a "second nuclear era" based upon ". . . reactors that were sufficiently safe to restore confidence in nuclear power, which had been shattered by the [Three Mile Island] accident." Their study concluded that incremental safety improvements in the current generation of light water reactors had rendered them quite safe and that new "inherently safe" reactor designs were also technically and economically feasible.[30]

Work on safer, cheaper nuclear power has continued throughout the 1980s as the utility industry anxiously awaits the dawn of the new era. A recent review of these developments by a researcher at the Electric Power Research Institute concluded:

> . . . nuclear power plants of the future will be designed to better fulfill their role as a bulk power producer that, if invulnerable to severe accidents, will be more broadly accepted and implemented. Their use will help stem the tide of environmental damage caused by air pollution from fossil fuel combustion products. The potential abundance and concentrated energy of nuclear fuel makes it practical to dedicate the design of future nuclear power plants to achieving that invulnerability . . .[31]

Calls for a nuclear power revival have been given additional impetus by the growing concern in recent years over potential global warming—the so-called greenhouse effect—due in large part to carbon dioxide emissions from the combustion of fossil fuels.[32] Indeed, Weinberg[33] projects that 5,000 large nuclear plants—more than twelve times the current global total—may be needed by the middle of the next century if a greenhouse world is to be avoided.

Although a second nuclear era could include safety and reliability improvements at existing nuclear plants as well as improved, "evolutionary" versions of the current generation of large, light water reactors, the cornerstone of the new era would be advanced reactor designs that are "inherently safe," that is, employing passive design features that rely on gravity and natural convection to assure safety. The advanced reactors, nuclear advocates claim, would also be simple, reliable, easy to operate, modular, and standardized in order to reduce costs and facilitate licensing.[30,31,34]

It is important, for our purposes, to make note of the risk messages contained in discussions of the advanced reactor designs. By implying that accidents are impossible,[24] the term "inherently safe" recalls the conventional model of risk communication wherein the experts assure the public that all is well. Implicit in its use is the mistaken notion that the public wants zero risk, and, therefore, the solution is to give them "inherent safety." Although increased public acceptance of nuclear power is a stated goal of the planners of the new era, one wonders whether the public would ever accept a claim of inherent safety by an industry whose credibility has been so heavily damaged by the failures of the first era.[35]

As obvious as it should be that the term "inherently safe" engenders mistrust of the nuclear industry, some engineers and applied scientists continue to use it with abandon. An engineering manager for a reactor vendor, for example, has referred to the already existing generation of reactors as "inherently safe".[36] Weinberg, criticizing those who would caution against use of the term, even argues that ". . . inherent safety . . . offers a technical fix for the public's anxiety" about nuclear power.[33]

"Technological fix" is a phrase invented in the 1960s by none other than Weinberg himself to describe the application of technology to the solution of social problems.[37] By implying that the public's anxiety needs "fixing," Weinberg demeans the layperson's point of view and displays an attitude which is all too typical of applied scientists and engineers: the public's response to risk is not legitimate since it is based upon emotions (anxiety) rather than facts (rationality).

Use of the term "inherently safe" to describe the next generation of nuclear reactors is only the most obvious exaggerated claim of nuclear advocates. The public is also given assurances that the new reactor designs will be cheaper than their predecessors. The industry claims that the changes in design and operating philosophy resulting from lessons learned in the first nuclear era "can achieve economic competitiveness".[31] As Walter Meyer[38], an energy researcher at Syracuse University, recently wrote in an op-ed piece for a major metropolitan newspaper: "We know that the next generation of nuclear power plants will be even better—smaller, simpler and less expensive, with a greater margin of safety." Morone and Woodhouse,[29] apparently persuaded by industry claims that "inherently safe" reactors are feasible, have gone so far as to suggest that safer reactor designs could be "engineered" for competitive economics.

Given that the technical feasibility of the proposed new reactor designs has yet to be demonstrated in a manner that even approaches commercial application,[39] such optimism is reminiscent of the heyday of the first nuclear era when advocates of nuclear power made unwarranted cost projections in light of the state of the art.[40] The implication in such messages that there need not be tradeoffs between economics and safety in the new generation of reactors, in addition to its questionable technical foundations, responds to the mistaken notion that the public is unwilling to pay for increased safety.

A final example of the exaggerated claims of the engineers and scientists who support a nuclear renaissance, which also highlights the quantitative/qualitative gap discussed earlier, is the misuse of probabilistic risk analysis (PRA) in estimating the likelihood of an accident occurring at a nuclear power plant. A PRA is conducted by using event trees and fault trees to anticipate all the ways in which component failures may lead to a system accident.[41] Based upon PRA, Weinberg[33] estimates that with today's reactor designs a core-melt accident will occur roughly one in every 10,000 to 100,000 reactor-years of operation. Incremental improvements to existing reactor designs, Weinberg estimates, will decrease the probability of such an accident by a factor ranging from ten to twenty times, to once in every 200,000 to 1,000,000 reactor-years. Weinberg is not alone in his expectations of safety improvements. Wolf Häfele,[42] a German physicist and energy analyst, predicts a 100-fold increase in reactor safety will occur, on the grounds that existing accident probabilities are "not acceptable" given a scenario of large-scale deployment of nuclear power. Now both of these risk estimates are extremely optimistic, especially in light of the fact that there have already been two core-melts—Three Mile Island and Chernobyl—in less than 10,000 reactor-years of operation. And although they are couched in quantitative terms, what they really amount to is the wishful thinking of the experts. And so we come to a double standard. The same experts who prescribe technical fixes for the public's anxiety continue to smuggle their own biases into the debate, cloaked in the "respectability" of numerical estimates.

CONCLUSION

While the proposed advanced reactor designs may prove to be substantial improvements over the current generation of nuclear reactors, I believe the second era of nuclear power is, like the first, doomed to failure unless the exaggerated claims for the promise of the second era are abandoned and unless engineers and scientists become truly responsive to the legitimate concerns of the public. Technical experts must learn to accept that the public's view of the risks of nuclear power and other potentially catastrophic technologies is far broader in scope than their own, and that Americans are willing to pay a price for decreasing such risks. And while people do not demand absolute safety, they do expect that risk estimates will be derived from actual design and operating experience, not extrapolations based upon the wishful thinking of nuclear planners or fabricated on the notion that the public needs assurances that all is well.

Technical experts interested in reviving the nuclear option must be willing to rebuild mutual trust by communicating honestly and by demonstrating a willingness to be responsive to public input.[5] Development of advanced reactors should proceed at a slow pace with every effort made to avoid unkept promises, as was the pattern in the first nuclear era. Technologists must learn to be flexible in siting, design and regulatory matters, even at the expense of purely technical efficiency.

In addition, more vigilance is called for in the operation of the current generation of reactors.[43] The industry that brought us Three Mile Island, and continues to bring us Peach Bottoms with operators asleep at the switch,[44] can hardly expect the public to be enthused about their claims that the next generation of reactors will be inherently safe. As Perrow[14] has noted, the construction and operation standards of the nuclear power industry are on a par with those of other industrial organizations. The public has made it clear, however, that a higher standard of care is expected of the nuclear industry. Perhaps the most effective way of communicating to the public a willingness to assume such a higher standard would be for the industry to voluntarily close down existing reactors with marginal safety performance. In addition to an expression of good faith, heeding the signal of public concern may also help prevent future Three Mile Islands from creating futher near-fatal setbacks for the industry.[10]

As the example of "inherently safe" nuclear reactors indicates, risk communication efforts are unlikely to succeed unless technical specialists begin to value non-technical perspectives on risk, and to incorporate such perspectives into their technological solutions. Only when mutual trust and respect have been established between expert and public as a basis of interactive risk communication will satisfactory resolutions be forthcoming to technological controversies which hinge upon questions of risk.

REFERENCES

1. Barry M. Casper and Paul David Wellstone. 1981. *Powerline.* The University of Massachusetts Press, Amherst, MA.
2. Wilson, Richard and E.A.C. Crouch. 1987. Risk assessment and comparisons: an introduction. *Science* 236:267-270.
3. Nair, Indira, M. Granger Morgan, and H. Keith Florig. 1989. *Biological Effects of Power Frequency Electric and Magnetic Fields.* Office of Technology Assessment, U.S. Congress, Washington, DC.
4. Fiorino, Daniel J. 1990. Citizen participation and environmental risk: a survey of institutional mechanisms. *Sci. Tech. & Hum. Val.* 15:226-243.
5. Covello, Vincent T. 1989. Informing people about risks from chemicals, radiation, and other toxic substances: a review of obstacles to public understanding and effective risk communication, pp. 1-49. In: William Leiss (Ed.), *Prospects and Problems in Risk Communication.* University of Waterloo Press, Waterloo, Ontario, Canada.

6. National Research Council, Committee on Risk Perception and Communication. 1989. *Improving Risk Communication*. National Academy Press, Washington, DC.

7. Plough, Alonzo and Sheldon Krimsky. 1987. The emergence of risk communication studies: social and political context. *Sci. Tech. & Hum. Val.* 12:4-10.

8. Leiss, William. 1989. Preface, pp. 1-49. In: William Leiss (Ed.), *Prospects and Problems in Risk Communication*. University of Waterloo Press, Waterloo, Ontario, Canada.

9. Finger, Harold B. 1985. Public approval of nuclear power: beyond the short term. *Pub. Util. Fort.* (February 7):15-19.

10 Slovic, Paul. 1987. Perception of risk. *Science* 236:280-285.

11. Rowe, W.D. 1989. Alternative risk evaluation paradigms, pp. 1-21. In: Yacov Y. Haimes and Eugene Z. Stakhiv (Eds.), *Risk Analysis and Management of Natural and Man-Made Hazards*. American Society of Civil Engineers, New York, NY.

12. Clarke, Lee. 1988. Explaining choices among technological risks. *Soc. Probs.* 35:22-35.

13. Douglas, Mary and Aaron Wildavsky. 1982. *Risk and Culture*. University of California Press, Berkeley, CA.

14. Perrow, Charles. 1984. *Normal Accidents*. Basic Books, Inc., New York, NY.

15. Krimsky, Sheldon and Alonzo Plough. 1988. *Environmental Hazards*. Auburn House Publishing Company, Dover, MA.

16. Covello, Vincent T., David B. McCallum and Maria T. Pavlova. 1989. *Effective Risk Communication*. Plenum Press, New York, NY.

17. Leiss, William (Ed.). 1989. *Prospects and Problems in Risk Communication*. University of Waterloo Press, Waterloo, Ontario, Canada.

18. Chess, Caron and Billie Jo Hance. 1989. Opening doors: making risk communication agency reality. *Environment* 31:11-15; 38-39.

19. Morgan, M. Granger. 1981. Probing the question of technology-induced risk. *IEEE Spectrum* (November):58-64.

20. Florman, Samuel C. 1987. *The Civilized Engineer*. St. Martin's Press, Inc., New York, NY.

21. Stanislaw, Joseph and Daniel Yergin. 1990. The latest political litmus test. *NY Times* (July 1).

22. Cook, James. 1985. Nuclear follies. *Forbes* (February 11): Cover; 82-100.

23. Diamond, S. 1986. Chernobyl causing big revisions in global nuclear power policies. *NY Times* (October 27).

24. Ahearne, John F. 1987. Nuclear power after Chernobyl. *Science* 236:673-679.

25. Schneider, William. 1986. Public ambivalent on nuclear power. *Natl. J.* 18:1562-63.

26. Greenpeace Action. 1990. *Nuclear Power*. Greenpeace Action, Washington, DC.

27. Campbell, John L. 1988. *Collapse of an Industry*. Cornell University Press, Ithaca, NY.

28. Tomain, Joseph P. 1987. *Nuclear power transformation*. Indiana University Press, Bloomington, IN.

29. Morone, Joseph G. and Edward J. Woodhouse. 1989. *The Demise of Nuclear Energy?* Yale University Press, New Haven, CT.
30. Weinberg, Alvin M. *et al.* 1985. The second nuclear era: a nuclear renaissance. *Energy* 10:661-680.
31. Taylor, John J. 1990. Improved and safer nuclear power. *Science* 244:318-325.
32. Lanouette, William. 1990. Greenhouse scare reheats nuclear debate. *Bull. Atom. Sci.* (April):34-37.
33. Weinberg, Alvin M. 1990. Engineering in an age of anxiety. *Iss. in Sci. and Tech.* (Winter 1989-1990):37-43.
34. Golay, Michael W. and Neil E. Todreas. 1990. Advanced light-water reactors. *Sci. Amer.* (April):82-89.
35. Herkert, Joseph R. 1987. High-risk technology and technological literacy. *Bull. Sci. Tech. & Soc.* 7:730-737.
36. Haggin, Joseph. 1986. New era of inherently safe nuclear reactor technology nears. *Chem. and Engr. News* (June 30):18-22.
37. Weinberg, Alvin M. 1966. Can technology replace social engineering? *Univ. Chicago Mag.* (October):6-10.
38. Meyer, Walter. 1989. Nuclear power is needed more than ever. *Phil. Inquirer* (March 26).
39. Fischetti, Mark A. 1987. Inherently safe reactors: they'd work if we'd let them. *IEEE Spectrum* (April):28-33.
40. Bupp, Irvin C. and Jean-Claude Derian. 1981. *The Failed Promise of Nuclear Power.* Basic Books, Inc., New York, NY.
41. Rasmussen, Norman C. 1981. The appliction of probabilistic risk assessment techniques to energy technologies. *Ann. Rev. Energy* 6:123-138.
42. Häfele, Wolf. 1990. Energy from nuclear power. *Sci. Amer.* (September):137-144.
43. Wald, Matthew L. 1991. Can nuclear power be rehabilitated? *NY Times* (March 31).
44. Stets, Dan and Joyce Gemperlein. 1987. PE nuclear plant closed; operators found asleep. *Phil. Inquirer* (April 1).

Natural and Technological Disasters: Causes, Effects and Preventive Measures. Edited by
S.K. Majumdar, G.S. Forbes, E.W. Miller, and R.F. Schmalz. © 1992, The Pennsylvania Academy
of Science.

Chapter Thirty-Two

COUNTY EMERGENCY MANAGEMENT SERVICES

LARRY PARKO
Former Director
Centre County Office of Emergency Services
Bellefonte, PA 16823

INTRODUCTION

This Chapter will describe one of the best kept secrets in government: The
Emergency Management Program. Though often unknown, or at best overlooked,
it is an essential function of government. Some have gone so far as to say that it
is the most important, though hopefully least used, governmental function, as
Emergency Management personnel prepare for and coordinate the response to a
major disaster. What sorts of emergencies do Emergency Management Agency
(EMA) personnel respond to? Where did Emergency Management come from? How
does it operate? Where is the Profession going? These are the primary questions
to be addressed below.

The term "Emergency Management" sounds contradictory: like "Rush Hour."
By definition, an emergency is out of control. Once one was able to gain total control of a situation and manage it, it would no longer be considered an emergency.
On the other hand, if one was able to manage every aspect of a situation from the
beginning, one would never let it get out of control to become an emergency. Well,
Emergency Management personnel do not manage "the" emergency itself. First
and foremost, they try to prevent emergencies. But if one does strike, they manage
the response to and recovery from that emergency.

Another source of confusion is the difference between Emergency and Disaster. The difference is often one of semantics and degree. Webster defines Emergency as an unforeseen combination of circumstances that calls for immediate action, while a Disaster is a sudden calamity causing great damage, loss or destruction. Emergency Responders (Fire, Ambulance, Police, etc.) handle house fires, injuries from traffic accidents, robberies and assaults on a daily basis. All are emergencies but well within the responder's capabilities. However, to those affected, they may seem disastrous. Emergency Management personnel respond when situations go beyond the capabilities of those Emergency Responders; when the emergency has truly become a community-wide disaster.

EMA RESPONSE IN PENNSYLVANIA

Pennsylvania is the most flood prone state in the Nation, averaging at least one serious flooding incident somewhere in the Commonwealth each year. In the last 20 Years, there have been 17 Presidential Declarations of Emergency or Major Disaster in Pennsylvania; 14 of these have been flood-related.

The most powerful of Mother Nature's storms is, of course, the Tornado. In Pennsylvania, tornadoes are not as rare a phenomenon as many think. They can strike at any time, though are most common in the late Spring and early Summer months. For example, on May 31, 1985, a wave of Tornadoes devastated the "Northern Tier" of the state and killed 65 Pennsylvanians. This was by far the worst outbreak of tornadoes in Pennsylvania history.

A Hazardous Materials incident has the potential to affect a considerable portion of the population. According to Statistics from the U.S. Dept. of Transportation, Pennsylvania again leads the way, experiencing more reported Hazardous Materials Incidents than any other state in the nation. During the 1980s, Pennsylvania led the nation five of ten years. That's a "National Championship" not to be envied. This is by far the most frequent incident in Pennsylvania.

And, of course, there is the Ultimate Disaster: Nuclear, Chemical, Biological or Conventional Attack. Hazards exist in every community. No one is immune from disasters.

HISTORY

Emergency Management, as it is known today, can trace its roots to World War II. Civil Defense Organizations were established to alert the civilian population in case of enemy attack. However, they rapidly dissolved after the war. Subsequently, the world went further into the Nuclear Age and the Cold War heated up with the possiblity of direct conflict between the United States and the Soviet Union. During that period, many Americans began to perceive the necessity for Civil Defense Organizations to exist on a permanent basis. This was accomplished in 1951, when President Truman signed the Federal Civil Defense Act. Pennsylvania soon followed suit by enacting the State Civil Defense Act.

Civil Defense Organizations emphasized safety during attack-related scenarios. The citizens viewed them as part of the military establishment. Civil Defense conjured up (and still does to some people) connotations of Air Raid Drills, Blast and Fallout Shelters, Block Wardens, etc. Fortunately, these Civil Defense Organizations never had to respond to enemy attack. While they still bore an association with the military, they began to use their resources and to assume a role in responding to "Peacetime" disasters. Their mission slowly evolved into an "all-hazards" concept, meaning that they would respond to any type of disaster, not merely an enemy attack. The term "Emergency Management" began to be used to reflect this, although the Civil Defense aspects were (and still are) a very important part of the overall program.

That evolutionary process culminated on July 20, 1979, when President Carter signed an Executive Order that created the Federal Emergency Management Agency. This consolidated responsibility for overseeing and administering the variety of both the Civil Defense and disaster related programs under a single agency. Pennsylvania, following the federal lead, enacted the Emergency Management Services Code of 1978. It repealed the State Civil Defense Act and it changed the name of the state agency from the Pennsylvania Civil Defense Council to the Pennsylvania Emergency Management Agency. More importantly, it outlines the shape of emergency management in the Commonwealth. They say, "What goes around comes around." President Reagan's signing of the National Security Directive in 1985 has caused Emergency Management Agencies to focus more of their efforts back toward attack preparedness. Actually, this was more of a return to a stricter interpretation of the provisions of the Federal Civil Defense Act rather than a change in Policy.

This law states that Federal Funds shall be used only for Attack Preparedness activities and capabilities or those with a "Dual Use." This means that such functions can enhance Non-Civil Defense aspects of the program as long as they do not detract from attack preparedness. However, the interpretation of "Dual Use" had grown quite lax during the 1960s and 1970s. At the same time, the Federal Government and its Budget both grew rapidly, with an accompanying decline in federal oversight activities.

The National Security Directive also coincided with his "New Federalism" Policy. That is, a decreasing amount of Federal support, particularly financial, with responsibility for these programs being shifted to the State and Local Governments. For example, Centre County, Pennsylvania will receive approximately 30% of its Emergency Management Budget from Washington in Federal Fiscal Year 1990. This is in sharp contrast to the nearly 45% which was received in Federal Fiscal Year 1981. Centre County is fortunate. In many other counties the reimbursement is even lower.

In Pennsylvania, the balance of the Emergency Management Budget comes from County Tax Dollars. There is no fiscal contribution from the Commonwealth toward a County's Emergency Management budget. There is help in the form of technical assistance and some equipment, however. Emergency Managers across the nation are waiting to see what the ultimate effects of the series of events that began in mid-1989 will be. The wave of democratization in Eastern Europe and Soviet Union, the apparent end of the "Cold War," and the war in the Persian Gulf will certainly have an impact. My opinion is that attack preparedness aspects will have to remain. However, their focus will change to Terrorist Attack and limited Nuclear Exchanges rather than a full scale Nuclear Holocaust.

CIVIL DEFENSE EMPHASIS

Part of the basis of the attack preparedness emphasis in the emergency management program at the federal level stems from the Constitution. Both Article I. Section 8. and Article IV. Section 4. give the Legislative and Executive branches of the federal government the responsibility to provide for the defense of the nation.

Part of this responsibility was addressed in the Civil Defense Act. So, aside from the fact that "it's the law," threats to our national security do exist. This includes not only nuclear attack, but chemical, biological, conventional, as well as terrorist attack. Furthermore, many of the things done to prepare for an attack related scenario are directly transferable to the preparation for, response to and recovery from natural and technological disasters. If you're prepared for the worst, it's easier to handle other incidents.

The threat of an all-out nuclear attack is quite small. There are many nations that have confirmed nuclear capability; there are other countries rumored to have such weapons; there are several more that appear to have the knowledge to develop nuclear weapons should they desire. However, as long as these weapons exist, so does that possibility. An unfortunate example of a multi-faceted threat is Iraq, based on their actions in 1990. There was the confiscation of Nuclear Detonators at Heathrow Airport in London in late-March indicating another potential nuclear threat. Then there was their invasion of Kuwait in early-August and subsequent humiliation at the hands of Allied Forces in early 1991.

Since the advent of the Nuclear Age, World Leaders have tried to prevent the spread of these weapons as well as reduce their total number. However, despite their best efforts, the number of Nuclear Warheads has increased steadily. This is a bit of a misnomer, however. While the number of Warheads has increased, the Gross Tonnage has not increased nearly as rapidly. Warheads are getting smaller as Delivery Systems become more accurate. This does serve to highlight that no matter how small it is, the nuclear threat certainly does exist.

Consequently, the Civil Defense aspects of the program are essential, even though an all-out nuclear war is unlikely. What President Kennedy said in 1961 is still quite true. Civil Defense, "is an insurance we trust will never be needed, but insurance which we could never forgive ourselves for forgoing in the event of a catastrophe." (Federal Emergency Management Agency, 1989. CIVIL DEFENSE SPEAKERS KIT. Office of Civil Defense. Washington, DC. Pg. 2-9).

This has been a short history of and the reasoning behind the existence of an Emergency Management Program. What follows will describe how Emergency Management is organized in Pennsylvania to handle all disasters.

EMERGENCY MANAGEMENT ORGANIZATION

The Federal Civil Defense Act mandates that an emergency management organization exists. Furthermore, Pennsylvania's Emergency Management Services Code states in Section 7501 that the governing body of each Township, Borough and County is responsible for ensuring that the organization persists. This Organization is generally charged by Resolution with implementing the Emergency Management Program for their jurisdiction. Consequently, they operate under the direction and control of the Elected Officials.

A viable Organization must have at least three basic components. These are the Emergency Operations Plan, The Emergency Operations Center and the Emergency Management Coordinator and Staff.

Emergency Operations Plan

The Emergency Operations Plan serves many functions. First, it must provide for the coordinated utilization of available resources. If there are no guidelines or priorities established for the use of resources before a disaster, then conflicts will arise over their distribution during the disaster. With limited resources, that's likely enough to happen anyway. Predetermined priorities and guidelines will reduce these tensions.

In addition, the Plan delegates authority to the extent possible. It gives the people who will be acting during a disaster the authority to do what they think is best for the citizens, to the maximum extent possible. Yet, on the other hand, it must remain consistent with the necessary control and responsibility legally assigned to the elected officials. Last, but not least, the Plan provides for continuity. A disaster will often require several days of non-stop operations. No single person can work that long without rest. The Plan must provide for back up personnel in some fashion. Furthermore, if primary personnel are not available, their functions must still be covered.

Emergency Operations Center

Facilities

The function of the Emergency Operations Center (EOC) is to provide a physical location and related facilities in which the Emergency Management personnel and Elected Officials meet so the coordination of activities can occur and support decisions can be made. In some Townships and Boroughs, there are only three or four people, a telephone, a few basic comfort facilities, and maybe a coffee pot. In sharp contrast, some counties have in excess of twenty-five people with an elaborate Communication System, Computers, a Full Kitchen, Bunk Rooms and Showers.

Communication

In the event of a major disaster, many agencies and individuals would respond.

The EMA is in essense a "Headquarters Operation." EMA personnel MUST be able to communicate both internally and externally.

External communications capabilities are a very important factor in the overall effectiveness of the operation of an EOC. "Rapid and accurate communications are the basis of effective emergency response. If you don't have adequate communications, you cannot effectively meet the other emergency response demands." (Lavalla, Rick and Skip Stoffel, Blueprint for Community Emergency Management. Olympia, WA: Emergency Response Institute, 1983: Pg 333.)

The EOC must also provide Communications facilities so that information can be gathered from the field to be used by the Elected Officials and Emergency Management personnel to help them make their decisions. Then, those decisions must be relayed back to the emergency workers in the field as well as the general public.

Another facet of a Communication System is the ability to advise and inform the public. Some disasters allow little, if any, time for Warnings. On the other hand, however, most disasters do not occur without some prior indication. After the citizens are warned, they must be kept informed of the status of the operation to prevent, or at least reduce, the impact of the "Rumor Mill." Communicating with the outside world during a disaster is very important to the ultimate outcome. However, all the communication equipment in the world will be of no use if the information is not effectively and efficiently used in the EOC. Therefore, some sort of Information Management System is necessary within the EOC as well.

First of all, the information must be received and recorded by the EOC Staff. This may be as simple as a TO/FROM*MESSAGE/REPLY Form. Once it has entered the system, it must be given to the proper persons. This is often the job of the Emergency Management Coordinator in smaller organizations while a separate staff person may be assigned this task in a large one. After the decisions are made, they must be documented. In this day and age, this may be nearly as important as external communication. In the event of a major disaster, there will be litigation. The EMA Staff and/or Elected Official who cannot show how and why a decision was made may well be liable for their decisions.

Emergency Management Coordinator and Staff

And last, but certainly not least, is the Emergency Management Coordinator and his/her Staff. The Coordinator works on behalf of the elected officials to oversee the administration of the ongoing Emergency Management Program and the work of the Staff as well as Emergency Response and Recovery operations if a disaster strikes.

This is obviously the most important part of the organization. The best Plans and the finest Emergency Operations Centers do not respond when there is a disaster. The people use the Plans in the Emergency Operations Center to make the system work. The collection and analysis of the information from all the responding agencies is far too much for one person, so the Staff members help out the Coordinator and Elected Officials. The Staff are responsible for supplying the primary decision makers with information and advice on matters related to their functional area of expertise (i.e. Fire & Rescue, Emergency Medical, Police, Transportation, etc.). They concentrate on their respective pieces of the puzzle; the Elected Officials and Coordinator concentrate on how all the piece fits together to form the "Big Picture."

While an emergency management organization must exist, there are no regulations as to the form it must take. Furthermore, there are provisions in the Pennsylvania Statutes whereby municipalities, or even counties, may join together to form that organization. The six Municipalities that form the Centre Region Council of Governments (Borough of State College, Townships of College, Ferguson, Halfmoon, Harris and Patton) recently completed a unique project that took full advantage of these provisions to consolidate their emergency management organizations. Each municipality has appointed the same person as Emergency Management Coordinator. In addition, they have developed a Region-wide Emergency Operations Plan. There is a single EOC for the region. The various Resolutions and Ordinances have been enacted by the Municipalities.

The Centre Region would be able to bring the resources of the five townships and one borough to bear on a problem, rather than each acting individually, as was previously the case. Now that this process is complete, it can be, and has been, used as a prototype for other municipalities, both in the County and across the State.

It is important to note that the emergency management organization, at any level, is by no means a replacement for, nor an addition to, the normal emergency response services (Fire, Police, Emergency Medical, etc.) and the many other important services and organizations (Red Cross, Salvation Army, etc.) that function during an emergency. Rather, it is that part of the system whereby the activities of these groups are coordinated, to prevent duplication of effort, and supported, to make sure they have as many of the resources as possible to function adequately when responding to a major disaster.

INTEGRATED EMERGENCY MANAGEMENT SYSTEM

The Integrated Emergency Management System (IEMS) is a strategy using a functional approach to Emergency Management as opposed to a hazard-specific approach. It is based on the fact that it is not practical to have a separate plan for every potential disaster. Besides, EMA Personnel generally would be performing many of the same basic tasks, no matter what disaster strikes. For example, the person in charge of overseeing the welfare of disaster victims does many of the same things no matter what situation arises, be it a flood, tornado or chemical incident. The IEMS strategy bases planning and response efforts on the fact that all emergencies have many common factors while allowing for the unique characteristics that each situation will present.

EMERGENCY MANAGEMENT PROGRAM

An Emergency Management Program has four phases: Mitigation, Preparedness,

Response and Recovery. While they are distinct for analytical purposes, they are closely interrelated.

Mitigation

Mitigation is any action taken to eliminate or reduce the impact of a hazard. Public Education is probably the most important mitigation activity performed by Emergency Management Personnel. A wide variety of pamphlets, booklets, films and video tapes are available to the public. News releases are prepared periodically on topics of general concern. Programs are presented for schools, civil or professional clubs and organizations. Citizens are informed of what the Emergency Management Agency can do and how they can help, as well as what they can do to help themselves in an emergency. EMA personnel also work with local and county planning agencies to prevent, reduce, or regulate the use of hazard-prone areas, particularly Flood Plains.

Preparedness

The bulk of their time is spend in the Preparedness phase. Important preparedness activities are planning and training. Planning involves keeping the Emergency Operations Plan up to date as well as maintaining a current inventory of resources and personnel that would be called on in an emergency. Keeping this information up to date serves two purposes. First, the information needed to make the decisions that have to be made during a disaster response will be available. Second, it develops a relationship with the people controlling the resources that Emergency Management personnel may be calling on during that time.

The County EMA also helps the Emergency Management Coordinator from each Township and Borough perform these same duties. Both are constantly updating the county and municipal plans and resource manuals to improve the coordination and cooperation between these branches of the emergency management family. The County is also responsible for training each Municipal Coordinator. In addition to "classroom training," various types of exercises are conducted periodically at both the municipal and county levels. These exercises apply the techniques learned in training to improve response and recovery capabilities.

Because experience shows that the way a community organizes itself before a disaster is the most important factor in how effectively it responds to a disaster. A good example is the response during the Loma Pieta Earthquake in October 1989. Most emergency responders in California had participated in an Earthquake Exercise earlier that year. Many reported that because of their training, they were better prepared to respond and were less confused than would have been the case otherwise.

Another important Preparedness activity is developing and maintaining systems to warn citizens of impending disasters. In Pennsylvania, many Counties are fortunate enough to have at least two such warning systems. The first, and most well known, is the Emergency Broadcast System. This is a Voluntary Program on the part of the Broadcast Media to accept and rebroadcast emergency information.

Second, many Counties have arrangements with their Cable TV providers to broadcast emergency information over their Cable Systems. In Centre County, the Emergency Warning Audio Override System was developed in cooperation with TCI of Pennsylvania, Inc., State College Borough and Centre County Governments. As the name implies, the Audio portion of the TV Signal can be overridden to broadcast emergency information.

Response

An Emergency Management Agency becomes most active and visible during the Response and Recovery phases of the program. As has been stressed throughout, the EMA performs a coordination and support role. They coordinate the wide variety of activities occurring in the field, to avoid duplication of effort, and support them, insuring that resources are used as efficiently and effectively as possible to alleviate pain and suffering and reduce property damage.

Recovery

Once the immediate threat has abated, Emergency Management personnel work to help the community recover from the disaster as quickly as possible. In the short-term, the goals are to restore basic utilities as quickly as possible, repair the transportation infrastructure and begin debris removal. During long-term recovery, they serve primarily as a liaison between the citizens and any State or Federal Agencies that may provide aid and assistance.

CONCEPT OF OPERATIONS

Intergovernmental Hierarchy

The emergency management system in the United States is built on the lowest level of government. Since Pennsylvania is a Commonwealth, this is the Townships and Boroughs. When disaster strikes, the response will start at that level. Fire, Ambulance, Police and other emergency responders will do what they do best: save lives and property and reduce pain and suffering. Without their dedication and courageous response, the core of the emergency management hierarchy would collapse. The rest of the system would soon follow into a "Black Hole" of confusion and chaos.

If the effects of the disaster exceed a local governments' capabilities to respond effectively, the Elected Officials and their Emergency Management Coordinator would request additional assistance from the County. In this instance, the County would not take charge of the situation, but rather, become another actor in the play, in a supporting role. If, on the other hand, the disaster affects more than one Township and/or Borough, the County, by law, takes a primary role but would by no means exclude the local governments from the operation.

If the magnitude of the disaster exceeds the County's capabilities to respond effectively, the County Board of Commissioners, with their Emergency Management Coordinator, would request assistance from the State through the Pennsylvania Emergency Management Agency. In similar fashion, if the resources of the State proved insufficient, the Governor would request assistance from the Federal government through the Federal Emergency Management Agency.

Thus, as the scope or severity of a disaster increases, progressively higher levels of government become involved. However, no matter how many levels or agencies are committed, the primary goal is to support the response efforts at the local level.

Emergency Operations

If the Elected Officials declare a disaster to exist, by law, they assume ultimate responsibility for the health, safety and welfare of their citizens. The Emergency Management Coordinator, becomes responsible for overall coordination of activities and distribution of resources under the direction of the Elected Officials and the Emergency Operations Plan.

At the County Level, Emergency Operations are far too complex for one person, or even a small group. The Emergency Operations Center (EOC) Staff is appointed to assist the Coordinator and elected officials. These volunteers provide the policymakers with information and advice related to their functional area of expertise. These Emergency Operations Staff Officers concentrate on their respective "piece of the puzzle," while the coordinator and elected officials concentrate on how these pieces fit together to form the "big picture."

All these people working together provide for the coordination and support of the emergency response at the various disaster scenes. They look at who is doing what to help the emergency responders avoid working against each other and/or avoid duplication of effort. They also support those operations with resources ensuring they are used as effectively and efficiently as possible. For example, if a Tornado, or series of Tornadoes were to strike in a populated area of the county, most Emergency Operations Staff Officers would be called into action. Other might be, depending on the specifics of the situation.

In Centre County, Pennsylvania, each 12-hour shift of the EOC Staff would consist of up to 24 individuals. Nine of these are the three members of the County Board of Commissioners, the Coordinator, Deputy Coordinator, and clerical/support staff. The others are the "resident experts" in their fields. The County Commissioners would first be called on to declare a Disaster Emergency. This would activate the Emergency Mangement Agency and put all staff members on "alert." It would also institute certain provisions of the Emergency Management Services Code, as amended. They may need to order an evacuation of areas that may have become unsafe due to the tornadoes. They would also approve emergency contracts for goods and/or services from the private sector that are needed to augment the Emergency Response by Expenditure of County Funds.

The Coordinator acts like the coach of a team. They help resolve any problems that may arise between members of the EOC staff. They can also bring the power of the Commissioners to bear on a problem that has arisen with people or situations in the "outside world." The Operations Officer supervises the flow of information through the EOC. Messages from disaster scenes must be routed to the proper staff officer. Furthermore, once a coordination and/or support decision has been made, that information must be relayed to the emergency workers in the field. In addition, this person ensures that graphic displays of information in the EOC are properly maintained and updated so all staff members are aware of the status of emergency operations throughout the county.

The person with the greatest impact on the public's perception of the emergency operations is the Public Information Officer. They help prepare, and often present briefings and releases to the news media. They are busy summarizing information on damage to the areas affected by the tornadoes as well as what is being done, and what will be done, to alleviate these problems.

The Communications and Warning Officer would determine what parts of the emergency communications systems were still operating and to what extent. They would then make arrangements to have as complete a communications system as possible by augmenting what remained with other communication resources available. This would be primarily amateur radio operators, many of whom have special training in emergency operations and communication. This person also monitors the status of the media to evaluate their ability to broadcast emergency information to the public.

The Fire/Rescue Services Officer monitors the status of and coordinates the use and relocation of fire and rescue resources. They would determine what, if any, fire equipment had been damaged by the tornadoes. They would also determine what equipment is committed to the response efforts. This person would then coordinate the relocation of equipment throughout the county to ensure that no area is without fire coverage.

The Health/Medical Services Officer provides information and advice on public health matters. They also coordinate the utilization of emergency medical services resources (ambulances, personnel, etc.). They also monitor the status of the health care facilities within the country. This person would also aid in the distribution of injured persons to those health care facilities so that no single facility was overwhelmed by the number of victims transported there.

The Emergency Welfare Officer is responsible for the care and well being of both disaster victims and emergency workers. They are the liaison with American Red Cross Chapter in the county to coordinate the opening, staffing, and stocking of mass care centers to house persons forced to leave their homes because of the tornadoes. They also serve as a point of contact, in cooperation with the Health/Medical Services Officer, for Critical Incident Stress Debriefing (CISD) teams. These teams help people deal with the psychological trauma resulting from disaster.

The Transportation Officer monitors the condition of the transportation infrastructure and coordinates the movement of equipment and/or evacuation of people. They would determine what roads and highways were closed as a result of the tornadoes and help ensure that as few people as possible use those roads. They would also coordinate the transportation of people and equipment to reduce traffic congestion to the extent possible.

The Hazardous Materials Officer is active during incidents involving chemicals. They would be the point of contact for outside agencies such as CHEMTREC (Chemical Transportation Emergency Center). This information is used to provide advice to minimize exposure to both emergency responders and the public. This person would also act as liaison if any outside response agencies were summoned to deal with a particular chemical incident.

The Radiological Officer provides information and advice for incidents involving radioactive materials, up to and including nuclear attack. They would provide information to minimize exposure to radiation as well as procedures to be followed for decontaminating persons that may have come in contact with radioactive materials.

The Agricultural Services Officer is the liaison to the agricultural community. They would provide information about the probable and expected impacts of a disaster on crops and/or livestock as well as advice on minimizing those damages.

The School Services Officer serves as the point of contact for all educational facilities. They would coordinate evacuation and relocation of students in the area affected by the tornadoes. They would also work with school district officials if school buildings were to be used as mass care centers.

The last two members are most active as the response activities are beginning to decrease and recovery activities are beginning to increase. The Public Works Officer monitors the status of the utility services and infrastructure. This person would help in developing priorities for their repair and/or replacement.

The Damage Assessment Officer coordinates the collection of damage estimate reports for properties affected by the tornadoes. Damage assessment information is sent to state and federal officials. They, in turn, use this information to determine whether or not a Gubernatorial or Presidential declaration of emergency is warranted.

WHERE EMERGENCY MANAGEMENT IS GOING

Technologically

Pennsylvania is leading the way with regard to using modern technology to enhance the Emergency Management Program. First, every County is using a Computer. Programs contain detailed lists of the resources that would be accessed during a disaster. They also have detailed maps of the Counties on which Emergency Management personnel can mark the location of these resources as well as map out the areas affected by a given disaster. Some now have Plume Dispersion Models in the event of a major hazardous materials incident to help decide what areas may need to be evacuated.

Secondly, every County has the ability to transmit, via Satellite, data to any or all of the 66 other Counties or the Pennsylvania Emergency Management Agency.

Satellite communication is far less subject to disruption during natural disasters than the Radio or Telephone systems. Pennsylvania is the first state in the nation to have installed both Computers and Satellite systems in every County. Many other states and even a few foreign countries have sent representatives to Pennsylvania to inspect these systems.

Professionally

As the emergency management programs has become more complex, the knowledge, skills and abilities required of those assuming the position of Emergency Management Coordinator have grown proportionally. As the qualifications have grown, so has the movement on the part of the practitioners to develop emergency management into a profession as opposed to just a job.

Toward that end, the National Coordinating Council for Emergency Management has been working for over two years to develop a Certification program for Emergency Management Coordinators. As this is a results-oriented profession, education will not and can not be the sole criteria for certification. The Certification process will include two phases: a Credentials Review and a Written Examination.

As currently devised, the Credentials Review will examine several areas:

1. Formal Education - After a phase-in period, a four-year college degree will be required.
2. Experience - The equivalent of three years' full-time experience.
3. Proficiency - Active involvement in actual events or exercises within the previous two years.
4. Continuing Education - Not only in Emergency Management but other areas as well including: general management, adult education, public relations, information management, etc.

Certification would be maintained by completing the second phase, a Written Examination, within five years. Recertification requirements beyond this phase are still being devised.

CONCLUSION

The Emergency Management Program is like an Insurance Policy. Policyholders (Elected Officials) pay their premiums (support the EMA) and talk to their Agent (Coordinator) periodically to make sure their coverage (Plan) is adequate. But, in the back of their mind, they hope and pray that they never have to collect on that Policy (implement the Emergency Operations Plan).

Emergency Management Personnel at all levels are training and exercising in preparation for disasters. They inform the public of what they need to do in case a disaster does strike. However, they would be all too happy if they never mobilized to respond to a disaster. Yet, they all know that disaster can strike at any time and they are constantly prepared to react.

Natural and Technological Disasters: Causes, Effects and Preventive Measures. Edited by S.K. Majumdar, G.S. Forbes, E.W. Miller, and R.F. Schmalz. © 1992, The Pennsylvania Academy of Science.

Chapter Thirty-Three

MAPPING A TECHNOLOGICAL DISASTER[1]

UTE J. DYMON[2]
and
NANCY L. WINTER[3]
[2]Department of Geography
Kent State University
Kent, OH 44242-0001
and
[3]Graduate School of Geography
Clark University
Worcester, MA 01610

INTRODUCTION

Maps play a critical role in coordination of emergency responses during a technological disaster. Actions and information flows necessary for successful emergency management are based on knowledge of spatial relationships within the crisis situation which are best presented through the medium of a map. This paper describes a Quick Response Study of the degress of map use during the response stage of a train derailment in Craigsville, Pennsylvania. A Quick Response Study must be conducted with great dispatch while a disaster and its immediate consequences are unfolding. Such timely investigation is essential in order to analyze how maps are utilized in the evacuation of humans from the danger zone, in efforts to control the physical agent causing the crisis, in communication with the media about the amount of risk involved, and in documenting key spatial aspects of the disaster.

[1]This research was supported by the Natural Hazards Research and Applications Information Center in Boulder, Colorado.

DISASTER MANAGEMENT

In the United States today, on site or in transit accidents involving hazardous materials have the potential to affect most of the 82,000 existing separate government units - towns, counties and states (Cigler, 1988). In the past decade, the frequency of this type of technological hazard has increased (Sorenson, Vogt and Mileti, 1987). With the passage of the SARA TITLE III "Community Right to Know Law" (USEPA, 1987), local governments must develop emergency planning for the handling of hazardous materials. Industries and businesses are required to report to the local government the quantities of hazardous materials that they store or transport within that community. A host of issues related to the routine transporting of hazardous materials on United States highways and railways now face the local Emergency Planning Committees established under this law. However, Cigler (1988) warned of "the intergovernmental paradox of emergency management" in which

"....local governments may be the least likely to perceive of natural and/or technological hazards as important problems. Consequently, emergency management becomes a low priority on local governments' formal agendas...the governments least likely to perceive emergency management as a key priority — local governments — are at centerstage in terms of responsibility for emergency management...The states have delegated the first-response functions for most emergency situations to their local governments" (Cigler, 1988).

Placing emergency preparedness responsibilities at the local level ignores two problems: a lack of financial resources and a lack of technical knowledge. To develop effective emergency planning and to garner resources for emergencies involving hazardous materials transportation, local leaders must accomplish interactions across town, county, state and federal governments. Even with state backup support and with federal agencies helping to coordinate disaster planning, few local communities have the necessary leadership skills. The effect of the "intergovernmental paradox" on the derailment disaster in rural Pennsylvania is detailed later in this chapter.

Public Choices in Evacuation

Dynes proposed a set of principles for emergency planning and warned that evacuation planning should be based on our knowledge of human behavior (Dynes, 1983). Questioning the assumptions underlying "command and control" type planning for evacuation, Dynes offered an alternative "emergent human resources model" highlighting the existing strengths in any local social system, along with human habits and established behaviors. He urged that emergency plans: 1) be built around existing patterns of social life, 2) use existing social units instead of constructing a new set of them, 3) synchronize incoming resources and policies with the local culture, 4) use existing authorities and patterns of power instead of trying to establish new ones, 5) use existing communication channels and broaden them instead of restricting information flow to "official messages," 6) aim to resume normal life by rebuilding and returning to many community routines quickly, and 7) adopt mitigation actions that do not alter dramatically the community's social traditions. Independent actions by citizens, such as self-evacuation and choosing shelter with friends and relatives, are expected and valued in this model of coordination. Historically, the public has always insisted upon the right to make private decisions about when and how to evacuate (Quarantelli, 1984; Zeigler and Johnson, 1984). However, most FEMA plans envision only command and control types of public evacuation. The history of evacuation shows overwhelmingly that people prefer to evacuate themselves and to choose their own shelters. We found the same to be true in Craigsville.

A Model of Evacuation

Quarantelli (1984) formulated an evacuation model which describes evacuation as one of the most profound effects of disaster on any community and as a process that involves more than one pattern of movement. Rather than being a single flight from a physical threat, evacuation is composed of a series of complex individual and group interactions with more than one focus. These complicated patterns of spatial movement are most often accomplished without the need for paper maps because people are moving over familiar territory as they carry out their responsibilities. Therefore, mental maps suffice for evacuation carried out within the local area.

Use of Mental Maps During Disasters

Relying on mental maps during disasters may decrease the efficiency of official and public responses to the crisis. Mental maps are defined by Dent as "mental images that have spatial attributes" (Dent, 1985). As humans grow, they develop such images from their environmental and spatial experiences (Liben, Patterson and Newcombe, 1981). These representations of reality may vary greatly between individuals, and they are affected by a person's social class and geographical location (Gould and White, 1986 and Downs and Stea, 1973). People who have lived in an area the longest will probably have more detailed mental images of it than newcomers (MacEachren, 1989). During a disaster, the disparity in the mental maps of decision makers may be a crucial negative factor in accomplishing effective response actions. Each emergency responder arrives at the disaster scene with a personal set of mental images which are constantly adjusted to include spatial aspects of the place of impact. The mental images of members of the public are similarly affected. Without paper maps for coordinated references, these varied mental maps may increase confusion or even cause misjudgements. Coordination of disaster responses requires accurate spatial references in the form of an image such as a written or printed map.

THE QUICK RESPONSE STUDY

Before, during and after a technological disaster emergency planning maps can play a vital role in fostering coordination of emergency response efforts between departments, between agencies and across jurisdictions. Delucia (1979) asserted that "maps are the fundamental media of communication for planning information." (Delucia, 1979). Our study assumes that coordination of emergency response actions during a technological disaster and any associated evacuation would be handled more effectively if a set of well-designed and integrated emergency maps were available for use by emergency personnel and the public. Key issues include what kinds of maps existed, how many of these were available, how they were employed, and who were the users of the maps?

Answers to these questions were sought through two research methods: on-site observation and administration of survey questionnaires. Within 36 hours of the derailment and with prior permission from the Pennsylvania Department of Environmental Resources (PADER), we began our investigations at the Emergency Command Center set up in the Worthington-West Franklin Fire Company Station in Worthington, PA. We had designed two questionnaires before the incident and were ready to administer them to evacuees and emergency personnel. Thirty evacuee interviews and twenty interviews with emergency personnel and representatives of volunteer agencies were carried out. Both questionnaires asked interviewees about personal and educational background, map availability and use, and map needs during the crisis. After the disaster, follow-up telephone calls were completed to locate evacuees whose whereabouts had to be established before they could be interviewed by telephone. Phone interviews were also conducted with emergency personnel who were active during the crisis.

During the interviews, adjustments were made to the questionnaire. It had been assumed that maps would be referred to by emergency personnel and the public when they carried out response actions, particularly those concerned with evacuation. However, neither emergency personnel nor evacuees used maps during this evacuation, so open-ended questions had to be added to the questionnaires.

A DERAILMENT DISASTER

The geographic setting of this disaster was the farming community of Craigsville, which is located thirty-five miles northeast of metropolitan Pittsburgh. Physically, Craigsville is situated amid a series of low hills and scarps drained by a third-order stream known as Buffalo Creek. In various places the land has been gashed by strip mines. In terms of built environment, Craigsville is little more than a group of houses extending between two places where its main road is bisected by railroad tracks (see Figures 1 and 2) which wind through the heights of the community along the crest of a steep ridge. The town is served by two highways: Route 422, which runs east-west from Kittanning to Butler and Route 28, which runs north-south through Kittanning to Pittsburgh. Politically, the community is under the jurisdictions of West

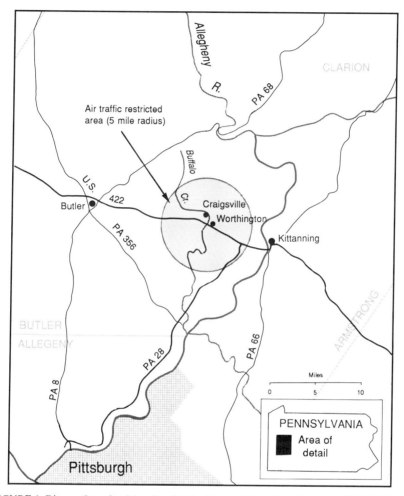

FIGURE 1. Disaster Location Map. Reprinted with permission from *Geoforum* Vol. 22, No. 4, pp. 377-389.

Franklin Township, the Borough of Worthington and the Armstrong County seat of Kittanning. Craigsville has its emergency services furnished by the Worthington-West Franklin Fire Company. This volunteer force and its very active Women's Auxiliary are housed in a fire station that provides the social center and is the scene of the annual social events for the Craigsville-Worthington community. Rural cooperation and cohesiveness characterize this tightly knit farm area where many families are linked by marriage. There is also a sense of control over the everyday environment because people know each other and the land intimately.

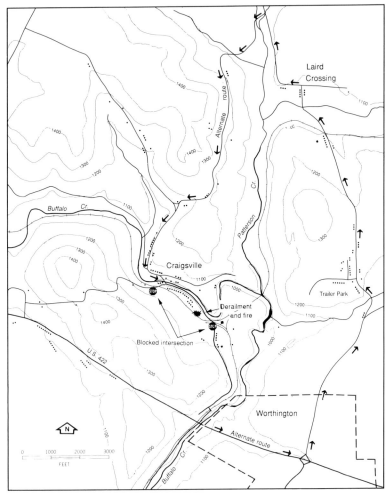

FIGURE 2. Craigsville Area Map. Reprinted with permission from *Geoforum* Vol. 22, No. 4, pp. 377-389.

As one of the oldest industrialized states in the nation, Pennsylvania has an extensive rail transportation system built to support heavy industries such as mining and steel-making. By a curious twist of irony, on the evening of Earth Day, April 22, 1989, this aging rail system produced a technological disaster. At 9:30 pm, 29 cars of a 96 car Buffalo and Pittsburgh Railroad (BPR) freight train being pulled by five locomotives derailed and fell into a ravine in the rural hamlet of Craigsville. "Harmonic rock" from moderate speed combined with slight dips in the rails has been identified by the BPR as the cause of this derailment. The physical conse-

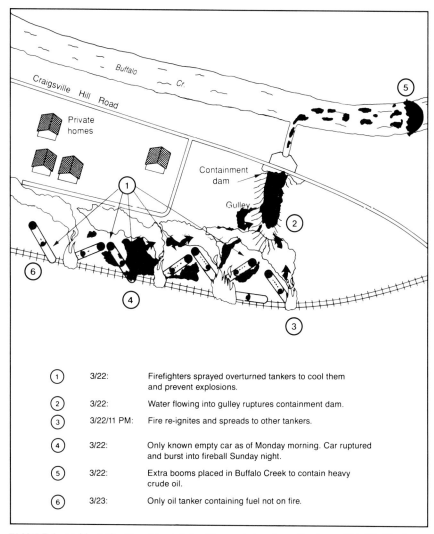

FIGURE 3. Accident Site Map. Reprinted with permission from *Geoforum* Vol. 22, No. 4, pp. 377-389.

quences included damage to the land, waters and air of this community. Fire and explosions were uncontrollable for several days. Extensive contamination of the hillside and of Buffalo Creek occurred as spilled crude oil and sodium hydroxide, a drain cleaner, mixed with water and chemicals that were hosed onto the wreck and poured down the steep slope into the creek. (See Figure 3). This threatened local farm businesses downstream, including a 3000-head dairy farm and the underground Moonlight Mushroom Farm which draws a 3 million gallon reservoir from Buffalo Creek for irrigation. A month prior to the accident, the Pennsylvania Fish Commission had stocked the Creek with 12,000 trout, and massive fish kills were reported following the derailment. Much farther downstream, Pittsburgh's water supplies drawn from the Allegheny River had to be monitored. A thick cloud of hydrocarbon particulates and caustic sodium hydroxide was trapped close to the ground by a weather inversion. This necessitated evacuation of nearby residents on the night of the disaster, an air advisory the second day to keep the young, ill and aged indoors, and a restriction on aircraft travel within a 5 mile radius of the disaster site as shown in Figure 1. Over the first three days after the incident, fourteen fire companies responded to the emergency, and three firefighters received chemical burns from the sodium hydroxide. Among the general public, no one experienced physical injuries.

During a technological disaster, one or more of the locally elected officials legally has command authority. In most cases, this authority is delegated to the fire or police chief who becomes the incident commander of any disaster. At Craigs ile, close communication took place between the Worthington Fire Chief, who was designated Incident Commander, the Pennsylvania Department of Environmental Resources (PADER) and the Pennsylvania Emergency Management Agency (PEMA). Advisors from other federal, state, regional, county and local agencies were also on hand.

As many as 580 people were served with evacuation orders during this emergency. When the train derailed, about 200 residents of Craigsville and nearby areas left, while another 200 people were alterted to the possibility that they might have to withdraw. In the early morning hours, when officials feared that the caustic cloud would drift until it extended over other areas, another 180 people from a trailer park across the valley and 200 people from a nearby, privately-owned town, Shadyside Village, were advised to evacuate. Two days later, on April 24, all but the 15 families with houses nearest the derailment site had returned to their homes. After three weeks had elapsed, three families still were not allowed back on their Craigsville properties due to contamination.

USE OF MAPS DURING EVACUATION

The survey of evacuees revealed that mental maps guided their evacuation. Not one person even considered using a printed map to aid in their movements when evacuating. However, 15% of the evacuees interviewed, all of whom were relative newcomers to the area, could envision the need to use a map during an evacuation. Even if they had wanted to use one, 30% of those interviewed said they own no maps at all. All the rest of the interviewees kept Pennsylvania and Pittsburgh road maps both in their cars and in their homes. During this disaster, the general public did not consider a printed map to be essential.

Decision makers had to issue the orders to evacuate without even one map to show the location of residents. Firefighters from the various volunteer companies of the surrounding communities were told to evacuate residents from certain areas. Using only their own mental maps, they notified people in a given area then reported back to the Incident Commander. Because no printed maps were available from the township, this system of collective mental maps had to be implemented. Both before and after the incident, the Fire Chief had tried to obtain a map of residences from the Supervisors of West Franklin Township, but to no avail. This lack of map availability is an example of Cigler's (1988) intergovernmental paradox of emergency management. The Fire Chief's limited local governmental position prevented him from receiving map resources essential for conducting safer evacuations. To acquire the necessary resources, the township should have responded to the expressed need for maps, but the political power of a local Fire Chief may not be strong enough to secure such action.

The risks involved in carrying out an evacuation without appropriate local maps are evidenced both by the evacuation experiences of two Craigsville residents and by a fire company videotape and raise a question about the scale of this disaster. Interviews revealed that the authorities overlooked two isolated residences. However, the occupants evacuated themselves after warnings from relatives. During the first vital moments of response, the audio portion of the official videotape recorded lengthy street location directions being discussed by emergency personnel. They had no street maps to refer to, and the delay caused by this time-consuming method of communicating spatial information may have delayed prompt actions. During the first night of the crisis, the Incident Commander personally directed nine fire companies and four ambulances to fight the explosive fire and to evacuate the public. His skills were sufficient to control this situation with mental maps alone, but what if the disaster had required evacuation of an area twice as large? A successful evacuation was possible because of three factors: the relatively limited area involved, the lack of severe toxics in the air, and the instant communication of news through privately-owned radio scanners. A train fire that stretched farther down the tracks or a more extensive or more toxic cloud could have exceeded the Incident Commander's abilities to carry out a successful evacuation without a township map that showed residences.

MAPS FOR EMERGENCY MANAGEMENT OF THE DISASTER SITE

It was possible for emergency personnel to refer to four maps in controlling the consequences of the derailment. During the first hours of the crisis, a privately-owned wetland map was used by the water manager of Armstrong County to advise PADER on strategies for protecting surface waters. One surprising finding was that during normal operations, no maps of any kind are posted in the Fire Station which served as the Command Center. During the crisis, the PADER staff brought three maps for use in the Commander Center: 1) a 1:24,000 USGS Topographical Map, revised in 1979; 2) a black and white 1″:1 mile Armstrong County General Highway Map made by the Bureau of Strategic Planning of the PA Department of Transportation in 1983; and 3) a 1″:1 mile Armstrong General Highway map produced in 1971. Outside the Command Center, the Armstrong County helicopter pilot used his aviation maps, and track cross sections and railroad maps may have been used by the BPR.

The map most used by decision makers during this disaster was the USGS Topographic Map. However, when interviewed, decision makers talked about using only one USGS Topographic Map. To show a total overview of the Craigsville-Worthington area, four such maps must be placed together. One quadrangle did show the actual accident site, but it did not encompass certain vital spatial relationships such as the locations of the Trailer Park and Fire Station. Federal agency officials expressed concern about the lack of an overview map of the whole disaster area.

CRISIS MAPPING

Crisis Maps to Control the Physical Agent

A map had to be produced on-the-spot in order to control the most dangerous aspect of the Craigsville derailment: explosions. This new type of cartographic endeavor is termed "crisis mapping." The production of this crisis map was prompted by safety concerns over the possibility of more tanker explosions. On Monday, the decision was made to stop spraying the derailed tanker cars while water containment dikes were dug at the foot of the hill to prevent further contamination of Buffalo Creek. Ten or fifteen minutes before spraying was again to commence, one of the derailed tankers exploded. Fortunately, all 15 to 20 firefighters previously hosing the wrecked cars had moved far enough away that no one was physically injured by the unexpected blast. To preclude the possibility of more explosions, throughout the rest of Monday and Tuesday, decision makers made their first priority to locate any existing fire or heat under the zigzagged tanker cars. A current site sketch of the tumbled tankers on the slope was drawn by hand from a neighboring hilltop. A PEMA staff member drew this "crisis map" on 17″ x 24″ posterboard (Figure 4). On Tuesday morning, the Incident Commander identified hot spots within the jumbled tank cars on this large sketch map while on a helicopter flight over the disaster site. Cars that were still in danger of igniting each other were identified, so that foam could be sprayed more accurately to eradicate explosion risks completely. The hand-drawn crisis map was a crucial aid in these tasks.

Crisis Maps for Risk Communication

Risk communication with the public can be facilitated by use of crisis maps. Because of the continuing threat of explosion and the degree of surface and air contamination, news media personnel were not permitted to visit the Craigsville derailment site for three days. A long-awaited news conference was held on Tuesday afternoon, the second day after the accident, for emergency managers to explain to reporters facts about the remaining risks from this accident. The key device for communicating these risks was the crude posterboard crisis map hand-drawn that morning to locate the remaining pockets of fire and heat in the wrecked tanker cars. As emergency personnel strived to convey the uncertainties driving their decision making, this simple visual image on posterboard became the center of attention. It had its limitations; the elevations of the slope at the site of the wreck were not protrayed. However, this crisis map greatly enhanced the capability of the emergency managers to communicate with the media about the spatial aspects of the continuing risks. The assumption can be made that this crisis map helped provide credibility and trust among reporters toward officials who spoke at the news conference (Kasperson, 1987).

Crisis Maps for Documenting a Disaster

Crisis maps, in the form of simple site sketches, provide lasting documentation of a disaster. In the Craigsville case, at least six of the organizations working from the Command Center had staff members produce site sketches of the accident: PADER, PEMA, Worthington-West Franklin Fire Company, Environmental Protection Agency (EPA), National Safety Transportation Board (NSTB), and the BPR. The uses for these rough maps highlight their value. The morning after the event, PADER designed their water sampling plan by employing a sketched crisis map. In order for PEMA staff at the Command Center to discuss the disaster with their headquarters the next day, a copy of their crisis map was faxed overnight to Harrisburg. Crisis sketches were also drawn to document the spatial relationships at the accident site in order to reconstruct the event later. This was a high priority for the EPA, NSTB and the BPR. Thus, crisis mapping constitutes a newly-recognized

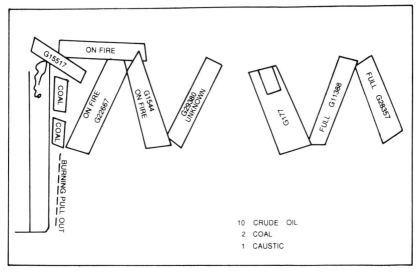

FIGURE 4. Crisis Map - Sketch Used By Incident Commander. Reprinted with permission from *Geoforum* Vol. 22, No. 4, pp. 377-389.

genre of cartography during a disaster and provides valuable documentation for review and recordkeeping.

WHEN MAPPING FACILITIES ARE NOT AVAILABLE

In this derailment disaster, the commonly held view that "the closer you get to the incident, the fewer the available maps" was upheld. At the state level in Pennsylvania, very advanced computer mapping systems exist. A one million dollar "TAGAVAN", an instrumented vehicle which can conduct chemical analyses and produce plume maps at the site of an emergency, was purchased by the state after the Three Mile Island nuclear event, but it was not considered to be suitable for use in the aftermath of the Craigsville derailment. Pennsylvania invested in this expensive system as a result of its potential to be the site of natural and technological hazards. The chief natural hazards include floods, a high number of tornados and severe storms, while the twelve nuclear power plants in the state pose potential technological hazards.

A statewide geographical information system (GIS) had been planned and work on it was already underway at the time of the Craigsville disaster. Pennsylvania counties had submitted information to be used in the GIS, and in return had received a GIS package to which they could add data to create updated maps as needed. However, this GIS system was not yet operational in most counties because of limited staffing and budget constraints. At the time of writing, training in use of these computerized data bases is still not complete, both among the counties and within PEMA.

CONCLUSIONS

Disaster Management in Craigsville

Both evacuees and emergency personnel expressed positive opinions about the management of the Craigsville disaster. Every evacuee interviewed voiced admiration and appreciation for what they judged to be a successful handling of the crisis, given the limited resources for dealing with technological problems that were available in such a rural area. An overwhelming majority of emergency personnel commented on the "lucky" aspects of the disaster mentioning the lack of rain, which would have brought the air contaminants to earth around Craigsville in more concentrated form and would have increased runoff into Buffalo Creek and the fact that no one was injured by the surprise tanker explosion. They also considered the disaster response to have been successful because of the high degree of coordination manifested in the Command Center.

From the perspective of this study, three major factors affected the quality of emergency management in the Craigsville disaster: the political structure, the social scene and the lack of appropriate maps. In the political realm, Cigler's intergovernmental paradox was seen clearly in the Township's inability to meet the Fire Chief's need for a map showing residences and in the richness of mapping facilities at the state level compared with the lack of maps in Craigsville. In addition, interviews with state officials revealed that over 90% of the major decision makers in emergency planning at the state level are former members of the military, many of whom worked with safety concerns while in the services. Their attitudes towards the role of the general public in disasters, especially disasters requiring evacuation, is conversant with FEMA's command and control approach (Quarantelli, 1988). In contrast, Craigsville residents evacuated on their own. Furthermore, attitudes expressed by those who had the greatest authority for emergency map production for the state revealed skepticism about the process of preparing for a technological disaster. Statements such as "We cannot have crisis management maps; we can't plan for manmade things" and "I don't think we can ever have evacuation maps because we don't know where the disasters will occur," may indicate a rigidity about mapping which will mitigate against the possibility of adequate supplies of maps at the local level, however badly they are needed (Kasperson, 1988).

Social aspects of this disaster fit positively and concisely into Dynes' "emergent human resources" model. Communication was quite open and broad, without official restriction of messages, and this allowed citizens to protect themselves. The outstanding social cohesion of the Craigsville-Worthington community was assisted by the remarkable and ubiquitous use of radio scanners and telephones by private citizens. Information flowed in lifesaving ways through the radio scanners owned by ordinary people. The existing social strengths of Craigsville meant that no new social forms were necessary. The emergency Command Center was in normal times the social center of the town. Authority was vested in the familiar Fire Chief, who controlled incoming resources and coordinated the response efforts. Self-evacuation was aided by the tightly-knit social fabric of citizens who felt responsible for the welfare of their neighbors. Many people evacuated on their own and chose shelter with relatives or friends. Evacuation movements followed the complex patterns suggested by Quarantelli's model of evacuation.

Evacuation efforts could have been more efficient, had adequate map resources been available. While mental maps employed during the crisis served extremely well, the videotape sound track reveals that time was wasted in describing street locations verbally. This leaves the question of how a larger disaster of greater geographical extent would have been handled. There are limitations to the application of collective mental maps to crisis management. Appropriately-detailed maps offer a hedge against faulty human memory. Also, not every community has a personal information network as good as that which existed in Craigsville. In place of a system of collective mental maps, emergency personnel expressed a strong need for large scale topographical maps and simple street maps that would provide details of residences. They felt that large scale maps of the local area would have been a useful aid in their decision making. In sum, in spite of the lack of printed maps, disaster management at Craigsville was relatively successful, but the emergency responders interviewed had visions of the future potential of emergency mapping.

Future Emergency Mapping

Improved emergency mapping systems were discussed by almost all of the local, state and federal emergency personnel who were interviewed. A veteran firefighter advocated a card system he had proposed years earlier for handling fires at the local level. The system he envisioned would provide numbers for each of the scattered farms throughout this part of the Pennsylvania countryside and would require owners to detail facts about number of residents and locations of water sources and hazardous materials on their properties. Information for these numbered cards would have to be kept up to date. He felt that his ideas were never acted upon "not from lack of funds, but from lack of incentive." For mapping at the state level, one state official outlined his vision of a real time mapping system capable of producing crisis maps. During any disaster, pertinent data could be added to a statewide GIS through an on-site computer terminal, resulting in a series of animated computer maps portraying dynamic changes at the disaster site. (See work of Belardo *et. al., Disasters* 7(3):215-220; *Interfaces* 14(2):29-39.) Ideas about future mapping possibilities were also aired by federal officials. One of these predicted that it was just a question of time before an interactive video mapping system became operational and standard in the field, replacing the hand-drawn site sketches of today.

Crisis Mapping

The newly recognized process of map production on site during a disaster has been titled "crisis mapping." This is any kind of creative on-the-spot map production used to capture the unique set of environmental circumstances and consequences of a technological disaster. A local, large-scale view is needed; thus, in the Craigsville disaster, hand sketches were vital resources for managing the emerency by giving this large scale presentation. They helped control the disaster conditions, communicate with the media about risks, document the history of the incident for improved record keeping, and reconstruct the disaster events and their consequences in order to learn lessons.

Attention should be given to the processes involved in crisis mapping. Answers are needed to the following questions:

1. How often are crisis maps being produced at technological disasters?
2. Who currently makes these maps and who should be responsible for them?
3. Should cartographic training be provided for staff members performing this task?
4. Should guidelines be established for the production of such maps?
5. What materials should be available on-site for emergency personnel to make crisis maps?
6. Would a computer graphics capability for crisis mapping at a disaster site serve better than hand drawings?
7. What role should crisis maps play in communicating risk to the public during a disaster?

The dynamic spatial relationships that exist during the response stage of a disaster point to the need for further study of emergency mapping.

BIBLIOGRAPHY

Belardo, S., A. Howell, R. Ryan and W.A. Wallace. 1983. A Microcomputer-based Emergency Response System. *Disasters* 7(3), 215-220.
Belardo, S., K.R. Karwan and W.A. Wallace. 1984. Managing the Response to Disasters using Microcomputers. *Interfaces* 14(2), 29-39.
Cigler, B.A. 1988. Emergency Management and Public Administration, *Crisis Management: A Casebook*. Charles C. Thomas Publisher, Springfield, IL. 10-12.
DeLucia, A. 1979. An Analysis of the Communication Effectiveness of Public Planning Maps, *The Canadian Cartographer*, 16(2), 168-182.
Dent, B.D. 1990. *Cartography: Thematic Map Design*. Wm. C. Brown, Dubuque, IA.
Downs R. and D. Stea. 1973. *Image and Environment*. Aldine, Chicago, IL.
Dynes, R.R. 1983. Problems in Emergency Planning, *Energy*, 8, 8-9. Pergamon Press, Oxford, 653-660.
Gould, P.R. and R.I. White. 1986. *Mental Maps*. Allen & Unwin, Winchester, MA.
Kasperson, R.E. 1987. Six Propositions for Public Participation and Their Relevance for Risk Communication, *Risk Analysis*, 6:275-281.
Kasperson, R.E. and J.X. Kasperson. 1988. Emergency Planning for Industrial Crisis: An Overview, *Industrial Crisis Quarterly*, 2:2, 84-85.
Liben, L., Patterson, A., and N. Newcombe ed. 1981. *Spatial Representation and Behavior Across the Life Span*. Academic Press, New York, NY.
MacEachren, A.M. 1989. Learning a City Using an Interactive Map: A Comparison of Route Versus Landmark Based Learning. Paper presented at the *14th World Conference of the International Cartographic Association*. Budapest, Hungary.
Quarantelli, E.L. 1988. Assessing Disaster Preparedness Planning: A Set of Criteria and Their Applicability to Developing Countries. *Regional Development Dialogue*, 9:48-69.
Quarantelli, E.L., B. Balsden and T. Bourdess. 1984. Evacuation Behavior and Problems: Findings and Implications from the Research Literature. *Book and Monograph Series #16,* University of Delaware Disaster Research Center, 23-32.
Sorensen, J. B. Vogt and D. Mileti. 1987. *Evacuation: An Assessment of Planning and Research* (ORNL-6376). Oak Ridge National Laboratory, Oak Ridge, TN.
USEPA, 1987. Review of Emergency Systems: Interim Report to Congress, EPA (U.S. Environmental Protection Agency), Washington, DC.
Zeigler, D.J. and J.H. Johnson. 1984. Evacuation Behavior in Response to Nuclear Power Plant Accidents, *Professional Geographer*, 36, 207-215.

Natural and Technological Disasters: Causes, Effects and Preventive Measures. Edited by S.K. Majumdar, G.S. Forbes, E.W. Miller, and R.F. Schmalz. © 1992, The Pennsylvania Academy of Science.

Chapter Thirty-Four

NATURAL HAZARD MAPPING: STATUS AND REVIEW

MARK MONMONIER[1]
and
GEORGE A. SCHNELL[2]

[1]Department of Geography
Syracuse University
Syracuse, NY 13244-1160
and
[2]Department of Geography
The College at New Paltz
State University of New York
New Paltz, NY 12561-2499

INTRODUCTION

This chapter begins with a few selected examples that attest to the map's important role in describing hazards and communicating risk. Although some illustrations are modern and others are over a hundred years old, these varied examples reflect the necessity of using maps to assess, estimate, and understand risks associated with natural hazards. The chapter then uses a review of the literature to explore the current status of risk and natural hazard mapping. Researchers in a variety of fields have indicated the importance of cartographic portrayal and analysis as basic steps in the improvement of a) understanding the geography of risk and natural hazards, and b) communicating that information. Indeed, cartographic communication is often the keystone of programs designed to assess risk and develop plans to prepare for natural disasters and other emergencies. In addition to the review of current literature, the chapter includes a summary of findings based on telephone interviews with ten experts. These findings provide an interesting comparison with a summary of key points gleaned from the literature.

MAPS OF HAZARD OR RISK:
SELECTED EXAMPLES

Although space limits the number of examples presented, at least a few maps portraying hazard or risk are needed to establish a context for this chapter. Any map of the atmosphere is a hazard or risk map since all elements of weather at extreme levels or in unfortunate combinations can result in hazardous circumstances creating serious risks for inhabitants and property. If not the first hazard maps per se, weather maps published in newspapers are certainly the earliest regularly published and widely circulated maps intended to inform readers of risk associated with myriad atmospheric phenomena. Although improved atmospheric measurement and record management[1] led to maps of temperature, pressure, and precipitation in the early 19th century, a reliable daily weather map awaited simultaneous observations over a number of locations and nearly immediate data collection.[2] In 1875 the *Times* of London became the first newspaper to publish regularly a daily weather map. As Figure 1 illustrates, these early weather maps depicted barometric pressure and its expected change, the condition of the sky and sea (described as clear-cloudy, smooth-rough), and wind direction and speed.[3] Although not specified, risk could be inferred.

Weather maps have become daily fare in newspapers. The launch of TIROS I (Television, Infra-Red Observation Satellite) began a new era in observing, forecasting, and mapping weather, and satellite maps have become a regular feature of weather reports in newspapers and on television.[4] In addition to forecasting the possible hazards of tomorrow's weather, maps also help viewers understand the processes and uncertainty of assessing risk associated with meteorological hazards.

In addition to collecting data and producing daily weather maps, federal agencies produce an impressive array of maps of the atmosphere.[5] Although comparatively short on electronic and graphic technology, earlier atmospheric cartography was also impressive in both its volume and its specificity in addressing risk. Perhaps the best known collection of non-contemporary examples appears in *Climate and Man*, the 1941 Yearbook of Agriculture.[6] This volume of more than 1,200 pages contains a section with numerous hazard maps that summarize considerable climatic data ranging from such general subjects as temperature and humidity to more specific hazards such as fog and sunshine.

Emergency management and planning, specifically the Federal Emergency Management Agency's (FEMA's) administration of the National Flood Insurance Program, is most relevant here given the broad importance of the Flood Insurance Rate map. Passed in 1968, the Flood Disaster Protection Act gained urgency after Hurricane Agnes in 1972. The upshot was a much greater effort to encourage municipalities to include flood-plain management in their zoning laws, in exchange for which the National Flood Insurance Program covers flood damage and FEMA offers technical assistance on flood-plain management and promulgates housing development in areas above the flood plain.[7] The map and key describe and delineate areas prone to theoretrical floods occurring every 100 and 500 years. As Figure 2 illustrates for a small section of the map for New Paltz, New York, FEMA's Flood

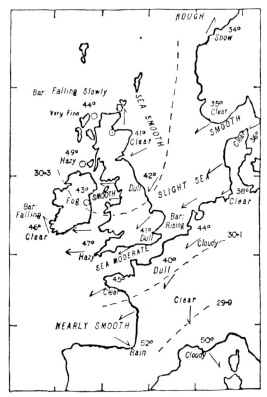

FIGURE 1. Weather map printed in the *Times* of London on April 14, 1875. (From "The Times' Weather Chart," *Nature*, 11, no. 285, April 15, 1875, 473-474.)

Insurance Rate maps also show base flood elevations and areas subject to minimal flooding.

FEMA uses these maps to determine which properties are within flood-prone areas and thus eligible for flood insurance. By limiting protection to municipalities enrolled in the program, the flood map effectively controls land use. As an example, Figure 3 shows the portion of the Town of New Paltz zoning map covered by the FEMA map in Figure 2. That the Open Space zone (OS on the zoning map) is identical to the area of 100-year floods illustrates the community's compliance.[8]

Among the oldest maps used by insurance underwriters to assess risk are fire-insurance maps, which depict the built environment and illustrate the role of private-sector cartographers in mapping risk. The most famous producer of maps used to establish fire-insurance rates is the Sanborn Map Company, which since 1867 mapped some 13,000 municipalities, almost all in the United States, showing in great detail all commercial, residential, and industrial structures. At a very large scale, Sanborn maps portrayed street names and widths; property lines, building use, and

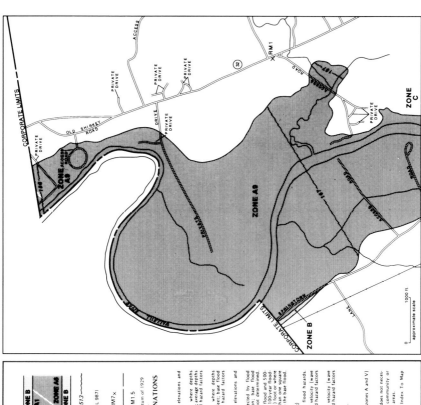

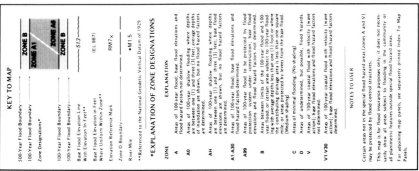

FIGURE 2. Part of Flood Insurance Rate Map, including map key, Town of New Paltz, New York (Photographically reduced.) Courtesy of the Federal Emergency Management Agency.

address for each parcel; the size, shape, safety, building materials, and construction features of each structure; and water mains, hydrants, and fire alarm boxes.[9] An employee training manual states in its introduction that "Customers depend on the accuracy of our publications, and rely upon the information supplied, incurring large financial risks without making personal examinations of the properties."[10]

Activity for the Sanborn Map Company peaked in the 1930s, but shifted to maps for the military during World War II. After the war, the National Bureau of Fire

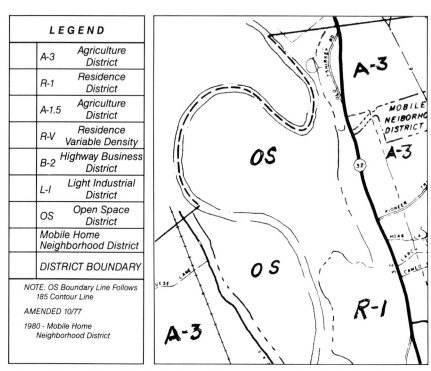

FIGURE 3. Part of Zoning Map, including map key, Town of New Paltz, New York. (Photograph-ically reduced.) Courtesy of the Town of New Paltz Building Inspector's Office.

Underwriters endorsed the need for fire-insurance maps of commercial and in-dustrial buildings but questioned the value of mapping residential structures.[1] Despite post-war problems, as the 1950 date of its last catalog attests, the company continues today, adding environmental anaylsis to its traditional activity of updating Sanborn maps for a number of American cities.[2]

Although a brief overview can do little more than describe the content and pur-pose of a few maps of hazard and risk, these examples suggest a broad array of applications. As computerized systems for the storage, retrieval, analysis and display of geographic data grow and improve, elected officials and the public are likely to use maps in increasing numbers to assess risk for a still wider range of both natural and technological hazards. The following section addresses the design and effec-tiveness of these maps.

DESIGN AND USE OF RISK MAPS

Natural-hazard and associated risk maps are not well covered in the literature, and this sparse coverge offers few novel insights for the seasoned cartographer or the specialist in risk communication. Yet several principles emerge, about which the environmental scientist with little or no background in cartography and risk communication must be aware. After discussing a representative sampling of published studies and essays, organized by topic, this section summarizes these key points. Where relevant to the design of natural-hazard maps, we also look at work concerned with technological hazards.

Risk Maps for the Media

An analyst preparing a risk map must give special consideration to the demands and limitations of the news media. With an overriding interest in newsworthy events, the news media might ignore or only mention briefly risk maps and other reports that are not seen as pressing or that lack an element of conflict or human interest.[13] For example, the media easily ignore large sheet maps, as McKay and Finlayson[14] noted in a paper on Australian urban-area flood-hazard maps. Mentioning the maps and their availability—free, no less—in a 26-item press release demonstrated that TV, radio, and the print media easily overlook maps mixed with other information. The press release did not include a sample map tailored for newspaper insertion or TV viewing. Although the reaction might be different for radioactive or chemical waste, the media and the public seem comparatively indifferent to some hazards. Because severe flooding occurs infrequently, for instance, the flood hazard is easily ignored.

Handmer,[15] who looked at the effect of flood hazard maps on public perception of risk from flooding, noted that risk maps reprinted in the media need have little beneficial effect on hazard perception. In one city he studied, the maps generated poor publicity when they had to be recalled because of errors. For another city, in which the maps received a sensationalist treatment, he credited the media, not the maps, with a heightened awareness that the city indeed had a flood problem. He also noted that flood-hazard maps were largely ignored and did not alter established attitudes; yet persons at risk who had seen the original maps did tend to know they lived in the flood-prone area.

Map Design and Information Content

Most writers addressing the use of maps for risk communication stress the need for simplicity. For instance, Handmer,[16] who found little useful guidance in the cartographic literature, offered a number of suggestions for the design of risk maps: make them "visually striking," preferably in color, but don't clutter them with data. Present information at a relatively large scale, show buildings and lot boundaries, and include not-yet-developed flood-prone areas so that the maps might influence future planning and development. Explanatory information printed on the map should be brief. Similarly, Ibrekk and Morgan,[17] who tested subjects' ability to interpret nine different statistical diagrams, caution that the most effective graphic is the one that presents information the viewer needs in the form he or she needs it. Wieczorek[18] demonstrated how the added cost of preparing interpreted landslide-inventory maps paid off in their increased use by planners and decision-makers. Pilkey and Neal,[19] who produced a straightforward safety guide for home-owners on North Carolina barrier islands, demonstrated the effectiveness of a coordinated collection of text and graphics to address the needs of nontechnical people.

A number of papers concerned with managing environmental hazards present or discuss risk maps without addressing directly their design or effectiveness. For example, Le Seur and her co-authors[20] described a risk-mapping project of the Illinois State Water Survey, which used risk maps to identify areas of high risk because of hazardous substances in ground water. Illinois mapped four factors (the density of industrial and commercial firms known to use hazardous substances, ground water withdrawals for public use, the likelihood of future groundwater development through potential yield of sand and gravel and shallow bedrock aquifers, and the susceptibility of these aquifers to contamination), set threshold limits for each, and produced overlays showing areas that exceeded the thresholds for one, two, three or all four of these risk factors. On an example map included with the paper, a gray scale based on parallel-line patterns represents relative risk, and the map key describes the risks associated with these respective areas as "low," "moderate," "high," and "greatest." The "greatest risk" areas are shown in solid black, blank areas are described as "lowest," and political boundaries are the only geographic frame of reference shown on the maps included with the paper.

Although their principal concern was sampling and temporal variation in the data, Doyle and Morse[21] presented some risk maps in their report on the use of National Geochemical Reconnaissance (NGR) maps to display Canadian data on uranium concentration in stream water. These maps shown the drainage network and use point symbols to represent sampling sites and uranium concentration. A small open circle represents a site with a negligible concentration, and range-graded black circles represent sites with higher concentrations. Although the maps appear to be designed for use by scientists, some of the example maps reveal clear regional patterns that reflect a good use of the data-ink concept.[22]

Bean,[23] in a useful general discussion of risk communication, presented an example of a simple map that would be useful in explaining the size of an area affected by an atmospheric contaminant. Accompanied by a cross-section/profile, the map shows wind direction and two risk zones in the vicinity of an incinerator. Small arrows, not a key, link the zones to their straightforward labels: "area of greatest concentration" and "area of lesser concentration," and two arrows show the general wind direction and north. Bean noted that the public might reject graphics perceived as instruments of propaganda, intended to befuddle. She cautioned against excessive detail—"when in doubt, don't"—but also warned that an overly simplistic schematic diagram must not be perceived as a cartoon, and rejected or ignored. Because available measurements (if any) seldom warrant statistical analysis, graphics might be useful for indicating the plausible range of outcomes.

Bean's article is a useful concise introduction to the problem of risk communication. She provided four basic guidelines to effective risk communication (know the risk communication problem, know the risk communication objectives, use simple language, and listen) and identified four fundamental risk communication tasks (explaining magnitudes, comparing risks, explaining risk versus hazard, and describing risk perception). Of these four basic tasks, maps are particularly suitable for indicating the areal extent of a risk or the location of a hazard.

Areal Scope of Hazards and Risks

Risk maps must reflect not only the shape and areal extent of a hazard but also the surrounding zone within which the public perceives a risk. Rowe[24] discussed the *spatial discounting function*, a concept that portrays perceived risk as a declining function of distance from the hazard. In his hypothetical function plot, Rowe represented perceived risk on a vertical arithmetic scale and distance on a horizontal logarithmic scale, to reflect a minimal decrease in perceived risk within the immediate neighborhood of the hazard and a sharper decline in risk beyond the limits of the community. A newspaper article on well contamination and the public's right-to-know indicated appreciable concern up to a half mile from a contaminated well: people up to a half mile away felt they should be notified and tested.[25] Radioactive hazards, because of greater uncertainty and less individual control, would seem to have a much wider areal impact.[26] Rowe noted that coverage by the mass media tends to shift the spatial discounting function to the right and thus broaden the geographic area within which citizens are apprehensive and eager for information about the proximity of their dwelling to the hazard. The author of a large-scale, detailed map of a hazard and its neighborhood must attempt to accommodate the public's innate perception of the spatial extent of a particular type of risk and the geographic compactness or dispersion of the community or neighborhood in question.

The question of areal scope is not merely an issue of risk perception or the size of a neighborhood. McMaster[27] used GIS-based modeling to estimate the hazard-zone geometry for hypothetical transportation accidents involving toxic materials. He demonstrated that computer modeling (and simulation) can explore the effects of terrain, air movement, and other factors on the geometry of risk zones. Natural hazards may have zones based on point features such as volcanoes; line features such as faults, coastlines, and rivers; or areas such as regions with a high risk of flooding, tornadoes, or earthquakes. But rarely is the zone at risk a simple geometric buffer around the point, line, or area source. GIS-based modeling of risk and hazard zones has been useful in studies of smelter-site remediation[28] and volcanic hazards.[29]

Evaluation of Map Design and Symbolization

During the 1970s a number of cartographers used a subject-testing/controlled-experiment approach to evaluate the comparative effectiveness of two or more symbolization strategies. A few of these studies are particularly relevant to the design of risk maps for use by the public and local officials.

Shurtleff and Geiselman[30] described a two-stage experiment in which they first asked undergraduate students to rank a variety of topographic map symbols according to "ease of identification," and then used subject-testing to evaluate several designs based on geometric and pictorial (which they call "derived") symbols, in both color and monochrome. Their evaluation is based on the percentage of correct responses for both locate and identify tasks. In general, the pictorial symbols performed slightly better then the purely geometric symbols, and the color symbols performed equally or less well. The authors suggest that monochrome pictorial symbols might serve effectively as a "background" (base-map) layer—to provide a relatively recessive spatial frame of reference—with color reserved for a thematic, "foreground" layer—to focus on the hazard or risk and attract the viewer's attention.

In another subject-testing experiment, concerned with maps prepared for presentation to local citizens at planning board meetings and public hearings, DeLucia[31] compared a traditional planimetric line map with an oblique air photo enhanced with labels and a few line symbols. Although the planimetric map was more geometrically accurate, there were no significant differences in response times, and the photomap presented more information and performed better on visualization tasks (locate-identify, area delimitation, verification). He recommended a fuller use of oblique-photo base maps, which can be shot from a light plane with a 35-mm camera and enlarged.

Risk Maps as Part of a Communication System

Design of effective risk maps requires, of course, an understanding of the intended audience and its limitations. Elected officials and the general public usually require concise, straightforward, simplified presentations. As Konheim[32] noted, legislators and public administrators often must absorb the essential elements of a complex analysis in 5 or 10 minutes—too short a time for a rambling, highly technical presentation of complex maps.

Ute Dymon[33] broadly examined the development, design, distribution, and use of the U.S. Geological Survey's Hydrological Atlas Series. Although called a "series" by the Survey's Water Resources Division, these maps vary in scale and content, and the HA program is designed to address needs identified by WRD scientists or a local or state cooperator. Dymon used an information-flow/feedback model to show ideal flows of information among WRD staff, local environmental scientists with some understanding of hydrogeology, planners and other administrators with little or no training in hydrogeology, and the general public. Her interviews with WRD scientists and others suggest that HA maps are not used as effectively as they might because their content is too technical, and because attempts are seldom made to produce easily understood, less intimidating generalized maps. Moreover, implementation of distribution policy might be inconsistent, especially for depository copies for local libraries, and professional cartographers have had little to say about the design and layout of the maps, which seem to be designed solely to serve hydrogeologists and persons with similar training. Dymon suggests that guidelines for interpretation be made available in a booklet or on the back of the maps. As Stallen and Coppock[34] have noted, risk communication to the public, the media, and public officials without the requisite technical expertise should not be mired in details important and fully comprehensible only to experts.

Brown and Kockelman[35] observed that the effective use of hazard maps might require a *mandated* disclosure of risk to home-buyers *before* they make the commitment to purchase. Like Dymon, they also noted that scientists must interpret and generalize the content of risk maps in order to serve the needs of non-scientists. They focused on the use of state and federal information about earthquake/geologic fault hazards and discussed six applications of risk maps to land-use planning in the San Francisco bay area. Considerable relevant information is available, but in order for it to be useful, the information must be organized and packaged in a form likely to be understood by planners and local officials. Although not directly addressing map design, they (1) noted the usefulness of color for highlighting hazard zones, (2) implied that risk information is not always distributed to those who might benefit from it, (3) noted the need for individual maps (and composites constructed therefrom) to focus on specific themes meaningful to decision-makers, and (4) observed that some applications require more detailed, larger-scale maps than those usually available for presentation.

Related Statistical Graphics

Risk maps are sometimes used with statistical diagrams that explain important concepts or relate the mapped information or status of a particular site to a wider context. A map author using aspatial statistical graphics with a risk map should be aware that a variety of strategies exist and that some designs are more visually effective and logical than others. For instance, despite its appeal to newspaper artists and developers of business graphics software, the pie chart performs poorly in presenting information about continuous probability distributions,[36] and almost always is less straightforward than a simple table or histogram.[37] Tufte reviews a range of common statistical diagrams and offers a lucid set of guidelines for their design and use.

Geographic Information Systems and Risk Mapping

Geographic information systems (GIS) hold considerable promise not only for analyzing the geography of hazards but also for communicating the spatial dimensions of risk. Beard[38] observed that geographic information systems will support an information-rich environment, which might promote a more informed (if not more intelligent) use of mapped information. She noted that a GIS can store much more information than might easily be shown on a conventional quadrangle map, and make available for inspection more detailed, disaggregated representations of the data, more extensive data documentation, and explicit statements of data resolution. The information can not only be more current than at present but also incorporate structures to prevent its illogical or illegal use. Berry[39] observed that a GIS is particularly useful to the analyst who needs to explore the data in a search for significant sites and revealing relationships. Weibel and Buttenfield[40] noted that expert-systems technology might afford a useful approach to developing software that will guide the evolution of a map's design and avoid inadvertent violations of established rules for map design.

SUMMARY OF KEY POINTS

- Maps should be "pitched" to the expected audience, and those intended for non-technical users should be simple, jargon-free presentations, designed to promulgate access to a carefully conceived message. By contrast, maps for specialists should be rich in detail.
- "Why" is as important as "how" a hazard or risk map should be used. A concise and "friendly" guide to map interpretation and use prepared by the map author will heighten the chances that a somewhat complex map will be helpful to the novice.
- Labels defining risk ("high," moderate," and "minimal") would improve the message by relating the hazard's location to the degree of risk.
- Authors of risk maps must be sensitive to the hazard's spatial discounting function and to the public's perception of the extent of neighborhoods and communities. Showing too much or too little area can reduce the risk map's effectiveness.
- Both the media and the public are likely to attach more importance to hazards related to, say, nuclear waste than to something as common as flooding—the former preceived as more pressing and thus more risky. Public attitudes can affect differently the success of risk maps of different hazards.
- To heighten the effectiveness of risk maps requires that they be distributed to the media, local libraries, and local officials, and that their availability be reported to the public.
- The quality and effectiveness of risk maps can be improved by adding well-designed and easily interpreted pictorial symbols, by replacing the map key with labels positioned near the item described or connected by arrows, and by fashioning oblique aerial-photos into base maps on which relevant streets and landmarks are highlighted and labeled.

TELEPHONE INTERVIEWS: SUMMARY OF FINDINGS

Telephone interviews inquiring about the design and use of risk maps were conducted with ten scientists or managers using a list of questions expanded into a six-page annotation form used for taking notes while talking with the informant. A tape recorder was used to record the interviewer's part of the conversation. Notes from the interviews were transcribed and expanded by the interviewer shortly after each interview.

Most of the informants were helpful, although some provided more useful insights than did others. A number of the informants revealed a surprising lack of concern with or interest in questions relating to the graphic design of risk maps, but this apparent ignorance was itself a useful revelation about the cavalier attitude of some environmental scientists toward cartographic communication. Existence of these attitudes suggests the need for formal guidelines for the design of risk maps. In addition, the interviews revealed no particularly important bibiliographic sources of information of which we were unaware in preparing the literature review. Yet, the respondents identified several important points, which follow:

- Risk maps often should be "translated products" that discuss the risk and interpret the analysis in simple, readily comprehended terms. For many cases, it would be useful for the risk maps to suggest or recommend an appropriate response, particularly if that response would also improve the perception of risk. Risk maps must address at least several questions—not only "What?" and "Where?" but also "So what?"
- The map's title should clearly and directly call attention to the risk itself, and to the message that the non-technical viewer should receive. Map titles that merely describe the measurements that underlie the mapped pattern can obscure the meaning of the risk map.
- It can be useful to show relative degrees of risk. In these cases, graytones rather than varying hues are useful as area symbols, unless a stop-light sequence (red, amber, and green) is appropriate. Maps showing only the locations of hazardous sites often are open to a wide and confusing range of interpretations.
- Map users must be warned (for some risk maps) that areas with a lower risk do not imply the absence of any risk.
- If a risk map is to be used only or largely by a specific group of individually identifiable persons, and if there is sufficient time, it can be useful to discuss the design and compilation of the map with the map's users while the map is being developed.
- Supplementary information is often necessary. This information should be direct and understandable. Cartoons might provide a useful vehicle for explaining the map and suggesting appropriate behavior. The supplementary information also should anticipate and counteract possible misinterpretations.
- The cartographic generalization inherent to small- and intermediate-scale maps might call for a caveat. In many cases the map viewer might incorrectly infer that the lines separating an area of high risk from an area of lower risk are drawn with precision. A fuzzy line symbol, a dashed line, or the word "approximate" might provide a suitable warning.
- Portrayal of more than one type of risk on a single map complicates the map. Where possible, use a separate map for each hazard. If various risks must be combined, the composite map might be supplemented by maps of the individual risks.
- Where color symbolization is possible, more information may be included. But red is best reserved for areas with the highest risk—areas where some activities should be banned.

CONCLUDING REMARKS

Maps are fundamental tools for describing and communicating information on natural hazards and their associated risks. When designed with both the message and the user in mind, the map is a valuable medium for disseminating information on risk and suggesting appropriate responses to the hazard. Moreover, when combined with geographic information systems, risk mapping can become a more effective method for understanding hazards and designing strategies for remediation or management. But scientists and officials who use maps to communicate with the public need to develop a fuller understanding of both the limitations of their audience and the principles of map design. And those who design mapping software and manage geographic data systems also need to understand these limitations and principles in order to provide effective support to map authors dealing with non-technical persons. Cartographic communication is a complex process, and map authors and their supervisors must pay attention to design, anticipate the skills of the target population, and agree on and understand the message to be sent.

ACKNOWLEDGEMENTS

The authors acknowledge the support of the New Jersey Department of Environmental Protection and the advice of Branden B. Johnson, and the assistance of D. Michael Kirchoff at the Syracuse University Cartographic Laboratory in preparing publishable copies of the illustrations.

REFERENCES AND NOTES

1. Robinson, A.H. 1982. *Early Thematic Mapping in the History of Cartography.* University of Chicago Press, Chicago and London, pp. 69-76.
2. Harrington, M.W. 1893. History of the weather map. *Bulletin of the U.S. Weather Bureau,* no. 11 [Paper presented at the Chicago Meteorological Congress, August 21-24], pp. 6-9.
3. Monmonier, M. 1989. *Maps with the News: The Development of American Journalistic Cartography.* University of Chicago Press, Chicago and London, pp. 112-113.
4. Whitnah, D.R. 1965. *History of the United States Weather Bureau.* University of Illinois Press, Urbana, pp. 238-239.
5. The National Oceanic and Atmospheric Administration (NOAA), National Climatic Data Center in Asheville, NC, publishes several products which include excellent graphics, many of which are hazard or risk maps. *Storm Data,* an especially relevant bulletin issued monthly, describes and depicts several atmosphereic hazards and their impact. Maps include, among many others, confirmed tornadoes (for both the month and the period 1916-1985), record cold, deaths due to cold for the U.S., and a series of regional maps of hurricane tracks.
6. U.S. Department of Agriculture. 1941. *Climate and Man, the Yearbook of Agriculture.* U.S. Government Printing Office, Washington, D.C., pp. 701-747.
7. U.S. Federal Emergency Management Agency. 1983. *This Is the Federal Emergency Management Agency.* L-135. Washington, D.C., offers an overview

of FEMA's responsibilities and operations.

8. According to the Town of New Paltz Local Zoning Law, the only permitted use in OS is agriculture (excluding farm animals). Uses permitted subject to additional standards include detached one-family dwellings, agriculture with farm animals, road stands provided they sell products from the same lot, recreation, golf courses, and the like. The district subject to periodic flooding is defined by a "natural" contour line, and additional standards and requirements are directed to building construction, potable water and septic systems, and appropriate access to public highways.

9. U.S. Library of Congress, Reference and Bibliography Section, Geography and Map Division. 1981. *Fire Insurance Maps in the Library of Congress*, with an Introduction by Walter W. Ristow. Library of Congress, Washington, D.C., p. ix.

10. Ibid, p. 5.

11. Ibid, pp. 6 and 8.

12. In addition to updating its attribute files annually for cities interested in the service, Sanborn Mapping and Geographic Information Service is heavily engaged in environmental analysis. Specifically, the company promotes the use of historic Sanborn maps in the identification and analysis of properties and structures containing potential environmental hazards.

13. Keeney, R.L. and D. von Winterfeldt. 1986. Improving risk communication. *Risk Analysis*, 6:417-424.

14. McKay, J.M. and B. Finlayson. 1982. Observations on mass media reporting and individual motivation to obtain a flood inundation map—River Torrens, Adelaide, South Australia. *Applied Geography*, 2:143-153.

15. Handmer, J.W. 1980. Flood hazard maps as public information: an assessment within the context of the Canadian Flood Damage Reduction Program. *Canadian Water Resources Journal*, 5 (4):82-110.

16. Ibid.

17. Ibrekk, H. and M.G. Morgan. 1987. Graphical communications of uncertain quantities to nontechnical people. *Risk Analysis*, 7:519-529.

18. Wieczorek, G.F. 1984. Preparing a detailed landslide-inventory map for hazard evaluation and reduction. *Bulletin of the Association of Engineering Geologists*, 21:337-342.

19. Pilkey, O.H. and W.J. Neal. 1981. Barrier island hazard mapping. *Oceanus*, 23 (4):38-46.

20. Le Seur, L.P., H.A. Wehrmann, S.C. Schock and J.M. Shafer. 1987. Prioritizing areas for statewide groundwater monitoring. *Journal of Water Resources Planning and Management*, 113:204-215.

21. Doyle, P.J. and R.D. Morse. 1987. The application of regional geochemical reconnaissance data for uranium in surface waters to identifying environmentally sensitive areas. *Journal of Geochemical Exploration*, 29:13-30.

22. Tufte, E.R. 1983. *The Visual Display of Quantitative Information*. Graphics Press, Cheshire, CT, pp. 96-105.

23. Bean, M.C. 1987. Tools for environmental professionals involved in risk communication at hazardous waste facilities undergoing siting, permitting, or

remediation. Paper presented to the 80th annual meeting of the APCA [Air Pollution Control Association], New York, June 21-26, 25 pp.

24. Rowe, W.D. 1977. *An Anatomy of Risk.* John Wiley and Sons, New York, pp. 130-131.

25. Linkous, J. 1988. Well tests and the right to know. *Asbury Park Press,* May 8, pp. A-16.

26. Zeigler, D.J., S.D. Brunn and J.H. Johnson, Jr. 1981. Evacuation from a nuclear technology disaster. *Geographical Review,* 71:1-16.

27. McMaster, R.B. 1988. Modeling community vulnerability to hazardous materials using geographic information systems. *Proceedings of the Third International Symposium on Spatial Data Handling, August 17-19, 1988, Sydney, Australia,* pp. 143-156.

28. von Lindern, I.H. and M.C. von Braun. 1986. The use of geographic information systems as an interdisciplinary tool in smelter site remediations. *Proceedings of the 7th National Conference on Management of Uncontrolled Hazardous Waste Sites, December 1-3,* Washington, D.C., pp. 200-207.

29. Wadge, G. and M.C. Isaacs. 1988. Mapping the volcanic hazards from Soufriere Hills Volcano, Monserrat, West Indies using an image processor. *Journal of the Geological Society, London,* 145:541-552.

30. Shurtleff, M. and R.E. Geiselman. 1986. A human-performance based evaluation of topographic maps and map symbols with novice map users. *The Cartographic Journal,* 23:52-55.

31. DeLucia, A.A. 1979. An analysis of the communication effectiveness of public planning maps. *The Canadian Cartographer,* 16:168-182.

32. Konheim, C.S. 1988. Risk communication in the real world. *Risk Analysis,* 8:367-373.

33. Dymon, U.J. 1988. The communication structure surrounding the groundwater maps within the USGS Hydrological Atlas series. *The American Cartographer,* 15:387-398.

34. Stallen, P.J. and R. Coppock. 1987. About risk communication and risky communication. *Risk Analysis,* 7:413-414.

35. Brown, R.D., Jr. and W. Kockelman. 1983. Geologic principles for prudent land use—a decisionmaker's guide for the San Francisco Bay region. *U.S. Geological Survey Professional Paper,* no. 946.

36. Ibrekk and Morgan, op cit., note 17.

37. Tufte, E.R. 1983. op cit., note 22, p. 187.

38. Beard, M.K. 1989. Designing GIS to control the misuse of spatial information. Paper presented at the annual meeting of the Association of American Geographers, Baltimore, March 19-22, 11 pp.

39. Berry, J.K. 1988. Maps as data: fundamental considerations in computer-assisted map analysis. *Proceedings of GIS/LIS '88, San Antonio, Texas, November 29 - December 3,* pp. 273-284.

40. Weibel, R. and B.P. Buttenfield. 1988. Map design for geographic information systems. *Proceedings of GIS/LIS '88, San Antonio, Texas, November 29 - December 3,* pp. 350-359.

Natural and Technological Disasters: Causes, Effects and Preventive Measures. Edited by S.K. Majumdar, G.S. Forbes, E.W. Miller, and R.F. Schmalz. © 1992, The Pennsylvania Academy of Science.

Chapter Thirty-Five

THE SAFETY AND SITING OF NUCLEAR POWER PLANTS WHEN FACED WITH TERRORISM AND SABOTAGE

STANLEY OPENSHAW
Centre for Urban and Regional Development Studies
Newcastle University
Newcastle upon Tyne NE1 7RU, UK

INTRODUCTION

Towards an All Nuclear World

Whether 'we' like it or not, the world is inexorably moving towards a nuclear power future. There are two reasons for this belief. First, it is, of course, well known that in the long term, viz. 500 years plus time, nuclear power is the only technically feasible source of bulk electricity supply currently known to man. When the fossil fuels become rare, then nuclear power from fast breeders may well be sufficient to last mankind another 10,000 years. However, a second and more compelling reason is that suddenly nuclear power is starting to look increasingly attractive in the short-term because of growing concern about global warming. If only Chernobyl in particular and to some lesser extent, Three Mile Island, had never happened, then the environmental attractiveness of nuclear power might well have appeared to be even greater. Yet despite Chernobyl, growing international concern about global warming may well soon result in a new surge of nuclear power plant building following curbs on the burning of fossil fuels for power generation. Electricity generation is a key area for action in that it is one of the few areas of human activity where there is a short-term option for a major reduction of CO_2 output.

The post-Chernobyl years have seen further reduction in nuclear power plant building activities with various moratoria on future plans (Openshaw, 1988a). However, it is possible that many of these may soon have to be reversed, especially as there are strong indications that the world is moving towards an energy famine. It is likely that the world energy production will have to double over the next 30 years and it may no longer be environmentally acceptable to meet most of the increase in electricity production via conventional plant. Furthermore, it is perhaps ironic, that the longer it takes to establish the details of global climatic change then the fewer degrees of atmospheric freedom that may remain. Increasingly, it will become not merely a leisurely management problem, with perhaps a target of zero growth in CO_2 loading over a 20-30 year period, to one of a potential global panic that urgent short-term and immediate action is needed. Of course fossil fuel combustion is only one source of the problem; however, it is one that might be most readily controlled. As the CO_2 computer models become more sophisticated and the uncertainties of global climatic change reduced, so it is likely that fossil fuel consumption will have to be curtailed, well before extinction of supplies forces this outcome. Under these circumstances, it is likely that nuclear power will have to play an increasingly important short-term role in meeting the world's needs for power generation.

This gradual realization that there is a strong, perhaps over-riding, environmental rationale for nuclear power was seemingly as much a shock to the nuclear industry as to the non-nuclear lobbies. Suddenly, the justification for nuclear electricity no longer has to be narrowly focused on economics and dubious accountancy, it no longer matters whether its cheap or not. For many countries there is no real alternative as the primary provider of bulk electricity supplies that is CO_2 free. The remaining questions concern planning its revival and particularly how nuclear power can be made publicly acceptable and safer.

A major strategic problem is that the nuclear option is extremely fragile but many countries have not yet appreciated the extent of this problem. Despite climatic change factors, the future of nuclear power is very dependent on securing public acceptance under open and democratic conditions; a major contrast with the first 30-40 years of nuclear history in many countries. If there is a surge of reactor building in the late 1990's then it cannot be a continuation of programmes that were postponed from the 1970's but has to be based on 1990's planning. So whilst the nuclear imperative still exists it will have to address rather than ignore public and political concerns.

The technology is fragile for a number of reasons and these issues need to be dealt with.

1. A major accident anywhere in the world has an impact on public opinion and nuclear neurosis levels everywhere. This is particularly true for the key generic reactor types; such as PWR or BWR or AGR; but it is also to a smaller extent reactor type invariant. The acceptability of nuclear power in a given country is also strong dependent on the absence of major accidents anywhere in the world, regardless of cause.

2. Additionally, as Chernobyl demonstrated so well, the impacts of major accidents are global and can extend far outside the originating country; in this case a region stretching from Greece to Scandinavia and Iceland, from Italy to Kazakhstan; see Gould (1990). Individual risks are related to the total global locational pattern of reactors and in the nuclear era no country is an island. Thus in Europe west of the Urals, there are 229 nuclear power stations and the total risk faced in any particular country is influenced by the total pattern and safety of plants in the neighboring countries.

3. Major accidents will continue to be possible events with repeat probabilities many orders of magnitude higher than what the safety authorities currently state or believe. This reflects the continued exclusion of key potential major accident causes from probabilistic safety assessments; for example, operator error and human factors are excluded yet this has been the principal cause of all the world's major reactor accidents so far. Yet the stated risks essentially refer to accidents caused by random component failure(s).

4. It will also be impossible to guarantee that more major accidents will not happen anywhere in the world due to a perverse variant of the multiple testing problem. The calculation is as follows. Assume each reactor has an annual major accident risk of 1 in a million (this is extremely conservative as it is doubtful whether most power reactors are that safe), that the reactor accident probabilities are independent (which they may not be), and that there are 1,000 reactors. The corrected annual whole world major accident risk is not one in a million but about one in ten thousand per year. If the analysis is repeated with a more pessimistic view of reactor safety, say accident risks of 1 in 100,000, then the whole world risk would increase to one in 1,000 per year. The same result would be obtained if there were 10,000 reactors (instead of 1,000). So the more reactors there are, the greater the statistical risk of there being major accidents somewhere in the world unless the reactors become increasingly safer. Note how these global accident probabilities bear no relationships to individual reactor risks and that an accident rate of one in ten thousand certainly does not imply an accident once every ten thousand years.

5. Finally, these major accident risk rates also exclude other major plausible accident generating factors with probabilities which cannot be estimated with any quantitative precision but which are qualitative neither incredible nor impossible. Terrorism and sabotage are recognized risks for nuclear power plant but for obvious reasons there is virtually no published studies. The same applies to war risks, although an exception is Ramberg (1980) who emphasizes that attacks on energy facilities are an increasingly attractive tactic in modern warfare.

Yet there are good grounds for believing that these unquantifiable risks, especially associated with terrorism, will increasingly come to dominate the risk assessments of modern nuclear plant as other causes of failure are removed by improved engineering and designs. So it is no longer adequate to simply exclude all discussion of terrorism and sabotage risks on the grounds of sensitivity and secrecy. This may merely foster a cozy status quo, in which it is convenient to delay any realistic response to these risks for as long as possible. Burton (1990) represents the prevailing industry view when he writes "It suffices to say that as yet no power plant has been subject to a serious terrorist attack. Inherently, the thick concrete radiation shielding around the more radioactive areas of a nuclear plant provides considerable protection against explosives" (p. 164). This may be correct, but catastrophic accidents may be caused by more subtle means than blowing up the pressure vessel by external explosives. It is this failure to give adequate credence to the terrorist risks that is perceived here to contain the roots of a significant future nuclear power dilemma.

It is argued that the world already faces a major potential nuclear dilemma and the rapid expansion of nuclear plant to combat global warming may well make matters considerably worse unless considerable care is taken. Yet it seems that we are increasingly dependent on an inherently fragile technology that is not safe because its safety is dependent on a mix of technological and societal factors which are not entirely controllable. Nuclear power is a Faustian bargin. It offers relatively clean, fairly cheap, and abundant electricity but at the same time it has the potential for catastrophic disasters of a historically unprecedent nature. Here are the ingredients for a continuing public nightmare, and yet from a State's point of view this is a technology that regardless of public fears, concerns, and opinions, may well have to be fostered and expanded. It is a major issue for both democracies and dictatorships, for capitalist and communist alike and a major problem for the world's management team (when one exists) to consider.

This chapter attempts to justify this pessimism. It is argued that by drawing attention to the problem then maybe the worst effects can be avoided before it is too late to do anything about it.

Putting the Nuclear Risks into Perspective

The nuclear industry has long faced problems in convincing the public that their activities are safe. Ironically, these problems may well have been created by the nuclear industry itself, as a byproduct of its technical sophistication. For instance, O'Riordan (1987) notes that in the UK "The total frequency of all incidents leading to such uncontrolled releases should be less than 10E-6 per reactor year" (p. 204). Despite the presence of highly dangerous substances, nuclear power was always thought to be extremely safe. The problem the experts faced was how to convince others in a reasonably rigorous scientific fashion. The uniqueness of the perceived dangers made the task of theoretical accident modelling an increasingly major activity. As it is impossible to guarantee 100% safety (after all nothing is that safe) and 100% freedom from accidents (indeed, no large industry is ever entirely without accidents), so it was necessary to demonstrate that first the nuclear risks are small compared with those of daily life and second that the really "big" high consequence accidents that matters are likely to be extremely rare events. The results are probability statements; for instance, that the risk of an uncontrolled release of radiation is less than 10E-7 per annum; or that the risk of a person being killed by such a rare event is less than one in a million. Table 1 is fairly typical of the usual statements that are made with the probabilities being converted into numbers per million. However, these attempts to explain what the numbers mean to lay people so that they can better appreciate the impressive safety characteristics of nuclear power causes immense problems. For example, Marshall *et al.* (1983) explains that the impact of the biggest accident they could imagine on London would be equivalent in risk terms to everyone in London compulsory smoking about 1/20th of a cigarette each Sunday. A different report estimated that the worst case accident scenarios at the Sizewell PWR station (120km away) would result in between 0 and 860,000 early deaths and from 56 to 440,000 additional cancers. If all 10 million people could be evacuated in 2 days then these would reduce to between 1 and 150,000 deaths and 420 to 40,000 fatal cancers (Kelly *et al*, 1983). All this is fine except that it is also horrific. No other industry could conceivably cause an equivalent scale of casualties, irrespective of frequency. The precision in the figures also works against the nuclear industry and increases nuclear fears, especially when subject to media amplification (Openshaw, 1988b).

There is also another problem which is much more serious. Quite simply these probabilistic studies are wrong! At best they are conditional probabilities; at worst they are biased by omission of key factors and are riddled with uncertainty.

The conditional nature of the estimates reflects:

1. the assumed accident scenario;
2. assumptions about the probability of failure for key components and safety systems;
3. assumptions about the subsequent release of radiation;
4. assumptions about the performance of safety systems and key personnel; and
5. assumptions about atmospheric dispersal, environmental impact, human behaviour, the effectiveness of untested preventive measures, and estimates of economic impact; and
6. the certain events namely war and terrorism affecting nuclear plant simply do not happen.

The multiplicative nature of the final estimates of frequency and personal risks tend to ensure vanishingly small numbers. If they were even broadly correct, then no one should worry about them. The problem is that these estimates are selective as well as conditional and since several impossible events have already happened then they have diminished public credibility, regardless of their scientific pedigree. Virtually all the world's major reactor accidents to date (Windscale, Chernobyl and Three Mile Island) would until they occurred have been derided as impossible events. They also illustrate a major weakness; that of selectivity. In nuclear safety assessments operators do not make major mistakes. As a result safety studies largely ignore operator errors; yet their efforts can range from trivial to Chernobyl. It is imagined, however, that better training and fail-safe systems will eventually preclude operator error. At the very least the domain for human errors should reduce with time.

TABLE 1

Risks of Death in Britain in the 1980's

Cause of of death	number per million per year
Average	11,900
All cancers	2,800
Violent causes	396
Road accidents	100
Gas	1.8
Lightning	0.1
Nuclear power	0
ICRP maximum radiation dose	1 to 10

Other exclusions: include major natural disasters and war. The former are supposed to be taken into consideration although predicting likely earthquake magnitudes on fault-line locations might well be far less precise than what is often assumed. Likewise, tidal waves (due to undersea earthquakes), forest fires (if relevant), secondary effects of other disasters elsewhere (i.e. dam failure), are probably excluded. The effects of war could be horrendous although, of course, deliberate attacks on nuclear power plants tends to be excluded from detailed consideration. For instance, Krass (1990) notes that ". . . a concern over intentional attacks on nuclear reactors must be tempered by the recognition that even when such attacks have been carried out in the past, no risk or radioactive release was incurred" (p. 25). Yet "intentional attacks on nuclear reactors, the purpose of which is to release large quantities of radioactivity, cannot be ruled out" (p. 26). The problem of course is that it is impossible to attach any quantitative estimates of the seriousness of the threat and neither is it clear as to what technical measures might be taken to avoid it.

The 1991 Gulf War has already demonstrated the obvious. If oil wells are a legitimate target despite the massive environmental damage it might cause, then nuclear reactors must also be a high priority military target. This is merely continuing a long established strategy for military forces to deliberately destroy entire environments; for example, the flooding of 17 percent of all Dutch arable land in World War 2 or the 1.2 million hectares that was destroyed in Norway; see Westing (1990). There are many historical precedents and equivalents. Gone also is the belief that strong condemnation by world opinion would have any major restraining influence. Likewise it is unlikely that popular adversion to radioactivity would preclude the use of radioactivity as a weapon in war. Indeed, common sense dictates that no country with a sizeable number of reactors can risk any kind of war that results in even conventional weaponry being targeted on their reactors. If the parties involved all possess nuclear targets that might be threatened, then some kind of balance of terror might be established; otherwise the party without nuclear facilities might well possess a real advantage. These arguments apply to both conventional as well as nuclear conflict.

The third major exclusion is terrorism. The Gulf War also clearly demonstrated that state sponsored terrorism is capable of virtually any outrage against a particular country, against a region, and against the entire world if need be. Iraq has demonstrated what is now obvious. Prior to 1991 the probability of all of Kuwait's oil fields being deliberately set alight, would have been zero. The implications that someday it will be nuclear reactors that are destroyed are obvious and need to be addressed prior to a manyfold expansion in their numbers brought about by environmental concerns. The damage, or the threat of nuclear radiation release, could even be self-inflicted! The options here for the unscrupulous, for the desperate, for the mentally insane, for the clever military strategist, for blackmailer, and for crude "doomsday" weaponry are virtually endless.

TERRORISM AND REACTOR SAFETY

Terrorism Risks In Current Safety Studies

Currently nuclear risk assessments give little or no mention of terrorist risks. The following are common characteristics:

1. terrorism is not regarded as a credible major risk factor in safety assessments;
2. no published accounts exist relating to reactor accident scenarios occasioned by terrorist or sabotage or war; and
3. the subject is not usually discussed in public, indeed in the UK the rules of public inquiries related to power stations states that "The Inspector shall not require or permit the giving or production of any evidence, whether written or oral, which would be contrary to the public interest" (HMSO, 1981; para 8.4).

Nevertheless, in Britain testimony at Public Inquiries often provides a useful source of otherwise unavailable material. Indeed, at the Sizewell PWR Public Inquiry the developer (the CEGB) stated that it was neither practical nor useful to quantify the risk from sabotage (Layfield, 1987; para 44.19). It was stated that sabotage is on the CEGB's list of potential hazards and that the design criteria require that protection is given against "unauthorized entry, deliberate maloperation and sabotage" (para 44.9). This was seen as involving special site security arrangements and plant safety systems, since the degree of redundancy, diversity and segregation in the design would require the saboteur to cause damage at a number of different locations throughout the plant if there was to be an uncontrolled release of radiation (para 44.9). Furthermore, there are contingency plans for dealing with criminal and terrorist threats against nuclear installations but "It would clearly be contrary to the public interest to disclose these plans" (para 44.12).

The CEGB regarded the probability of a terrorist attack as small and noted that there are many other less well-protected targets that would provide an easier means of damaging a country. This of course ignores the uniqueness of the reactor as a major source of harm. Nevertheless, the CEGB further stated that if an attack took place, the probability of serious damage was small. In the case of Sizewell, the segregation of safety systems and the massive shielding around the reactor would make it unlikely that there would be an uncontrolled release of radiation (para 44.15). Naturally, no nuclear developer would dare say otherwise.

As reactors become intrinsically safer with greater protection against random component failure and operator errors, so terrorist risk factors may well start to dominate the "big" accident scenario. The risks are real enough. The Gulf War witnessed the growing importance of environmental terrorism. The world is seemingly at risk of becoming much safer from a global nuclear war perspective and simultaneously far more sensitive to the effects of localized or regional disputes that could nevertheless still cause environmental consequences of global significance. It would seem that the attractiveness of nuclear terrorism based on the sabotage of power plant will increasing become a potential weapon.

Some Myths

There are a number of key myths or mistaken assumptions regarding terrorism and nuclear power plant safety. The principal ones can be enumerated as follows:

1. Nuclear power is fail-safe. At the moment of an attack the reactor is shutdown and put into an intrinsically safe condition. The fission process would be stopped by the insertion of control rods.
2. It is often claimed that the secondary containment structure will withstand a crashing aircraft so the entire complex would appear to be an extremely hard structure to damage. This strong containment defense mainly applies to PWR reactors. In the UK the flimsy secondary containment on the MAGNOX and AGR sites is pidgeon but not plane proof. On the other hand, the AGR's massive reinforced concrete primary pressure vessels gives the impression of immense strength.
3. In the UK, there was a public relations exercise involving an express train being crashed into a spent fuel flask to demonstrate the safety of these fuel flasks. The unanswered question is what can terrorists do that an express train travelling at over 90 mph could not do? The impression is once again of immense strength and thus safety.
4. It is often assumed that nothing less than a direct hit by a nuclear weapon would be needed to disperse the contents of a reactor. Under conditions of nuclear war, there would be other more pressing concerns; see Openshaw *et al* (1983). In conventional war, the military might well wish to avoid attacking reactors because of the radiological consequences.
5. Nuclear sites are already subject to special site security measures. For example, the UK Atomic Energy Authority sites have their own, legal, independent armed police-force.
6. The complexity of nuclear power and the presence of various safety mechanisms would prevent terrorists from entering a control room and deliberately causing a major accident.
7. There is an assumption that no terrorist group would deliberately wish to create a major nuclear disaster that could affect millions of people for many

generations. There is also no perceived benefit that might be gained.
8. The resources needed to successfully attack a reactor are not available to terrorists.
9. There is no obvious way by which terrorists could destroy or severely damage nuclear plant.
10. There is no history of terrorist attacks on reactors which suggests that the future probability of such an occurrence is zero.

Sadly these presumptions are almost certainly incorrect.

Myth 1 ignores the effect of decay or residual heat. After shut-down, up to 20% of the thermal output of the reactor needs to be removed by cooling systems, else it might easily melt; cf. Three Mile Island.

Myth 2 assumes that structures that can withstand a few pounds of overpressure might also be resistant to either a large nearby explosion (viz. a lorry bomb) or anti-tank weapons. Resistance to such things was not a design specification and in the UK protection against aircraft impacts was not considered relevant for the MAGNOX and AGR reactors. It is not a problem because aircraft do not fly overhead or near.

Myth 3 is an irrelevant distraction. Even an obsolete anti-tank weapon would probably be extremely good at doing what the express train failed to do. Indeed there have been suggestions as to the need to fit tank armour to spent fuel carriages.

Myth 4 is arguably incorrect. Power plant constitutes a major strategic target and the destruction of the Iraqi reactor in the Gulf War, despite being close to Baghdad, proves the military point. Larger reactors might have been ignored unless the situation was perceived to be desperate or there was massive concern about nuclear bomb making. Radiological consequences might well be regarded as an extremely useful byproduct, creating a major internal crisis for the country concerned which would significantly reduce their war making capabilities. Additionally, it is also clear that the environmental damage or the threat of environmental damage is itself a useful terrorist weapon.

Myth 5 concerns the untested abilities of armed police to cope with an attack by a well equipped professionally trained group of terrorists, as distinct from anti-nuclear protestors. One imagines that the necessary weaponry would not be available on site. Entrances to the key buildings are not fortified and a quick response from security forces might be too late.

Myth 6 has to some extent been exploded by unintentional accidents caused by operator errors. Certainly, the ignorant terrorist would probably be unable to create an accident, although widespread damage of control equipment might eventually result in a major release of radiation. However, why assume that the terrorist is ignorant of reactor control systems. Fully automated, hands-off, control systems with no prospect of manual over-rides do not exist. So control room complexity may not be a good anti-terrorist device. Indeed, a US Nuclear Regulatory Commission document states that "the major threat of sabotage to a nuclear power plant is associated with the insider or employee of the plant who has access to the vital areas of the plant . . . protecting nuclear power plants from insider threats is an extremely difficult and necessary undertaking" (NRC, 1983).

Myth 7 has to do with terrorist psychology. There is no reason to believe that rational thinking or fear of radiation are relevant constraints. Is murdering millions any worse than murdering a few people? Will not the aims of terrorism be better enhanced by big effects rather than small ones? When State sponsored terrorism is involved there are seemingly no limits to anything.

Myth 8 concerns the nature of the threat. There is no reason to suppose that the real dangers come from amateurs or part-time terrorists with crude "home-made" weaponry. Instead it should be assumed that the latest and best equipment will be available. It is only a matter of money or State sponsorship and training. Likewise it is not possible to rule our either air attack (cf Israeli bombing of Iraq's reactor) or missile attack or trained terrorist or mercenary groups intent on maximum economic or military or civil sabotage.

Myths 9 and 10 are not true. Myth 9 requires faith in many of the myths numbered 1 to 8, whilst 10 is a matter of perspective. When does a military strike to delay the acquisition of bomb making material against a country not at war, count as terrorism? Additionally, there have been some limited acts of terrorism and sabotage already; see Steadman and Hodgkinson (1990). Sadly, it is only a matter of time.

MANAGEMENT OPTIONS

Protecting nuclear plant against terrorist attacks is not easy. Gould (1990) writes "The possibility of a plane crashing into an atomic plant seems remote, but in a world of suicidal terrorists prepared to blow themselves up with trucks loaded with explosives the chance of such a deliberate terrorist attack has made one highly distinguished proponent of nuclear energy change his mind" (p. 128). In fact the problem is even harder than this. For instance, an attack on the nuclear plant might be designed to cause a meltdown by disrupting vital systems. For example, simultaneous destruction of the power lines going out and of the standby diesel or gas turbine power supplies on site might well cause most reactors to meltdown and thereby very effectively generate a most catastrophic disaster. Of course, the probabilities of these events happening by chance are miniscule but they could be caused by terrorists relatively easily. Additionally, suppose by some miracle such an attack failed, the very fact that it had happened at all and might well have succeeded would probably be sufficient to create a major crisis. Should this event occur when there is a heavy committment to nuclear power on environmental grounds, then the world could be plunged into a major dilemma.

The problem becomes worse as less stable and well developed countries develop nuclear power facilities. They may in the near future have no choice. Maybe it is here where the unstable political environment may well foster the first major terrorist attacks on nuclear plant. Unfortunately, it is a generic issue. It does not matter whether the attacks are successful or where or under what cirumstances they occur. The situation becomes critical once they do occur, anywhere on the planet. The impact will be felt everywhere. The usual "it cannot happen here" smokescreen will be applied in many countries to disguise the realities of the situation. It is not unlikely that the response of many States will be to take steps to ensure that it cannot happen. Given the nature of the threat, there is only one 100 percent successful solution; abandon nuclear power. The unacceptability of such a response will result in the loss of civil liberties (justified on the grounds that under no circumstances can a major attack be tolerated) and the gradual but re-location of nuclear plant to more defensible locations. This cannot be done quickly and it really needs to be built into nuclear planning rather than emerge as an afterthought. Additionally, it will be no easy task yet the risks and costs of ignoring the problem and gambling on it never happening anywhere in the world are horrendous.

There are five obvious responses.

1. Nuclear plant in accident intolerant locations should be phased out. This is a variant of Openshaw's (1986, 1988c) argument that to preserve the viability of nuclear power it is important to seek sites that do more than optimise the short-term economics of power transmission. Of particular importance are really remote locations where only relatively small numbers of the public might feel themselves threatened should a major accident occur. Table 2 shows that for many of Britain's current sites evacuation is simply not feasible. The fairly large numbers of people living within the Chernobyl evacuation zone of 30km does not always adequately represent the marginal nature of some of the sites, if judged from a "what if a major accident happened here" scenario. Nevertheless, it gives an indication of the effects of locating nuclear plant near to major population concentrations. It is noted that even in the UK, it is possible to find genuinely remove sites. The problem here is that the nuclear industry has historically never had any need for real remote siting. This situation is acceptable only whilst accidents can be guaranteed not to happen. Unfortunately, current guarantees are too limited and conditional to offer much hope of public acceptance once terrorism is considered a viable threat, or if other major accidents continue to occur elsewhere in the world. At risk is the entire nuclear infrastructure! Clearly, many of the sites in Table 2 need to be phased out. They are not accident tolerant locations. Remoteness also needs to consider neighboring countries and siting nuclear plant may well have to be organized on a supra-national scale. The nuclear planting decision is not a 30 or 50 year investment but is likely to be a 200 to 500 year decision because of inertia and the difficulties of decommissioning (Openshaw, 1990). Neither can it remain the perrogative of individual countries to plant their reactors anywhere within their territories.
2. Develop accident scenarios that reflect plausible and informed terrorist attacks. It is becoming vitally important to harden the key components against sabotage and terrorism as the world becomes more dependent on nuclear power and terrorists less afraid to attack them. It should be recognized that nuclear plants are prime terrorist targets with both plant design and the safety studies being modified accordingly. It is no use waiting until after the predictable but unthinkable has happened either in Britain or Europe or elsewhere in the world.

3. Alter design specifications to harden the critical systems against terrorist attack. Underground control rooms, backed-up underground power supplies, blast resistant buildings, and fortified entrances would all seem to be extremely important.

4. Improve zonal off-site security. A full frontal armed assault is only one possibility. Rocket, mortars, short-range and intermediate range missiles, and aircraft are all realistic possibilities. Defensive measures need to be taken accordingly. For example, it is surely absurd that the high level waste tanks at Sellafield are not protected against anything modern or sophisticated weaponry. There are no anti-aircraft batteries, no anti-missile precautions, and the site is overlooked. Yet here is sufficient long lived radiation to contaminate and render uninhabitable a vast area of Britain or Europe. Urgent action is needed to fortify the place and then dispose of the waste underground out of reach of terrorists (Openshaw et al, 1989).

5. The urgent institution of more broadly based citizen monitoring and control systems based on computer technology. Satellite surveillance around key installations, computer eavesdropping to monitor movements of suspected terrorist groups, and better intelligence to forewarn of attacks.

However, none of these strategies can be assured of complete success against all possibilities. The geographer would again emphasize the benefits of seeking consequence minimizing locations.

TABLE 2

Populations near to UK reactor sites in 1981

Power	Population within:	
Station	16 km	30 km
Berkeley	125,316	876,304
Bradwell	128,637	731,143
Calder Hall	54,258	123,670
Chapelcross	26,678	185,441
Dounreay	10,975	15,644
Dungeness	18,256	240,510
Hartelpool	430,941	852,272
Heysham	146,258	524,538
Hinkley Point	78,937	407,205
Hunterston	87,555	409,367
Oldbury	168,017	969,989
Sizewell	29,524	130,204
Torness	9,611	44,759
Trawdfynydd	18,201	64,032
Winfrith	75,660	392,047
Wylfa	23,952	64,040

CONCLUSIONS

It is admittedly not usual to write about terrorism and nuclear power. If any detailed "official" risk assessment has ever been made then they are almost certainly unpublished or restricted. Nevertheless, this is clearly an important subject with wide potential ramifications on a global scale. It is a problem that affects every country with nuclear power plant and many neighboring ones as well. It is a global problem. Indeed, as nuclear power looks set to be increased because of one global problem (global warming) it is ironic that the solution creates another global problem that is simply not soluable via technology alone. It is important that the nuclear countries face up to the risks before events make it necessary. Early recognition is far better than late, especially whilst there are still management options available. Delayed recognition could be disasterous and could conceivably persuade many countries that the risks of global warming would be preferable. It is hoped that the relatively poorly informed speculations of a geographer will manage to strike an acceptable balance between the need to draw attention to a major potential problem without increasing the risks of it actually happening. The worrying thought is that, if a geographer can identify seemingly plausible scenarios whereby it might actually happen, then the professional in this field should be able to do so much better.

REFERENCES

Burton, B. 1990. Nuclear Power, Pollution and Politics. Routledge, London.
Gould, P. 1990. Fire in the Rain: the Democratic Consequences of Chernobyl. John Hopkins University Press, Baltimore.
HMSO. 1981. The Electricity Generating Stations and Overhead Lines (Inquiries Procedure) Rules 1981. HMSO, London.
Kelly, G.N. Charles, D. Broomfield, M. Hemming, C.R. 1983. The radiological impact on the Greater London population of postulated accidental releases from the Sizewell PWR', National Radiological Protection Board Report 146. HMSO, London.
Krass, A.S. 1990. The release in war of dangerous forces from nuclear facilities. In A.H. Westing (Ed.) Environmental Hazards of War. Sage, London, pp. 10-29.
Layfield, F. 1987. Sizewell B Public Inquiry, Volumes 1 to 8. HMSO, London.
Marshall, W. Billington, D.E. Cameron, R.F. Curl, S.J. 1983. Big nuclear accidents, UK Atomic Energy Research Establishment Report 10532. HMSO, London.
Nuclear Regulatory Commission. 1983. Operational response to events concerning deliberate acts directed against plant equipment, IN83-27. Washington, DC.
Openshaw, S., P. Steadman, O. Green. 1983. Doomesday: Britain after nuclear attack. Blackwells, Oxford.
Openshaw, S. 1986. Nuclear Power Siting and Safety. Routledge, London.
Openshaw, S. 1988. Post Chernobyl prospects for nuclear power in the UK, Environment and Planning C: Government and Policy 6: 251-268.

Openshaw, S. 1988b. Making nuclear power more publicly acceptable. Journal of the British Nuclear Energy Society 27:131-136.

Openshaw, S. 1988c. Planning Britain's long term nuclear power expansion programme. Land Use Policy 5:7-18.

Openshaw, S., J. Fernie, S. Carver. 1989. Britain's Nuclear Waste: Siting and Safety. Belhaven Press, London.

Openshaw, S. 1990. Nuclear archaeology: the influence of decommissioning on future reactor siting in the UK. In M.J. Pasqualetti (Ed.) Nuclear Decommissioning and Society. Routledge, London. pp. 143-158.

O'Riordan, T. 1987. Assessing and managing nuclear risk in the United Kingdom. In R.E. Kasperson and J.X. Kasperson (Eds.) Nuclear Risk Analysis in Comparative Perspective. Allen and Unwin, Boston pp. 197-218.

Ramberg, B. 1980. Nuclear power plants as weapons for the enemy: an unrecognized military peril. University of California, Berkeley.

Steadman, P., S. Hodgkinson. 1990. Nuclear Disasters and the Built Environment. Butterworth, London.

Westing, A.H. 1990. Environmental hazards of war in an industrializing world. In A.H. Westing (Ed.) Environmental Hazards of War, Sage. London, pp. 1-9.

Natural and Technological Disasters: Causes, Effects and Preventive Measures. Edited by S.K. Majumdar, G.S. Forbes, E.W. Miller, and R.F. Schmalz. © 1992, The Pennsylvania Academy of Science.

Chapter Thirty-Six

HUMAN DECISIONS AND NATURAL HAZARDS: A CASE OF THE EAST RIFT ZONE OF KILAUEA VOLCANO ON THE ISLAND OF HAWAII

MUNCEL CHANG

P.O. Box 960
15416 Forest Ranch Way
Forest Ranch, CA 95942

INTRODUCTION

Every human settlement is subject to the risks imposed by some type of natural hazard. Most settlements are places of choice, although these locations often seem to be dictated by necessity. The reasons for settlement most often include water, soil and/or mineral availability, trade opportunities, favorable climate conditions, land speculation, or simply "the view." Whether the risks imposed by natural hazards are fully recognized or understood prior to settlement by either the settling individual or the involved governmental agencies is often a confusing matter of personal and institutional perceptions and responsibilities. Individual and community behavior patterns suggest that after settlement has occurred, the location is generally considered to be "worth the risk."

The human choices and compromises that have been made in adapting to living in a physically hazardous environment differ from place to place. The relationships between humans and their environment can be exceedingly complex. Moreover, perceptions of the choices which are made by one culture may not be well understood by those living in another. While accepting one's own natural hazard, it is common to criticize the foolishness of someone else who might be living under the threat of a different hazard. Thus, understanding a hazardous situtation in one context may not necessarily give one a greater understanding of how and why people adapt and cope with hazardous situations elsewhere.

A large portion of the world's population lives in regions that have evolved from volcanic processes. The hazard imposed by the presence of dormant or inactive volcanoes on "desirable" land is of considerable concern. Examination of the historical geography of a specific example may shed some light on how to adapt and cope with similar future situations. The case under consideration is the East Rift Zone of Kilauea Volcano on the island of Hawaii and the implications which the recent destruction of property by lava flows may have for the risks to life and property posed by future eruptions elsewhere on the island.

THE PHYSICAL SETTING AND HISTORICAL BACKGROUND

Unlike the "classic" volcanoes of the Pacific Rim, the West Indies, or the Mediterranean, the eruptive nature of Hawaiian volcanoes is vastly different. Classified as "quiet" or non-violent volcanoes, their eruptions have historically threatened property, not life. This "gentle" characteristic was among the primary factors in selecting Kilauea as a site for what was to become the world renowned Hawaiian Volcano Observatory (HVO).

Thomas A. Jaggar, the former chairman of the Department of Geology at the Massachusetts Institute of Technology, was instrumental in this development. His efforts, begun in 1909, resulted in the construction of the initial volcano observatory in 1912, where he served as director (scientist-in-charge) from its beginning until 1940. Jaggar noted from the outset that his goals were more than just scientific investigation: "The main object of all the work should be humanitarian - earthquake prediction and methods of protecting life and property on the basis of sound scientific achievement." (Bevens, 1988). This human concern was central to Jaggar's research throughout his life. Until recently, however, much of the gathered data has not been utilized for the stated humanitarian objective.

Located on the southeastern side of the island of Hawaii, the Kilauea volcano complex is one of the most active in the world (Figure 1). The frequency of volcanic activity in this region was among the primary reasons for Jaggar's decision to establish the HVO at this site. The summit of Kilauea is at an elevation of 4,000 feet. To the northwest, the enormous volcanic shield of Mauna Loa (elevation 13,677 ft.) looms over Kilauea. A large caldera, or circular depression in the landscape, occupies the summit of Kilauea. This caldera is two-and-a-half miles long by two miles wide. Within the caldera and close to its southwest wall is the large crater called Halemaumau. Three-quarters of a mile in diameter and four hundred feet deep, Halemaumau is almost a perfect circle.

Two rift zones spread outward from the caldera of Kilauea. Both run off the island into the ocean and define where lava originates from Kilauea. The first, the Southwest Rift Zone, is eighteen miles long. The area on either side of this rift zone, extending to the sea, is generally known as the Ka'u Desert. It is characterized by low rainfall and sparse vegetation. No roads or settlements exist in this region today. Even in prehistoric times there were apparently few native Hawaiian settlements on the *makai*, or seaward, side of this rift zone. Significant volcanic activity along this rift occurred most recently in 1974. The resulting lava flows did no more damage than cover the land that was not being utilized by people. The second rift zone, the East Rift Zone, is thirty-five miles long and runs through the Puna district of Hawaii. This rift zone has seen considerable volcanic activity since 1955 with lava flows affecting the coastal region between Apua Point and Cape Kumukahi (Figure 1).

Early nineteenth century documents and maps indicate that there were a number of native settlements along the Puna coast. In describing this area in the early 1820s, Reverend William Ellis expressed surprise at the size of the population found here. Excellent fishing and an established trade network with inland communities helped to make this area a desirable region for settlement (Ellis, 1827). The attractions of climate, vegetation, and general lure of the landscape have led to growth and development in more recent times.

In the area of Kalapana, the land slopes upward from the sea at the rate of approximately four percent for a mile or so. Behind this sloped plain, or on what the Hawaiians call the *mauka* or mountain side, rise the *pali* or cliffs. From an elevation of a thousand feet or more, the view overlooking the landscape and the ocean is spectacular. Some sections of the *pali* are not steep enough to discourage construction.

The land's boundary with the sea is nothing short of dramatic. With the exception of a few small black sand beaches, the imposing coastline is made up of volcanic cliffs which reach heights of a hundred feet or more. Waves pound relentlessly against these cliffs, creating towering columns of spray which dwarf the cliffs and etch the scene into the viewer's mind.

The vegetation and the rainfall of the area vary with elevation and northeast-southwest location. Between Kalapana and Cape Kumukahi, the land is generally lush with both native and exotic species. Numerous large mango trees and various other tropical lowland bushes, plants, vines, and grasses cover most of the land. The heavy annual rainfall averaging one hundred inches is a major factor in producing the abundant growth. Prior to the lava flows of 1990, the coconut groves which formed the background to the black sand beach at Kaimu were photogenic landscape signatures. No rivers or streams flow in this area as the land is mainly composed of layer upon layer of old, porous lava flows.

Southwest of Kalapana the climate patterns begin to change rather abruptly with markedly lower rainfall. Dryland brush and low grasses mark this as the transition zone into the Ka'u Desert and the region downslope from the Southwest Rift Zone.

In Puna, the heavy cover of vegetation is deceptive. Most of the region has little or no topsoil; with heavy rainfall, native plant species can rapidly grow to maturity directly on a lava substrate. However, there are areas on both sides of the rift zone in the northeastern section of Puna where the soil is relatively free of rocks and deep enough to have attracted sugar cane growers.

The Puna Sugar Company was established in the late 1800s at Kapoho. By 1900, a rail line linked this region to Hilo, the island's main port. Besides promoting the agricultural development of the area, the railroad also served the short-lived Hawaiian Mahogany Lumber Company at Pahoa. Both of these commercial activities have ceased to exist.

Containing about 17 percent of the Big Island's population, Puna has been a rapidly growing area in recent years. Most of the 21,000 people in this region live on the northern side of the East Rift Zone. Many work in Hilo, the island's most populous town and the main shipping port, several miles north of Puna.

Pahoa, with a population of less than a thousand, is the only sizable town in the Puna area. It is located almost directly on the East Rift Zone. The population living below the rift zone is mixed. The ethnic Hawaiians trace their occupation of the land to pre-missionary days. Those of Japanese and Filipino ancestry trace their heritage to the sugar cane laborers of the early 1900s. As mechanization occurred and sugar declined, land owners switched to other agricultural pursuits such as growing papayas, vanda orchids, anthuriums, and macadamia nuts.

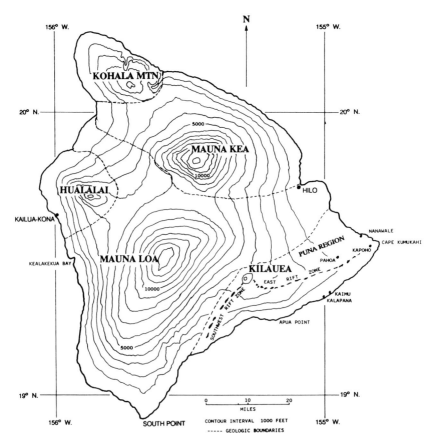

FIGURE 1. Island of Hawaii (After Macdonald and Abbott, 1970).

In recent years, real estate development has attracted a different population, many of whom have dreams of a vacation or retirement home. Some have sought a primary residence away from "civilization." A number of these people are from the Mainland and are comparatively recent "natives."

ERUPTION HISTORY

Prior to 1955, the only historical eruption of any consequence along the East Rift Zone occurred in 1840, at the extreme northern end of the rift zone. It resulted in the destruction of the coastal village of Nanawale, northwest of Kapoho (Figure 1). The people who have lived in this region have always been aware of the volcano. Nevertheless, although evidence of the land's geological formation is everywhere, fear of volcanic destruction has not been of as much concern as one might expect in such a situation. Ever since the early 1800s, eruptions had been largely centered in Halemaumau at the Kilauea summit. When asked by Reverend Ellis in 1823 about the historical eruptive activity at Kilauea, the natives said, "mai ka po mai." In Hawaiian this means "from a time of chaos until now," or since the beginning of the world (Ellis, 1827). Throughout the nineteenth century and into the twentieth, the pattern of almost continual activity in Halemaumau remained unchanging.

Although Jaggar warned that more eruptions along the East Rift Zone were highly probable, one hundred and fifteen years of volcanic inactivity in the region resulted in many residents overlooking any such warnings (Macdonald, 1970). In fact, when the area became the focus of real estate development in the 1950s and 1960s, support for settlement in the region was heavily influenced by political and economic considerations which overrode any opposition based upon volcanic hazards (Aleshire, 1990).

The century of quiet along the East Rift Zone came to an end with the Pu'u Ki'i and I'ilewa eruptions of February 28 - May 26, 1955. Most of the new activity took place in forested areas. Lava covered some six square miles, including 1100 acres of sugar cane and other crops. Lava flows entered the sea in three places along the coast. Iwasaki Camp, a small plantation community, was overrun with lava. Including an area on the outskirts of Kapoho, more than twenty homes were destroyed and approximately forty others were rendered uninhabitable (Macdonald and Eaton, 1964).

Five years later, on January 13, 1960, fountains of lava lit the evening sky only a half mile northwest of the town of Kapoho. By the time the eruption ended on February 19, the entire village of Kapoho with approximately seventy structures, including homes, stores, and a school, had been covered by lava. A number of homes along the coast two miles away were also destroyed.

During the next twenty-two years, between 1961 and 1982, a number of significant eruptions occurred along the East Rift Zone. Most of these were clustered along the rift a few miles southeast of Kilauea (Figure 2). Although many of these eruptions were spectacular, of long duration, and high in volume output, the lava flows they produced were generally confined with the boundaries of Hawaii Volcanoes National Park. Consequently, these flows did not destroy agricultural land, nor, with the exception of the 1977 eruption, did they threaten any communities. On January 3, 1983, the longest sustained Hawaiian rift eruption in historic times began. At the time of this writing in January, 1992, the eruption continues to pour lava out at the rate of more than a half a million cubic meters per day. Known as the Pu'u O'o-Kupaianaha eruption, lava flows have covered in excess of thirty-five square miles, most of which lie outside the eastern edge of Hawaii Volcanoes National Park. More than 180 structures have been lost as numerous flows passed through the communities of Kalapana and Kaimu and the adjacent subdivisions of Royal Gardens and Kalapana Gardens (Figure 3).

HUMAN PERCEPTIONS

Human perceptions of a hazard are often culturally-biased and misunderstood. One of the most prevalent criticisms heard regarding volcanic hazards centers around the belief that such hazards are "avoidable."

In the legends of ancient Hawaii, Pele, the goddess of the volcano, is considered to be one of the more powerful deities. Hawaiian history is replete with accounts of Pele's power. It is a story that every *kama'aina* or native resident has grown up with. Pele established her home in the crater of Halemaumau after a series of bitter conflicts with one of her sisters who chased her from one island to another. She would periodically visit her other "houses" or craters, announcing her travels, and her displeasures, with the earthquakes of her stamping feet. Defiling and desecrating her houses or showing disrespect to her in any manner would bring sure destruction.

Belief in Pele is still strong today. Her residence is still considered to be Halemaumau, and offerings of food and flowers may be seen at her "house" or before her lava flows. Stories of Pele appearing before and during an eruption as a beautiful young girl or an old woman persist to the present. Meeting Pele and being rude to her or refusing her a simple request is believed to result in a person's property being inundated with lava.

In religious matters, little has changed since Reverend William Ellis noted that in a conversation with a priestess of Pele in the early 1820s, "She did not dispute that Jehovah was a God, but that he was not the only God" (Ellis, 1827). This integration of religious beliefs is not viewed as being contradictory to the many *kama'ainas* and native Hawaiians who are Christians and who regularly attend church on Saturday or Sunday. It is a culturally harmonious response to the supernatural.

Regardless of religious or even educational background, the generally philosophical response to property destruction by Pele is, "If she want 'em, she can take 'em." The belief is that humans are permitted to live on and utilize the land which was created by Pele. She has the right to reclaim it at any time and for any reason.

Over the years there has also been the perception by some that since the *haole* scientists were not really part of Hawaii, they did not understand the workings of Pele. Although this perception has changed somewhat, one can still hear it being expressed from time to time.

While the *kama'ainas* accept the supernatural and rely on fate or the uncon-

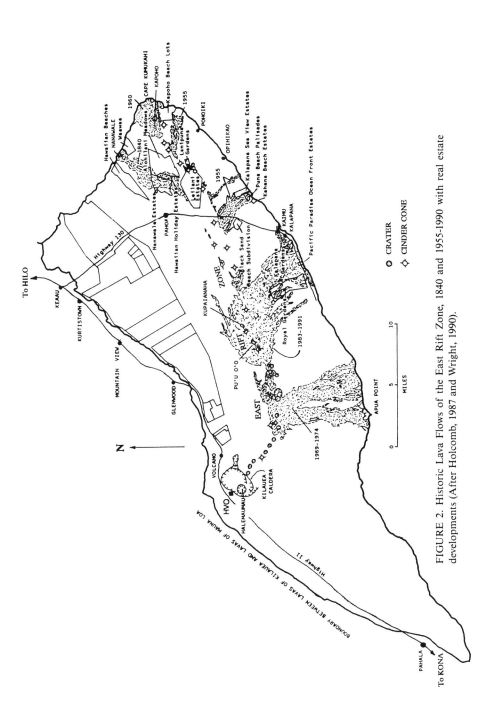

FIGURE 2. Historic Lava Flows of the East Rift Zone, 1840 and 1955-1990 with real estate developments (After Holcomb, 1987 and Wright, 1990).

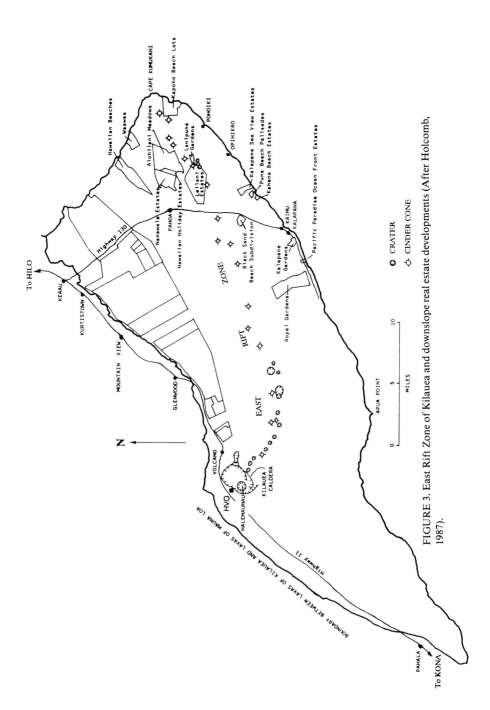

FIGURE 3. East Rift Zone of Kilauea and downslope real estate developments (After Holcomb, 1987).

trollable forces of nature, the perceptions of the *malihini haole,* or newcomer Caucasian, are somewhat different. Some embrace local tradition and belief, but there is a greater reliance on the pronouncements and predictions of science (Murton and Shimabukuro, 1972). Regardless of personal backgrounds or group identification, many are naive in regard to scientific and geographic principles.

The longer period of volcanic inactivity between 1840 and 1955 led many to believe there was no real danger along the East Rift Zone. This belief was strengthened by the fact that during this same period, activity was almost continual in Halemaumau. Even after the 1955 and 1960 rift zone eruptions, the perception persisted among some that these eruptions were unique and not likely to be repeated. The eruptions of the late 1960s and 1970s also seemed to suggest that such activity would be confined to that section of the rift zone closest to Halemaumau and within the boundaries of the national park. These perceptions were evidenced by the agricultural expansion and real estate development that not only continued, but increased in the region.

The natural vegetation of the Puna region also aided in camouflaging the true nature of volcanic hazard in the area. High rainfall and excellent drainage combined with a tropical climate conducive to rapid growth, produce a lush landscape within a very short time. In 1991, many parts of the 1955 lava flows exhibit remarkable vegetation coverage. Instead of evoking a response of caution toward the possible dangers that would be suggested by a black, jagged landscape, one is drawn to the beauty of an area softened by greenery.

Yet it is erroneous to conclude that people living in the East Rift Zone region have failed to perceive volcanic eruptions as hazardous. A 1972 study of area residents indicated that most people in the area were well aware of the geological realities of the landscape. A majority stated that the hazard was to property and not to life. In spite of the threat and understanding that there were other places on the island which were considered safer, more than ninety percent of those responding stated that the advantages of the region outweighed the disadvantages (Murton and Shimabukuro, 1972). Personal conversations in 1990 and 1991 with a number of people living both in and out of the area confirm that those same perceptions continue.

HUMAN DECISIONS

Prior to the 1983 outbreak at Pu'u O'o, the main human response to a volcanic eruption has been to evacuate. Given the perceptions, attitudes, and cultural values of the population in general, leaving one's house and land behind was part of the initial pact one made with nature. Prayer and/or an appeal to Pele was also high on the list of actions. There were no other significant adjustments made toward the emergency, either at the time of an eruption or prior to one (Murton and Shimabukuro, 1971).

Previous eruptons have seen some human attempts to mitigate the hazard. In 1935, and again in 1942, bombs were used on the source end of Mauna Loa eruptions, whose lava flows threatened the town of Hilo. The results of these efforts to break long lava flows into several shorter ones or to rechannelize them were largely inconclusive. Initial assessment gives some credibility to the utilization of this method, but the eruptions ceased shortly after the bombing and before sustained change in flow behavior could be observed. (Jaggar, 1936, Macdonald, 1942).

In 1937, the construction of embankments for the protection of Hilo was proposed (Jaggar, 1937). No action was taken then. The idea was revived in 1960 at Kapoho. Almost every bulldozer on the island of Hawaii was mobilized to construct earthen walls in an attempt to divert the flow of lava away from the community. Six separate walls twenty to thirty feet high were built in different places. Their combined length was a little more than three miles.

The effectiveness of the walls is still in dispute as, in reality, the effort failed to accomplish anything except to buy some time for those evacuating. Observers in 1960 witnessed that lava either overflowed these barriers or, in at least one case, melted its way under and through the barrier. All barriers were eventually either destroyed or carried away by the flows.

The feasibility of diversion barriers may never be known. Legal considerations have since put such projects on hold. Any interference of the natural flow of lava might result in the destruction of property that would have otherwise been untouched. The responsibilities and liabilities involved in these decisions are complex and would require legal and legislative attention.

The human response to volcanic eruptions in Hawaii reflected no change until the 1970s. Change was initiated by the fact that human populations, and their property, were more affected than at any other time in Hawaiian history. The explosion of tourism and land development following statehood in 1959 resulted in dramatic increases in real estate prices. While speculation investments were driving prices higher everywhere in the state, the Puna region contained properties which were considered "affordable." A number of subdivisions were started here during the 1960s. Royal Gardens was laid out on the *pali* slope to the northwest of Kalapana. Farther downslope and closer to the sea was Kalapana Gardens, then known as Kalapana Vacation Lots (Figure 3). Lured by lots selling for an average of less than $2,000 at $100 down and $15 a month, the Hawaiian property seemed like a speculator's dream come true. In fact, the value of many lots increased to more than $20,000 before the lava flows of the 1980s rendered them temporarily valueless (Figure 4).

An examination of local real estate developments reveals that these projects appear to have been driven by the all-too-familiar economics of the "fast buck." For example, the 159-acre subdivision of Kalapana Gardens had an original price of $53,200 when it began in 1959. At least $4.8 million in estimated sales was realized before the subdivision was covered with lava in 1990. Those involved in the various subdivision developments included a former governor of Hawaii, several state legislators, and a number of other high-ranking political figures who also had other interests in companies related to the infrastructure of the state.

The real estate subdivision boom eventually resulted in the creation of about 80,000 lots on the Big Island; 60 percent of these lots were located in the Puna district, on or near the East Rift Zone. A 1975 survey found that 88 percent of the land owners in the Puna area lived off the island of Hawaii, and a majority of those were on the Mainland. At the time of purchase, many were unaware of the seriousness of the local volcanic hazards.

The advertised use of Hawaiian properties as "vacation lots" or "retirement properties" was apparently never the objective either. Hopes for spectacular returns on land investment were fueled by real estate prices elsewhere in the state. During the decade of the 1980s, Honolulu led the nation in appreciation of single-family dwellings at 145.3 percent.

For those who actually decided to build on the land, development conditions provided few essentials. Most lots had no access to utilities. Water was provided through individual catchment systems. Total lack of sewer hookups necessitated the added expense of blasting out cesspools in lava rock. These problems, combined with a number of other considerations, resulted in less than 5 percent of the nearly 50,000 lots in the Puna region having residences built on them (Cooper and Daws, 1985).

Until the 1970s, responses to volcanic hazards were initiated only after an eruption began. In 1974, the release of a volcanic hazard zones map of the island of Hawaii played a major role in changing that (Insurance company interviews). Revised in 1987, the map prepared by the U.S. Geological Survey caught the attention of real estate developers, financial institutions, and the general public (Figure 4). Approximately 60 percent of all speculative subdivisions lots were located within the zones of highest risk. Economic controls on the marketplace evolved based on hazard map perceptions and influenced land use decisions where previous arguments and policies had not. Land sales were still permitted, but construction on land within the high risk zones was severely curtailed by several other economic factors.

Although the Puna region has been among the least expensive real estate areas in Hawaii, construction costs are still very high. In 1990, the median price for a single-family dwelling on the island of Hawaii was $136,000. By comparison, it was $355,000 on the island of Oahu. Lacking the financial resources to build a home outright, most people attempt to obtain financing through a bank loan. Such loans are directly linked to an insurable property. Beginning as early as 1971, insurance policies were being refused on properties within the zones of highest volcanic risk. Having no insurance meant having no loan. Consequently, unless a person was willing and able to personally commit such funds and become involved in a "do-it-yourself" construction project, not many substantial structures were built. To be sure, a number of construction projects were undertaken by individuals acting as their own builders and contractors. While some dwellings were large and of considerable value, many were not.

During the Pu'u O'o-Kupaianaha eruption of 1983-91, some of the smaller dwellings in the Kalapana Gardens subdivision were raised off their foundations and moved by truck to safer locations. Roads of inadequate width and construction made it impossible to move larger dwellings. A number of property owners dismantled their homes board by board, hoping to rebuild elsewhere. The most dramatic move involved the Star of the Sea Painted Church in May, 1990. The entire church was jacked up and trucked to a temporary site on the shoulder of Highway 130, awaiting relocation.

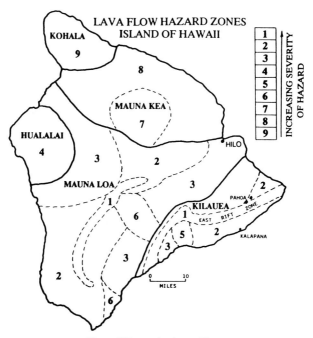

Hazard Zones for Lava Flows

Zone	Percent of area covered by lava since 1800.	Percent of area covered by lava in last 750 yrs.	Explanation
Zone 1	greater than 25 pct	greater than 65 pct	Includes the summits and rift zones of Kilauea and Mauna Loa where vents have been repeatedly active in historic time.
Zone 2	15-25 pct	25-75 pct	Areas adjacent to and downslope of active rift zones.
Zone 3	1-5 pct	15-75 pct	Areas gradationally less hazardous than Zone 2 because of greater distance from recently active vents and/or because the topography makes it less likely that flows will cover these areas.
Zone 4	about 5 pct	less than 15 pct	Includes all of Hualalai, where the frequency of eruptions is lower than on Kilauea and Mauna Loa. Flows typically cover large areas.
Zone 5	none	about 50 pct	Areas currently protected from lava flows by the topography of the volcano.
Zone 6	none	very little	Same as Zone 5.
Zone 7	none	none	20 percent of this area covered by lava 3,500-5,000 yrs. ago.
Zone 8	none	none	Only a few percent of this area covered in the past 10,000 yrs.
Zone 9	none	none	No eruption in this area for the past 60,000 yrs.

FIGURE 4. Lava Flow Hazard Zones (After Heliker, USGS, 1990).

In early 1991, the state government was in the process of obtaining relocation property for the displaced residents of Kalapana. The state legislature was also working on a solution to the availability of volcano insurance.

Local governmental agencies have been intimately involved with hazard and disaster management ever since eruptions began along the East Rift Zone in 1955. The Director of Civil Defense has been responsible for everything from organizing evacuations and directing traffic to comforting residents and conducting news interviews. Besides having to cope with the 24-hour job of any volcanic eruption, the responsibilities of the office require overseeing all other emergencies both natural and human. Hawaii's location makes it subject to other natural hazards, such as tsunamis and hurricanes, which impose additional demands on the Civil Defense Agency. To its credit, this agency has managed to maintain a high level of efficiency and respect. Its greatest asset appears to be the perceived psychological value of genuine concern it projects to local residents.

Given the existence of active volcanoes and the frequency of various other natural hazards, one would expect an office of the Federal Emergency Management Agency (FEMA) to be located in Hawaii, yet as of 1991 none existed. The closest FEMA office is in San Francisco, where it is ironically located almost on top of the San Andreas Fault. Hawaii's state government has been attempting without much success to get a FEMA office located in Honolulu.

CONCLUSIONS AND FUTURE IMPLICATIONS

Since 1955, approximately 30 percent of the land area downslope from the East Rift Zone has been covered with lava (Figure 2). Consequently, hazard experiences of the past few decades should provide some valuable lessons for the land use policies and decisions that have to be made in the next few years. The new real estate projects which have been started and the future developments that are planned require careful scrutiny and consideration. There are some projects seeking approval which exhibit the type of planning which brought disaster to the developments of Royal Gardens and Kalapana Gardens. It is evident that decision makers need to better utilize the information and tools at their disposal. The general public also needs to be more aware of the natural ecological cycles of the region, the nature of volcanic eruptions and their hazards, and have a clearer understanding of geologic time and sequence.

Various agencies and business institutions have also tended to consider the volcanic hazard zones as being absolute, with well-defined boundary lines separating each one. These perceptions ignore the complexities of approximations and scientific probabilities. Most importantly, responsible political and social decisions need to be driven by more than a quick profit.

In May, 1990, President Bush declared Hawaii County a major disaster area as a result of the Kilauea eruptions. Responding to that declaration, FEMA issued a Hazard Mitigation Team Report for the Kilauea volcano eruption in October of that year. The report identified, evaluated, and reviewed the various aspects of the volcanic activity. Recommendations were made for the reexamination of state and county land use policies in Hazard Zones 1 and 2. The report expressed particular concern over development and increased population density within these zones.

Past performance has demonstrated that the land on the downslope side of the East Rift Zone is suitable for agricultural use. Papayas, macadamia nuts, and various horticultural crops do extremely well, even on lava flows that have been broken up and planted. Although there might be damage from both solid and gaseous material during an eruption, personal grief and property losses are likely to be far less than if the land were covered with dwellings and resorts.

While the two most populous areas on the Big Island, Hilo and Kona, are in no danger from Kilauea, both lie in the direct path of lava flows which could emanate from Mauna Loa and Hualalai. In 1931, Thomas Jaggar expressed concern over the fate of Hilo and called for disaster preparations. The danger is no less imminent today. As the island's population continues to grow and as future developments are considered, land use policies need to reflect a consideration of historical evidence and thoughtful concern. Society will have to decide not only the costs and benefits of such undertakings, but to determine who pays.

BIBLIOGRAPHY

Aleshire, Ilene. 1990. *Honolulu Star-Bulletin & Advertiser,* At Kalapana, Lava was a Minor Worry, August 5.

Armstrong, R. Warwick, ed. 1983. *Atlas of Hawaii,* Second Edition. Honolulu: University of Hawaii Press.

Bevens, Darcy, Taeko Jane Takahashi and Thomas L. Wright, eds. 1988. *The Early Serial Publications of the Hawaiian Volcano Observatory,* Vols. 1-3. Hawaii National Park, Hawaii: Hawaii Natural History Association.

Big Island Insurance Agency, Inc. 1991. Hilo, Hawaii. Interview by author, April 2.

Brigham, William T. 1909. *The Volcanoes of Kilauea and Mauna Loa on the Island of Hawaii.* Honolulu: Bishop Museum Press. (1974 reprint).

Carlquist, Sherwin. 1970. *Hawaii: A Natural History.* New York: The Natural History Press.

Continental Insurance Agency of Hawaii, Ltd. 1991. Hilo, Hawaii. Interview by author, April 2.

Cooper, George and Gavan Daws. 1985. *Land and Power in Hawaii.* Honolulu: University of Hawaii Press.

Decker, Robert W., Thomas L. Wright and Peter H. Stauffer, eds. 1987. *Volcanism in Hawaii.* Vol. 1. Washington: United States Government Printing Office.

Department of Business, Economic Development & Tourism. 1990. *The State of Hawaii Data Book. 1990.* Honolulu: State of Hawaii.

Ellis, William. 1963. *Journal of William Ellis.* Honolulu: Advertiser Publishing Co., Ltd. (Reprint of the London 1827 edition).

First Insurance Co. of Hawaii, Ltd. 1991. Hilo, Hawaii. Interview by author, April 2.

Fiske, Richard S., Tom Simkin and Elizabeth A. Nielsen, eds. 1987. *The Volcano Letter,* (1925-1955). Washington, DC: Smithsonian Institution Press.

Fitzpatrick, Gary L. 1986. *The Early Mapping of Hawaii.* Honolulu: Editions Ltd.

Hawaii Tribune-Herald. 1983-1991.

Hawaiian Insurance Group. 1991. Hilo, Hawaii. Interview by author, April 2.

Heliker, Christina. 1990. *Kilauea: The Newest Land on Earth.* Honolulu: Bishop Museum Press.

Heliker, Christina. 1990. *Volcanic and Seismic Hazards on the Island of Hawaii.* Washington, DC: U.S. Government Printing Office.

Hewitt, Kenneth, ed. 1983. *Interpretations of Calamity from the Viewpoint of Human Ecology.* Boston: Allen & Unwin Inc.

Hilo Tribune-Herald. 1955.

Holcomb, Robin T. 1987. Eruptive History and Long-Term Behavior of Kilauea Volcano. *Volcanism in Hawaii.* Vol. 1. Washington: United States Government Printing Office.

Honolulu Star-Bulletin & Advertiser. 1983-1991.

Kane, Herb Kawainui. 1987. *Pele: Goddess of Hawaii's Volcanoes.* Captain Cook, HI: The Kawainui Press, 1987.

Kates, R.W. 1978. *Risk Asessment of Environmental Hazard.* New York: John Wiley & Sons.

Macdonald, Gordon A. and Agatin T. Abbott. 1970. *Volcanoes in the Sea: The Geology of Hawaii.* Honolulu: University of Hawaii Press.

Macdonald, Gordon A. and Douglass H. Hubbard. 1989. *Volcanoes of the National Parks in Hawaii.* Ninth Edition. Honolulu: Hawaii Natural History Association.

Mullineaux, Donal R., Donald W. Peterson and Dwight R. Crandell. 1987. Volcanic Hazards in the Hawaiian Islands. *Volcanism in Hawaii*, Vol. 1. Washington: United States Government Printing Office. pp. 599-621.

Murton, Brian J. and Shinzo Shimabukuro. 1972. Human Adustment to Volcanic Hazard in Puna District, Hawaii. Professional paper presented at 22nd International Geographical Congress. July 24-30.

Smathers, Garret A. and Dieter Mueller-Dombois. 1974. *Invasion and Recovery of Vegetation after a Volcanic Eruption in Hawaii.* Washington, DC: U.S. Government Printing Office.

The State and Federal Hazard Mitigation Team. 1990. *Hazard Mitigation Team Report for the Kilauea Volcano Eruption Hawaii County, Hawaii.* FEMA-864-DR-HI, October.

Tilling, Robert I., Christina Heliker and Thomas L. Wright. 1987. *Eruptions of Hawaiian Volcanoes: Past, Present, and Future.* Denver: U.S. Geological Survey.

Viola, Herman J. and Carolyn Margolis, eds. 1985. *Magnificent Voyagers: The U.S. Exploring Expedition, 1838-1842.* Washington, DC: Smithsonian Institution Press.

Westervelt, William D. 1963. *Hawaiian Legends of Volcanoes.* Rutland, VT: Charles E. Tuttle Company, Inc. (Reprint of 1916 edition).

White, Gilbert F., ed. 1974. *Natural Hazards: Local, National, Global.* New York: Oxford University Press.

Wright, Thomas L. and Taeko Jane Takahashi. 1989. *Observations and Interpretation of Hawaiian Volcanism and Seismicity, 1779-1955.* Honolulu: University of Hawaii Press.

Natural and Technological Disasters: Causes, Effects and Preventive Measures. Edited by
S.K. Majumdar, G.S. Forbes, E.W. Miller, and R.F. Schmalz. © 1992, The Pennsylvania Academy
of Science.

Chapter Thirty-Seven

MORAL ISSUES AND DILEMMAS IN HIGH RISK TECHNOLOGY

RACHEL M. RANKIN and JOSEPH R. HERKERT

Bachelor of Arts in Engineering Program
Lafayette College
Easton, PA 18042

INTRODUCTION

More than 2,000 dead and over 200,000 injured by a chemical leak; a nation mourns the loss of six astronauts and a teacher; a culture that has existed for hundreds of years faces extinction due to fallout from a nuclear accident; thousands at risk each day because of the industrial plant right next door—all of these outcomes have resulted from the use of technology. Individuals, corporations and governments all make decisions concerning how, where, when and why to use technology. The decisions and their consequences pose moral dilemmas, ". . . those moral problems in which two or more moral obligations, duties, rights, ideals, or applications of a single principle come into conflict in a situation in which not all of them can be respected or fulfilled."[1] Often, these dilemmas are disregarded or kept from the public.

High risk technology is defined by Perrow as technology having catastrophic potential; the ability to take or in some way alter the lives of a large number of operators, passengers, innocent by-standers and members of future generations in a single accident. The characteristics of many high risk systems, such as interactive complexity and tight coupling, suggest that ". . . there is a form of accident that is inevitable", regardless of the presence of safety devices.[2] A more conventional or mainstream term is "low probability—high consequence" risk. This implies that there is a low probability of an accident occurring; but if or when it did, there would be high consequences, for example the 2,000 plus killed and the 200,000 plus injured by the chemical leak in Bhopal, India.[3] The continued use of such technology and the castastrophes that result suggest that closer scrutiny be directed toward the related moral issues and dilemmas. The aim of this paper is to inquire about these issues and dilemmas that surround the use of high risk technology.

Moral Issues and Dilemmas in Risk Assessment

Risk assessment, sometimes called risk-benefit analysis, is a field that evolved in large part to assist in the decision making process regarding high risk technology.[4,5] A risk assessment, which is based on the results of fault trees, failure mode worksheets, and mathematical models, is used to determine the probability of certain risks and the consequences of those risks. The four main steps of a risk assessment include defining the conditions of exposure ("Who will be exposed? To what? In what way? For how long?"); identifying the adverse effects ("What is the effect?"); relating the exposure with the effect ("How much adverse effect results from how much exposure?"); and finally, estimating the overall risk.[6] In this step:

The several effects are compared in order to identify which are the strongest, the most undesirable, and the most likely to affect many people. This judgement edges up to being political as well as scientific, and its outcome often becomes the principal input to the heavily value-laden public tasks of judging the acceptability of risks and setting standards . . .

The Challenger space shuttle accident is a strong case illustrating the moral issues and dilemmas resulting from this political aspect of risk assessment. The risk assessment presented to the public regarding the likelihood and severity of an accident involving the Challenger was altered to present a lower failure probability. There was very little historical data on which to base a risk assessment as a result of the limited number of shuttle flights and of NASA's "management methodology" for obtaining data and calculating risk. This methodology was laid out in NASA's 1985 safety analysis of the Galileo nuclear powered space craft which was to be launched from the space shuttle. Management held the belief that the use of reliability or probability numbers was not practical because of the amount of testing needed to verify predictions and the expense and "bookkeeping" involved.[7] They stated that, "[e]xperience has shown that with the safety, reliability, and quality assurance requirements imposed on manned spaceflight contractors, standard failure rate data are pessimistic."[7]

NASA needed to prove to Congress and the public that the shuttle was justified and that it would soon be ". . . cheap and routine rather than large and risky, with respect to both technology and cost."[7] Adelbert Tischler, a retired NASA manager, stated that, as a result of what NASA felt was a need to justify the shuttle in a time of political unpopularity, ". . . some NASA people began to confuse desire with reality . . . One result was to assess risk in terms of what was thought acceptable without regard for verifying the assessment."[7] Therefore, while management was quoting a very low probability of catastrophic failure, 1 in 100,000, the working

engineers were stating much higher chances of 1 in 100. These numbers originated
when the Interagency Nuclear Safety Review Panel required NASA to carry out
risk assessments before it would allow the Galileo launch from the shuttle.[7] Bell
and Esch reported one risk assessment, which was completed by J.H. Wiggins Co.,
that noted,

> . . . that the history of other solid-fuel rockets showed them as undergoing
> catastrophic launches somewhere between 1 time in 59 and 1 time in 34, but
> the study's contract overseers, the Space Shuttle Range Safety Ad Hoc Com-
> mittee made an "engineering judgement" and "decided that a reduction in
> the failure probability estimate was warranted for the Space Shuttle SRBs
> . . ." The Ad Hoc Committee therefore "decided to assume a failure prob-
> ability of [1 in 1,000] for each SRB." The Committee also decided that a
> second probability of 1 in 10,000 should be proclaimed due to improvements
> in the motors.[7]

A second study by Teledyne Energy Systems, Inc. pointed out that the Wiggins
analysis disregarded data and arbitrarily assigned risk levels " 'as per sponsor direction' with 'no quantitative justification at all.' "[7]

In the case of the Challenger, NASA's management claimed to have but did not
actually use true risk assessment. Ignoring actual "engineering judgement", they
arbitrarily chose probability numbers that were overly optimistic.[8] It seems that the
risk assessment they presented was solely for the purpose of justifying the high risk
technology to the skeptical public, which Perrow[2] and other critics argue is an all
too frequent use of risk assessment.

The risk assessment figures quoted by the nuclear power industry also illustrate
how probabilities put forth in risk assessments are often manipulated to justify high
risk technology. For example, as Ian Stewart, a professor at the University of Warwick, notes,

> According to the old Central Electricity Generating Board, the probability
> of a catastrophic accident in a nuclear power station was one every 10,000
> years . . . A probability of one in every 10,000 years sounds very reassuring,
> but it is worth taking a closer look. What it means is that for each nuclear
> reactor, the probability of a catastrophic accident in any given year is one in
> 10,000; that is, 0.0001 per year. There are roughly 40 nuclear power stations
> in Britain, so the probability that at least one will have a catastrophic acci-
> dent in any given year is the sum of the 40 probabilities, which is 0.004. The
> probability of at least one catastrophic accident in Britain during the next
> 25 years is 25 times this, or 0.1. That is, the chances are one in 10. This does
> not sound as reassuring as "one every 10,000 years." But it is just a different
> way of saying the same thing.[9]

The British nuclear power industry apparently uses the "one in 10,000" probability to reassure the public, to convince them that nuclear power is the "safest
form of energy". One critic argues that formal assessments, such as those presented
by NASA and the nuclear power industry, have been used by ". . . officials not as

a tool to aid rational decision making, but as a tool of legitimation to set some choices in a context that made them seem optimal."[10]

A related issue is the presentation of risk assessments as being completely objective and all inclusive when in fact they are not. In high risk technology, assessors often lack the experimental data upon which to base their analyses. Assessors must therefore make valuative judgements.[11,12] As a result, all risk assessments, ". . . are inherently subjective. Someone, relying on his or her own judgement, must structure an analysis to determine the various ways that failures might occur, their relative importance, and their logical interconnections."[11] In this subjective process, certain key risk factors may be overlooked or underestimated.[11]

The Value of Life in Risk Assessment

One task of risk assessment that clearly has a moral dimension is the valuing of human life in determining which risks ae most acceptable. To determine risk acceptability, assessors weigh the costs against the benefits. They compare the cost of saving a life, possibly by adding an expensive safety feature, to the cost of injury or death expected from not adding the feature. They must determine the answer to the question that Perrow asks, "What is a life worth?"[2]

The dilemma of, ". . . whether it is morally permissible to place any 'price' on human life"[13] exists because of the two options available to those who make decisions regarding benefits and risks. The options are to conduct risk benefit analysis, which includes economic valuation of human life, or to only use subjective judgement. Both seem equally morally appalling.[13,14]

The methods used in placing a value on life raise some daunting moral questions. For example, analysts often use one's economic worth, future earning power, occupation and social status to determine the value of life. Many believe that this practice is morally unacceptable because a person's worth is not just an economic issue. Other questions to be considered include social aspects, such as who will be affected by the loss of that life, differences in the way life is viewed by different cultures, the belief that human life is "unique and priceless" and the fact that occupation and social status may be the result of economic and social constraints.[12,13,14]

The 1984 catastrophe in Bhopal, India illustrates the human consequences of implicitly valuing life on the basis of economic worth. As critics point out, citizens of Bhopal, India were subject to higher "technological risks" and "poorer safety standards" than faced by citizens of the USA or more favored countries.[3,15] According to Castleman and Purkavastha, it is very obvious that Union Carbide valued the lives of its workers and residents near its plant in Institute, West Virginia more than the lives of those in Bhopal. Their argument is based on the following facts: "The Bhopal plant was designed less safely than the Institute plant . . ."; discrepancies existed between the two sites in plant design and operation; there were repeated cases of executive management decisions that exemplified the attitude that safety was not an important issue in the Bhopal plant; the citizens of Bhopal were not informed of the hazardous materials used and the risks they faced.[15]

The Bhopal catastrophe illustrates that the value of life issue is closely related to questions concerning who shall decide the value of life and the risks to be imposed upon others. For example, Donaldson asks, "What moral obligations underlie, what extra-national responsibilities should inform the behavior of global actors such as Union Carbide and the United States?"[3] And, ". . . what about the 'White Man's Burden'? Isn't it morally arrogant of us to prescribe levels of risk for other sovereign nations?"[3]

Distribution of Risks and Consequences of High Risk Technologies

As Bhopal illustrates, while some may benefit from the use of one high risk technology or another, there are those who are placed at much higher risk and face more serious consequences because of where they live or the time and location of their conception and birth. The risks and consequences of high risk technology do not hesitate to cross geopolitical, cultural, or even generational boundaries.

Another good illustration of the risks and consequences of technology crossing such boundaries is the Chernobyl catastrophe. Outside of the Soviet Union, most radioactive fallout was deposited in Switzerland, Austria, northern Italy, Sweden, and Poland where it polluted much of the grazing and farm lands. Therefore, milk and agricultural products were poisoned and unfit for consumption.[16,17] The people of Europe were contaminated by breathing in and being exposed to radioactive substances from the fallout. Many were also affected by consuming the "contaminated food and drink".[6] One recent review of the impacts of Chernobyl notes, ". . . worldwide dispersion of core material is estimated to be responsible for as many as 28,000 delayed cancers in the next 50 years."[18]

The consequences of high risk technology are also not limited by cultural boundaries. The fallout from the explosion at Chernobyl is threatening the extinction of the Sami culture that has existed for approximately 2,000 years.[19,20] The Sami people of Lapland, also referred to as the Lapps, inhabit northern parts of Norway, Sweden, Finland, and the extreme northwest of the Soviet Union. Of the total Sami population of approximately 70,000, ten percent are herders. For those Sami herders, especially the South Sami of Norway and Sweden, their culture and way of life are jeopardized by the Chernobyl accident.[20] Their entire culture is tied to reindeer, which before Chernobyl, provided them with food, clothing, materials for shelter and transportation, and a means of economic exchange. As one herder stated, "Sami culture begins with the reindeer. In some ways it would also end with the reindeer."[19]

The nuclear fallout from Chernobyl brought very high levels of iodine-131 and caesium-137 raining down on the reindeer's food source, lichen. Since this plant absorbs its nutrients from the air it became highly contaminated and in turn contaminated most of the reindeer. In 1986, the year of the Chernobyl accident, 70,000 out of 100,000 reindeer slaughtered were condemned.[19] The Swedish and Norwegian governments paid the herders the market value for the condemned reindeer. However, the Sami say that, ". . . the losses could not be compensated by any amount of money."[20]

The Sami have overcome obstacles and adapted to imposed changes in the past and they have the conviction to do so again. However, as Martin Linton notes, "It is bitter injustice to them that the ultimate accident of modern industrial technology, Chernobyl, should threaten the one people in Europe who still live in harmony with nature and the environment."[19]

The risks and consequences of Chernobyl and other high risk technologies may also extend well into the future. Members of future generations that are affected by the consequences of high risk technology, such as stillborn or deformed children, are classified by Perrow as "fourth-party" victims.[2] He argues that,

> Fourth-party victims potentially constitute the most serious class of victims. Chemical or radioactive contamination of land areas could have far-reaching effects upon the health of future generations . . . Future generations carry the burden; the present generation reaps whatever rewards there may be from the activity.[2]

The number of people exposed to radiation as a result of the Chernobyl accident is staggering. *Izvestia*, the Soviet government's newspaper, stated that, ". . . as many as 3 million people are living on irradiated land."[21] The effects on these people will most surely extend to their children in some form or another, including a change of lifestyle, mental and or physical handicaps and the spread of cancers. These effects can already be seen in Palessie, in southern Byelorussia. There, ". . . between 50 to 70 percent of children now have health problems. About 8 per cent have thyroid complications in forms [not observed] before Chernobyl. The incidence of cancers and of congenital deformities was significantly higher . . ."[22]

There are a number of moral issues related to the distribution of risks as illustrated by these three categories. First, should thousands of people have to suffer the consequences of an accident that, one, was not in their country and two, was caused by a system that they did not ask for, approve of, or receive any benefits from? Is there a moral obligation to protect and preserve cultures and is that more important than the continued use and development of high risk systems? A controversial moral dilemma also exists because of the conflict between the obligation to try and make life the best it can be for people today and the obligation to look out for the well being of future generations as reflected in the world we pass on to them.

Technical Experts, Managers and Complex Technology

In his article, "Return Technology to Human Hands", Manley discusses the increasing complexity of technology and its affect on humans:

> Successful technologies rapidly grown more complex . . . At the same time, as technological complexity increases, more humans become involved, with each possessing a specialized responsibility and purview . . . Complexity thus leads to an inherent paradox: it demands greater interaction between people and their technical systems, and among the people involved as creators, operators, and users. Yet the complexity generates an environment that makes this rapport more difficult.[23]

The paradox created by the inherent complexity of high risk technology has led to disagreements between technical experts and managers that pose some moral questions. Take for example the Challenger accident. A disagreement between the engineers and managers at Morton Thiokol Inc., the manufactures of the space shuttle's solid rocket boosters, and NASA occurred over the safety of the booster rockets' O-rings. The O-rings were used to seal the joints of the rockets. Since at least 1980 and up until the explosion, NASA and Thiokol had known that the O-ring sealing system was a safety concern.[24] In a report dated December 17, 1982, this sealing system was listed by NASA as a critical item that had the potential to cause "loss of mission, vehicle and crew due to metal erosion, burn-through, and probable case burst resulting in fire and deflagration."[24]

At a teleconference the evening before the fatal Challenger launch, representatives of Thiokol and NASA discussed this safety issue. Engineers for Thiokol warned against the launch because of the possible failure of the O-rings to seal and the catastrophic consequences that would result. Initially, Thiokol managers sided with their engineers. However, under pressure from the NASA representatives, they took off their "engineering hats" and decided that it was safe to launch the Challenger! A management only vote was held and it resulted in the company's official finding, which stated ". . . that the seals could not be shown to be unsafe."[1] Although the decision to reverse Thiokol's initial decision was a management one, it was conveyed to NASA as an "engineering assessment".[8] The NASA managers present at the teleconference knew of the potential catastrophe but it seems that the desire to alleviate launch schedule and budget pressures outweighed the obligation to safety. There was testimony after the accident that engineers from Morton Thiokol argued with both Thiokol management and NASA not to launch the Challenger, but their warnings were not heeded.[24,25]

The Challenger case is not the only example of management overruling the judgement of technical experts. As Rosemary Chalk notes, ". . . situations in which scientists or engineers have raised serious concerns which have been ignored or suppressed by company or agency managers and superiors . . ."[26] are common. Engineers and scientists in this situation must decide whether or not to "blow the whistle". As Martin and Schinzinger note, "This really involves two questions: When are they morally permitted, and when are they morally obligated, to do so?"[1]

Martin and Schinzinger characterize whistle-blowing as an activity which consists of the revealing of new information "outside the approved organizational channels" with the intent of drawing attention to what the whistle-blower believes is a moral problem! The main moral dilemma for someone contemplating blowing the whistle is to determine which of these often conflicting obligations should have top priority: obligations to the public, to clients or customers, to one's family, to one's profession, and to one's employer![27]

Until recently, whistle-blowers were regarded as disloyal and legal protection for them was almost nil. In many cases, they were singled out and made objects of scorn by their peers and of retaliation by their employers. There are several cases involving high risk technology that illustrate the consequences of whistle-blowing. In the Challenger case discussed above, the engineers at Morton Thiokol who argued against the fatal launch of the Challenger were accused by some for not blowing the whistle soon enough and by others for blowing the whistle at all. The engineers who did finally blow the whistle at the Rogers Commission hearings on the Challenger accident, were retailiated against by Morton Thiokol. Thiokol reportedly, ". . . stripped them of their responsibilities, and . . . reassigned them to lesser projects."[28]

In the nuclear industry, there are several examples of whistle-blowers.[29] One of the most famous is the case of Karen Silkwood, who died in an automobile accident while working to expose hazards at an Oklahoma plutonium processing plant.[29] Another that is quite similar to the Silkwood story, is the case of Judith Penley, an employee of the Watts Bar nuclear plant in Tennessee. Penley was shot and fatally wounded in October 1985. She had been working with an outside firm to mediate employees' concerns about safety. Another employee of the Watts Bar plant had his life threatened several times following his appearances before the Tennessee Valley Authority in which he complained about a ". . . damaged cable leading to the Watts Bar nuclear core and bad plant welding."[29]

Nonetheless, attitudes toward whistle-blowers are slowly changing.[28] On April 10, 1989, President Bush signed into law the "Whistleblowers Protection Act of 1989" to enhance the protection of federal employees.[30] Although this law does not protect all whistle-blowers, it sets a precedent for the way in which whistle-blowers should be treated. Louis Clark, executive director of the Government Accountability Project, has noted, "It's far more socially acceptable now. Public officials say great things about whistle-blowing . . ."[28] However, as long as, ". . . the conditions that provoke whistle-blowing are stil prevalent,"[25] there will likely be retaliation against whistle-blowers, thus discouraging others from acting in the public's interest. As Stephen Unger of the Institute of Electrical and Electronics Engineers has stated, "If technology is to be used in a beneficial manner, the conditions under which engineers operate must be changed . . . Decision makers cannot be allowed to overrule engineers' professional judgements in a peremptory manner."[25] Many believe that corporations and government agencies have a moral obligation to establish a system in which an employee would be free to discuss his or her concerns related to safety and in which legitimate concerns would be taken seriously.[27]

CONCLUSIONS

During the past decade, moral philosophers have begun to wrestle with the dilemmas posed by high risk technology. MacKinnon, for example, sees a way out of the dilemma involved in pricing human life by appealing to the distinction between the positive duty to save lives and the more compelling negative duty not to take lives. This may require spending a very large amount to avoid placing others at risk![3] Donaldson suggests that it is immoral for multinational corporations and their home countries to impose risks upon developing nations that would be unacceptable at home, were the home country at the same stage of development as the developing nation. In response to the "White Man's Burden" problem, Donaldson asserts that we have a responsibility not to impose a ". . . moral burden on the shoulders of societies still adolescent in the age of technology."[3]

In an effort to avoid the misuse and inequitable consequences of conventional risk assessment, Schrader-Frechette has proposed "ethically weighted [risk analysis] parameters" and "a judicial procedure of adversary assessment," known as the "technology tribunal", designed to consider the social, political and ethical aspects of technological controversies, in addition to the scientific dimensions.[2] Werhane suggests that conflicts between managers and technical experts could be minimized if both parties were ". . . to take personal moral responsibility for decision-making . . ." grounded upon ". . . the process of questioning, the development of a moral imagination, and testing one's decisions as precedents and against moral minimums . . ."[31]

Indeed, a personal responsibility is perhaps the single most powerful concept in dealing with the moral issues raised by high risk technology. Perrow has noted that ". . . as long as national goals are served by risky systems, we will continue to have them and their catastrophies." [32] To this thought we would add that humans will also continue to be confronted with the moral dilemmas posed by such technologies.

REFERENCES

1. Martin, Mike W. and Roland Schinzinger. 1989. *Ethics in Engineering.* McGraw-Hill, Inc., New York, NY.
2. Perrow, Charles. 1984. *Normal Accidents.* Basic Books, Inc., New York, NY.
3. Donaldson, Thomas. 1986. The Ethics of Global Risk. *IEEE Technology and Society Magazine* (June):17-21.
4. Wilson, Richard and E.A.C. Crouch. 1987. Risk Assessment and Comparisons: An Introduction. *Science* 236:267-270.
5. Slovic, Paul. 1987. Perception of Risk. *Science* 236:280-285.
6. Lowrance, William. 1976. *Of Acceptable Risk.* William Kaufmann, Inc., Los Altos, CA.
7. Bell, Trudy and Karl Esch. 1989. The Space Shuttle: A Case of Subjective Engineering. *IEEE Spectrum* (June):42-46.
8. Herkert, Joseph R. 1991. Management's Hat Trick: Misuse of "Engineering Judgement" in the Challenger Incident. *Journal of Business Ethics.* 10:617-620.
9. Stewart, Ian. 1990. Risky Business. *New Scientist* (19 May):1-4.
10. Clarke, Lee. 1988. Explaining Choices Among Technological Risks. *Social Problems* 35:22-35.
11. Sills, David, C.P. Wolf and Vivien Shelanski, eds. 1982. *Accident at Three Mile Island: The Human Dimensions.* Westview Press, Boulder, CO.
12. Schrader-Frechette, K.S. 1985. *Science Policy, Ethics, and Economic Methodology.* D. Reidel Publishing Company, Dordrecht, Holland.
13. MacKinnon, Barbara. 1986. Pricing Human Life. *Science, Technology, & Human Values* 11:29-39.

14. Rhoads, Stephen, ed. 1980. *Valuing Life: Public Policy Dilemmas.* Westview Press, Boulder, CO.
15. Castleman, Barry I. and Prabir Purkavastha. 1985. The Bhopal Disaster as a Case Study in Double Standards, pp. 213-221. In Ives, Jane, ed. *The Export of Hazard: Transnational Corporations and Environmental Control Issues.* Routledge & Kegan plc., Boston, MA.
16. Park, Chris C. 1989. *Chernobyl: The Long Shadow.* Routledge, New York, NY.
17. Megaw, James. 1987. *How Safe? Three Mile Island, Chernobyl and Beyond.* Stoddart Publishing Co. Limited, Toronto, Canada.
18. Hohenemser, Christoph, Robert L. Goble and Paul Slovic. 1990. Institutional Aspects of the Future Development of Nuclear Power. *Annual Review of Energy* 15:173-200.
19. Linton, Martin. 1988. Lappland: Living With Nuclear Fallout. *New Statesman* (22 April):16-18.
20. Stephens, Sharon. 1987. Lapp Life after Chernobyl. *Natural History* (December):33-39.
21. Bogert, Carroll. 1990. Chernobyl's Legacy. *Newsweek* (May 7): 30-31.
22. Rich, Vera. 1990. Concern Grows Over Health of "Chernobyl Children". *New Scientist* (21 April):23.
23. Manley, John. 1987. Return Technology to Human Hands. *Bulletin of Atomic Scientists* (December):7-8.
24. Biddle, Wayne. 1986. What Destroyed the Challenger. *Discover* (April):40-47.
25. Chalk, Rosemary. 1988. Making the World Safe for Whistle-Blowers. *Technology Review* (January):48-57.
26. Chalk, Rosemary. 1982. The Miners' Canary. *The Bulletin of Atomic Scientists* (February):16-22.
27. Wilson, Glenn. 1984. Ethics: Your Company or Your Conscience?. *Working Woman* (June):62-64.
28. Asbrand, Deborah. 1987. The Whistle-Blower's Burden: Public Approval, Corporate Exile. *EDN* (January 8):296-298.
29. Karlen, Neal and Ginny Carroll. 1985. Nuclear-Powered Murder?. *Newsweek* (November 4):29.
30. Israel, David and Anita Lechner. 1988. Protection for Whistleblowers. *Personnel Administration* 65:6.
31. Werhane, Patricia H. 1991. Engineers and Management: The Challenge of the Challenger Incident. *Journal of Business Ethics* 10:605-616.
32. Perrow, Charles. 1986. The Habit of Courting Disaster. *The Nation* (October 11).

Natural and Technological Disasters: Causes, Effects and Preventive Measures. Edited by
S.K. Majumdar, G.S. Forbes, E.W. Miller, and R.F. Schmalz. © 1992, The Pennsylvania Academy
of Science.

Chapter Thirty-Eight

WHY DO THEY MAP GNP PER CAPITA?

LAKSHMAN S. YAPA

Department of Geography
Pennsylvania State University
University Park, PA 16802

INTRODUCTION

Modern economic development is universally understood to be the solution to
the problems of underdevelopment and poverty in the Third World. Progress along
the path of development is commonly measured by, GNP per capita and its annual
rate of growth, measures that have remained popular among academics and policy
makers despite serious criticisms of their continued use (Ekins, 1986: pp. 22-40).
Almost all undergraduate textbooks on human, economic and cultural geography
of the world have a map of the distribution of GNP per capita, this being one of
the basic geographic "facts" of our modern world (Figure 1). The map is widely
used in high schools for teaching students where the poor countries are. The map
is also used throughout the schools and universities of the Third World to educate
their own young people concerning the "facts" of underdevelopment and the steep
ascent to development. I have argued here that the map of GNP per capita offers
little help to think about the problems of poor people; in fact it only helps confirm
popular misconceptions about poverty and development.

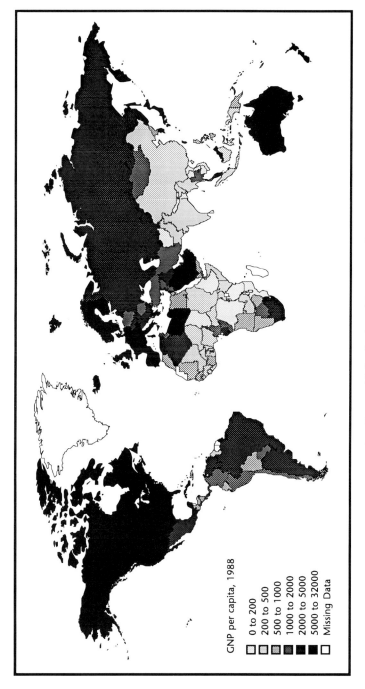

FIGURE 1. World distribution of GNP per capita.

GNP per capita, 1988

0 to 200
200 to 500
500 to 1000
1000 to 2000
2000 to 5000
5000 to 32000
Missing Data

MAP AS IDEOLOGY

The problem that I refer to does not lie in the cartography of the mapping exercise, but rather in the epistemology of development theory that lies behind the construction of such maps! There is a small but growing literature that argues that poverty and malnutrition are not caused by underdevelopment; on the contrary, they reflect social consequences of the very path of modern economic development (Lappe and Collins, 1977; Timberlake, 1986; Illich, 1978; and Esteva, 1987). It is beyond the scope of the paper to develop this argument in depth; however, I wish to comment on some aspects of it using the map of GNP per capita as a point of departure.

The map of GNP per capita is a good example of Brian Harley's (1988) argument that maps represent a means by which dominant classes extend their ideology, power and influence in society, a position he has developed over several years following the leads of Foucault (1980) on the relation between knowledge and power. The following quotes from Harley (1988) refer to some of the themes I have developed in the paper.

. . . The specific functions of maps in the exercise of power also confirm the ubiquity of these political contexts on a continuum of geographical scales. These range from global empire building, to the preservation of the nation state, to the local assertion of individual property rights. In each of these contexts the dimensions of polity and territory were fused in images which— just as surely as legal charters and patents—were part of the intellectual apparatus of power (p. 300).

. . . It has not proved difficult to make a general case for the mediating role of maps in political thought and action nor to glimpse their power effects. Through both their content and mode of representation, the making of and using of maps has been pervaded by ideology (p. 300).

. . . The way in which maps have become part of a wider political sign-system has been largely directed by their associations with elite or powerful groups and individuals and this has promoted an uneven dialogue through maps. The ideological arrows have tended to fly largely in one direction, from the powerful to the weaker in society (p. 300-301).

. . . The practical actions undertaken with maps: warfare, boundary-making, propaganda, or the preservation of law and order, are documented throughout the history of maps. On the other hand, the undeclared processes of domination through maps are more subtle and elusive. These provide the 'hidden rules' of cartographic discourse whose contours can be traced in the subliminal geometries, the silences, and the representational hierarchies of maps (p. 303).

---

¹Epistemology is a branch of philosophy that deals with the conditions of knowing: how do we know what we know and why is that we do not know what we do not know.

To summarize the main points from Harley: (1) map knowledge is a social product and is often used as an instrument in the exercise of power and domination;
(2) wielders of such power are the elites and dominant classes of society who have
used maps to extend their ideologies of domination; (3) the means employed for
the ideological deployment of maps are subtle and they include what Harley has
called "subliminal geometry", "silence by omission", and "representational hierarchies." By subliminal geometry he has meant the location on which maps are
centered or the projection that is used to amplify the political impact of the image.
Silence by omission refers to the exertion of influence by leaving out certain features
and names. Representational hierarchy describes the use of symbols to depict an
ordering of space as in the depiction of towns and villages on maps. I have argued
in this paper that the map of GNP per capita is a very good example of Harley's
argument concerning maps, ideology, knowledge, and power.

The primary purpose of the map of GNP per capita is to "rank order" nations
of the world according to the size of their economic product. This ordering principle comes from the imposition of a very specific, narrow, socially constructed view
of the world, a view that actually plays a part in the general oppression of the poor.
It would be false to suggest the problem is in anyway cartographic because the ordering logic of GNP per capita does not originate in mapping, but in the theories of
development. The power of the map of GNP per capita to suggest and persuade
comes from the reductionist logic of development theory; however, the map
reproduces the original reductionism, confirms it, extends it, and communicates
it to a larger public in powerful graphic ways.

MAP OF GNP PER CAPITA

The gross national product is the total monetary value calculated at market prices
of all goods and services produced in an economy over a given period, typically
one year (Todaro, 1985, p. 411). Income per capita is the total GNP divided by the
total population, that is the amount of GNP each person would have if GNP were
divided equally. Countries with high GNP per capita are considered to be wealthy
and developed, and those with low per capita incomes, underdeveloped and poor.
The map of GNP per capita is an ordering of the world's countries using per capita
income as the criterion for ranking (Figure 1). One purpose of the comparison is
to suggest that poor nations need to expand their GNP in order to catch up with
the more developed countries. It is believed that a GNP growing at 3 per cent per
year is healthy, less than this is worrisome, and zero or negative growth poses a
serious problem. A 3 per cent growth rate will yield a doubling of GNP every twenty-
five years. The primary assumption driving this thinking is that growth is good
because it leads to development, and lack of it, to poverty and hunger.

W.W. Rostow (1960), the American economic historian, formalized these ideas
in his celebrated model of "the stages of economic growth." He divided the countries of the world into five groups according to their per capita income, and argued

that there were five stages in the transition from underdevelopment to development through with all countries must pass.

It is possible to identify all societies, in their economic dimensions, as lying within one of five categories; traditional society, the pre-conditions for take-off, the take-off, the drive to maturity, and the age of high mass-consumption (p. 4).

The advanced countries of the world had during earlier periods of their history passed through the stage of take-off into self-sustaining growth, and today, the underdeveloped countries are in stages before the take-off. Rostow's stages of economic growth has been reproduced in a number of economics and geography textbooks. Though it cannot be proven I believe that the popularity of Rostow's stages of growth contributed much to popularizing the use of the GNP per capita map with its usual four or five income classes. Rostow's five stages of growth has long since been discredited (Baran and Hobsbawm, 1973); however, the idea that nations can be ranked along a measure of economic progress is very much a part of our contemporary public and intellectual views of the world, enjoying support from a wide section of the political spectrum. For example, it was the declared intent of the Chinese government to reach a per capita GNP of $1000 by the year 2000. The official environmentalist position on development can be gleaned from the U.N. World Commission on Environment and Development report, *Our Common Future*, in which they argued that the problems of poverty and underdevelopment could not be solved without a new era of growth in which the Third World countries played a stronger role.

HEGEMONY OF DEVELOPMENTALISM

Economic development as we know it today in the West is not a realistic goal for nations of the Third World. To attain US levels of per capita energy consumption, India would have to increase her commercial energy production by a factor of 35 and Black Africa by a factor of 38.[2] One fourth of the World's population, those living in the West, USSR, and Japan, consume about three-fourths of the World's resources to maintain their standards of living. It is clear that minerals, materials, and energy are simply not here for the majority of people in China, India, Indonesia, Brazil, Bangladesh,Nigeria, and Pakistan to emulate Western styles of living. The idea that there are real "limits to growth" is a very old argument (Meadows, 1972). And yet, we have not explored its implications for the feasibility of development. Why is that?

There is near universal agreement among the elites of the world on the desirability of development, with support coming from all sectors of the political spectrum. Conservatives, liberals, radicals and greens who disagree with each other on a range of basic issues, find no disagreement on the need for economic development. This

---

[2]Calculated from World Bank, *World Development Reprot 1988*, Table 10.

is because development is an instrument of the elite in exercising authority in society and serves important political, economic, and social functions.

Politically, the idea of development provides consensual goals and, therefore, stability to society. In India, it is not possible for the vast majority of people to ever attain the living standards of the top fifth of the consumers; but why has there not been an open discussion of this point? As elsewhere in the world, many in India believe, and are constantly socialized to believe, that they are poor because their country is underdeveloped, and that their poverty can be eradicated through development. This belief in the possibility of development serves the ideological needs of the Indian elites quite well as an important tool in the arsenal of political control. Not unlike the Hindu belief in rebirth, the idea of development encourages poor people to live in hope that life will get better, if not for them during their lifetime, then, at least, for their children or grandchildren. Development serves the purpose of social control of the masses, keeping them in line by exploiting a precious human resource, namely, hope. Of course, the means employed are more populist and humanitarian than those employed by authoritarian repressive regimes. Political parties compete with each other on the basis of whose platform is best able to deliver "development to the people," allowing the modern state in the Third World to use development as the principal means of legitimizing state power.

Economically, development is an important instrument of surplus extraction which provides a means of using public funds to enhance private accumulation. Ministers of state and their agents are permitted to raise development loans on behalf of the government and public. It is commonly alleged that a part of these funds are secretly appropriated for private use by those who negotiate the loan contracts. Other sums are appropriated "legally" through sub-contracts given to companies that are owned by loan negotiators or agents of their families. And all the while the loan remains part of the public debt. Dam construction in south Asia provides numerous examples of this practice. Since independence, multi-purpose dams have been seen as symbols of economic modernization; in fact India's first Prime Minister Nehru is supposed to have once said, "Dams are the modern temples of India." Over the years the massive dams have caused widespread social dislocation and ecological degradation, added heavily to a vast public debt, and yet, in the name of progress, the construction of new dams continues unabated. Dogra (1986) writing on the Indian experience with dams has said the following:

> The Indian experience with large dams has been disastrous. Yet that experience is consistently ignored by the government, which continues to approve new dam projects despite the lessons of the past. Why is this so? If one wishes to answer this question honestly, it is difficult to avoid the conclusion that large dams are chiefly built to satisfy the vested interests of construction companies, senior officals and politicians. Certainly they are the ones who have reaped the benefits of the large dams constructed so far: the peasants whose health and welfare the projects are supposed to enhance, have generally ended up worse off economically and demoralized socially (p. 207).

Another source of the ideological mystification surrounding development is the nature and outlook of the post-colonial political leadership in the Third World. Nehru of India, Jinnah of Pakistan, Nkrumah of Ghana, Sukarno of Indonesia, and Bandaranaiyake of Sri Lanka were all inveterate modernizers. As Harrison (1990) has commented on this point:

> More serious than anything else, the elites they [the colonial powers] handed over power to were products of the colonial education system and were schooled in western ways. Instead of pursing indigenous models of development, almost all of them set to construct imitation western societies. So modern industry was put before agriculture, modern skyscrapers before the masses were housed, modern-sector employees had to be paid enough to enjoy imitation western consumer lifestyles while the majority languished in poverty (p. 46) . . . The aim was not only to show the old imperialists, but to impress other Third World leaders in the only way everyone would recognize: the western way (p. 50).

FAILURES OF DEVELOPMENT

The theory and practice of economic development is in a serious crisis today. After four decades of development planning, hunger and malnutrition persist among large segments of the world's poor. Over a billion people lack basic needs of nutrition, water supply, and shelter.[3] The impressive increases in food production by many countries since the late 1960's have not translated into less hunger. India, for example produces a food surplus while malnutrition persists throughout the country. In the very regions of chronic hunger environmental degradation now poses a serious threat to the conditions of production (Timberlake, 1986; Goldsmith, Hilyard, McCully, and Bunyard, 1990). Prestigious development projects begun a few years ago with much publicity are mired in debt and trouble: Green Revolutions leading to soil erosion, water pollution, loss of genetic diversity, and crop diseases; cattle ranches laying waste to the tropical forest; and tube-well irrigation that mines the groundwater and causes salinization of the soil (Glaeser, 1987; Cowell, 1990).

More than any other fact, the staggering size of the Third World debt exemplifies the depth of the crisis of development theory (George, 1988). The foreign debt of the Third World countries exceeds the figure of one thousand four hundred billion dollars (World Bank, 1988). Several Third World nations spend from one fourth to one half of their annual export earnings simply to pay the interest on their debt. Some nations are being loaned more money to pay interest in order to avoid default on previous loans. Distressingly, much of the loan capital cannot be used for productive investment because it is needed to make the interest payments on previous loans.

The crisis in development also includes the economic and political institutions that are engaged in development. Many states in the Third World are run by the military where elected bodies are weak such as in Latin America and Africa, and

---

[3] The estimate is quoted in Conway and Barbier (1990) on pp. 17-18.

many states are steeped in bribery, corruption, and nepotism. Even states with civilian authorities have massive military budgets that starve their economies of development and social welfare funds. Democratic movements in Eastern Europe, USSR, and China are mounting effective challenges to the once monolithic power structures in the socialist states. The programs of bilateral aid are a thinly disguised extension of foreign policy and are severely constrained by the political, economic, and strategic needs of the donor nations. Multilateral agencies like the World Bank are not in the business of eradicating poverty despite the public relations rehetoric. Their main interest has been in promoting export-led economic growth, a policy that often conflicts with the food needs of the poor and conservation of the environment. More than any other, the Third World debt crisis shows the bankruptcy of the international financial systems in their role as agents for the eradication of poverty. And what of the multinational corporations? They are undoubtedly the most dynamic instruments ever devised by mankind for the develpment of the productive resources of the earth. It is clear that they will continue to play an important role in the Third World, and an increasingly larger role in the socialist countries as well. Useful as they are we must not look to the multinationals as appropriate institutions for the eradication of mass poverty. The legitimate interests of multinationals are not compatible with the task of meeting the basic minimum needs of the poor. The breakfast cereals, processed meats, carbonated beverages, infant formula feeds, brand name drugs, robotics, and labor-saving machines are useful products but they are not the means for eradicating malnutrition nor solving problems of mass unemployment. Indeed, as Illich (1970, p. 179) has said, modern poverty is a by-product of a world marketing catering to the ideologies of an industrial middle class.[4]

DEVELOPMENT AS DESTRUCTION

The failures of development that I have stated so far are not "mistakes" or "accidents." Contrary to what we have been asked to believe development is not a part of the solution to the problem; in fact it is one of the basic causes of mass poverty.

Production is commonly defined as the creation of use values. But under certain circumstances production not only creates use values but also destroys them, a notion that I call "the two faces of production." Poverty is a relation that grows out of this twin characteristic of production. The study of the history of production has been reduced to the separate histories of technology, economics, and ecology. It is this dismemberment of the story of production into separate histories that has concealed the destructive dialectic of modern production. Indeed modern poverty is born in the womb of production, and is a direct result of its destructive dialectic. It is beyond the scope of this paper to argue this in detail.[5] In this paper

---

[4]Almost twenty years ago, Illich, a brilliant social critic, was one of the first to articulate the idea that modern economic development actually causes poverty. See also Illich (1978, 1973).

[5]A more detailed version of this argument appears in Yapa (1991).

I look at how the map of GNP per capita helps to perpetuate the false notion that more GNP is necessarily better than less, and that the growth of GNP will help to eradicate hunger and poverty. I have looked at two examples to illustrate the argument - the Green Revolution and the construction of large dams.

The Green Revolution was a massive campaign launched by the FAO in 1960s to increase food production. The spread of high yielding varieties (HYVs) of hybrid seeds in wheat, rice, and corn is credited for averting massive food shortages in the Third World that were predicted in the seventies (Paddock and Paddock, 1967). "Per capita food production in the developing countries has risen by 7% since the mid 1960s, with an increase of 27% in Asia. Only in Africa has there been a decline" (Conway and Barbier, 1990: p. 20). However, if we go beyond the impressive production statistics and look at the Green Revolution from a holistic view point of social, ecological, and cultural relations, it is evident that it has left in its wake a devastating trail of destruction, and an ecologically unsustainable mode of agricultural production which will aggravate problems of hunger and malnutrition in years to come.

HYVs do best in well endowed physical environments, which explains why they have not done well in Africa. HYVs require irrigation and large doses of fertilizer. In south Asia the irrigated land belongs almost exclusively to the more wealthy farmers. HYVs did not benefit the vast majority of farmers who depend on rain-fed cultivation or work marginal areas. Because of the need to buy commercial inputs farmers cannot grow HYVs just for consumption, they have to grow for the market. Of course, the purchase of inputs and the sale of farm produce in the market help boost GNP but that does not necessarily mean farmers eat better. The wealthy farmers who can afford costly inputs buy out smaller peasants leading to increasing inequity in size of holdings. Ecologically, the HYVs have been an unmitigated disaster. Genetically uniform varieties of rice, wheat, and corn growth in monocultural stands are quite vulnerable to pests and pathogens. For example, severe outbreaks of brown planthoper that were reported from rice paddies in Indonesia led to the banning of the use of pesticides in some areas. Excessive use of chemical pesticides has aggravated pest problems by destroying non-target insects, particularly the natural predators. This has created a vicious treadmill of chemical agriculture: the continued use of pesticides increases pest hazards by destroying natural predators, thus necessitating the use of more pesticides. Moreover, the evolution of pesticide resistant insects has meant the use of new and more powerful pesticides. Likewise, the long use of chemical fertilizer has affected soil quality adversely, and increased soil erosion. And to counteract the consequent decline in yields farmers are forced to apply more fertilizer. This is the treadmill of chemical farming. In addition, fertilizer and pesticide run-off have contaminated ground-water and streams. Prior to the adoption of HYVs, fish living in rice paddies were an important source of protein for poor farmers in south Asia, but this is no more. The diet of poor farmers has deteriorated due to repeated monocropping of cereals, and the elimination of the polyculture of cereals, legumes, and vegetables.

HYVs have done much for integrating Third World farms with markets and agribusiness of fertilizers, pesticides, machinery, fuel, and seeds—a transformation that has been justified as necessary for eradicating hunger in the world. Critics have argued that agricultural systems designed for the eradication of hunger require very different structural and technological characteristics (Chambers, 1977). Consider the technology of hybrid seeds: the basic property of the seed to reproduce itself had always acted as a barrier to companies who wished to sell improved seeds; a major intent of modern plant breeding was to convert seed into a saleable commodity by eliminating its self-reproducing capacity. Thus "improved seed" which creates value for seed companies has eliminated the value previously derived by farmers from seeds which reproduced naturally as a free good (Kloppenberg, 1988).[6] Modern agricultural scientists have been aware of "low-input" agriculture for years from the writings of King (1973; first printing in 1911), Howard (1973; first printing in 1940) and others. Altieri (1987) and his associates have argued that indigenous techniques can produce high yields of varied crops while maintaining soil fertility and reducing farmer's reliance on expensive and destructive chemcial inputs. For example, in Mexico one hectare planted in maize, beans, and squash can produce as much food as 1.7 hectares planted to maize alone (Altieri, 1991, p. 95). Unfortunately, such techniques have received little official sponsorship and research funds (Glaeser, 1987). Hewitt de Alcantara (1973-74) has written a fascinating story about the early history of the Green Revolution in Mexico in which she describes the circumstances of decisions taken to disband an existing program of research for the improvement of rain-fed corn and beans in favor of research into the commercial cultivation of high-yielding irrigated wheat.

Based on her studies in the province of Punjab, Vandana Shiva (1991), the noted Indian environmentalist, has summarized the destructive aspects of the Green Revolution:

> The Green Revolution has been a failure. It has led to reduced genetic diversity, increased vulnerability to pests, soil erosion, water shortages, reduced soil fertility, micronutrient deficiencies, soil contamination, reduced availability of nutritious food crops for the local population, the displacement of vast numbers of small farmers from their land, rural impoverishment, and increased tensions and conflicts. The beneficiaries have been the agrochemical industry, large petrochemical companies, manufacturers of agricultural machinery, dam builders and large landowners.

The second example I have chosen to illustrate the destructive aspects of development is the construction of giant multipurpose river dams, which are popularly seen as playing a vital role in economic development because they provide cheap electricity, supply water for irrigation and reduce flood hazards. The editors of *Ecologist* have commented on the down side of dam construction in the following words:[7]

---

[6]On the political economy of agrarian research see also the essays in Levins and Lewontin (1985).

[7]This quote is taken from p. 2 of a briefing document titled, "The Social and Environmental Effects of Large Dams" included as a supplement in *The Ecologist*, Vol. 14, No. 5/6, 1984.

Unfortunately, there is another side to the dam-building coin, a side which is rarely shown to the public. It portrays a picture of massive ecological destruction, of social upheaval, disease, and impoverishment.

The first victims of dams are the thousands of people who are displaced due to the flooding of their villages and homes. Invariably these "development refugees" are resettled in marginal inhospitable areas with little hope of rebuilding their previous communities. The resistance of local people to forced evacuation is sometimes met with official violence as in the Chico dam project in the Philippines (Drucker, 1986). In large scale water projects vast areas of agricultural and forested land are lost to submergence. In Ghana, a land area the size of Lebanon was submerged behind the Volta dam causing very serious problems of resettlement (Graham, 1986). In Sri Lanka the construction of the Victoria Dam submerged one of the most productive, densely settled agricultural valleys in the central highlands (Alexis, 1986). The Narmada Valley project in India will uproot a million people and submerge about 350,000 hectares of forest lands and 200,000 hectares of cultivated land (Alvraes and Billorey, 1987).[8] Dams also take their toll in the pro-liferation of diseases such as malaria and schistosomiasis. Gilbert White believes that the invasion of irrigation schemes by schistosomiasis is so common that it is now the rule rather than the exception.[9] After the building of Aswan the infection rate from schistosomiasis in some communities reached 100 percent.[10] The most serious problems associated with dams and irrigation are the loss of cultivable lands due to salinization and water logging. Perennial irrigation raises the water table; in some areas this is due to seepage from irrigation channels. Lining miles and miles of channels is expensive; so it is rarely done in Third World countries. Irrigation schemes in dry lands invariable affect the delicate water-salt balance in adverse ways. According to the FAO at least 50 percent of the world's irrigated land now suffers from salinization. Rapid sedimentation of reservoirs which reduces the useful lifetime of dams is another serious problem. Dogra (1986) claims that in most In-dian dams the rate of siltation far exceeds official rates; in one instance 60 percent of storage capacity was silted in forty years. The siltation problem in Egypt has a double-edge—not only are the rates of siltation behind the high dam excessive, but the lower Nile suffers from the lack of beneficial siltation effects of the annual floods resulting in a staggering bill for chemical fertilizer. Larger-scale dam projects are economic only if the land can be farmed in capital-intensive ways. Moreover, the project has to earn foreign exchange to repay the loan taken to build the project in the first place. Therefore, peasants producing food for local consumption are not important actors in the "superdam scene."

Goldsmith and Hilyard (1984a, p. 220), who have surveyed a number of dam projects throughout the world, have concluded:

---

[8]A detailed description of the Narmada project appears in Kalpavriksh, 1985, and a description of popular resistance to the scheme is in Esteva and Prakash, 1991.

[9]Quoted on p. 6 of the briefing document on dams.

[10]Quoted on p. 6 of the briefing document on dams.

[If] . . . dams were only built when they could be certain to provide water on a sustainable basis and without incurring intolerable social and ecological costs—then very few, if any, would be built.

Why, then, do dam projects continue to be funded? The answer is that dams are very much a part of the hegemonic idea of development. Again to quote Goldsmith and Hilyard (1984b, p. 231):

[there is an] entrenched belief that large-scale water development schemes are an essential part of the process of economic development—a process which we have been taught to see as the only means of combatting poverty and malnutrition, . . . To challenge dams is to challenge a fundamental credo of our civilization.

Dams are also an integral part of pork barrel, politics, bribery, corruption, and a means for the private appropriation of public funds.[11]

The launching of the Green Revolution and the construction of dams contributed to the rate of growth of GNP in several countries, but that did not necessarily lead to the eradication of hunger and poverty. In fact, the examples I described were directly implicated in the creation of poverty. Economic activities are too often evaluated by the quantity of commodities they generate. As we have seen it is important to look at production from a holistic viewpoint taking into account technological, social, ecological, and cultural relations of production activity.

THE MAP AS PART OF THE PROBLEM

The map of GNP per capita must be viewed in the context of an uncritical intellectual milieu where the hegemony of developmentalism reigns supreme. Although the problem is by no means cartographic, the map makes its own contribution to the perpetuation of uncritical reasoning along the lines argued by Harley (1988) of map as ideology. The map, as part of the ideology of development, is used widely in books and reports in extending that ideology.

In the map of GNP per capita, the basic unit of analysis, representation and comparison is the nation. Treating the nation as a homogeneous unit of discourse conceals the destructive aspects of national development by ignoring the plight of "development refugees"—Amazon Indians and rubber-tappers, displaced peasant farmers, urban immigrants, resettlers from dam projects, victims of urban renewal and slum clearance, and so on. Using the nation as the basis of discourse helps strengthen the ideology of a "national interest" which is used by elites to implement policies that serve their own narrow interests as we have already seen in the cases of the Green Revolution and the construction of super dams. To oppose such projects is to stand in the way of progress, modernity and the national interest.

Great care must be exercised in the use of maps to avoid falling into reductionist,

---

[11]For example, in the Mahaweli dam project in Sri Lanka nearly a third of all aid money may have gone into bribes.

ahistorical, superficial modes of spatial reasoning. The map of GNP helps to construct intellectually the notion of a Third World and represents it as a contiguous group of nations lying between the two tropics. It was undoubtedly the suggestive power of spatial reasoning that persuaded Harrison (1990) to title the first chapter of a popular book on the Third World. "The Cruel Sun: The Curse of the Tropics." He has written:

> Let us do a little map reading. If you open any decent atlas at those nice, blotchy maps on temperature, rainfall, soils and vegetation, you begin to notice some very curious things. Very roughly speaking, the problems of underdevelopment appears to be confined to the tropics, between thirty degrees north and south of the equator (p. 21).

By problems of underdevelopment Harrison meant of course the state of those countries with low per capita incomes. Harrison continued with his cartographic logic:

> A schoolboy could be forgiven for taking one look at the map and proclaiming the theory that an average annual temperature of 20 degrees or over was the cause of underdevelopment. Would he be very far from the truth with his little discovery? (p. 22).

Harrison goes on in the book to suggest that the schoolboy's conjecture is not far from the truth (Figure 1). Harrison's ahistorical, spatial reasoning would have gone unchallenged in the 1940s, but is definitely inexcusable in the 1980s when it continues to reappear in his popular book on the Third World that has gone through six reprints already. I shall not digress to comment on Harrison's thesis of climatic determinants of poverty other than to say schoolboys may have such thoughts because they are socialized to do so by adults who have succumbed to reductionist modes of superficial map reasoning.

Still another way in which the map of GNP per capita contributes to the myths of poverty and development has to do with the anti-dialectical mode of map reasoning (Harley's "silence by omission"). Since hungry malnourished people live in Bangladesh it is easy for us to conclude that the problem must be physically located within the boundaries of that nation. We equate Bangladesh with the problem because we can obviously see that this is where the starving people are. By contrast the geographic space of the First World, with its capital and know-how, is the realm of "the non-problem" and the locus of the "solution." The map helps to confirm this static, ahistorical, dualistic conceptualization of the world. What the map does not show is the evolution of the historical geography of the global system of capital where the hegemonic imperial powers developed the production forces in the colonies and incorporated them to meet their domestic needs for raw materials, food, and markets. In the colonies food cultivation had to compete with the production of commercial export crops (Stavrinos, 1981; Wallerstein, 1987). Kept active by local elites and multinational corporations, the circuits of surplus extraction continue to function today through a series of mechanisms like deteriorating terms of trade, terms of investment, and charges for debt service. Through the "silence of omission" we are not taught to see poverty as a "relation"—between First and Third World nations, and between classes withing a Third World nation.[12]

The map of GNP per capita also illustrates what Harley has called "representational hierarchies." The main purpose of the map of GNP per capita is to compare nations, i.e., rank them according to the size of income per capita. The use of this ranking principle also helps us define a group of nations as the Third World, behind the First and Second, which the map formalizes by giving the Third World a concrete geographic location. The exhortation made to Third World nations to catch up with living standards of the west is patently irrational. Consider a few statistics: a citizen of an industrialized nation consumes in six months as much energy as a citizen in a poor country does over his entire life; North America, Western Europe, and Japan with a quarter of the worlds' population use three-quarters of the world's 10,000 million kilowatts of electricity; the US with 4 percent of the world's population produces 24 percent of the global carbon dioxide emissions; the number of cars in the world have risen from 50 million in 1946 to 386 million in 1986 and production is increasing by 3 million every year with large sales going to the cities of the Third World.[13] Urbanization, air pollution, water pollution, destruction of forests, chemical contamination of soil, water, and food, destruction of agricultural land, migration to unhealthy, bloated cities, and poverty—these are essential consequences of development.

The idea that nations need to catch up because they are backward helps to foster a sense of ethnocentric condescension towards all people of the Third World. When Harley's principle of hierarchical representation of space is applied to the ranking of nations, there occurs an interesting cultural transformation from the nation to the individual, whereby people themselves become ordered giving rise to the firmly held belief that residents of the Third World are traditional, backward, and in dire need of modernization and development. This is one reason why we discount the indigenous techniques of Third World farmers, and view non-consumerist simpler lifestyles with disdain or with condescending sympathy.

CONCLUSION

The world map of GNP per capita is widely used in textbooks and reports because it is considered a basic "fact" of economic geography. What do we really communicate when we use this map?: that it is reasonable to compare whole nations to each other according to the exchange value of commodities; that developed countries are advanced because they have a higher GNP per capita; that underdeveloped countries need to expand their GNP rapidly if they hope to solve the problems of hunger and poverty, and catch up with the rest of the advanced world. But growth in GNP has no necessary relation to the eradication of hunger. In fact, as the previous examples from the Green Revolution and dam construction showed modern forms of poverty are a direct result of activities that are carried out in the name

---

[12]For a description of this history in Bangladesh see Hartman and Boyce (1988).

[13]All of these statistics are taken from Goldsmith, Hilyard, Bunyard, and McCully (1990), pp. 241-271.

of development. To suggest that the poor of the Third World need to develop and catch up to profligate, energy-intensive modes of living is ecologically irrational, culturally insensitive, socially irresponsible, and academically absurd. But the hegemony of development reigns supreme among academics, policy makers, and politicians. This is because development is an ideology, and part of the power apparatus in the elite exercise of authority over people and domination of nature. But unlike other modes of domination, the idea of development is culturally subtle because domination is exercised with the full acquiescence of the dominated. As Harley has argued maps are a part of the nexus of ideology, knowledge, and power; the map of GNP per capita is an excellent example. The routine use of this map by teachers and other academics is most unfortunate. I hope this paper will stimulate readers to think about what this map really means and serve as a warning against its uncritical use.

CITED LITERATURE

Alexis, L. 1984. The Damnation of Paradise - Sri Lanka's Mahaweli Project, *The Ecologist*, Vol. 14 No. 5/6, pp. 206-215.

Altieri, M.A. 1987. *Agroecology: The Scientific Basis of Alternative Agriculture.* Boulder: Westview Press.

Altieri, M.A. 1991. Traditional Farming in Latin America, *The Ecologist*, Vol. 21, No. 2, pp. 93-96.

Alvares, C. and R. Billorey 1987. Damning the Narmada: The Politics Behind the Destruction, *The Ecologist*, Vol. 17, No. 2, pp. 62-73.

Baran, P. and E.J. Hobsbawm. 1973. The Stages of Economic Growth: A Review, in C.K. Wilber (ed) *The Political Economy of Development and Underdevelopment.* New York: Random House.

Chambers, R. 1977. Challenges for Rural Research and Development, in B.H. Farmer (ed) *Green Revolution?* New York: Macmillan.

Conway, G.R. and E.B. Barbier. 1990. *After the Green Revolution: Sustainable Agriculture for Development.* London: Earthscan Publications.

Cowell, A. 1990. *The Decade of Destruction.* New York: Henry Holt.

Dogra, B. 1986. The Indian Experience with Large Dams, in E. Goldsmith, N. Hilyard (eds) *The Social and Economic Consequences of Large Dams.* Camelford: Wadebridge Ecological Centre, pp. 201-208.

Drucker, C. 1986. Dam the Chico: Hydro Development & Tribal Resistance in the Phillipines, in E. Goldsmith, N. Hilyard (eds) *The Social and Economic Consequences of Large Dams.* Camelford: Wadebridge Ecological Centre, pp. 304-313.

Ekins, P. (ed). 1986. *The Living Economy: A New Economics in the Making.* New York: Routledge & Kegan Paul.

Esteva, G. 1987. Regenerating People's Space, *Alternatives*, Vol. XII, pp. 125-152.

Esteva, G. and M. Prakash. 1991. Learning to Damn the Dams: The Narmada Story and Beyond, Paper prepared for the Annual Meetings of the American Geographers held in Miami, Florida.

Foucault, M. 1980. *Power/Knowledge.* New York, Random House.

George, S. 1988. *A Fate Worse than Debt: The World Financial Crisis and the Poor.* New York: Grove Press.

Glaeser, B. 1987. *The Green Revolution Revisited.* London: Allen & Unwin.

Goldsmith, E., N. Hilyard, P. McCully and P. Bunyard. 1990. *Imperiled Planet: Restoring Our Endangered Ecosystems.* Cambridge Mass.: The MIT Press.

Goldsmith, E. and N. Hilyard. 1984a. The Myth of the Benign Superdam, *The Ecologist,* Vol. 14 No. 5/6, pp. 217-220.

Goldsmith, E. and N. Hilyard. 1984b. The Politics of Damming, *The Ecologist,* Vol. 14 No. 5/6, pp. 221-231.

Graham, R. 1986. Ghana's Volta Resettlement Scheme, in E. Goldsmith, N. Hilyard, (eds) *The Social and Economic Consequences of Large Dams.* Camelford: Wadebridge Ecological Centre, pp. 131-139.

Harley, J.B. 1988. Maps, Knowledge, and Power, in D. Cosgrove and S. Daniels (eds) *The Iconography of Landscape.* New York: Cambridge University Press, pp. 277-312.

Harrison, P. 1990. *Inside the Third World.* New York: Penguin Books, Publications.

Hartman, B. and J.K. Boyce. 1983. *A Quiet Violence: View from a Bangladesh Village.* San Francisco: Institute for Food and Development Policy.

Hewitt de Alcantara, C. 1973-74. The "Green Revolution" as History: The Mexican Experience, *Development and Change,* Vol. 5 , pp. 25-44.

Howard, A. 1973. *An Agricultural Testament.* Emmaus, Pa: Rodale Press. First printing in 1940.

Illich, I. 1973. *Tools of Conviviality.* New York: Harper & Row.

Illich, I. 1970. *Celebration of Awareness.* Berkeley: Heyday.

Illich, I. 1978. *Towards a History of Needs.* Berkeley: Heyday.

Kalpavriksh and the Hindu College Nature Club, 1986. The Narmada Valley Project: Development or Destruction, in E. Goldsmith, N. Hilyard, (eds) *The Social and Economic Consequences of Large Dams.* Camelford: Wadebridge Ecological Centre, pp. 224-244.

King, F.H. 1973. *Farmers of Forty Centuries.* Emmaus, Pa: Rodale Books. First printing in 1911.

Kloppenburg, J.R. 1990. *First the Seed: The Political Economy of Plant Biotechnology 1492-2000.* New York: Cambridge University Press.

Lappe, F.M. and J. Collins. 1977. *Food First: Beyond the Myth of Scarcity.* New York: Ballantine Books.

Levin, R. and R. Lewontin. 1985. *The Dialectical Biologist.* Cambridge, Mass.: Harvard University Press.

Meadows, D.L. 1972. *The Limits to Growth.* New York: Universe Books.

Paddock, W. and P. Paddock. 1967. *Famine - 1975! America's Decision: Who Will Survive.* Boston: Little, Brown & Co.

Rostow, W. W. 1960. *The Stages of Economic Growth: A Non-Communist*

Manifesto. Cambridge, Mass.: Cambridge University Press.

Shiva, V. 1991. The Green Revolution in the Punjab, *The Ecologist*, Vol. 21, No. 2, pp. 57-60.

Stavrinos, L.S. 1981. *Global Rift: The Third World Comes of Age.* New York: William Morrow.

Timberlake, L. 1986. *Africa in Crisis.* London: Earthscan Publications.

Todaro, M.P. 1985. *Economics for a Developing World.* Singapore: Longmans.

Wallerstein, I. 1987. *The Capitalist World Economy.* Cambridge: Cambridge University Press.

World Bank, 1988. *World Development Report.* New York: Oxford University Press.

World Commission on Environment and Development. 1987. *Our Common Future.* Oxford: Oxford University Press.

Yapa, L.S. 1991. Innovation Diffusion and Paradigms of Development, in C. Earle and M. Kenzer, (eds) *Concepts in Human Geography.* Lanham, MD: Rowman and Littlefield (in press).

Natural and Technological Disasters: Causes, Effects and Preventive Measures. Edited by S.K. Majumdar, G.S. Forbes, E.W. Miller, and R.F. Schmalz. © 1992, The Pennsylvania Academy of Science.

Chapter Thirty-Nine

THE PSYCHOLOGICAL AFTERMATH OF TRAUMA: POSTTRAUMATIC STRESS DISORDER

RUBEN J. ECHEMENDIA

Department of Psychology
314 Bruce V. Moore Building
The Pennsylvania State University
University Park, PA 16802

INTRODUCTION

Disasters create inordinate amounts of stress in the lives of the people they touch. The stress is not limited to the "direct" victims but extends to rescue workers, mental health workers, community planners, reporters and possibly even those who might be watching the drama unfold on television. Viewed in this light, disasters and other traumatic events take on a significant level of importance. As has been indicated elsewhere[1] the pervasiveness of disasters is underscored by the fact that between 1947 and 1973 there were over 836 major disasters worldwide in which greater than 100 people were killed or injured and which resulted in one million dollars of damage. In roughly the same timespan, the United States was involved in three wars which claimed the lives of over 10 million and injured over one million more. At the time of this writing, the U.S. recently completed its campaign to liberate Kuwait and the psychological consequences of this action on theatre combatants and civilian populations will not be fully examined for many years to come.

The purpose of this chapter is to provide an overview of the psychological impact of disasters, whether caused by man or by nature. The idea of providing a comprehensive overview of the psychological sequela of traumatic events is a Herculean task for a book length volume. It is an impossibility for a chapter length discussion. In light of this, the text which follows will attempt to acquaint the reader with the major features of posttraumatic stress reactions in general and Posttraumatic Stress Disorder (PTSD) specifically. The goal is to focus on those components which are central to any discussion of posttraumatic stress and to provide enough references so that the interested reader will have a place to begin a more comprehensive exploration. Rather than focus on a narrow band of research, e.g. Vietnam War Theatre veterans, a rather broad range of traumatic events will be discussed. In short, a focus on breadth rather than depth has been employed in order to entice the reader into further study.

BACKGROUND

While it is generally accepted that disasters are situations which invoke significant stress, there has been considerable debate as to the effects of this stress on adults and children.[2] Some studies report little or no significant mental health consequences[3,4,5] while others document significant behavioral and emotional difficulties.[6,7,8,9,10] Questions arise as to whether the symptoms that surface are transient and short-lived or whether they are chronic in nature.[11]

The advent of the Vietnam War heralded significant interest and attention in the psychological consequences of sustained stress and trauma. In 1980, the American Psychiatric Association published the third revision of the Diagnostic and Statistical manual (DSM-III)[12] which introduced the diagnostic entity entitled Posttraumatic Stress Disorder (PTSD). The introduction of PTSD as a formal diagnostic category helped to organize much of the thinking and research in the area.

While PTSD is a relative newcomer to psychiatric nosology, the existence of stress response syndromes has been recognized since the time of Freud[13] who suggested that victims of trauma attempt to remember or repeat the trauma and that they attempt to defend against or avoid the memories and repetitions.[14] In the first Diagnostic and Statistical manual (DSM-I) responses to stress were grouped under "gross stress reaction".[15] It was believed that this disorder was transient and would resolve rapidly unless it was maintained by preexisting personality disturbance.[16] DSM-II[17] provided two categories for stress disorders: "transient situational disturbance" was used when the symptoms were of short duration while "anxiety neurosis" was used if the symptoms were more persistent. As Green and her colleagues[18] point out, these diagnostic categories imply that responses to stress or trauma are short lived unless the individual suffers from other pathology. Also inherent in these descriptions is the notion that individuals who have a protracted response to stress do so because of difficulties in their early history. The publication of DSM-III represented a shift in thinking whereby trauma in adulthood may yield significant psychological disturbances *independent* of earlier difficulties.

PTSD - THE SYNDROME

The most recent revision of the Diagnostic and Statistical manual, DSM-III-R,[19] classifies PTSD as an anxiety disorder which has a characteristic pattern of symptoms that arise after exposure to a "psychologically distressing event that is outside the range of usual human experience" (p. 247). It is believed that this event would be distressing to the vast majority of people and that it would be experienced with fear, terror and hopelessness. Most commonly, the traumatic events include a significant threat to one's life or property; significant threat of harm (or actual harm) to one's children, spouse or other loved ones; sudden destruction of a home; catastrophic community event; or witnessing another person(s) being seriously injured or killed. The stressors may be natural disasters (e.g. tornados, floods, earthquakes), accidental disasters (airplane crashes, fires, structural collapse) or disasters which are deliberately caused (e.g. bombing, torture, concentration camps).

The symptoms associated with PTSD are grouped into three broad categories: (a) reexperiencing of the event, (b) persistent avoidance of stimuli associated with the event or an emotional numbing, and (c) a set of miscellaneous symptoms. The trauma may be reexperienced in a variety of ways including intrusive recollections of the event, persistent dreams about the trauma, sudden "flashbacks" to the trauma where the individual experiences a sense of reliving the event, and significant emotional distress when confronted with stimuli that are associated with the trauma or may be symbolic of it (e.g. anniversaries). Avoidance may take the form of avoiding thoughts of the trauma, avoiding events that may remind the individual of the trauma, amnesia for important components of the trauma, significantly decreased interest in activities, feelings of detachment or estrangement from others, restricted range of emotional experiences, and a sense of a "foreshortened future." Additional symptoms include irritability, anger outbursts, decreased concentration ability, hypervigilance, exaggerated startle response, physiologic responsivity to events that resemble or symbolize the trauma (e.g. car accident victim experiences heart palpitations on hearing car tires squeal) and sleep difficulties. Indeed, sleep disturbances have been advanced as the hallmark of PTSD.[20]

PATHOLOGIC VERSUS "NORMAL" RESPONSE

Thus far the diagnostic criteria for PTSD have been outlined. However, by virtue of the fact that PTSD is included in the DSM-III-R, it is considered to be a "mental disorder." When does a "normal" response to a disaster or other significant trauma turn into a "disorder?" Is PTSD an inevitable consequence to trauma? Much debate exists around both of these questions. From a diagnostic perspective, the symptoms outlined above must persist for at least thirty days in order to be legitimately diagnosed as PTSD according to DSM-III-R. Inherent in this criteria is the recognition that individuals exposed to catastrophic trauma experience myriad psychological symptoms which may or may not become persistent or chronic in nature. As such, these "transient" symptoms are considered to be part of a "normal" response to a traumatic event rather than a disorder *per se*. Additionally, a victim may experience only a subset of the symptoms which are manifest in PTSD and hence not meet criteria for the disorder. As MacFarlane points[16] out, "intrusive imagery is commonly observed in victims of disasters who do not have any numbing or other disturbance of mood arousal or attention and may be as much an indicator of distress due to exposure to extreme adversity as a marker for PTSD" (p. 5). Others may experience symptoms after exposure to trauma which are not necessarily related to those of PTSD. For example, in a study of tornado victims[21] it was found that victims did not typically experience "incapacitating" emotional problems, yet 75% reported subjective distress characterized by tension, nervousness and anxiety, and "minor" somatic complaints. Similarly, no differences were found in illness rates, duration of illnesss or self-perceived impact of a disaster when flood victims were compared to non-flood groups.[4]

In short, the current diagnostic nosology allows for the expression of "normal" posttraumatic stress reactions. If the symptoms persist and are manifest according to the published criteria, a *diagnosis* of PTSD is applied. In the pages that follow, studies will be discussed which alternately use the terms "posttraumatic stress" and "PTSD." Since PTSD is a relative newcomer, many early studies do not correspond to current diagnostic distinctions. When possible, an indication will be made to specify the studies that refer to DSM-III/DSM-III-R diagnoses and those that do not.

PREVALENCE OF POSTTRAUMATIC STRESS

The literature which examines the prevalence of posttraumatic stress reactions in general or Posttraumatic Stress Disorder more specifically is fraught with contradiction and controversy. While some report a common occurrence of stress disorders following traumatic events, others report little or no significant mental health complications.[22] In response to the difficulties present in the extant literature, Green[23] concluded that the data were so contradictory that no definitive conclusions could be drawn. Nevertheless, the issue remains central to any discussion of the effects of disasters on the mental health of individuals. In light of this, a sampling of reported prevalence rates is presented below for a variety of natural and man-made disasters. These data stand in contrast to the prevalence rate of PTSD in the general population which is estimated to be approximately 1%.[24]

Much of the research on PTSD has concentrated on Vietnam Theater Veterans. Data from the National Vietnam Veterans Readjustment Study (NVVRS[25]) estimate that approximately 479,000 men suffer from PTSD while current prevalence rates for female theater veterans are estimated at 8.5% or approximately 610 cases. NVVRS data estimate that the *lifetime* prevalence of PTSD is 30.9% for male veterans and 26.9% for the females. Additionally, it is estimated that 22.5% of the men and 21.2% of the women had a lifetime prevalence of "partial" PTSD. Therefore, more than half of the men (53.4%) and almost half of the women (48.1%) in the

Vietnam theater experienced clinically significant stress-reaction symptoms. It is of significance that the rates of PTSD varied according to the level of war-zone stress that the veteran was subjected to; those veterans exposed to high levels of war-zone stress had rates that were "dramatically" higher than those exposed to low or moderate war-zone stress. This would suggest that the intensity of exposure to a traumatic event or the intensity of the traumatic event itself is related to the type and severity of symptoms exhibited. However, this hypothesis has not been fully supported by the empirical literature. Also of interest is the finding that Hispanic veterans have higher current prevalence PTSD rates (27.9%) than Blacks (20.6%) or White/ "Other" (13.7%). The implications of this finding have not been fully explored.

Individuals involved in "body handling" and recovery during disasters are at increased risk of PTSD up to six months following the exposure with estimates of up to 40% of body handlers experiencing significant levels of distress.[26] In his study of an Australian bush fire disaster, McFarlane[27] found that approximately 50% of the firefighters involved in the disaster suffered from some form of PTSD (158 "no disorder" group and 157 in disorder subgroups). Eight months after the fire, 50 firefighters who were identified as a "high risk" subgroup were reassessed. McFarlane[28] found that of this group, nine developed chronic or delayed PTSD, two experienced acute PTSD which had resolved and five were classified as having "borderline-chronic" PTSD. Thus 32% of this high risk subgroup developed symptomatology significant enough to warrant a diagnosis of PTSD.

In a study of the effects of a tornado which devastated a rural North Carolina community[2] it was found that 59% of the respondents qualified for a diagnosis of acute PTSD according to DSM-III criteria. Of these, 16% were reported to have been suffering from a "severe" form of the disorder. Eighty-two percent of the sample reported experiencing intrusive thoughts, 81% reported an exaggerated startle response, and over 50% of the sample reported increased tension when reminded of the event, decreased concentration, memory difficulties, feelings of estrangement and insomnia.

In 1972, a huge wave of sludge and black water was released from the failure of a sludge waste dam and devastated the Buffalo Creek Valley in Southern Virginia. It has been reported[29] that "traumatic neurotic reactions" were found in approximately 80% of the survivors while it is estimated that over 90% of the children were experiencing "disabling psychiatric symptoms" two or more years after the disaster. However, caution must be used in interpreting these data since all of the victims were involved in a lawsuit in which they stood to gain financial compensation for the difficulties they were experiencing.

Kinzie and his colleagues[30] surveyed a sample of Indochinese refugees and found that an outstanding 70% of the sample met diagnostic criteria (DSM-III) for PTSD. An additional 5% were found to meet the criteria for past PTSD. Of the total group, it was found that the Mein experienced the highest rate (93%) while the Vietnamese had the lowest rate (54%). These data are in contrast to other studies which estimate a prevalence of PTSD at 50% among a southeast Asian population[31] and 50% among Cambodian adolescents.[32]

Rape victims have also been shown to experience high prevalence rates. It has been reported that up to 70% of rape victims meet the criteria for PTSD.[35,34,35] Donaldson and Gardner[36] found that 96% of women psychiatric patients with a history of incest reported symptoms of PTSD.

CHRONICITY OF POSTTRAUMATIC STRESS

As with prevalence data, the literature on the course of posttraumatic stress reactions is often contradictory and lacks a cohesive theoretical framework to guide research endeavors. In part, the difficulties in documenting the natural course of the disorder stem from the observation that the psychological effects of exposure to trauma often manifest themselves over a broad timespan.[37] Additionally, the pattern of the symptoms themselves creates difficulty. Horowitz[38] proposed a model which characterizes the course of stress related difficulties as cyclical in nature with periods of intrusive thoughts, relative dormancy and emotional numbing. Green[18] has suggested the possibility that those symptoms which represent enduring patterns of attitudes and behaviors towards oneself or others (e.g. alienation, estrangement, excessive guilt) are less cyclical than those which represent intrusions (e.g. nightmares, reenactments). These may also differ from those symptoms which are physiological in nature (hypervigilance, hyperarousal). Hence, the diagnosis of PTSD may be a function of *when* the individual is interviewed in relation to the trauma. For example, in a study of unsolicited psychiatric patients following a bush fire,[39] it was found that the majority of cases estimated the onset of symptoms at a point two months after the disaster. The author notes that 24 months after the fire, new cases were still presenting themselves for treatment. Similarly, while some individuals may experience all of the component symptoms of PTSD during the course of their illness, they may not experience them as a group in close enough proximity to each other to meet the criteria for the diagnosis of PTSD.

The DSM-III included three distinct forms of PTSD: acute, chronic and delayed. In the subsequent revision (DSM-III-R), the differences between the acute and chronic forms were eliminated due to a lack of substantive arguments for maintaining the distinction, as well as an attempt to reduce the overall number of disorders.[4] A "delayed onset" category was retained and is to be used if the onset of symptoms occurs at least six months post trauma (DSM-III-R).

Despite the methodological difficulties noted above, many published reports lend credence to the belief that PTSD is a chronic rather than acute dysfunction. Data from the Buffalo Creek disaster suggest that significant symptoms of anxiety continued to be characteristic of victims seventeen years after the flood.[40] Three Mile Island victims continued to be bothered by intrusive thoughts and engaged in avoidance of thoughts five years after the accident. They also demonstrated performance decrements in a cognitive task and exhibited elements of hyperarousal.[41] McFarlane[27] found that of those firefighters that experienced posttraumatic symptoms, 42% reflected a chronic pattern while 39.5% were delayed onset. In short, 68% of the firefighters who experienced symptoms shortly after the fire (4 months) developed chronic forms of the disorder. McFarlane points out that these findings stand in contrast to the early (DSM-III) statements that acute PTSD has a good prognosis.

Cambodian refugees who survived up to 4 years in concentration camps were found to be experiencing PTSD a minimum of three years after internment.[42] Southeast Asian refugees continued to experience symptoms of PTSD 10 to 15 years after the trauma. In fact, only 6% of those patients who had a past diagnosis of PTSD no longer met the criteria.[30] In a study of 62 World War II POWs, it was found that 50% met the criteria for PTSD the year after repatriation and 29% of these met the criteria for PTSD 40 years later.[43]

Leopold and Dillon[44] reported on the effects of an explosion aboard a gasoline tanker that collided with a freighter at sea. It was found that all but six of the 27 men interviewed immediately following the accident experienced significant symptoms of posttraumatic stress. In a follow-up conducted 3.5 to 4.5 years later, it was found that 71% of the men experienced an "appreciable deterioration" in symptoms with those in the older age group (above 36) reflecting the most deterioration. Similarly, in an interesting report on the coping strategies of seven men who survived a shipwreck, it was noted that five developed a "substantial psychiatric disorder" 12-24 months after the incident.[45]

POSTTRAUMATIC STRESS IN CHILDREN

Brett and her colleagues[14] have examined diagnostic issues with respect to PTSD in children and report that while many of the symptoms that pertain to the adult manifestation of the disorder are appropriate for children, several characteristics are specific to children. Specifically, children often reexperience the trauma by engaging in repetitive play which contains themes or components of the trauma. Children may manifest the loss of recently developed skills and regress to more developmentally primitive levels. The sense of a foreshortened future is manifest in the fear of not reaching adulthood or a decreased expectation of attaining particular life goals (e.g. career, family). Children may also exhibit omen formation in which they mistakenly believe in an ability to prophesy future untoward events. Other symptoms noted in DSM-III-R include: occasional muteness and refusal to discuss the event, the presence of physical symptoms (e.g. stomachaches, headaches), and distressing dreams which may generalize to nightmares symbolically related to the trauma or experiences related to the trauma.

A group of 10 children ranging in age from 2 to 6 years were treated and evaluated for PTSD after reportedly having experienced sexual abuse in a daycare setting.[46] It was found that the children exhibited a variety of behaviors that appeared to be trauma related: trauma related fears, mundane fears, sleep disturbances, aggressive behaviors and depressed withdrawn behaviors. Many of the children appeared to be reexperiencing the trauma by reacting with "panic" behaviors to stimuli related to their experience. They evinced enduring interpersonal difficulties characterized by a mistrust of people. Also found was a difference between the boys and girls with the boys initially presenting with more "clinically significant" reactions. Yet the girls appear to be more symptomatic at a one year follow-up.

In a longitudinal study on the effects of an Australian bush fire on 808 schoolage children, McFarlane[47] found that approximately one third of the children were experiencing preoccupation with the fire 26 months after the disaster. No significant "working through" was found as time passed between the 8th and 26th month post disaster. At 2 and 8 months after the fire the intensity of anxiety and behavioral disturbances exhibited by a child in school was significantly correlated with the intensity of posttraumatic phenomena at 26 months post disaster. These data are supportive of the ability of acute behavioral distress to predict latter posttraumatic symptomatology, particularly if the difficulties are expressed in a setting separated from the reassurance of the parents. In addition, the author also finds support in these data for the contention that a child's response to a traumatic event may be more a function of the parents' response to the trauma than the intensity of the danger experienced. This finding is consistent with those obtained in a study of a regatta accident in which it was found that the severity of PTSD symptoms was not commensurate with the seriousness of any injuries sustained.[48]

Eth and Pynoos[49] propose four developmental considerations in understanding the effects of traumatic events in children: (1) the presentation of symptoms and content of PTSD in children will vary with age although the general phenomena appears consistent across age groups; (2) the child's early efforts to cope with traumatic anxiety and helplessness vary as a function of maturity (e.g. evolving ability to regulate intense affects and formulate cognitive reappraisals); (3) developmental influences can either augment or impede the recovery process—depending on age, children are more or less susceptible to intrapsychic, parental or societal pressures; and (4) the interplay between the trauma resolution process and other childhood tasks must be monitored—e.g. schoolwork, play and other interpersonal relationships are immediately affected.

As with adults, it appears that the development of PTSD in children and adolescents requires the understanding of a complex interaction of variables. However, with children, it is imperative that the symptoms are understood in the context of developmental level and family functioning.

ETIOLOGICAL FACTORS IN PTSD

There is little question as to the proposition that catastrophic events can lead to the development of significant mental health symptoms. However, not all individuals exposed to trauma develop significant trauma related disorders. What factors combine to produce a disorder in some individuals and not others? Are some individuals predisposed or more vulnerable to the development of PTSD?

It has been argued that while exposure to a disaster or other extreme event is required for the diagnosis of PTSD, it is not sufficient to explain its onset.[27] In light of this, the development and maintenance of PTSD must reflect a multidimensional framework that includes biological, psychological and social components. Several etiological models of PTSD exist including biological,[50] neuropsychological,[51]

Psychodynamic,[52] Cognitive - behavioral,[53] and Behavioral.[54] A review of these models is beyond the scope of the present paper (see 55, 56 for thorough reviews), but a brief discussion of a "psychosocial" framework is warranted.

Green and her colleagues[1] have proposed a psychosocial framework which advocates that psychological responses to traumatic events are multiply determined. In this model, the central feature of the determination of outcome is the nature and intensity of the traumatic event. As the intensity of the trauma increases, it is hypothesized that greater numbers of individuals will develop symptoms. If the event is severe enough, virtually all individuals exposed to it will manifest symptoms. Whether a disaster is man-made or natural has been a consideration in determining differential impact on psychological well-being. It has been speculated that the effects of man-made disasters are more severe and long lasting than naturally occurring disasters yet this has received little empirical support. In the Green model, the characteristics of the event are seen as interacting with both the characteristics of the individuals and the characteristics of the recovery environment.

The contribution of individual attributes to the development of PTSD has been a controversial and often emotional subject. Some feel that by implicating personality or premorbid (prior to the onset of trauma or symptoms) characteristics, one is denigrating the effect of the catastrophic event and in essence "blaming the victim".[57] As can be expected, the findings in this area yield contradictory results. For example, in a study of supper club fire victims, Green[58] found that 60% of the variance in psychological functioning was attributable to event characteristics with premorbid characteristics accounting for a much smaller percentage. McFarlane's firefighter studies[16,27] suggest that event characteristics (e.g. threat experienced, losses incurred) decreased over a 29 month period. However, the more chronic the posttraumatic symptoms, the more important premorbid individual factors became ("neuroticism," family or personal history of psychiatric illness, tendency to avoid thinking through unwanted or negative experiences). Similar results were obtained in a study of Norwegian factory paint fire victims (59 cited in 16) where the occurrence of acute PTSD was associated with the initial intensity of exposure. However, as time went on, the prognosis was related more to premorbid psychological functioning than to intensity of exposure.

Among a sample of Vietnam veterans, Card[60] found that the intensity of combat experience was a "strong contributory factor" in which veterans developed PTSD. The only two "background characteristics" significantly associated with PTSD development were low self confidence at age 15 and heavy liquor consumption during military service. Similarly, Foy and Card[61] found that combat exposure accounted for a much larger proportion of variance than other predictors among Vietnam vets. Lastly, in a study of POWs the authors conclude the "severe trauma experienced as an adult can precipitate psychopathology, particularly PTSD, independently of predisposing factors"[43] (p. 150).

Returning to the Green *et al.*[1] model, characteristics of the recovery environment have received relatively little attention. Of those characteristics studied, social supports have received the most attention. It appears the social supports are involved in the moderation of symptoms in PTSD in much the same way as they moderate the effects of other emotional disorders.[55] Other recovery environment variables include cultural differences in the way survivors are expected to respond, demographic characteristics (age, social class, education level), and attitudes of society!

TREATMENT CONSIDERATIONS

If, as most researchers and theoreticians believe, the onset and maintenance of PTSD results from a complex interaction of multiple factors, then the challenge faced by clinicians in the treatment of PTSD is monumental. Here are but a few of the challenges that the clinician must face. First, there is diagnostic uncertainty. What constitutes an event "outside the range of usual human experience?" In whose eyes is the event judged to be traumatic or not—the victim, the clinician, society? Second, given the increased expression of dissociative symptoms (e.g. depersonalization, derealization, psychogenic amnesia)[62] in PTSD, is the victim able to access or even remember the event? Third, given the time delay in which PTSD can manifest itself, both clinician and victim may not associate the current symptoms to the precipitating trauma. Fourth, many victims are hesitant to seek treatment or feel shame with respect to the trauma (e.g. rape). Fifth, while the symptoms of PTSD may be easily detected in their "pure" form, there is a significant number of PTSD sufferers with comorbid disorders (e.g. personality disorders, drug/alcohol addiction, another anxiety disorder). The symptoms of these other disorders must be treated in tandem in order to achieve a successful therapeutic outcome. Sixth, clinicians must carefully examine their own reactions to the trauma being presented and their ability to sensitively yet directly probe the experience of the trauma.[63] Lastly, the clinician must be keenly aware of cultural and subcultural norms when assessing PTSD in a diverse, multicultural society.[30]

As with most disorders in the mental health field, there are various treatment approaches to PTSD: pharmacologic,[64] behavioral/cognitive,[53,54] psychodynamic,[65] psychoanalysis,[66,67] hypnosis,[68] play therapy[49] and integrated approaches.[69] Scurfield[63] has reviewed the treatment literature and isolated four "key factors" in facilitating the recovery process: (1) an exploration of the trauma itself with attention paid to the initial (emergency) coping mechanisms; (2) the subsequent intrusion or reexperiencing of the negative aspects of the traumatic event; (3) coping attempts to control, reduce or eliminate the unwanted intrusions or reexperiencing; and (4) the integration of the traumatic experience and its positive and negative impact on the individual, relationships with significant others, and society.

In the acute phase of symptom manifestation, a crisis intervention approach is usually adopted whereby the thrust of the intervention is aimed at helping the individual return to a premorbid level of functioning as quickly as possible. This approach takes advantage of the weakened state of the individual's defenses (coping mechanisms) in order to make rapid therapeutic gains.[63] The defensiveness which is usually seen is significantly diminished allowing the clinician easier access to disturbing material. A subsequent reorganization or reconstitution takes place which may be either adaptive or maladaptive.

Scurfield also delineates five key principles which he believes are involved in the treatment of PTSD: (1) the establishment of a therapeutic trusting relationship; (2) education with respect to the recovery process in which the victim learns what to expect in the way of symptoms, the process of treatment, and the belief that PTSD is responsive to treatment; (3) stress management/reduction focused on managing the expression of distressing symptoms; (4) a regression back to or reexperiencing of the trauma in such a way that the trauma is experienced in the present to the fullest extent possible, thereby allowing the client access to feelings and conflicts that were previously unavailable; and (5) an integration of the traumatic experience such that all components of the trauma, both positive and negative, are consolidated with the survivor's notions of who he or she was before, during, and after the trauma.

In addition to individual forms of treatment, group therapy has been found to be successful in the treatment of PTSD, with some arguing that it is the treatment of choice.[63] Family approaches have also been used successfully.[63] While the present discussion does not allow for a review of disaster preparedness or community/organizational response from a mental health perspective, the reader is referred to Wright and his colleagues[26] for an interesting case study of an aircraft disaster.

CONCLUSIONS

While the nature and extent of the psychological effects of traumatic events remains a matter of debate, few would argue that disasters and other catastrophic events touch the lives of many people in a variety of ways. For some, the event represents just one of a number of challenges which life throws at them and which must be conquered. For others, the event represents an insurmountable obstacle which has shattered their sense of self, trust in others, and even eliminated their will to live. The literature reviewed above doesn't help answer many question. In fact, it creates many more: What are the psychological ramifications of trauma? Is there a "normal" response to trauma? Why is it that some people develop severe psychological symptoms in response to trauma and others do not? How are premorbid personality characteristics related to symptom manifestation? Conversely, what premorbid characteristics help innoculate the individual from the development of symptoms? What is the natural course of PTSD? Which symptoms develop when and why? Can treatment provided early arrest the progression to more serious forms of the disorder? If so, how do you identify the individuals who should be treated?

The answer to these and many more questions will not come easily nor cheaply. However, there are some things we do know. First, *some* individuals do develop severe posttraumatic reactions which exhibit a relatively well defined cluster of symptoms. Taken together, these symptoms represent what is referred to as PTSD. Second, a relationship must exist between individual characteristics and the development and onset of PTSD. If not, it would be virtually impossible to explain the differential effects of a given traumatic event on a variety of people. Our task is to isolate those characteristics whether they are biological, cognitive, intrapsychic or characterological in nature. Third, it appears that PTSD is not simply an acute phenomena in that symptoms tend to persist and, at times, intensify. The course of symptom reduction and exacerbation remains largely unknown. Fourth, the symptoms of PTSD may take time to develop. As such, the mental health community must be prepared to provide treatment for long periods of time following trauma. Fifth, many individuals are reluctant to seek treatment while others are so involved in denial that they are unaware they need help. Outreach efforts must be extensive and vigorous. Lastly, children exposed to traumatic events manifest symptoms in different ways at different developmental levels. Similarly, they appear to exhibit different symptoms at different developmental levels. A developmental perspective must be incorporated in working with children exposed to trauma.

Clearly, much work needs to be done. Yet it appears that a solid foundation has been laid for future work. The introduction of PTSD has helped to focus much of the thinking in the area and delineate those components which are in need of further investigation. The proliferation of literature in this area in recent years is a hopeful sign that there is interest and energy available to understand this phenomena and thereby help those individuals whose lives are so severely disrupted.

REFERENCES

1. Green, B.L., J.P. Wilson and J.D. Lindy. 1985. Conceptualizing Post-traumatic Stress Disorder: a psychosocial framework, pp. 53-69. In: C.R. Figley (ed). *Trauma and its wake: the study and treatment of Post-traumatic Stress Disorder.* Brunner/Mazel, New York.
2. Madakasira, S. and K.F. O'Brien. 1987. Acute Post-traumatic Stress Disorder in victims of a natural disaster. *J. Nerv. Ment. Dis.* 175:286-290.
3. Bromet, C., H.C. Schulberg, and L. Dunn. 1982. Reactions of psychiatric patients to the Three Mile Island Nuclear accident. *Arch. Gen. Psychiat.* 39:725-730.
4. Melick, M.E. 1978. Life change and illness: Illness behavior of males in the recovery period of a natural disaster. *J. Health. Soc. Beh.* 19:335-342.
5. Quarantelli, E.L. and R.R. Dynes. 1977. Response to social crisis and disaster. *Annu. Rev. Sociol.* 3:23-49.
6. Burke, J.D., J.F. Borus, B.J. Burns, K.H. Millstein and M.C. Beasley. 1982. Changes in children's behavior after a natural disaster. *Am. J. Psychiat.* 139: 1010-1014.
7. Logue, J.N. and H. Hansen. 1980. A case control study of hypertensive women in a post-disaster community. Wyoming Valley, PA. *J. Human Stress.* 6:28-34.
8. Logue, J.N., M.E. Mellick and E.L. Struening. 1981. A study of health and mental health status following a major natural disaster. *Res. Comm. Ment. Health.* 2:217-274.
9. Newman, C.J. 1977. Children of disaster: clinical observations at Buffalo Creek. *Ann. Prog. Child Psychiat Child Dev.* 10:149-161.

10. Ollendick, D.G. and M. Hoffman. 1982. Assessment of psychological reactions in disaster victims. *J. Comm. Psychol.* 10:157-167.
11. Adams, P.R. and G.R. Adams. 1984. Mount Saint Helen's Ashfall: evidence for a disaster stress reaction. *Am. Psychologist.* 39: 252-260.
12. American Psychiatric Association. 1980. *Diagnostic and statistical manual of mental disorders (3rd ed.).* Washington, D.C.
13. Freud, S. 1939. Moses and monotheism: three essays. In: *Complete psychological works, standard ed., vol. 23.* Hogarth, London.
14. Brett, E.A., R.C. Spitzer and J.B.W. Williams. 1988. DSM-III-R criteria for Post-traumatic Stress Disorder. *Am. J. Psychiat.* 145:1232-1236.
15. American Psychiatric Association. 1952. *Diagnostic and statistical manual of mental disorders.* American Psychiatric Association, Washington, D.C.
16. McFarlane, A.C. 1990. Vulnerability to post-traumatic stress disorder, pp. 3-20. In: M.E. Wolf & A.D. Mosnaim (eds.). *Posttrautamic Stress Disorders: etiology, phenomenology, and treatment.* American Psychiatric Press, Washington, D.C.
17. American Psychiatric Association. 1968. *Diagnostic and statistical manual of mental disorders, 2nd ed.* American Psychiatric Association, Washington, D.C.
18. Green, B.L., J. Lindy and M.C. Grace. 1985. Post-traumatic stress disorder: Toward DSM-IV. *J. Nerv. Ment. Dis.* 173:406-411.
19. American Psychiatric Association. 1987. *Diagnostic and statistical manual of mental disorders, 3rd edition, Revised.* American Psychiatric Association, Washington, D.C.
20. Ross, R.J., W.A. Ball, K.A. Sullivan and S.N. Caroff. 1989. Sleep disturbance as the hallmark of Post-traumatic Stress Disorder. *Am. J. Psychiatry.* 146:697-707.
21. Penick, E.C., B.J. Powell and W.A. Sieck. 1976. Mental health problems and natural disaster: Tornado victims. *J. Community Psychol.* 4:64-67.
22. Quarantelli, E.L. 1985. An assessment of conflicting views on mental health: the consequences of traumatic events, pp. 173-215. In: C.R. Figley (ed.) *Trauma and its wake: The study and treatment of Post-traumatic Stress Disorder.* Brunner/Mazel, New York.
23. Green, B.L. 1982. Assessing levels of psychological impairment following disaster. *J. Nervous and Mental Disease.* 170:544-552.
24. Helzer, J.E., L.N. Robins and L. McEvoy. 1987. Post-traumatic Stress Disorder in the general population: Findings of the epidemiologic catchment area survey. *N. Engl. J. Med.* 317:1630-1634.
25. Kulka, R.A., W.E. Schenger, J.A. Fairbank, R.L. Haugh, B.K. Jordan, C.R. Marmar and D. Weiss. 1990. *Trauma and the Vietnam War generation.* Brunner/Mazel, New York.
26. Wright, K., R.J. Ursano, L. Ingraham and P. Bartone. 1990. Individual and community responses to an aircraft disaster, pp. 127-138. In: M.E. Wolf & A.D. Mosnaim (eds.). *Posttraumatic Stress Disorders: etiology, phenomenology and treatment.* American Psychiatric Press, Washington, D.C.
27. McFarlane, A.C. 1988. The longitudinal course of post-traumatic morbidity: The range of outcomes and their predictors. *J. Nerv. Ment. Dis.* 176:30-39.

28. McFarlane, A.C. 1988. The phenomenology of Post-traumatic Stress Disorders following a natural disaster. *J. Nerv. Ment. Dis.* 176:22-29.
29. Titchener, J.L. and F.T. Kapp. 1976. Family and character change at Buffalo Creek. *Am. J. Psychiatry.* 133:295-299.
30. Kinzie, J.D., J.K. Boehnlein, P.K. Leung, L.J. Moore, C. Riley and D. Smith. 1990. The Prevalence of Post-traumatic Stress Disorder and its clinical significance among Southeast Asian refugees. *Am. J. Psychiatry.* 147:913-917.
31. Mollica, R.F., G. Wyshak and J. Lavelle. 1987. The psychosocial impact of war trauma and torture on Southeast Asian refugees. *Am. J. Psychiatry.* 144:1567-1572.
32. Kinzie, J.D., W. Sack, R. Angell, *et al.*. 1986. The psychiatric effects of massive trauma on Cambodian children, I: the children. *J. Am. Acad. Child Psychiatry.* 25:370-376.
33. Kilpatric, D.G., L.J. Veronen and C.L. Best. 1985. Factors predicting psychological distress among rape victims, pp. 113-141. In: C.R. Figley (ed.). *Trauma and its wake: The study and treatment of Post-traumatic Stress Disorder.* Brunner/Mazel, New York.
34. Frank, E. and B.P. Anderson. 1987. Psychiatric disorders in rape victims: past history and current symptomatology. *Compr. Psychiatry.* 28:77-82.
35. Coons, P.M., C. Cole, T.A. Pellaw and V. Milstein. 1990. Symptoms of Post-traumatic Stress and dissociation in women victims of abuse, pp. 205-221. In: R.P. Kluft (ed.). *Incest related syndromes of adult psychopathology.* American Psychiatric Press, Washington, D.C.
36. Donaldson, M.A. and R. Gardner. 1985. Diagnosis and treatment of traumatic stress among women after childhood incest, pp. 356-377. In: C.R. Figley (ed.). *Trauma and its wake: the study and treatment of Post-traumatic Stress Disorder.* Brunner/Mazel, New York.
37. Horowitz, M.J. and G.F. Solomon. 1975. A prediction of delayed stress response syndromes in Vietnam veterans. *J. Soc. Issues.* 31:67-80.
38. Horowitz, M.J. 1976. *The stress response syndromes.* Jason Aronson, New York.
39. McFarlane, A.C. 1986. Post-traumatic morbidity of a disaster. *J. Nerv. Ment. Dis.* 174:4-14.
40. Simpson-Housley, P. and A. deMan. 1989. Flood experience and Posttraumatic trait anxiety in Appalachia. *Psychol. Reports.* 64:896-898.
41. Davidson, L.M., A. Baum. 1986. Chronic stress and Post-traumatic Stress Disorders. *J. Cons. Clin. Psychol.* 54:303-308.
42. Kinzie, J.D., R.H. Fredrickson, R. Ben, J. Flick and W. Karls. 1984. Post-traumatic Stress Disorder among survivors of Cambodian concentration camps. *Am. J. Psychiat.* 141:645-650.
43. Speed, N., B. Engdahl, J. Schwartz and R. Eberly. 1989. Post-traumatic Stress Disorder as a consequence of the POW experience. *J. Nerv. Ment. Dis.* 177:147-153.
44. Leopold, R.L. and H. Dillon. 1963. Psychoanatomy of a disaster: A long term study of post-traumatic neuroses in survivors of a marine explosion. *Am. J.*

Psychiatry. 119:913-921.
45. Henderson, S. and T. Bostock. 1977. Coping behaviour after shipwreck. *Brit. J. Psychiat.* 131:15-20.
46. Kiser, L.J., B.J. Ackerman, E. Brown, N.B. Edward, E. McColgan, R. Pugh and D.B. Pruitt. 1988. Post-traumatic Stress Disorder in young children: A reaction to purported sexual abuse. *J. Am. Acad. Child Adolesc. Psychiatry.*
47. McFarlane, A.C. 1987. Post-traumatic phenomena in a longitudinal study of children following a natural disaster. *J. Amer. Acad. Child Adolesc. Psychiatry.* 26:764-769.
48. Martini, R.D., C. Ryan, D. Nakayama and M. Ramenofsky. 1990. Psychiatric sequelae after traumatic injury: The Pittsburgh Regatta accident. *J. Am. Acad. Child Adolesc. Psychiatry.* 29:70-75.
49. Eth, S. and R.S. Pynoos. 1985. Developmental perspective on psychic trauma in childhood, pp. 36-52. In: C.R. Figley (ed.). *Trauma and its wake: The study and treatment of Post-traumatic Stress Disorder.* Brunner/Mazel, New York.
50. Van der Kolk, B.A., H. Boyd, J. Kaystol and M. Greenbury. 1984. Post-traumatic Stress Disorder as a biologically based disorder: Implications of the animal model of inescapable shock, pp. 124-134. In: B.A. Van der Kolk, (ed.). *Post-traumatic Stress Disorder: psychological and biological sequelae.* American Psychiatric Press, Washington, D.C.
51. Kolb, L.C. 1987. A neuropsychological hypothesis explaining Post-traumatic Stress Disorders. *Am. J. Psychiatry.* 144:989-995.
52. Horowitz, M.J. 1986. *Stress response syndromes* (2nd ed.). Jason Aronson, Northvale, N.J.
53. Foa, E.B., G. Steketee and B.O. Rothbaum. 1989. Behavioral/Cognitive Conceptualizations of Post-traumatic Stress Disorder. *Beh. Therapy.* 20:155-176.
54. Keane, T.M., R.T. Zimering and J.M. Caddell. 1985. A behavioral formulation of Post-tramatic Stress Disorder in Vietnam veterans. *The Beh. Therapist.* 8:9-12.
55. Jones, J.C. and D.H. Barlow. 1990. The etiology of Post-traumatic Stress Disorder. *Cl. Psychol. Rev.* 10:299-328.
56. Fairbank, J.A. and Nicholson, R.A. 1987. Theoretical and empirical Issues in the treatment of Post-traumatic Stress Disorder in Vietnam veterans. *J. Clin. Psychology.* 43:44-53.
57. Reich, J.H. 1990. Personality Disorders and Post-traumatic Stress Disorder, pp. 65-79. In M.E. Wolf & A.D. Mosnaim (eds.). *Posttraumatic Stress Disorders: etiology, phenomenology and treatment.* American Psychiatric Press, Washington, D.C.
58. Green, B.C., M.C. Grace, J.D. Lindy, J.L. Titchener and J.G. Lindy. 1983. Levels of functional impairment following a civilian disaster: The Beverly Hills supper club fire. *J. Cons. Clin. Psychol.* 51:573-580.
59. Weisaeth, L. 1984. *Stress reactions in an industrial accident.* unpublished doctoral dissertation, Oslo University, Oslo, Norway.
60. Card, J.J. 1987. Epidemiology of PTSD in a national cohort of Vietnam veterans. *J. Clin. Psychol.* 43:1-18.

61. Foy, D.W. and J.J. Card. 1987. Combat-related Post-traumatic Stress Disorder etiology: Replicated findings in a national sample of Vietnam-era men. *J. Clin. Psychol.* 43:28-31.

62. Spiegel, D. and E. Cardena. 1990. Dissociative mechanisms in Post-traumatic Stress Disorder, pp. 23-34. In: M.E. Wolf & A.D. Mosnaim (eds.). *Posttraumatic Stress Disorders: etiology, phenomenology and treatment.* American Psychiatric Press, Washington, D.C.

63. Scurfield, R.M. 1985. Post-trauma stress assessment and treatment: Overview and formulations, pp. 219-256. In: C.R. Figley. *Trauma and its wake: The study of and treatment of Post-traumatic Stress Disorder.* Brunner/Mazel, New York.

64. Fiedman, M.J. 1990. Interrelationships between biological mechanisms and pharmacotherapy of post-traumatic stress disorder, pp. 205-225. In: M.E. Wolf & A.D. Mosnaim (eds.). *Posttraumatic Stress Disorders: etiology, phenomenology and treatment.* American Psychiatric Press, Washington, D.C.

65. Horowitz, M. 1974. Stress response syndromes: Character style and brief psychotherapy. *Arch. Gen. Psychiat.* 31:768-781.

66. Haley, S. 1974. When the patient reports atrocities. *Arch. Gen. Psychiat.* 30:191-196.

67. Haley, S. 1978. Treatment implications of post-combat stress response syndromes for mental health professionals, pp. 254-267. In: C. Figley (ed.). *Stress disorders among Vietnam veterans.* Brunner/Mazel, New York.

68. Brende, J. and B. Benedict. 1980. The Vietnam combat delayed stress syndrome: Hypnotherapy of "dissociative" symptoms. *Am. J. Clin. Hypnosis.* 23:34-40.

69. Friedman, J. 1981. Post Vietnam syndrome: Recognition and management. *Psychosomatics.* 22:931-943.

Natural and Technological Disasters: Causes, Effects and Preventive Measures. Edited by S.K. Majumdar, G.S. Forbes, E.W. Miller, and R.F. Schmalz. © 1992, The Pennsylvania Academy of Science.

Chapter Forty

THE DISASTER OF DEFORESTATION IN THE BRAZILIAN RAINFOREST

ROBERT H. STODDARD

Department of Geography
University of Nebraska
Lincoln, NE 68588

INTRODUCTION

In 1987, a major disaster occurred when an estimated eight million hectares of tropical forests in Brazil were destroyed (World Resources Institute 1990, 102). This event is considered a disaster because it was only the annual portion of an on-going process having immense spatial and temporal effects. The temporal impact is expected to remain virtually forever. In contrast to many disasters having a limited temporal impact because restoration is possible, the extermination of several biotic species associated with rainforest destruction is permanent. Likewise, some of the spatial effects have reached their potential areal maximum because they have affected the entire Earth.

In some respects, it may be misleading to refer to "the disaster of 1987" because the expression implies the tragedy happened only during a single year and that rainforest destruction no longer occurs. It should be made clear that many of the forces that led to the widespread cutting and burning of forests in the Amazon in 1987 had produced similar results in previous years and they continue to create conditions that encourage the destruction of forests (Figure 1). Nevertheless, comments here focus on a particular year because such a time constraint aids in describing the multitude of interrelated events that affect the Amazon region.

The magnitude of this disaster is revealed by noting the trend in destruction of tropical forests throughout the world. Prior to the industrial revolution, more than 1400 million hectares were probably in rainforests; by 1980 somewhat over 1000 million hectares remained; now their areal extent is approximately 800 million hectares (Wolf 1991, 13). This disaster is especially critical in Brazil because about a third of the world's rainforest is in this country and this is where the current rate of destruction will lead to the forest's complete destruction within a century (Shukla, Nobre, Seller 1990, 1322.)

In spite of the magnitude of forest destruction, it might be argued that such is not necessarily a disaster. Afterall, one could declare, vast temperate forests were destroyed in East Asia, Europe, and North America in previous centuries without major calamities resulting. Furthermore, according to this perspective, forests, which are composed of living matter, can be rejuvenated through purposeful plantings or by human abandonment that allows natural regrowth.

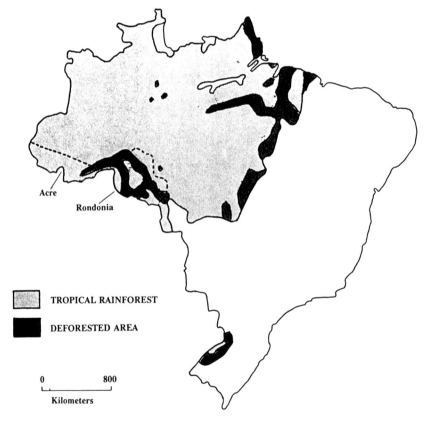

TROPICAL RAINFOREST

DEFORESTED AREA

0 _____ 800
Kilometers

FIGURE 1. Areas of Deforestation in the Rainforest of Brazil. Recent deforestation has been especially prevalent in the provinces of Acre and Rondonia. (*After* World Resource Institute 1990, p. 104).

The current destruction of the tropical forest, however, is not the same as previous tree clearings. The difference lies in the magnitude and permanence of biological extinctions and alterations of the atmosphere. To clarify the detrimental consequences of this disaster, each of these global effects is discussed in greater detail.

GLOBAL EFFECTS OF DEFORESTATION

The possibility of permanently losing much of the biological diversity is a critical concern because the rainforest is an extremely rich storehouse of the biota. According to current knowledge about the Earth's biological species, the rainforests hold 50 percent of our total genetic heritage, including 67 percent of all known plants, 80 percent of the world's insect species, and 90 percent of the non-human primates (May 1988; Shulka, Nobre, Sellers 1990). To destroy the rainforest habitat, therefore, results in the extermination of a major form of the Earth's wealth.

Some of the direct benefits from the rainforest are known: it provides fruit, nuts, resins, and latex, as well as drugs used to treat cancer, malaria, heart disease, and high blood pressure. If these were to be the only products that would be lost with the destruction of the rainforest, the term "disaster" might not be appropriate because some people might regard the costs of losing these few products as less than the benefits gained from clearing rainforests for other uses. This is not the case, however.

Humans know very little about the multitude of species living in tropical forests, which means it is impossible to know the potential benefits future generations might obtain from this huge storehouse of biological forms. No one can predict which additional sources of food and medicinal products may be discovered from yet unknown species. Humans depend heavily on about 20 food species, but an estimated 75,000 plant species are known to be edible, some of which are known to be superior to crops currently in use (Wilson 1989, 114).

In spite of our known present and potential dependence on many species, humans are causing the total extinction of many rainforest species by destroying their habitat. It has been estimated that four to six thousand plant species are disappearing per year—a rate much faster than that from natural extinction (Wilson 1989, 112).

Because of the complex interdependency of various species, the destruction of a few affects the environment of many others. Major superstructures of ecologically related species may be destroyed in a short time. Once destroyed these interrelated biological communities are almost impossible to reassemble. Reconstructed forests, for example, are often vulnerable to greater damage from pests and diseases than diversified virgin forests.

Also, the destruction of habitats in Brazil affects the wildlife in other areas. For example, some migratory birds that spend most of their time in North America depend on the Brazilian rainforest for their winter habitat. The disruption of these species, in turn, affects other life forms in an ever widening circle of alterations.

Furthermore, the effects are not proportional to the amount of habitat destroyed. According to the theory of "island biogeography," the number of species found on an island corresponds normally to the fourth root of the area (Wilson 1989, 111). This means that clearing much of the forest while leaving several isolated reserves of virgin forest is not a viable option because such "islands" would not provide the habitat necessary to sustain the diversity of existing species.

Another critical concern associated with the destruction of the rainforest is its atmospheric effect. Climatologists reckon that recent burning in the Amazon accounts for 15 - 30 percent of the global carbon-dioxide emissions (Repetto 1990, 36). Many scientists believe the increase of carbon dioxide in the atmosphere may contribute to "greenhouse" conditions and thence to global warming. Although such a relationship has not been accepted by all scientists, the potential calamitous effects of global warming would be severe enough that very few policy-makers are willing to proceed as if there were no connection. If, indeed, global warming is occurring, tremendous changes in coastal inundation, precipitation patterns, and biological habitats would result in many areas of the world.

Even if long-range, global climatic modifications cannot be predicted with certainty, local climates are expected to change with deforestation in the Amazon. According to the results obtained from numerical models, replacing the forest vegetation with pastures will increase surface temperatures and decrease evapotranspiration and precipitation over the Amazon region (Shukla, Nobre, Sellers 1990). The decreased precipitation and the lengthening of the dry season would, in turn, make it very difficult to reverse conditions and reestablish a tropical forest. Thus, although trees would return if pastures were to be abandoned, they would not re-create the diversity of the original rainforest.

In summary, the deforestation occurring in the Amazon is a disaster because of the biological exterminations and the atmospheric modifications that can permanently affect life throughout the world. Given the seriousness of such a scenario, it would seem logical that humans would choose to preserve the tropical forests. What is logical in the long run and for a population in general, however, often does not coincide with the immediate needs of particular individuals. It is the combination of many persons, each with self interests, that in the aggregate creates the forces which are destroying large sections of the Brazilian rainforests.

It is not possible to study the motives of all individuals associated with the Brazilian Amazon, but groups of people with similar interests can be examined meaningfully. Some of the major groups involved with utilizing the resources of the Amazon are the indigenous populations, the rubber tappers, the small farmers, the ranchers, the lumber companies, foreign investors, and the Brazilian government. To understand factors that lead to rainforest destruction, it is helpful to study the varying power these groups have in exploiting or preserving the forests.

COMPETITORS FOR THE RESOURCES OF THE AMAZON

One element in the mix of competitors for the resources of the Amazon is the *indigenous population*. Numerous Indian communities have been living in an overall ecological balance with the rainforest for centuries, but they have been continually threatened by the invasion of other groups. Ever since the arrival of the Portuguese in the 16th century, the Indian populations have declined in number. The number of Indians living in the area that is now Brazil probably exceeded three million, but by 1960 the total was approximately only 200,000 (Branford and Glock 1985, 182). Death from European diseases and the collapse of several Indian cultures have diminished the size of many Indian forest communities.

Another main contributor to the decline of Indian communities has been the appropriation of their traditional territories and, hence, their source of livelihood. Through most of Brazilian history, Indian communities have suffered from the imposition of a fundamentally different view of the land. According to governmental law, land is legally owned and can be utilized as the owner wants. Usually these wants are commercial, which often depend upon "development" of the land. In contrast, virtually all Indian groups have viewed the land communally, with its resources available to those with long traditions of occupancy. From the Indian perspective, it is difficult to believe that individuals who obtain a sheet of paper—i.e., a land title—become sole possessors of the land and all its resources.

This conflict has resulted in the disposition of Indians from many regions of the Brazilian forests. Although government agencies have been established to protect Indian rights, these were generally ineffective in the past. In more recent years, however, actions by religious organizations (e.g., the Missionary Indian Council), anthropologists and other scholars, and assertive Indian leaders have led to the establishment of national parks in which land is preserved for Indian communities. Nevertheless, the discovery of gold within a designated park, the building of a highway nearby, or other changes having commercial benefits for various non-Indian groups jeopardize the continued preservation of Indian territories.

The indigenous population of Brazil must be considered one of the competing groups for the resources of the Amazon, but it certainly is not one of the forces leading to the destruction of the forests. The Indian peoples are among those wishing to preserve the rainforests. Nevertheless, as certain groups who oppose the Indian way of life and seek to destroy that culture and as various commercial forces gain access to Indian territories, the forests are also endangered.

The *rubber tappers* and other extractors of forest products also depend directly on the existing rainforest. This group consists primarily of people who occupied forest areas early in the 20th century to collect latex from wild rubber trees, but currently members also gather Brazil nuts and other products that can be sold. Although there have been some conflicts between groups of Indians and rubber tappers, both are vitally interested in preserving the rainforests and have recently joined forces to work toward such conservation.

The communities of extractors have also suffered from more powerful commercial interests in recent years. The plight of these people received considerable publicity when Chico Mendes was honored by the United Nations in 1987 for his attempt to protect the rainforest and again when he was assassinated in 1988. His death was not an isolated event; many hundreds of rubber tappers, along with Indians, were killed in the 1980s (World Resources Institute 1990, 110).

A third category of people wanting to use the land that is naturally covered by rainforest consists of *small farmers*. Within the last two decades, an estimated 24 million persons have left their homes in the coastal regions of Brazil in hopes of making a living in the sparsely settled interior of the country. Factors that push migrants from the long-settled regions are the extremely inequitable ownership of land in Brazil and the general economic conditions that have increased the number of poor families. Between 1981 and 1985, for example, agricultural wages declined almost 40 percent in real terms (Repetto 1990, 41).

Factors encouraging migration into the rainforest, especially into the provinces of Rondonia and Acre, are government programs that have encouraged settlement in the Amazon and the building of new highways. Moving to the Amazon is regarded by many as an opportunity for acquiring land and thereby achieving a better life in a frontier region. New highways cut through the rainforests and provide access to previously isolated regions for millions of migrants wanting to own a piece of virgin land.

One of the first tasks undertaken by these aspiring farmers is the clearing of a plot of land, which is accomplished by cutting or girdling and then burning trees. Crops planted in the ash-enriched land grow fairly well during the first two or three years, but then the fertility of the cleared land declines rapidly. Because traditional farming methods are at ecological odds with the rainforest environment, within a few years crops fail and farmers are forced to abandon the land. In some situations, pressure from cattlemen accelerates the rate at which small farmers flee their cleared plots. After abandoning one area, farm families move to other virgin lands to repeat the process.

Ranchers form a fourth group of people competing for the use of the rainforest. As with the small farmers, they need the forests cleared so the land can be used for an alternative product, namely, grasses for pasture. Cattlemen destroy the rainforest either directly by burning trees or indirectly by scaring away farmers who have already completed that task. The forage grasses also suffer after a few years because of declining soil nutrients, which results in the invasion of shrubs and nonforage grasses. Although ranchers may then expend the costs of cutting and burning this undesired vegetation, the quality of pastures is rarely restored completely, which means that ranchers seek larger landholdings capable of supporting their cattle herds.

Ranchers who seek additional land do not experience the same constraints that apply to the Indians, rubber tappers, and small farmers who attempt adjustments to deteriorating conditions. Ranchers are usually able to obtain the financial backing necessary to acquire land as the need arises. Furthermore, this economic power is accompanied by political power, especially at the level of local and regional governments. Such power provides considerable leverge in conflicts with farmers, tappers, and other local groups over land ownership or utilization of forest resources.

During the period of greatest deforestation, ranchers were aided by the government through long-term loans, tax credits covering most investment costs, and tax write-offs. Ranchers typically lost more than half their invested capital within 15 years, but land could be repeatedly resold as tax shelters (Repetto 1990, 41). Most of these governmental policies were discontinued in 1989, but in 1987 they contributed significantly to the magnitude of forest destruction.

The ranchers' greater economic and political power arises partly from their linkages with distant markets. In contrast to farm families who attempt to survive by growing crops for their own subsistence and for local or regional markets, the ranchers have the economic support of a marketing network that reaches metropolitan Brazil and buyers in Europe, Japan, and North America.

The fifth group of competitors considered here includes all persons associated with the *lumber industry.* In many countries, including Brazil, large corporations are cutting trees, primarily hardwoods, for distant markets, especially in Japan and the United States. At first glance, this activity might be regarded as similar to the harvesting of a renewable resource that occurs commonly throughout the world. It is not the same, however, because current logging practices destroy approximately half of the trees while only 10 percent are extracted and used (Repetto 1990, 37). The relatively few trees that are obtained are acquired at a tremendous sacrifice of the unused trees.

Wastefulness is also evident in the form of the final products. Rather than utilizing the tropical hardwoods for furniture or other items depending on distinctive qualities of the wood, much of the production goes into panelling, plywood, cardboard, pulp, and other materials for which numerous sustainable alternatives are available. Within Brazil, some trees have been used only as a commercial fuel, with one example being the making of charcoal for the iron smelters at Carajas.

The destruction of tropical forests may be more permanent than the cutting of trees in other vegetative zones. Efforts at reforestation of rainforests have generally failed because they do not replicate the wide diversity and extensive distribution of species. Without a freeze season to kill pests, blights, and diseases that attack trees, the wide dispersion of species is essential. Attempts to replace the forests with tree plantations consisting of only one or a few species, therefore, have generally failed.

In addition to these five groups of people living and operating within the Brazilian Amazon, other non-local forces affect the use of the forests. As already noted, the national government regulates land ownership and tax rates, which affect decisions about land utilization. The building of national highways greatly influences the accessibility of places and the economic feasibility of commercial ventures. Likewise, foreign investments and importation of Brazilian products provide the financial backing for activities that promote exports. For example, decisions made by the directors of a corporation in Tokyo can directly affect the rate at which lumber is extracted from distant rainforests.

PROSPECTS FOR IMPROVEMENTS

What are the prospects for diminishing the magnitude of this reoccurring disaster? An answer depends on the degree that the various forces contributing to deforestation are changing and the likelihood that they will continue to reduce destructive activities. Any such prediction, of course, requires a fairly accurate assessment of the principal "causes" for the existing destruction.

Efforts to determine "the cause" for the deforestation in the Brazilian rain-forest are thwarted because of the multiplicity of forces involved with its utiliza-tion and the varying power of these contending forces. For example, although it is easy to observe the actual burning of a section of forest by a small farmer, such action does not constitute the primary reason for the disappearance of tropical forests. Only when this act is repeated millions of times does it become a signifi-cant contributor to forest destruction. Even so, it can be argued logically that the clearing of land by small farmers is merely a symptom of an economic system that causes rural poverty and leads people to do whatever is necessary to eke out an existence. To declare that "an economic system" is the root cause, however, does not identify any causative elements because of the intricately interwoven com-ponents of a modern economy.

The difficulty in identifying factors that ultimately result in deforestation is illustrated by the complexity of international finances. In the 1970s, United States banks and other foreign financial institutions loaned money to the Brazilian military government with floating interest rates. As the United States budget deficits increased, interest rates rose, which then made it more difficult for Brazil to make repayments from export earnings alone. Brazil then sought money from the Inter-national Monetary Fund (IMF), which required the government to cut spending on health, education, housing, food subsidies, public transportation, and similar public benefits. These budgetary restrictions on social expenditures and the con-tinual outflow of debt payments were followed by the expansion of poverty. These conditions of poverty, in turn, contributed to the migration to the Amazon and the resultant deforestation.

The Brazilian national debt also put more pressure on the government to en-courage exports, particularly those with international marketing networks, such as associated with beef and lumber. Any expansion in the exportation of these prod-ucts, however, is accomplished by more rapidly clearing the tropical forest. Again, as with the problem of assessing the true "cause" for burning trees by land-hungry migrants, there is little agreement about the primary "cause" for clearing the forest for rangeland. Is it the rancher who strives to make a living by producing a marketable commodity, the government that encourages the production of this export item, or the consumers in distant countries who buy Brazilian beef?

Without agreement on basic underlying conditions that have created the disaster of deforestation, it is difficult to assess the merits of current and prospective changes. Several factors have contributed to a reduction in the amount of forest destroyed in Brazil since 1987. Some changes have occurred since the return of a democratic government, which is more receptive to the interests of a diverse population.

One policy that was only partially implemented in the past but is now being en-forced with greater vigor is the reservation of specified areas for Indians. In recent years, several million hectares have been designated as "extractive reserves" where Indians and rubber tappers, and hence the forest, are assured protection from encroachment.

Change is also occurring partly from the reevaluation of the costs and benefits of using the forest resources in particular ways. For example, studies in Acre show that because pastures quickly lose their productivity and carrying capacity for cattle, the revenue from collecting wild rubber and Brazil nuts is four times as high as that from cattle ranching (Repetto 1990, 38). Similarly, research in the Peruvian Amazon found that the value of edible fruits, latex, and very selective logging can yield more than twice the income achievable from ranchers (Peters, Gentry, Mendelsohn 1989).

Since 1988, the Brazilian Institute for Natural Environment and Renewable Resources has been monitoring forest fires by examining imagery obtained by satellites. As soon as a fire is spotted on images, the site is checked by helicopter. Then the persons responsible for the burn are fined by an enforcement patrol arriving in trucks. The tremendous reduction in fires from 1989 to 1990 is believed to be largely attributable to this kind of immediate response.

Outside Brazil, a growing awareness about the problems resulting from the destruction of tropical forests has generated public pressure to make changes. Adverse publicity and direct protests seem to have encouraged world lending agencies to give more weight to the possible environmental impact of proposed development projects. The abandonment of highway extensions in Acre province illustrates what appears to be a modified lending policy.

These changes have reduced the amount of annual deforestation that has occurred since 1987, but they do not negate most of the basic forces that contribute to the destruction of the forests in Brazil. The economic factors that entice people, individually and collectively, to cut or burn a portion of the forest are still operating. As long as individuals benefit—or at least believe that they benefit—from clearing and cutting trees, this kind of activity will persist.

This "disaster," therefore, is an on-going one. Although it results from human decisions and consequently is solvable by human action, the intricate and complex characteristics of the national and world economic systems make it very unlikely that deforestation will be stopped in the near future. The radical and rapid changes necessary to stop deforestation will occur only when the costs of biological extermination and atmospheric modification are deemed unacceptable by the major centers of economic and political power.

REFERENCES

Branford, Sue and Oriel Glock. 1985. *The Last Frontier: Fighting Over Land in the Amazon*. London: Zed Press.

May, Robert M. 1988. How Many Species Are There on Earth?, *Science* 241:1441-49.

Peters, Charles M., Alwyn H. Gentry and Robert O. Mendelsohn. 1989. Valuation of an Amazonian Rainforest, *Nature* 339:655-56.

Repetto, Robert. 1990. Deforestation in the Tropics, *Scientific American* 262:36-40.

Shukla, J., C. Nobre and P. Sellers. 1990. Amazon Deforestation and Climate Change, *Science* 247:1322-25.

Wilson, Edward O. 1989. Threats to Biodiversity, *Scientific American* 261:108-116.

Wolf, Edward C. 1991. Survival of the Rarest, *World Watch* 4:12-20.

World Resources Institute. 1990. Forests and Rangelands, *World Resources 1990-91*, 101-20. New York and Oxford: Oxford University Press.

Natural and Technological Disasters: Causes, Effects and Preventive Measures. Edited by S.K. Majumdar, G.S. Forbes, E.W. Miller, and R.F. Schmalz. © 1992, The Pennsylvania Academy of Science.

Chapter Forty-One

THE JOHNSTOWN FLOODS: CAUSES AND CONSEQUENCES

MARY P. LAVINE

Department of Geography
210 Krebs Hall
University of Pittsburgh at Johnstown
Johnstown, PA 15904

INTRODUCTION

Johnstown, Pennsylvania has a long history of flooding. Nathan Shappee, in his seminal analysis of the Great Johnstown Flood, identifies 16 occasions on which flooding occurred there during the 73 year interval between 1816 and 1888. In 1889, the worst flood Johnstown ever experienced caused the death of more than 2,200 people and the destruction of more than half the city's buildings. Because the 1889 flood was one of the major news stories of the second half of the nineteenth century, it is not surprising that media coverage of subsequent major floods in 1936 and 1977 was accompanied by comparisons with and retrospectives on the flood of 1889. All of this attention has contributed to Johnstown's lingering image as the "flood city."

THE "GREAT" JOHNSTOWN FLOOD OF 1889

In the annals of American disasters, "the tragedy of the Conemaugh" holds a position of prominence comparable to that of the Chicago Fire (1871) or the San Francisco Earthquake (1906). It earned this distinction as a result of the failure of the South Fork Dam, located about 14 miles upstream from Johnstown on the South

Fork of the Little Conemaugh River. In less than an hour after the dam was breached, the entire contents of the one mile by two mile lake moved down the narrow, winding riverbed into Johnstown itself, causing almost unimaginable destruction.

At the time of the 1889 flood, the South Fork Dam was nearly 50 years old. An earthen structure constructed between 1840 and 1852, it was built to insure a reliable source of water for the canal portion of the Pennsylvania statewide system of canals and railroads. Although the portage rail and canal system was abandoned after the Pennsylvania Railroad's Main Line was completed between Philadelphia and Pittsburgh, the Western Reservoir and dam were left in place. For years after, the dam suffered from poor maintenance, leaks and general neglect. In the 1870s, its discharge pipes were removed and sold as scrap metal.

In 1879, the dam and lake, now renamed Lake Conemaugh, became the property of the South Fork Fishing and Hunting Club of Pittsburgh. Prominent men such as Andrew Carnegie, Henry Phipps, Jr., Philander Chase Knox, Robert Pitcairn, Andrew Mellon and Henry Clay Frick built summer homes and a club house overlooking Lake Conemaugh. The dam underwent several changes intended to make it more useful to the vacationing Pittsburghers. It was lowered several feet at the breast so that a roadway could be constructed to carry carriages over the dam. Screens were placed across the spillway to prevent game fish from escaping. Repairs to and modifications of the dam made in the course of the Club's ownership were apparently undertaken without engineering supervision or consultation.[2,3]

On May 30 and 31, 1889, Johnstown experienced an unusually heavy rainfall. Although Johnstown's rain gauge was destroyed in the flood, rainfall has been estimated at 6.2 inches, based on precipitation reports from nearby locations.[4] In other sites nearby, even more precipitation fell. By midmorning on the 31st, the river had already risen 20 feet above low water level, and by noon it was higher than local residents ever remembered it being. The streets filled with water just as they had on many previous occasions, leaving much of Johnstown covered with three to six feet of water.

Flooding from the rainstorm was exacerbated by several factors. Decades of encroachment on the Little Conemaugh and Stonycreek Rivers upstream and at Johnstown had reduced the rivers' widths, causing water levels to rise. Runoff from surrounding hillsides was accelerated because of years of cutting timber for mine supports and charcoal to use in making iron.

The same rainstorm that caused the streets of Johnstown to fill with water also filled Lake Conemaugh, finally causing it to overflow the South Fork Dam. Water spilled over the breast of the dam, eroding away and cutting through its face until, despite efforts to save it, the dam was breached along its mid-section. An estimated 640 million cubic feet of water, or about 20 million tons of water roared downstream, reaching Johnstown in less than an hour after damaging or destroying a succession of settlements along the way (Figure 1). Johnstown experienced the highest mortality, with more than 1,000 deaths, followed by Cambria City with at least 360 and Woodvale with over 270.[5]

The extraordinary damage was due in large measure to the height and force of the water as it moved downstream. The difference in elevation between the breast of the dam and the Stone Bridge across the Conemaugh River in Johnstown was about 450 feet. This dramatic drop in elevation over a relatively short distance caused flood waters to travel quite rapidly—22 feet per second down the channel to Johnstown.[3,4] The narrowness of the stream bed further raised the height of the water so that, by the time it reached Johnstown, it was a "wall" of water 30 feet high. Water from the dam then combined with the three to six feet of flood water already covering city streets.

Survivors compared the flood waters to a rolling "ball" of water in which the upper portion of the wave rolled over the slower moving underlayers of water, carrying along with it everything from locomotives, boxcars and trees to houses, livestock and bales of barbed wire.

One of the many vivid eyewitness accounts of the flood described it this way:

> It came like a thief, and was upon us before we were aware. Already when it reached us it had numbered its victims by the hundreds. Mineral Point and East Conemaugh Borough were gone, a passenger train was engulfed. Woodvale was swept away. Conemaugh Borough was shaved off as if by the sharp surface of an avalanche; in a moment Johnstown was tumbling all over itself; houses at one end nodded to houses at the other end and went like a swift, deceitful friend to meet, embrace, and crush them. Then on sped the wreck in a whirl, the angry water baffled for a moment, running up the hill with the town and the helpless multitude on its back, the flood shaking with rage, and dropping here and there a portion of its burden—crushing, grinding,

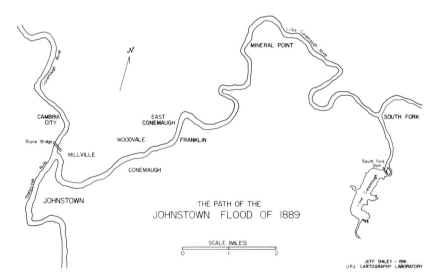

FIGURE 1. When the South Fork Dam was breached on the afternoon of May 31, 1889, it took less than an hour for the flood waters to move down the Little Conemaugh River to the city of Johnstown. A number of smaller settlements along the route were damaged or destroyed.

pulverizing all. Then back with the great frame buildings, floating along like ocean steamers, upper decks crowded, hands clinging to every support that could be reached, and so on down to the great stone bridge, where the houses, piled mountain high, took fire, and burned with all the fury of hell you read about—cremation alive in your own home, perhaps a mile from its foundation; dear ones slowly consumed before your eyes, and the same fate your own a moment later.[6]

The fire referred to in the preceding quotation involved one of the most vivid images of the flood of 1889. The Pennsylvania Railroad's Stone Bridge over the Conemaugh River trapped flood refuse, forcing water to flow up the Stonycreek River and briefly retarding its removal from the city. As a result of this dam effect, flood waters rose higher and covered even more ground than otherwise would have been the case. Worse yet, the debris trapped by the Stone Bridge caught fire, burning several days before it could be extinguished (Figure 2). David McCullough,[7] author of the most well known account of the 1889 flood, estimates that between 500 and 600 people survived the flood itself only to become entangled in the rubble of the Stone Bridge, as many as 80 of them fatally.

The tragic 1889 flood produced some enduring consequences for Johnstown and surrounding communities. The flood provided the impetus for suburbanization

FIGURE 2. Refuse from the 1889 flood, at the site of the Pennsylvania Railroad's Stone Bridge on the Conemaugh River.

above the floodplain. It facilitated a rapid expansion of Johnstown's population and area by making consolidation with other boroughs and villages appear more attractive than before. No less important, it helped create the enduring perception of Johnstown as a flood-ravaged city, an image which subsequent floods have certainly reinforced.

THE SAINT PATRICK'S DAY FLOOD OF 1936

Johnstown's second major flood occurred at the end of winter in 1936. An especially thick snow mantle covered the Allegheny highlands, the result of a substantial accumulation of snow and a cold winter in which little melting occurred. Prior to March 17, up to 14 feet of packed snow was reported in upland areas. By late February city officials, already anticipating the consequences of a spring thaw, ordered the destruction of parts of the ice flow on the Stonycreek, fearing that the ice would jam up the bridges and cause flooding. Temperatures rose well above freezing on March 14, and were accompanied by several days of heavy rain, which subsequently caused flooding in locations throughout Pennsylvania and beyond.[8] In the Conemaugh drainage basin, warm rains caused the snow pack to melt quickly. By midafternoon on March 17, the Stonycreek and Little Conemaugh Rivers began to overflow their banks. Flood waters reached a height of 17 feet at City Hall in downtown Johnstown, flooding the entire downtown area plus adjacent wards (Figure 3). 77 buildings were destroyed and nearly 3,000 more were damaged. 25 deaths were attributed to the flood, although twelve of these were caused by heart attacks and shock rather than drowning. Damage in the city of Johnstown, excluding public works, was estimated at $40.8 million.[9]

President Franklin D. Roosevelt visited the city on August 14, 1936, promising residents that "the federal government is determined to keep you from facing these floods again." In keeping with that goal, the Corps of Engineers proposed constructing a series of flood control reservoirs in Western Pennsylvania to protect cities like Johnstown and Pittsburgh. The plan to build a reservoir on the Stonycreek was subsequently abandoned, and at Johnstown only a channelization program was implemented. The Corps spent more than $8 million deepening, widening and relining portions of the Stonycreek, Little Conemaugh and Conemaugh River channels, in an effort to speed flood waters through the city before they could overflow the river banks. For more than 35 years after the Corps of Engineers completed the channelization project, Johnstown had no severe floods. Even when Hurricane Agnes flooded Harrisburg and other cities along the Susquehanna River, Johnstown was untouched. This helped reinforce the locally popular but fatally flawed perception of Johnstown as "the flood free city."

THE 1977 FLOOD

The most recent severe flood in Johnstown occurred on July 19-20, 1977. Torrential downpours associated with a succession of thunderstorms resulted in heavy rainfall in parts of Bedford, Cambria, Indiana, Somerset and Westmoreland counties. Parts of Cambria and Indiana counties received 8 to 12 inches of rainfall over an 8 to 9 hour period from early evening on July 19 to early morning on July 20.[10] The National Weather Service recorded 8.5 inches of rainfall for Johnstown between 9 p.m. and 4 a.m.[11] One location in Johnstown recorded 2.2 inches of rainfall during a single 40-minute period between 2:50 a.m. and 3:30 a.m., but the storm was so localized that no precipitation was recorded as little as 20 miles away to the southwest of Johnstown.

A brief chronology of events for the 1977 flood[12] reveals how ineffective warning systems proved to be in this instance. During the afternoon of July 19, the Pittsburgh office of the National Weather Service (NWS) issued a series of statements about flash flood warnings for northern Crawford County and other areas in northwestern Pennsylvania, and noted that a thunderstorm had passed through southwestern Pennsylvania. At 7:30 p.m. the NWS issued its first weather statement for the Johnstown area. This statement, which was not a flash flood warning, was based on radar observations and some reports of brief but heavy rains and minor flooding in urban areas.

The severity of the thunderstorms caused electrical and telephone services to be distrupted over an increasingly wider area from mid-evening onward. At midnight,

FIGURE 3. Downtown Johnstown during the 1936 flood, as seen from the top of the Incline Plane.

streets in Johnstown were covered with water but still passable. By 12:45 a.m. Johnstown police were attempting to evacuate city residents. Communities in Cambria County were without phone service after 1 a.m. During the middle of the night, a succession of streams overflowed their banks and did substantial damage. The Solomon Run overflowed its banks and rushed through a public housing project in the Walnut Grove area of Johnstown and Dale Borough. Elsewhere, along the border of southern Cambria and northern Somerset counties, the Elton Run and Paint Creek overflowed their banks, completely overwhelming the flood-control project on the Paint Creek and causing water to rush through the boroughs of Scalp Level and Windber.

At 2:40 a.m. the National Weather Service, apparently unaware of the severity of local conditions, issued a flash flood warning for Indiana and Cambria Counties, noting that "heavy rain and some flooding has been reported in this area. Radar shows heavy rainfall continuing thru the area for the next hour or so. Person (sic) should move to higher ground immediately if near flooded streams."[12]

About 4 a.m. the Laurel Run Dam burst, sending 101 million gallons of water down the Laurel Run and killing 36 in the Middle Taylor Township settlement of Tanneryville.[13] Water from the Laurel Run Dam backed up the Conemaugh River and into Johnstown neighborhoods below the downtown area. Throughout the evening and early morning hours, flooding from overfilled streams occurred in such disparate places as Clymer, Homer City, Indiana and Cherry Tree (all in Indiana County), scattered sites in Bedford County, Seward and New Florence (Westmoreland County), and a variety of locations in Cambria and Somerset Counties.[14]

In an assessment of the flash flood warning system, a report to the Administrator of the National Oceanic and Atmospheric Administration notes that a timely announcement of flood watches and warnings for the affected area failed to occur in part because "our capability to predict heavy or extreme rainfall amounts over small areas is limited . . . ." The report found flaws in the interpretation of satellite and radar information and in the system of local reporting of weather information. It concludes that "on the disastrous night of July 19-20, 1977, neither the National Weather Service component of the Flash Food Warning System nor that part of it involving local communities and Civil Defense did much good for anyone in the Johnstown, Pennsylvania, area . . . ."[12]

A BRIEF COMPARISON OF THE THREE FLOODS

Tables 1 and 2 summarize some pertinent information about Johnstown's three most severe floods. The most common criteria for comparing the magnitude of hazard events are mortality and property damage. Additional dimensions examined here include causal factors, water height and areal extent of flooding. An examination of these attributes suggests that the three floods have little in common except for their association with Johnstown.

Causal factors

The immediate cause of the 1889 flood was the failure of the South Fork Dam. Although the cluster of small communities along the Little Conemaugh and Conemaugh Rivers had already experienced some flooding because of heavy rains, this situation was familiar to Johnstowners and probably would not have resulted in significant loss of life or exceptional property damage, had the dam not failed and released some 640 million cubic feet of water.

The 1936 flood was the result of quite different circumstances. The heavy rains which caused flooding in the drainage area of the Conemaugh River were part of a larger weather system extending throughout much of the northeastern United States. The storm caused extensive damage elsewhere, including Pittsburgh's worst ever flood. In Johnstown, flood waters rose slowly and, except for the extraordinary depth (17 feet at City Hall), the situation locally with regard to the effects of spring rain and snow melt was not unfamiliar. City officials had anticipated the likelihood of flooding weeks before the event occurred, and had taken some measures to reduce the severity of flooding.

The 1977 flood was the result of unusually severe, localized thunderstorms which, unbeknownst to weather forecasters, had stalled over Johnstown and vincinity, producing rainstorms of such intensity that the rapid runoff quickly exceeded the capacity of small streams and dam spillways. Nearly half the deaths were the result

TABLE 1

A Comparison of Causes, Height and Mortality of Three Major Floods in Johnstown, Pennsylvania

Date	Causes	Height of water at present site of City Hall	Mortality*
May 31, 1889	Heavy rains estimated at 6.2″, combined with failure of earthen South Fork Dam (640 million cubic feet of water)	21 feet	2,209
March 17, 1936	Heavy rains and warm temperatures caused rapid melting of a 14′ snow cover	17 feet	25
July 19-20, 1977	Heavy localized thunderstorms, releasing up to 12″ of rain over a 9 hour period, and the failure of 7 earthen dams, including Laurel Run Dam (101 million gallons, or about 13.5 million cubic feet of water)	8 feet	85

Note: *Figures for the number of lives lost include all deaths attributed to each flood, not just deaths occurring within the city of Johnstown. The 1936 figure includes 12 "flood-related" deaths not attributed to drowning.

of a single dam failure, while others occurred as normally placid streams quite suddently became like rivers. This flood illustrates the continuing difficulty of forecasting or reporting from afar the ongoing nature of severe localized storms. The breakdown of communications systems, the inadequacy of local reporting mechanisms and the complications of nighttime and severe weather conditions all hindered the deployment of timely warnings and effective evacuation measures. The fact that a number of flood control channelization systems in the Johnstown region proved to be inadequate for the severe weather conditions of that night serves as a reminder that any flood control project has certain built-in limitations which nature will occasionally exceed. Finally, vigilance against flooding may have faltered because of confidence in the Corps of Engineer's channelization project which, having prevented flooding for more than 35 years, helped reinforce the local image of Johnstown as "the flood free city."

Areal Extent

Loss of life and property damage in the 1889 flood were confined to low-lying areas along the Little Conemaugh and Conemaugh Rivers and that portion of the Stonycreek River receiving a backwash of water from the temporary damming of

TABLE 2

A Comparison of Property Damage Losses for Three Major Floods in Johnstown, Pennsylvania (All Values Expressed in Millions of Dollars)

Date	Johnstown estimated losses, in then current dollars	Johnstown estimated losses, adjusted to 1977 equivalent dollars	Flood area estimated losses, in then current dollars	Flood area estimated losses, adjusted to 1977 equivalent dollars
May 31, 1889*	16	97-145	17	103-154
March 17, 1936	41**	179-221**	50-80	219-269; 350-431
July 19-20, 1977	117	117	200-240	200-240

Notes: These values correspond to commonly cited loss estimates associated with each flood.[7,10,11,15] Values are given for the city of Johnstown and for the overall areas affected by each flood. These figures should be viewed with considerable caution, because of the lack of consistency in the way in which losses are estimated, and because of the widely differing definitions of the affected areas.

1889 and 1936 losses have been adjusted to their 1977 dollar equivalents, using both the GNP Deflator Index (source: *Historical Statistics of the United States*, Volume 1) and the Consumer Price Index (sources: *Economic Report of the President* and *Survey of Current Business*). Because these two indices produce different values, the 1977 equivalents for prior years are presented as ranges. However, given the uncertainties associated with the original data and the questionable accuracy of these conversion indices when applied to real estate and infrastructure, even these range values should be viewed with great caution, particularly for the 1889 flood.

*Most of property damage in the 1889 flood occurred in areas which, if they were not at the time, are now part of Johnstown.

**The 1936 estimate for Johnstown excludes public works.

the Stone Bridge. The 1936 flood in Johnstown was part of a much larger regional pattern of rainstorms and spring flooding in which other cities suffered more damage and loss of life. What is commonly defined as the flood of 1977 involved portions of five Pennsylvania counties, with loss of life widely dispersed, excepting only the cluster of deaths in Tanneryville.

Mortality

Loss of life is the most common criteria by which we measure a disaster's severity. In the U.S. flood experience, only the Galveston hurricane of 1900, with its 5,000 + fatalities, surpassed the Johnstown flood of 1889 in mortality. Apart from these two most severe flood experiences, only another dozen or so floods in the United States, with causes ranging from tidal waves, hurricanes and other tropical storms to flash flooding, persistent rainstorms and dam failures, have resulted in more than 100 fatalities. This makes the flood of 1977, with its 85 deaths, a major flood mortality experience although in no way comparable to the flood of 1889. This is not the case for the 1936 flood; indeed, had the 1889 flood not already established Johnstown's flood reputation, it is not likely that the 13 deaths by drowning in 1936 would be considered noteworthy.

Economic losses

The financial dimensions of property loss for the three floods are difficult to compare, for several reasons. First, substantial differences in the sizes of the affected areas makes establishing a basis for comparison difficult. Second, there is reason to believe that the criteria for estimating flood damage in each of the three years differs, perhaps significantly, thus rendering published damage estimates difficult to compare. Third, even assuming that the damage estimates for each flood are reasonably accurate, adjustments must be made for differences in the value of the dollar over time.

Table 2 contains estimates of property damages due to the three floods and conversions of the 1889 and 1936 figures to their 1977 dollar equivalents. These adjustments were made using both the GNP Deflator Index and the Consumer Price Index. Neither measure is without its flaws. The composition of the Consumer Price Index varies over time and, given what it measures, is somewhat questionable when applied to flood damage estimates dominated by losses in real estate, infrastructure and major capital investments. Comparable reservations are appropriate regarding use of the GNP Deflator Index, which is based on the value of goods produced. Nevertheless, if one accepts original flood damage estimates as being reasonably on target and reasonably comparable, and if one accepts their conversions to a common year value (1977) as "being in the ballpark," then the results are quite surprising.

The 1889 flood, the nation's most infamous flood and its second worst ever in terms of mortality, does not tower above the other two floods when property losses are compared. Instead, it is the St. Patrick's Day Flood of 1936, which had the least loss of life and deep but not turbulent waters in the city itself, which accounts for the highest dollar losses, even though many more buildings were destroyed in the 1889 flood.

What explains these findings? Simple or single answers are not forthcoming, but several contributing factors immediately suggest themselves. First, more people and more firms occupied the floodplain in 1936 than in 1889, and thus there was more investment in real estate. By 1977, city population had fallen significantly and businesses had also begun to outmigrate. Nevertheless, significant investment remained in Johnstown even though the central city was a declining economic unit. Second, over a 100 year period, the level of material wealth grew considerably, as did the extent of public and corporate investment in infrastructure. More recent floods are more expensive floods because, over time, more individual and societal wealth has been accumulated and thus there is more to lose. Third, the 1936 flood caused more damage than the 1977 flood because the water rose to a greater height and stood in place for a longer period of time. Despite the deeper waters, loss of life was less in 1936 because the element of surprise (e.g. dam failure and rapid, unexpected rise in stream height at nighttime) was absent.

CONSEQUENCES OF THE JOHNSTOWN FLOODS

The physical evidence of these three severe floods has been largely eradicated, but some significant and enduring consequences remain. Three are discussed here: the changing political geography of the city of Johnstown; the rapid suburbanization of areas above the floodplain; and the popularization of an image for Johnstown which was synonymous with flood disaster.

Growth of Johnstown by Consolidation and Annexation

One almost immediate consequence of the 1889 flood was a dramatic change in the political geography of Johnstown. Prior to the flood, Johnstown was a borough of slightly more than 10,000. It shared its modest floodplain and the immediately adjacent upland areas with a number of other settlements whose population totalled nearly 30,000.

In May of 1889, Johnstown's Borough Council rejected the petition of the unincorporated settlement of Moxham to consolidate with Johnstown, but agreed to reconsider the question on May 31. The flood on that same date delayed further discussion of the annexation, but in the months immediately following the flood the move to consolidation took on a new intensity and broader popular support. A number of communities now sought consolidation into a single, larger unit.

On November 6, 1889, barely five months after the flood, residents in Johnstown, Millville, Cambria City, Prospect, Woodvale, Coopersdale, Grubbtown, and Conemaugh all voted in favor of consolidation (although the courts later turned down Coopersdale's petition because it didn't share a common boundary with Johnstown) (Figure 4). Only East Conemaugh and Franklin voted against consolidation. The unincorporated village of Moxham petitioned to join the city, and was annexed in

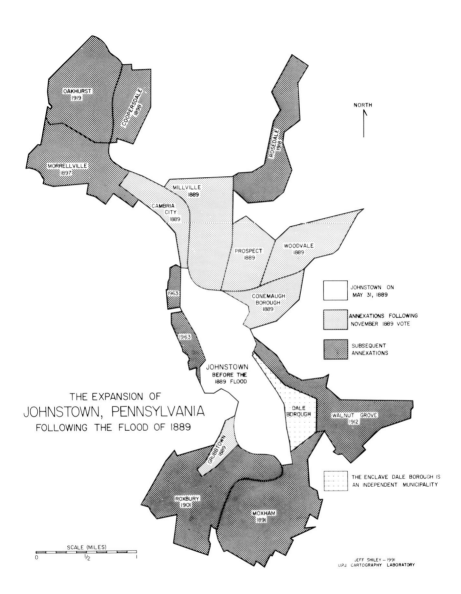

NORTH

JOHNSTOWN ON
MAY 31, 1889

ANNEXATIONS FOLLOWING
NOVEMBER 1889 VOTE

SUBSEQUENT
ANNEXATIONS

THE ENCLAVE DALE BOROUGH IS
AN INDEPENDENT MUNICIPALITY

THE EXPANSION OF
JOHNSTOWN, PENNSYLVANIA
FOLLOWING THE FLOOD OF 1889

OAKHURST
1919

COOPERSDALE
1949

ROSEDALE
1918

MORRELLVILLE
1897

MILLVILLE
1889

CAMBRIA
CITY
1889

PROSPECT
1889

WOODVALE
1889

1963

CONEMAUGH
BOROUGH
1889

1963

JOHNSTOWN
BEFORE THE
1889 FLOOD

DALE
BOROUGH

WALNUT GROVE
1912

GRUBBTOWN
1889

ROXBURY
1901

MOXHAM
1891

SCALE (MILES)
0   1/2   1

JEFF SHILEY – 1991
U.P.J. CARTOGRAPHY LABORATORY

FIGURE 4. The political geography of Johnstown changed as a result of the 1889 Flood, when six previously independent boroughs and villages voted to consolidate with Johnstown. The outline of Johnstown shown here is based on its 1991 boundaries. Also shown are the approximate boundaries of the 13 boroughs and villages annexed between 1889 and 1919. Reflected in the city's boundaries but not shown in detail are 11 additional annexations ranging from 0.2 acres to 33.74 acres. The 1963 annexation of 84.82 acres consists of a steep hillside on either side of the Incline Plane.

1891. Morrellville and parts of Stonycreek and Upper Yoder Townships also petitioned to join the city, and were subsequently annexed. By 1891, less than two years after the flood, the much expanded city of Johnstown had a population of 22,539, more than double that of the pre-flood period!

Consolidation's popularity, according to Johnstown newspaper articles and editorials from the summer and fall of 1889,[16] seemed to stem from the perception that the many small, separate municipalities were handicapped in their efforts to secure flood recovery assistance or otherwise act effectively on their own behalf. A case in point was sanitation control, which was difficult to implement on a municipality by municipality basis. The multiplicity of municipalities was perceived as impeding recovery efforts because so many different officials had to be consulted before any agreement could be reached on common actions. Smaller communities also complained that public relief efforts overlooked them in favor of the larger and more visible city of Johnstown. Consolidation was seen as a way of overcoming these obstacles.

For several decades Johnstown continued to expand by annexation, adding Morrellville (1891), Coopersdale (1898), Roxbury (1911), Walnut Grove (1912), Rosedale (1918) and Oakhurst (1919).[17] Other boroughs created by the Pennsylvania legislature declined to join with the city, and indeed have resoundingly defeated every consolidation proposal put forward.

Suburbanization

A second consequence of the 1889 flood was rapid suburbanization in locations above the floodplain. Almost immediately following the flood, the Cambria Iron Company, dominant employer in Johnstown and predecessor to Bethlehem Steel Corporation, built the Borough of Westmont on a bluff overlooking the city of Johnstown. Westmont was intended to house Cambria Iron Company employees in a model community serving all classes. Located about 500 feet above the city, Westmont had easy access to downtown Johnstown via an inclined plane, which began operation in 1891 and continues its service more than one hundred years later.

Many flood survivors rebuilt their homes on the floodplain, but others were attracted to higher elevations in places like Westmont, Roxbury, Daisytown, Upper Yoder Township, Brownstown, Ferndale, Dale and Moxham. Over the next hundred years, other municipalities also attracted population and reinforced the early post-flood pattern of upland suburbanization.

Johnstown's Image as "The Flood City"

A third consequence of the 1889 flood was the popularization of Johnstown as the flood city, a view that subsequent floods in 1936 and 1977 only served to reinforce. The 1889 flood was the most devastating disaster of the nineteenth century, and as such was extensively covered by the print media. Reporters and photographers crowded into Johnstown to record that "epitome of horror for the Victorian Age" (Figure 5).

The greatest natural disaster of the century, it touched the emotions of all levels of society. The rush of the waters on unsuspecting Johnstown, the violation of happy homes, the cruel drownings and horrors at the bridge, the plight of orphans and widows, the recovery of the dead—all these became subjects of conversation, poetry, novels, legends and song. However incredible the descriptions coming from Johnstown may have sounded, the photographs soon showed gruesome evidence that the calamity was real![18]

As Selvaggio notes, "the country was deluged with fake histories, pathetic songs, pulp novels, bad verse, and vivid photographs, each, in its way, commemorating the disaster."[19]

News accounts of the 1936 and 1977 floods inevitably contained references to and comparisons with the events of 1889, reinforcing the notion that Johnstown and flooding were synonymous. That this image persists is verified by much anecdotal evidence provided by residents of the Johnstown area, who have become accustomed to hearing strangers automatically link Johnstown with its flood history.

The other side of the "Johnstown flood image" is reflected in the *local perception* of the flood history, in which the city's recovery from three devastating floods

FIGURE 5. "The Flood at Johnstown—The Scene at the Bridge." This drawing by W.A. Rogers appeared in Harper's Weekly (XXXIII, 1695), June 15, 1889. The 1889 flood produced an outpouring of sensational and sentimental drawings, photographys, books, commentaries and poetry.

in less than one hundred years is seen as proof of its resilience, its "unquenchable spirit," its ability to "triumph over adversity." This experience has produced an almost automatic response locally; its theme is the community's faith in its ability to recover from whatever natural or economic disaster may befall it.

The communal flood history experience now combines local pride with a strong entrepreneurial interest, as institutional and private sector forces combine to market the flood history. The 1889 flood is now a heavily promoted tourist attraction. The Johnstown Flood Museum, located in a former library built with funds donated by Andrew Carnegie, contains flood memorabilia and is one of the area's two major "interpreters" of the flood. In March 1990, its documentary film on the 1889 flood won a prestigious Oscar award. The other major interpreter of the 1889 flood is the National Park Service, which operates at the site of the infamous South Fork Dam. Marketing the flood history is also being linked to plans for America's Industrial Heritage Project, which is intended to preserve working examples of coal mining and iron and steel making as they were in the second half of the nineteenth century.

CONCLUSIONS

More than 100 years after the event, identification with a notorious disaster continues to have an impact on Johnstown. The 1889 flood changed the political geography of the valley, fueled the move to the upland suburbs, and created an indelible link with the flood image. While differing from the 1889 flood in cause, areal extent, mortality and economic impact, the subsequent major floods in 1936 and 1977 helped reinforce the popular image of Johnstown as the flood city. More locally, the community's successive flood recovery efforts are seen as evidence that the community is resilient in the face of adversity. This "triumph of the human spirit" has most recently become a vehicle for marketing a local tourist initiative based on the flood history combined with the area's nineteenth century experiences in basic steel and coal mining and its richly diverse ethnic heritage. Therein lies the hope of parlaying the tragic event of 1889 and its successor floods into something of lasting benefit to the community.

Note: Some portions of this chapter which deal with the 1889 flood events and consequences draw upon the author's previous article about the 1889 Johnstown flood, "The Legacy of the Johnstown Flood" (*The Pennsylvania Geographer*, Volume XXVIII, No. 2 [Fall/Winter 1990], 68-80), and papers presented at the 1990 Annual Meeting of the Association of American Geographers (April 20, Toronto, Ontario, Canada) and the Applied Geography Conference (Charlotte, North Carolina), October 25, 1990.

ACKNOWLEDGEMENTS

Photographs used with permission of the Johnstown Area Heritage Association,

Johnstown, Pennsylvania. The Association's archival files on the 1889, 1936 and 1977 floods provided extensive background material. Maps were prepared by Jeffrey Shiley, University of Pittsburgh at Johnstown Cartography Laboratory. The author acknowledges the helpful comments or other assistance generously given in the preparation of this manuscript by Norm Bothwell, City Engineer, Johnstown; Richard Burkert and Robin Rummel, Johnstown Area Heritage Association; and Thomas McGahagan, University of Pittsburgh at Johnstown.

LITERATURE CITED

1. Shappee, Nathan Daniel. 1940. A History of Johnstown and the Great Flood of 1889. Thesis (Ph.D.), University of Pittsburgh.
2. Bcalc, David J. 1890. *Through the Johnstown Flood.*Edgcwood Publishing Company.
3. Committee on the Failure of the South Fork Dam, Report of the Committee on the Cause of the Failure of the South Fork Dam. June 1891. *Transactions* of the American Society of Civil Engineers. 24:431-469.
4. Ludlum, David M. April, 1989. The Johnstown Flood: Our Most Infamous Natural Disaster. *Weatherwise*, 42, No. 2, 88-92.
5. Storey, Henry Wilson. 1907. *History of Cambria County, Pennsylvania.* Volume 1. New York: The Lewis Publishing Company.
6. Johnstown*Tribune.* June 14, 1889.
7. McCullough, David M. 1968. *The Johnstown Flood.* New York: Simon and Schuster.
8. The Pennsylvania Railroad Company. 1937. *History of the Floods of March, 1936 and January, 1937.* The Cuneo Press, Inc.
9. Cooper, Ramon. *The Flood and the Future: The Story of a Year in City Government at Johnstown, Pennsylvania, 1936.* Johnstown, Pennsylvania: McKeown Printing Company.
10. National Oceanic and Atmospheric Administration, Environmental Research Laboratories. October 1978. Meteorological Analysis of the Johnstown, Pennsylvania, Flash Flood, 19-20 July 1977. U.S. Department of Commerce.
11. Watts, J. Dan, Editor. 1977. *The Johnstown Flood July 20, 1977.* C.F. Boone, Lubbock Texas.
12. National Oceanic and Atmospheric Administration. October 1977. Johnstown, Pennsylvania Flash Flood of July 19-20, 1977. A Report to the Administrator. Natural Disaster Survey Report 77-1. U.S. Department of Commerce. Rockville Md.
13. Johnstown *Tribune-Democrat*, July 20, 1978, pp. 11-12 and other issues in July and August, 1977.
14. The Great Flood of 1977: A Story of Catastrophe in the Conemaugh Valley. August 1977. Mirror Printing Company, Altoona, PA.
15. U.S. Army Corps of Engineers, Pittsburgh Division. The 1977 Southwestern Pennsylvania Flood . . . A 500 Year Flood . . . . Public Affairs Office. 75 pp.

16. Johnstown *Tribune*. Various dates. Johnstown Area Heritage Association archives.
17. The Cambria County Historical Society. 1954. Cambria County Sesquicentennial 1804-1954.
18. Degen, Paula and Carl Degen. 1984. *The Johnstown Flood of 1889: The Tragedy of the Conemaugh*. Philadelphia, Pennsylvania: Eastern Acorn Press.
19. Selvaggio, Marc. May/June 1989. After The Flood. *Carnegie Magazine*. LIX, No. 9:22-28.

Subject Index